The Founder of Opus Dei

The Life of Josemaría Escrivá

Vol. I

The Early Years

The Founder of Opus Dei

The Life of Josemaría Escrivá

Vol. I

The Early Years

Andrés Vázquez de Prada

Scepter Publishers
Princeton, NJ

This edition of *The Founder of Opus Dei: The Life of Josemaria Escriva, Vol. I: The Early Years* is published in the United States by Scepter Publishers, Inc. PO Box 1270, Princeton, NJ 08542. The title of the Spanish original is: *El Fundador del Opus Dei, Vol. I: Señor, que vea!* The translation is by Bernard Browne. The entire English text was edited at various stages by John Coverdale, Mary Gottschalk and Russell Shaw. Additional editorial input for this translation was provided by Michael Adams and Father Martin Heneghan. Page footnotes are by John Coverdale.

Scepter Publishers   ISBN: 1-889334-25-1 hb
                    ISBN: 1-889334-26-X pb

Library of Congress Cataloging-in-Publication Data

Vázquez de Prada, Andrés.
  [Fundador del Opus Dei. English]
  The founder of Opus Dei : the life of Josemaría Escrivá / Andrés Vázquez de Prada.
     p. cm
  Includes bibliographical references and index.
  Contents; 1. The early years
  ISBN 1-889334-25-1 (hb : alk. paper) -- ISBN 1-889334-26-X (pbk. : alk. paper)
     1. Escrivá de Balaguer, Josemaría, 1902-1975. 2. Catholic
  Church—Spain—Clergy—Biography. 3. Opus Dei (Society) I. Title.

BX4705.E676 V39 2000
267'.182'092--dc21
[B]

                                                        00-061238

Contents

TABLE OF ABBREVIATIONS

AGP	General Archive of the Prelature (*Archivo General de la Prelatura*)
Apuntes	Personal Notes (*Apuntes íntimos*)
AVF	Assorted writings of the Founder (*Autógrafos Varios del Fundador*)
C	Correspondence (personal letters of the Founder, cited by number and date)
D	Document
IZL	Section of AGP corresponding to the Servant of God Isidoro Zorzano Ledesma
Letter	Letters written to all the members of the Work, cited by date and section number
P01, P02 etc.	Collections of printed documents (sections within AGP)
PM	Madrid Process of beatification (*Proceso Matritense*), followed by folio number
PR	Roman Process of beatification (*Proceso Romano*), followed by page number
RHF	Historical Register of the Founder (*Registro Histórico del Fundador* [section within AGP])
Sum.	*Summarium* of the Cause of beatification and canonization. *Positio super vita et virtutibus*, Rome, 1988. The name of the witness, followed by the corresponding section number of the *Summarium*.
T	Testimonial

Introduction

What is a biography? In the strict sense of the term it is the story of a particular life. And it falls within the academic field of history. But a life does not exist in isolation, like a small island lost in a vast ocean. It is born and grows to maturity in a community. The individual is tied to a place, participates in a particular culture, and has a homeland. And the events of whatever time and place the subject lives in have an effect on his or her life. Thus the biographical focus necessarily transcends those things that affect only the person in question. The researcher, as well as the reader, has to keep in mind many other cultural and social circumstances to completely understand events and set them in their historical context.

Method of research. The biographer usually adopts a chronological structure, first studying the historical roots, and then proceeding to follow the subject's life from cradle to grave. The author will probably begin by describing the subject's family, home atmosphere, early life, and schooling to show the sources of the subject's personality. But one must avoid fiction and fantasies, and must work according to the methodology of research and the rules for evaluating sources. Thus any biography intended to boast scholarly objectivity represents a serious challenge, since the biographer must first find the testimonies and other relevant documents and then subject them to critical evaluation. (No matter how credible the sources found, the researcher is never dispensed from the arduous task of choosing testimonies, evaluating their significance, and fitting them into the historical picture.)

Abundance of sources. When I felt I had completed the task of collecting testimonies and other historical records and tried to sketch out the structure of this book, I was surprised to see how much material I had collected. To reduce it to manageable proportions, I found I had to concentrate on the founder himself and not get sidetracked into secondary matters. Thus those aspects of Opus Dei that are intimately linked to his personal mission are dealt with fully; other subjects, important in themselves, such as the origins of the spirituality of Opus Dei, the expansion of its message throughout the world, salient features of the cultural and social milieu in which the founder worked, and so forth, are only touched upon. All of that, undoubtedly, will be material for future studies. But here I have confined myself narrowly to biographical matters, to keep the narrative from straying from its subject. Meanwhile, as the notes demonstrate, I have subjected myself to the rigorous rules of documentation and the other critical requirements for historical credibility.

An objective view of historical reality. In this research effort, we can be particularly thankful for one quality of the founder and his writings. I refer to his objective view of events. Father Josemaría possessed in a high degree the intellectual gift of being able to evaluate historical realities objectively and clearly. He was always on the alert to see things and situations in the light of God's designs, setting aside his personal tastes and inclinations and detaching himself from personal interests. In relation to God, the track of his life runs straight, simple, and deep. One might summarize it by saying that he dedicated himself body and soul to fulfilling the plans of God with regard to Opus Dei. On October 2, 1928, after ten years of waiting, and of having premonitions of something that was going to come, he was led by the hand of God into the saga. The young priest received the mission of carrying out Opus Dei, and was granted the corresponding charism. From this date on, God and Josemaría—Josemaría led by the hand of God, that is—will have together one long and amazing adventure.

The two themes of this biography. Here, then, is one basic theme of this biography: to follow step by step the development of Opus Dei, to the point where the man chosen to carry out this great enterprise puts the final period to his work. Father Josemaría devoted his whole life to this effort. This is as much as to say that the charism he received worked, during all those years, within his soul, identifying his person with Opus Dei, making him—the man himself—Opus Dei. That is the other theme of this biography.

Divine logic and human logic. As a father with his child, God taught Josemaría a divine logic, at times very disconcerting, that is far different from any human logic. Human logic judges and operates according to earthly criteria. God's judgments, on the contrary, are lovingly grounded in the sense of divine filiation; in the cross, the joyful sign of Christ's victory; in the unlimited power of prayer; in the hidden fruitfulness of setbacks . . . That objective view that the founder had of historical reality was something more than just clear-sighted discernment; it was the gift of being able to penetrate the essence of history, its wise governance by Divine Providence. He applied to religious realities and supernatural events the categories proper to divine logic, in accordance with his divine and universal mission within the Church.

The stature of the founder. To properly appreciate his greatness, one must go back in time and accompany him as he gradually acquires spiritual maturity. His path of interior growth is at the same time a stream of love and a Way of the Cross of suffering, through a progressive identification with Christ. There is, then, no need for hagiographic panegyrics, since his sanctity is obvious and rises so impressively before us.

Shortly after receiving his divine mission, Father Josemaría (in entry no. 244 of his journal, *Apuntes íntimos*) compared himself to a "poor little bird" which can only fly a short distance. An eagle snatches it up, "and in his powerful claws the little bird soars, soars very high, above the mountains of earth and the snow-capped peaks, above the white and blue and rosy clouds, and higher yet, until he is looking directly at the sun . . .

And then the eagle, letting go of the bird, tells him, 'Go on—fly!' " In the pages of this book we will also try to project a vision of the mystical path of a soul.

The father of a large family. God raised up a man, in this world of our time, to bring about a great good for the Church and for souls. This is a divine gift for which thanks are due, primarily to God, and also, in part, to Father Josemaría, for cooperatively taking it upon himself to carry out God's plans. Far from turning his back on the world, he was interested in its development and progress. He put daring and optimism into his apostolic enthusiasms and ceaselessly proclaimed that sanctity is not just for the privileged few. With his message he in fact opened "the divine paths of the earth"—paths of sanctification for all those who in the midst of the world identify themselves with Christ, working for love of God and neighbor.

Within the mission of the founder was included the charism of paternity: he was father and shepherd of a portion of the People of God. Like the patriarchs of old, he already in his life-time had many descendants—spiritual descendants. On May 17, 1992, the day on which the Church officially raised him to the altars, an immense multitude of children of his spirit, people of all races and all conditions of life, packed St. Peter's Square in Rome.

*   *   *

I wish to express my gratitude for the extremely valuable help I received from the late Bishop Alvaro del Portillo, former prelate of Opus Dei; from his successor, Bishop Javier Echevarría, its present prelate; and from all those who have been so kind as to check for accuracy some of the data included in this book.

Finally, I must confess that, led by a desire not to leave any loose ends in this story, no matter how small they might appear, I am continuing to revise my drafts of the two remaining volumes.

1

Barbastro Years (1902–1915)

1. Family background

Josemaría Escrivá de Balaguer was born in the Spanish city of Barbastro on January 9, 1902, and died in Rome on June 26, 1975. A few weeks before his death, trying to bring his life into sharp focus, he expressed a deep awareness of Divine Providence: "Our Lord has made me see how he has been leading me by the hand."[1] There was for him just one pivotal date between the years 1902 and 1975: October 2, 1928, the day Opus Dei was founded. This supernatural event marked his life so profoundly that almost every autobiographical reference reflects an indelible consciousness of a personal mission. Describing his arrival into the world, he says, "God our Lord was preparing things so that my life would be normal and everyday, nothing extraordinary. He had me born in a Christian home, as was typical in my country, of exemplary parents who practiced and lived their faith."[2]

Josemaría was born near the end of a winter's day, at about ten o'clock at night. For this reason he used to say, with a twinkle in his eye, that his first moments had been like the footsteps of "a sleepwalker," for he had begun life with a whole night ahead of him. But in saying this he probably also was making a veiled allusion to the long night of obscurity that for years enveloped his spiritual mission.[3]

On the next day, January 10, he was entered into the city register of births. These facts were recorded there:

5

That said boy was born at 10:00 P.M. yesterday in the home of his parents, at 26 Calle Mayor.

That he is the legitimate son of Don José Escrivá, merchant, 33 years old, and of Doña Dolores Albás, 23 years old, of Fonz and Barbastro respectively.

That he is the grandson, on his father's side, of Don José Escrivá, deceased, and of Doña Constancia Cerzán [*sic*], natives of Peralta de la Sal and Fonz respectively.

And on his mother's side, of Don Pascual Albás, deceased, and of Doña Florencia Blanc, natives of Barbastro.

And that said boy has been registered with the names of José María, Julián, and Mariano.[4]

A few days later, on January 13, the Octave of the Epiphany and the feast of the Baptism of our Lord, he was baptized in the cathedral of Barbastro with the names that were already inscribed in the city register: José, for his father and grandfather; María, out of devotion to the Blessed Virgin; Julián, for the saint on whose feast day he was born; and Mariano, in honor of his godfather.[5]

Through the years, Josemaría showed deep gratitude toward the priest who had conferred this sacrament on him. His name was Angel Malo [bad angel]—a name not easily forgotten! Father Josemaría remembered him every day in the Memento of the Masses he celebrated over the course of half a century.[6] He showed the same kind of gratitude to his godparents.

The baptismal font of the cathedral of Barbastro was an elegant and beautiful piece, one of the works of art described in the cathedral chapter's *Liber de Gestis* for the year 1635.[7] But its antiquity and beauty did not afford it much protection. In 1936, when iconoclastic fury raged through the city, it was broken into pieces and thrown into the river.* Thousands of Christians had received their baptism in this font—including Josemaría's

* During the Spanish Civil War (1936–1939) many churches were sacked. The cathedral of Barbastro was among them.

mother. As a boy he had seen his little sisters baptized in it. Its remnants were worthy of respectful treatment. So, when in 1957 the bishop and the cathedral chapter presented him with the fragments salvaged from the wreckage, he decided to have them sent to Rome to be reassembled and set up in a place of honor. In 1959 he wrote:

> The fragments of the baptismal font of Barbastro's cathedral, which Your Excellency and the Most Excellent Cathedral Chapter have been so good as to donate to Opus Dei, have arrived in Rome. I cannot fail to express my thanks to Your Excellency—and I will also directly thank the Chapter—for this generosity, which has so moved me.
>
> Those venerable stones of our holy cathedral church, once well restored here in Italy by these sons of mine, will occupy a place of honor in our central headquarters.
>
> Thank you once again, Your Excellency, for this act of kindness. We will forever remember it with profound appreciation.[8]

The baptismal font was not the only casualty of that Marxist barbarism. The city register of Barbastro suffered even greater harm. Documents and entire archives were reduced to ashes. The birth certificate now in Barbastro is not, then, the original of 1902, but, rather, a certified copy made in 1912.[9] One might note that this copy has a few slight errors with regard to names and places. This would have meant little to Josemaría's father were it not for the fact that a particular spelling mistake was injurious to him and his family.

The fact is that in some documents the name "Escrivá" shows up misspelled as "Escribá."[10] This spelling error is really quite innocent and not at all surprising, given the fact that in Spanish there is no phonetic difference between the letters *b* and *v*. The trouble is, though, that if the name is pronounced without the accent being put on the final syllable, it immediately suggests something very different: the Gospel's pairing, not at all complimentary, of "scribes and Pharisees."

When his classmates flippantly joked about the *"escribas and Pharisees,"* these little taunts made Josemaría blush.[11] Nor did his sister Carmen escape these digs. The situation continued until one day their indignant father rose in defense of the family name and insisted that Josemaría never put up with such an affront. This advice became so deeply engraved in the mind of the son that he waged war on the offending *b*. In May or June of 1935, in a note about his interior life, he said regarding the special care he took with his signature, "Around 1928 I began to exaggerate the *v* in my family name just so that nobody would write 'Escrivá' with a *b*." And a few years later, in a note written in October 1939, he said, "It was my father (who is now in heaven) who ordered me not to tolerate having that *b* put in my family name. He said something to me about our heritage . . ."[12]

Even the priest who baptized him at the cathedral did not avoid that spelling error. Monsignor Escrivá did not discover the mistake on his baptismal certificate until 1960, as we can read in a letter he wrote to someone who had just sent him a photocopy of it. "I was happy," he says, "to receive the photocopy of my baptismal certificate, but I notice that the good Father Angel Malo made a mistake in the name 'Escrivá,' writing it with a *b*. Would it be possible—I'm sure it would be—to add a marginal note correcting this?"[13]

Similar complaints show that Josemaría's defense of his family name was a campaign of long duration. This manifestation of family loyalty reveals, too, a deep understanding between father and son.

But who were the Escrivás? Where did their ancestors come from? During the twelfth century, forebears of theirs came from Narbonne and crossed the Pyrenees to settle in the Catalonian region of Balaguer, in the district of Lérida, which borders on Upper Aragon. The branch of the Escrivás which remained in that region attached the place name "de Balaguer" to the family name, while another part of the family established themselves in Valencia after Jaime I the Conquistador took that city in 1238.[14] Josemaría Escrivá, being a descendant of the Catalonian branch, in 1940 requested and obtained legal permission to use "Escrivá de Balaguer" as his last name to distinguish him from the other branches of the family.[15]

Josemaría's great-grandfather José María Escrivá Manonelles, who was born in Balaguer in 1796, studied medicine in Perarrúa, settled there, and married Victoriana Zaydín y Sarrado.* The couple had six children, one of whom became a priest. Their second child, José Escrivá Zaydín, married Constancia Corzán Manzana, a native of Fonz, uniting illustrious names of the Ribagorza lineages with some of those of the Somontano Aragonese. This couple also had six children. The youngest, José, became the father of our Josemaría.[16]

Don José Escrivá Zaydín—who, since he died in 1894, never knew his grandson—held positions in local government from time to time, having to ride out the fluctuations and misfortunes of that era. As we know, there were fierce ideological and partisan battles, various Carlist wars, and, on several occasions, blatant persecutions of the Church. Judging by the anecdotes about him that have come down to us, he seems to have been a man who was very conservative in his habits and deeply rooted in the village in which he had established himself, since Fonz, the ancestral home of his mother, is where all the family remained—all, that is, except the youngest son, the father of Josemaría.[17]

Perhaps the crises which the farming country of Upper Aragon suffered in the years around 1887 forced young José to earn his living away from Fonz. The persistent droughts, the severe snowstorms, and, as a finishing touch to those disasters, the plant lice in the vineyards forced many to abandon

---

* In Spain it is customary to use both the father's and the mother's last names, at least in formal situations. In the case of José María Escrivá Manonelles, his father's last name was Escrivá, and his mother's maiden name was Manonelles, and so, when he wanted to give his name in short form, he called himself José Escrivá.

their lands. At any rate, it is clear that by some time in 1892 the young man had already established himself in Barbastro, a short distance from Fonz.[18] He lived on Rio Ancho Street, in a house owned by Cirilo Latorre, on the ground floor of which was a textile business actually named Cirilo Latorre, but more commonly known in the village as Casa Servando. Shortly after the death of his father, young José joined with Jerónimo Mur and Juan Juncosa to create a company called Successors of Cirilo Latorre. Later, when Señor Mur retired in 1902, the other two partners set up a new company called Juncosa & Escrivá.[19]

*   *   *

Doña Dolores Albás y Blanc, Josemaría's mother, belonged to a family originally from Aínsa, the capital of Sobrarbe, which is halfway between Barbastro and the peaks of the Pyrenees. In the eighteenth century the Albás family became part of the rural nobility of the region, but they did not establish themselves in Barbastro until well into the nineteenth century, when, in 1830, a certain Manuel Albás Linés married Simona Navarro y Santías.[20] Four children were born of this marriage. The older two, Pascual and Juan, married on the same day two sisters: Florencia and Dolores Blanc. The two couples apparently got along quite well, since they occupied adjoining apartments in the same building (at 20 Via Romero). Soon, because of all the children living there, the building became known as "the children's house."[21]

Pascual and Florencia already had twelve children (nine surviving) when Florencia gave birth to twin daughters in 1877. The girls were baptized with the names Dolores and María de la Concepción. The latter died two days after birth. The other grew up and became the mother of Josemaría. And when he, as a priest, wanted to emphasize the great spiritual benefit of early initiation into Christian life through baptism, he cited the case of his parents, "who were baptized on the very day they were born, even though they were born healthy."[22] This is corroborated by their baptismal certificates. His mother's reads, "I . . . solemnly baptized a girl born at two o'clock in the afternoon of this same day [March 23, 1877]." And his father's reads, "I . . . solemnly baptized a boy born at twelve o'clock noon of this same day [October 15, 1867]."[23]

As we see, the family was large and solidly Catholic. Thus it is not surprising that at the time of his reception into the bosom of Holy Mother the Church, the infant Josemaría had three uncles who were priests: Father Teodoro, a brother of Don José; and Vicente and Carlos, brothers of Doña Dolores. He also had, on his mother's side, two aunts who were nuns: Cruz and Pascuala. And that is to say nothing of more distant relatives.[24]

On January 10, 1938, during the Spanish Civil War, when the founder was in Burgos, he met a parish priest from Madrid who told him with great delight that he was a friend of Carlitos, Alfredo, and José, three priest relatives of his mother.[25] This anecdote was usually capped off with the remark, "You see, my mother's family has acquaintances even in Siberia!"[26] This was, of course, just an expression, simply a reference to the number of his mother's relatives. Don Carlos, Don Alfredo, and Don José were three priests related to those two brothers who married sisters on the same day.

On September 19, 1898, Don José Escrivá, "a bachelor, native of Fonz, resident of Barbastro, merchant," contracted marriage with Doña Dolores Albás, "a single woman, native and resident of Barbastro." The groom was thirty; the bride was twenty-one. The marriage was celebrated in the chapel of Santo Cristo de los Milagros (Christ of the Miracles) in the cathedral. The priest was Father Alfredo Sevil: uncle of the bride, vicar general of the archdiocese of Valladolid, one of those relatives known "even in Siberia."[27]

The Christ of the Miracles was a beautiful medieval wood carving kept in a chapel within the cathedral precincts. Originally, in 1714, the chapel had been constructed on one of the bastions of the old fortress. This fusion of cathedral with rampart, so frequently found in the many fortress cities of the Middle Ages, was a symbol reflecting the history of the city's inhabitants.

The saga of Barbastro began with the rising of the native population against the Romans on the death of Julius Caesar. This was followed by a siege of the town by the legion of Sextus Pompey. Later there came successive and unstoppable waves of invaders: Visigoths, Franks, and Muslims. Barbastro grew, and in the eleventh century it became an important and well-fortified garrison town of the Moorish kingdom of Saragossa. An Arab historian called it "the country's citadel." It was a rich and populous city, with good gardens and even better walls. In 1064 Christians laid siege to the fortress, since it was a wedge that extended Moorish power as far as the valleys of the Pyrenees. Pope Alexander II proclaimed a crusade, and troops from Italy and Burgundy answered the call. Near Barbastro they were joined by Norman soldiers under the command of the duke of Aquitaine, by the forces of the bishop of Vichy, and by Catalonians led by the count of Urgel.[28] In August of that year the Christian troops broke into the fortified town, but they were forced out the following year after a brief siege led by Moctádir, the Moorish king of Saragossa. In that passing victory of the Christians, legend found a basis for elaborating a heroic epic poem (having little to do with history) entitled *Le siège de Barbastre*.[29]

In 1100 the city was definitively reconquered by King Pedro I of Aragon, who then granted it a municipal charter. The main mosque was converted into a cathedral, to which the old episcopal see of Roda was transferred. It was in the cathedral of Barbastro that the union of Aragon and Catalonia was forged, through the marriage of Doña Petronila, daughter of King Ramiro "the Monk," to King Ramón Berenguer IV of Catalonia. Barbastro was granted the rank of a city of nobility and was the seat of a royal court convoked in 1196. Its glory would not last long. The cities of Upper Aragon would become shadows of the past as the military and commercial frontiers moved south. But the Aragonese historian Jerónimo Zurita mentions that after the taking of Barbastro, the rough mountaineers of the north "made war on the Moors, not in the measured, step-by-step way that they had done this before, but with incredible fury and excess."[30]

Time went by. The walls and turrets which for so many years had encircled the two old castles of Barbastro were demolished in 1710 by the duke of Atalaya. And, it is said, it was on the site of one of those castles that the chapel in which the parents of Josemaría were married was built. The moat was filled with earth, which made it easier for the city to spread out, and the bastions were flattened.

Barbastro enjoyed centuries of peace, disturbed only on rare occasions. But in its heart there remained embedded the thorn of historic unrest.

King Pedro I, after taking Barbastro, created there a diocesan see which rivaled that of neighboring Huesca. This caused interminable ecclesiastical conflicts. In 1500, to reaffirm their independence from the diocese of Huesca, the citizens of Barbastro built a cathedral of their own. Stubbornly insisting on its claims, they finally succeeded, through petitions and pressure brought to bear by King Philip II, in getting Pope Pius V to establish the diocese of Barbastro. But just when the diocese got to the point of "rocking serenely in the shade of its glorious memories and traditions," laments a historian of the last century, it was once again incorporated into the diocese of Huesca, by virtue of the Concordat of 1851 between Spain and the Holy See, and the cathedral was sadly relegated to the category of a collegiate church.[31]

The whole city felt hurt and insulted by that deed. And this created a certain understanding between Barbastro's ecclesiastical and civil authorities. Thanks to the tenacity of the city's administrators, application of this provision of the Concordat remained suspended. Later, in accord with the wishes of the Holy See and by a royal decree enacted in

1896, an apostolic administrator was appointed for the diocese.[32]

*   *   *

Soon after their wedding, José and Dolores Escrivá moved into a house on Calle Mayor—a house facing the impressive Argensola building. The apartment they lived in was a large one. Some of its balconies looked out onto the corner of the adjacent plaza, which was in the very center of the city, not far from General Ricardos Street, on which was located José's business—the one bearing the trade name Sucesores de Cirilo Latorre.

In 1899, on the feast of Our Lady of Mount Carmel (July 16), a daughter was born to the young couple. She was given the names María del Carmen, Constancia, and Florencia (the last two in honor of her grandmothers). On the baptismal certificate of their daughter, the parents are described as "residents and merchants" of Barbastro.[33] The term "merchants" did not call into question their social position, notes the Baroness of Valdeolivos (with some obvious concern for status distinctions), because "the merchants, in those days in Barbastro, were the city's aristocracy." She adds that the couple's financial situation was "good and comfortable" and that they were "highly esteemed in the town."[34]

Don José, an enterprising and methodical type of person, had within a few years of establishing himself in Barbastro a network of commercial contacts that extended throughout the entire region, although his center of operations continued to be the building on General Ricardos Street. Barbastro, the chief town in the district, was the commercial center for many of the surrounding villages, and had over seven thousand residents. Because of its good location—between Huesca and Lérida, two provincial capitals—and because of its railroad connection with the Barcelona-Saragossa line, it was the center of trade and other business transactions for the whole region. Its periodic agricultural and cattle fairs kept this activity alive.

After eight years of permanent residence, Don José Escrivá already had a well-established place in the social life of Barbastro. He was a familiar sight at church, on the street, and at the club. His elegant appearance alone was enough to attract attention. From afar one could see the careful way he dressed—conservative, and very tasteful. He wore a derby hat and carried a walking stick, as was the custom at the time. He was a gentleman, courteous, agreeable, and kind, although not overly outgoing, and somewhat sparing in his speech. He always showed fairness toward his subordinates, generosity toward the needy, and piety toward God. His time was basically divided between business and home.[35]

Both business and home prospered. When 1902 arrived, the couple had another child: a boy, born on January 9. He was given, as his first name, the name of his father. (Years later he combined his first two baptismal names to form "Josemaría," because of his devotion to Saint Joseph and the Blessed Virgin Mary. He always thought of them as being together.[36])

With a new baby in the house, Doña Dolores ("Lola" to her family) had another person to look after; and there was also the nanny. The lady of the house, almost ten years younger than her husband, was a woman of medium height, genteel manners, and a serene beauty. Graced with a natural dignity, she was sincere and easygoing in her conversation. Those who knew her considered her outstanding for her "patience and balanced personality," inherited, perhaps, from her mother, Florencia, who did such a good job rearing her own large family, of whom Doña Lola was the second to youngest child.[37]

Following the obstinate tug-of-war between the episcopal sees and then the reestablishment of peace by the royal decree of 1896, in 1898 (the year of the wedding of Josemaría's parents) Bishop Antonio Ruano y Martín was installed as the first apostolic administrator of Barbastro. The new prelate found himself faced with such a backlog of work that he set out to handle it with sweeping measures. On April 23, 1902, using broad criteria and implementing a traditional and legitimate practice of the Spanish churches (a practice dating back to the Middle Ages), he administered the sacrament of Confirmation to all the children of the city: 130 boys and 127 girls.[38] In the parish record of this collective Confirmation, the names of all the children are entered, in alphabetical order. In the boys' group appears Josemaría, who was then three months old, and in the girls' group, his sister Carmen, who was not quite three years.[39]

When the boy was about two years old, his parents felt the time had come to start making a historical record of his childhood. But when they tried to take, for the family album, a photo of him naked, he cried so hard and threw such a fit that they gave up that idea. Doña Lola, with resignation and patience, put his clothes back on him. The photo taken for posterity catches him in a moment in which he can't decide whether to cry or not, with something between a pout and a smile on his face.[40]

Around that time he came down with a serious illness, possibly an acute infection, and nearly died. Relatives and acquaintances remember this episode in detail. The doctors had given up on the child; they had "already predicted a fatal outcome, inevitable and imminent."[41] One evening, Dr. Ignacio Camps Valdovinos, the family doctor, came to visit the child. He was an experienced physician with a good clinical eye, but in those days there was no way to stop the course of a virulent infection. Given the seriousness of the situation, another doctor who was a friend of the family—Dr. Santiago Gómez Lafarga, a homeopathic physician—had also come to the Escrivá home. But there came a moment when Dr. Camps had to say to Don José, "I'm sorry, Pepe, he won't make it through the night."

With much faith, the parents went on asking God to cure their son. Doña Dolores, with great confidence, began a novena to Our Lady of the Sacred Heart, and the couple promised our Lady that if their child recovered, they would take him on a pilgrimage to her shrine of Torreciudad.

Early the next morning, assuming that the child had died, Dr. Camps called on the family again, to share their sorrow. "What time did the boy die?" was the first question he asked when he came in. Don José joyfully answered that not only was he not dead, but he was completely cured. The doctor went into the little one's room and saw him in his crib, holding on to the bars and jumping around like any healthy child.

The parents kept their promise. On horseback, along winding mountain trails, they traveled the fourteen long miles. Doña Lola, riding sidesaddle and carrying the boy in her arms, was frightened by all the jolting they experienced between the crags and deep gorges which plunge to the Cinca River. Perched on a steep hilltop is the shrine of Torreciudad. There, at the feet of our Lady, they offered the child in thanksgiving.[42]

Recalling this episode years later, Doña Dolores repeated more than once to her son, "My son, it must be for something great that our Lady left you in this world, because you were more dead than alive."[43] For his part, Josemaría left written testimony, in 1930, of his conviction that he had been cured by the Blessed Virgin: "My Lady and my Mother! You gave me the grace of my vocation; you saved my life when I was a child; you have listened to me so many times!"[44]

2. *"Those fair days of my childhood"*

Not a trace of that illness remained. Josemaría enjoyed very good health. He was, in fact, "the envy of all the mothers of Barbastro," who day after day saw the boy sitting on the balcony, legs dangling between the bars, and happily waving to the passers-by.[45]

Strong and lively, the little boy also had a great capacity for observation, thanks to which he forever retained in his memory things from very early in his life. Among those first memories were the prayers that he learned from the lips of his mother, and which, with the help of Don José or Doña Dolores, he recited upon awakening or when going to bed. These were children's prayers, short and simple, to the Child Jesus, our Lady, or his guardian angel. Here is one of them:

> O Guardian Angel, to you I pray,
> Desert me not, by night or day.
> If you were to leave me, where would I be?
> O Guardian Angel, pray for me.[46]

He also learned some prayers from his grandmothers. Here is one example:

> Yours am I, I was born for Thee.
> What is it, O Jesus, you want of me?[47]

Later he learned to recite the "Blessed Be Your Purity" prayer* and this act of self-offering to our Lady:

> O my Lady, O my Mother, I dedicate myself entirely to you. As proof of my filial affection, I consecrate to you this day my eyes, my ears, my tongue, my heart—in a word, my whole self. Now that I am entirely yours, O Mother of Goodness, guard and defend me as something of your very own.[48]

Throughout his life he felt very grateful to his parents for those prayers, which were forever engraved in his mind and heart. He recited them frequently and returned to them in moments of spiritual dryness.[49]

He had not yet attained full use of reason when he started to enjoy taking part in the family Rosary, going to Mass with his parents, and attending Saturday services at Saint Bar-

---

*In English the prayer goes as follows: "Blessed be your purity, may it be blessed forever, for no less than God takes delight in such exalted beauty. To you, heavenly Princess, Holy Virgin Mary, I offer on this day my whole heart, life, and soul. Look upon me with compassion. Do not leave me, my Mother."

tholomew's (an oratory, close to their house, where the Escrivás went each Saturday to pray the Hail Holy Queen).[50] And he had very fond memories connected with the family's Christmas celebrations. Together with Carmen, he would help his father put up the Nativity scene. And the whole family sang Christmas carols together. He remembered in particular the one which begins, "Mother, there's a little boy at the door." This carol has a verse in which the Child Jesus repeats, "I have come down to earth to suffer." The song stayed with him from the cradle to the grave. "When I was three years old," he would tell us, "my mother would take me in her arms and sing me that song, and I would very happily go to sleep."[51] In his last years he would be visibly moved, and would become totally absorbed in prayer, whenever he heard this song at Christmastime.

* * *

Doña Lola devoted herself completely to her household. Together with her husband, she centered her efforts on the education of Carmen and Josemaría, creating a family environment to which those children whom the Lord later would send would be added. The mistress of the house was a strong-minded woman with lots of common sense. So when her son, who like all other children had his whims and little likes and dislikes, stubbornly refused to eat something, she would calmly say to him, "You don't want to eat this? All right, don't eat it"; but she did not give him anything else in its place.[52]

One day they set before him a dish he did not like. Realizing he would then have to go hungry, he threw it against the wall, which was papered. They did not change the paper. For several months the splotch remained there, so that the memory of his tantrum would be impressed on the child.[53]

The fine pedagogical gifts of his mother sometimes included a judicious use of proverbial sayings or moral axioms. To instances of carelessness, such as throwing clothes on the

floor or leaving things in a mess, she would respond by saying, "It's not somebody else's job to put back in order what
we mess up." She never ill-treated the domestic help or
considered it beneath her dignity to serve others. "My rings
won't fall off!" she used to say, and her example was a
gentle and continual invitation to her children. She also
warned her children against making rash judgments, saying to them, "We can easily misunderstand what other people say." She said this so that they would never be scandalized on the basis of a mere suspicion.[54]

Through the years, wise words heard from Doña Dolores
appear here and there in Josemaría's reflections on human behavior. He tells us, for example:

> When I was a child, two things bothered me a lot: hav-
> ing to kiss my mother's women friends who came to visit,
> and wearing new clothes.
>
> When I was dressed up in new clothes, I would hide
> under the bed and stubbornly refuse to come out. My mother
> would give a few gentle taps on the floor, with one of the
> canes that my father used, and then I would come out—for
> fear of the cane, not for any other reason.
>
> Afterward my mother would say to me affectionately,
> "Josemaría, be ashamed only of sin." Many years later it
> dawned on me what a depth of meaning was in those
> words.[55]

It should be said on the boy's behalf that he had ample reason for finding it distasteful to be kissed by those good
women—especially one very elderly lady (a distant relative of
his grandmother) who had developed a bit of a mustache,
which scratched the child's face. His mother, of course, realized how much discomfort these kisses caused Josemaría,
whose face was often left smudged with powder and lipstick.
So when one of these visitors was announced, Doña Dolores
would tell her son with a mischievous wink, "Mrs. So-and-So

is coming well stuccoed, so we can't make her laugh or else her face will peel off."[56]

The children never heard their parents quarrel. In their home there was always affection, respect, and good treatment of the household staff, who were like part of the family. When any of the maids got married, the couple would provide her with a trousseau, as if she were their own daughter.[57]

The parents were early risers, even though they went to bed after the rest of the household. In the morning, Don José left for work with such strict punctuality that one always knew where he was and when he would come home. The boy would wait with great impatience and excitement for his return. Sometimes he was too excited to wait, and would go out to meet him. At times, Josemaría would go to the store on General Ricardos Street and entertain himself by counting the coins in the cash register, and his father would take advantage of the occasion to explain the basics of addition and subtraction. And on the way home, in the fall, Don José would buy roasted chestnuts and put them in the pocket of his overcoat. Then Josemaría, standing on tiptoe, would put in his little hand in search of the chestnuts, and would get a tender squeeze from his father's hand.[58]

For many years the people of Barbastro saw them take walks together. That intimate relationship of confidence and friendship between father and son was due to the solicitude of Don José, which bred in Josemaría generosity and sincerity. He never spanked him, though once he did give him an affectionate slap. This was when the boy stubbornly refused to sit in a high chair in the dining room because he wanted to be like the grown-ups.[59]

His father invited him to open his heart, and to share with him all his concerns, in order to help the child learn to control the impulsive outbursts of his budding personality and sacrifice personal preferences and whims. Don José listened to him unhurriedly and answered to the boy's satisfaction the questions that arose from a child's curiosity about life. Josemaría was happy to see that his father made himself available to be consulted, and that whenever he asked a question, "he always took him seriously."[60]

Both husband and wife taught their children to practice charity with deeds and without ostentation, sometimes simply by the giving of spiritual counsel, at other times with the addition of some alms. At that time it was customary in many Spanish towns and villages for the more well-to-do households to give weekly alms on a particular day. A nephew tells us that the Escrivás practiced that custom. "Don José," says Pascual Albás, "was a great almsgiver. Every Saturday there was a long line of poor people who came looking for alms, and he always had something for each of them."[61]

Young Josemaría retained a vague memory of a Gypsy woman who did not come on Saturday like the other poor people. From time to time he saw her enter the house, at his mother's invitation, with a quiet self-assurance. The Gypsy, as if wrapped in mystery, went in to speak with Doña Dolores where they knew they would not be interrupted: in her bedroom, where not even the closest relatives were invited. The boy never found out the reason for these unusual visits. He only knew, in a very vague way, that this Gypsy woman (whose name was Teresa) was someone who made great sacrifices for her people and came to his mother for comfort and guidance.[62]

For the boy it was a real pleasure to give to the beggars asking for alms at the entrance of the cathedral the coins Don José gave him as they set out for Mass on Sundays and holy days.[63] When they arrived at the cathedral, which was a dauntingly austere mass of stone, Josemaría compassionately rushed to help a poor disabled man stationed near the entrance. Then, once inside, he looked up—by the light sifting in through the high windows—from the intricacies of slender columns to ornate ribbed arches in a vaulted ceiling. As he passed one of the side chapels, he was always captivated by a beautiful image there: a recumbent statue of our Lady. There was something about her expression that the boy found gently fascinating. On the feast of the Assumption this statue was presented for the veneration of the faithful, since it depicted the Dormition of our Lady.

When this same feast came around a quarter of a century later, on August 15, 1931, these deeply felt childhood memories welled up in his heart. This is how he described it:

> Feast of the Assumption of our Lady, 1931. . . . I truly rejoice, feeling like I'm there, with the Blessed Trinity, with the angels receiving their Queen, with all the saints acclaiming our Lady and Mother.
>
> And I remember those fair days of my childhood: the cathedral, so ugly on the outside and so beautiful within . . . like the heart of that land—good, Christian, and loyal—hidden under the rough exterior of the Aragonese peasant.
>
> Then, in the middle of one of the side chapels, there stood a catafalque on which rested a recumbent image of our Lady. The people went by, respectfully kissing the feet of the Blessed Virgin of the Bed.
>
> My mother, my father, my sisters, and I always went together to Mass. My father gave us the alms that we happily brought to the disabled man who leaned against the wall of the bishop's house. After that, I went on ahead to get holy water to give to my family.* Then, Holy Mass. Afterward, every Sunday, in the chapel of the Christ of the Miracles, we prayed the Creed. And on the feast of the Assumption, as I've already mentioned, it was obligatory to "adore," as we used to say, the Virgin of the Cathedral.[64]

* * *

In his parents' home, Father Josemaría recalled, "I was given a Christian upbringing. I received more formation in the

---

*He is referring here to the custom, practiced in many countries, of dipping one's hand in the holy water and then, by touching their fingers, passing it along to friends or relatives entering behind one.

faith there than at school, even though at the age of three I was taken to a school run by nuns, and then, at the age of seven, to one run by a religious order of priests."[65]

The nuns were Daughters of Charity. Their preschool and kindergarten, which Josemaría attended from 1905 to 1908, consisted of a single room with several levels. On the bottom level, the younger children were entertained with toys and songs and were taught the alphabet. Meanwhile, in the back of the room, the part at higher levels, the nuns divided the older children into separate groups and taught them catechism, Bible stories, and some "Basic Ideas of the Natural Sciences." (These last classes were also known by the less lofty title of "Lessons about Things.") Josemaría stood out in the kindergarten, not so much by his own merits as by the fact that his parents had already taught him some catechism and arithmetic, and had taught him to read. It was, however, a nun who initiated him into the first stages of writing.[66]

From those years in preschool and kindergarten, he would always particularly remember one painful thing that happened when he was just three. His memory of this incident resulted largely from the kind of impression that is produced by intense feelings or any too rough collision with reality. It was no blind impression. The boy's sensitivity, which was rather extraordinary, moved him to try to understand the meaning and consequences of things.

The incident was this. His nanny, when she came to pick him up at the end of the school day, was told that Josemaría had hit a little girl. This was not true, but he nevertheless was given a sharp reprimand, and the unfairness of the accusation hurt him deeply. Such an understanding of the meaning of justice did the experience give him that, from that day on, he remained firmly convinced of the importance of not judging until one has heard both sides of the story.[67]

The nuns had a good opinion of the youngster. In fact, in June 1908, when he completed kindergarten, they proposed him as a contender in the competition for the "Virtue Prize." This contest was part of a program of events set up by the apostolic administrator of Barbastro, Bishop Isidro Badia y Sarradell, to celebrate the golden anniversary of Pope Pius X's ordination to the priesthood.[68] A panel was selected to award the prizes. The children were vying for the "thirty pesetas of spending money" promised to "the child in each of the elementary schools of this city who best serves as a model for the others because of his or her application and good conduct."

October 4, 1908, was the date of the evening ceremony at which the bishop handed out certificates to the contestants. In the virtue contest there were four winners: one from the municipal elementary school, two from the Piarists' school, and Josemaría from the school of the Daughters of Charity.

At the close of the ceremony, a telegram was sent to Rome relaying to Pope Pius, for his jubilee, expressions of the filial love the whole diocese felt for him. It brought this response: "Rome, the 6th. To the Apostolic Administrator: The Holy Father thanks you for your filial homage on the occasion of his jubilee and with all his heart blesses Your Excellency and all the authorities, clergy, and faithful of Barbastro. Cardinal Merry del Val."[69]

3. *First Communion*

In October 1908 Josemaría became a pupil of the Piarist Fathers. Their school in Barbastro was the first that this religious order opened in Spain.[70] Its founder, Saint Joseph Calasanz, had been born in the very town in which Josemaría's paternal grandfather lived: Peralta de la Sal, which is about ten miles from Barbastro. The entrance to the school was not far from the Escrivá home.

Two days after receiving the telegram from Cardinal Merry del Val, the bishop of Barbastro started a pastoral visitation of the diocese. In the preceding month the people of the cathedral parish, Our Lady of the Assumption, were reminded that it would be good for adults and all children able to do so to receive the sacrament of Penance, so that they could receive the indulgences attached to the pastoral visitation. It was during that school year of 1908–1909, when the boy was attending the school of the Piarist Fathers, that Doña Dolores personally prepared her son for his First Confession. She then took him to her confessor, Father Enrique Labrador.[71] Josemaría was six or seven at this time.

In those days it was customary for men and boys to make their confession kneeling in front of the half door behind which the priest sat, while women and girls used the grille on the side. When the good Piarist greeted him, the boy knelt down, but he was too short to see over the half door. The priest had to open it and let him kneel inside. As the penitent confessed his sins, Father Labrador listened to him with a smile. For a moment the boy felt a little discouraged because he thought he was not being taken seriously, as he always was by his father. But then the confessor gave him a little advice and imposed on him a penance.

That first confession brought great peace to his soul. He ran home to announce that he had a penance to do. His mother offered to help him. "No," said the little one, "I have to do this penance all by myself. Father told me you should give me a fried egg."[72]

*   *   *

By this time Josemaría already had two younger sisters: María Asunción, born on August 15, 1905, and María de los Dolores, born on February 10, 1907. A third, María del Rosario, arrived on October 2, 1909.[73]

With five children, the mother had acquired plenty of experience in managing a flock of noisy offspring. As did most women of her social position in those days, she had a good staff of servants. Besides the cook and a cleaning woman, she had a nanny and also a young man who came in from time to time to do the jobs that were less suitable for women. Doña Dolores, a very hardworking woman with a great deal of practical sense, could always be seen putting order in the house. When the children came home from school, often with friends, they had a room set aside for their games—a room they called "the lions' den."[74] In dealing with them, she was discreetly flexible—or, on the contrary, inflexible, depending on the situation. Sometimes the little ones would get very noisy at table on special days, when chicken was served. Everyone had to have a leg! Doña Dolores, without getting upset, would simply multiply chicken legs: three, four, six, as many as were needed. But she didn't allow anyone to be unduly picky. Nor did she let the children go into the kitchen to eat between meals. The kitchen was, of course, a constant temptation for the children whereas Doña Dolores herself only went there occasionally, to see how things were going or to prepare some special treat.

One of these special treats was *crespillos* (little crepes), which showed up on her name day and on a few other special occasions.[75] This was a dessert anyone could afford and involving no culinary secret except knowing how to present it just right. It consisted simply of some spinach leaves coated with a batter of flour and eggs, fried with a little boiling oil, and then sprinkled with sugar and served hot. In the Escrivá home any "crespillos" day was a thrill.

Apart from sweets and fried potatoes and such, there was another reason for the boy to prowl the kitchen. The children would often be told little jokes or stories by the girls who worked there—especially María, the cook. She knew a story about thieves. It had no tragedy or violence, and it was the one and only story she knew. But she told it in such a masterful way that the child never tired of hearing it.[76] Listening to María was what started awakening his own gifts as a storyteller.

Some afternoons when Carmen came home from school with friends and they went to play in the "lions' den," Doña Dolores would graciously and affectionately entertain them or give them some old clothes to play with. "Often," recalls Esperanza Corrales, "we were invited to stay for snack time, and I remember that we were given bread with chocolate bars and oranges."[77]

If Josemaría was not out with his friends, he would come to the "lions' den" to amuse the girls. "He liked to entertain us," says the Baroness of Valdeolivos. "Often we would go to his house and he would take his toys out for us. He had lots of jigsaw puzzles."[78] He also had tin soldiers, and ninepins, and a large horse (made of heavy-duty cardboard) on wheels. The girls would take turns climbing onto it, and he would pull them around the apartment by the halter. And if one of them got too noisy, the owner of the horse would pacify her with a little pull of her braids.

"But what he liked best when he was with us," remembers Adriana, Esperanza's sister, "was to sit on a rocking chair in the living room and tell us stories—usually scary ones, intended to frighten us—that he made up himself. He had a vivid imagination, and we—this included his sisters Chon and Lolita, who were younger than Josemaría by three years and five years, respectively—listened to him attentively and were a little bit frightened."[79]

*   *   *

From 1908 to 1912, the year he started secondary school, Josemaría received his "primary education." According to the regulations then in effect, the school day consisted of six hours of class: three in the morning and three in the afternoon. But Josemaría had a more extended schedule. In the evening he did his homework under the supervision of a tutor, so that he would get more out of it. Year after year the pupils studied the same subjects, but in greater depth each year. The curriculum was an encyclopedic combination of different subjects ranging from basics of hygiene and rudiments of law to singing and drawing.[80]

The most specialized and outstanding instruction given in that school was in the art of handwriting. The Piarist Fathers were well known for the "Piarist script"—an elegant, distinctively Spanish style of lettering characterized by tall, thick strokes and a lack of any ornamentation or eccentricity.[81] You had to work at it a lot to master the skill. Beginners spoiled sheet after sheet of paper. Their lines veered off into capricious curves like the contours of a mountain range, while they stained their fingers dunking their pens in the ink wells. Then the teacher would come over and correct the children. He would show them how to hold the pen, and, to help them keep their lines straight, would put sheets of heavily lined paper under their writing sheets, so that they could follow the neat parallel lines that showed through the translucent paper.

Years later, these memories summoned up supernatural metaphors in Josemaría's mind. God in his omnipotence, he once said, does not need lined paper or even a pen. "As people write with a pen," he said, "our Lord writes with a leg of the desk, so that we can see that he's the one doing the writing."[82]

Josemaría soon acquired a handwriting that was readily recognizable throughout his life. His personality comes through in the energetic outlines, large and simple, that make even his earliest writing unmistakably identifiable, its strokes revealing a decisive, frank, and generous temperament.

From early childhood, his sister Carmen once said, "he was very careful not to violate the rights of others; he preferred to lose rather than have a classmate treated unfairly."[83] One of those classmates says something similar: Josemaría "was not quarrelsome; he readily gave in rather than quarrel."[84] That is not to say he was timid. That he wasn't can be deduced from a fight he had with a classmate nicknamed "Pig Foot." For reasons no one has recorded, the two of them fought it out until both were entirely satisfied. However, Josemaría learned from the experience that violence never changes the mind of one's opponent, so from then on he refused to have recourse to it.[85]

In his tendency to be generous with his companions we can see an incipient magnanimity joined to a great delicacy in his treatment of people, as appears from the fact that his fight with "Pig Foot" was so exceptional. One thing that made a lasting impression on him was an incident in which some children in Barbastro nailed a bat to the wall and mercilessly threw stones at it. Josemaría, whose natural sensitivity prevented him from taking part in such a cruel diversion, would never forget that terrible incident.[86]

He would also recall two occasions, when he was peacefully walking down the street and a dog came up from behind and bit him, with no warning or provocation. He bore the pain bravely and went to the house of his aunt Mercedes to have the wound treated, so as not to upset his mother.[87] Such occurrences toughened his character, enabling him to withstand greater moral and physical difficulties later on.

Never, though, did he manage to get over his natural dislike of wearing new clothes or calling attention to himself in any other way. Since he no longer could crawl under the bed, as he had done when he was small, he now adopted a new tactic. If, for example, the students were told to come to school dressed up for a class photo, Josemaría would not mention this at home. Later, when the photo was sent to his parents, Doña Dolores was caught by surprise, but there was no need for questions. She could see for herself that all the other mothers had made sure their children were appropriately dressed. Her child was the only one not wearing Sunday clothes. "Josemaría," she would say to him, "do you want us to buy you secondhand clothes?"[88]

Although the Escrivás were well-off, they economized, using things others might have considered no longer serviceable. Order prevailed. If a child broke a vase or some other valuable object, it would immediately be glued back together or sent out for repair. There were several clocks in the house, and they all told the same time. Don José, without being fanatic about it, loved punctuality, holding that with a lack of order one never knows where he will end up. The mistress of the house would often use a popular saying to get across this truth. When reminding her daughter Carmen to clean up after doing her needlework, for example, she would say, "With threads left lying around, the devil makes a rope."[89]

Josemaría's father was always his best friend. The boy would go to him for the solution to any kind of problem or difficulty, knowing that Don José would provide an answer that would satisfy him. Thus he came to understand, for instance, why his parents gave him very little money, and that, at the same time, they had a lot of respect for him and his decisions. They did not open his letters to or from his friends, nor did they spy on him. This confidence shown him by his parents contributed more than a little to making him self-controlled and responsible.

From Don José he learned about the "social question": about relations between labor and management, associations for the defense of the common interests of employees, and the much-debated issue of the just wage for workers.[90] There were no major social conflicts in Barbastro. It had no big industries, nor even any large estates. The petite bourgeoisie, the landholders who spent their time working in the fields, and the local merchants all peacefully shared their bread and their good manners with their employees. But despite all that and even though that city, following centuries-old tradition, remained practicing and pious in matters of religion, the country as a whole was being fragmented by ideological strife.

Barbastro was not exempt from the social conflicts taking place in the rest of the country. Differences found expression at the meetings of its various circles and clubs,
which had such names as "The Union," "The Future," "The
New Century," and "Friendship." (Don José was a member
of this last one.) The regional press reflected the currents of
opinion of the different groups. Newspapers of the time included *La Cruz del Sobrarbe, La Epoca, El País, El Eco del Vero,*
and *El Cruzado Aragonés.*[91]

Spanish Catholics found it very difficult to agree on how
to resolve the "social question." Pope Leo XIII, in his encyclical *Rerum Novarum* (May 15, 1891), had clarified doctrinally the ethical principles of the economic order, thus awakening the consciousness of the faithful. However, the
program of social renewal was a long time coming; the example of other countries pulled Spaniards along.[92]

Between 1902 and 1915, the people of Barbastro, and in
a special way Don José Escrivá, did seek a solution to the
problem. In 1903 they founded a newspaper, *El Cruzado
Aragonés* (The Aragon Crusader); in 1907 they created the
"Salón de Buenas Lecturas" (Good Publications Reading
Room); and in 1909 they set up a "Centro Católico Barbastrense" (Barbastro Catholic Center), whose purpose was to
"promote the defense and realization of a Christian civi-
lization and social order, in accord with the teachings of the
Church."[93] And undoubtedly all these projects brimmed
with good will. But the big battle was taking place in loftier
intellectual environments—the universities and the various
academic fields. Catholics soon suffered the consequences
of a regrettable intellectual laziness that had persisted for
centuries.

Don José was responsible for the employees of Juncosa &
Escrivá, and also for those of the chocolate shop attached to
the textile business. He was a good employer, not only paying
his workers a just wage but also tending to their spiritual

needs. Every year he arranged for them a series of Lenten conferences, paid for out of his own pocket, and adjusted the
work schedule so that everyone who wanted to attend these
conferences could, although, out of consideration, he himself
did not, lest they feel pressured to do so.[94]

* * *

In Spain, as in many other countries, children had not, as a
rule, been making their First Communion before the age of
twelve or thirteen. By a decree issued in 1910 by Pope Saint
Pius X, the age requirement was lowered to when the use of
reason is acquired, "which is at about the age of seven."[95] The
timing of this ruling coincided with preparations for the International Eucharistic Congress to be celebrated in Madrid in
June 1911. An intense catechetical effort was launched in all the
parishes of Spain, so that the greatest possible number of children could receive Holy Communion.

A Piarist priest named Manuel Laborda de la Virgen del
Carmen, or "Padre Manolé," as he was affectionately called by
his students, prepared Josemaría for his First Communion.
Some time before the long-awaited day arrived, he taught the
boy a prayer to use to keep that desire for the Eucharist ever
alive: "I wish, my Lord, to receive you with the purity, humility, and devotion with which your most holy Mother received
you; with the spirit and fervor of the saints."[96] From that time
on, Josemaría recited this prayer very often.

On the evening before the appointed day a hairdresser was
called in to give him a nice, elegant look; but while gathering
up some hair to make a curl, he burned the boy's scalp with
the hot curling iron. Josemaría suffered it in silence, to avoid
the hairdresser being taken to task or anyone getting upset.
His mother did eventually find out about it, but only much
later, when she discovered the scar left by the burn.[97] Thereafter he would find that on his special days, our Lord would

announce his presence with a touch of pain or a twinge that felt sweet, "like a caress."[98]

He made his First Communion on April 23, 1912, exactly ten years after his Confirmation. It was the feast of Saint George, patron saint of Aragon and Catalonia, and the traditional day for the First Communion ceremonies in the church of the Piarists' school. At the moment of Communion, Josemaría prayed for his parents and sisters and asked Jesus for the grace of never letting him lose him.

He would always observe with an unabashed fervor the anniversaries of that wonderful day on which our Lord, as he put it, "chose to come and take possession of my heart."[99]

4. *Family misfortunes*

On June 11, 1912, Josemaría went to the city of Huesca, the provincial capital, to take his entrance examination for secondary school.[100]

Upon his return, he found out that his sister Lolita was sick. Five years old, she was now the youngest child in the house, another of the girls, Rosario, having died two years earlier, on July 11, 1910, at the age of only nine months. On the eve of the second anniversary of the death of her sister, Lolita went to join her, leaving a sad void in the family.[101] There remained Josemaría and two sisters: Carmen, his older sister, and Chon (Asunción). Their parents accepted the misfortune very calmly, with no rebellion or turning away from God. Infant mortality was high in those days, though this did not make it any less sad for the children's families.

As they did every summer, the Escrivás went on vacation to Fonz, which, as was said earlier, is a village on the other side of the Cinca River, about ten miles from Barbastro. Situated on a small hill—the church at the very top, and the houses scattered along the sides—the town had a few well-to-do families still living in their ancestral homes. In one of these lived Josemaría's grandmother Constancia with two of her children: Josefa and Father Teodoro. A visit from her third son, accompanied by her daughter-in-law and the grandchildren from Barbastro, was always a thrill.

In those summer days Josemaría's childish curiosity, though never totally satisfied, was captivated by the things of nature. He absorbed the landscapes and scenes so full of color and movement, storing in his memory the wonderful little surprises he experienced every day. Years later, when it came time for him to teach about the interior life, the memories flowed warm and clear:

> During my summer vacations, when I was little, I loved to watch bread being made. Back then I wasn't trying to get any supernatural meaning out of it—I was only interested because I knew the cook would give me a little rooster made out of that dough. But I now enjoy the memory of the whole ritual. It was a real rite, first of all, just to prepare the yeast well. They would take a little lump of fermented dough from the previous batch and add it to the water and the sifted flour. After the mixture was made and kneaded, they covered it with a towel and, with it thus sheltered, let it rest until it swelled up as much as it possibly could. Then they put it in the oven, a portion at a time, and there came out that good bread that's full of little holes—marvelous. Because the leaven was well preserved and prepared, it let itself be dissolved—disappear—in the midst of the mixture, that large mass, which owed its quality and value to it.
>
> May it fill our hearts with joy to think about our being just that: leaven which makes the mass ferment.[102]

The family made excursions to the mountains—to the Buñero Mountains, among whose foothills Fonz is located, or even higher yet, through valleys climbing gradually up to the Pyrenees:

One of my most vivid childhood memories is of seeing, up in the mountains near my home, those signposts they planted alongside the hill paths. I was struck by those tall posts usually painted red. It was explained to me then that when the snow fell, covering up everything, paths, seeded fields and pastures, thickets, boulders and ravines, the poles stood out as sure reference points, so that everyone would always know where the road went.

Something similar happens in the interior life. There are times of spring and summer, but there are also winters, days without sun and nights bereft of moonlight. We can't afford to let our friendship with Jesus depend on our moods, on our ups and downs.[103]

He later attached what he called "supernatural inferences" to everyday events, to the kinds of work the people did at home and in the fields, and to the customs of the village. In his poetic recalling of these everyday things, spiritual pleasures and sufferings come to life:

I remember how in my country, when harvest season came and they did not yet have these modern agricultural machines, they lifted the heavy bundles of wheat by hand and loaded them on the backs of mules or poor little donkeys. And come a certain time in the day, around noon, the wives, the daughters, the sisters would come—with scarves gracefully draped over their heads, so that their more delicate skin would not get sunburned—and bring them cool wine. That drink refreshed the tired men, encouraged them, strength- ened them. . . . That is how I see you, O Blessed Mother. When we struggle to serve God, you come to encourage us through- out this journey. Through your hands all graces come to us.[104]

Finally, in his Gospel commentaries we find images pre- serving intact some memories from the times and places of his childhood:

I remember seeing, as a child, the shepherds all bundled up in their sheepskin jackets in the bitter days of winter in the Pyrenees, when all was covered with snow, coming down through the ravines of that homeland of mine with those very faithful dogs and that donkey loaded with all the provisions. At the top of the load were some pots, for preparing their meals, and also medicinal concoctions for any wounds that their sheep might get.

If one of the sheep did get injured—if it got a broken leg, for example—the old picture from the Gospel came to life. The shepherd carried it on his shoulders. I also saw how the shepherd—shepherds are rough men who don't look like they're capable of any tenderness—would lovingly carry in his arms a newborn lamb.[105]

From this attentive observation of people and things he extracted all sorts of lessons: for example, about the apparent foolishness of scattering seed that will then be buried in the ground and lost to view, and about the constant, indispensable work of the donkey who keeps walking around and around in circles to turn the waterwheel. But he incurred a special spiritual debt to his grandmother Constancia. Seeing her with a rosary constantly in her hands made it easier for him to understand that all our efforts must be based on unceasing prayer.[106]

* * *

That fall of 1912, Josemaría began his secondary-school studies. Class hours were from nine to twelve, and then in the afternoon from two to five. But the students arrived an hour earlier every morning, to attend Mass in the school chapel. They wore jackets of navy blue with metal buttons and caps with patent leather visors.

Classes for the first year included Spanish, Geography, Arithmetic and Geometry, and Religion. When Josemaría took his exams at the Institute of Lérida, the grades he got were exceptionally high.[107]

The boy's character was maturing, which meant, among other things, that he was becoming less talkative and more thoughtful. By all indications it was during that school year of 1912–1913, not long after he had lost those two little sisters, that he did something most astonishing. One afternoon his sisters Carmen and Chon were playing with some friends in the "lions' den," making castles out of a deck of cards. "We were just finishing one," relates the Baroness of Valdeolivos, "when Josemaría reached out with one hand and knocked it over on us. We started crying and asked him, 'Why did you do that, Josemaría?' And he, in a very serious tone of voice, answered us, 'That's exactly what God does with people. You build a castle, and when it's almost finished, God knocks it over on you.' "[108]

Thoughts long repressed may just then have violently burst into his consciousness. In any case, a new realization had dawned on him: God is the proprietor of souls, and he disposes of them unconstrained by any personal plans of ours.

At the end of the next summer, Chon fell gravely ill. She was eight years old. One day, says the Baroness of Valdeolivos, Josemaría "was playing with me and the other kids, and he said to us, 'I'm going to go see how my sister is doing.' He asked about her, and his mother answered, 'Asunción is already well—she's already in heaven.' "[109]

It was October 6, 1913. The parents did not want Carmen or Josemaría to go into the bedroom where the body of little Chon, wrapped in a shroud, was laid. But at a moment when no one was looking, the boy went in to pray and to say goodbye to his little sister. It was the first time he saw a dead body.[110]

He thought a lot about all that: about the innocence of the little girls; about their disappearance, going from youngest to oldest; and about the disturbing proximity of the three deaths. Slowly reviewing the facts of the case in his imagination, he concluded that, following the natural course of the deaths, after Chon's recent departure he would be the next to die. And he did not hesitate to say so quite openly. "Next year it's my turn," he would say.[111] Then Doña Dolores, to calm him down, would remind him how our Lady had saved him when he was little, and how they had taken him on that pilgrimage to Torreciudad. "Don't worry," she would finish reassuringly, "I offered you to our Lady, and she will take care of you." After a while Josemaría stopped talking about his approaching death, because of the confidence his mother's words instilled in him and because of the suffering these dire prophecies were causing her.

The school year of 1913–1914 was a sedative for his soul, a brief break before coming tribulations. He threw himself completely into his studies.

The Piarists were very devout and well trained as teachers. Josemaría felt a sincere affection for them. He admired their patience. And just as he would forever remember the little tunes the nuns had taught him in kindergarten to help him memorize the alphabet and certain prayers, that school year of 1913–1914 would leave the Latin ditty *Qui, Quae, Quod* engraved in his mind.[112] His favorite subject, however, was mathematics, in which he won first place every year. Its exactitude, the mental discipline involved, the logic of the deductions, the method of reasoning, all so tidy and precise, appealed to him. He got along well with the teacher, and he was the best student in the class. But the teacher had no idea of the fire that the boy had in him, that would make him impetuously explode against the slightest injustice. One day he summoned him to the blackboard to be quizzed about some material supposedly previously covered. The question had not yet been covered in class, but the teacher insisted that he answer it. The student was infuriated. He slammed the eraser against the blackboard, did an about-face, and on his way back to his desk loudly protested, "We've never had that question!"[113]

The story doesn't end there, though. As he himself tells it, "A few days later I was walking down the street with my father, and we ran into this very same friar. I thought, uh-oh, now he's going to tell my father what I did. . . . But in fact he just stopped, made some kind of pleasant remark, and said good-bye without saying a word about it. I was so grateful to him for his silence that I still pray for him every day."[114]

At the end of that school year Josemaría went to Lérida with his classmates to take the state exams. In those circumstances, far from school and without any supervision, students sometimes drifted into inappropriate conversations. Josemaría would try to change the subject or else go off by himself to say the Rosary in reparation. On more than one night he fell asleep saying the Rosary.[115]

He did spectacularly well in his examinations. *Juventud*, a weekly paper published by the diocese of Barbastro, actually reported the marks he received.[116]

*   *   *

At first sight, the financial ruin which now came upon the Escrivás seems like just one more calamity in an uninterrupted series of family calamities. One person who witnessed all these events sums them up this way: "Within a few years they went from a comfortable financial situation to the collapse of the business which supported them. And in those same years the three girls born after Josemaría died, one after another."[117]

Later, Josemaría would find a supernatural key and a deeper significance to those events which fell like a deluge on the whole family:

I have always made those I had around me suffer a lot. I haven't brought on catastrophes, but the Lord, to hit me, who was the nail (pardon me, Lord), landed one blow on the nail and a hundred on the horseshoe. I saw my father as the personification of Job. He lost three daughters, one after the other in consecutive years, and then lost his fortune. I suffered scorn from my little colleagues, because children don't have a heart, or don't have a head, or perhaps lack both head and heart....[118]

Carmen and her brother did not find out about the trouble their father's business was in until Don José and Doña Dolores no longer had any choice but to tell them. Don José did not want to make his children share in his sufferings any sooner than necessary, so he kept back the news for a time—but only a short time, as it turned out, because it was impossible to hide for long the imminent ruin of his business. It all happened in the brief interval between two autumns: between October 1913, when Chon died, and the last weeks of 1914, when Juncosa & Escrivá definitively collapsed.

During that year the entire region was hit by an economic recession which caused the closing and liquidation of many businesses, including that of Mauricio Albás, one of Doña Dolores' brothers. But the case of the collapse of Juncosa & Escrivá was different.[119]

First there was a failure on the part of Jerónimo Mur, an old business partner of Don José, to honor certain commitments. Don José "suffered a terrible financial blow," says Martín Sambeat, "owing, as I heard it from my parents, to the fact that a business partner of his did not act as a good partner." Adriana Corrales, echoing the rumors that circulated around Barbastro, relates that "the family's friends thought it was ultimately the result of a dirty trick played on that good man, Don José Escrivá."[120]

At any rate, within a few months the setbacks began to do away with whatever superfluous comfort there might have been in Josemaría's home. The process was visible and rapid. Friends of Carmen have described it. From the beginning, says one, "they had to give up a lot of things."[121] Soon after Chon died, the nanny was let go, and then their cook, and later the maid. Carmen helped her mother with the household chores, and the two of them adapted to their straitened circumstances without complaint. Indeed, compared to the moral suffering and humiliation they had to put up with, the disadvantages of being relatively poor in material terms were a very minor inconvenience. The couple explained to their children the importance of accepting joyfully this new financial situation that the Lord had allowed to befall them. One day Don José called the whole family together and explained how they should deal with this poverty. "We must look at everything with a sense of responsibility," he said. "On the one hand, we must not live beyond our means. But on the other hand, we must live this poverty with dignity, even though it is a humiliation. We must live it without others noticing it and without telling them about it."[122]

The surprising thing in this turn of events was not the fortitude shown by Don José, or the spirit of sacrifice shown by all the Escrivás in their serene acceptance of their reversal of fortune. After all, the collapse of the business was at least in part a result of circumstances, including a general economic crisis, that existed all over the country. What was really surprising, to relatives and outsiders alike, was a heroic decision made by Don José. Having lost his business, his son tells us, he "could nevertheless have remained in a very comfortable situation for those times, had he not been a Christian and a gentleman."[123]

That Christian gentlemanliness lies in the fact that he forgave, right away and with the best will, those who caused his financial ruin. He prayed for them and refrained from ever bringing up the subject, lest the family feel resentment toward them. In addition, once the company had been legally decreed bankrupt and it was obvious that its assets were not sufficient to pay off the creditors, he checked to see if he had an obligation, in strict justice, to compensate them from his private funds. And although he was told that he definitely had no moral obligation to do this,[124] the honorable man nevertheless acted according to his own sense of justice and "sold all that he had in order to pay the creditors."[125]

He disposed of his goods, sold the house, paid off all his debts, and ended up ruined. Not to the point, however, of not having enough to eat or not having a penny to his name. Yet Josemaría's friends heard such rumors at home and took them quite literally, as appears from this story told by the Baroness of Valdeolivos: "I remember things I heard that got stuck in my mind and caused me to be surprised when I saw Josemaría, one afternoon, having a snack of bread and ham. I said to my mother, 'Mama, why do they say that the Escrivás are so bad off? Josemaría had a very good snack today.' My mother explained to me that actually they were not that bad off, not so bad off that they couldn't have a decent snack."[126]

Some of Doña Dolores' relatives, deeming her husband's conduct naïve, were unsympathetic and critical. What, after all, did he think would really be accomplished by this romantic, extravagant, heroic feat of giving up things the family needed?

Josemaría, comments Pascual Albás, "had to suffer plenty, because his family went through very difficult and sad times. Some of his uncles purposely distanced themselves so that they would not have to give them any help."[127] One of these uncles was Father Carlos Albás, a brother of Doña Dolores. He went around referring to the conduct of his brother-in-law as colossal stupidity. "Pepe has been a fool," he said. "He could have retained a good financial position, and instead he's reduced himself to misery."[128]

These hardships, however, brought the Escrivás even closer together. His wife and children felt proud of the noble decision made by the head of the family. Such Christian behavior aroused in Josemaría feelings of admiration that made him exclaim many years later, "I have a holy pride: I love my father with all my heart, and I believe he has a very high place in heaven, because he managed to bear in such a dignified, marvelous, Christian way all the humiliation that came with finding himself out on the street."[129]

At the same time, though, the boy did feel a strong inner rebellion against the hardships that resulted from this trial, and especially against the painful humiliations that it brought him. Later, in fact, he would ask forgiveness from the Lord, confessing his resistance to accepting the situation of the family: "I rebelled against that situation. I felt humiliated. I ask pardon."[130]

Again and again he pondered those designs of Divine Providence which dashed to the ground the plans of human beings and which, showing no consideration, sent financial ruin and other sorrows to faithful Christians. Only the deep, exemplary faith of the parents enabled the son to rise above these trials.

*   *   *

During 1914, months before bankruptcy was officially decreed, Don José was worried about the future of his family. The Escrivás' financial position had descended to a level which was incompatible with their traditional social status. Within the privacy of their home they were ready to live in poverty, but circumstances outside the home prevented them from going on as before. Barbastro was a small city in which it would be difficult to rebuild a business right after its collapse. Don José did not have savings or family money that he could use. Living with all those misunderstandings, or having to face those who had abused his trust and led to the downfall of himself and his family, would have been very hard on the dignity of such a gentleman. So, after discussing the matter with his wife, he looked for a way to open up new horizons for his family, thinking mainly about the future of his children.[131]

He had no trouble finding employment elsewhere, since he had many friends and acquaintances in the textile trade. In addition, Don José's integrity—the fact that the loss of his property was the result of a praiseworthy generosity—was common knowledge. He promptly reached an agreement with Don Antonio Garrigosa y Borrell, the owner of a textile business in Logroño. The position offered him involved a great deal of responsibility in terms of running the business and dealing with customers. But it was far from a partnership.[132]

Early in 1915, Don José left Barbastro to work in Logroño. For the first time, he and his wife lived apart: Doña Dolores stayed in Barbastro with the children, until the end of the school year. Inevitably, the financial misfortune had taken a toll on that long-suffering woman. "I very well remember Doña Lola in those last days that she was in Barbastro, now without any household help, doing the household chores herself," says Adriana Corrales. "I saw her ironing, sitting on a low little chair. We thought at the time that she was not in good health, that maybe she had a heart problem."[133]

But what Doña Dolores was suffering from had nothing to do with a heart ailment.

2

1. "The Great City of London"

During his last months in Barbastro, Josemaría conscientiously applied himself to his studies. "He left good memories among his classmates and teachers. Everyone hated to see him go," says one of those old schoolmates.[1]

In June 1915 he went to the Institute of Lérida to take his exams. He received good grades in French and in Spanish history, and the highest possible grade in geometry. But despite his teachers' high hopes, he got only a passing grade in Latin, because he became nervous and did not express himself well.[2]

As usual, most of the family went to Fonz for summer vacation at the beginning of July. Lacking the company of his father, who was far away in Logroño, Josemaría immersed himself in reading to help him forget recent problems. This enjoyment of reading had begun when he was very young: his father had bought him lots of storybooks and had even gotten him a subscription to *Chiquitín* (Little Folk). Don José was himself an avid reader who liked to keep up with what was going on in the world—events of all kinds, political, religious, economic, cultural. His favorite newspaper was *La Vanguardia*, and his favorite magazines were *La Ilustración Española* (The Spanish Pictorial) and *Blanco y Negro* (White and Black).[3]

With all this free time ahead of him, the boy steeped himself in the novels of Jules Verne. Those fantastic adventures, with their continual parade of exotic lands and customs, fabulous inventions, and mind-boggling dangers, held him spellbound. But when the author got bogged down in tedious scientific details, Josemaría flipped rapidly through the pages to find where the story picked up again.[4]

At the beginning of September, as soon as they returned from Fonz to Barbastro, the family got news that Don José had an apartment ready for them in Logroño. Immediately they moved all the furniture and other objects out of their home on Calle Mayor—the home where all the children had been born, but which for several months now had no longer been theirs.[5]

From the fourth to the eighth of that month, Barbastro celebrated the feast of the Birth of the Virgin Mary. It was during those days that the Escrivás made their preparations for moving. They said their good-byes—probably painful ones. Recently, however, Doña Dolores had made it her rule of conduct to act as if nothing had happened. She hated melancholy farewells and nostalgia. So one morning in the middle of September, very early, the Escrivás took the stagecoach that made the run to Huesca, and apparently none of the relatives came to see them off.

"I remember that they left early in the morning," relates Esperanza Corrales. "I know the school year had already started, because we went from there to class. Doña Lola did not like farewells, so just we friends of Carmen were there."[6]

* * *

In Barbastro the boy left relatives, friends, childhood memories, and the graves of his three sisters—all of them unforgettable ties to his hometown. He would never again live there, yet he would always keep up with the events going on there. The saddest of all would occur twenty-one years after the Escrivás had left, in the summer of 1936. Under Marxist rule the diocese of Barbastro was constantly in mourning, paying a heavy tribute of blood. Of the 140 diocesan priests, 123 were martyred. So was the bishop who served as Barbastro's apostolic administrator. And the religious-order priests fared no differently. Nine Piarist priests, 51 Claretian priests, brothers, and novices, and 20 Benedictines of the monastery in Pueyo were assassinated. The Escrivá family had to mourn the deaths of several relatives.[7]

Later, having suffered nine centuries of instability, conflict, and violence, the diocese found itself facing problems of a new kind. The vacancy of sees whose bishops had been martyred and the destruction wrought by the civil war made necessary a reorganization of the Church in Spain. Among the proposals was a suppression of the diocese of Barbastro. In 1945 the people of Barbastro asked Father Josemaría to intercede on their behalf with the papal nuncio in Spain. Never before had he agreed to do any mediating, not even for members of his own family. This case was a notable exception.[8]

The diocese managed to survive that crisis. But twenty years later the same threat again arose. Serious, well-founded rumors started circulating about suppression of the see. Again the people of Barbastro went to their illustrious townsman, and he interceded in writing with Pope Paul VI, setting out the historical, social, and pastoral reasons why maintaining the diocese would be in the best interests of the Church and of souls. At the end of his letter he said to the Holy Father, "And, finally, I wish to emphasize once more that it is only love for the Church and for souls which moves me to write these lines humbly beseeching the Holy Father not to suppress the diocese of Barbastro."[9]

With the passage of time, his love for his little hometown became even more obvious. "Every day that goes by," he wrote, "I feel more closely united to my beloved city of Barbastro and to all Barbastrans. My memories and my affection run very deep."[10] This was not mere nostalgia. Those memories had deep roots in the difficult circumstances that obliged the family to leave that area. And the affection that Josemaría felt was intensified by the fact that the memory of Barbastro brought with it memories of his father. On March 28, 1971, from Rome, he wrote to the mayor of Barbastro:

> I am very much a Barbastran, and I try to be a good son of my parents. Let me tell you that my mother and my father, even though they had to leave that place, did instill in us, along with faith and piety, a great affection for the banks of the Vero and the Cinca. I remember specifically some things about my father that fill me with pride and have not faded from my memory at all even though I was only thirteen when we moved away: stories of a generous and hidden charity, an upright faith without ostentation, abundant strength at the time of trial, a strong union with my mother and his children. It was thus that our Lord prepared my soul—by way of those examples so imbued with Christian dignity and hidden heroism always accompanied by a smile—so that later, by God's grace, I could become a poor instrument for the carrying out of a work of Divine Providence that would not separate me from my beloved city. Please forgive me for letting go like this. I cannot hide from you the fact that these recollections fill me with joy.[11]

Logroño celebrated the feast of Saint Matthew for a whole week, from September 20 to 27. A few days before the festivities began, the Escrivás moved into the apartment rented by Don José: number 18 on Sagasta Street. (The number was later changed to 12.) It was on the fourth floor, and above it there were attics and garrets making it extra cold in the winter and hot in the summer. Señor Garrigosa, the owner of the company where Don José worked, lent them a hand during the difficult first days. According to Paula Royo, a daughter of one of the employees, Señor Garrigosa "came to my father and asked that he, with his family, volunteer to help out Don José Escrivá and Doña Dolores Albás, who had come from Barbastro, where they had suffered a reversal of fortune."[12]

The business of Don Antonio Garrigosa y Borrell was doing well. Its name was Grandes Almacenes de Tejidos (The Great Textile Department Store) and there were two stores in Logroño. One, on Station Street, was "a wholesale store which exported goods to the provinces." The other was at 28 Portales Street, near San Blas; called La Gran Ciudad de Londres (The Great City of London), it provided its Logroño clientele with the latest fashions. Señor Garrigosa was a very enterprising businessman, as one might suppose from the rather grandiose names of his stores. The company lasted for many years, although the name of that second store was eventually changed to the more modest "La Ciudad de Londres."[13]

Logroño, seat of the province of the same name (now the Comunidad Autónoma de la Rioja), was enjoying a period of growth. Its population had increased considerably: by 1915 it had about 25,000 inhabitants. Its demographic expansion, which was due largely to immigration, was accompanied by economic growth. The surrounding district, stretching along the upper right bank of the Ebro River, owed its fertility to the river and its tributaries. The agricultural riches consisted principally in large vineyards and olive groves, grain fields and orchards, and irrigated vegetable gardens. With most of Europe involved in World War I, Spain, a neutral country, experienced boom times selling raw materials and manufactured goods to the warring nations, especially France.

Logroño benefited from a hefty amount of exportation of not only its agricultural output but the products of its wineries, flour mills, fruit and vegetable canneries, and olive oil, sausage, and tobacco processing plants.

The people of Logroño were provincial, isolated, not troubled by great social tensions or political upheavals. Tradition and work gave the place order and tranquillity. There was a certain social equality. Political predominance belonged to the liberals, whose chief medium of expression was the newspaper *La Rioja*. Its rival, the *Diario de la Rioja*, characterized itself as "independent Catholic" and conservative.

In keeping with the provincial environment, Don José accustomed himself to going on Sunday outings with his family. Elegantly dressed, with his derby hat and walking stick, he would take them for a stroll along the banks of the Ebro. Says Paula Royo, "Our two families would go out together almost every Sunday afternoon, around four o'clock, to get some sun. Usually we would meet on Sagasta Street, where they lived, and cross the iron bridge over the Ebro and walk down the road that goes to Laguardia, or the one to Navarre, just taking a stroll. . . . Afterward we would all go inside and end the afternoon with a snack or some games."[14]

Sagasta Street, where the Escrivás lived, was intersected by Mercado [Market] Street, which ran all the way through Logroño from east to west. Along the central stretch of Mercado stood buildings with large continuous arcades; this was the zone for stores and businesses. Here is where The Great City of London was located—at 28 Mercado, more popularly known as 28 Portales [Arcade]. The distance from the Escrivá apartment to the building where Don José worked was short, even by Logroño's modest standards. Being the punctual, methodical, and dependable individual that he was—and this he remained to the day he died—he had fixed habits. Almost every day he set out at a few minutes before seven to attend Mass at the nearby church of Saint James.[15] He returned home for breakfast, and left again at about 8:45 to go to work.

At The Great City of London he worked as a sales clerk, waiting on customers.[16] It was a constant, poignant reminder for him of the days when he was proprietor of a similar business in Barbastro. In recognition of his knowledge, social distinction, age, and experience, he was given a higher position than that of the other employees of the store, but his salary was modest. That the Escrivá family was short on money showed itself in a thousand ways.

Doña Dolores devoted herself to taking care of the household tasks, and was "in those difficult times of financial crisis, in which they felt somewhat lost in Logroño, a great support to her husband and children."[17] A classmate of Josemaría's who got to know his mother in Logroño tells us "she was a woman who always maintained a dignified environment in accord with that of the family from which she came and in which she was brought up."[18] Evidently this lady was now doing household jobs that she was not accustomed to doing, since she used to have domestic help and now did not, but she did them gladly.

According to the recollections of Josemaría, those were "very hard times," and especially for his father, who for the rest of his life had troubles and problems to cope with.[19] However, his father "was very cheerful and bore his change of position with great dignity."[20] And for that reason Josemaría's family environment, hard as it was on the boy in some ways, was not poisoned by the sadness of adversity, nor marked by mere stoic resignation. On the contrary, the Escrivá home exuded a humble joy, an atmosphere of courteous manners and discreet silences. The tone was set by the head of the family, who has been called "a real saint."[21] It is easy to believe that people who knew both his past in Barbastro and his present in Logroño actually said this, because the gentleman "had a great patience and agreeableness in everything, always looked cheerful, and was always unassuming and unpretentious in his conversations. He lived his whole life with a trusting and cheerful acceptance, despite the reversal of fortune that he had suffered. He never talked about his worries or complained about his situation."[22]

2. The Institute of Logroño

Regardless of the cost, it was essential to give the children a good education. Don José Escrivá had decided that before he left Barbastro.

Logroño, as a provincial capital, had the corresponding institutions and administrative services. When it came to schools, it had an official center for secondary education (the General and Technical Institute), two teachers' training colleges (one for men, the other for women), and a "School for Trades, Arts, and Crafts."

Josemaría still had three years to go to finish secondary school, so his records were transferred from the Institute of Lérida to that of Logroño and he was enrolled as a nonofficial student for the 1915–1916 school year.[23] Going from a Catholic school like that of the Piarists to a public institution might well have been a rather abrupt change for Josemaría, and quite possibly Don José saw it that way. But the majority of the students at the Institute went in the afternoon to a private school for a review of the material they were being taught. Two private schools vied for top honors: Saint Joseph's, which was run by Marist Brothers, and Saint Anthony's, which, since it was not run by religious, was considered a secular school despite its name.

The strong competition between Saint Joseph's and Saint Anthony's showed up very conspicuously in newspaper ads and articles.[24] Saint Joseph's prided itself on having "a Laboratory of Physics, Chemistry, and Natural History; a spacious chapel for liturgical functions; a large, comfortable, and well-ventilated dormitory for the boarding students; and a large recreational patio with a magnificent recently renovated handball court." Saint Anthony's responded by flaunting its academic potential, for besides the regular secondary-school classes, it offered "special classes in calligraphy, drawing, French, English, German, and popular Arabic." The effect of that kind of advertising, with its impressive listing of languages and implicit reference to the countries then at war, was not to be underestimated.

In the end, though, the rivalry between the two schools came down to a simple question of examinations results—pure numbers. And going solely by academic results, it seems that Saint Anthony's was better than Saint Joseph's.[25] But the weightiest factor in the couple's thinking, and the one that led them to enroll Josemaría in Saint Anthony's, was simply that they wanted to head off the possibility of a rivalry between him and another student, a cousin. "His parents rejected the possibility of his going to the school of the Marist Brothers in Logroño," we are told, "because a cousin of his was already studying there and they did not want any tension or unhealthy competitiveness to come up between them."[26]

Josemaría attended classes at the Institute in the morning and went over the lessons at Saint Anthony's in the afternoon. Meanwhile, his sister Carmen was studying at the teachers' training college in Logroño.[27]

*   *   *

The Institute of Logroño was new, having recently been built on a site formerly occupied by a Carmelite convent.[28] It had good classrooms, excellent chemistry and physics labs, and a natural history section. It faced a street called Muro de Cervantes, which was a continuation of Mercado

Street. Behind it there was a promenade with gardens. The large building also contained the provincial library, the art museum, a teachers' training college, and the school of arts and crafts.

During his three years there, Josemaría worked hard and progressed intellectually. The faculty, overall, was of a very high caliber both professionally and personally. Josemaría learned not only from the explanations that his teachers gave in their classes, but also from their example, their moral conduct. In his final exams he did exceptionally well, as the records attest.[29] His report card for the fifth year (1916–1917), the least impressive that he got in Logroño, consists of three "Outstandings" and two "Notables"—a set of marks which seems a bit low only in relation to his generally excellent performance.[30]

One of these "Notables" was for Psychology and Logic, a course taught by Father Calixto Terés y Garrido, a diocesan priest who had been teaching philosophy since 1912. He had an aura of prestige because, it was said, he had taken his qualifying exams for a professorship before a tribunal that did not take a friendly view of clerical cassocks. He was chaplain to the Brothers of the Poor and lived with his mother in a humble little house with a small garden. Simple, hardworking, and good-natured, he had no hesitation about giving a passing grade, but was a lot tougher when it came to an "Outstanding" or even a simple "Notable." So it is noteworthy that in the following year Father Calixto gave Josemaría the grade of "High Honors" for a sixth-year course, Ethics and Law.

The priest had excellent teaching skills. His student would particularly remember the in-depth explanation of Marxism that he gave in that Ethics and Law course of 1917–1918, because he did such a good job of putting the subject and its absurdities in terms that the students could understand.

Teacher and student had a mutual affection. Despite their differences in age, they soon became friends. And even after Josemaría was ordained, Father Calixto provided him counsel in times of difficulty. Many years passed without their seeing each other, but then one day, during a visit to Logroño, the former student went to see Father Calixto. Pointing to the desk where Josemaría used to sit, the old man said in a husky voice, "That's where you used to sit, little one, that's where you used to sit."[31]

That second "Notable" was in Physics, a subject taught by Don Rafael Escriche. He had come from the Institute of Mahón and at that time had not been in Logroño more than a couple of years. He too was very sparing with good grades. But former students still chuckle about his chemistry lab experiments and the suspense of waiting to see if liquids would precipitate and substances change color. Truth to tell, the textbook predictions did not always come true.[32]

Don Rafael was, however, a methodical man with a lot of common sense. On the first day of class, in the fall of 1917, he found the lab in a state of incredible disorder and filthiness after the months of vacation. Instruments were scattered. Cabinets were dirty and covered with dust. Not wanting to lose a day of class, Don Rafael suggested that the students wash only the test tubes or other objects they needed, and then, when they were finished with them, clean them well and put them back where they belonged. After just a few classes every piece of equipment was bright and shining and in its proper place again. With his knack for retaining whatever was useful in any incident, Josemaría never forgot the lesson of that chemistry class. Whenever, later in life, he encountered a similar situation of urgency or disorder, he applied the method of Don Rafael.[33]

*   *   *

Leaving Barbastro was a painful uprooting for the whole family, but it was especially hard on Josemaría, whose character was beginning to be solidified. His parents led the way in making the difficult adjustment to new surroundings and a new lifestyle. By their example they made things easier for Carmen and Josemaría.

Other than that one cousin of Josemaría's who was studying with the Marists, the family did not have any close relatives in Logroño. Fortunately, Don José was already establishing friendships through his work. Thanks also to his good manners and personal distinction, he soon widened his circle of acquaintances. However, he could not mix with them socially. There were several social clubs—the Rioja Literary Club, the Friendship Circle, the Catholic Circle—but financial constraints kept him from joining them. Finding themselves in a strange city, parents and children centered their lives on their home, in an instinctive movement of affection and defense. Josemaría thus came to understand "the importance of confronting difficulties well united"—another lesson learned from his father.[34]

Paula Royo recalls that when he started at Saint Anthony's, "Josemaría was very tall for his age—about fourteen—and rather stocky. He still wore short pants.* I remember him in a dark gray outfit, black socks up to the knees, and a little beret. He was very good-looking—I can still see him now as he was back then. He was always cheerful and had a contagious laugh."[35] His teachers at once held him in high esteem, says another friend of the family, and he won friends among his classmates through his natural capacity for adjustment and by "his loyalty to his companions."[36]

He exemplified generosity, loyalty, and a spirit of service to such an extent that with no holding back or hesitation, he would forgo for the sake of others even things that he needed. In view of this, Doña Dolores, who knew him better than anyone else,

---

*At that time it was customary in Spain for preadolescent boys to wear short pants year round. Putting on long pants was a sign of having outgrown childhood.

felt obliged to warn him that he would suffer a lot in this life if he kept giving of himself to people in that way.[37]

Later in life he now and then would run into old friends and they would exchange big hugs and reminisce about school days. One of these friends was a boy with whom Josemaría had patiently reviewed class material he had been unable to grasp.[38]

In the end, his mother's prediction came true. Life brought the boy innumerable letdowns and sorrows. But Josemaría never regretted being the way he was or tried to rein in his big heart. In 1971, with the bitter taste of a recent disillusionment with a "friend" still in his mouth, he wrote, "Why is it that, in spite of my miseries, I'm usually more of a friend to my friends than they are to me? Yet surely this does do me a lot of good, if I accept—*fiat!*—their lack of affection."[39]

His basic character did not change much with the years. He gave himself with unlimited loyalty and generosity, unreservedly, with an overflowing warmheartedness. Some of the friendships he made at that time with classmates at the Institute would just keep growing ever closer, on into eternity, as was the case with Isidoro Zorzano.[40] When in 1918 the bishop of the diocese of Calahorra and La Calzada requests information about Josemaría's studies, the response conveys—within its concise formality—high praise for the boy. "The young man in question," writes the rector of the Logroño seminary, "resides in Logroño, is studying at this Institute, and serves as a model for the other students by his application and conduct."[41]

3. *The maturing of an adolescent*

The blows to the family were followed by a long series of moral sufferings and physical privations that would deeply affect Josemaría's transition from childhood to adolescence. This may have been one of the most difficult periods of his life. He was in a state of crisis, waging a tenacious and painful battle with himself, apparently for several months. Veiled hints, made years later, indicate that for a time he no longer had those friendly chats with Don José in which son opened his heart to father and asked his advice.

After the death of his sister Chon, an idea kept running through his head which pierced him like a thorn. Whenever he saw the innocent suffer, he was nagged by the thought, Why, Lord, why? Still a boy, and one with an acute sense of justice, Josemaría lost himself in painful meditations, searching for a ray of light that would clarify what to him made no sense. It was wasted effort. His feelings were too strong for him to see any possible explanation. This is how he tells it:

> Even back when I was a child, I thought so often about the fact that there are many good souls who have to suffer so much in this world—sorrows of every type: reversals of fortune, family calamities, the trampling of their legitimate pride. At the same time, I could see other people who did not seem to be good (though I'm not saying they weren't, because we don't have a right to judge anyone), for whom everything was going just great. But then, one fine day, it occurred to me that even the very evil do some good things, although they don't do them for supernatural motives, and I realized that God in some way has to reward them on earth, since he won't be able to reward them in eternity. Then I thought of the old saying, "They also feed the ox that will go to the slaughterhouse."[42]

In Logroño Josemaría began to feel uneasy about the new situation and resistant to accepting it. His generosity, the impulse to give of himself without holding back, seemed at odds with the cutting back and financial calculating the family had to do. The boy had a hard time catching on to the fact that moral riches are much more important than material goods.

With Carmen's help, his mother worked hard at the household tasks: cooking, sewing, cleaning, washing clothes, and bargaining when she went shopping at the market. We know—and perhaps Josemaría did too—some more personal details about his father. To save money at afternoon break time, he would have just a small piece of candy to stave off his hunger. Though he did not give up smoking, he imposed on himself a daily ration of six cigarettes, which he rolled himself and then placed carefully in a silver cigarette case, a souvenir of better times.[43] The household economy was ruled by thrift, and expenditures were subject to a prudent scrutiny, in line with a saying of Doña Dolores, "Don't extend your arm further than your sleeve will go."[44] In Josemaría's eyes, everything in the house bore the seal of a practical poverty, which was frustrating to his impulsive spirit. It aroused in him feelings of rebellion which he could restrain only with difficulty. Magnanimous and disposed to sacrifice as he was, he suffered from the silent suffering of his parents.

When the clouds lifted, and a little later he could see clearly the Christian dimension of that poverty, he took pride in the very thing that as a boy he had considered a disgrace to his family. And when speaking of it to his spiritual children, he cheerfully said so. "If they throw in my face my parents' poverty," he once said, "you should all rejoice, realizing that our Lord wanted it that way so that our Work—his Work—would be built without human means. That's how I see it. And furthermore, my parents, my quietly heroic parents, are my great pride."[45]

At the time, though, he could not see it that way. The family's poverty, no question about it, brought with it all kinds of humiliation. To the many relatives of Doña Dolores, Logroño was an exile for the Escrivás, and according to some, an exile they deserved.

For Josemaría the hardest trial, more painful than the deprivations, was the quiet suffering of his parents. Their smiling serenity showed the inner self-control with which they accepted all these adversities. But through that humble cloak of amiability one could also see the many renunciations it covered. And instead of calming the boy, this upset him terribly. The waves tossed painfully in his soul. He did not dare discuss this with Don José—those heart-to-heart talks during their

Sunday walks were broken off for the time being, and they just talked about other things—because to Josemaría it would have been unjust and ignoble to make "comments that might have wounded the sensibilities of his parents."[46]

From the happier days of his childhood Josemaría kept in his memory a lithograph that became part of his spiritual treasury. It had on it two Japanese drawings. One of them, entitled "The Pretentious Man," showed "a family gathered around a table which had above it a big lamp on top of a pole. From afar that light attracted one; it called attention to itself. But when one got closer, one could see that the family was cold—without light, and without the warmth of a home. The other drawing, entitled 'The Wise Man,' showed another family, with a lamp very close by—right on the table, in the midst of everything. It did not call attention to itself; it was not at all ostentatious. But coming closer, one found there a family atmosphere."[47]

God wanted his saving help to come to Josemaría by way of his family. Among his own, he found the warmth of affection. Time calmed his anxieties and feelings of anger. And later he came to see the profound significance of those events. What had been a cause of shame and humiliation now shone with the radiance of virtue, and he saw the providential order and divine logic behind it all. "God made me go through all kinds of humiliations, things that seemed shameful to me, but which I now see were just so many instances of virtue on the part of my parents. I say this with joy. Our Lord had to prepare me, and since what was right around me was what could make me suffer the most, that's where he struck. Humiliations of every kind, but borne with Christian nobility—I see it now, more clearly every day, and with more gratitude to our Lord, to my parents, to my sister Carmen. . . ."[48]

Later, with the definitive development of his personality, the boy began to acquire a maturity beyond his years. With his friends he was serious and thoughtful, but was also living proof that these qualities are not incompatible with cheerfulness and a lively sense of humor. Doña Dolores had a good way of putting it: she used to say that Josemaría "was always a grown-up child."[49] It was by swimming against the current, not letting misfortune hold him back, that he got through his adolescent crisis.

And so his spirit opened up very early to the idealism of youth. For this reason, when he looked back to that long-ago stage of his life, he had words of forgiveness and gratitude for everyone. "Our Lord," he once said, "was preparing things. He was giving me one grace after another, overlooking my defects, my mistakes as a child and my mistakes as an adolescent."[50]

*   *   *

By themselves, his school records tell us little about Josemaría as a person and only indicate how his intellectual abilities were rated. But even so, they indirectly provide some valuable information about the boy's character and interests.[51]

In his final exams for the fourth year of secondary school (1915–1916) he earned an "Outstanding, with Prize" (also called "High Honors") for Literature and Composition. The prize was not a merely honorary one: it was the waiving of the tuition for one course to be taken in the following year, with the student allowed to choose, according to personal taste and convenience, which course it would be. Josemaría wrote the principal of the Institute on September 1, 1916, asking that his prize for Literature and Composition be applied to the course "General History of Literature."[52]

The teacher of this course was Don Luis Arnaiz, a man of literary sensibilities and esthetic feelings which he readily expressed.[53] According to Josemaría, he became particularly emotional when reading Cervantes aloud. That brought back to the boy some distant memories of his own, for among the books the Escrivás had brought from Barbastro, most of which were classics, was a beautiful and very old edition of *Don Quixote*, in six volumes. He had begun to read it, as well as enjoy the illustrations, at a very early age.

In his literature classes Josemaría was able to savor to his heart's content the classics, from medieval writers to those of the Spanish Golden Age.[54] Years later, literary and historical anecdotes (some in prose and some in verse) came readily to his mind as illustrations of Christian doctrine.

One Holy Thursday, making his personal prayer aloud, Monsignor Escrivá brought into it some of these things he had learned as a boy.

> From childhood, O Lord, from the first time I got to leaf through that Galician poetry of Alfonso the Wise, I have been moved by the memory of some of his verses.
>
> I was really touched by those ballads—for instance, the one about the monk who in his simplicity asked our Lady to let him contemplate heaven. He went up to heaven in his prayer—this is something all of us understand, all my children understand it, all, because we are contemplative souls—and when he returned from his prayer, he did not recognize a single monk in the monastery. Three centuries had passed! Now I understand this in a special way, when I consider that you have remained in the tabernacle for almost two thousand years so that I could adore and love and possess you; so that I could eat you and nourish myself with you, sit at your table, become divinized! What are three centuries for a soul that loves? What are three centuries of suffering, three centuries of love, for a soul in love? An instant![55]

What he read as a child took root deep in his soul, saturating it with beauty. On many occasions he would make use of literary recollections to explain his plans or ideas. Take, for example, a letter written in Rome on June 7, 1965, half a century after his graduation from the Institute of Logroño:

> I am now reviving some of my childhood interests, reading old Spanish literature, which our Lord also used to confirm me in his peace. I'll explain this with an example: You know how often I've said, all those far too many times when

people have attributed to me, who am a sinner, things like revelations and prophecies (no less!), that all this is not true. Faced with people's belief, I'll grant at most, because it seems right, that if by any chance what they are saying is true, it's a fruit of the goodness of God, who is rewarding the faith and other virtues of those people. But I'll also admit that *io non c'entro per niente* [I have nothing to do with it].

Well, then, I was reading Gonzalo de Berceo's *Life of Saint Dominic of Silos*. (I'll gladly concede to him that, as he says, the book is "well worth, I think, a good glass of wine.") And taking into account the difference between the thirteenth and the twentieth centuries, and even more the difference between a saint and a sinner, I felt consoled as by a great light from God when I read, "He prophesied the thing that was to come, / Maguer prophesied it, but he didn't understand it." Isn't it a blessing from heaven that, even in our diversions, we can draw divine wisdom poured out by a good clergyman who lived over seven hundred years ago?

Now, to entertain you still further, I want to tell you another literary anecdote, if you can call it that—it might be better to say it comes from my literary confusion.

Not infrequently, when speaking of spiritual things, I used to like to mention a verse I thought came from *Cantar del mío Cid*: "And the prayer rode on horseback to heaven." Now, you can't tell me that's not expressive! But lately I've reread that song, and I've had to recognize that my elderly memory committed in good faith an error that could almost be called unpardonable. Because the original, if you really think about it, is more realistic and even has more of *our theology*. Here's what it says: "Having prayed, he then rode off." First you pray, then you ride. Riding means working, fighting, getting ready to fight. And working and fighting, for a Christian, are praying. I understand this verse from the epic poem as fitting in very well with our epic of ordinary contemplative Christians. Better than that other idea which came, foggily, from an impression made on my adolescent imagination.[56]

* * *

Carmen considered her brother "a normal boy with an outgoing personality."[57] When it came to having fun, however, Josemaría felt a little inhibited in the presence of girls. He did not go to dances, in part because he had never gotten around to learning how to dance. His father, on the other hand, had been an excellent dancer. "Your father," Doña Dolores used to tell Josemaría, "could dance on the tip of a sword."[58] But in any case, wanting to prepare her son for what would naturally be expected, that he would someday fall in love with a girl, she gave him good advice in the form of a popular saying: "If you're going to marry, find you a woman neither so beautiful that she bewitches, nor so ugly that she causes twitches."[59]

Josemaría lost much of his shyness and pensiveness in early adolescence, revealing a nature full of youthful enthusiasms. Extremely orderly and punctual, he could not tolerate disorder. It made him nervous, and he was not tactful about it.[60] This may have had some obscure connection with his liking for geometry and other branches of mathematics. It is clear, though, that the exact sciences were not responsible for his forceful character.

Throughout his life Josemaría had to struggle against the natural impetuosity of his temperament, to rein in that torrent of healthy energy and turn it into a controlled force and a strength of spirit with which to confront obstacles.[61]

His youthful excitability also showed up, although in a different way, in another aspect of his character: his romantic idealism. This would find expression in poetry writing, in patriotic fervor, and sometimes in exalted sentiments about freedom and justice, in connection, for instance, with Ireland's bid for independence.[62]

Each week the family received the magazine *Blanco y Negro*, which gave extensive reports, complete with photographs, of developments in the First World War. Spain, although it remained neutral, was sharply divided in its sympathies; everyone was for one side or the other. Don José strongly backed Germany, perhaps because of the enmity toward France that had persisted in Upper Aragon as a result of the invasion and excesses perpetrated by Napoleon's troops.

But in the case of Ireland, what really stirred up the boy was the issue of religious liberty. "I was then about fifteen," he says, "and I eagerly read in the newspapers everything about the events of the First War. Most of all, though, I prayed a lot for Ireland. I wasn't against England; I was for religious freedom."[63]

*   *   *

In the summer of 1917, father and son resumed their long walks together and discussed Josemaría's plans for the future. In the year ahead he would graduate from secondary school, and he needed to decide what professional path he then would follow. The boy had no doubts. He had already made up his mind to be an architect, since he was so gifted in mathematics and drawing.

Realizing that his son spoke very well, liked history and literature, and was good with people, Don José gently tried to steer him in the direction of law. But Josemaría could not be budged. When his father said that what he was aspiring to be was nothing more than a "glorified bricklayer," it was not just a little dig.[64] Becoming an architect involved long and costly studies, and would require of the family a heavy financial sacrifice. Probably he did not realize this at the time, but many years later he had to recognize it. "So that I could have a university-level career," he said, "my parents continued my education in spite of the family's financial ruin, when they would have had every right to make me get a job—just any kind of job—right away."[65]

A few months remained before a decision would have to be made. Don José grew more uneasy with each passing day. But God would speak, and God would have the last word.

In 1934, looking back from the perspective of his priestly vocation, Josemaría thought about where his professional dreams of 1917 would likely have gotten him. "The priestly vocation! If you hadn't called me, where would I be now? I would probably be a conceited lawyer, an arrogant writer, or an architect enamored of my buildings. (I thought of all this even back then, in 1917 or 1918.)"[66]

4. *Some footprints in the snow*

Up to then God had intervened in his life in a silent way. All the hard lessons he had learned had come by way of painful events concerning his family. Now, as though playing, God set out to meet him, yet still without showing himself openly. He did so through little things that for a person with a less sensitive spirit would have lacked any special significance, but that for a simple soul alert to the touch of grace were tangible signs of God's love. In such ways our Lord kept the boy's soul alert. Years later he would write, "Our Lord was preparing me in spite of myself, using apparently innocuous things to instill a divine restlessness in my soul. Thus I came to understand very well that love, so human and so divine, that moved Saint Thérèse of the Child Jesus when, leafing through the pages of a book, she suddenly came upon a picture of one of the Redeemer's wounded hands. Things like that happened to me too—things that moved me and led me to daily Communion, to purification, to confession, and to penance."[67]

In the Escrivá home the Rosary was prayed daily and the traditional devotions of Barbastro continued to be practiced. The Escrivás joined the parish of Santiago el Real, whose pastor, Father Hilario Loza, knew the whole family very well. The boy went to confession and Communion here, although on Sundays and feast days during the school year he mostly attended Mass at Saint Anthony's. Don José continued to give alms to the poor, and especially to a community of Daughters of Charity which from time to time let him keep in his home a statue of Our Lady of the Miraculous Medal that was enclosed in a glass case.[68] By turn, families were allowed to take this little statue home for their devotions.

Another church the Escrivás attended was Santa María de La Redonda. Going from their house down to Mercado Street, and then turning left, one would face Constitution Plaza, the site of the church. It was the most beautiful building in the city, its façade a huge vaulted niche between two towers and capped by a semidome. Like a gigantic shell in splendid baroque style, the niche served as a canopy when one was entering the church. The pastor was Father Antolín Oñate. A very good friend of Don José, he was also the highest-ranking ecclesiastical authority in the city, since he was the superior of the collegiate church of Santa María de La Redonda and the archpriest of the three parishes of Logroño.[69]

Because the restructuring of ecclesiastical territories stipulated by the Concordat of 1851 between the Spanish government and the Holy See had never been put into effect, Logroño still belonged to the old diocese of Calahorra and La Calzada. By virtue of the Concordat, Logroño was to have become the seat of the diocese. But the ecclesiastical authorities were opposed, while the government, for its part, would not give in either. So for a long time (from 1892 to 1927) Logroño was in episcopal limbo under apostolic administrators, who resided in Calahorra. From 1911 to 1921 the diocese was governed by the Most Reverend Juan Plaza y García, titular bishop of Hippo.[70] The clergy of Logroño included, besides the parish priests, the canons and holders of benefices at La Redonda, chaplains at hospitals and other institutions, seminary professors, and military chaplains.[71] Religious communities in Logroño included the Marist Brothers who ran Saint Joseph's School, the Jesuits at Saint Bartholomew's Church, and quite a few women's communities: Discalced Carmelites, Augustinians, Religious of the Mother of God, Daughters of Charity, Adoration Sisters, Servants of Jesus. . . .

Such was the situation in the autumn of 1917, before the

Carmelite nuns approved (in a chapter resolution dated October 23) the coming of two Carmelite priests to minister to the convent.[72] Father Juan Vicente de Jesús María arrived in Logroño on December 11, and a few days later came Father José Miguel de la Virgen del Carmen. The two of them, together with a Brother named Pantaleón, made up the community in charge of the convent church.

The official inauguration of their pastoral and liturgical services was celebrated on December 19, in a solemn ceremony. The weather, however, contributed nothing to the splendor of the occasion. Since the beginning of the month, rain and snow had been pouring down on Logroño, and although on Tuesday, December 18, much of the snow melted, the slush refroze overnight and the faithful who came to the solemn inauguration of this new era for the Carmelites had to risk slips and tumbles.

Father Juan Vicente did the preaching. He "greeted the city with great feeling and offered everyone in it the spiritual services of the new Carmelite community."[73]

Some very rough days followed, with stormy skies and intense cold covering the whole Rioja region. On Friday, December 28, it started snowing steadily; for two days, great quantities of small but dense flakes kept falling. The New Year came in with glacial temperatures. The thermometer fell to -15 °C (5 °F). Travel became impossible. Stores stayed closed. A number of people actually froze to death.

Beginning on January 3, the city's street-cleaning crew, reinforced by about a hundred extra workers hired by the city government, spent several days removing snow from streets and sidewalks. On Wednesday, January 9, Josemaría's birthday, they finished their work, helped by the rains that had arrived on the previous evening. But the cold returned and the snow season lasted another week.[74]

In the meantime, our Lord anticipated Josemaría's birthday with a surprise that would change the course of his life. Walking down the street one morning during those Christmas holidays, he came upon prints in the snow made by bare feet. His curiosity piqued, he stopped and stared at those white imprints so obviously left by one of the Discalced Carmelite fathers. Moved to the very depths of his soul, he asked himself, "If others can make such sacrifices for God and neighbor, can't I offer him something?"[75]

The footprints had been made by Father José Miguel. Following that snowy trail, the boy sought out the Carmelite for spiritual direction. He now had, very deep inside, "a divine restlessness" that moved him to a more intense life of piety, manifested in prayer, mortification, and daily Communion.[76] "When I was scarcely an adolescent," he will tell us, "our Lord cast into my heart a seed burning with love."[77]

This sharp change was, however, just a brief prelude to greater demands on the part of our Lord:

> I began to have intimations of Love, to realize that my heart was asking for something great, and that it was love. . . . I didn't know what God wanted of me, but it was evident that I had been chosen for something. What this was would come later. . . . Realizing, at the same time, my own inadequacies, I made up that litany, which is a matter not of false humility but of self-knowledge: "I am worth nothing, I have nothing, I can do nothing, I am nothing, I know nothing. . . ."[78]

He was set on fire with love, yet at the same time left in the dark. By the light of our Lord's grace he could see that he had been chosen, but for what remained obscure.

Three months passed. Father José Miguel, seeing the dispositions of that soul, suggested that he join the Carmelites.[79] The boy brought this to his prayer, asking heaven to let him hear clearly that mysterious call resounding in his heart.

Looking back, he could see that from the very morning when he saw those footprints in the snow, something had been leading him directly toward Love.[80] Our Lord had been preparing him. He had made a "divine restlessness" spring up in his soul, such that when he came upon those footprints of a Carmelite religious in the snow he recognized in them the footsteps of Christ, and an invitation to follow him.

During the weeks between that day and the one on which the Carmelite invited him to enter his order, Josemaría had undergone a major interior change of direction. How could such a small event have moved him to put his whole will into a firm desire to offer himself entirely to our Lord, without knowing exactly what he was committing himself to? The disproportion between that event and the reaction shows us the caliber of the boy's temperament—vehement and noble—and his great capacity for love. The carpet of snow soon turned to slush. Josemaria, however, remained firm in his determination. His generous responsiveness to grace only enlarged that wound of love.

By now it was spring. In a couple of months, classes finished, he would take his exams and graduate. He had to make a decision. He thought of the difficulties a strict religious life would present to carrying out the plans of God that he was starting to sense. If he renounced the pursuit of a secular career and became a religious, would he be able to help his parents financially? The monastic life did not appeal to him, nor did the idea of becoming a religious calm his inner restlessness. Besides, shouldn't he be free, with no attachments, when he discovered what that something was that God was asking of him and that was already simmering in his soul?[81] He thereupon came to a quick decision: he would become a priest and thus be prepared for whatever was coming. He then told Father José Miguel his decision and stopped going to the Carmelite for spiritual direction.[82]

All this was obviously not the result of a chance encounter with the footprints of a discalced friar. There was nothing accidental about this encounter, as Josemaría well knew. It was a gift from God. Therefore his commitment had to be a total self-giving, without asking for a proof or extraordinary sign. And immediately, after he made it, he began receiving an outpouring of graces that shortly brought his soul to a state of manifest maturity, to judge by his spiritual director's invitation to him.

It was not, however, to religious life that God was calling

him. He soon saw this clearly, and said so to the Carmelite. And then, with an incredible generosity and a gigantic faith—not at the instigation of grace, but, so to speak, apparently jumping ahead of our Lord—he decided to become a priest. It was a heroic step, an extravagant response that no one had expressly invited him to make. Nor did he make any apologies when he let it be known that he was not being called to a monastic life. He chose the priesthood as a base of operations for attaining an ideal; as the most appropriate means, given his personal circumstances, for identifying himself with Christ in anticipation of a vocation he was beginning to intuit but could not yet see. It would be up to the Lord to provide the new impetus that the future priest could not foresee. For now, from within the darkness of his faith, like the blind man in Jericho, Josemaría just kept crying out to the Lord, begging him to manifest his will. He had a strong intuition that he was about to enter upon the adventure of his life. In 1931 he wrote:

> For years, starting back when my vocation first came about in Logroño, I constantly had on my lips, as an aspiration, "Domine, ut videam!" [Lord, that I may see!]. I was convinced that God *wanted me for something,* even though I didn't know what that something was. I am certain that I expressed this several times to Aunt Cruz [Sister María de Jesús Crucificado] in letters that I sent her at her convent in Huesca. The first time I ever meditated on the passage in Saint Mark about the blind man whom Jesus cured, the passage where Christ asks him, "What do you want me to do for you?" and he answers, "Rabboni, ut videam" [Lord, that I might see], this phrase became deeply engraved in my mind. And despite the fact that I (like the blind man) was told by many to keep quiet . . . , I went on saying and writing, without knowing why, "Ut videam! Domine, ut videam!" And at other times, "Ut sit! Let me see, Lord, let me see. And let it be."[83]

Having made up his mind to become a priest, he communicated this decision to his father. He relates Don José's reaction:

My father answered me, "But, my son, are you taking into account that you will not have a love here on earth, a human love?"

My father was mistaken. He realized it later on.

"... You won't have a home"—he was mistaken!—"but I will not stand in your way."

And two tears came to his eyes. This was the only time I ever saw my father cry.

"I will not oppose it. In fact, I will introduce you to someone who can give you some guidance."[84]

A disturbing thought then crossed the boy's mind: what about his obligations toward his parents? Being the only son, he was bound in justice to plan for the day when he would have to support the family—a day that could not be far off, since his parents were getting up in years and worn out by life. Doña Dolores, after all, had not had any more children for the past ten years.... And at that very moment, without thinking twice, with the confidence that comes from great faith, plus the consciousness of having handed over everything our Lord had asked of him, he prayed that his parents might have another son, to take his place. That was it; he made the one request, he took the matter as settled, and no longer concerned himself with it.[85]

*   *   *

By now it was May. The news that Josemaría was going to become a priest spread quickly among the family's friends and acquaintances. Father Antolín Oñate, the archpriest, was thrilled. At the request of Don José, he met with the boy, and afterward was able to confirm to the father his son's vocation.[86] So did Father Albino Pajares, another priest whom the boy consulted at his father's suggestion.[87] But the news took the family's acquaintances by surprise. "Even his parents," says Paula Royo, "sounded amazed when they told my parents about it, but they never for a moment put any obstacles in his way. We just never thought he would want to be a priest."[88]

At that time Josemaría often went to Santa María de La Redonda for Mass, long periods of personal prayer, and confession. His confessor was Father Ciriaco Garrido, the canon of the collegiate church who was specifically assigned to hear confessions. Father Ciriaco was as physically slight as he was rich in virtue. Don Ciriaquito, as they affectionately called him because of his short stature, was one of the first "to encourage my budding vocation," Josemaría would write.[89]

On May 28 he finished his exams. At last he was a graduate. Having escaped the dreaded prospect of his son's pursuing a career in architecture, Don José once again counseled the boy to study law—something that would be compatible with ecclesiastical studies—although the first order of business was to find out what they needed to do to get him into the seminary.[90]

5. *At the seminary of Logroño*

Father Antolín knew all about everything having to do, either directly or indirectly, with the running of the diocese. He informed Don José of the steps to be taken. First the bishop had to be asked to validate the courses taken in secondary school. And without losing any time, it would be good for the new graduate to get some preparation in Latin and philosophy, because he would have to take a preliminary examination in those fields before starting his theological studies. Don José was very grateful to the archpriest and to Father Albino, both of whom took it upon themselves to find teachers for the boy—although, of course, the teachers' fees would have to come out of his own pocket.[91]

The summer of 1918 was a time of severe drought. Special litanies were prayed, and the bishop ordered that the prayer "Ad Petendam Pluviam" be said at Mass "for the purpose of obtaining from Almighty God a remedy for the prolonged drought which is parching the fields and threatening to destroy a great part of the agricultural products that constitute the principal resource of our beloved diocese."[92] On August 29, the bishop set the first of October as the date of the official opening of the academic year 1918–1919, both for the seminary in Logroño and the one in Calahorra.[93] The history of the diocese having been, as we have seen, a somewhat checkered one, it should come as no surprise that it had two seminaries. From 1917 on, teaching responsibilities were divided between them, with the seminary in Logroño offering courses in ecclesiastical studies only up to third-year theology.[94]

Before the start of the school year, the diocesan *Boletín Eclesiástico* published a list of requirements for admission to the seminary. One, as Father Antolín had anticipated, was that secondary-school graduates had to pass an examination in Latin, logic, metaphysics, and ethics. But the school year could not begin on October 1, as planned, not so much because of the drought as because of something even more terrible: a severe flu epidemic. The days went by, and on November 6 Josemaría sent the bishop a letter saying, "Since I feel that I have a Church vocation, and since I have completed my secondary-school years and passed all my secondary-school examinations, I request that Your Excellency deign to allow me to take the examination in Latin, logic, metaphysics, and ethics that is a prerequisite for first-year theology."[95]

Because of the terrible epidemic, which spread through the entire region, the seminaries did not open until November 29. When the epidemic ended, the bishop ordered that in all parishes a *Te Deum* be sung and an Our Father be prayed "for the victims, and especially for those priests of ours who died as heroes of charity, going beyond the call of duty in the carrying out of their ministry."[96]

While the flu was wreaking havoc and Josemaría was taking his examinations, he also had to fulfill an additional requirement for entrance to the seminary—a special one for students from other dioceses. These students had to obtain permission from their respective bishops. Josemaría sent a request to the bishop of Barbastro, and on November 12 that bishop sent to the bishop of Calahorra this response:

> Don José María Escrivá Albás, sixteen years of age, a native of this city and for the past three years a resident of Logroño, living with his family, and having, as he declares, a vocation to the ecclesiastical state, has requested permission for a transfer to the Diocese of Calahorra. We, therefore, taking into consideration the reasons expressed by said youth, and assuming his acceptance by that diocese, hereby excardinate him from the Diocese of Barbastro and transfer all of the jurisdiction that we have over him *ratione originis* [by reason of origin] to the Most Excellent Bishop of Calahorra. He may, if he sees fit, confer upon him all the minor and major orders.[97]

*   *   *

The "Old Seminary" of Logroño owed its name both to the length of time it had been a center of ecclesiastical studies and to its sheer age. The dilapidated building dated back to 1559. In that year the Jesuits established a school in Logroño. When they were expelled from Spain it passed into the hands of the diocese. In 1776 it began to be used as a seminary, but academic operations suffered notable interruptions. From 1808 to 1815 Napoleon's troops used it for a barracks and set up stables there. On several occasions later, it was a military hospital or a prison for captured Carlists.

The decrepit building, which did not have electric lighting until 1910, was an immense rectangular structure with an interior patio and five floors. Its rooms and halls, which were far larger and more numerous than necessary, were in shamefully poor condition. Moreover, the ground floor was occupied in 1917 by a company of artillery with a full allotment of men and horses.[98]

The code of conduct of that venerable establishment had

been drawn up according to norms promulgated on January 1, 1909, by Cardinal Gregorio Aguirre of Burgos, who was also the apostolic administrator of the diocese of Calahorra and La Calzada. The official text was entitled "Discipline to Be Observed by the College Gentlemen Who Are Residents of the Seminary." Here were spelled out the resident seminarians' daily schedule, "principal duties," and "special prohibitions." The latter included "all communication with the day students."[99]

There was a disciplinary reason for keeping residents and nonresidents separate: so that the nonresidents would not poke fun at the strict rules observed by the residents. At that time the nonresidents were all students whose families lived in Logroño; these young men ate and slept at home. But with this one exception the regimen of education and spiritual life was the same for everyone.

Josemaría entered the seminary at 6:30 each morning. First there was a period of private prayer, then Mass. Sometimes a Jesuit priest came in to give the homily. After Mass the day students went home for breakfast, and those taking theology returned to the seminary at 10:00. At 12:30, when class ended, they went home again and ate lunch with their families. By 3:00 they were back at the seminary for another class, followed by free time. The day ended with the Rosary and either a talk or spiritual reading.[100]

Josemaría did not abuse his freedom as a day student. Máximo Rubio, a fellow seminarian who also lived in Logroño with his family, says, "He was most punctual and exemplary. From all appearances, he had a real desire for perfection."[101] The resident students had special duties, among them giving catechism classes on Sundays, something the day students were not required to do. One of the resident seminarians, Amadeo Blanco, remembers Josemaría particularly well because he was the only day student who showed up on Sundays and volunteered to help out.[102]

The seminary was on Sagasta Street, not far from the Escrivás' first home in Logroño. Recently, in 1918, the family had left the old apartment and moved into a new building on Canalejas Street, where they also had a fourth-floor apartment, though not as centrally located as the previous one.[103]

One day Josemaría got a big surprise. Doña Dolores called him and Carmen aside to announce that she was expecting a baby. Although her pregnancy was already showing, her children had not thought of it as even a possibility. But then Josemaría remembered his prayer of several months earlier, and at once he was sure it would be a boy.[104]

Those winter weeks were ones of quiet family closeness. On February 28, 1919, Doña Dolores gave birth to a son, which for Josemaría was an obvious confirmation of his vocation.

> In answer to my petition, and even though it had been many years since my parents had had any children and they were not young anymore—in answer to my petition, I repeat, our Lord God (just nine or ten months after I asked him) saw to it that my brother was born. . . . I had asked for a baby brother.[105]

Two days later the boy was baptized at the church of Santiago el Real by Father Hilario Loza with the name Santiago Justo. The godparents were Carmen and Josemaría.[106]

During his two years at the seminary of Logroño (1918–1919 and 1919–1920), Josemaría completed all his first-year theology courses with great ease, receiving in all but one the outstanding evaluation of "Meritissimus" (Highest Honors).[107] He left only one of these courses (Theological Principles, also called Fundamental Theology) for the 1919–1920 school year—he had to leave at least one because, being not yet twenty-one, he was not permitted to take first-year theology on the fast track.[108] In this second year, he therefore had considerable free time, which he used to go more deeply into philosophy and improve his Latin.

6. *Priesthood and ecclesiastical career*

The testimony of his fellow seminarians is short, to the point, and strikingly consistent. Josemaría "was very careful about his outward appearance," says Amadeo Blanco. "He wore a blue jacket, a shirt with a high collar, and a tie." Luis Alonso says basically the same thing: "He always dressed very elegantly, in a complete suit, dark and well tailored."[109]

Pedro Baldomero Larios remembers him as being "very open and communicative, friendly, fun, cheerful, and very agreeable." "The thing about him that really stood out," observes Amadeo Blanco, "was his open, friendly smile; it clearly reflected an inner joy."[110] Máximo Rubio describes him as "a man of character, with a strong personality," and tells us that "he had a great influence on the piety and spirituality of his fellow seminarians."[111]

These reminiscences look especially significant alongside the opinions the superiors of the seminary expressed. The rector, Father Valeriano-Cruz Ordóñez, once made this brief report: "Said person is a graduate of the Institute with a diploma in the arts, a boy of very good disposition and very good spirit."[112] For confession, Josemaría probably went to the school principal, Father Gregorio Fernández Anguiano, whom he would always remember as "that holy priest."[113] Besides being devout, Father Gregorio had a surprising amount of administrative talent. In 1921 he was named vice-rector of the seminary, and within a short time he began to cultivate the souls of the seminarians with a firm hand, since their spiritual direction had been neglected for some time.

Within the seminary, discipline was very strict. The day students, on the other hand, had a somewhat different life. For them, weekends were free times when they could get together with friends and indulge in their favorite pastimes.

Josemaría lived an intense spiritual life. A classmate remembers "seeing him go on walks with a rosary in hand."[114]

In the evening, on his way home from the seminary, he often stopped at the church of Santa María de La Redonda to make a visit to the Blessed Sacrament.[115] His life of piety was in no way saccharine. It was a fruit of that divine restlessness consuming him, and it made him draw his companions along apostolically. "His way of thinking and acting also had an impact on the seminarians themselves," by example.[116]

His weekdays were devoted to study. Sundays he devoted to children's catechism classes in the morning and walks with his family in the afternoon, avoiding any occasion of socializing or conversing alone with Carmen's friends. "Despite our association," says Paula Royo, whose parents used to go on walks with the Escrivás, "I never got to be friends with Josemaría."[117] Referring specifically to those years in the seminary, Máximo Rubio, a classmate, speaks of the exquisite care with which Josemaría protected the purity of his feelings. "Everyone had a high opinion of him in this matter of purity. I did too."[118] But his cultivated delicacy did not go against common sense, as the following story, with nothing in it of prudishness, makes clear.

Military establishments were as common a sight in Logroño as ecclesiastical ones, with monasteries and barracks giving the whole city a somber uniformity. There were two infantry regiments (Bailén no. 24 and Cantabria no. 39), a mounted artillery regiment (no. 13), a military hospital, and military trading posts. In addition to the military and ecclesiastical establishments, there was a tobacco factory with a motley crew of women cigar makers about a block from The Great City of London, on Mercado Street.

At La Redonda, and also at the church of Santiago el Real, Josemaría saw among the devout faithful certain individuals who looked familiar. He recognized women from the tobacco plant and officers from the regiments. Those gray-haired officers and those cigar makers, who had lost their youthful looks, set the boy's imagination roaming. He saw officers and cigar makers on the verge of old age, erasing old frivolities and mistakes with their repentance. His reflections may well have sparked the devotion he would always have to Mary Magdalene, the penitent saint, the exemplar of contrite love.

> When I was starting to get intuitions about the Work, but did not yet know with clarity what it was that our Lord wanted of me, I started going to daily Mass. At the church I attended, I soon noticed quite a few women cigar makers who were up in years, and also quite a few military men with white mustaches. I surmised that both groups were making up for sins of their youth. Those repentant cigar makers and colonels made me think of Mary Magdalene.[119]

Josemaría's good appearance and other outstanding qualities—his good manners, cheerfulness, intelligence, and so forth—gave him a definite prestige among the seminarians. Outside the seminary, though, things were a little different. The young seminarian would sometimes run into old classmates. They might exchange greetings, a friendly gesture; but sometimes he met with a taunting look of derision or scorn that pained his soul.

In his journal he wrote, "I remember the look of pity, the sense that they were looking down their noses at me, that I got from my classmates at the Institute when, after finishing secondary school, I entered the service of the Church."[120] This simple observation—a very sad one for a seminarian—reflects the social status that the clerical state (and, indirectly, the whole Church) had in Spain in the early years of the twentieth century. Those sardonic looks from former classmates evidently did not come from any personal animosity. Along with a slight touch of anticlericalism, they expressed the general sense of superiority that the liberal bourgeoisie had toward seminarians. In those days, one rarely encountered a seminarian with a secondary-school degree. Even rarer were priests with a college degree in a secular field. Children from families of a higher intellectual, social, or economic position, if they

happened to feel a vocational call, preferred to enter a prestigious religious order or institute.[121]

Given all that, it is understandable why so many diocesan
clergy felt themselves tacitly and unfairly held in contempt by
sectors of society that, along with their religious unbelief, held
certain kinds of secular learning in fatuous esteem. Humanly
speaking, entering the seminary meant for many giving up all
hope of being materially well off. It was a safe assumption that
they would all end up as village priests, pastors in a city, chaplains for convents, or military chaplains. At best, by virtue of
their greater intellectual capabilities or other personal gifts,
they might manage to secure the position of a canon in a
cathedral, a professorship, or some other benefice. For Josemaría, entering the seminary meant renouncing the socially
and financially rewarding career he could have had as an architect or lawyer. He saw quite clearly what his ecclesiastical
prospects would be once he entered into the dynamics of clerical life after ordination. This, he wrote, was what typically happened to people in the seminary:

> They went from there to pursue their career. They be-
> haved well and tried to go from one parish to another, bet-
> ter one. Anyone who had the preparation would take the
> examinations for the position of canon. In time they would
> be admitted to the cathedral chapter, from whence came
> those needed to help out in the governing of the diocese, or
> in the formation of clergy in the seminary. . . .[122]

For some clerics, in other words, being a priest was something of an administrative job. This was an idea Josemaría did
not share in the least. The seminarian felt himself called to no
such career.

> That was not what God was asking of me, and I told
> myself, I don't want to be a priest just to be a priest, or "el
> cura," as they say in Spain. I had a lot of respect for

priests, but I didn't want for myself that kind of priest-hood.[123]

When Josemaría decided to become a priest, it was be-cause he judged that this would make it easier for him to carry out the hidden plan of God, and also because he sensed that it would be a good way to get to know God's will in this regard.[124]

It was not the example he got in his family—the fact that on both sides he had uncles who were priests—that brought him to the priesthood.

> I had never thought of becoming a priest, or of dedicat-ing myself to God. That problem had not presented itself to me, because I thought the priesthood was not for me. Even more, I was so bothered by the thought of possibly becom-ing a priest someday that in a way I felt anticlerical. I loved priests very much, because the formation I received in my home was profoundly religious; I had been taught to respect, to venerate, the priesthood. But not for me—for others.[125]

From a "divine restlessness," an inner agitation, Josemaría had moved to a certitude that our Lord wanted him for some-thing. He was getting inklings of Love, and in conformity with this love he totally surrendered himself, sacrificing all human yearnings. Actually given the readiness and joy with which he decided to become a priest, he may have seen that surrender not as a sacrifice, but, rather, as a joyful giving of his whole self.

His *Ut videam!* was an impatient lover's prayer, a wish to know more so that he could give all that was asked of him, a petition for the light he needed in order to set out on the right path toward accomplishing the will of God. He under-stood his vocation to the priesthood as an integral part of an-other vocation—one not yet in sight. He found himself, then, not at the end, the goal, but at the beginning of the path along which the will of God would become manifest. His life thus moved into the "premonition" stage, as he puts it. In his journal he writes, "I had premonitions from the beginning of 1918. Then I kept *seeing*, but without being able to tell exactly what it was that our Lord wanted. I could *see* that our Lord wanted something of me. I asked, and kept asking."[126]

Ever an enemy of mediocrity, Josemaría had thoroughly disposed himself to receive the specific fullness of his vocation to the priesthood, which he conceived as an ideal of love. And so, just as some of his classmates did not understand his entering the seminary, some of his fellow seminarians were amazed later at his indifference to everything concerned with "carving out a career." His high regard for the priesthood never lost any of its vigor. Witness this journal entry from 1930:

> A few days ago, someone had the nerve to ask me, when, of course, I hadn't said anything to invite such a question, if those of us in the priesthood get a pension when we reach old age. . . . It made me angry. Since I didn't give him an answer, the impertinent fellow asked me again. Then an answer occurred to me which to my way of thinking isn't changing the subject. "The priesthood," I told him, "is not a career—it's an apostolate!" That's the way I feel about it. And I wanted to write it in these notes so that, with the help of the Lord, I'll never forget the difference.[127]

Now we can better understand that earlier reaction of Don José, who, knowing the boy and his youthful ardor, counseled prudence and reflection. "My son," he said, "you need to really think this through. It's very hard not to have a house, not to have a home, not to have a love here on earth. Think about it a little more—but I will not oppose it."[128]

The news—the suddenness of it, the realization of all the changes and adjustments it would mean for the family, and especially the glimpse he got of the shining ideal that seemed to infuse his son—brought tears to his eyes. He had to get hold of himself inside and make a decision: "I will not oppose it." Perhaps he was thinking of the heroic sacrifices that perseverance on that path of holiness would require of his son. In any case he did not live to see, in this world, Josemaría's ordination to the priesthood.

Several years later, on January 23, 1929, in Madrid, at the bedside of a dying woman who had lived a very holy life, Josemaría gave her this commission: "If I am not going to be a priest who is not just good, but holy, tell Jesus to take me as soon as possible!"[129]

*   *   *

Everything seemed to indicate that Saragossa was the best place for him to study law, as Don José had suggested he do. Doña Dolores had two brothers, a sister, and a niece living there: Mauricio, whose wife's name was Mercedes; Carlos, a canon and archdeacon of the cathedral; and, living with Carlos, Candelaria, a widow, and her daughter Manolita Lafuente. Saragossa had both a pontifical university and a secular university. Even its geographical closeness and good connections with Logroño seemed to make it the best place for Josemaría to do his ecclesiastical and secular studies.

According to the Baroness of Valdeolivos, the move from Logroño to the seminary of Saragossa was worked out during 1919.

> Some later summer, possibly the summer of 1919, Don José, Josemaría's father, came to Fonz to see his brother and sisters. He brought photos of his children: Santiago (who had just been born), Carmen, and Josemaría. He showed them to us, very proud of his children. . . . Then, pointing to Josemaría, he said thoughtfully, "He has told me he wants to be a priest but also wants to study law. This will be a bit of a sacrifice for us. . . .[130]

Paying for studies away from Logroño would be a financial sacrifice affecting the whole family. But it would have been an even greater burden on the family if he had gone to Barcelona or Madrid to become an architect.

Later in the school year, Josemaría expressed his intentions to the seminary rector. Knowing the intellectual capabilities and the good vocational disposition of the student, he offered his support. Later, in the first half of June 1920, and possibly through the mediation of his uncle Carlos, whom his mother had asked to intercede for him, Josemaría obtained permission from the cardinal archbishop of Saragossa for his eventual incardination into that archdiocese.

The next step was to request permission to transfer from Logroño to Saragossa and continue his ecclesiastical studies there. He applied to the bishop of Calahorra and La Calzada for excardination.*[131] The application was approved, on the basis of a favorable report from the rector of the seminary of Logroño, who, as mentioned, characterized him as "a boy of very good disposition and very good spirit."[132] With this he was transferred to the authority of the archbishop of Saragossa. The *Libro de Decretos Arzobispales* (Book of Decrees of the Archbishop) contains the following entry, dated July 19, 1920: "Dn. José María Escrivá Albás.—Decision as to his incardination in this Archdiocese, in his favor."[133]

Dated September 28, 1920, there is another concise entry in which the cardinal archbishop gives the student permission to enter the seminary of San Francisco de Paula.[134] Thus begins a new stage in the seminarian's life.

---

*At that time, if a man wanted to study for the priesthood and be ordained for a diocese other than the one in which he was born, he needed the permission not only of the bishop of the diocese for which he wished to be ordained but also of the bishop of his diocese of origin.

3

Saragossa (1920-1925)

1. *San Carlos Seminary*

In 1960, in the address he gave upon receiving an honorary doctorate from the University of Saragossa, Monsignor Escrivá reminded his listeners of what were for him some "unforgettable memories of long-ago times": "Years spent in San Carlos Seminary, on my way to the priesthood, from the clerical tonsure I received from the hands of Cardinal Juan Soldevila, in a secluded chapel of the archbishop's residence, up to my first Mass, said very early one morning in the chapel of the shrine of Our Lady of the Pillar."[1]

He was at San Carlos Seminary until the day of his ordination. In the records there is a note, handwritten by the rector, saying he entered the seminary on September 28, 1920.[2] He was, then, at San Carlos for exactly four and a half years, since he was ordained to the priesthood on March 28, 1925.

At that time Saragossa had two seminaries preparing candidates for the priesthood: the conciliar seminary (San Valero y San Braulio)* and San Carlos (also known as San Francisco de Paula). Students of both schools took their ecclesiastical courses at the pontifical university, whose classrooms occupied the ground floor of a building on La Seo Plaza, next to the archbishop's residence. The history and character of the large, rambling building

*The Seminary of San Valero y San Braulio was referred to as the "conciliar" seminary because it was founded in response to a decree of the Council of Trent calling for the establishment of diocesan seminaries.

where Josemaría lived from 1920 to 1925 are strikingly similar to those of the old seminary of Logroño. San Carlos started out in 1558 as a Jesuit residence with four floors and a spacious interior patio. A large church, with beautiful baroque stucco decorations, was later attached to it.[3] The entire complex, including the church, was seized by the government after the expulsion of the Jesuits in 1767 and then ceded by King Carlos III for the founding of the Priestly Seminary of San Carlos [Saint Charles] Borromeo. But the purpose of this foundation was not to educate boys and turn them into virtuous seminarians. This royal seminary had a much grander aim: improvement and enlightenment of the clergy—an enterprise very appropriate to the Age of Enlightenment. Its staff members were all well-educated diocesan priests with prestige and expertise. Answerable directly to the archbishop, they were given such special assignments as organizing his pastoral visits, preparing the examinations to be taken by the ordinands, and assisting in the granting of ministerial faculties.

About a century later, the light of the Enlightenment having faded and money become scarce, the old institution was reduced to a half dozen priests who lived on the second floor and presided at the church's services.[4] That was how things were when, in 1885, Cardinal Francisco de Paula Benavides became head of the archdiocese. Deciding to create a seminary for boys from poor families, he saw that besides financial assets, San Carlos had several corridors of empty rooms—easily enough space for a hundred boys. Such an enormous number of rooms was far more than that small group of prestigious clerics (called by some "the gentlemen of San Carlos") could possibly use.

The cardinal carried out his plan with great speed. The new seminary opened with an enrollment of fifty-two students on October 4, 1886. Unfortunately, though, his calculations proved overly optimistic. Cardinal Benavides was not an administrator and had no business experience, just praiseworthy intentions. Unforeseen expenses and other difficulties began to rain down on him. He had not concerned himself with the question of the faculty, so the authorities hurriedly agreed that the seminarians would for the time being attend classes at the conciliar seminary.[5] This temporary arrangement would, over time, become a permanent one.

After attaining this "charitable purpose of providing a place for the many youngsters from poor families who, inspired by God, knock at the doors of the sanctuary with the noble aspiration of being enlisted in the clerical ranks," the cardinal realized that his protégés needed a code of conduct. This problem had an easier solution. The cardinal himself drew up a set of regulations, which appeared in January 1887. In its preamble, addressed to "the Rector, Directors, and students of our San Francisco de Paula Seminary for the Poor," he expressed his wish that the rules serve for the good governance of said seminary, "which is giving such great encouragement to our disheartened spirit with the well-founded hopes that it offers us."[6]

But the "seminary for the poor" dragged along in a languid way. When Cardinal Benavides died in 1895, his successor, Archbishop Alda, decided to put the finances on a sounder basis. He did away with the scholarship examinations and began also to admit seminarians who could pay their way. From then on San Francisco de Paula, or the Seminary for the Poor, was known by the more generic name San Carlos, as it will be called here for simplicity's sake. [San Francisco de Paula was one of several smaller, individual seminaries of the General Seminary of San Carlos.] It differed from the conciliar seminary very little, if at all, except for the number of students, their place of residence, and their uniform.[7] The conciliar seminary had about one hundred fifty seminarians, counting both residents and day students; San Carlos, fewer than forty. Students at the conciliar seminary wore a blue cape with a pink sash. The San Carlos uniform was a sleeveless black cape, a red sash with a shield (a sun, with rays, with the word "Caritas" ["charity"] in the center), and a four-pointed black cap with a purple tuft in the middle.[8]

*   *   *

The theology students lived on the third floor of San Carlos. Above, on the fourth floor, were the bedrooms of the youngest students, those taking courses in the humanities and philosophy. The rooms were small, but more space was not needed, since the only furnishings were a bed, a table and chair, a washstand with a water jug, a nightstand with a candlestick, and a coatrack. Clothes, books, and other belongings were kept in the suitcase or trunk the seminarian had brought with him.

The plumbing reflected the antiquity of the building. The kindest word for it is "deficient." The seminarians had no more than one rudimentary bathroom per floor, plus a faucet for filling the water jugs for their washstands. There was electric light, but the wiring was so poor and inadequate it had to be supplemented with candles. Chapel, dining room, study hall, corridors, and stairways all had electric bulbs, but bedrooms did not, so weekly each seminarian was given a number of candle stubs for his candlestick.[9]

The seminarians rose at 6:30 and had thirty minutes for washing up and getting dressed. It was at this point in the schedule that Josemaría suffered his first unpleasant surprise, for nowhere could he find any kind of shower or bathtub. At 7:00 began the half hour of meditation, in a private chapel on the third floor—a room with a vaulted ceiling where Mass was said only on very rare occasions and the Blessed Sacrament was not usually reserved.[10] After that they went down to attend Mass in the church of San Carlos, entering from the seminary patio. They would sit in the first pews, which were reserved for them. Usually the Mass was celebrated by the seminary president.

They ate breakfast in silence, listening to a reading from *The Imitation of Christ* or some other spiritual book. Then, in line, they walked to the university. Avoiding the main road because of the traffic, they made their way, under the watchful eyes of the prefects, through the labyrinth of back streets and alleyways leading to the cathedral of La Seo.

The pontifical university and the conciliar seminary shared the same building. The conciliar seminary, San Valero y San Braulio, was founded in 1788. After various vicissitudes, it moved in 1848 to a new location where once had stood the royal council chambers, which had been reduced to rubble by Napoleon's armies. In 1897 its school component was raised to the level of a pontifical university, a distinction it kept until 1933.[11]

At the pontifical university the San Carlos students (who never did have a faculty of their own) had two hours of class in the morning, with a break for study and recreation. At about 12:30 they returned to San Carlos for lunch. They maintained silence in the dining room while one student read aloud from some martyrology or from Scripture, until the presiding prefect gave them permission to talk.[12]

After lunch they had a period of recreation and then set out again for the university, taking the same back streets and alleyways as in the morning. After an hour of class they returned to the seminary for an afternoon snack and a period of study. There was one communal study hall, with desks, monitored by a prefect. The study sessions were broken up by the Rosary and spiritual reading.[13]

At 9:00 they had supper, and immediately afterward said night prayers, made an examination of conscience, and went to bed.

2. The book of "life and customs"

The president of the Seminary of San Carlos was Bishop Miguel de los Santos y Díaz de Gómara. Its vice president was Father Antonio Moreno Sánchez. Among the priests belonging to this illustrious foundation was the rector of San Francisco de Paula; in 1920 this was Father José López Sierra. He had under him two prefects who helped him maintain order and discipline. These prefects were chosen from among the students in the last two years of theology.[14] One of their main duties was to note any disciplinary action, or anything else having to do with the conduct of the seminarians, in monthly reports that would be examined by the rector and then transferred to the official records. The judgments of the rector, once written, were indelible.

The record book's title page reads, "*De vita et moribus* de los alumnos del Seminario de San Francisco de Paula" ("Of the life and customs of the students of the Seminary of San Francisco de Paula"). This famous book, containing in summary the history and exploits of the seminarians, begins in February 1913.[15] It has large foldout pages, one for each seminarian, with a section on his family and, below, five columns: "Piety," "Application," "Discipline," "Character," and "Vocation." On one side of each column are grades, on the other "General Observations." Josemaría's page is 111. The section for background information says, "He was recommended by Father Carlos Albás Blanc." Uncle Carlos, the archdeacon, a man of influence among the clergy of Saragossa, was for the seminarian both good luck and bad. At first he welcomed his nephew with open arms, and probably he had a lot to do with what the rector wrote two lines below: "He has a half scholarship." There is no reason to doubt the good disposition of the archdeacon with respect to his family's affairs. Still the fact is that at that time there were only half a dozen paying seminarians at San Carlos.

During the first weeks, Josemaría often went out to eat with his uncle on Sundays and feast days, as regulations allowed. He also accepted the invitations of another of his mother's brothers, his uncle Mauricio, who had recently been widowed and had a large family. He preferred, however, to space out his Sunday visits, so as not to be a nuisance to his uncles. Besides, he did not want to be singled out and excused from the rules, something that might arouse his companions' envy.[16]

Ten days after entering the seminary, Josemaría was put in charge of the Association for the Apostolate of Prayer for the 1920–1921 school year. That may have been because it was obvious that he had a solid spiritual life. "He was the only seminarian I knew who would go down to the church during free time," says one of his classmates.[17] In fairness to the other seminarians, it should be mentioned that there was no shortage of religious exercises. Jesús López Bello, a classmate of Josemaría's, gives us this very conservative (by no means exhaustive) list of the daily devotions: "In the morning, in common, Morning Offering, meditation, and Holy Mass. Before and after meals, visit to the Blessed Sacrament. In the afternoon, Holy Rosary and spiritual reading. At night, visit to the Blessed Sacrament and examination of conscience. On Saturday evening, Benediction and Salve Regina. During the days of May, the 'Flowers of Our Lady,' with sermon. The Seven Sundays of Saint Joseph. The novena to the Immaculate Heart of Mary. The Seven Sorrows of our Lady. Octave of the Child Jesus, at Christmas. Every month we had a day of recollection, and once a year, a retreat."[18]

Within the tight rhythm of the schedule, already filled with religious activities, personal piety was usually shown, says Aurelio Navarro, "in the intensity and application with which each one tried to live the common devotions."[19] Another seminarian, Arsenio Górriz, remarks that Josemaría "was pious, very pious," and that this was evidenced "not so much by what he did as by how he did it."[20] But he also continued his custom of praying all three parts of the Rosary, and his heart beat impatiently with repeated aspirations—*Domine, ut videam! Domine, ut sit!*—that kept alive in his soul the call he had received from our Lord in Logroño. And as if to reinforce that alertness, he took advantage of free time to go to the nearby Basilica of Our Lady of the Pillar and make a similar request before her statue: *Domina, ut sit!* ("My Lady, let it be!").[21]

Feast days provided a welcome break in the routine succession of days in the Church calendar. On feast days the seminarians got up a half hour later, had no classes, and enjoyed a walk. There was a good amount of extra food and wine on the tables and the students were served an especially substantial meal, including what we would now call an additional

entrée.[22] (However, the hierarchical principle was always preserved. The priests at San Carlos usually had two entrées a day,
one of meat and the other of fish. For this reason, among others, the seminarians' nickname for the prestigious priests of
this house—"the gentlemen of San Carlos"—did not lack a
touch of envy-inspired sarcasm.)

* * *

Josemaría entered the Seminary of San Carlos with a
spirit of detachment. He knew that living with other seminarians would require changing some habits and giving up
many comforts of home. As a way of symbolically expressing
that renunciation, when he arrived at the seminary he gave
the custodian the tobacco, pipe, and other smoking para-
phernalia he had brought with him, and, with this definitive
gesture, gave up smoking.[23] But what he could not have foreseen was that this stage of his priestly vocation would be a
real trial by fire.

There was, to begin with, the lack of the culture and good
hygienic standards to which he was accustomed. Still, in an effort to accommodate himself to the mentality and customs of
his fellow seminarians, he made it a point to be sociable with
all of them and to be of service to them.[24]

His efforts to adapt began on the very first day. At home he
had gotten into the habit of washing himself from head to toe
every day, summer or winter, with cold water, and now he had
to fetch several jugs of water every morning to keep up that
practice.[25]

Women never came into the seminary. A few male servants
took care of the general cleaning. (Needless to say, the appearance of the buildings left something to be desired.) As for personal clothing and changes of bedclothes, each seminarian
took care of these things as best he could. It was Josemaría's
good luck that his clothes were washed at the house of his
uncle Carlos,[26] but he took care himself of the meticulous pol-

ishing of his shoes and brushing of his cassock that the regulations required.[27]

If his classmates had been surveyed concerning his most notable characteristics, responses would no doubt have focused on his friendly courtesy and impeccable grooming. "Josemaría was a gentleman from head to foot, in every way: in his manner of greeting people, in the way he treated people, in the way he dressed, in his table manners," says one of his classmates. "Without trying, he presented a striking contrast to what was typical back then."[28] Another seminarian mentions something that happened on one of their excursions, when they visited the mental hospital: "We saw many mentally ill individuals, some of them really out of their minds—a man, for instance, who claimed he was more powerful than anyone else because he was the king. Well, at the end of our visit there was an old woman who kept insisting that Josemaría was her fiancé, because he looked so good and was so well dressed. Truth is, he always looked very elegant."[29]

As the years went by, it became obvious that the son was taking after the father in terms of refinement and good manners. What had become of the child who hid under the bed when he had to wear something new? Where was the boy who refused to put on his Sunday best when school pictures were taken? Things had changed a great deal for the family since then. Fortune had turned its back on the Escrivás, and poverty now obliged him to care for an old suit as if it were new.

His carefulness about personal hygiene, and especially his morning ablutions, soon earned him a nickname. "When I entered the seminary," he tells us, "I went on keeping my shoes and clothes very clean, as I had always done before. I don't know why, but I became for that reason 'el señorito' [the little gentleman] to some people who had treated me with the utmost politeness before I entered the seminary. Another cause of surprise and curiosity for those good seminarians—all of whom were better than I was, and most of whom became exemplary priests, several even dying as martyrs—was that I washed myself, that I tried to take a sponge bath, every day. Again I was called 'el señorito.' "[30]

The term "señorito" is obviously a euphemism. Some gave him the more openly insulting nickname of "pijaito," an Aragonese expression more or less along the lines of "rich little daddy's boy."[31] Knowing how much he disliked any lack of hygiene or cleanliness, one of the more uncouth and aggressive students—one who was very sparing in the use of soap and water—used to rub up against him, saying, "You need to smell like a man!" One day, dripping with sweat, he rubbed his sleeve on Josemaría's face. Josemaría nearly exploded, but controlled himself and put an end to the other's shamelessness with a remark that was, considering the situation, rather mild: "Being dirtier doesn't make you more of a man."[32]

But the ridicule did not stop there. Very soon there were also taunts about his spiritual life. His daily visits to the Basilica of Our Lady of the Pillar brought him the additional nickname of "Mystical Rose"—an epithet of exceptionally poor taste, coming from seminarians and being so irreverent toward our Lady.[33] Josemaría was also an object of criticism because of his lengthy visits to the Blessed Sacrament in the church of San Carlos and because of the apostolic zeal he showed in his conversations. "Here comes the dreamer!" some of his fellow seminarians would say in a loud voice, quoting the words of Jacob's sons concerning their brother Joseph. Some habitually referred to him as "the dreamer."[34] Josemaría tried to turn a deaf ear, but the nicknames hurt him deeply because they were such cutting insults and showed such deliberate malice, and especially because they broke the ties of fellowship and friendship.[35]

This behavior of some of his fellow students was due mainly to a lack of good manners, to envy, or to ignorance, but in any case it left painful memories in his soul. Ten years later, writing with notable restraint, he unburdened himself to our Lord. He begins by lamenting the generally lower-class background of priestly vocations and the deficient level of culture and manners among some seminarians:

About vocations of seminarians, I say: What a shame that families, even very devout ones, hold back from sending their sons to the seminaries! In many regions of Spain, with rare exceptions, one sees in the seminaries only the sons of poor farmhands. . . .

After pointing out that in our seminaries magnificent examples of virtue can be seen . . . , I must also say, to be entirely truthful, that those who live there are likely to be quite holy but very bad-mannered, though there will be exceptions. Someone born and brought up in a different kind of environment really suffers.[36]

On February 14, 1964, while taking another look at those thorns on his path to his priestly vocation, he said to a sizable audience:

Time went by, and many hard things, terrible things, happened. I will not tell you about them, because although they no longer cause me any pain, they probably would cause you pain. They were axe blows that our Lord God gave in order to make—from that tree—the beam that would serve, in spite of itself, for the constructing of his Work. Almost unconsciously I would repeat, "Domine, ut videam! Domine, ut sit!" I didn't know what it was that I was praying for, but I kept going forward, forward, not responding to God's goodness, but waiting for what I would have to receive later on: a string of graces, coming one after the other, which I didn't know how to classify, but which I called "operative" because they dominated my will in such a way that I almost didn't have to make any effort.[37]

Those "hard things, terrible things," those "axe blows," evidently were not the crudities or insults coming from a few seminarians. The proof is that the echo of those events was so poignant that forty years later it was still resounding in his memory, whereas usually the stream of life numbs and smooths school memories as a current does the rough edges of pebbles. With the passing of time, in fact, he would call those hurtful nicknames "trifles," tiny things, in comparison to the great good done to his soul by his stay in that seminary, of which "he remembered only good things."[38] No; more bitter roots must be sought for that other memory of San Carlos.

The priest who in 1964 was reluctant to dredge up personal events from the past hinted at those "axe blows" when in July 1934 he took a reflective look at the course of his priestly vocation in a text meant to be read only after his death. "Where would I be now, had you not called me?" he silently asked our Lord. And then he gave our Lord his own answer:

> Had you not prevented my leaving the seminary of Saragossa when I believed I had mistaken my path, I would perhaps be traipsing around the Spanish parliament, as some of my classmates from the university are doing . . . and not exactly at your side, since . . . there was a point when I felt profoundly anticlerical—I who love my brothers in the priesthood so much![39]

In this confession we can glimpse Josemaría's resistance to adopting the clerical model imposed by the environment. A terrible storm broke out in his soul as a result of the difficulties he experienced, but he still felt that he was on the right path. And finally a saving intervention came from our Lord that confirmed him in his vocation.

Not surprisingly, many of his classmates came to a wrong conclusion about the future of the seminarian from Logroño. They thought Josemaría, being so cultured and well-mannered, would not become a priest, since, as one of the seminary employees put it, "he had possibilities for a better career."[40] But this idea was both naive and off-base, it showed a total lack of awareness of his high-mindedness. He saw from the start that there was only one way for him to go: to ignore the impertinences of this or that seminarian, while at the same time trying to detach himself from certain tastes and in-clinations, as he had in one day rid himself of tobacco. Other, very different obstacles would be the ones that actually got in his way.

What was unusual about Josemaría's vocation was that priesthood was a step toward its fulfillment, but was not the whole thing. The ultimate reason for his presence at San Car-los was a desire to respond to those "inklings of Love" he had been experiencing over the past three years. Neither the seminary atmosphere, which he never got used to, nor the taunting of some of his companions, nor their vulgarity, could cause a vocational crisis that would put to the test the boy's fidelity to God's call. But he did suffer intense inner turmoil due to anticlerical feelings surging in him and fo-menting a holy rebellion against any attempt to debase the pure concept of the priesthood to a lucrative "ecclesiastical career." On this point he kept his thoughts and feelings strictly to himself, yet to some extent the struggle did show through. "One could see that he had something within him that made the seminary too narrow a framework for his in-terests," says one of his companions.[41] At heart he was a "dreamer," of things divine. This he remained all his life, so those who called him by this name were not entirely wrong.

As the school year went on, the rector, Father José López Sierra, began to get perplexing reports about the seminarian from Logroño. The independent behavior of this nephew of the archdeacon, his singular piety, his offbeat ideas and comments about the ecclesiastical career, and vague rumors of nicknames, insults, and conflicts—all these things caused the rector to form a far-from-favorable opinion. To his way of thinking, Josemaría was living and acting too differently from the ma-jority of the seminarians.

At the end of the school year, in the summer of 1921, the rector put his opinion in writing. On Josemaría's page in the book *De vita et moribus*, he wrote, "Piety: Good. Application: Average. Discipline: Average. Character: Inconstant and haughty, but well-mannered and courteous. Vocation: he seems to have one."[42]

The "Average" for application, for dedication to study, does not seem to square with Josemaría's excellent examination grades—which, of course, are recorded, one by one, by the rector himself, immediately after these evaluations. The "Average" for discipline is contradicted by the monthly reports of the prefect in charge. Josemaría was one of the few students who did not have a single punishment imposed on him in that whole school year. As for character, the evaluation is thought-out and balanced, but not consistent with the testimony of his fellow seminarians.[43]

As far as vocation is concerned, there is no reason to doubt the rector's sincerity. However, that "seems to have one," innocuous as it appears, conveys misgivings and implies some doubt. The prefect Santiago Lucus, on the other hand, assessed Josemaría's likelihood of having a vocation as "Good," which does not fit in too well with the rector's guarded statement.[44] What could account for that unconscious prejudice on the part of Father José López Sierra? Was he perhaps disturbed by the small commotion the new seminarian was causing? Was there something about the boy's appearance and demeanor that made him uncertain he would persevere? All we know for certain is that the Lord permitted the rector to misinterpret the facts. But what doubts assaulted Josemaría himself, to make him admit "I believed I had mistaken my path"?

Josemaría kept this terrible interior trial to himself and did not even mention the obstacles that he encountered. But although he had a solid certainty of his vocation, he did not know what to make of those hints God was giving him.

And I, half blind, was always waiting for the answer. Why am I becoming a priest? Our Lord wants something; what is it? And in Latin—not very elegant Latin—using the words of the blind man of Jericho, I kept repeating, "Domine, ut videam! Ut sit! Ut sit! What is this thing that you want and that I don't know? Domina, ut sit!"[45]

At the beginning of the 1921–1922 school year the rector may still have had his doubts, for on October 17 he wrote to the rector of the seminary in Logroño asking for information on Josemaría.

> Please be so good as to inform me, as briefly as possible, . . . as to the moral, religious, and disciplinary conduct of a former nonresident student of the seminary that you so worthily direct: José María Escrivá y Albás, native of Barbastro, legitimate son of Don José María Escrivá and Doña Dolores, residents of Logroño. Please also mention anything else you consider relevant concerning his vocation to the priestly state and his personal qualities, returning this communication with the corresponding report. God grant you a long life. Saragossa, October 17, 1921. José López Sierra, Rector.[46]

By return mail he received the following response: "During his stay in this seminary, I saw his moral, religious, and disciplinary conduct as being beyond reproach and as giving clear proof of a vocation to the ecclesiastical state. God grant you a long life. Logroño, October 20, 1921. Gregorio Fernández, Vice-rector."[47]

Years later, thinking back on the persons Providence had placed at his side to nurture his "incipient vocation," Josemaría would write:

> In Logroño . . . there was that holy priest, the vice-rector of the seminary, Father Gregorio Fernández. In Saragossa, Father José López Sierra, the poor rector of San Francisco whom our Lord changed in such a way that, after really doing everything he could to induce me to abandon my vocation (he did this with the best of intentions), he was my one and only defender against everyone else.[48]

These brief lines provide the key to the meaning of those events, and the role assigned to the seminary rector, in God's plans. The change in him was truly miraculous. That is how Josemaría saw it: as an answer from heaven to his prayers and a confirmation of his vocation to the priesthood. Freed of his prejudices against that "inconstant and haughty" seminarian, as he had so pejoratively described him, the rector was later to write, "A first-rate seminarian, distinguished among his classmates by his polished manners, his friendly and simple demeanor, and his obvious modesty; respectful toward his superiors and obliging and kind toward his companions, he was highly regarded by the former and admired by the latter."[49]

3. *Study and vacations*

The world of the seminary, already turned in on itself, was still more tightly hemmed in by the list of regulations. Fortunately, however, those in charge of San Carlos softened the rigors by a rather lenient interpretation of the text. For example, while the categorical prohibition against smoking was applied literally to the younger seminarians, or "philosophers," the "theologians" were allowed to smoke behind closed doors.[50]

It was also against the rules to look out the windows or to socialize on the terrace.[51] But there was no better site for recreation and games than the spacious fourth floor, which had large windows looking out onto the small plaza of San Carlos. This was the favorite place for handball. But Josemaría preferred to take walks along the corridors around the courtyard. One of them was in almost total darkness, and an inspired joker had written on the wall the psalm verse *Per diem sol non uret te, neque luna per noctem* ("The sun shall not smite you by day, nor the moon by night").[52]

As for other prohibitions, we have already seen how the seminarians observed the rule against the use of epithets or nicknames.[53]

Students at the conciliar seminary were under even tighter control than those at San Carlos, since they lived and studied in the same building, going out only on excursion days. Those at San Carlos got to walk through the old downtown area every day; they got fresh air, sunshine, and as much contact with the city's life as was permitted by the "composure, order, and symmetry" that the seminarians were required to maintain on their way to and from the university.[54]

The Pontifical University of San Valero y San Braulio was situated in the historic heart of Saragossa, which was originally a Roman colony. According to an ancient tradition, during her lifetime our Lady visited that prosperous city in Tarraconensis to encourage the apostle Saint James in his work of evangelization, and a church was built in her honor. During the Muslim occupation the practice of the Christian faith continued without interruption, and when the city was reconquered in 1118 the Church hierarchy was reestablished.[55]

The archdiocese of Saragossa covers a large territory and has several suffragan sees, among them Barbastro. Starting in 1902 the diocese was run by Archbishop Juan Soldevila, a man learned in ecclesiastical studies and a skillful speaker and administrator. He was well known for his pastoral dynamism and the reforms he introduced into the diocesan system of government. He pushed ahead with the renovation of the Basilica of Our Lady of the Pillar and spread this Marian devotion to Latin America. In 1919 he was named a cardinal.[56]

At that time Saragossa had some 140,000 inhabitants, half of whom had moved there from other parts of the country in the past twenty years. Its industrial growth—sugar beet refineries, flour mills, textile plants, and metal shops—produced major social changes setting the stage for labor–management confrontations and anarchist agitation.*[57]

The seminarians did not read newspapers. What happened outside the seminary either did not concern them or took them by surprise. Generally speaking, only those whose families

---

*In the early twentieth century, many Spanish workers belonged to anarchist trade unions. Saragossa was one of the cities where anarchist unions were most powerful.

lived in Saragossa were informed about what was going on in the world. During the autumn of 1920 Josemaría had occasion to travel through the city, because of his Sunday visits to his uncles, but that situation did not last long.

A glance at his study program shows the impressive list of courses he had to tackle as soon as he arrived from Logroño. In the first year he took five second-year-theology courses— On the Incarnate Word and Grace, Acts and Virtues, Homiletics, Patristics, and Liturgy—plus another four courses, since Saragossa's curriculum did not coincide with Logroño's.[58] Two (Greek and Hebrew) were in the humanities, and the other two (Introduction to Sacred Scripture, and New Testament Exegesis) were first-year-theology courses.

He was a diligent student but did not have to put out too much effort, although, as with all students, when it was time for an examination, "I never felt what you could call calm."[59] His grades that year in Greek and Hebrew ("Average") are an exception in his otherwise brilliant academic record.[60] His uncle the archdeacon made him see the importance of Greek for the study of patristics, and the nephew, "on his own initiative, when the course was over, put a lot of time into reviewing the material until he got up to a really acceptable level."[61]

* * *

The professors were a diverse lot: some wise and some not so wise, some blessed with great pedagogical gifts and others woefully lacking in them, some with a lot of initiative and a few who were sticklers for routine. Josemaría tried to assimilate the positive qualities he saw in each, with the result that his recollections include many edifying anecdotes.

Of his moral theology professor, a wise and prudent man, he says that at the beginning of a lesson about the virtue of chastity and the vices opposed to it, he gave his students this piece of advice from Saint Alphonsus Liguori: Commend yourself to the Blessed Virgin and be at peace.[62]

From Father Santiago Guallart, his homiletics professor, he learned not to rely on improvisation, the spontaneity of a mind either conceited or lazy. On one occasion Father Josemaría said to a group of people, "I don't improvise anything, and don't you believe that anyone does. I remember that I had a homiletics professor who was very well known and admired, particularly for his improvisations. Well, one day eight or ten students were chatting with him, and he said to them, 'Not once have I ever improvised. Whenever I am invited anywhere, I know I'm going to be asked to say a few words, and I prepare myself well.' "[63]

But Josemaría's intellectual horizon was not limited to ecclesiastical studies. He stood out among his companions at the seminary for his "broad culture," and especially for his interest in the human side of events. As one classmate puts it, "He was very human. Gifted with a great sense of humor, he had the critical capacity to pick apart all kinds of incidents in a nice way and see the funny side of things. I had a great admiration for the little epigrams he would write in a little notebook that he carried in his pocket. These were clever phrases, very ingenious, either jovial or satirical, showing a great understanding of human nature. They were also surprising in that they showed both a mastery of contemporary Spanish and an impressive familiarity with classic authors. Recalling them later, I have sometimes been reminded of Aristophanes' style in *The Wasps*. They were full of a very human philosophy of life and always had a moral at the end."[64]

By one of those flukes that life is full of, Josemaría got a chance to demonstrate his oratorical and literary gifts. For the students' entertainment it was customary to celebrate some events in a more intimate setting, free of academic rigidity.[65] For one of those events—one held in honor of Bishop Miguel de los Santos, president of San Carlos—the rector had to ask the help of Josemaría. The nature of the occasion and the status of the honoree called for a rather lofty literary presentation. Don Miguel, who had just a few months earlier been appointed titular bishop of Tagora and auxiliary bishop of

Saragossa (he was consecrated December 19, 1920), was a very learned man, having earned a doctorate in theology in Saragossa and a doctorate in canon law and philosophy at the Pontifical Gregorian University in Rome. He also had secular degrees: a licentiate in law from the University of Saragossa and a doctorate in law from Madrid's Central University.[66]

Josemaría at first demurred but finally gave in. The topic he chose was the bishop's motto, *Obedientia Tutior* (Obedience Is the Safer Way). He delivered his discourse in Latin, in the form of a poetic composition. His reflections on the special security attained by adhering to the counsels of one's superiors, and the elegance of his presentation, were greatly appreciated by the bishop and by the half dozen priests of San Carlos who took part in the celebration.[67]

There is another academic anecdote from his second year in Saragossa. One of his courses in the school year of 1921–1922 was *De Deo Creante* (On God the Creator), which was taught in Latin by Father Manuel Pérez Aznar. This professor liked to give very involved theoretical explanations during the first part of the course. Then, having reached the summit, he would begin his descent in the second semester through a more pragmatic system of questions and explanations. He put great emphasis on orthodoxy. A declared Thomist, he critically confronted errors and heresies, at the same time giving his students the "antidote to the venom." It was from him, in fact, that Josemaría learned the right use of antidotes when one has to read doctrinally contaminated books. That kind of poison is, after all, as he would later put it, transmitted "as though through osmosis."[68]

One day, indulging in a little casuistry, Father Manuel asked Josemaría about the rib of Adam mentioned in the Bible, *utrum costa Adami fuerit supererogatoria an naturalis*—was this an extra rib or one of the regular ones? Caught unawares, Josemaría tried to buy time. First he gave a long, drawn-out discourse in Latin about our father Adam, then did the same with Eve. But no matter how many ways he approached the subject,

no idea came to his rescue. He kept expanding on the subject
until finally the professor ran out of patience and said to him
in Spanish, "Fine, but what about that rib?"[69]

* * *

The seminary's bookkeeping was done by the rector and
could not have been simpler. The general expenses of the
house were taken care of by the Royal Seminary of San Carlos,
and since almost all the seminarians either had a scholarship or
provided services in lieu of tuition, calculations of income
were not very complicated either. For the school year of 1920-
1921, for example, the income consisted in four and a half
board payments and the proceeds from the sale of a dozen
emblems for students' academic robes. Four seminarians paid
in full; the half payment was for Josemaría, who had a partial
scholarship.

The rector's scrupulous thoroughness in computing days
of boarding at the seminary and amounts to be paid is helpful
to us. According to the accounts sheet for that year, Josemaría
paid 157 pesetas and 50 centimos for 252 days of room and
board. (Full payment was one peseta and twenty-five centimos
per day.)[70] The 252 days were, exactly, the total from his arrival
on September 28, 1920, up to the closing of accounts on June 7,
1921. Seminarians usually stayed uninterruptedly from September to June, as the regulations required.[71]

In those long months spent far from his family, the seminarian kept up a frequent correspondence with his loved ones.
He told them of his studies and youthful dreams, and tried to
cheer them up. The Christmas of 1920 was his first away from
home. He remembered with nostalgia those Christmases in
Barbastro, and in particular an old carol Doña Dolores used to
sing to him, that she would now sing as a lullaby to his brother,
Guitín (as Santiago was usually called in the family): "Mother,
at the door there is a little boy, more beautiful than the shining
sun, who says he is cold. . . ."[72]

On receiving news from home and rereading accounts of little household events, he could glimpse between the lines the family's hardships and his father's sufferings.[73] When the time came for summer vacation, his presence at home filled everyone with joy. He visited Father Hilario, the pastor of Santiago el Real, and put himself at his service.[74] He spent time with his father and took his mind off his problems, and helped his mother with her work. He went on walks with little Guitín, holding him by the hand. There is a picture of the two of them on a park bench, taken in the summer of 1922, when his brother was three and a half. Josemaría is wearing a dark gray suit, a black tie, and a straw hat. Guitín has on a white outfit, with a hat pulled down almost to the eyes, and has assumed a serious expression for the photo.

Josemaría and his friend Francisco Moreno, a fellow seminarian, exchanged visits during vacation, each spending some time with the other's family. When Francisco came to Logroño, the two seminarians made excursions along the banks of the Ebro River and afterward often showed up at Don José's store, The Great City of London, to accompany him on the short walk home. "The walk was pleasant, but it made me suffer more than a little to see this man who, though still relatively young, was aging prematurely," says Francisco Moreno, who had taken Don José for much older than his actual age of fifty-five. "After those long hours of standing behind the counter at the store," he recalls, "his feet were so swollen that he had to take off his shoes as soon as he got home."[75]

During these visits, Doña Dolores' motherly heart was manifested in little domestic attentions—for example, in the care and affection with which she prepared breakfast for the two seminarians. "In this and other things," says the guest, "she wanted to give us what we couldn't have when we were in Saragossa."[76]

We have more information about their stays at the Moreno house, since a group of friends of their age often got together with them there. This group included Francisco's brother Antonio, who was studying medicine in Saragossa and was an acquaintance of Josemaría's, and another set of brothers, Antonio and Cristóbal Navarro. Francisco Moreno tells us: "I'm not sure if it was during two summers or three that Josemaría spent several days—fifteen or twenty—with my family in Villel, a town near Teruel, where my father was a doctor. My whole family liked Josemaría very much because he made himself liked: he was courteous, discreet, and prudent, but at the same time very affectionate and sociable. Furthermore, his down-to-earth and wonderful sense of humor was always in evidence. His arrival at Villel was a great joy to that house, and when he left, it felt like there was a big vacuum. To my mother he was another son."[77]

He wore dark suits and a black tie, so as not to disguise the fact that he was a seminarian. He went to Mass every day and filled in as altar server whenever necessary. The village priest was a holy man, but he suffered from narcolepsy, which made Josemaría feel very sorry for him. The man could hardly carry out his duties. Sleep would come upon him at the most inopportune times—during his homily, for instance, or even during the Consecration.[78]

In the mornings the group of friends would go for a walk along the shores of the Turia River. If his companions went skinny-dipping, Josemaría, for modesty's sake, did not join them. They would go back to the house to eat, and then spend the hours of suffocating heat in those long summer afternoons organizing excursions to nearby places of interest, such as La Peña del Cid (the Rock of El Cid) or the shrine of Our Lady of Fuensanta, which was in the mountains. When some girls joined the excursion, as happened from time to time, the seminarian always found a pretext for staying home working. His absence did not go unnoticed by the girls. Concerning his relationship with the female friends of his friends, Carmen Noailles remarks that "the resoluteness and firmness of his vocation to the priesthood was very obvious."[79]

When the group went to the town's recreation center to play cards, Josemaría went to his room to read or write. He translated the incidents of the day into comic verses that he entered, complete with illustrations, in a notebook entitled "Adventures of Some Boys of Villel in Their Comings and Goings from Saragossa to Teruel."[80]

During those long periods back at the house, he would also chat with Francisco's mother, who had not yet recovered from the recent death of her husband. It was a great consolation for the poor woman to talk with Josemaría. When the subject of her loss came up, as often happened, Josemaría would say, "I don't want to see you so sad. Please don't cry, Señora Moreno. We just need to pray a lot for him. As soon as I am ordained, I will say a Mass for him."[81]

4. A "molder" of future priests

The president and other priests of the Royal Seminary of San Carlos soon became aware not only of the good appearance, piety, and good manners of the seminarian from Logroño, but also of the insults some of his companions offered him; as a result, he became known even beyond the walls of San Carlos. The truth of the old saying "There is no evil that does not lead to good" was a constant in the life of Josemaría. At each stage, a seemingly endless series of lamentable episodes proved ultimately providential, always culminating in joy. He liked to put his experiences in a Christian light by saying, "God writes straight with crooked lines."[82]

Somehow, whether by way of comments made by the president or in chats with the rector of San Carlos (now turned into a staunch defender of the seminarian), Josemaría's name reached the ears of the cardinal. From the windows of his residence he could see the students filing daily into the foyer of the university. Becoming interested in Josemaría, he had him summoned. On several occasions, when coming across the ranks of San Carlos seminarians on the street or in church, he asked Josemaría about his life and studies. A classmate reports having once heard the cardinal tell him, "Come see me when you have some time."[83]

With his extensive ecclesiastical experience, the cardinal soon saw in the seminarian exceptional gifts of piety, maturity of judgment, and leadership. Just before the summer vacation of 1922, he announced to the rector his decision to make Josemaría a prefect of San Carlos, thus filling one of the imminent vacancies. He proposed this with a touch of humor, subtly teasing Josemaría about one of his nicknames. "I will give you the tonsure,"* he said, "because I don't want the seminarians to see you dressed like a 'señorito' [little gentleman]."[84] (As long as he was not yet a cleric, he could still wear ordinary clothes and thus be dressed "like a señorito.")

The school year of 1922–1923 began on September 28. On that day, Josemaría—only he—received the tonsure, in a chapel in the cardinal's residence. And on that same day he became a prefect of San Carlos, a position he retained until his ordination as a priest on March 28, 1925.[85]

Through the years, he would always remember this event, "my receiving of the clerical tonsure from the hands of Cardinal Juan Soldevila, in a private chapel in his residence," as one of the big milestones on his path to the priesthood.[86]

The prefects at the conciliar seminary were all priests. At San Carlos, however, it was customary that one prefect be a deacon and the other only in minor orders. The prefects, also called directors or superiors, were responsible for seeing to it that the regulations were followed, and for taking disciplinary action when necessary. They also presided at some community activities in the name of the rector, and carried out functions delegated by him. The First Prefect took charge in the absence of the rector. This was the post held by Josemaría. Juan José Jimeno was his assistant, the Second Prefect.[87]

That a seminarian who had not yet received even the minor orders occupied the position of head prefect, with no one over

---

*At the time, the ceremony in which a man became a cleric included a shaving or clipping of the hair on the crown of his head. This was called tonsure.

him except the rector, gives some idea of the cardinal's daring. First he had to give Josemaría the tonsure ahead of schedule, so that this position would fall to a cleric. Then there is the unusual amount of confidence placed in this recently tonsured young man: the confidence implied in making him a guardian of discipline among people who not so long ago had made seminary life difficult for him. The prelate must have felt very sure of his appointee.

The position brought with it certain material advantages, such as having a "servant" and getting special meals, a special room, free room and board, and fifty pesetas per year. In addition, the examination fee at the university was paid by the seminary.[88] Each priest at San Carlos was assigned a "servant": a student assistant who provided some domestic services, though not of a servile nature. This was how some seminarians paid for their tuition and room and board. Out of respect for the custom, the new prefect accepted the services of the assistant assigned him, but as much as possible he avoided asking him to do anything, since he found it embarrassing to have a fellow seminarian as a servant. The assistant, José María Román Cuartero, gives us some idea of the behavior of his director:

> I was always impressed by the kindness and patience he showed me. I remember, for instance, that when I was making his bed for him and he could tell I was upset about something by the slipshod way I spread the sheets, he would make some affectionate remark or tell me a joke. I also remember how he would share his meals with me—because the prefects got special meals—without making a big deal of it. I realize now that he was purposely doing these mortifications in a very natural way so that they would not be noticed.[89]

Josemaría now had more freedom to carry out his devotional practices and leave the seminary premises. His position also allowed him to associate more with the priests of San Carlos, who lived on another floor of the building. He developed such a close relationship with the president, Bishop Miguel de los Santos, that until the day he died the bishop kept not only his letters but also some notes from conversations with his young friend.[90]

Now and then on Saturday or Sunday afternoon, Josemaría got together with certain friends of his, the nephews of Father Antonio Moreno, vice president of San Carlos, in the visiting room of this good priest. Thus the young companions from the summers at Villel were able also to meet at the seminary.[91]

Father Antonio had been at San Carlos for many years. In a manuscript on the history of the foundation of the seminary of San Francisco de Paula he is mentioned as having been the preacher for the seminarians' days of recollection in the school year of 1892–1893, when Cardinal Benavides was still alive.[92] Now, in his old age, he enjoyed a robust constitution, a wealth of priestly experience, and some small hobbies. Often he sought out the company of Prefect Escrivá, who enjoyed listening to him talk and who would graciously let him win when they played dominoes, to avoid putting him in a bad mood. (Father Antonio was one of those people who can't stand to lose.) Later, the priest would take some kind of "treat" out of his closet which, unappetizing as it was, Josemaría would courteously accept.

The vice president had done some traveling, and like all old people, he liked to recall memorable events from his trips. In particular, he enjoyed sharing anecdotes about the pastoral visits of the archbishop of Saragossa to the villages of his diocese. Some were quite astonishing to a seminarian. But when it was time to draw the moral of the story, Father Antonio would say, "Josemaría, don't take anything for granted—not anything at all."[93]

Early on, Josemaría learned Christian precautions drawn from worldly wisdom. One is that it is best to break off and flee from occasions of sin in good time. A companion of Josemaría's at San Carlos tells us that one day when they were all walking in line to class through the back streets in the center of the city, two girls who happened to cross their path tried to attract Josemaría's attention. The next day, they planted themselves in the same spot, waited for the seminarian, and boldly tried to tempt him. The day after that, seeing that he wasn't going to pay them any attention, they tauntingly said to him, "Are we so ugly that you can't bear to look at us?" Still not looking at them, Josemaría bluntly replied, "What you are is shameless!"[94]

This incident seems to have reached even the ears of his father, in Logroño.[95]

* * *

The cardinal, as we have seen, had conferred the tonsure on Josemaría ahead of time. His first opportunity to receive the minor orders was in Advent, shortly before Christmas. On November 20, therefore, he sent a letter to the cardinal "humbly requesting the honor of being admitted, during the forthcoming ember days of Saint Thomas the Apostle, to the minor holy orders."[96]

The necessary inquiries were made into various aspects of the life, scholastic achievement, and conduct of those requesting ordination. One question was whether the seminarian "has demonstrated a solid vocation to the ecclesiastical state."

The rector gave a response, dated November 23, covering all those requesting ordination at San Carlos: "The above-named gentlemen have, without exception, observed good moral and religious conduct, . . . evidencing in their external behavior a vocation to the priesthood. They have in my judgment done nothing to deserve unfavorable mention with regard to any of the matters in question."[97]

On December 17 Cardinal Soldevila conferred on Josemaría the orders of porter and lector, and four days later, those of exorcist and acolyte.[98]

* * *

The main concern of the prefects, if not to say the only thing that mattered to them, was maintenance of discipline. At San Carlos, as opposed to the conciliar seminary, the prefects were still students. Thus, on account of their duties, they often found themselves between a rock and a hard place. Jesús López Bello tells us that the role of the prefect "was not at all easy, because he was at the same time a director and a student and because the seminarians tended to act their youthful age."[99] Josemaría had to learn to maintain the right balance between, on the one hand, the demands of the seminary regulations, which obliged him to keep in check youthful impulses, and, on the other hand, the friendship uniting him with his fellow seminarians. Those who served as prefects in the following year (1925–1926), Agustín Callejas and Jesús Val, testify that Josemaría's spirit of fellowship with everyone "was as strong as the sense of responsibility with which he carried out his duties." He "never left any seminarian in a bad situation," they say. "He exercised his authority in a friendly way, without going too far. He did not make arbitrary demands, as do so many people who govern."[100]

Josemaría tried to be tactful, not making a big issue of prohibitions in the Regulations that had to do with matters of little importance, so that he could get a more willing compliance in the things that really mattered. For example, he allowed the older students to smoke; he tried to keep short the readings in the dining room, maximizing time to talk; and as soon as anyone showed a sign of repentance for an infraction, he readily rescinded that person's punishment.

One day he found an abandoned and dusty piece of cardboard on which, in gold letters on a red background, were three words from Saint Paul's canticle on charity: *Caritas omnia suffert* (1 Cor 13:7, "Love bears all things"). Probably it had been a decoration for one of the seminary's feast days, but it also had a connection with the emblem on the seminarians' robes, which was a sun with rays and with the word "Caritas" in the center. "On my work table," noted the young prefect of San Carlos, "I put this reminder: *Caritas omnia suffert.* I wanted to learn to do everything out of love and to teach this to the other seminarians by example."[101]

Along with the rector, he was responsible for forming the seminarians both humanly and spiritually, since there was no spiritual director at San Carlos at that time. Each week some confessors came in from outside, and, for anyone who wished to go to them, the priests of San Carlos made themselves available in the confessionals of the church while Bishop Miguel de los Santos celebrated Mass in the morning.[102]

As head prefect, Josemaría gave his fellow seminarians little talks in the study hall about special feasts or devotional practices. It was he who initiated the custom of a weekly Saturday visit to the Basilica of Our Lady of the Pillar by the prefect and his fellow seminarians.[103]

The rector once described him with a lapidary phrase—"a molder of young aspirants to the priesthood"—and said that clearly "his motto was to win everyone for Christ, that all might be one in Christ."[104] In all his actions the prefect took charity as his guide, trying to make his fellow future priests true "men of charity." He once put it this way:

> This preoccupation of mine is nothing new; I've been preaching and trying to live it with all my strength since I was twenty-one. It is possible that at the Seminary of San Carlos they still have some papers of mine—because I've always been fond of putting things in writing—from when I was prefect, with reflective observations, praising the changes for the better in the seminarians, speaking of charity and of the need to give an example of charity.[105]

These writings were indeed found, after his death, in the archive of the Royal Seminary of San Carlos.[106] They are the reports that he, as prefect, handed in each month to Father José López Sierra. They cover the period from October 1922 to March 1925, with breaks only for summer vacations. The most remarkable thing about them is the total absence of routine formulas. Because the section for "Conduct" also covered "Vocation," the other prefects usually left it blank, or at most wrote in, a couple of times a year, a vague and noncommittal adjective. By contrast, Josemaría entered notes showing that he paid close attention to each seminarian. If others, not wanting to get really involved, salved their consciences with a "Good" or an "Average," this prefect conscientiously weighed his judgments and expressed them in clear terms, but always with friendliness. In the seminarians he saw souls for the priesthood.

On the back of the report it was customary to note "Punishments Imposed by the Prefect," as well as "Punishments Imposed by the Rector," in a rather dry fashion: for example, "So-and-so one day on his knees in the dining room, for smoking and for lying to the rector." Josemaría would make his notes more complete, adding background, immediate causes, and subsequent circumstances. For instance: "Since being punished (as of the 12th) by the rector until the end of the month, Mr. R. P. has been acting like a different person: he is obedient, respectful, and desirous of fulfilling his duty."[107]

The first hurdle for him was how to be accepted as director—how to have his authority respected. Immediately he had to deal with challenges and dissension coming from a group of rebels. In his report for November 1922, referring to four unruly seminarians, Josemaría writes, "They have very little of the respect due to a superior, and whenever they are reprimanded, no matter with how much affection the reprimand may be given, they respond badly. Some, like Mr. C., make faces so that the community will laugh."[108]

The troublemakers were a little slow coming around, but eventually the director's patience won out, as we see in his report for February 1923: "During the five months of this school year so far, I am happy to note, both Mr. A. and Mr. C. have changed from being unmanageable to being very cooperative and courteous students. The same is happening with Mr. L."[109]

Generously, he looked for excuses for everyone. We often find statements like "I am revoking his punishment because he promised, with tears in his eyes, to improve," or "Mr. M. and Mr. L. often—*usually*, in fact—are disrespectful without realizing it."[110]

But empathy did not cloud or bias his judgments, especially where the priestly vocation was concerned. In that same report for February 1923 he wrote, "On the other hand, I don't know what to say about the vocations of these other gentlemen: M. M., P. R., and C. M. The first two, as can be seen from the reports for previous months, have been doing what they please since the beginning of this school year. I'm always inclined to judge in a person's favor, and for that reason I have said that they show signs of a vocation. Today, though, I feel obliged to state clearly and objectively how I really see things. Mr. C. M. has gotten worse and worse since the beginning of the year, his major defect being a lack of respect for the superior. Finally, I note that all these gentlemen receive Communion daily or almost daily."

A year later, in February 1924, the seminarians at San Carlos had changed so much that Josemaría writes with satisfaction, "I would like to record, because it gives a good, clear idea of the current spirit of the seminary, that when I punished the students as a group, not only was there no protest, but they accepted the reprimand with good grace, acknowledging it as very well deserved."[111]

Father José López Sierra, says Jesús Val, came to have such confidence in this director that "in effect he delegated his own duties to him" to the point that he "practically left the seminary in the hands of Josemaría."[112]

The seminarians' progress reflected the prayer life of their prefect, who closely accompanied them. "With what joy did I note the progress of those boys! I often talked with the Lord about them, asking that he, with his Mother, take good care of them."[113]

The "molder of young aspirants to the priesthood," to borrow the rector's rather grandiose expression, was already a subdeacon when he made the following commentary in November 1924:

> I didn't dare write this last year, fearing that it might be just a temporary change, but thanks be to God, that has not

been the case. I therefore want to say it now. Especially after the feast of the Purification in 1923, the novena for which was made by everyone with great fervor, there has been an admirable change in *all* the old students—a change that is having an impact on the young ones coming in. It is undoubtedly our Lady who has done this, and, I repeat, since this is surely my last year to be in this beloved seminary, I can't refrain from giving a very brief summary.

He then mentions by name a few seminarians who not long ago were straying quite far from the paths of piety, but now were very courteous and devout. "They are so totally changed, they're different persons," he says with obvious joy. Did he sense that this would be his last time to take the pulse of the seminary, and that he should therefore make a brief farewell summary? In any case, this is it:

All in all, there is a lot of fervor. The crucifix on the fourth floor was missing its crown, and they put one on it! The missions, the decorating of our oratory, the hymns for First Friday, for the nineteenth, for the Saturday devotions. . . . One detail: more than once they asked my permission to cut their recreation short so they could have more time to spend in the oratory for the Sacred Heart devotions, and last year for the Immaculate Conception novena. The monthly quota for apostolic work has increased. From the way they treat one another, one can see that it is not in vain that Saint Francisco de Paula is the father of the house: they are charitable, always charitable. If someone does something wrong, he admits it and accepts the punishment. It is now a sure thing that when reprimanded they will not answer back, and that they will accept—even joyfully!—the medicine of punishment. I could say more, but I think this will suffice. It's clear to me that whenever any bad element made its appearance, our Blessed Mother went to work and everything worked out to the greater glory of God and herself. Now, in writing this, I don't mean to say that our boys are angels. The fact that they're *boys* is evident from the punishments meted out every month. All of us here have our faults.[114]

The little placard that he kept in his prefect's office, the one saying "Love bears all things" served him as a reminder to do all he could to give unity in Christ to all of those seminarians. Constantly during his two and a half years of participating in their formation, he felt most of all the joyful responsibility of preparing future ministers of the Lord. It was a real challenge for a seminarian like himself—not just because of his youth, but also because of his lack of experience in an ecclesiastical environment. But he threw himself totally into the task, once again confirming the truth of something Doña Dolores had said to him several times: "Josemaría, you are going to suffer a lot in life, because you put your whole heart into whatever you do."[115]

Indeed he did put body and soul into whatever he was engaged in. At this time in Saragossa he also gave himself over to poetic inspiration. "I wrote some really bad poems," he would later recall, "and signed them—putting into my signature everything I had in me—'The Priestly Heart.' "[116]

With a temperament like that, he had no need to work up some plan of action. It was enough to follow literally that of Saint Paul. He once said, "I am moved whenever I recall those words of Saint Paul's first letter to the Corinthians that I kept at hand so long, back when I was director at San Carlos Seminary in Saragossa: 'Love is patient and kind; love is not jealous or boastful; it is not arrogant or rude. Love does not insist on its own way; it is not irritable or resentful; it does not rejoice at wrong, but rejoices in the right. Love bears all things, believes all things, hopes all things, endures all things.' "[117]

From that long process of helping form his brothers in the seminary, he himself emerged transformed. For he had tried always to live that litany of human and supernatural virtues—patience, prudence, courtesy, sacrifice, charity, and so forth—which as director he promoted for over two years. The virtues of the others were continually boosted by the example, good manners, counsel, affection, and prayer life of Josemaría. As a result, by the end of that arduous process he himself had been enriched with invaluable experience in the field of spiritual direction, the exercise of authority, and the art of governing.

The title of "director" or "head prefect" may sound a little grandiose or exaggerated when applied to a young seminarian with several years of study still ahead of him. But we have to look at the facts. The saying that no one can give what they don't have is especially true of the work of formation. Based on the transformation that he brought about in the seminarians of San Carlos, it seems undeniable that Josemaría had a precocious maturity directly resulting from the superabundance of his interior life and his exercise of the virtues of government.

5. *A regrettable incident*

His literary bent led Josemaría to spend much of his free time reading. Often he was seen jotting down interesting expressions or ideas. As director he had access to the library of the Royal Seminary of San Carlos, which had inherited "the famous collection assembled in Rome, at great expense and with great intelligence, by the most excellent Don Manuel de Roda, and later augmented by him in Madrid, where he served as Secretary of State to His Majesty."[118] Josemaría was in his element, and not about to pass up the opportunity offered him by his ready access to so many choice books. It awakened in him a tremendous appetite for culture—an appetite fed by the literary and spiritual classics but costing him many hours of sleep. Beneath the door of the prefect's room other seminarians would see the flickering light of a candle, since not all the rooms of San Carlos had electricity.[119]

Josemaría enjoyed a fruitful two years of reading. Later he would not have much time or opportunity for this, except for when he had to consult some classical author. But now he read in depth especially the mystics and the ascetics, studying the hidden operations of grace. He particularly liked the works of Saint Teresa.

In June 1923 he passed—with the highest grades—all his courses for fourth-year theology, thus completing the requirements for a licentiate at the pontifical university.[120] It was now time to begin his secular studies, as had been agreed upon before he left the Logroño seminary to finish his ecclesiastical studies in Saragossa. His transfer had carried with it implicit permission from the bishop of Calahorra and La Calzada to study law in Saragossa, it having been the bishop's prerogative to grant or deny permission for clerics to attend secular universities since the time of Pope Leo XIII. More recently, on April 30, 1918, the Sacred Consistorial Congregation had issued norms "guarding against the great dangers that, as shown by long and sad experience, threaten the sanctity of life and purity of doctrine of priests who attend the above-mentioned universities."[121] Cardinal Soldevila had given Josemaría the necessary permission because he felt fully confident of his fidelity to his priestly vocation and of the firmness of his doctrinal convictions, and also because he knew the University of Saragossa was no nest of heretics.[122]

Very suddenly, unexpectedly, and tragically, Cardinal Soldevila was removed from the scene. On the afternoon of June 4, 1923, as he was going by car on a visit to the outskirts of the capital, anarchists riddled the cardinal with bullets, at the same time wounding the driver and a lay assistant. Josemaría went to the cardinal's wake and prayed for his soul. The news filled the front pages for days. But neither the identity of the assassins nor their motive was known at the time. The archdiocese of Saragossa remained without a bishop for nearly two years.

In the summer of 1923, in Logroño, Josemaría took two courses that were prerequisites for studying law: Spanish Language and Literature, and Basic Logic. In the mornings he and another student, José Luis Mena, went over the material together, asking each other questions on literary subjects.[123] In the middle of September they went to Saragossa to take the exam.

Father Carlos, the archdeacon, saw his nephew often at that time and enjoyed talking with him. That same friend from Logroño recalls how nice he was and especially how he used to invite him and Josemaría to his house for an afternoon snack. "Father Carlos was," he says, "a priest who made quite an impression. I even remember what he gave us for our snack: Spanish hot chocolate with candy."[124]

Following his uncle's advice, Josemaría decided to enroll in the law school as a "nonofficial" student so that he could go to classes when he was able, but would not have to attend them all.* This way he could do his studies with a certain freedom and take his exams either in June or during the special sessions held in September.** Actually, to say that he did his secular studies "simultaneously" or "alternately" with his ecclesiastical studies is not quite accurate, since he began his law studies only after finishing his fourth year of theology. The schedule of his ecclesiastical studies was normal and continuous, but there was something a bit hit-or-miss about his pursuit of a secular degree, since it was subject to the pressures of the moment and done under circumstances impossible to foresee at the start.

On the recommendation of his uncle, he went to Don Carlos Sánchez del Río, at that time provost of the university, to discuss his studies. From that first meeting, the seminarian impressed Don Carlos with his "outstanding personality." He also visited

---

*At the time, "official" students were required to attend classes. But it was also possible to register as a "nonofficial" or "free" student. Nonofficial students were free to attend classes if they wished, but were not required to do so. They received credit for a course if they passed the exam, even if they had not attended any classes.

**Spanish universities at the time normally did not function on the basis of semesters. Classes ran from early October until June. Exams, which were usually oral, were held in early summer, and again in September. Students were free to take the exam at either time, and if they failed an exam in early summer, they could take it again in September.

the professor of natural law, to whom his uncle introduced him. The professor received him "with surprise and pleasure at seeing that a seminarian already advanced in his seminary studies wanted also to earn a secular degree, along with the ecclesiastical one. That was certainly a rare thing in those days."[125]

Among the courses Josemaría chose for that first year were Elements of Natural Law, taught by Don Miguel Sancho Izquierdo; Principles of Roman Law, taught by Father José Pou de Foxá; and Principles of Canon Law, taught by Don Juan Moneva y Puyol.[126] These three professors made up a triumvirate of an exceptional intellectual caliber. They had a profound influence on the development of Josemaría's personality and were largely responsible for his acquiring an astute juridical mentality. The student soon established a warm and steadfast friendship with each of them.[127]

Also providential for his future tasks as a founder was the fact that in 1923–1924, he studied canon law at two schools, a secular one and an ecclesiastical one, simultaneously. The chairs were held by two intellectually outstanding professors: Don Juan Moneva at the law school and Father Elías Ger Puyuelo as part of the program for fifth-year theology.[128]

Along with their prodigious knowledge, both had a flair for wittiness and for the use of proverbial sayings. Father Elías had a unique teaching style that communicated an amazing amount of priestly wisdom in a very colorful way. Josemaría would forever remember some of those sayings of his that were so funny and so full of common sense.[129]

Don Juan Moneva's witticisms were no less wise and to the point. Both in Saragossa and elsewhere he became something of a celebrity, although his eccentricities sometimes rose to the level of the bizarre. He nicknamed Josemaría "el curilla" (the little priest) and continued to remember him until he died. In fact, Father Josemaría got notice of his death by mail addressed to him in the old professor's handwriting. Apparently, Don Juan, a character to the day he died, had addressed the envelopes for his death announcements and instructed his family to mail them when the time came.[130] These moving words in the speech his former student gave upon receiving an honorary doctorate at Saragossa on October 21, 1960, sound like a funeral eulogy:

> I would like to mention today, with affectionate respect, the names of so many outstanding jurists who were my teachers here. Let me mention just one of them, to sum up in him the grateful recognition I owe to each and every one of them. I am speaking of Don Juan Moneva y Puyol. He was, of all my professors back then, the one that I was closest to. There developed between us a friendship that remained active until his death. Don Juan showed me on more than one occasion a deep affection, and I've always had a deep appreciation of that whole treasure-house of robust Christian piety, of profound uprightness of life, and of charity as discreet as it was magnificent, which he hid beneath that sometimes deceptive cape of shrewd irony and the jovial wittiness of his imaginative mind. For Don Juan and for my other teachers I have the most heartfelt regard. May he, and all the others who have passed on from this world, have received from our Lord the reward of eternal happiness.[131]

Josemaría's friendship with Father Elías was brief, for the priest died in November 1924. However, Josemaría would never forget a little story that he told in class at the beginning of the previous school year, in October. It was about a cinnamon merchant who bought the stuff raw and had it ground to a fine powder in a stone mill. One day the mill stopped working. The stones were worn out; it was time to order some more. These stones were imported from Germany.

Weeks went by, but the new stones did not arrive, and the cinnamon was just piling up there, waiting to be milled. Seeing how worried he was, a friend suggested to the merchant that he go to a nearby stream and find some round stones about the size of the old ones, put them in the mill, and let them revolve for several days without grinding any cinnamon.

The merchant did this, and after two weeks he found that the stones had become so smooth by grinding against each other that they were as good as the ones from Germany.

The professor paused for a moment, and then, turning to Josemaría, he said, "That's how God treats those whom he loves. Do you understand me, Escrivá?"[132]

From this story Josemaría drew the moral that God uses our abrasive encounters with our neighbors to polish away the roughness of our characters. In the years that followed, he would keep an absolute silence about what the professor was referring to, except for making a vague allusion to a "major unpleasantness" that occurred when he was a seminarian in Saragossa.[133] But everything leads us to suspect that this anecdote of the cinnamon miller conceals something quite serious and very painful. One of his companions, Jesús López Bello, speaks of "rumors of a fight" with another seminarian.[134] A student at the conciliar seminary, Francisco Artal Ledesma, who hastens to rate the incident as "something of little importance," tells us that "another seminarian, from Rioja, an older man, of over forty who claimed to have been secretary to the governor of Buenos Aires when he lived in Argentina, provoked Josemaría, and there was a violent encounter."[135] Evidently Artal knew this Riojan, for he adds that "what happened in this incident was due to the characteristics of the two protagonists." The Riojan was insolent and "capable of getting anyone angry," while Josemaría, "despite his youth, was incapable of instigating any act of violence."

The most reliable eyewitness is the rector. In *De vita et moribus*, on the page for Josemaría, he sums up the event as he saw it, and then its consequences:

> He had a fight with Julio Cortés, and I gave him the appropriate punishment. But the acceptance and carrying out of it was really a glory for him, since in my judgment it was his adversary who had struck first and most, and he had spoken to him in gross language improper for a

cleric, and, in my presence, had insulted him in the Cathedral of La Seo.[136]

To understand why this incident was so upsetting to Josemaría, we need to consider not only his natural sensibilities, but also that he was a director of San Carlos and had already received minor orders. The last time he had gotten into a fist fight was in Barbastro, with "Pig Foot." The Riojan's insults must have driven him beyond the breaking point. He fought back with words, and the other man turned it into a physical fight.

Although he had legitimately defended himself, Josemaría had lost his composure, both in word and in deed. This hit him so hard that he lost his spiritual peace and had to pour out his soul in a letter to Father Gregorio Fernández, his old spiritual director, the vice-rector of the seminary of Logroño. On October 26, 1923, Father Gregorio sent him the following response:

> I feel very badly about your encounter with Julio—not so much for him, since he has very little to lose, as for you. I realize that it was unavoidable on your part, but I wish you had never had to find yourself in the position of having to defend yourself with such forceful arguments. I know the nobility of your sentiments, and I'm sure that by now you do not hold in your heart the slightest trace of resentment. . . . You should not discuss this matter with anyone other than God.[137]

Josemaría took this advice and buried the matter in his heart. Only after his death, upon looking through his papers, did someone come upon other details which completed the story. "We found among some papers," says Bishop Javier Echevarría, "a calling card from the seminarian who provoked the incident in La Seo. On this card was printed the name of the place where he was working: a Red Cross hospital in a city in the south of Spain. The man had written a few words beneath his name, Julio Cortés: 'Repentant, and in the most humble and absolute way possible. Mea culpa!' "[138]

6. *"Domina, ut sit!"*

On the banks of the Ebro stands the splendid Basilica of Our Lady of the Pillar. An earlier church had stood there during the Muslim era. The basilica's construction began during the Renaissance, continued through the Baroque period, and ended in the middle of the eighteenth century with some neoclassical embellishments. Inside is the Chapel of Our Lady of the Pillar, a magnificent little structure housing a column upon which, according to tradition, our Lady set her feet.* This pillar, covered with bronze and silver, supports a statue of our Lady wearing a voluminous cloak and holding the child Jesus in her arms.

Upon his arrival in Saragossa, Josemaría adopted the custom of making visits to the Pillar, taking the time out of his free periods between classes. As long as he was in Saragossa he practiced that custom daily, as he himself tells us:

My devotion to Our Lady of the Pillar goes back to very early in my life, since my parents, with their Aragonese piety, instilled it in the soul of each of their children. Later on, during my studies for the priesthood and also when I studied law at the University of Saragossa, my visits to the Pillar were a daily event.[139]

Later, as head prefect, he would bring his fellow seminarians with him to pray together a Salve Regina. However, even though his devotion to Our Lady of the Pillar suffused his interior life, his memory of those years was that of a mediocre effort to respond to the divine call. To him, he had

---

* According to an old tradition, when the apostle Saint James was preaching in Spain, the Blessed Virgin appeared to him on top of the column or pillar preserved in the chapel of Our Lady of the Pillar.

"worked with only medium intensity."[140] Perhaps this was because he was thinking of a past that was free of the terrible ascetical struggles that would follow. But even back then his devotional practices were validated by the cheerful suffering of involuntary mortifications: snubs, insults, vulgarities. There was corporal penance, too, since he made use of a cilice.[141] Surrounded by darkness, he continued to cry out untiringly for clarity in his vocation.

I had hints that our Lord wanted something, but many years passed before I found out what it was. In the meantime I thought of the blind man in the Gospel, because I was blind with regard to my future and the service that God wanted from me. Like him, I kept repeating, *Domine, ut videam! Domine, ut sit!* [Lord, that I may see! Lord, let it be!]. I repeated this for years: "Let it be. May this thing that you want come about. Let me know what it is. Give light to my soul." The light did not come, but evidently prayer was the right path.[142]

More than for any other advantage connected with his position, the prefect was thankful for the freedom of time and movement it gave him, since it allowed him to converse more with the love of his life. An assiduous and devoted reader of Saint Teresa of Avila, Josemaría smiled at something the saint had said: namely, that "the Lord had given this person [i.e., herself] such a lively faith that when she heard people say they wished they had lived when Christ walked on this earth, she would smile to herself, for she knew that we have him as truly with us in the Most Holy Sacrament as people had him then, and wonder what more they could possibly want."[143]

Even back in Logroño, at Santa María de La Redonda, Josemaría used to make long evening visits to the Blessed Sacrament. Now he continued those visits at the church of San Carlos, even when his obligations as head prefect did not leave him much free time. Love always finds a way. Soon he found himself a nice spot near the main altar, where the tabernacle was.

As soon as the seminary lights went out, Josemaría went from the second floor to the area where the priests lived, and from there to the upper level of the church. This level was supported by the arches of the side chapels and had spacious balconies for the faithful, built between the buttresses of the church, below ribs that crisscrossed the ceiling. Josemaría would kneel in the balcony to the right of the main part of the church, looking down on the sanctuary. He would greet our Lord with that lively faith spoken of by Saint Teresa, and through the latticework fix his eyes on the tabernacle, while the flickering sanctuary lamp lighted up the gold of the reredos and made shadows dance in the baroque profusion of niches, statues, and medallions.[144]

With the night ahead of him, free from interruptions, and alone in an empty church, the seminarian would carry on long conversations with our Lord in the tabernacle—conversations always the same and always different. In the past few years Josemaría had intensely cultivated his relationship with our Lord. He knew how to unburden himself with confidence and simplicity in a lengthy dialogue without a lot of words. He spoke easily, with the intimacy with which close friends speak to one another.

Sometimes his thoughts were a torrent of supplication; at other times his soul was inflamed with affection for our Lord and our Lady. We know for certain that his prayer was constant and that for several years he kept repeating the same petitions: *Domine, ut videam! Domina, ut sit!* The petitions were not being granted, yet he kept on asking the same things, day and night, without doubt or discouragement. And it concerned something that was not even a promise, but only a matter of "inklings of Love." Josemaría understood perfectly the language and pain of lovers.

In those vigils he asked for strength for the ascetical struggle, light for his tasks of government, and promptness in responding to grace. Even details of his notes on the progress of the seminarians served, he tells us, "for dialogue with the Lord."

opff

The nocturnal visits to the church increased; this rendezvous with our Lord became more and more frequent. From that time on, when for any reason at all his soul needed to speak at length with our Lord after a hard day's work, he knew when and where he could be alone with him. So he spoke from experience when later on, as spiritual director, he gave this Gospel-based reproach, *"Pernoctans in oratione Dei*—'He spent the whole night in prayer to God,' says Saint Luke of our Lord. And you? How many times have you persevered like that? Well, then . . ."[145]

* * *

On May 14, 1924, the office of archbishop being vacant following the assassination of Cardinal Soldevila, Josemaría wrote to the vicar general of the archdiocese expressing his desire to receive the subdiaconate "since I believe I am called to the priestly state."[146] The vicar general, as was his duty, asked the rector for a character reference. The response was that the candidate had shown "good moral and religious conduct, receiving the sacrament of Penance frequently and Communion daily."[147]

On June 14, in the church of San Carlos, the subdiaconate was conferred on Josemaría by Bishop Miguel de los Santos.[148]

Shortly before, Josemaría had taken his fifth-year-theology examinations, receiving a "Meritissimus" (Excellent) in all of them. His academic records, now completed, show twenty courses: sixteen with that highest grade, "Meritissimus," two with the next highest grade, "Benemeritus" (Good), and in Greek and Hebrew a simple "Meritus" (Average).[149]

Now that he was a subdeacon, "he felt he was already a minister of God."[150] His proximity to the priesthood filled him with joy. But probably it was the reason why the relationship with his uncle Carlos began to deteriorate. In the beginning, the archdeacon had taken him under his wing, helping him get into San Carlos with a partial scholarship, frequently inviting him to his home, providing other small services. Nevertheless, as a close friend of Josemaría notes, the nephew "was never able to have very cordial relations with his uncle."[151] Father Carlos was one of those relatives who had criticized Don José's heroic, profoundly Christian gesture of paying off business loans, after his business was legally declared bankrupt, by selling family possessions and thus bringing his family to the brink of poverty. As the years went by, relations between the archdeacon and the seminarian also became more and more difficult because Josemaría did not agree to the plans for his future career that Father Carlos had worked out in his mind.

Sixta Cermeño, the wife of a cousin of Josemaría's at that time living in Saragossa, explains that the archdeacon, "well aware of the importance of his position in the diocese, considered himself something of a leading figure in the family and responsible for it."[152] Accompanying this role of protector and counselor was a notion of an ecclesiastical career which was quite different from his nephew's idea of the priesthood. The one felt he "had made it to the top," whereas the other "did not have the least interest in making the priesthood a career."[153]

During his summer vacations Josemaría studied for the law school examinations. These covered quite a few subjects. Professor Sánchez del Río gives some details:

> It would have been in the month of September, in 1923 or 1924, that I was on the tribunal which gave him his exams in canon law and Roman law. (The nonofficial students always took their exams before a tribunal.) Both tribunals were made up of Don Juan Moneva, Father José Pou de Foxá, and myself. I remember that at the start of the exam in canon law, Professor Juan Moneva, the teacher of this course, asked him in Latin if he wished to take the exam in that language. Without a moment's hesitation he answered yes, and so he did. His answers were very good, very specific and concise. He answered

quickly in correct Latin, in a clear and brief manner; it was a brilliant examination. And the one in Roman law showed the special liking he had for this discipline.[154]

* * *

When he went to visit the Basilica of Our Lady of the Pillar, he often had to stand in line with the other faithful to get to kiss the part of the column that was exposed and was worn down by the lips of many generations of Christians. There, in the Holy Chapel, he repeated his insistent aspirations, "Domine, ut sit! Lord, may that which you want be done, though I don't know what it is!" and the same to the Blessed Virgin, *Domina, ut sit!* (My Lady, let it be!).[155]

But kissing the column was not enough for him; he wanted to kiss the image itself. As he tells it, months earlier he had hit on a way to pull this off, since usually no one except children and the authorities was allowed to kiss even the cloak in which the image was dressed. "Since I was good friends with some of the clerics who took care of the basilica," he says, "I was able to stay in the church one day after the doors were locked. With the complicity of one of those good priests (now deceased), I climbed the few steps so well known to those who escort the little children, and getting up close, I kissed the image of our Mother."[156]

In his room at San Carlos the prefect had a plaster reproduction of that statue. Monetarily and aesthetically it was worth practically nothing. But it was given him by one of Cardinal Soldevila's servants, and gazing upon it, he kept asking our Lady to intercede for him so that God's will could be carried out as soon as possible. "Before a little statue of the Virgin of the Pillar," he says, "I confided to her my prayer in those years, that our Lord would let me understand what he was already hinting at in my soul. 'Domina!' I said to her, in a Latin that was not exactly classical, but embellished by affection, 'Ut sit! May whatever God wants me to do be done!'"[157]

So constant was this prayer, in fact, that he finally engraved it in the base of the statue, with the point of a nail. When Josemaría left Saragossa, the statue stayed behind, and he did not see it again until 1960, in Rome, when one of his daughters in Opus Dei showed him a statue of Our Lady of the Pillar which until then had been in the home of some relatives of his in Saragossa. They had sent it to him, he tells us, because it had been his.

> "Father, there has arrived here this statue of Our Lady of the Pillar which you had in Saragossa." I answered, "No, I don't remember it." And she said, "Yes, look at it—there's something written on it by you." It was such a horrible statue that it didn't seem possible that it could have been mine. But she showed it to me: under the statue, with a nail, was written on the plaster "Domina, ut sit!"—with the exclamation point, which is how I always used to write aspirations in Latin. "My Lady, let it be!" And a date: "24-5-924."
>
> Many is the time, my children, that our Lord humbles me. While he often gives me plenty of clarity, many other times he takes it away from me, so that I can never trust in myself. And then he comes and gives me a dab of honey.
>
> I have spoken to you about those inklings many times, even though on occasion I have thought, Josemaría, you are a fraud, a liar. . . . That statue was the concrete manifestation of the prayer I prayed for years—the prayer I have related to you so many times.[158]

7. *The death of Don José*

On November 27, 1924, Josemaría received a telegram from his mother asking him to come to Logroño because his father had come down with a serious illness. He took the train that very afternoon. At the Logroño station he was met by Manuel Ceniceros, a godson of Señor Garrigosa's who worked as a clerk at The Great City of London. It was Manuel who had sent the telegram, at the request of Doña Dolores.[159] From its tone and the urgency with which it was given him by the president of the seminary, Bishop Miguel de los Santos y Díaz de Gómara, Josemaría knew before he left Saragossa that his father had died. As soon as he entered the house he saw the body, already piously enshrouded by his mother and sister, laid out on a crimson bedspread on the living room floor. The son wept freely, and then prayed with great Christian serenity.

They told him what had happened. Early in the morning, just after breakfast, Don José had played for a short time with little Santiago. Then he had knelt for a moment in front of a statue of Our Lady of the Miraculous Medal, to whom he was very devoted and whose confraternity had brought it to the Escrivás' home, this being their week to have it. He then said good-bye and turned to leave, but before reaching the door he was stricken. Crying out in pain, he grabbed hold of the door jamb, and then collapsed. Carmen and Doña Dolores rushed to his side. They got him into bed and, realizing the seriousness of his condition, immediately called the doctor and the parish priest. But there was nothing the doctor could do. Two hours later, having received the last sacraments but not having regained consciousness, Don José died.[160]

At nine that morning when The Great City of London opened for business, the other employees were surprised that Don José was not there. It was most unusual for this meticulously punctual man to be late. On a hunch, the owner sent Manuel to the Escrivá home on Sagasta Street to find out what had happened. Don José died soon after Manuel got there.[161]

A heartbroken Josemaría comforted his family. Little Santiago, who was then about six, would never forget the expression his brother had on his face when, facing the body, he promised to take over his father's responsibilities for them. "He said in front of my mother, my sister, and me— these are the words I remember—that he would never abandon us and would take care of us."[162]

He immediately took charge of the preparations for the funeral and burial, making the arrangements for the coffin, the grave, the services, and the incidental expenses. But the family did not have sufficient savings. In this painful predicament, Josemaría had to request assistance from Father Daniel Alfaro, a military chaplain who was an acquaintance of the family. This priest would forever be remembered for his charitable loan. The money was soon paid back, but Josemaría never ceased to remember him with gratitude in his Masses. For several years he did this in the Memento of the Living, and later in the Memento of the Dead.[163]

A wake was held throughout the night. Friends from Logroño and Don José's coworkers were there. But the relatives did not come.

The burial took place the following day. Before closing the coffin, Josemaría removed the cross that lay in his father's hands: a poor, worn cross which had also lain in the hands of his grandmother Constancia.[164]

The funeral party crossed a bridge en route to the cemetery. Josemaría walked in front, apart from the rest, as the only relative of the deceased who was present. His mother and sister had remained at home, since it was not customary then for the women of the family to attend the burial. At the grave site the traditional prayer for the dead was recited, and then Father Daniel Alfaro, at Josemaría's request, said some additional prayers.

The coffin was lowered into the grave, and the son threw on it the first handful of dirt. The grave digger handed him the key with which he had locked the coffin. Crossing the bridge over the Ebro on the way back to Logroño with the funeral party, the son reflected on his loss. He put his hand in his pocket and pulled out the coffin key. Resolutely, as though ridding himself of a symbolic attachment that could distract him from his vocation, he threw the key in the river. "Why," he thought to himself, "should I want to keep this key, when it could be for me an undue attachment?"[165]

Days of mourning and of family privacy followed. During this time, on the first of December, a city census reached their neighborhood. Perhaps no documentation could be more simply eloquent of the change in the Escrivá home than the signature given on the census form for "head of the family": "Dolores Albás, Widow of Escrivá."[166]

Although officially it was the widow who was head of the family, it was the elder son who took charge of everything. He decided that within a few weeks, as soon as he could manage to rent an apartment in Saragossa, they would go live with him. Overnight, there had fallen on the shoulders of the young seminarian the heavy responsibility of financially supporting his family. His hopes in that little brother of his—that other son whom he had asked our Lord to send to take his place since he was becoming a priest—had collapsed. Now he had to be more of a father to Santiago than an older brother.[167]

He took a long, hard look at his situation. He was now a subdeacon. As such, he was bound by certain commitments he had made to the Church, including that of remaining dedicated to the service of God in celibacy. True, he could apply for a dispensation, and in view of his new obligations, who would be surprised if he did? Nevertheless, despite the recent misfortune, he felt interiorly strengthened, as if all the more confirmed in his vocation. His unlimited trust in Divine Providence led him to see the issue as entirely resolved. Whereas if his father's death had occurred before he took the subdiaconate, might there not have been some doubt about whether he should continue to seek the priesthood?[168]

Now, in compensation for this new family misfortune, he was able to see more clearly the meaning of his life and the hand of God accompanying him through all his sufferings. On the path of suffering his life was being stripped of human encumbrances, material resources, and whatever might have represented support in the future. He thought of the three little sisters who had died in Barbastro, the collapse of his father's business, the financial constraints, and the family left in his care. All this became part of the history of his soul. Our Lord was forging it by means of these family woes.

I have always made those around me suffer a lot. I haven't brought on catastrophes, but the Lord, to hit me, who was the nail (pardon me, Lord), landed one blow on the nail and a hundred on the horseshoe. I saw my father as the personification of Job. He lost three daughters, one after the other in consecutive years, and then lost his fortune.[169]

Don José died worn out by work and worries. But from him his son had learned something he would never forget:

I saw him suffer with cheerfulness, without showing the suffering. And I saw a courage that was a school for me, because later I would so often feel as if the ground was falling out from under me and the sky was falling on me, or as if I was being squeezed between two sheets of iron.
With those lessons and the grace of the Lord, perhaps I did lose my peace occasionally, but not very often. . . .
My father died exhausted, but still with a smile on his lips and a special congeniality.[170]

With deep gratitude he recognized the roles played by his parents in God's plans for him, and how exemplary their virtues were. The memory of Don José, patient and serene in the face of adversity, forgetful of himself in service of his neighbor, grew in a holy way in his son's mind to involve something more than filial affection. "Logroño! Very dear memories," he wrote in a letter dated May 9, 1938. "In that cemetery are the remains of my father, which for me—for many reasons—are relics. I hope to *recover them* someday."[171]

8. *The first Mass*

Two weeks before his father's death, Josemaría had requested ordination to the diaconate because "I believe I am called to the priestly state."[172] Shortly thereafter, the chancery secretary prepared the request for ordination, and on December 5 the vicar general sent it to the diocese of Calahorra and La Calzada. Several witnesses, including the pastor of the parish in Logroño (Father Hilario Loza) and the military chaplain Father Daniel Alfaro, attested to the subdeacon's good conduct and reputation. The paperwork completed, Bishop Miguel de los Santos conferred the sacred order of the diaconate on Josemaría on December 20, in the church of San Carlos.[173]

It is very probable that he spent a few days in Logroño before going back to San Carlos to receive the diaconate, since Paula Royo recalls his relating to her some humorous incidents connected with his search for an apartment in Saragossa.[174] The family situation obviously made the move advisable. Within a few months Josemaría would be ordained a priest for the diocese of Saragossa. Maintaining two homes would not be financially feasible, and, given the new circumstances, it would not be right for Josemaría to be far from his family.*

So first he rented, on a temporary basis, an apartment on the third floor of a cramped and stuffy building on Urrea Street. And from there they moved, a few weeks later, to a modest apartment at 11 Rufas Street.[175]

Already Doña Dolores' relations with some members of her family had been not entirely cordial, but they became even worse following the death of Don José, turning cold and strained. This abrupt change took place when the Escrivás decided to move to Saragossa. Actually the reaction of Father Carlos, who was rather imperious and pompous on account of his ecclesiastical preeminence, is not entirely surprising. He had, after all, not even attended his brother-in-law's funeral. But he was downright indignant when he learned that the Escrivás would soon be showing up in Saragossa. According to Pascual Albás, one of his nephews, Doña Dolores' brothers even thought of giving her a small pension if she would stay in Logroño. Sixta Cermeño tells us the archdeacon was of the opinion that "what

---

*At the time, urban parishes in Spain did not normally have rectories for their priests. Priests often lived with their families.

Josemaría should do was give up any other studies, get ordained and settled, and support his mother and siblings."[176]

Perhaps it was at bottom a question of vanity or worldly shame on the part of the uncles, at the idea of having to mix socially with relatives who had come down in the world. But to make matters even worse, the archdeacon had living with him a niece, Manolita, who managed to make him downright hostile toward his nephew.[177] That became apparent in a terrible family incident that took place shortly after the Escrivás moved to Saragossa. With the best of intentions, Josemaría and his sister Carmen went to visit their uncle Carlos. The archdeacon welcomed them with expressions that were crude and more than rude—words to the effect of, "Why the devil have you come to Saragossa? To parade your poverty?" Not dignifying this with an answer, Carmen said to her brother, "Josemaría, let's get out of here, since in this house we are not approved of."[178]

The archdeacon neither backed down nor offered any excuse for those insults, which were like a slap in the face. But Josemaría never complained about the treatment he had received. On several occasions he even tried again to approach Father Carlos, but to no avail.

Only the sad events of the war made the archdeacon forget his old prejudices. At the beginning of the 1940s Father Josemaría went to visit his uncle in Saragossa. "He did not want him to think," says a person who accompanied him on that visit, "that he was harboring any resentment."[179] He left happy about how the visit had gone. It was not he who had changed, but his uncle.

His attitude toward his mother's brother was always one of exceptional charity. On January 6, 1948, having just received news of Father Carlos' death, he quickly wrote these brief lines to his sister and brother, Carmen and Santiago: "I hear that Father Carlos has died. I ask you to pray for his soul, especially since he acted so badly toward Mama and us—I feel this obliges us all the more to pray for him. If you do, you will please our Lord God and I will be grateful to you."[180]

(The news, however, was erroneous. His uncle would die two years later.)

* * *

The family adjusted to its new life without complaint. The better-off relatives did not, indeed, offer them any help. However, a little while after they moved to Rufas Street, a nephew of Doña Dolores who worked at a bank came to stay with them, which gave them a little financial relief, since he paid 150 pesetas a month for room and board.*[181]

Josemaría's duties as prefect and his participation as deacon in liturgical services at the church of San Carlos kept him away from home much of the time. The exercise of his diaconate had an unforgettable emotional impact on him. So great was the yearning with which he looked forward to those moments, and so great his reverence for Jesus in the Blessed Sacrament, that his hands and sometimes his whole body trembled when he touched the Sacred Host. The first time this happened to him was during a solemn Benediction, when he had to put the small glass case containing the Sacred Host into the monstrance. At that moment he interiorly asked our Lord never to let him get used to handling him; and to the end of his life he felt the impact of this blessed encounter. In 1974 he confessed that his hands sometimes still trembled as they had that first time.[182]

At San Carlos he gave Communion to the faithful, including his mother. "In this house of San Carlos," he would comment years later, "I received my priestly formation. Here, at this altar, I came up, trembling, to take the Sacred Host and for the first time give Communion to my mother. You can't imagine. . . . I go from emotion to emotion."[183]

---

* In these years, the income of an average middle-class family in Spain was somewhere around 7,500 pesetas a year. A laborer was paid about 6 pesetas a day, on which it was very difficult to support a family. A modest boarding house in Madrid charged about 7 pesetas a day for room and board.

Time seemed to drag as he dreamed of being a priest. He was only twenty-three, ten months short of the age required by canon law, so he had to request a dispensation from the pope. On February 20, 1925, a positive response arrived from Rome.[184] So on March 4 Josemaría sent to the vicar general this formal request: "Desiring to receive the holy order of the priesthood during the coming ember days of the fifth week of Lent, since I believe I am called by God to the priestly state, I entreat Your Excellency to deign to grant me the requisite dimissory letters, upon fulfillment of the requirements of canon law."[185]

The procedure was carried out in accordance with the canonical requirements and with a certain sense of urgency, since Ember Saturday that year would come soon—on March 28. The documents in the ordination file begin with the examination for suitability (given at the Royal Seminary of San Carlos) and include the required letter from the vicar general of the diocese of Calahorra, the public banns proclaimed in Logroño, and the response from the pastor of Santiago el Real, complete with four sworn statements expressing the judgment that "Don José María Escrivá y Albás is worthy of being admitted to what he is requesting." This last document, dated Logroño, March 23, was sent on to Calahorra. From there, with the approval having been secured, the papers were returned to the secretary of the chancery office of the archdiocese of Saragossa.[186]

On Ember Saturday, March 28, 1925, the ceremony of priestly ordination was celebrated in the church of San Carlos, with Bishop Miguel de los Santos presiding.[187]

The ordinand put his whole self into the liturgical ceremonies: the anointing of the hands, the *traditio instrumentorum* [the giving to the priest of a chalice and some of the other items he will use in his priestly ministry], the words of the Consecration. . . . Deeply moved and bewildered by the goodness of the Lord, he dismissed as nothing the difficulties he had experienced since his calling, and offered thanks like a youth in love.[188]

As for his first Mass, it would be not a solemn one, but a Low Mass, since it would be celebrated on the Monday of Passion Week, with purple vestments, for the repose of the soul of his father. The newly ordained priest sent notices to only a small number of persons, since the family was still in mourning and the celebration was to be a private one. Some holy cards of our Lady were sent out with the following announcement on the back.[189]

The Priest
José María Escrivá y Albás

will celebrate his first Mass in the Holy Chapel of Our Lady of the Pillar in Saragossa on March 30, 1925, at 10:30 in the morning, for the repose of the soul of his father, Don José Escrivá Corzán, who went to his rest with the Lord on November 27, 1924.

A.M.D.G.
Invitation and memento

It had not been easy to get permission to use that chapel, but he very much wanted to celebrate his first Mass there, in the place where he had gone every day to cry out his "Domina, ut sit!" But, that aside, the Mass was more sorrowful than the celebrant could have foreseen, although he would hide the memory and circumstances of the ceremony in a very simple statement: "In the Holy Chapel, in the presence of a handful of people, I quietly celebrated my first Mass."[190]

Santiago, who was six at the time, remembers the simplicity of the ceremony and the small congregation: "It was a Low Mass, attended by my mother, my sister Carmen, myself, and a few others." Their cousin Sixta Cermeño gives a more detailed report:

My husband and I were the only members of the Albás family who joined his mother in attending that first Mass. . . .

The people there were Josemaría's mother (Aunt Lola), his sister, the little boy (who was then about six), ourselves (my husband and I), two neighbors from Barbastro whose last name was Cortés (they were close friends of his sister Carmen, and of about her age), and a few others that I didn't know. I seem to recall two or three priests, and possibly there were some other friends from the university or the seminary. It's hard to say, since, as you know, that chapel of Our Lady of the Pillar is always full of people.[191]

The conspicuous absence of the priests of Doña Dolores' family and the small number of people present left an impression of loneliness. "His uncles Carlos, Vicente, and Mariano Albás were not at his first Mass, in 1925," says Amparo Castillón. "I was there, and to me it felt like he was very much alone."[192]

The rector, Father José López Sierra, adds that two priests who were friends of the family assisted the new priest at the altar. Moved with pity, he describes the scene in the chapel. The mother "was dissolved in a sea of tears and at times seemed close to fainting," while everyone else, kneeling the whole time, "without even blinking, remained immobile through the entire Mass, contemplating the sacred gestures of that angel on earth."[193]

Doña Dolores, who had gotten up that morning feeling sick, became especially emotional at the thought of the many sacrifices she and her husband had made to see this ceremony. The same thought must also have crossed the mind of her niece Sixta Cermeño, since she recalls that "together with the feeling of intimacy there was a note of sadness," and that the priest's mother was crying, "perhaps thinking about the recent loss of her husband."[194]

Good son that he was, the new priest was hoping his mother would be the first person to receive from his hands a host he had consecrated, but he was denied that joy. Just as he was about to distribute Communion, a woman got ahead of Doña Dolores and knelt down on the prie-dieu, and so the priest felt obliged to give the first host to that good woman, so as not to snub her.[195] After the Mass came the customary kissing of the new priest's hands, congratulations in the sacristy, and farewells to the small group of attendees. For Josemaría, the memory of that first Mass would always have a taste of sacrifice. He would see it as "a picture of sorrow, with his mother dressed in mourning."[196]

At the altar, celebrating the Mass, the priest exercised his liturgical ministry in the most sublime way, in the offering of that same Victim who offered himself on the cross to redeem humanity. Now personally and definitively identified with Christ in virtue of the sacrament of Holy Orders, Josemaría made the Eucharistic Sacrifice the center of his interior life. And just as on the evening before his First Communion he had received as a memento the painful caress of a burn caused by the carelessness of a barber, now he had the memory of being denied a pious dream—to give Communion first, at his first Mass, to his mother. Our Lord was drawing him closer to the cross with these little signs of predilection.

At the apartment on Rufas Street there was a small reception. Doña Dolores' nephews and nieces, Carmen's two friends from Barbastro, and some other close friends were invited. The modest dinner combined poverty with good taste, since the lady of the house had prepared an excellent rice dish.[197]

When they had eaten, the priest retired to his room. He had just been notified of his first assignment in his priestly career. Reviewing the events of the past few months and the most recent blows, he realized that there was good reason to think the Lord was still hammering away in the same way as before: "one blow on the nail and a hundred on the horseshoe." Dejected and sobbing, he filially protested to the Lord, "How you treat me! How you treat me!"[198]

4

A Young Priest (1925–1927)

1. *The parish of Perdiguera*

The parish of Perdiguera, of which Father Josemaría had been appointed temporary administrator, was in a village about fifteen miles from Saragossa.[1] Although not far from the capital, it was rather out of the way and in an area with poor roads. Its pastor, the only priest in the village, had been away for some time due to a serious illness. This appointment was a heavy blow for the new priest, who had not expected an assignment away from his family, nor one announced so suddenly, since it was taken for granted in clerical circles that newly ordained priests would be sent to parishes where they could get pastoral experience under the eye of other priests—and Saragossa had no shortage of priests.[2] But Father Josemaría obeyed promptly and without complaining, and on the very next day, Tuesday, March 31, he set out for his new post, in a mule-drawn carriage.

Perdiguera had about eight hundred inhabitants. It was situated on an elevation in a plain just south of the Monegros district, in an area of unirrigated farm land. Above its tiled roofs arose, massive and heavy, the great bulk of its church, while on the horizon lay the Alcubierre mountain range. The parish sacristan, Urbano Murillo, had been sick in bed for several days, so it was his son Teodoro, a bright young boy, who accompanied Father Josemaría to the house in which he would stay.[3]

The new priest immediately inspected the church, which was named Our Lady of the Assumption. It was well preserved, despite the centuries, and its masonry was as solid as it looked, offering sightseers a peculiar mixture of Gothic elements with Moorish traceries and projections, all in brick. It had a single nave and a fairly good Renaissance altarpiece, featuring a statue of the Blessed Virgin. But the newly arrived priest was distressed by the obvious neglect and dirtiness of the interior, and especially by the pitiful condition of the sanctuary and altar. He had to do a lot of sweeping and scrubbing before he could say Mass there the next day.

The house he stayed in belonged to a family of honest country people, and was very modest, indeed very poor. Like most houses in the village, it consisted of a ground floor which included the kitchen (and which had right behind it a chicken yard), and a second floor with bedrooms. The family consisted of Saturnino Arruga, his wife, Prudencia Escanero, and their son, who was ten or twelve.[4]

Father Josemaría was surprised to find that these good people had provided magnificent sleeping accommodations for him. On a large bed with gilded headboard and legs lay two soft mattresses and a multicolored down quilt.[5] He joked that he would have to make a running jump to get into bed, but this was to disguise with good humor his penitential practice of sleeping on the floor. The bed was surely an imposing-looking and cumbersome piece of furniture: at the slightest movement it shook and creaked, making a "festive noise" that could jolt one out of the soundest sleep. To judge by his jokes, he must seldom have slept in it.

The day after his arrival in Perdiguera, he celebrated his first Mass there, and then set to work organizing a schedule. There were only a few days left before Holy Week, and he wanted all the parishioners to receive the sacrament of Penance so that they could fulfill their Easter duty. With the help of the sacristan and his son, he carried out his resolution to get acquainted as soon as possible with all the families of the parish. Teodoro, who was his altar server, testifies that even though this meant going to almost two hundred homes, "within a short time he visited all the families in the village."[6] As he got to know his parishioners, he came to realize that the adults had very little doctrinal knowledge and that their children were absolutely ignorant of the catechism. Immediately he set new goals: to organize catechism classes for adults and for children, and to prepare the children for First Communion. Once Holy Week, with its lengthy liturgical services, was behind him, Father Josemaría (accompanied by his altar server) went to visit all the shut-ins. He heard their confessions and offered to bring them Communion later on, if they so desired.

Evidently the young priest wanted the Mass to have as much solemnity as possible, because feast day or not, and regardless of how few people were present, he celebrated a sung Mass every day.[7] Most of the villagers got up at dawn to go out and work in the fields, vineyards, and olive groves. Much of the land was hard to cultivate, but there was some pasture land used by the villagers' flocks of sheep and goats.

If Father Josemaría found any free time, he spent it reading or studying. At midday he sat at the table of his hosts and ate, happily and with a good appetite, whatever Prudencia had prepared. The food was not elegant, but it was plentiful and substantial: good bread, vegetables, and pork or mutton, all with lots of olive oil and peppers. After lunch, when the rest of the village was taking a siesta, he took a walk through the neighborhood with his altar server. While getting his exercise, he also took the opportunity to give his young companion some religious instruction. They started out on what was called "the priests' path"—every village had one, and Perdiguera was no exception—and returned by way of "the Olive Plantation." Teodoro has forgotten what they chatted about, but not an odd habit that the priest had. "During those walks" he says, "we would always be talking, but the only thing I remember is that he used to pick up pebbles and put them in his pocket." With a respectful simplicity, he adds, "I never had the nerve to ask him why he was doing this."[8] (The Murillos of Perdiguera were discreet both by nature and also in keeping with a parish tradition. In sharing his reminiscences Teodoro said, "My father, Urbano Murillo, who died some years ago, was the sacristan of the parish of Our Lady of the Assumption in Perdiguera, which is in the province of Saragossa. Before him, my grandfather had been the sacristan. In Father Josemaría's day I was an altar server, but in time I became the sacristan, and I hope to continue serving in this capacity as long as our Lord keeps me alive."[9])

Had the priest been asked the reason for his odd habit, he might have been embarrassed. For it was not a mania for collecting, but, a simple way of keeping track of prayers and mortifications. Of course that can be dangerous, because it can lead to vanity. Very soon, in fact, experience and time taught the young priest to leave the counting to his guardian angel.[10]

Father Josemaría spent his evenings in the church. He held exposition of the Blessed Sacrament, led a Rosary, and on Thursdays conducted a holy hour. Before and after the holy hour he waited patiently in the confessional for penitents. Usually these were children or old women, but from time to time a teenager or a grown man would show up. The priest was happy to see that the numbers were increasing. But one day, on his way out, he was surprised to overhear in the vestibule a boy saying to his friends, "What a priest! If I hadn't been careful, he would have found out everything!"[11] Only ignorance—a failure to realize that in the sacrament of Penance the confessor is, besides a judge, an instrument of mercy—could have led that boy to commit such a sacrilege. But the priest's sorrow at this lack of sincerity in confession led him to offer, for several years, prayers and mortifications in reparation. As earlier, when upon his arrival in Perdiguera he had discovered the state of neglect of the sanctuary, his priestly sensibilities were upset. From that day on, whenever he caught sight of a church, he made an act of love to our Lord eucharistically present there.

About three weeks after his arrival, when he had the parish functioning in regular fashion, he received a surprise visit. The father of the sick pastor suddenly showed up and demanded for his son the stipends received by the substitute priest for the Masses he had celebrated, the collections taken up at those recently organized holy hours, and any other parish income. Father Josemaría wrote to his uncle Carlos asking for his thoughts and suggestions regarding this claim which he considered unjust and impudent. He could, of course, have gone directly to the diocesan authorities, but he saw in this incident an opportunity to repair, very tactfully, his damaged relations with the archdeacon.

Soon he received an official response from the chancery office, dated April 24, which seems to reflect a certain lack of interest in him on the part of the archdeacon:

Chancery Secretary of the Archdiocese of Saragossa

Father José M. Escrivá / Perdiguera

My esteemed friend:

Your uncle Carlos, who left today for Burgos, left me the letter you wrote him. I answer it as follows:

1. You can and should sign the sacramental certificates.

2. Since you are the one responsible for whatever takes place during the absence of the pastor (who left without asking anyone's permission), you should not let his father or any other member of his family collect the monies given you by the faithful as stipends.

3. The parish income belongs to you absolutely. Since presumably it will be a while before he returns, you could, out of charity and for a short time, offer the pastor half of it, but making it clear that all of it is yours.

4. Show this letter to the pastor's father, if necessary, so that he knows he must completely refrain from any interference in the parish. This means, among other things, that he had better not try again to collect for the holy hours and the Masses you celebrate.

5. Anything irregular that you observe in the parish must be reported to the vicar general and not to your uncle, although the archdeacon's views are highly respected in the vicariate.

Yours truly,

Juan Carceller
April 24, 1925.[12]

There is nothing in the chancery secretary's files to indicate how this story turned out. Father Josemaría was softhearted, but he also had a family to feed. In all likelihood he took the secretary's suggestion and shared the parish income with the other priest's family.

Taking almost scrupulous care to avoid tying spiritual care to material contributions, however, he rejected anything even remotely resembling a payment for ministerial services. Those country people, seeing that he would not take gifts, wanted to at least bring something to his family in Saragossa when they went there to sell produce or livestock. But he refused to tell anyone where Doña Dolores lived, even though, as his brother Santiago says, gifts of cheese, fruit and poultry would have been very welcome at the Rufas Street apartment.[13]

Saturnino and Prudencia, his host and hostess, enjoyed many conversations with their guest. Father Josemaría wanted to repay their kindness in some way, and it was a special sorrow to him that their son could not take part in the classes he was giving to a group of children to prepare them for First Communion. The boy left the house very early, with his goats, and did not return until twilight. The priest ended up teaching him catechism at night. After a short time, to see if he was ready, he asked him, "If you were rich—very rich—what would you want to do?" Before venturing an answer, the boy wisely protected himself by asking, "What does being rich mean?" The priest explained this to him as best he could. He said being rich means having lots of money, lots of clothes, lots of land, very fat cows, and very splendid goats. "And so," he repeated, "what would you do if you were rich?" The boy had a sudden inspiration. His eyes lighting up, he exclaimed, "I would have big bowls of wine soup!"

The priest became very serious when he heard this answer. He thought to himself, "Josemaría, the Holy Spirit is speaking."[14] For all earthly ambitions, however grand, really amount to no more than a bowl of soup.

He thought of writing down this and other anecdotes from his weeks in the village under the title "Tale of a Village Priest," with the idea of opening the eyes of some inexperienced priest and helping him in his spiritual life.[15] Thirty years later, in a meditation, he sketched for his listeners an event that undoubtedly occurred during his stay in Perdiguera. It would surely have found a place in the "Tale," had he ever gotten around to writing it. Its basic elements are obviously autobiographical: A recently ordained priest comes to a country village which has few houses and very few inhabitants. One fine day, as he is walking to the church, he comes across some priests playing cards.

They invite him to join the game, but the young cleric courteously excuses himself. Telling them he does not know how to play that game, he quietly makes his escape. He goes into the church to spend some time with our Lord in the Blessed Sacrament, as he does every evening and also most mornings. The cardplayers are not offended, but naturally they smile at the simplemindedness of this young priest, who could just as well be taking it easy after breakfast, and then, like any respectable pastor, taking a sunny stroll in the winter or a shaded one in summer. And when the young priest comes out of church, the cardplayers call out to him from where they are sitting, "Mystical Rose! Mystical Rose!"[16]

As we have seen, this was one of the nicknames Father Josemaría had been given by some of his classmates at the seminary in Saragossa. Not surprisingly, the story and the nickname spread through the neighboring villages. Now a few people even began to call the acting administrator by that name.

Father Josemaría found consolation in serving souls. Great was his joy when he prepared a group of children for First Communion. But this, like many of his other pastoral accomplishments, is not recorded in the parish books. Were we to judge exclusively by what was entered there, it would seem that the acting administrator did very little. During his stay in Perdiguera only one death took place. The baptismal certificates are somewhat more numerous: he baptized four boys, named Isidoro, Pascual, Mariano, and Carmelo.[17] The small size of the parish and the administrator's short stay there do not permit one to draw any valid statistical conclusions, even about life in a rural parish.

At any rate, Father Josemaría's assignment to this parish ended on May 18, 1925, the day after Cardinal Soldevila's successor, Bishop Rigoberto Doménech, arrived in the archdiocese.[18]

In 1975 Teodoro Murillo, the parish sacristan, gave Perdiguera's fomer administrator this eulogy:

> Of all the priests who have passed through this village, Father Josemaría was for me the most unforgettable, though I don't know that I could say exactly why. He was very cheerful, had a wonderful sense of humor, was very well-mannered, down-to-earth, affectionate. In the short time he was here I grew very close to him, and when he left I took it very hard.[19]

2. *The study of law*

In Perdiguera, Father Josemaría had not had a moment's rest. But since he was young and naturally resilient, his trials, corporal penances, late-night vigils, and nights of sleeping on the floor all left no trace of fatigue. When he got home, his sister spontaneously greeted him with the comment, "How nice and filled out you've gotten!"[20] His healthy appearance had a lot to do with Prudencia's cooking, especially the bread, and the potatoes and other vegetables cooked in all that olive oil.

Things had been tight for years, but since his father's death the situation had verged on dire poverty. Sixta Cermeño, who visited the apartment on Rufas Street fairly often, says her aunt Dolores "suffered a lot in those days, though she tried not to show it." By tacit agreement, the family did everything possible to make sure visitors did not notice the financial straits the household was in. "I remember, for example," Sixta continues, "that one Sunday afternoon we were together and my aunt said she would make us some hot chocolate. She gave me the impression that she was doing it to give me a treat, but now I feel sure that this was their supper."[21]

Faced with such pressing need, the young priest could hardly allow himself the luxury of making sunny long-range plans. First of all, he had to resolve the question of his relationship with the chancery, a question pending since his ordination and for which, given the events leading to Perdiguera, a happy solution did not seem likely. It was also more or less obvious that the letter sent to him in Perdiguera by the chancery secretary contained between the lines a rather strong message that he should refrain from bothering his uncle Carlos. So why try asking him for anything!

Josemaría finally had to confront, not on a theoretical or ideal level, but as a very real and urgent problem, the question of "the ecclesiastical career." He was not sure what path to take. On the one hand, he loved the exercise of his ministry; he felt off-center when far from the altar, and he was ready for any sacrifice. But, he had to consider his personal circumstances and particularly his family obligations. All these things, no doubt, greatly shortened the list of possible church positions he could request. And of course he would not make any decision without first meditating on it in the light of his "inklings of divine love."[22]

Failing, despite much searching, to come up with anything substantial and definite to cover his pressing financial needs as head of the family, he finally obtained a position that could at least accommodate his priestly zeal. Somehow or other, he ended up at Saint Peter Nolasco—a Jesuit-run church better known as Sacred Heart. He began to work there on a provisional basis in May, shortly after leaving Perdiguera. The stipends, as might be imagined, were not enough to cover the family's expenses.

But Doña Dolores was worried about something else: that her son might be given another assignment outside of Sara- gossa. With a mother's boldness, she decided to request a rec- ommendation from her brother the canon. Santiago would never forget the sorry incident that occurred when his mother, dressed in mourning clothes and holding him by the hand, showed up at Uncle Carlos' house to ask him to do something for Josemaría. "Once he was ordained a priest," he says, "my mother wanted him to be allowed to stay in Saragossa with us. She went to ask this of her brother Father Carlos, who had a lot of influence in the chancery. I went with my mother. But her brother Father Carlos—I remember it as though it were hap- pening now—treated her very badly. In fact, he rudely threw us out of his house."[23]

Another unresolved issue for the newly ordained priest was that of his secular career. Hardly a year after he had begun his legal studies, the family's situation was so changed that he felt obliged to finish them as soon as possible. He could see that the only way he could support his family—at least the only one compatible with his vocation as a priest—would be by teaching.

On April 29, while still in Perdiguera, he had written to the dean of the law school explaining that, having completed on his own the required studies in political law and civil law, he would like to take the examinations for those subjects in June, so that he could get academic credit for them.[24] In 1924–1925 there had been so many big changes in Josemaría's life—the death of his father, his ordination to the diaconate, his family's move, his priestly ordination, the assignment to Perdiguera, and, most recently, his assignment to Saint Peter Nolasco—that he had had very little time for studying. Now, with great en- thusiasm and tenacity he buckled down to study political law and civil law. But soon he saw that he had bitten off more than he could chew, so he presented himself only for the examination in civil law, which he passed by a comfortable margin.[25]

Thanks to his efforts the previous year—when, in a single set of examinations taken in September 1924, he had managed to pass six subjects—he was now halfway through his law studies.[26] Filled with optimism, he drew up a new plan of attack: he intended to cover two more subjects, penal law and administrative law, during the summer of 1925. But in September, he took neither exam.[27] Perhaps his new liturgical and pastoral duties at Saint Peter Nolasco made preparation impossible. Or perhaps his sense of responsibility kept him from trying his luck without having actually mastered the subjects.

In any case, neither studying nor prudence kept him from getting a failing grade in Spanish history—a subject in which he had thought he was well prepared, because he liked it so much and had done such extensive reading in it.[28] The Spanish history professor was known among the students for his touchiness, his air of self-importance, and the magisterial tone of his lectures. As an unofficial student, Josemaría was not obliged to attend the classes. But the professor took his absence very badly, ascribing it to a lack of appreciation of his erudite discourses. When the time came for the examination, he had someone tell Josemaría not to bother showing up, since he was going to fail him no matter what. And so he did.

Naturally the student was upset by this blatant injustice. To head off any repetition of such arbitrariness, he sent the professor a note with a reasoned explanation as to why, before again presenting himself for the exam, he would like a guarantee that he would be allowed to pass it. Recognizing the injustice of what he had done, the professor assured Josemaría that he need only show up for the exam, since he had already demonstrated his mastery of the subject.[29]

His law studies were becoming for him an exhausting obstacle course. By all indications, it would take a lot of sacrifice to finish. But he had made this commitment to his father when he was still living, and the veneration Josemaría felt for his memory gave him the strength to persevere. Also, out of gratitude and loyalty, he felt bound to do this for God, whose call he continued to experience in the form of presentiments.

In part, that explains the spirit of inner certitude and exuberant optimism with which he began the school year of 1925–1926. He made a firm resolution to complete the courses still needed for his law degree, though realizing that he would have to wait until June and September for the exams.

A companion of Josemaría's who also attended the ecclesiastical university and studied at the law school was a little surprised to find that in the two institutions the social values were so different. Josemaría, who at the seminary was considered an oddball because of his "cultural interests," now had no problem adapting to his environment, those same inclinations served him wonderfully at the secular university; he "fit absolutely perfectly" into its milieu.[30]

Possibly the cassock helped give him an aura of prestige, since it was such a novelty among these students. Certainly his clerical attire, which he wore very naturally and always kept neat and clean, never constituted a barrier between Josemaría and his classmates. One of them, Juan Antonio Iranzo, says that he and some other friends saw it as a reflection of two things: "his concept of the dignity of the priesthood, and his apostolic spirit."[31]

From the first moment, he was at home in the university. Father José López Ortiz tells us that in June 1924, just after his own ordination to the priesthood, he went to take an examination in Saragossa, and there he struck up a friendship with the head prefect of San Carlos, who gave him useful information on the law school. "Josemaría was very well prepared and very much at home in what was to me a foreign environment," he tells us. "Generously, as if it were the most natural thing in the world, he gave me valuable advice on various aspects of my studies."[32] He adds that "everybody at the school knew him, and . . . because of his outgoing and cheerful personality he was very well liked. Since he was the only seminarian, some friends affectionately called him 'the little

priest' [*el curilla*]—the nickname given him by that canon law
professor, Moneva y Puyol, who liked him so much."³³

The young priest was never alone. His personal charm and
engaging conversation made students gravitate to him. They
would crowd around him "to hear him speak" because "they
felt drawn by his personality." Luis Palos, recalling this in his
old age, still has fresh in his memory nostalgic pictures of the
"little priest." "I can still see him, in the halls of the old university, or in Magdalena Plaza, or on his way to the Cerbuna Library (which is now gone), walking always with a group. No
doubt about it, he exerted over all of us a very strong human at-
traction. He had a very open mentality, a universal outlook."³⁴

That broadness of outlook and feeling was in great part a
result of his priesthood. For him, this was the vocation from
within which our Lord would summon him to carry out a divine plan of a very far-reaching scope, leading him to grasp
that elusive something not yet revealed to him. Josemaría had
been chosen to participate as a priest in the eternal priesthood
of Christ for the benefit of *all* his brothers and sisters—the
whole rest of the human race. Through the sacrament of Holy
Orders, an indelible mark had been conferred on him that
bonded him to the mission of the Church, making him another
Christ and a minister of his sacraments.

So lofty a view did he take of this tremendous dignity, his
friends tell us, that it transformed his way of acting and his appearance; these reflected his awareness of being, as it were, a
new person. The young priest was extraordinarily sensitive to
any kind of joking or teasing about the clerical state, especially
when he was in the company of students. One of them tells us
that Josemaría "quietly put up with the mere indiscretions—
the crude words, the low-class jokes—of his companions, and
knew how to gracefully extricate himself from situations that
for others would have been embarrassing."³⁵ But if the conversation slipped into actual impropriety, if there was the slightest
hint of salaciousness or anything that showed a lack of respect
for the priesthood, he would emphatically put a stop to it,

without losing his decorum or self-possession, though perhaps not without blushing.

He himself showed in an exemplary way the reverence due the priesthood by trying his best to make sure his contact with the world of students did not compromise his self-possession and dignity. The need for circumspection comes up over and over in his notes. Eventually it would be expressed, against an obviously autobiographical background, in a piece of advice offered to all faithful Christians:

> Don't ever make a priest run the risk of losing his dignity. It is a virtue which, without pompousness, he simply must have.
>
> How hard that young priest—a friend of ours—prayed for it: "Lord, grant me . . . eighty years of dignity!"
>
> You too should pray for it for all priests, and you'll have done something good.[36]

He redoubled his efforts not to give rise to any gossip, going beyond what prudence and discretion would have required. He even took care not to be seen in public in the company of his mother or sister, to avoid any possibility of scandalizing those who did not know they were related. Toward the young ladies who were studying at the law school (very few in those days), he showed a guarded friendliness, not going too far in the courtesies he showed them.[37]

His clerical garb, we repeat, was no barrier for him. Whether on the street or at the university or in the exercise of his ministry at Saint Peter Nolasco, Father Josemaría acted quite naturally while being well aware of the value of the cassock. As one of his classmates puts it, "he never disguised the fact that he was a priest."[38] The young clergyman was proud to possess this treasure and dignity. He loved his brothers in the priesthood wholeheartedly, defended the honor of ministers of the altar tenaciously, and sought to restore this dignity when it was sullied.

Father Josemaría was witness to a sad incident of this sort; a close friend of his from the seminary soon abandoned his priestly ministry. His conversion required long prayers and vigils. José Romeo says that in about 1930 Father Josemaría "asked me to pray for that man, and told me in strict confidence something of his prayer and mortification for that intention."[39] Several years later, another person testifies, he "still often thought of that man, prayed for him, and tried not to lose contact with him, always thinking that he might yet be salvageable."[40] A third person says that he "kept admonishing him, by spoken word and in writing, trying to get him out of that bad situation," and that finally, at the end of his life, the sinner, now reconciled, saw that Josemaría "had been his most faithful friend and the instrument used by God to return him to the Church."[41] At other times the individual in question was an older man. After mortifying himself and praying for a long time, the young priest would approach him armed with charity and sympathy.[42]

*   *   *

On April 25, 1926, out of a commendable desire to take a big step forward in his secular studies, but with excessive optimism, he sent to the dean of the law school a request to be allowed "to take, the next time they are given, the examinations in the following subjects: political law, penal law, administrative law, public international law, business law, and judicial procedure. . . ."[43] He had decided to push ahead with this difficult bunch of subjects even though he knew that his apostolic zeal, coupled with the rigorous obligations of his ministry at Saint Peter Nolasco, would not leave him much free time.

Seeing the tight spot he was in when the time came for examinations, he did some quick calculating and put off the ones for penal law and judicial procedure to the September session. He took the rest of the exams in June and came out with one "Special Honors," two "Notables," and one "Passed." At the end of the summer he took and passed the other two exams, plus those in public finance and private international law. Now he had just one more course to take.[44]

3. *Ministry at Saint Peter Nolasco*

Father Josemaría underwent many privations on account of pursuing his ideal of priestly ministry while awaiting orders from on high. The presentiments of his hidden calling remained that—presentiments. Having promptly responded to God's summons in Logroño at the beginning of 1918, he was in 1925 still wondering about his mysterious vocation. The anticipation of something sublime helped him cope with the hard realities of daily life, one of which was his having to be the family breadwinner.

Had Providence arranged things differently, by now Father Josemaría would have been enjoying an ecclesiastical benefice or a well-paid position, thanks to the help of Cardinal Soldevila or of some relative. But the cardinal was dead, and the uncles who were canons and holders of benefices seemed to have turned their backs on their nephew. As for his priestly faculties, on the day of his ordination these were granted for a six-month period by Father José Pellicer, the vicar general of Saragossa.[45] The first extension of this authorization "to celebrate and to absolve" was granted by Bishop Rigoberto Doménech.[46]

The new prelate had been consecrated in 1916 and for the next eight years had served as bishop of Mallorca. In 1926, not long after coming to Saragossa, he launched a reform of the seminary and made sweeping changes in chancery office personnel. It may have been all this commotion that led an experienced priest, with the best of intentions, to advise Father Josemaría not to work too hard and especially not to write anything that could get him in trouble by clashing with the opinions of others, since backtracking would be very difficult.[47]

The battering to which life would subject him would make Father Josemaría see the wisdom in that advice: the truth that renewers and reformers can expect enmities and obstacles. At present, though, nobody envied the young priest his good luck. He was, if anything, an object of pity.

Upon his return from Perdiguera, as we have seen, he looked about for priestly work and found nothing except the position at Saint Peter Nolasco Church. But as later attested by Father Celestino Moner, S.J., he carried out his duties there to everyone's satisfaction. "I certify," says Father Celestino, "that Father José M. Escrivá, from April or May of 1925 until March of 1927, served at Saint Peter Nolasco Church as an assistant priest, to celebrate Holy Mass, administer Holy Communion, and expose and reserve the Blessed Sacrament, and that he always comported himself to the edification of all and without giving the slightest grounds for complaint with regard to the fulfillment of his duties."[48]

So eager was he to celebrate the Holy Sacrifice that he would have considered a lifetime of dedication and work well spent if that was what it took to get to be ordained and say Mass. His good pastoral dispositions and diligence were much appreciated by the rector of the church. In September he offered him a provisional contract—provisional in that it did not establish a lasting connection and in that it did not fully cover his financial needs. Father Josemaría accepted it, since he had no other offer of a remunerated priestly position. The contract reads:

> Duties and rights of the assistant priest at Saint Peter Nolasco Church:
>
> On feast days, First Fridays, and other solemn days, he is to be at the service of the church from 6:00 to 10:30 in the morning; on other days, from 7:00 to 9:30 or 10:00 in the morning.
>
> Whenever there is a sung Mass, and also during Holy Week, he is to be on hand to help out as needed.
>
> On First Fridays, during Forty Hours Devotion, on every day in the month of June, and on any other occasion

that includes exposition of the Blessed Sacrament, he is to show up punctually at the time of the service to do the exposition and to help out in any way needed.

When necessary, he will wash the purificators.

He will say Holy Mass at the assigned times.

He will receive a fixed stipend of 3 pesetas for each Mass.

For the other services described above, he will receive 2 pesetas a day.

On feast days he will have breakfast in the sacristan's office.

On days when for any reason he does not fulfill his duties, he will not receive either stipend unless he sends a substitute who fulfills all of those duties.

The father superior of the church can, if he sees fit, appoint a different assistant priest, giving the undersigned eight days' notice.

Agreeing with these conditions, I accept them, in Saragossa, on September 10, 1925. José María Escrivá, Priest.[49]

(How much did the monthly stipends of the assistant priest come to? A sheet of paper was saved which enumerates the Masses and other services for the month of October, and the total revenue was 155 pesetas.[50])

The church was located in one of the older sections of Saragossa, not far from San Carlos. Architecturally it was nothing special, but it was a very busy place, which is why the Jesuits needed the help of a diocesan priest. Its activities were numerous and varied: Saturday devotions and monthly days of recollection for the Daughters of Mary; Masses on the third Sunday of each month for the Archconfraternity of Christian Mothers; services on the third Friday of each month for the Good Death Association; catechetical instruction every Sunday at the nine o'clock Mass; services for women's Saint Vincent de Paul conferences; First Sundays for men; Sunday Mass for the Annunciation and Saint Aloysius Gonzaga fraternities; a

monthly service for the Saint Stanislaus Fraternity; Mass on
first Sundays for household employees of the Congregation of
the Daughters of Mary and Saint Zita; evening rosaries and
talks. Rounding out the schedule of services were days of
recollection for blue-collar workers, for white-collar workers,
for members of the Saint Vincent de Paul conferences, for an
association of women teachers. . . .[51]

Out of all this bubbling activity came also many other services
not specified in his contract, but which he cheerfully took on his
shoulders: teaching catechism, caring for the sick, filling in for
someone at the last minute, hearing the confessions of all kinds of
people. As in Perdiguera, Father Josemaría sat in the confessional
for hours on end, when not needed somewhere else.[52]

Even before his ordination he had had a deep veneration
for the sacrament of Penance. He himself tells this story:

> When I was studying at the University of Saragossa, I
> had a friend who was leading a messed-up life, and it took
> several of us to do this, but we did manage to get him to go
> to confession.
>
> This was so many years ago that I can now speak freely,
> since it would be impossible to identify the priest, who was
> in any case actually a very good one.
>
> Well, this friend went to the shrine of Our Lady of the
> Pillar, went to confession, and came back very happy. But
> he commented to us, "That priest should have been a rail-
> road signalman."
>
> "Why?" we asked him.
>
> "For my penance he told me to do seven stations a day
> for seven days."[53]

Father Josemaría had to explain to the student what these
"stations" were.* And from this incident he learned to impose

---

* A "station" here means three Our Fathers, three Hail Mary's, and three
Glory Be's."

easy penances, which he would afterward supplement with his own prayer and mortification.[54]

His caution in dealing with women did not prevent him from acquiring a knowledge and understanding of feminine psychology by way of his penitents. From the confessional he directed many consciences, and, according to one of his friends, for some time he heard the confessions of nuns.[55]

Apart from liturgical services and other activities connected with his ministry, he always found time to get to know and become friends with those around him. The university circle in which the young priest moved was quite broad, since he offered his friendship with open arms, without concern about differences in personality or viewpoint. "I can still remember," says Luis Palos, "the names of some of those who hung around Josemaría and were good friends with him: for instance, Pascual Galbe Loshuertos, who had a reputation for being a nonbeliever; Juan Antonio Iranzo, who was a couple of years behind us; the Jiménez Arnau brothers—José Antonio, the ambassador, also a writer and the head of the Diplomatic School, and his brother Enrique, now a prominent lawyer in Madrid. . . ."[56]

Accompanying his congeniality and gracious, outgoing demeanor were other qualities much appreciated by the students. "I remember his constant cheerfulness: he was always smiling," says Domingo Fumanal. "He was very good-natured and very generous with his friends."[57] He was always ready to do favors. During his first semester at the law school, a group of students of Don Juan Moneva, the canon law professor, asked Josemaría to give them classes in Latin; they wanted to know enough to be able to translate the canons. He taught them three days a week, free of charge. They were, needless to say, very grateful.[58]

The "little priest" focused his natural way with people on apostolic concerns. Says David Mainar, "He took part in our get-togethers perhaps because he already had in mind some plan, his plan."[59] But his intentions—which were nothing less than to bring those souls to Christ—were as obvious as his cassock. "In our conversations," says Domingo Fumanal, "Jose-maría never said anything that was out of place. He respected our way of being."[60] He had to learn, of course, to keep the composure called for by his clerical attire, and how far to let a conversation go. But this did not keep him from accompanying his friends after school to the Abdón Bar on Independence Boulevard, when invited along for some wine and a snack. On the street and in the bar, he would continue to chat with them about the things of God as well as everyday matters.[61]

Once he was a priest, his relationships at the law school took on, in the school year of 1925-26, a more elevated spiritual tone. Not obtrusively, but as the most natural thing in the world, he began to use his prestige and friendliness to encourage his companions in devotions, such as making a daily visit to Our Lady of the Pillar. For some, too, he became not only a trusted friend but their confessor and spiritual director.[62] Domingo Fumanal says that in this priest, so full of optimism and energy, the students saw "a Christian romantic: someone head over heels in love with Christ; a man with total faith in the Gospel."[63] The ideal of his youth was very much alive—indeed, redoubled; it consisted of love, of the essence of love, and it sparked and ignited all those he dealt with. His was more than a life of dedication; it was a life of radical self-giving, a life saturated with love.

One of his close friends—Francisco Moreno, from Teruel—mentions that "he established relations with professors of a high intellectual caliber and kept up real friendships with them for life."[64] His relationship with such prestigious professors as Juan Moneva, Father José Pou de Foxá, and Miguel Sancho Izquierdo developed into a friendship based on equality. The genial Don Juan Moneva showed his student an affection that was both fatherly and friendly.[65] Don Miguel Sancho Izquierdo, the natural law professor, felt "a great veneration for him, despite their difference in age," as Bishop Javier Echevarría says; he was to leave a glowing testimonial concerning the kind of student he was.[66] Other teachers regarded him the same way, in particular the penal law professor, Inocencio Jiménez Vicente, and the legal history professor, Salvador Minguijón.[67] And Father José Pou de Foxá became an especially close friend—"a loyal and noble and good friend," Father Josemaría called him in his journal—who gave him counsel and moral support on several occasions over the years.[68]

In time, those classmates at Saragossa were dispersed—some marrying, moving to other provinces, entering various professions; some disappeared during the war. Now and then the young priest would run into some of these old friends: Father José López Ortiz, Juan Antonio Iranzo, Luis Palos, the Jiménez Arnau brothers. . . . In the fall of 1937, as he was preparing to cross the Pyrenees secretly and in very hazardous circumstances during the civil war, he met one of his professors and one of his classmates in Barcelona. At the height of the religious persecution, in fact, at great risk to himself, he searched through that Catalonian city for Father José Pou de Foxá, just to talk with his old friend and make his confession to him.[69]

During those same days, he also met with another old friend—that young man who among his classmates had had a reputation for being an atheist, since he did not practice the faith. Father Josemaría tried to revive his half-extinguished faith, basing himself on the mutual affection that the two of them had felt ever since their days in Saragossa. When the war ended, Father Josemaría found himself in Madrid, but the other man emigrated to France, where his estrangement from the faith led him to depression and, finally, to despair and suicide. After his friend's death, the priest performed the only act of friendship he could: "he kept praying for him, thinking about the mercy of God."[70]

* * *

Perhaps recalling the catechism classes he had given in Logroño and Perdiguera, Father Josemaría now began an apostolate among humble folk. He got together a small group of young men who in their free time on Sundays would go teach Christian doctrine to poor children in the neighborhood of Casablanca, which is at the edge of Saragossa along the old highway to Teruel. Most of these young men were college students who either belonged to Marian sodalities or else went to Mass at Saint Peter Nolasco.[71]

4. *Providential injustices*

The violent rupture that Don José's sudden death produced in the Escrivás' family life inevitably had an impact on their future. On the one hand, the loss reaffirmed the son's vocation, while obliging him to reorganize his life for the sake of his mother and siblings. On the other hand, his legal studies, begun with such ease and finished in such a hurry, became a heavy burden for him instead of a liberation. After 1926, and especially after he finished law school, his dedication to teaching was continual. This was a matter not of a professional vocation, but of necessity: it was the only way he could make a living for his family. It made him feel consigned to the galleys. "I am a galley slave to teaching!" he exclaimed.[72]

The Escrivás lived in want in Saragossa, without hope of relief. It got so bad that Father Josemaría, doing an inventory of their resources, had to write, "I don't know how we are going to live. . . . Really—I'll spell this out when I have more time—we have lived this way since I was fourteen, but the situation has gotten even worse since Papa's death."[73]

In the privacy of their home, the Escrivás bore their hardships with dignity maintaining at all costs the old family traditions and customs practiced in Don José's time. There is a story about Guitín, little Santiago, that shows the lasting impact left by the head of the family, a man who had been known as "quite an almsgiver." "A holy little nun came, holding by the hand a little girl being raised in the orphanage run by that venerable community. When she asked for alms, the little boy gave her the small sum that his mother used to give each month, saying with innocent simplicity to the little nun—who was so amused that she just had to laugh—'Sister, for the both of you.' "[74]

Squeezing hours out of the day and stealing hours from sleep, Father Josemaría managed to finish his studies. He kept going—but without abandoning in the least his idealistic vision of the priesthood. If we look for an explanation of why he had such a hard time making ends meet, we come up against a reality of his first years as a priest that seems strange, not to say bizarre. Two days after being ordained he was given an assignment in a very abrupt way, and from there he went to residing in Saragossa for two long years as a priest incardinated in that diocese, but provided no means of financial support.[75]

Certainly he did not sit around twiddling his thumbs. On his own initiative, appealing to friends and other contacts, he sought positions where he could exercise his ministry. This search led to his temporary position as assistant priest at Saint Peter Nolasco. Not much is known about his efforts, but there does exist a curious paper trail of later attempts that failed.

On December 19, 1925, the archbishop of Saragossa wrote to the president of the Provincial Assembly the following letter:

My dear and distinguished friend:

In answer to your esteemed letter recommending Father José Escriba [*sic*] for the chaplaincy of the Reparatrix nuns, I must with great regret inform you that this position was offered a week ago to Father Manuel de Pablo, and he has accepted it.

I will be most happy to be able to serve you on another occasion. You know you can always feel entirely free to count on your good friend and Prelate, who blesses you.[76]

A perfect "other occasion" to "be able to serve" this man presented itself at the end of March, and this is the response, dated April 3, 1926, that the archbishop sent him:

My dear and distinguished friend:

By the time I received your esteemed letter recommending Father José Escrivá for the chaplaincy of the nuns of the Incarnation, I had already appointed another priest to that position and signed the letter of appointment. I am truly sorry not to be able to oblige you in this matter. You must understand that it is not for lack of good will.[77]

These letters imply that the chaplaincies were denied Father Josemaría because there were so many candidates, or because some of them were better qualified.[78] But the behavior of the diocesan authorities tends to support the explanation given by some who knew the ins and outs of clerical life in Saragossa: that someone very influential was doing everything possible to get him out of the diocese, diplomatically or not.[79]

This judgment fits the facts and is not mere speculation. Based on his many contacts with the diocesan authorities and the clerical in-group, Father José Pou de Foxá had no doubt about it. Well aware of the circle of isolation drawn around the young priest, and realizing that he "had no future" in Saragossa, he advised him to go to Madrid.[80]

There is a journal entry from 1931 in which Father Josemaría gives an indication of his strained relations with the diocesan authorities: "I could mention here some very interesting things that happened with my testimonials in Saragossa, but I won't go into all that."[81] He made just one charitable comment on the subject: that the Lord had allowed "some providential injustices" to be done him.[82] They were providential in that, by opening some doors and closing others, God was leading him step by step to the appointed place and moment for responding to that cry of his, "Domine, ut videam!" At this time he was still like a poor blind man, taking steps without knowing where he was going.

It was probably in September 1926 that he made a trip to Madrid—which would explain why he did not take the Forensic Practice examination at this time. His intention was to look into the possibility of studying for a doctorate at the University of Madrid, then known as Universidad Central.[83] A doctoral degree would make it easier for him to work as a teacher, and it would be the ultimate fulfillment of his father's wishes. But around this time he was offered an opportunity to give classes at a new academic center in Saragossa, which was always better than giving them at home. The center was called Instituto Amado.

For some time, Don Santiago Amado Lóriga, an infantry captain who had a science degree, had been planning to open in Saragossa a school preparing students for various career programs, and especially for entrance into the military academies. The institute bearing his name opened in October 1926. On its flyers, in the list of faculty members, appears "Don José María Escrivá, Priest."[84] Judging from a letter written him by one of his students on May 26, 1927, Father Josemaría worked with a small group of students in the law department of the Institute, where law school graduates were prepared for their bar exams and undergraduates were assisted in reviewing class material.

The letter is from Nicolás Tena. In a cheerful and very free and easy tone of voice, he tells Father Josemaría how he did in his canon law exam. And particularly in his closing sentence one can see the closeness and apostolic zeal that the priest maintained with his students: "Father, I have gone to confession and received Communion—I'll have to write you a very long letter about this."[85]

Taking advantage of a royal ordinance of 1926, Father Josemaría presented himself for the Forensic Practice examination given at the extraordinary session of January 1927. He passed it, and thus completed his studies for the law degree.[86] In the second issue of *Alfa-Beta*, the magazine of the Amado Institute, the news gets a prominent paragraph written in a rather grandiose style: "Our beloved priest and fellow professor Don José María Escrivá has brilliantly completed his legal studies. Since he is too modest to allow us to congratulate him, we congratulate ourselves, sure that his culture and talent will always be one of the most solid promises of triumph for our Institute."[87]

The third issue (March 1927) features "a collection of writings by our law professors." Among these is "Marriage in Current Spanish Law," by "José María Escrivá y Albás, Priest and Lawyer, Professor of Canon Law and Roman Law at the Amado Institute."[88]

The following month, his name no longer appears on the list of professors.

5. *From Saragossa to Madrid*

Moved by his presentiments, Father Josemaría began keeping letters and other papers very early. Were it not for that commendable solicitude, the biographer would lack material needed for analyzing important events of his life. However, many of those with whom he dealt did not have the same concern for the future. As a result, situations must often be reconstructed from the answers he received to his letters.

That correspondence includes several letters, written in February and March of 1927, that shed a bit more light on those "providential injustices" in Saragossa. The first, dated Segovia, February 7, is from Father Prudencio Cancer, a Claretian, and begins as follows:

My dear friend:

With joy, as always, I received and read your letter of February 4, and from that I understand your situation. . . . I remember perfectly what we spoke about in Saragossa, during those pleasant hours that I spent with you. Consequently, when I arrived in Madrid I spoke of you to one of our priests stationed there, to see if I could interest him in speaking on your behalf to the bishop of Madrid, who definitely owes him some big favors. But I didn't see him as being very likely to make a recommendation once I found out how bombarded he is by petitions and bids from clerics wanting to relocate to Madrid.[89]

Father Cancer had been good friends with the Escrivá family for some time. Possibly this had to do with his being from Fonz or Barbastro, or with his having exercised his ministry in Barbastro.[90]

During the trip he had made to Madrid at the end of September to investigate the possibility of earning a doctorate in law, Father Josemaría had seen that he had a lot of loose ends to tie up before he could establish himself in Madrid with the aim of bringing his family there. The Claretian was definitely aware of the Escrivá family's financial situation, since he told the young priest of his desire that "your poor mother and good sister and brother" might "go through this life freed of the anxieties and troubles they have had to live in on account of the straits to which the wise Providence of God has seen fit to subject them."[91]

The following letter from Father Cancer is dated Segovia, February 28, 1927:

My esteemed friend:

I received in Madrid your first letter, with the certificates from your exams, and now, in Segovia, I've received your second one. In Madrid I highly recommended you to two priests and gave them a note stating your intentions and desires. Both of them are on friendly terms with a number of bishops and one of them mentioned a couple of very prominent individuals in Saragossa who could help you with what I used to think would be the easiest thing to get: that is, a position in Saragossa provided by your bishop. The two or three priests with whom I spoke about your situation found it very strange that, given your gifts and talents as I described them, the bishop would not give you a position and would let you leave his diocese. It seems incredible that C. A. has so much influence with such a high-ranking and relatively new prelate that because of him this prelate does not dare give you a position. It would seem simplest for them to find a solution allowing you to stay in Saragossa.

That of your coming to Madrid will surely involve some serious difficulties. . . .[92]

Evidently the new information the Claretian had received concerning Father Josemaría's status in Saragossa's ecclesiastical circles had opened his eyes to the difficulties in the way of the young priest's obtaining a position there—something he "used to think would be the easiest thing to get." Even the mysterious reserve with which he refers to the archdeacon, Father Carlos Albás (C. A.), who, preempting the authority of the bishop, had declared his nephew *persona non grata* in the diocese, hints at those "providential injustices." Quite possibly it was Father José Pou de Foxá who opened Father Cancer's eyes, since at the end of this letter he sends him regards as though he were another member of the family: "Regards to Dr. Pou, to your mother, and to your sister and brother. Yours truly, Father Cancer."[93]

Father Cancer seems confident that skillful management of friendships and contacts will remove most of the obstacles to his friend's coming to Madrid. But his optimism collapses before the worst of them. In view of this one he says to Father Josemaría in this letter of February 28, "I believe it would be easier for you to find a position in some diocese that has either a new bishop or a bishop who is a friend of the above-mentioned priests." What was that fearful obstacle?

*   *   *

Administrative centralization, population growth, and other historical circumstances had made the capital of Spain a magnet for the whole country. Adventurers, parasites, and simple, honest folk flocked there. Some sought bread and work; others, power, fame, or riches. Priests from other dioceses came too. So great, in fact, was the influx of clerics into

Madrid that the Holy See found it necessary to intervene. The papal nuncio sent the Spanish bishops a circular letter stating:

> The grave harm which the capital of this monarchy is suffering because of the concentration here of priests of less regular and orderly conduct from the different dioceses of Spain has placed the Holy See in the position of having to prohibit, and therefore it does henceforth prohibit, all the ordinaries of this kingdom from giving permission to priests under their jurisdiction to transfer to Madrid and its diocese, unless there is a special reason for such transfer and they have made it known to the ordinary of said diocese.[94]

This prohibition was issued in 1887 to limit the influx of extradiocesan priests into Madrid. In later years the Spanish bishops had to be given official reminders because, as we read in a circular letter of 1898, "the serious problems which counseled the above-mentioned dispositions have not disappeared."[95] In 1909 Madrid's diocesan synod made these provisions law. Successive bishops had to restate, again and again, that any priest who needed to transfer to the diocese of Madrid must present written permission from his ordinary to reside there and must also obtain the consent of the bishop of Madrid.[96]

In the midst of this problematic situation, Father Josemaría received a letter from Father Cancer, dated Segovia, March 9, 1927, in which his friend jubilantly says:

> My dear friend:
>
> Can we now sing a *Te Deum*?* I think we can! So you can understand what I'm saying, I will tell you that I accidentally found out that Saint Michael's Church in Madrid—which is near Calle Mayor, is under the jurisdiction of His Excellency the Nuncio, and is run by the

---

* A solemn hymn of praise and thanksgiving.

Redemptorists, who have a house there—has an opening
for someone to say Mass there every day at 5:50, and that
to obtain this position you only need the permission of
His Excellency the Nuncio. I saw the heavens open when
I learned this, because the great difficulty, as I see it, in
getting you into Madrid, even with good recommendations, is to get permission from this bishop. Look how
our Lord is smoothing out your path![97]

The solution to his problem did really seem heaven-sent,
since the Pontifical Church of Saint Michael was not subject to
the bishop of Madrid—who, as will be seen, was extremely
sparing in granting permission for priests to transfer into his
diocese—but, instead, was directly under the jurisdiction of
the nuncio. Father Cancer enclosed with his letter a note to him
from the rector of Saint Michael's, clarifying some points:

> The priest you recommended will, of course, be able to
> get the permission of the papal nuncio to celebrate Mass in
> this church. . . . This position is not a chaplaincy, but it does
> assure that he can continue celebrating Mass and receiving
> the stipend for as long as he remains in Madrid.
>
> To obtain faculties from the nuncio, he must have in
> order the ministerial licenses from his own prelate and
> must also present a document authorizing him to live in
> Madrid with that prelate's blessing. His Excellency the
> Nuncio also wants the prelate to say in that same docu-
> ment at least a word testifying to the priest's good conduct.
> This is what is always required, and with this it's no prob-
> lem—he can come.[98]

Father Josemaría had to make a quick decision, especially in
light of what the rector of Saint Michael's wrote at the end of his
note: "If he can come right away, we will accept him at once." He
talked the matter over with his family, and together they decided that until he could get settled in Madrid and find them an

apartment, his mother and sister and brother would go to Fonz to live with Don José's brother Teodoro.[99]

The first step was to get the archbishop of Saragossa's permission to go to Madrid to study for the doctorate, and the necessary letters of recommendation. Father Josemaría made clear his desire to obtain a doctorate in law, but also his firm determination to attend to his ministerial obligations before all else. On March 17 he was granted permission for two years of study at the University of Madrid, and five days later he obtained the necessary letters of recommendation.[100]

With these authorizations in hand, he took care of the academic formalities. He paid his fees, had his Licentiate in Law diploma sent to him, and arranged for a transcript of his school records to be sent to the University of Madrid.[101] The fees amounted to 37.50 pesetas, the equivalent of a week's worth of minimal household expenses. (In Saragossa, that is. In Madrid the cost of living was higher. The Mass stipend at Saint Michael's was not enough to support even one person. Father Cancer was aware of this; he remarked that "a family can't live on 5.50.")

On one of those days Josemaría ran into a former classmate and told him about his upcoming move. "What will you do in Madrid?" asked this man. "I'll get a job as a tutor, or give classes," he responded.[102]

Although Father Josemaría had obviously already given a lot of thought to this possible way of earning the extra money he needed, the friend felt he should give him some advice on this matter, since along with knowledge of the subject and pedagogical skills, teaching requires congenial social interaction and skill in dealing with people. Josemaría did not lack these gifts, but he did have a reputation for not bending his moral principles to suit social convention. For him this was especially important because he was a priest: priests must not give the slightest occasion for scandal.

Around March 20, things began to get complicated. Suddenly the chancery office notified him that he was assigned to the parish of Fombuena for Passion Week and Holy Week; that is, April 2 to 18.[103] Simultaneously, the rector of Saint Michael's urgently requested that he be there those same two weeks. "If he could come right away," he wrote in a letter, "it would be very much appreciated, because this is the time when we need priests the most."[104]

Everything was going too well for the devil not to meddle. A promising opportunity like this, making permission for residence in Madrid practically certain, was not likely to come up again. Should Father Josemaría go to the chancery office and turn down the assignment to Fombuena? Fortunately, he decided to ask his mother's advice, and on that basis accepted the temporary assignment. "Mama seldom got involved in my affairs," he would write in his journal, "but when she did (as at my first Mass, and in my going to Fombuena) her suggestions seem to have come from God. She was always right."[105]

Henceforth there could be no accusing him of lack of interest in his ministry or lack of loyalty to his diocese. And if it was God who was offering him the position in Madrid, couldn't he save it for him for two or three weeks? He wrote, then, to the pastor of the parish of Badules, on which Fombuena depended, and to the rector of Saint Michael's.

In his letter of reply the rector excuses himself for not having answered right away and stresses the urgency of the situation and the eagerness with which he is awaiting his arrival. "I would appreciate it very much," he says, "if you do not delay your coming beyond the time that you indicated, because we need your Mass. We expect you, then, during the first days of Eastertide."[106]

The pastor's reply is much more explanatory and genial, although his rambling letter takes a relaxed approach to the use of commas:

Badules, March 26, 1927

Father José M. Escrivá, Saragossa

My dear fellow priest:

I have received your letter telling me that you are coming to help out at the parish of Fombuena, from the first of the month until Easter and in reply I am happy to tell you that I have already found you a place to stay while you are there which is the best and which is the safest bet since the village teacher who is the pastor's niece lives there and most assuring of all this is the house of the village judge who is a straightforward person as is the rest of his family. You come by way of the Cariñena station where you ask for a ticket to Daroca that includes the price for an auto which picks up passengers from Cariñena and then you hold on to the train ticket just showing it when leaving the station and they will ask for it in the auto, and although the ticket is for Daroca, you get out at Mainar and go find the rural postman who comes by here and then goes to Fombuena which you will already be able to see when you get out of the car and you can come on horseback since he rides a horse and can load up on it whatever you might have such as a suitcase, valise, etc. In those days there will not be much to do just giving the Sunday homily and on Fridays the Stations of the Cross and during Holy Week the Good Friday service and teaching catechism to the children from 11 to 12 and saying Mass in the morning and hearing some confessions which are no more than ten or twelve on any day and in the evening a novena, a Rosary and nothing more and anyway when you come I will give you more details, the village is small and shabby but you can get through 15 days here just fine, for more time no.

That's all that can be told you by your affectionate colleague who greets you and very much looks forward to meeting you.

> Leandro Bertrán
> Pastor

The letter carries this postscript:

P.S.   Since the trip is long because you leave at 9 from there and arrive here at 3 be sure to bring yourself something to snack on along the way. . . .

Could you come on Saturday the 2nd to celebrate the
Mass for Passion Sunday?[107]

* * *

The Escrivá family left for Fonz, and the young priest for
Fombuena, on Saturday, April 2, 1927. For two full weeks, until
Easter Sunday, he filled in for the pastor in that village of two
hundred fifty souls, which was far from Saragossa and about
four miles from Badules, the village in which the pastor normally resided. The church of Fombuena, like that of Perdiguera, was named Our Lady of the Assumption.

No account has come down to us of Father Josemaría's pastoral activities, but it seems safe to suppose that his priestly zeal
led him to do the same sorts of things he had done in Perdiguera: visit families, conduct liturgical services, teach catechism,
and spend long hours in the confessional. The sacramental
records of the parish show no trace of his stay there, but that is
not the fault of its temporary pastor. Presumably, in that brief period there were no new babies to baptize and no dead to bury.

We do nevertheless know one detail of his stay at Fombuena that at first sight might seem insignificant: he always
carried with him, as a family relic, the crucifix that lay in his father's hands during the hours before his funeral.[108]

The memory of those far-off days of his ministry in Perdiguera and Fombuena would always fill him with joy. "I was in
country parishes twice," he once wrote. "What joy whenever I
recall it! They sent me there to upset me, but they did me a big
favor. Even back then some people were out to give me a hard
time. They did me a colossal, colossal, colossal amount of
good! With what happiness I remember that!"[109]

With the passing of time he saw more and more clearly
the deeper meaning of those assignments and how God
had allowed him to be moved around, from one place to another, like a little donkey. "I have tried always to fulfill the will
of God," he would say. "They moved me from one place to an-

other like one moves a donkey, pulling on the halter and often using a stick."[110]

On Easter Monday, April 18, he returned to Saragossa. That night he slept at the Barrio Hotel. He kept the bill as a souvenir of that historic milestone on his path toward the capital.[111]

*   *   *

When Father Josemaría reviewed his life in prayer, he saw it as a vast landscape that changed with time. Within that vision the big events of his life fit together providentially, contrasting but not conflicting with one another, in line with a divine logic that directed things in orderly fashion.

What could he have understood of this logic when, as a child in Barbastro, he suddenly knocked down that house of cards with one swipe of his hand? Was that how God treated people? Did he let them build something just so that he could dash it to the ground when it was almost finished?

What painful thoughts went through the head of that boy as he sought an explanation of why so many good souls suffered reversals of fortune, losses of family members, and the thwarting of noble ambitions! And where was the justice in God's heaping success and other goods on people who broke all his commandments? Why, Lord, why?

From the time of his baptism, God had been at work in his soul in a marvelous hidden way. Later, at First Communion, the child made Jesus the Lord of his heart, asking that he grant him the grace of never letting him lose him. Having already given him exemplary parents, the Lord poured down more favors by confirming the whole family in the way of the cross. Josemaría did not understand this way as a child, since the call to the cross always entails suffering and sacrifice. The family's misfortunes in Barbastro and the poverty and humiliations of Logroño brought the boy to the verge of rebellion. But the inspirations of grace tempered his soul, maturing it. And soon, from a very early age, he had within it a divine restlessness.

On the day he saw those footprints in the snow, he unhesitatingly threw himself into the arms of God. Henceforth he wanted only to fulfill the divine will. Later he came to understand, once and for all, that detachment and generosity are essential to love. He could see the point of that divine logic by which the Lord takes away goods from those who are dear to him, and comforts from those he loves. And so he voluntarily and joyfully transformed himself by means of detachment. Giving himself over totally to the desire to be identified with Christ, he decided to become a priest.

Later came a long and difficult trial. In the years of his stay at San Carlos, God continued sculpting in him the image of Christ. Don José died at a critical moment, when Josemaría could still turn back. Instead, as the funeral party returned from the cemetery, he flung the coffin key into the river, a gesture signifying determination to be rid of all human attachments, no matter how legitimate, that might be obstacles to his ordination as a priest.

The Lord purified him with pain, laying on the blows where they would hurt him the most, not sparing those around him, particularly his family. Josemaría was so convinced of this that he expressed it in a formula that he would often repeat throughout his whole life: "The Lord, to hit me, who was the nail (pardon me, Lord), landed one blow on the nail and a hundred on the horseshoe."[112]

This way of forging saints requires of them enormous humility and fidelity, a willingness to let the Lord do his work without getting in his way. The silence of the young priest about the axe blows God gave him in Saragossa signifies not that he buried them in forgetfulness, but that they were so deeply engraved in his memory that he preferred not to speak of them. He derived a powerful image from God's use of hammer and chisel on him to make him a pillar on which the Work could rest: Those who try to dodge the will of God, he would say, suffer in vain and end up as a formless pile of gravel.[113]

Through experience after experience, at great cost and with great speed, he learned the ways of wisdom. Eventually, with time and the intense activity of the Holy Spirit in his soul, he developed a kind of supernatural instinct for discerning, in the heart of history and the concatenation of events, that ineffable quality which is the unmistakable signature of Providence. He sensed a secret purpose in the circumstances that had driven the Escrivás to move from Barbastro to Logroño, in the family's move from there to Saragossa, and in the difficulties that now besieged him, forcing him to leave Saragossa. Having decided to go to Madrid, and finding himself shoved out of Saragossa yet simultaneously guided by the hand of God, he felt certain that a hidden divine plan awaited him in Spain's capital. That continual moving from one place to another—from Barbastro to Logroño, from there to Saragossa, and finally to Madrid—was not, in other words, an erratic or circuitous route but a disciplined, step by step, ascent to the summit at which he would be shown the enterprise God had in store for him. (It was also, as it turned out, a foreshadowing of the second great itinerary of his life: the one he would have to travel in order to carry out his role as founder.)

The priest kept waiting for a reply to his *Domine, ut videam!* [Lord, that I may see!]. By faith he sensed that the fulfillment of his *Domine, ut sit!* [Lord, let it be!] was imminent. Among the signs indicating its nearness were some that he recorded in a small cloth-covered notebook that Agustín Callejas, a classmate at the seminary in Saragossa, mentions. "I was about eighteen, maybe younger," Father Josemaría recalls, "when I felt impelled to start writing, without rhyme or reason."[114] In these pages were open-hearted verses signed by "The Priestly Heart," brief outlines and phrases for his projected "Tale of a Village Priest," and quotations from classical authors, Saint Teresa, historians, poets, and novelists. But this haphazard accumulation also included some notes of a more personal sort. These first ramblings of an adolescent writer had the transparency of pure water. His depth of soul showed clearly in phrases glowing with spiritual ambition and ardent sentiment.

From time to time, within or outside of prayer, Josemaría felt obliged to put in writing an idea, an apostolic suggestion, a sign from heaven. Many notes unquestionably were divine inspirations. Some were explosions of light opening new paths in his understanding. For some time now, divine favors had been so abundant that the shower of graces had become a downpour. It was probably during this last period in Saragossa that he began to receive the divine locutions that would remain imprinted, as though by fire, in his soul. He reverently transcribed them, as a written testimony to what had happened and as material for his prayer.

Perhaps the growing frequency of those supernatural occurrences reinforced his presentiments that something lay ahead whose coming would be heralded, like the sunrise, by the gradual dispelling of the darkness.

There was still another indication that he would soon reach his goal. No one looking at his life closely can help marveling at what he accomplished as a young seminarian. He himself was amazed, for example, by the sudden infusion of piety into a whole seminary. "It is undoubtedly our Lady who has done this," he says. To him that is the only possible explanation for the change in the piety and conduct of the seminarians.

He carried that same apostolic spirit into the ecclesiastical university and the secular university. He exercised his ministry in rural and urban parishes with incomparable zeal. He carried out apostolic tasks and spiritual direction among all kinds of people and in various places. At twenty-five, ready to leave for Madrid, he saw with amazement that our Lord had enriched him with an abundance of ministerial experience difficult to acquire in so short a time. God had made use of his generous availability to bring him quickly through a spiritual apprenticeship which normally would take a lifetime.

Father Josemaría also noticed that this dizzying pastoral career had some very peculiar characteristics. First of all, the fields in which his apostolate had developed included social sectors which up to then had been neglected. Secondly, his zeal was directed equally at priests and laity, monks and nuns, ecclesiastics and nonecclesiastics, people of every social class and profession. In this sense he was a self-taught person led by the hand of God; and consequently he was deeply convinced that his father's advice to study law in Saragossa was literally providential.

In his head teemed a multitude of suggestions—ideas that had not come from books or sages—for initiatives so specific that the developing of each would require a special, separate effort. These were not just theories. The young priest had already started doing these things—in the country and in the city, in the confessional and in intellectual settings. Spiritual direction of lay people, for example, was not a very widespread practice. Never satisfied with mediocrity, Father Josemaría tried to raise the sights of his friends and directees, making every effort to get them to bear the fruit that they were capable of bearing.

The many divine inspirations were like luminous sparks that kept his soul on the alert, ready for action. Through them came an influx of more graces, efficacious, abundant, full. He felt an inexhaustible energy. Obviously he would have obstacles to contend with. He would have to overcome resistance and fight against fatigue, lack of means, scarcity of time. But despite all that, his path proved more feasible than might have been expected, since it was what the Lord wanted. For that reason Father Josemaría gave a special name to this flood of graces reinforcing his faculties in such a manifest and tangible way. He called them "operative graces," since they took such complete possession of his will that, compared with how things usually are, "I almost didn't have to make any effort."[115]

Looking back on his early life, he could easily see how frequently God had made providential provision to prepare him for the mission he was to receive. The closer he looked the more he saw. Had it, for instance, really been stupid of him not to get his doctorate in theology while he was in Saragossa, before the ecclesiastical program of university studies was changed?

"On account of that change," he said in December 1933, "I thought a lot about my stupidity in not having graduated in due time in Saragossa. However, apart from merely human considerations, I see some supernatural good reasons for this. If I'd gotten my doctorate in theology back then, I undoubtedly would have taken the canonry examination, or else one of those jokes that passed for qualifying exams for teaching high school religion in the time of Primo de Rivera.* In that case, I would not have gone through all that I went through in Madrid, and who knows if God would have finally given me that inspiration of the Work! He led me along, making use of countless adversities and even of my laziness."[116]

---

* General Primo de Rivera governed Spain as a dictator from 1923 to 1930.

5

The Foundation of Opus Dei

1. Madrid, the capital city

Sensing an ultimatum in the rector's note telling him he was expected in Madrid during "the first days of Easter Week," Father Josemaría presented himself at Saint Michael's as soon as he arrived in the capital, on Easter Tuesday, April 19, 1927. He showed the rector the documents entitling him to receive priestly faculties and to celebrate Mass there.[1]

He then moved into a boarding house on Farmacia Street, in the labyrinth of little side streets off the San Luis crossing. From there he could walk to Puerta del Sol. Formerly there had been two churches a short distance from the Plaza Mayor: San Miguel de los Octoes, where Lope de Vega was baptized, and San Justo; but both had been demolished, and a new church built on the site of the latter. In 1892 it was turned over to the papal nuncio. This was the Pontifical Church of Saint Michael.[2]

Despite Madrid's importance as the capital ever since the era of Philip II,* the ecclesiastical territory of Madrid depended for centuries on the see of Toledo, and was not an independent diocese. The Concordat of 1851 provided for its becoming a diocese dependent on Toledo, but even this did not take effect until 1885.[3] The inevitable result was that king, nobility, and churchmen founded monasteries, set up charitable foundations, and endowed churches and chapels outside the jurisdiction of the

---

* King of Spain from 1555 to 1598.

ordinary, at that time the archbishop of Toledo. In this way there grew up in Madrid, sheltered by privileges and exemptions, a variety of jurisdictions, such as the personal jurisdiction of the nuncio, the court jurisdiction of the king, and the jurisdiction of the military.

The recent arrival sought information about academic procedures, with the intention of taking the law exams the next time they were given. His file indicates that on April 28 he requested permission from the dean of the law school to take the examination in History of International Law, a subject required for the doctorate. At the top of his request is written, "Don José María Escrivá y Albás, native of Barbastro, in the province of Huesca, 25 years of age, living in Madrid at 2 Farmacia Street. . . ."[4] The request is accompanied by a certificate with the seal of the "Official Medical School." It is signed by Dr. José Blanc Fortacín, and reads as follows: "Don José Ma. Escrivá y Albás, 25 years of age, has been vaccinated and revaccinated. Madrid, April 29, 1927."[5] Dr. Blanc Fortacín was from a family related by marriage to Doña Dolores, and the certificate shows every sign of having been obtained in a hurry.

Like some other priests coming into the capital, Father Josemaría found himself quite alone. Accustomed to the apostolic activity of Saint Peter Nolasco, he did not find any opportunity or enthusiasm for this kind of service at Saint Michael's. It was not the fault of the rector, who had told him from the start that this was not a matter of a chaplaincy, properly speaking, but of celebrating Mass daily, with the right to a stipend of five and a half pesetas.[6] But this sum did not even cover daily room and board at the Farmacia Street place, which came to seven pesetas.[7]

Hoping to find more modest and suitable lodging, Father Josemaría continued his search and learned that a thirty-room "Priests' House" had recently opened, on Larra Street. This was a charitable establishment for priests, run by the Congregation of Apostolic Ladies (Damas Apostólicas) of the Sacred Heart of Jesus. One of the monthly bulletins of this religious order con-

tains the following item: "Priests' House: It has been functioning all year, and very well. The priests residing there seem
happy with it. . . . They pay five pesetas, the usual stipend for a
Mass, . . . and enjoy excellent treatment in terms of meals, cleaning services, etc. . . . The bishop was so kind as to inaugurate it
himself, and the vicar general, who so much appreciates this endeavor, has offered to say Mass for us so that we can have the
Blessed Sacrament reserved in the very lovely chapel. . . ."[8]

Father Josemaría's move most likely took place on April
30. But in any case, although little is known with certainty of
his doings and studies prior to the first weeks of May, it looks
very much as if something had gone wrong with the plans so
optimistically sketched out by Father Cancer when he proposed singing a *Te Deum* and advised his protégé: "I recommend that, without yet actually moving here, you come to
Madrid and negotiate the matter, accept it, speak with the nuncio, and see how things open up for you."[9]

By two weeks after his arrival in Madrid none of these
things had happened. That can be deduced from this letter
written on May 9 by Father Luis Latre, vice-president of San
Carlos Seminary in Saragossa, in response to one from Father
Josemaría:

My dear friend:

On the very day that I received your welcome letter, I
sent a special-delivery letter to my brother in Madrid, so that
he could find out more about what you want and could explain it better to Don Inocencio, who was in Cercedilla that
day, but who learned of your desires as soon as he returned
to Madrid. . . . I needn't tell you how happy I am to know
that you are well situated for the moment. I say "for the moment" because I don't believe your present situation is really
satisfactory, since your separation from your mother and
brother and sister under these conditions can't, I'm sure, be
good for any of you. The good little friar has acquitted

himself very badly. The least he could do now is to find you some contacts who could enable you to give classes, and to recommend you to the bishop, either directly or through someone else, so that you could be attached to some church where you might receive good stipends and other income.

In the meantime, try to be patient and, above all, to be very good and to avoid companionships that could do you an enormous amount of harm. Study what you can, so that if God does allow that the gates of the capital be closed to you, you can return here as soon as possible and place yourself at the disposition of our prelate, who is so much in need of personnel.

I often speak of you with Father José Pou; he is sorry that you have had so little luck. He says he will write you in a few days.[10]

How could Father Josemaría be helped by Don Inocencio Jiménez, his old penal law professor? A look at his student records shows that he did not take any final exam in either June or September of 1927.[11] This was quite detrimental to his financial situation, since enrollment cost 42 pesetas, the equivalent of eight days' room and board. And he had not yet found a way to earn a living by giving classes.

*   *   *

A good number of the priests at the Larra Street residence were middle-aged, but there were also a few younger ones: for example, Fathers Fidel Gómez and Justo Villameriel, who were preparing for exams for military chaplaincies; Father Avelino Gómez Ledo, who had been ordained in Madrid; and Father Antonio Pensado, who, like Father Josemaría, was from outside the Madrid diocese—he was from Santiago de Compostela.[12]

Father Antonio's case tells a lot about the policy of the bishop of Madrid on granting faculties to priests from other dioceses, and it taught the young priest from Saragossa what to watch out for. With the permission of his bishop, Father Antonio had studied philosophy and literature in Madrid from 1922 to 1926. Then his odyssey began. On October 26, 1926, he was notified by the Madrid chancery office that his faculties for that diocese would not be renewed, since he had completed the studies that made it necessary for him to reside there. He got around this problem by obtaining a one-year permit to celebrate Mass at Incarnation Monastery, a royal foundation not under the bishop's jurisdiction.[13] But in February 1927 the bishop of Madrid successfully urged the bishop of Santiago de Compostela to also revoke his faculties if he refused to return to his diocese, so that the directives of the Holy See regarding extradiocesan priests moving to the capital would not be treated as a joke. Now deprived of the faculty to say Mass, but still determined to stay in Madrid, Father Antonio promptly sought a position at the Provincial Hospice. In April he sent a formal request to the chancery office that his faculties be reinstated for this purpose. The petition was denied.[14]

To function as a priest in a particular diocese, one must have authorization, or "faculties," from its bishop. These faculties are the rights to hear confessions, to preach, and to celebrate Mass, and may be granted either for a limited time or permanently. If a priest lacks faculties, or they are revoked by the Church authorities, his situation is critical. He cannot administer the sacraments licitly, and so cannot receive stipends and other sacrament-related offerings. This was the dead-end in which Father Antonio Pensado found himself.

In May 1927 Father Josemaría and Father Antonio struck up a friendship at the Larra Street residence, but they were comrades for a short time only, since Father Antonio soon found himself forced to leave Madrid.

Father Josemaría had been at the residence for a month when word of his zeal, and his desire to find an outlet for his ministry, reached the ears of Doña Luz Rodríguez Casanova, the foundress of the Apostolic Ladies. The problem was that he lacked permission to celebrate Mass in Madrid, other than at

Saint Michael's. Doña Luz saw something special in him that made her want him appointed chaplain of the church of the Foundation for the Sick; but first he would have to get that hard-to-come-by diocesan permission. On June 10, therefore, he sent in the following request:

> Father José Ma. Escrivá y Albás of the Diocese of Saragossa—with permission of his Ordinary, granted on March 17, 1927—desiring to remain in this capital, at the Priests' House at 3 Larra Street, for a period of two years, requests that Your Excellency deign to grant him the necessary authorization for celebrating the Holy Sacrifice of the Mass in the church of the Foundation for the Sick.
>
> May God preserve Your Excellency for many years to come.
>
> —Madrid, June 10, 1927.[15]

Later on, he said about the obtaining of these faculties: "The first time they were granted me in the diocese of Madrid, at the request of Mother Luz Casanova they were general, if I remember correctly: to celebrate, to absolve, and to preach."[16] The background of this transaction makes the influence of Doña Luz appear all the more remarkable. An enterprising woman with a deep spiritual life, the daughter of the Marchioness of Onteiro, she had founded the Congregation of Apostolic Ladies in 1924, in Madrid.[17] The congregation's specific end was works of charity and instruction among the poor.

At that time the bishop of Madrid was Leopoldo Eijo y Garay. His life up to then had been little different from the lives of other bishops of the time, but it is of particular interest to us because it was soon to become linked with that of Father Josemaría. Born in Vigo in 1878, he studied at the seminary in Seville and the Gregorian University in Rome, and was ordained in 1900. He became bishop of Tuy in 1914, bishop of Vitoria in 1917, and bishop of the diocese of Madrid-Alcalá in 1923.[18] He was a very spiritual and cultured man, and his style of government showed it. An official letter of his concerning the situation of priests in Spain's capital gives an idea of his character. A member of the Roman Curia, a cardinal, had interceded on behalf of a certain priest from outside the diocese, Father Jerónimo Muñoz, asking that he be granted faculties for Madrid. In reply, Bishop Leopoldo sent this handwritten memorandum, dated Madrid, February 18, 1933:

> I received the estimable letter of Your Eminence on the 9th of this month . . . and am honored to be able to provide the following information.
>
> It has always been the wish of a great part of the Spanish clergy to come and live in Madrid. There is no need for more priests here. In fact, there are already more than there should be.
>
> In fulfillment of my duty to comply with the wishes of the Sacred Congregation, which does not want a crowding of extradiocesan priests into the great capitals, I have always taken the utmost care to avoid granting faculties to those who want to move to Madrid without sufficient canonical reason to do so. . . .
>
> This constitutes a real cross in this diocese, where almost every day we have to turn down four or five similar petitions. . . . Father Jerónimo Muñoz, of the diocese of Avila, is in that situation. The Count of Santa Engracia brought him here to be his chaplain, and when he asked me to grant faculties to this priest, I told him that I could not do so because the Holy See forbids me to. . . . Now, then, my humble request to the Sacred Congregation is that in the case of Father Muñoz, as in that of all others who ask for the same thing, the Sacred Congregation would deign to answer *non expedire* [do not proceed]. Otherwise, all of the extradiocesan priests aspiring to live in Madrid will direct their petitions to the Holy See, and if they are granted, half the clergy of Spain, especially in these times we are living in, will come here, with really serious detriment to the diocese and the Church.[19]

Obviously Bishop Leopoldo was not afraid to speak his mind. The letter is strikingly firm and clear and is proof that he never gave in to any kind of pressure when it came to enforcing the Holy See's restrictions on the granting of faculties. The permit he gave Father Josemaría in 1927 was for only one year. Extensions would be granted only very stintingly, through periodic negotiations with the chancery office, which meant that the priest was in constant suspense and apprehension. Against this backdrop one can appreciate the unstable situation of extradiocesan priests in Madrid. Bare-bones entries in the diocesan "Books of Ministerial Faculties" hint at anxieties concealed between the lines. Thus on folio 53 of book 8 we read:

> Escrivá Albás, Father José María.—Saragossa—
> On June 8, 1927, one year Foundation for the Sick. On June 11, 1928, until March 22, 1929, plus give absolution. On March 23, 1929, four months. On July 23, 1929, until the end of June 1930.

And on folio 55:

> Escrivá Albás.—Father José. Saragossa.
> On July 15, 1930, six months Foundation plus hear confessions. On January 14, 1931, six months. On June 23, 1931, one year Santa Barbara.[20]

The entries had to be brief, because priests kept pouring into the capital. In 1927 the bishop had in his charge 533 extradiocesan priests and 648 diocesan ones, and since the latter were spread through the whole province, the majority in the city proper did not belong to the diocese.[21]

Always extraordinarily faithful in complying with Church regulations, Father Josemaría had to request an extension of his ministerial faculties from Saragossa, since they were on the point of expiring. Also, to comply with canon 130 of the Code of Canon Law then in force which required that every priest take an examination in sacred studies annually during the first three years after ordination, he requested permission to have the examination given him by the rector of Saint Michael's.[22] The authorities in Saragossa granted the request. The chancery office assistant secretary sent him a letter to this effect, and Father Santiago, rector of Saint Michael's, gave the examination to the young priest.[23] He had him choose topics in moral and dogmatic theology, and then administered a long written examination on those topics. In his evaluation, which he handed over to the examinee so he could send it on to Saragossa, he set forth his reasons for giving him the highest possible mark.[24]

In a letter dated July 9, the priest received the ministerial licenses from Saragossa. His faculties were granted for one year. After that, they would be renewed annually until 1931, at which time they would be granted for five years. In 1936 they were granted him generally and in perpetuity.[25] Father Josemaría was always very diligent about keeping his residence permits current and thus keeping his dimissory and commendatory letters from Saragossa from being invalidated. All these documents were needed to justify his presence in Madrid, outside his diocese, and to enable him to exercise his ministry there. As will be seen, the chancery office books contain no record of the many annoyances these regulations caused him. But compared to the sufferings that his situation as an extradiocesan priest in Madrid would bring him, those things were of little importance.

2. *The residents at the Priests' House*

To go from the lack of assignments at Saint Michael's to the chaplaincy of the Foundation for the Sick was like going from starvation to surfeit. The Foundation was the Apostolic Ladies' headquarters, and it had a public church attached to it. During the summer of 1927 the chaplain entered little by little into the charitable and apostolic activities of that institution, even though, at that time, they were not part of his job. One of the Ladies explains:

The chaplain of the Foundation for the Sick was responsible for the religious services at the house: he was expected to say Mass every day, give Benediction, and lead the Rosary. His position did not require him to get involved in the additional work being done from the Foundation among the poor and sick—in general, the needy—of the Madrid of that time. Nevertheless, Father Josemaría took advantage of his position as chaplain to give of himself generously, sacrificially, and disinterestedly to the huge number of poor and sick who came within reach of his priestly heart.[26]

Following the example of the other young residents at the Larra Street residence, which was near the Foundation, Father Josemaría soon was taking care of small repairs and doing a multitude of favors for his confreres. Summer vacation began a few weeks after his arrival, and some of the priests left Madrid. In the summer of 1927 there were not many permanent residents at Larra Street, but priests passing through Madrid often spent a few days there. One of these visitors, Father Joaquín María de Ayala, stayed four days, from June 15 to 19.[27] At the end of the month, needing to ask a favor of someone in Madrid, he thought of the generous spirit of service of that friendly Aragonese priest he had met there. Father Joaquin was rector of the seminary in Cuenca; his age and position entitled him to ask a favor of the young priest. He wrote Father Josemaría from Alange, in Badajoz, on June 30, beginning by invoking the all-powerful virtue of kindness and its broad scope and then noting its "disadvantages." "One of these," he says, "is the abuse of it which can be made by those upon whom it is exercised. The proof thereof is this letter. You were extremely kind to me when I had the pleasure of being with you on the occasion of the Franciscan Congress, and now I am going to abuse that kindness."[28]

He then proceeds to request that a cassock he had left behind to have the collar repaired be picked up. And speaking of favors, could Father Josemaría also be so kind as to buy him some flints for his cigarette lighter, since one cannot get these in Cuenca? He closes with greetings to the residents, "especially . . . Fathers Plans and Pensado."

Of Father Plans is known nothing, and of Father Antonio Pensado, not much more than what has already been mentioned. With the bishop of Madrid breathing down his neck, he did finally return to Santiago de Compostela, and from there he wrote on July 30 to his friend Father Josemaría, asking him to tell Doña Aurora, who was in charge of household services at the residence, that he had carried out the request she had made to him. He was writing Father Josemaría because he was the only priest he knew for sure would be spending the summer there. "I suppose," he says, "that you are almost alone in that house, since the ones on summer vacation have already left. Of course, the number of those passing through has probably increased."[29]

Of the correspondence from the summer of 1927 there also remains a letter from Father Prudencio Cancer, dated July 19, replying to one from Father Josemaría. The young priest had evidently learned very soon to trust exclusively in God's help and not in recommendations from human beings, including fellow clergymen. From his questions and conjectures, one can tell that the Claretian is full of curiosity in the face of the discreet silence of his former protégé. He writes:

> Your silence had me worried. How must things be going in Madrid for that poor little priest who doesn't tell me anything? You must be going through a bleak time, a very bleak time.
>
> Your last letter reassured me somewhat. However, . . . it seems to me that you are keeping a lot from me, to keep me from worrying. . . .
>
> I would have thought that by this time you would have already found something more than the chaplaincy of the pontifical church—maybe some tutoring, or a teaching position at an educational center; a job as an assistant to some important lawyer; some supplementary work, helping out

in a parish or at a religious house. Of this you tell me nothing, nor of your reception by or relations with the nuncio, nor of the efforts of Father Ramonet, who is so experienced, so worldly-wise, and so well-connected, nor of your situation with respect to the diocesan bishop, to the seminary, to your prelate in Saragossa. Have you by any chance completely left the pontifical church in order to serve Doña Luz Casanova? . . .

I was thinking that by now you would already have some chancery position, with a professorship attached, provided by some well-placed friend of Father Ramonet. . . . Let's see if we can get together soon.[30]

In his letters to his family, Father Josemaria informed them of the efforts he was making. He tried to lift their spirits, but was still in no position to think of bringing them to Madrid. Even from that distance, however, they could feel the tenderness of his love. Santiago remembers how each week his big brother would send him the same children's magazines that Don José had bought for Josemaría when he was little and the family was living in Barbastro.[31]

Father Josemaría stayed at the Larra Street residence from May through November of 1927. Although it was only six months, his stay is well remembered by two of the priests who then made up the group of "the youngsters," Avelino Gómez Ledo and Fidel Gómez Colomo. Living under the same roof with older, and sometimes elderly, priests, notes Father Avelino, demanded "a special patience and understanding, of which Father Josemaría set an example."[32] Now elderly themselves, Father Fidel describes him as "a cordial, transparent, loyal person,"[33] while Father Avelino highlights a particular indication of his human warmth and priestly sensibility: namely, that he remembered him on his feast day. Saint Andrew Avelino was not very popular in Spain, and most people did not know when his feast day was. Father Josemaría was the only one to congratulate Father Avelino, and he did so "affectionately and supernaturally."[34]

The Foundation for the Sick ran many charitable programs. The Larra Street residents were only marginally involved in that apostolate, with one notable exception: the young chaplain. By the end of the summer he was fully immersed in those works of mercy. Father Fidel points out that he was never ostentatious about it, but that with his natural friendliness and apostolic enthusiasm he did try to get other priests to come with him on visits to the poor and sick in the slums. Obviously he had some success, because Father Avelino recalls: "I remember how one day, in one of those slums, Father Josemaría took in his arms a little boy who was dirty and covered with sores, and gave him a couple of kisses."[35]

The residents celebrated Mass in the morning at different hours and in different places, and in the afternoon they usually worked at different parishes or chapels or carried out other diverse duties. The only time they came together was for the midday meal. But after eating they spent some time just talking, and in these get-togethers they touched on all sorts of subjects. The young priest took advantage of these occasions to inject some apostolic fervor into the conversation or give an interesting twist to some news in the paper.

In one of those conversations, says Father Fidel, "we were discussing some event that I don't now recall, and he commented to me that we needed also to do apostolate with intellectuals, because, he said, they are like snow-covered mountain peaks: when the snow melts, down comes the water that makes the valleys fruitful. I have never forgotten this image that so well reflects that ideal of his of placing Christ at the summit of all human activities."[36]

Father Avelino says the participants in these get-togethers were struck by "the sincerity with which he spoke, and especially by his cheerfulness, which reflected not just his youth (he was then twenty-five), but an inner joy—that of a priestly vocation lived totally from a supernatural outlook."[37]

So, despite his problems, the young chaplain was not "going through a bleak time," as Father Prudencio imagined. On the contrary he was enjoying a splendid optimism which for him was like a second nature, because, as he would later write, he found himself under the influence of "those inspirations, those impulses of grace, that wanting something while not yet knowing what it was."[38] Without knowing where he was going, and without feeling too wearied by the journey, he pressed forward, repeating, as he had for nine long years, "Domine, ut videam!"

3. *The Cicuéndez Academy*

In November 1927 Father Josemaría rented a small apartment at 46 Fernando el Católico, not far from the Foundation for the Sick. Now, at last, the Escrivás could be reunited. This good news also cheered up Father Cancer. On December 9, from Segovia, he wrote: "I was overjoyed by your letter. My congratulations to your mother and brother and sister. Always trust in the Lord."[39] Wanting to lift their spirits, he then proffered some wholesome spiritual considerations.

The Lord, in his mercy, gave them no hint of the tribulations to come. For the third time the Escrivás reorganized their life in a strange city, not knowing that they had put themselves in the very eye of a tempest that was on the verge of breaking out. After a long period of national stability under the Constitution of 1876, tensions began to simmer. Social, labor-related, and economic problems, together with a malaise in the army, led in 1923 to the establishment of the dictatorship of General Primo de Rivera. Within a short time order was restored, the conflict in Morocco was resolved, public works were initiated, the peseta was strengthened, and the standard of living was raised—but at the cost of political and civil liberties.

The Primo de Rivera regime enjoyed a brief period of popularity, but after seven years this was exhausted; and when the first economic disasters came, the general had to resign. The dictatorship apparatus now had no governmental basis, and so in 1930 the monarchy entered a dead-end street.[40] But that is getting ahead of the story. . . .

The Escrivás were barely settled in Madrid when Father Josemaría found himself once again caught up in the grind of teaching. As he had done in Saragossa, he was giving private lessons under the watchful eyes of Doña Dolores. Santiago recalls that first home in Madrid: "Josemaría gave several private classes, some in the apartment on Fernando el Católico. A girl came there to take a class, and Josemaría saw to it that my mother was always present, sewing. He also gave classes to some boys, older than me, whom we called 'the great-aunt's boys' because they were accompanied by a very nice great-aunt, whose name I don't recall."[41]

So, too, taking the place of the Amado Institute was the Cicuéndez Academy, where he taught Roman law and the fundamentals of canon law, just as he had in Saragossa. But there were also significant differences. In an advertisement placed in the newspaper *ABC* in 1918, the Cicuéndez Academy is described as "Specializing in law: A study center, with boarding facilities, directed by priests."[42] The bylaws stated that the object of the Academy was "to be a private school of juridical studies, providing painstaking preparation for the legal profession alone." Its director and owner was Don José Cicuéndez, a priest and lawyer with a licentiate in theology.[43]

The Academy occupied the first floor of a building at 52 San Bernardo, at the corner of Del Pez, close to Universidad Central and well known to the university's students. As a professor, Father Josemaría raised the prestige of the Academy. In his classes, he did not remain on the theoretical level but tried by practical examples and real-life cases to fix the lessons in students' minds. He was profound, but also pleasant. One of his students, Mariano Trueba, says that they always looked forward to his classes "because the atmosphere there was so nice and family-like."[44]

Still, he was demanding in his educational work and eager to get the most out of his students. As he had done with his students at the Amado Institute in Saragossa, he proposed that they study the canons in the Latin text known as the Codex. This suggestion was greeted with skepticism, the students' weakness in Latin being notorious. But months later, they discovered to their surprise that, thanks to Father Josemaría's teaching method, they had acquired a certain fluency in Latin.[45]

His former students speak eloquently of his conduct and character. "He was very pleasant, down-to-earth, and fatherly," says Manuel Gómez-Alonso. "It was easy to make friends with him, and so, quite often, when classes were over, I would walk with him part of the way back to his home."[46] Julián Cortés Cavanillas says that the students "felt drawn to this professor because he was such a good teacher, and also because he was so human and priestly."[47]

For the most part, the students at the academy were boys who for one reason or another were not able to attend classes at the law school. Nonetheless, they could enroll at the university as unofficial students. Often they would take the exams given in September, since that gave them the summer vacation as study time. Father Josemaría took a truly paternal interest in them. We know from a letter from his own former professor of Roman law that Father Josemaría did not hesitate to ask him to send notes and syllabuses from Saragossa. A group of students at the Academy had to go to Saragossa to take their Roman law, history of law, and political economy exams, and Father Pou de Foxá made the arrangements for them. His letter, dated June 27, 1928, reads: "Dear José María: I received your letter of the 21st. . . . I think we can register your students here for the three subjects you indicate. I'm sending you the three sets of notes, background information, and syllabus. . . . Affectionate greetings to your mother, sister, and brother."[48]

Among those taking classes at the Academy was an older man, a good father of a family, who was trying to earn a university degree to improve his financial situation. His professional work took so much out of him that he ended his workday exhausted and with hardly any time left for his family and for studies. Father Josemaría felt a special compassion for him, perhaps seeing in him a reflection of what he himself had gone through in Saragossa. And so, out of pity and a feeling of kinship, he gave him extra classes, receiving nothing in return except the satisfaction of seeing him get his degree.[49]

From the director to the office boy, there was a good rapport among everyone who worked at the Academy. Indeed, the office boy, whose name was José Margallo, has a small part in this story. Father Josemaría saved a little sheet of paper from him with a Christmas greeting and the signature, "The Academy Office Boy."[50]

The young priest was always trying to cultivate good relations with everyone for apostolic purposes. He devoted time each day to writing letters and sending or giving greetings for special occasions. For example, on March 18, 1930, he went to congratulate the director of the Academy, Father José Cicuéndez, on the occasion of the feast day of his patron saint, Saint Joseph, the day itself (March 19) being a holiday. Father Cicuéndez accepted the greeting with pleasure, and only later remembered that Saint Joseph was also one of Father Josemaría's patron saints. Since Father Josemaría had already left, the director sent him the following note the next day:

My dear friend:

Yesterday you came by to congratulate me. . . . When you were already out the door and I was talking with Chacón, I suddenly remembered that there was another José besides myself, and I called out to you two or three times, but you didn't hear me. The prayer that you said you offered for me in your Mass has kept resounding in my ears, so I have not forgotten to pray for you at Mass; "oremus pro invicem ut salvemini" ["let us pray for each other that we may be saved"]. My most cordial felicitations. . . .

—Madrid, March 19, 1930.[51]

Father Josemaría's first year of teaching at the Academy was 1927–1928. His contract was renewed annually until perhaps 1933.[52] He gave his classes during the afternoon, with the rest of his day being taken up with priestly duties and other activities connected with his being chaplain of the Foundation. Even during the bits of free time between classes, he did apostolate with the students. Mariano Trueba describes him as "a dynamic man, with a robust appearance and good color in his face, very straightforward, with a desire to get involved in everyone's life."[53]

At the end of the school day, some of the students would accompany him part of the way home, discussing all kinds of subjects with him. One day one of them complained that it was impossible to go on believing when so many priests were making a mockery of religion by living double lives, negating what they preached in public by what they did in private. Father Josemaría responded with a beautiful metaphor. The priesthood, he said, is a priceless liqueur which can be put into vessels either of porcelain or of clay.[54]

His interior dispositions were so transparent to his students that, while observing the distance proper to the teacher-student relationship, they treated him as a friend and companion. They were also very impressed by the neatness of his appearance and elegance of his manners. And so that they were greatly surprised when he showed up in class one day with white splotches all over his cassock. They insisted on hearing what had happened, says Mariano Trueba, so he told them. He was just stepping into the streetcar when he saw coming toward him a construction worker, overalls covered with lime, whose malicious intent the priest could see in his eyes. Beating him to the punch, he gave him a big hug, saying in a disarming tone of voice, "Come here, my son, coat me with as much of that stuff as you like! Are you pleased with the effect?"[55]

"In my heart," says Mariano Trueba, "I felt that that was something that could only have happened if Father Josemaría was a saint, and I said so to my companions."[56]

They were even more astonished by a comment by one of the professors at the Academy. Apparently that young priest, distinguished and professorial as he appeared, interspersed his lectures on the Codex and on Roman law with visits to the poor and the sick in the slums. They only half believed it, and placed bets on whether it was true or not. Following him secretly, some of the students found themselves in the extreme north of the city, in the slum of Tetuán de las Victorias; and on another day, in the slum area of the town of Vallecas, in the south.[57]

4. *The Foundation for the Sick*

The Foundation for the Sick, of which Father Josemaría was head chaplain, was at 13 Santa Engracia Street. (The assistant chaplain was Father Norberto Rodríguez García.) The building had been constructed with the idea that it would be the headquarters of the foundation established by Doña Luz Rodríguez Casanova. The construction records include a statement of the principles inspiring its architectural plan: "It should be simple but well made, without decorative extravagances but with authenticity and permanence, as charity should be, for that is the principal idea behind this building."[58] The result was a solid and simple building combining brickwork with stone masonry, and featuring a cheerful and beautiful arrangement of glazed tiles from Talavera.

The Foundation for the Sick was based on charity, and from that solid trunk shot out various branches in which nested a multitude of charitable and apostolic works: the Work of Preservation of the Faith in Spain, the Work of the Holy Family, the Charity Dining Halls, the Protection Society, the Saint Joseph Clothes Distribution Center, and so on.[59] The young chaplain laughingly summed it up by saying: "The work of Doña Luz is the fourteen works of mercy."[60]

The Foundation for the Sick waged war on ignorance and misery, through schools, soup kitchens, clinics, chapels, and catechetical programs scattered all through Madrid and the surrounding areas. On the ground floor of Santa Engracia there was a public dining room, and on the second floor, a twenty-bed infirmary. The parlors and bedrooms of the Foundation looked out onto a large courtyard with a public church attached. There, early each morning, the chaplain said Mass, celebrating it, says one of the Apostolic Ladies, "thoughtfully and devoutly, taking up to three quarters of an hour."[61] (Later, out of consideration for the congregation, he tried to keep it to half an hour, and for this purpose would place his watch on the altar.) Pedro Rocamora, a law student who sometimes served him at the altar, says that when he celebrated Mass, "there came about in him a kind of transfiguration."

> I am not exaggerating. For him the liturgy was not a formal act but a transcendent one. Each word held a profound meaning and was uttered in a heartfelt tone of voice. He savored the concepts. At that time many of us knew the Latin Mass by heart, and so I could follow one by one the words of the liturgy. Josemaría seemed detached from his human surroundings and, as it were, tied by invisible cords to the divine. This phenomenon peaked at the moment of Consecration. At that instant something strange happened in which Josemaría seemed to be disconnected from the physical things around him (the church, the sanctuary, the altar) and to be catching sight of mysterious and remote heavenly horizons.[62]

When the altar servers returned to the sacristy, and the intensity of the Mass was relaxed, tears came to their eyes.

One of the altar servers, Emilio Caramazana, a seminarian, served Father Josemaría's Mass during his summer vacations, in August of 1927, 1928, and 1929. He was struck by "the exquisite way" this priest performed the liturgy. One could see, he says, that he was "very absorbed, lost in thought, especially during the Canon," but despite his obvious immersion in the Mass, "he enunciated the prayers very well. One could understand his Latin from the very back of the chapel, which was fairly large."[63] His piety kept his altar servers awake and attentive.

José María González Barredo, then a young student living with his parents near the Foundation, mentions that at home they called the chaplain "the boy priest," because of his youthful appearance and contagious cheerfulness, and because they didn't know his name.[64]

On weekdays the Mass in the chapel was attended by Catholics of the neighborhood and some of the poor and sick who lived at the Foundation. On weekends and on holy days of obligation, however, the chapel was packed, and to make room for everybody the partition separating it from the dining room had to be removed. Everyone listened enthusiastically to the chaplain's homilies, which were simple but well prepared. María Vicenta Reyero, one of the Apostolic Ladies, says that Father Josemaría "was a serious and rigorous preacher and catechist."[65]

Another of the Ladies, Asunción Muñoz, recalls that after Mass he would teach catechism to, and speak with, young and old alike, "always ready to listen to them and to resolve their doubts and difficulties." The chaplain, she says, made a habit of walking through the dining room to get to know everyone. He cared about everyone's problems and "what was inside of each person. He was a friend and a holy priest."[66]

There were all kinds of activities went at the Foundation on weekends. As a prelude to his other pastoral ministrations, the chaplain started off in the confessional. On Saturdays the poor and sick from the surrounding neighborhoods came to Santa Engracia—that is, those whose ailments did not prevent them from getting there—for physical and spiritual care in the clinic and the chapel. On Sundays, it was the turn of the boys and girls of the schools that the Apostolic Ladies conducted. They all gathered at Santa Engracia, and Father Josemaría heard their confessions. So many people showed up there on the weekends that one of the Ladies' lay auxiliaries remembers that a cousin of hers, Pilar Santos, "upon seeing the number of sick persons who were tended to, or of children who came for confession or to make their First Communion, used to say, 'Here at the Foundation, everything is done by the ton.' " [67]

In 1928, these were the actual numbers: 4,251 sick persons tended to; 3,168 confessions; 483 anointings of the sick; 1,251 weddings; 147 baptisms.[68] But beyond that, it took more than one meeting—in fact, it took a lot of persuasion and Christian struggle—to prepare people who had lived in an irregular situation for years for sacramental marriage, or to get individuals who had been away from the Church for years to go to confession. The bare statistics leave all that out.

Father Josemaría voluntarily involved himself in the charitable works of the Foundation. First he took part in the works of doctrinal formation, such as the Work of the Holy Family, which were carried on at Santa Engracia.[69] Then, little by little, he became involved also in some of the activities that took place outside of that center. Among these was the Ladies' pet project, the Work of Preservation of the Faith in Spain, which they themselves described as "difficult, thankless, costly, and consequently a great struggle."[70] This was an apostolate carried out on the streets of the slums to combat the blatant anti-Catholic propaganda that was rapidly spreading in the poorer areas of Madrid. Sheds serving as secular or anti-Catholic schools were cropping up overnight. The Ladies accepted the challenge and started up schools in the same neighborhoods, adopting the other side's tactics in an effort to keep them from seducing the tender souls of children.

By 1928 the Ladies had fifty-eight schools in Madrid, with a total of 14,000 children. (To a certain extent, these numbers reflect that apostolic competition in the face of the growth of anti-Catholic schools.) Indirectly, therefore, without being part of his job description, it became the chaplain's responsibility to prepare some 4,000 children a year for First Communion. This eucharistic catechesis consisted in three days of in-depth explaining of what is involved in the reception of the Sacrament and chatting with each child to evaluate his or her understanding and dispositions.[71]

Father Josemaría did not, of course, go to all fifty-eight schools individually. Children who lived not too far from the Foundation came to Santa Engracia for Mass, confession, and catechesis. But in the outlying areas there were six other small churches or chapels dependent on the Apostolic Ladies, and none of these had a priest assigned to it; and so the chaplain took care of them too.[72] "He was very good," says one of the Ladies' auxiliaries. "He was always available for anything and everything—never caused us any problems."[73] He himself would never forget all the time he spent hearing the confessions of those poor children.

> [I went for] hours and hours all over the place, every day, on foot, from one area to another, among poor people ashamed of their poverty and poor people too miserable to be ashamed, who had nothing at all; among children with runny noses—dirty, but children, which means souls pleasing to God. How indignant I feel in my priestly soul when they say now that small children should not go to confession! That's not true! They should make their personal confession, speaking one on one to the priest in secret, just like everyone else. What good, what joy it brings them! I spent many hours in that work, and I'm only sorry that it was not more.[74]

*   *   *

Many poor people came to Santa Engracia, either to be treated in the clinic or admitted to the infirmary; but the Ladies and their auxiliaries also traveled the streets of Madrid visiting the sick and dying, while trying to alleviate the spiritual misery of people lacking the most elementary religious instruction.

To fully appreciate the apostolic zeal of the young chaplain, one must consider not only the activities already mentioned but also his visits to homes. Sometimes the help of the priest was indispensable and urgently needed—to hear a confession, or perform a wedding, or prepare someone for a good death. Besides being on call for emergencies, which came up all the time, Father Josemaría also had fixed times for regular visits. On the eve of every First Friday, he went to the homes of many sick people to hear their confessions, and next day brought them Communion. In the other weeks he made a eucharistic round on Thursday, in a car lent him by Doña Luz Casanova; on other days he made his visits by streetcar or on foot.[75] Many of the sick lived in remote or hard-to-find places. But distances were never a problem for him. Without waiting to be asked, he cheerfully went from one end of Madrid to the other. It was all the same to him, says Josefina Santos, whether he "brought Communion to the sick who lived in Tetuán de las Victorias or to those in the area of Paseo de Extremadura, or in Magín Calvo, or in Vallecas, Lavapiés, San Millán, Lucero, or Ribera del Manzanares."*[76]

Ordinarily he took no time off. His hours were overloaded with pressing tasks. Before or after classes at the Academy, he would go see some sick person. Asunción Muñoz, the Apostolic Lady in charge of emergencies and particularly difficult cases, gives this testimony: "Often it was necessary to regularize their situation, get them married, solve urgent social or moral problems, help them in all sorts of ways. Father Josemaría pitched into everything, at whatever hour, with constancy, with dedication, with not the least sign of being in a hurry to get it over with, but as someone fulfilling his vocation, his sacred ministry of love. And so, with Father Josemaría, we were sure of help at all times. He would always give people the sacraments, and so we did not have to bother the parish priest at inopportune times."[77]

His graciousness in accepting assignments made it a certainty that he would be deluged with tasks. He took them with a smile and, in the words of one Apostolic Lady, carried them out "gladly, with pleasure, lightheartedly, promptly, without

---

* These were outlying neighborhoods situated all around Madrid.

making any objection." The fact was, says another, that "the sick were for him a treasure: he carried them in his heart."[78]

On one occasion one of the Apostolic Ladies was deeply concerned about a dying man who had a history of being rabidly anticlerical. She went to Father Josemaría, thinking that he might be able to do something, even though the man had already lapsed into a coma. "When I got near the house of this poor man," the chaplain relates, "when I got to his street (Cardinal Cisneros), I remembered how, when they gave me the note about him, I protested, saying, 'It's crazy to think I can do anything. If he's delirious, what chance is there that I'll find him in any condition to go to confession? But, all right, I'll go and I'll give him conditional absolution.' "

Following his "custom of saying something to the Virgin Mary when going to visit each sick person," he recited a Memorare, asking that the dying man be able to receive unconditional absolution. When he reached the house, the neighbors told him there was nothing he could do. A priest from the parish had just been there, and had had to leave without hearing the man's confession, since he had not regained consciousness.

Undeterred, the chaplain called the old man by name.

"Pepe!"
Immediately he gave me a very favorable response.
"Would you like to go to confession?"
"Yes," he told me.
I threw everybody else out. He went to confession—with me helping him a lot, naturally—and received absolution.[79]

Margarita Alvarado says of Father Josemaría, "We liked him a lot and were always happy to be with him, because he always solved our problems." Asunción Muñoz notes that if a delicate situation arose—if a sick person in danger of death refused the sacraments—the case was turned over to him, in the

certainty that "he would gain the good will of that person and
open to them the gates of heaven."[80]

One such situation involved a critically ill man of whom
the religious of the Foundation had anxiously told the chaplain
because he refused to see a priest. Father Josemaría recorded
what happened next with that dying, stubborn sinner:

> I came to the man's house. With holy, apostolic shame-
> lessness, I sent his wife outside and was then alone with
> the poor man. "Father, those women from the Foundation
> are such nuisances, so impertinent. Especially one of
> them. . . ." (He was talking about Pilar, who could be can-
> onized!) "You're right," I told him. And then I was quiet, so
> that he could go on talking. "She told me I should go to
> confession . . . , because I am dying. Well, I will die, but I
> will not go to confession!" Then I said, "Up to now I
> haven't said anything to you about confession, but tell me,
> why don't you want to go to confession?" "When I was
> seventeen I swore that I would never again go to confes-
> sion, and I have kept that promise." That's what he said.
> And he told me also that not even when he got married—
> the man was about fifty years old—had he gone to confes-
> sion. . . . About fifteen minutes after saying all this, he went
> to confession, in tears.[81]

God's grace never failed to do its work among the hundreds
of sick people whom he had to attend during his years as chaplain. "I can't remember a single case," says Asunción Muñoz, "in
which we failed in our effort."[82] Such a categorical statement is
hard to believe. But the chaplain himself reports that in his visits to the sick during his time at the Foundation, "by the grace of
God we always managed to have everyone go to confession before they died."[83]

The usual practice was that he was given a sheet of paper
with the day's date and the names and addresses of the sick to
be visited. And as can be seen from the sheets that have been

preserved, the priest, who was always short of time, would study the list and rearrange it, to come up with an efficient and economical plan of travel. Those lists, which usually included five or six names, called for hiking for several miles through inhospitable neighborhoods, sloshing through mud in the winter, trekking through dust clouds in the summer, stepping in manure, and tromping through piles of garbage. Many trips started in the center of the city and wound up in the outskirts, among ragged rows of shacks, built with no particular order or plan. There are pages that give the addresses but not the names of the sick persons. In other cases the addresses are not complete. And in others the trajectory looks like that of a knight on a chessboard.

Some of the lists are incredible. The one for March 17, 1928, a day devoted to the hearing of sick people's confessions, has thirteen names. The distances are amazing. The addresses go from downtown Madrid (the embassy area) to the neighborhood of Delicias in the south, then to Ribera de Curtidores, and from there way over to Francos Rodríguez, in the area now known as Tetuán de las Victorias, in the northern part of Madrid. Walks of more than six miles were not unusual.

The page for July 4, 1928, is typical. It does not give the name of sick person no. 6, but does say where this person can be found: "10 Zarzal, the Chamartín road, a little before you get there, right-hand side, where there's a gas tank." The priest must have had a problem with these directions, because there is added in his own writing, "First there's a fish market." It seems probable, given the kinds of notes he added and the corrections he later made of names and addresses, that he kept the sheets to help him in making subsequent visits.[84]

After reading the list, the young chaplain went on foot or by streetcar even to the outlying districts of the capital, often crossing the whole Madrid area from one end to the other in search of these sick or dying souls. With all this exercise, his shoes wore out very quickly. His joy, on the other hand, grew in proportion to the increase of his pastoral duties.

To God's grace, which he had in abundance, Father Jose-maría united a lot of astuteness. As María Vicenta Reyero observes, everyone was happy, "and the sick people whom we visited at home asked that he, and no one else, come back to hear their confessions."[85] When complications arose, the Ladies would always call on the chaplain, as is suggested by this note on the sheet for February 2, 1928: "He has serious problems, and wants to go to confession. It would be good for Father José María to go out there."[86]

Sometimes out on the street he would run into emergency situations not included on the list. One day he was walking by Retiro Park, which is not far from the zoo. A zoo attendant who had just been mauled by a bear was being rushed into a first-aid station. The chaplain managed to get in just behind him. The man communicated by signs that he wanted to go to confession, and was absolved then and there.[87]

These were years of exhausting work that tested to the limit not only his strength and stamina but also the endurance of his stomach, for often all he could offer the beggars who asked alms on the street was the sandwich he had brought along for lunch.[88] But at the end of the day, when the Ladies passed by the chapel, they would see the chaplain kneeling at the altar, head in hands, praying beside the tabernacle for hours.[89]

Among the notes from the Foundation for the Sick which Father Josemaría saved, is one written in large, bold letters, unmistakably by the chaplain: *Fac, ut sit!* ("Do it, let it be!").[90] Through all those months of 1927 and 1928, the young priest kept pleading for the accomplishment of the divine ideal that he was glimpsing in his supernatural presentiments. He also received divine locutions announcing the imminent approach of that something he desired so ardently.*[91] With apostolic longings burning inside him, he sang out at the top of his lungs, as he himself tells us:

---

* "Locution" is a technical term for a message in words from God. Some locutions involve hearing a voice. Others are "heard" only within the soul.

When I had presentiments that our Lord wanted something and I didn't yet know what it was, I said—shouting,
singing, whatever way I could!—some words that surely,
if I did not pronounce them with my mouth, I savored in
my heart: *Ignem veni mittere in terram, et quid volo nisi ut accendatur!*—"I came to cast fire upon the earth; and would
that it were already kindled!" (Lk 12:49). And this answer:
Ecce ego, quia vocasti me!—"Here I am, for you called me!"
(1 Sam 3:5).[92]

The walls of the apartment on Fernando el Católico rever-
berated with his songs. And his little brother, Santiago, who
heard him and didn't want to be left out, would try to sing the
same verses, butchering the Latin.[93]

Those words of our Lord, recorded by Saint Luke, filled
many hours of meditation for the young priest. Undoubtedly
they caused him a special tension of soul, judging by the tone
of voice in which he describes the interior commotion he felt.
Fire, in Sacred Scripture is a symbol of God's ardent love, come
down from heaven to earth to enkindle human beings. From
the urgency and insistence with which Father Josemaría kept
repeating that cry uttered by our Lord, it is obvious that he res-
onated with its words and fully identified with God's desire to
offer his love to all people. He saw the redemption as a marvelous divine adventure to be completed in history, an adventure which demands on our part a radical commitment to unite
ourselves with Christ, to try to feel as he did toward all humanity, and to take up his redeeming cross.

Father Josemaría first jotted down such inspirations on loose
sheets of paper, and then gleaned from them practical suggestions or apostolic orientations, which he entered in a notebook.
Unfortunately in looking around him, he did not need his
wealth of pastoral experience to note a lack of unity of purpose
and integration in souls. He saw with sorrow that the beliefs of
many Christians were, in terms of actual practice, unconnected
with their personal, familial, and social lives. Nor was there anywhere offered to the faithful the possibility of developing a life

that was fully Christian in all its dimensions. As for infusing society with the fire of Christ, that task had been put on the shelf.

In fact, the historical process was moving in the opposite
direction. On all sides there were attempts to eject God from
society and relegate him to the churches or to a corner of the
individual's consciousness. As Father Josemaría would later
put it, "Apostolate was conceived of as a different kind of
act, an act separate from the normal actions of everyday
life—certain methods, organizations, advertising cam-
paigns, and so forth, superimposed on one's familial and
professional obligations (sometimes preventing one from
carrying out these obligations perfectly) and constituting a
separate world, one not rooted in or interwoven with the
rest of one's existence."[94]

For directing souls to God, was there perhaps a way of proceeding that took seriously the universal invitation to love? Was
it possible to Christianize society and apostolically rouse the
world? Inspirations darted through Father Josemaría's mind
like arrows shot in the dark at an invisible target. The stream of
illuminations given him by our Lord left in their wake, in his
loose notes, answers to many of the problems he had thought of.
Father Josemaría knew that these answers came not from his
own understanding or reflections, but from a divine source.

Astounded by the lights he was receiving, and by the
apostolic panoramas unfolding before his eyes, he promptly
answered the Lord, "Here I am, for you called me." He had
been saying this since 1918, but now this "Ecce ego, quia vocasti me!" had a special resonance. It was a new way of
telling the Lord that he was entirely at his disposal, awaiting
that imminent something that he could tell was a loving plan
of God for all humanity. He sensed that in some way he
would play a major role in it, but what that role would be he
could not yet imagine. As he would later put it, "Although
before October 2, 1928, I didn't know what it was, I could
vaguely make out a new foundation, which, it seemed,
would not have any very specific purpose."[95]

5. *October 2, 1928*

The district of Chamberí, in which the Foundation for the Sick was located, was a northward extension of the old downtown area of Madrid. Dominated by middle-class apartment buildings of four or five stories, it was an area of growth that still had large open spaces surrounding monasteries, mansions, and administrative buildings. There were many turn-of-the-century brick structures of mixed style, featuring Moorish adornments with Gothic traceries.

Doña Dolores' apartment was some distance from the Foundation and was in keeping with the family's financial situation, which depended entirely on the income of Father Josemaría. Needless to say, things were tight, though exactly how tight is not known. One of the Apostolic Ladies offers the very conservative speculation that the Escrivás "must not have been very prosperous, since they lived simply."[96] The priest's income from teaching is unknown. But one fact from the summer of 1928 gives some idea of the straits the household was in.

On August 31 Father Josemaría signed up for three courses needed for a doctorate in law which meant that he suddenly had to come up with 150 pesetas.[97] Considering the amount of money, one would hardly expect him to skip one of the exams. Nevertheless, on September 15 he skipped the one for History of Spanish Juridical Literature, taking (and passing) only the other two exams.

If he lacked time to study for the exam, or money to pay the fee to take it, how could he have laid out those 150 pesetas? Very likely they came not out of his own pocket, but rather from the generosity of Father José Cicuéndez, who knew that his professor of canon and Roman law was nearly broke.[98]

Once the September examinations were over, the university and the academies closed for a couple of weeks before beginning the new term. Father Josemaría, who usually made a weeklong retreat each year, used this academic break for that purpose. He made all the arrangements for going on a retreat for diocesan priests, including asking the assistant chaplain of the Foundation to cover for him.[99] The Vincentians' headquarters, where the retreat was to be given, was near the Foundation. It was a large, four-story brick building with simple and austere rooms opening into corridors, and with a large interior patio garden. Next to that building, at the corner where García de Paredes Street begins, was Saint Vincent de Paul Church, now the Basilica of La Milagrosa (Our Lady of the Miraculous Medal), built in 1904. Behind it was "a large kitchen garden—fertile, verdant, colorful, and luxuriant—with various flower beds separated by walkways covered by leafy fruit and shade trees."[100] As the years went by, these enormous open spaces of vegetable and flower gardens—which extended to Cuatro Caminos, alternating with ancestral homes and built-up areas—were eaten up by the city's expansion.

The retreat began on Sunday, September 30, and lasted through October 6. Father Josemaría arrived Sunday evening, bringing with him personal effects and a good stack of papers, including his loose notes on, among other things, the extraordinary graces that the Lord had been giving him for the past ten years, mainly in the form of inspirations and illuminations.[101]

Later he explained the origin and content of those notes, which afterward became some of the entries in his journal (*Apuntes íntimos*) that he called "Catherines" (in Spanish, "Catalinas"), in honor of Saint Catherine of Siena. "I don't know," he said, "if I have mentioned somewhere in the Catherines how these notes came about. In case I haven't, I would like to put on record that I was at most eighteen, possibly younger, when I felt impelled to just start writing, without rhyme or reason. . . . Now I remember that this is spoken of in the early pages. Enough, then."[102]

This explanation whets the appetite of curiosity but leaves it unsatisfied, since those "early pages" no longer exist. He transcribed them into the first notebook of the *Apuntes,* the one he later burned. In it were recorded many events of a supernatural character. Fearing, with good reason, that they might lead someone reading them to consider him a saint, he decided to destroy them.[103] More than anything else, they revealed the really extraordinary thing about his life: his fidelity to his pre-sentiments of love, which proved to be, after ten long years of self-denying responsiveness to grace, truly heroic. His faith was gigantic; his hope, unshakable; his love, superabundantly expressed in deeds. But, forgetting the delay and his troubles, the young priest considered himself far more than repaid with the graces he was receiving.

At this point the Lord, who had been preparing him from birth for the day when he could place in his hands a divine task capable of changing the course of history, deemed him mature enough. Father Josemaría was only twenty-six years old, but he had walked at the pace set for him by God, with no reservation or delay. And the Lord did not let himself be outdone in gene-rosity; in the midst of those presentiments of love he kept filling him with graces. The young priest was conscious of the hidden working of the extraordinary gifts he was receiving, though not of all of them. He was also aware of the serenity and cheerfulness he was communicating to those around him, and of his gifts as a counselor and guide of souls. He could see the hand of God in the fortitude with which he confronted adversity, in the apostolic effectiveness of his speech, in the docility with which all kinds of people—the poor and sick of the Foundation, children preparing for First Communion, university students—responded to the warmth of his priestly ministry. It seemed as though obstacles gave way as he approached, and were simply marking out his route toward what God wanted of him.

The cry *Domine, ut videam! Domine, ut sit!* brought him at last to the summit from which he could see a divine plan— A plan that did not originate yesterday or ten years ago, but in the eternity of God's love.

* * *

Six priests were making the retreat. Wake-up time was 5:00 A.M., and bedtime was 9:00 P.M. In between there were exami-nations of conscience, Mass, talks, the Divine Office. . . .[104]

On the morning of Tuesday, October 2, feast of the Guardian Angels, after celebrating Mass, Father Josemaría was in his room, reading the notes he had brought with him. Suddenly an extraordinary grace came over him, and he understood that our Lord was responding to those insistent petitions, *Domine, ut videam!* and *Domine, ut sit!*

He would always maintain a reserve about this event and especially its more personal elements.[105] Three years later, he described the gist of it like this: "I received an illumination *about the entire Work,* while I was reading those papers. Deeply moved, I knelt down—I was alone in my room, at a time between one talk and the next—and gave thanks to our Lord, and I remember with a heart full of emotion the ringing of the bells of the Church of Our Lady of the Angels."[106]

Under the powerful and ineffable light of grace he was shown the Work as a whole; "saw" is the word he always used when relating this event. This supernatural vision absorbed into itself all of the partial inspirations and illuminations of the past, variously recorded in the individual notes he was then reading, and projected them toward the future with a new unity and fullness of meaning.[107]

These were moments of indescribable grandeur. As he prayed he saw displayed within his soul the historical panorama of human redemption, illuminated by God's love. At that moment, he comprehended in a way that could not be expressed in words the divine core of the exalted vocation of Christians who, in the midst of their earthly tasks, are called to the sanctification of themselves and their work. In this light he saw that the Work (as yet unnamed) was destined to promote the divine plan of the universal call to holiness; that from within its heart as an instrument of God's Church would radiate the theological principles and supernatural spirit needed for the renewal of peoples. With immense astonishment he understood, deep in his soul, that that illumination was not only the answer to his petitions, but also an invitation to accept a divine commission.

Immediately following that torrential outpouring of grace, he was invaded by the special feeling of uneasiness that souls feel in the sovereign presence of the Lord. But in the midst of that fear and apprehension, he heard in his soul a comforting "Do not be afraid!" About this experience he later wrote:

> Those are divine words of encouragement. In the Old Testament and in the New, God and celestial beings spoke them to raise people out of their misery and dispose them for a dialogue of illumination and love, and for a confidence about things that are seemingly impossible or so difficult that creatures cannot carry them out. . . .
>
> I can assure you, my children, that those souls do not look or wish for the manifestations of that *extraordinary ordinary providence* of God, and that they have a profound awareness of not deserving it. I repeat to you once more that their sentiments in the face of such things are feelings of fear, of terror. But afterward our Lord's encouragement, *Ne timeas!* ["Do not be afraid!"], communicates to them an indestructible security, sparks in them impulses of faithfulness and dedication, gives them clear ideas about how to fulfill his most lovable will, and inflames them to hasten toward goals beyond merely human reach.[108]

Now disposed for "a dialogue of illumination and love," he burst into acts of thanksgiving while feeling the "Domine, ut sit!" become more insistent than ever. Now, before this panorama of total clarity, beyond premonitions and presentiments, he joyfully surrendered himself to his vocation as founder in order to bring God's plan to fruition.[109]

Into the room, at this moment of prayer, flooded the jubilant sound of the pealing of the bells of Our Lady of the Angels, a church in the nearby neighborhood of Cuatro Caminos. That sound would stay with him forever. "Still resounding in my ears," he said in 1964, "are the bells of the Church of Our Lady of the Angels, announcing the feast of its patroness."[110]

*   *   *

October 2, 1928, had a very precise meaning for the young priest: it was the date of the foundation of Opus Dei. In all his accounts, he is very precise in the language he uses to describe what happened. To avoid any ambiguity or possibility of misinterpretation, he deliberately isolates the supernatural event from other, merely personal circumstances. For instance: "And then came October 2, 1928. I was making a retreat, because I had to, and it was then that Opus Dei came into the world."[111]

The historical event was unforeseen and surprising. Although in a way it was the begetting of a human enterprise, it was a product of God's entrance into history. In one of his meditations, the founder put it in this impersonal way: "The Work burst into the world on that 2nd of October of 1928."[112]

Father Josemaría was always unshakably clear that the Lord was protagonist of that event, its principal author, the one who dominated the situation with his majesty and took the initiative, imperiously bursting into the soul of his servant. "On that day," he says, "the Lord founded his Work; he started Opus Dei."[113]

Putting himself in the background, he avoided the use of the word "founder." He always attributed to himself a secondary role, as recipient of that divine illumination, as one gratuitously chosen by the Lord, as one with whom the Lord chose to play as a father plays with a little child. In the year he died, he said: "Once more was fulfilled what Scripture says: that that which is foolish, which is worth nothing—which, one might say, almost doesn't exist—the Lord takes all that and places it at his service. Thus he took that little child as his instrument."[114] And, more explicitly, he wrote in 1934: "The Work of God was not dreamed up by a man. . . . Many years ago our Lord gradually revealed it to an inept and deaf instrument, who saw it for the first time on the feast of the Holy Guardian Angels, the second of October of nineteen twenty-eight."[115]

That illumination forever constituted for him the moment when the Work began. To him, October 2 was the date of an invitation and of his response to that foundational call.[116] On one October 2 he said:

> It is reasonable that I should say a few words to you today, when I begin a new year of my vocation to Opus Dei. I know you're expecting it. But I must tell you, children of my soul, that I feel a great difficulty, a sort of embarrassment, about appearing in public on this day. It is not natural modesty; it is the constant conviction, the clear-as-day obviousness, of my own unworthiness. Never had it entered my head, before that moment, that I should carry out a mission to humanity.[117]

*   *   *

October 2 was the milestone marking the exact historical moment in which the mind of the founder was illuminated with a "clear general idea" of his mission.[118] Surprisingly, another highly significant event was attached to that one: the inspirations that the young priest had been receiving with a certain regularity were suddenly discontinued. As of October 2, 1928, it was as if the well had dried up at its source. "The first inspirations were over," he later wrote in his *Apuntes*. That silence of God would continue until November 1929, when "there started up again that special, very specific help from the Lord."[119]

The loose notes that the retreatant had brought to meditate on concerned ideas that up to then had been disorganized. In the remaining days of the retreat he put them in order, on the basis of the general illumination he had just received "about the Work as a whole." That unitary vision of God's project gave new depth to the earlier, fragmentary inspirations, and from that perspective of vast historical dimensions "he 'saw' Opus Dei just as our Lord wanted it and as it must be throughout the centuries."[120]

The notebook he destroyed contained all the foundation-related journal entries written before March 1930. But what he had seen on October 2, 1928, never left his mind or heart. From then on, the light he had received from God about the universal call to sanctity, and about seeking the fullness of Christian life in the midst of the world and through professional work, made up the substance of his preaching. He also began to draft documents that he would later present to his children in Opus Dei.

In the opening lines of the earliest of these writings, a long letter dated March 24, 1930, the founder seems to be hearing a faint echo of that cry, *Ignem veni mittere in terram, et quid volo nisi ut accendatur?* and telling the world of the divine mission entrusted to him. "Our Lord's heart," he says, "is a heart of mercy which takes pity on people and draws close to them. Our dedication to the service of souls is a manifestation of that mercy of our Lord, not only toward ourselves, but toward all of humanity. For he has called us to attain sanctity in ordinary, everyday life."[121]

This universal call to Christian perfection is a clear proof of the infinite love of the Lord, who "satisfies the desire of every living thing" (Ps 145:16). The founder, therefore, proclaims aloud, in his own name and in the names of those to follow him, the daring and imperious words of one who has received a personal mission from God of historic significance:

> We must always keep in our sight the multitude, for there is no human being that we are not to love, that we are not to try to help and to understand. Everyone is of interest to us, because everyone has a soul to be saved, because we can bring to everyone, in the name of God, an invitation to seek Christian perfection in the world, repeating to them, *Estote ergo vos perfecti, sicut et Pater vester caelestis perfectus est*: "You, therefore, must be perfect, as your heavenly Father is perfect" (Mt 5:48).[122]

God does not discriminate among souls—he himself assures us of this—nor does he make exceptions. Therefore, no one can offer the excuse of not having beeen invited. Barriers and prejudices have fallen.

We have come to say, with the humility of those who know themselves to be sinners and of little worth—"Homo peccator sum" ["I am a sinful man"], we say with Saint Peter (Lk 5:8)—but also with the faith of those who let themselves be guided by the hand of God, that sanctity is not something for a privileged few; that our Lord calls every one of us, that he expects love from everyone: from everyone, no matter where they are; from everyone, whatever might be their state in life, their profession, or their position. Because that ordinary, everyday life, with nothing showy about it, can be a means of sanctity. It is not necessary to abandon one's state in the world to seek God, if God does not give the soul a vocation to religious life, for every path of life can be the occasion of an encounter with Christ.[123]

God meets people right where they are, usually without removing them from their place: from the area they live in, the job they work at, the family situation they are in. God awaits everyone in the little, ordinary things. The extraordinary is rare; God must be found in ordinary, everyday tasks.

The extraordinary for us is the ordinary: the ordinary done with perfection. Always with a smile, ignoring—in a nice way—the things that bother us, that annoy us; being generous beyond measure. In a word, making our ordinary life a continuous prayer.[124]

There is always a hidden treasure in small things done with love and perfection—in difficulties and joys, in a job well done, in service to society or one's neighbor. Professional work and social relations are the milieu and the matter that Christians must sanctify; they must become saints in and through the fulfilling of their family and civic obligations. The universal call to sanctity implies, in other words, the sanctifying value of work offered to God and the Christian value of secular activities—the reality that one can be detached from this world without being absent from it, that mundane things can be used as a means for becoming sanctified, for becoming divinized.

In that ordinary life, as we go along through the world with our professional colleagues or coworkers (as the old Castilian saying goes, "every sheep with its mate," for such is our life), God our Father gives us the opportunity to exercise ourselves in all the virtues: charity, fortitude, justice, sincerity, temperance, poverty, humility, obedience. . . .[125]

Thus the sciences and the arts, finance and politics, crafts and industry, housework, and all other honorable fields of endeavor no longer are indifferent or "profane." Any activity carried out in union with Christ—with an upright spirit of sacrifice, love of neighbor, and perseverance, and with the intention of giving glory to God—is thereby ennobled and endowed with spiritual value.

The founder wrote in his journal, "Christ our King has manifested his will." Later, in a few short words, he summarized his whole teaching about how to attain sanctity. We can do it, he says, by "being always in the world, in ordinary work, in the duties of our own state in life, and there, by means of everything, saints!"[126]

The essence or nucleus of this divine message about love and sanctification called for an apostolic mission to spread this good news throughout the world, and a foundation or institution to ensure the mission's continuity. On that October 2, God gave Father Josemaría both the mission and the means to carry it out. "From that day," he tells us, "the mangy donkey *was aware* of the beautiful and heavy burden that the Lord, in his inexplicable goodness, had placed on his back. That day the Lord founded his Work."[127]

The burden was a beautiful one because the young priest was to be the herald of a message for humanity as old and as new as the Gospel itself. But he saw himself as, at best, a humble, worthless donkey upon whom a precious and very heavy load had suddenly been placed.

If you ask me how one recognizes a divine calling, how one comes to a realization of it, I will tell you that it is a new view of life. It's as if a light was lit within us: it is a mysterious impulse which urges one to devote one's noblest energies to an activity which, with practice, begins to take on the nature of an occupation. That vital force, which is something like an avalanche sweeping everything before it, is what others call a vocation.

Vocation leads us, without our realizing it, to take up a position in life and maintain it with eagerness and joy and a fullness of hope right up to the very moment of our death. It is a phenomenon which gives our work a sense of mission and which ennobles and gives value to our existence. Jesus, of his own accord, enters the soul—yours, mine. . . . That is the call.[128]

For more than ten years he had been praying for two things, and now they were a reality. His "Domine, ut videam!" was answered when the divine plan for his life, for the good of all humanity, was revealed to him. And from the moment when God accepted him as his instrument for realizing the Work, "an entity with a divine core," he had his reply to his *Domine, ut sit!*

Jesus undoubtedly wanted me to cry out from my darkness like the blind man in the Gospel. And I did cry out, for years, without knowing what it was that I was asking for. Often I shouted out the prayer *Ut sit!* which seemed like a request for a new being. . . .

And the Lord gave light to the eyes of the blind man, in spite of himself (the blind man), and announced the coming of an entity with a divine core, a being that would give God all the glory and promote his kingdom forever.[129]

In Logroño he had dimly glimpsed that "a something" would overtake him that "was both above me and in me."[130]

Now the presentiment was fulfilled. The divine plan was above him, and the foundational grace necessary to overcome all difficulties and carry it to fruition was within him. He had, then, capacity and experience enough to carry it out, as appears from the fact that God entrusted the founding of the Work entirely to him. He was graced with supernatural and human virtues; he lived a contemplative life in the midst of work and hardships; he had apostolic drive, leadership skills, and a zeal for souls. In short, he already had, in essence, the spirit that this foundation would need. With no teacher except the Holy Spirit, he incarnated the Work as founder. The seed planted by God in his mind and heart would in time blossom into its whole spirit and reality.

The supernatural mission entrusted to Father Josemaría was fully part of the mission of the Church. It was to make tangible, for all time, the reality of God's plan of a universal call to holiness.

> Our Lord has raised up in these years his Work because he wants it never again unknown or forgotten that all are called to strive for sanctity, and that the majority of Christians are called to do this in the world, in ordinary work. For that reason, as long as there are people on this earth, the Work will exist. There will always be persons of every profession and position who seek sanctity within their state of life, within that profession or position of theirs; contemplative souls in the midst of the world.[131]

The Work came to be, in the Church, a means of apostolic outreach aimed at proclaiming the good news and giving witness to the possibility and urgency of seeking sanctity in the midst of the world.

> Jesus Christ himself has chosen us so that in the midst of the world—in which he placed us, and from which he does not wish to separate us—each of us will seek sanc-

tity in our own state of life and, teaching with the testimony of life and word that the call to holiness is universal, promote among persons of all walks of life, and especially among intellectuals, Christian perfection in the very heart of civil life.[132]

The Work was to be a response to Jesus' cry "I came to cast fire upon the earth," an apostolic means for announcing this burning desire of his everywhere, by example and teaching. But in carrying out that mission, members of the Work act as ordinary Christians and citizens, sharing customs, jobs, and social concerns with everyone else. They fulfill their mission with complete naturalness, with no desire to stand out. Like leaven in dough, they strive from within society to lead the world to God, to place the labor and affections of their fellow human beings at his feet. "You and I know and believe," writes the founder, "that the world has as its sole mission to give glory to God. This life only has a reason for existing insofar as it projects the eternal kingdom of the Creator."[133]

From the moment of the Work's appearance, one hears a new note in his life and writings. "Soon will arrive," he says, "the Pentecost of the Work of God. . . . and the whole world will hear, in all of its languages, the delirious acclamations of the soldiers of the great King: *Regnare Christum volumus!* [We want Christ to reign!]."[134]

* * *

God asked and received Father Josemaría's wholehearted yes to his divine plan. Indeed, with great humility, the founder turned his response into a joyful "*Serviam!* I will serve!" Every day for the rest of his life he would pray that aspiration as an expression of complete submission to the will of God, an affirmation of readiness to make the Work a reality, and a rejection of all rebelliousness. For "one hears," he would say, "in personal life, in family life, in the workplace, and in public life, what amounts to a colossal *non serviam* ['I will not serve']."[135]

On that October 2 he was fully aware of his poverty, and of how much help he would need. But, instead of backing out, he asked for light and strength, for "a will of iron that, united to God's grace, will bring us to complete his Work for the glory of God, so that Christ Jesus will really reign, because all will go with Peter to him, by the one path, Mary!"[136]

Seeking to sum up in a few words what were to be the guiding principle and end of his foundation, he turned to three aspirations which mark out the path of holiness of its members.

> Jesus is our model: let us imitate him! Let us imitate him, serving Holy Church and all souls. *Christum regnare volumus* ["We want Christ to reign"]. *Deo omnis gloria* ["All glory to God"]. *Omnes cum Petro ad Iesum per Mariam* ["All to Jesus with Peter, through Mary"]. These three phrases summarize the three goals of the Work: Christ really reigning; all glory to God; souls.[137]

From the very beginning he understood that great things for the Church and for the world depended on his personal conduct in carrying out this divine enterprise. Knowing that he had a precious charism, he also knew that, like the "good and faithful servant" of the parable, he had to make it fruitful, opening up with personal effort and grace a path that did not yet exist. He could foresee that as the Work grew with the exercise of apostolate and the seeking of sanctity in the world, a new pastoral and ascetical phenomenon would appear which would require new practical and theoretical models. The process of foundation would be a long and difficult journey— one which, as it turned out, would not end until the day he died. Bearing within him the spirit of the Work, he was the trunk from which its branches and fruit were to sprout.

The founder did not then see the specific details of the long, painful path leading to the goal. He did, however, see the Work projected against the background of centuries, as a plan providentially realized by God. He wanted to start work as soon as possible, for he was sure from the beginning that it would cost him blood and tears. "I know very well," he says with assurance, "that we first ones to set to work will have to mix with tears of blood that cement of which I speak. But we will lose neither our faith nor our joy. We can do all things in him who comforts us."[138]

* * *

During that retreat with the Vincentians, he came to see how the Lord's providential hand had prepared the foundation's cornerstone by means of those sad events that had forced his family to move from Barbastro to Logroño, from Logroño to Saragossa, and from Saragossa to Madrid. In that light his life took on a new and full coloring. God had brought him to the capital city to plunge him into the very depths of the problems of humanity. "Yesterday evening, while walking down the street," he would write in his *Apuntes*, "it occurred to me that Madrid has been my Damascus, because it was here that the scales fell from the eyes of my soul . . . and it was here that I received my mission."*[139]

He took an inventory of the material means on which he could count for this mission, and found that he had none at all. As his life progressed, the Lord had been divesting him of all impediments. "I found myself then alone, equipped with nothing but my twenty-six years and my good humor," he says.[140] On another occasion he expressed it this way: "We started the Work, when our Lord wanted, with a complete lack of material means. I had only twenty-six years of age, the grace of God, and good humor. But that was enough."[141]

---

* It was on the road to Damascus that Saint Paul was converted and called to be an apostle.

6. *A campaign of prayer and mortification*

When the retreat was over, Father Josemaría resumed his activities at the Foundation, but he also immediately set about looking for persons who would share his eagerness to communicate the message of the universal call to holiness.[142] He went over the list of young men he knew, some of them students at the Cicuéndez Academy. One of the first to whom he spoke of his apostolic ideal was Pedro Rocamora, whom he met in that same year, 1928. They were introduced by José Romeo Rivera, an architecture student whose brother Manuel had been a classmate of Father Josemaría's at the law school in Saragossa. Soon they were joined by Julián Cortés Cavanillas and another student at the Academy.[143]

Strolling and chatting with these friends, the priest would explain his spiritual ambitions. To Pedro Rocamora they sounded too ambitious. He spoke "like someone inspired," he says. "He amazed us, all of us who were with him, with his total conviction that he had to give over his life to that ideal. He took up that enterprise like someone who knows he has to fulfill a kind of determined destiny in his life. I asked him, 'But do you think that is possible?' And he answered me, 'Look, this isn't something I've thought up; it's an order from God.' "[144]

The conversations did not always take place during a walk. Sometimes the priest would find a quiet place, gather his companions around a table, and read them things he had jotted down in the notebook he carried with him. If the weather was good, when school let out at the Academy they would walk over to La Castellana,* at the corner of Riscal, and sit outside on the terrace of a bar. Most of the time the group would go to the "Sotanillo" [little basement]. This establishment—a chocolate shop, bar, and cafeteria, all in one—was in a very central location: on Alcalá, between Cibeles Plaza and Independencia

---

* La Castellana is one of the main streets of Madrid.

Plaza. Its entrance was at street level, but from there one had to go down a few steps, because it was in a semibasement. Father Josemaría greatly enjoyed the atmosphere of the Sotanillo and the company of his friends. The proprietor, Juan, and his son Angel got used to seeing the priest accompanied by students. Whichever of them would first see him come in, would call out, "Here he is, with his disciples."[145]

In working up an inventory of his friends, Father Josemaría went back to his years as a student in Logroño. A letter dated December 9, 1928, from Isidoro Zorzano asks for news about his life, indicating that the priest had lately resumed contact with that classmate from the Institute of Logroño.[146] Zorzano, having gone on to study engineering in Madrid, now lived in Cádiz and worked at the naval shipyard in Matagorda. His letter was followed by a lengthy correspondence that would bring some surprises to both of them.

Father Josemaría's field of possible apostolic collaborators soon expanded to include some priests. His youthful appearance did not seem the best suited to winning him a hearing in a society with numerous clerical exponents of centuries-old customs and traditions. Nor could he ignore the precariousness of his situation as a priest from outside the diocese of Madrid, which made him feel like a fish out of water.[147] But he would let nothing stop him.

One of the first priests he tried to get enthused was Father Norberto, the other chaplain of the Foundation. At first he acted purely and simply out of charity. Father Norberto was about fifty at the time and suffered from a nervous condition that kept him from carrying out regular ecclesiastical duties. He had gotten better for a while, but then had suffered a relapse. For the rest of his life was a sick man. Yet he had a good supply of apostolic zeal and a healthy spiritual life.[148] The Apostolic Ladies, who had known him since 1924, had observed the growing friendship between the two chaplains and knew what it meant when they saw the two go together on visits to the sick and to children in the schools. "Father Josemaría," says one, "brought him along in order to help him. It was so that he would feel useful and appreciated."[149]

Another priest with whom he undoubtedly discussed his vocation in depth early on was Father José Pou de Foxá. The Roman law professor at Saragossa wrote to Father Josemaría from Avila on March 4, 1929, asking him to meet him at the station and to make a hotel reservation for him. The last lines of his letter give one an idea of how eager he was to see his former student face to face. "Since we'll be seeing each other soon," he writes, "I won't say anything more, except that your friend will soon give you a hug, José."[150]

Father Pou de Foxá stayed in Madrid several weeks, and spoke at length with his friend. Professor Carlos Sánchez del Río, who happened also to be in Madrid at this time (to take the competitive examination for a chair of Roman law), says that the three of them went together "almost every afternoon, rather late, to a chocolate shop called 'El Sotanillo,' which was on Alcalá. We had very enjoyable get-togethers there in which we exchanged ideas and feelings on all kinds of subjects."[151]

Never one to pass up an opportunity to make new friendships with priests, Father Josemaría also kept in touch with the residents of the Priests' House on Larra Street, sowing there, too, hopes for the future. That is how he met, for example, Father Manuel Ayala, who came through Madrid in 1929. Father Manuel would always cherish the memory of that brief conversation in which the chaplain shared with him some of his ideas. "At that time I confided to him something of the Work," Father Josemaría wrote, "and he remembers it fondly."[152]

In the summer of 1929 Father Rafael Fernández Claros, a young priest from El Salvador studying at the Catholic Institute of Paris, showed up one day to say Mass at the Foundation. Afterward, having finished his thanksgiving, he went to see the chaplain, and they spoke for a while. "It only took me a few minutes," says the Salvadoran, "to fully appreciate, in all its superlative value, the treasure of sanctity so carefully guarded by that exquisitely priestly soul."[153] Their closeness continued for years and gave rise to a bond of a higher order. "How, Father, can I reciprocate your kindnesses?" wrote Father Rafael on November 4, 1929, from Paris. "In no other way than by accepting—and I do accept—without any restriction, your beautiful proposal of a priestly spiritual pact."[154]

Father Rafael said more about this fraternal pact in another letter, dated March 20, 1930: "My repeated thanks for your faithful fulfillment of your promise to remember me in Holy Mass. I, for my part, remember you every day in the august Sacrifice."[155]

The chaplain of the Foundation began to organize a mobilization of souls and prayers. "Starting in 1928," he says, "I made it a point to approach holy souls—even persons that I didn't know, who had, as I used to say, 'the look of good Christians'—and ask them for prayers."[156]

On the street one day in 1929, at six in the morning, he encountered a priest he did not know, and he stopped him and asked him to pray for an intention of his. The priest was Father Casimiro Morcillo, who years later would become archbishop of Madrid.[157] This was not the only such instance. Father Avelino Gómez Ledo well remembers the zeal with which Father Josemaría, "in a lively, stimulating way," requested prayer and penance from him when the two of them were living at the Larra Street residence. Later, when the chaplain was no longer living there, he happened one day to run into Father Avelino at Cibeles Plaza. Father Avelino recalls, "He was wrapped up in a cloak, and I noticed how extraordinarily recollected he was. There was no doubt that he was praying as he walked along the street. I got the impression of having had suddenly appear to me one of those souls who live to an unusual degree in union with God. And again he spoke to me of what he was counting on for his apostolic work: prayer and mortification."[158]

Months went by, and the priest continued to beg for help. "I go on asking prayer and mortification from many people. What fear people have of expiation!" he exclaimed with sorrow and surprise.[159]

One of the Apostolic Ladies' auxiliaries notes, with cheerful simplicity, that no one could escape his prayer campaign. "Pray hard for me, pray hard for me," the chaplain told her. "What is Father Josemaría going to do, that he's asking so much prayer for?" she wondered.[160]

In January 1929, as one of the Ladies lay dying, the chaplain begged her to intercede for him in the next life. He wrote in his journal:

> I recall—sometimes with a certain fear, that it may have been tempting God or done out of pride—that as Mercedes Reyna was dying, . . . without my having thought of this ahead of time, it occurred to me to ask her, and I did ask her, "Mercedes, ask our Lord, from heaven, that if I am not going to be a priest who is not just good, but holy, that he take me young, as soon as possible." Later I made the same request to two lay persons, a young lady and a boy, and every day, at Communion, they make this prayer for me to the good Jesus.[161]

Having attended this Apostolic Lady in the last days of her illness, he afterward sought her protection and often visited her grave. That summer he made a novena to her for his intentions, praying the Rosary daily on his knees before her tomb.[162]

The Work was taking root, and the founder felt moved to give himself totally, as a holocaust, though never as a "victim soul." The idea of making a spectacular self-sacrifice, as if disdaining to offer to God the little sufferings and crosses of everyday life, was far removed from his way of being and thinking. In fact, he so disliked it that he found the very term "victim soul" repugnant.

Yet he did seek something special to offer by way of expiation. Three days after finishing his novena in the cemetery, feeling spiritually prompted to do this, he unhesitatingly asked our Lord to take from him his health, as an expiatory offering.

In his journal he writes, "On August 11, 1929, according to a note that I wrote that day on a holy card that I keep in my breviary, while giving Benediction in the church of the Foundation for the Sick, without having thought of this beforehand, I asked Jesus for a serious, painful illness, for expiation." Later he adds, "I believe that our Lord granted it to me."[163]

7. *February 14, 1930*

Recapitulating his apostolic desires since October 2, Father Josemaría says with great simplicity, "From the first moment, there was an intense spiritual activity and I started looking for vocations."[164] But where had he gotten the idea of asking the Lord, at the deathbed of that Apostolic Lady, to make him a holy priest, if not from the fact that he saw himself as being plunged "in tepidity and negligence"?[165]

There was this much basis for it in fact, that he perceived an enormous discrepancy between his apostolic efforts and the magnitude of the enterprise entrusted to him, and this made his conscience uneasy. "What can a little child do," he says, "who has a mission to carry out but lacks the necessary means, age, knowledge, virtues, and whatever else? Go to his mother and to his father; go to those who can do something; ask help from his friends. . . . That is what I did in the spiritual life. Keeping time, of course, with the blows of the discipline. But not always: there were times when I didn't."[166]

When he saw the huge gap between his mission and his resources, it seemed to him as if his soul had fallen into a stupor that he could not shake off.

> After 1928, although I set to work immediately, I also slept. *Ego dormivi, et soporatus sum; et exsurrexi, quia Dominus suscepit me* ["I lie down and sleep; I wake again, for the Lord sustains me"] (Ps 3:5). I slept, I felt like I was in a stupor; it was the Lord who led me and got me to work with more intensity each day.[167]

Years later, he remained convinced, in his heroic humility, that he had put up resistance, and he continued to reproach

himself for it. "The Lord well knows that I started my work
in Opus Dei reluctantly, and for this I ask your pardon many
times over," he would apologetically say to members of the
Work.[168] It seemed to him as if his will had failed and he had
been inwardly divided once God answered his prayers.

> I wanted, and I did not want. I wanted to carry out
> what was a definite mission, and from the first day an in-
> tense spiritual labor began. But at the same time I didn't
> want to, despite the fact that from the age of fifteen to the
> age of twenty-six I had been constantly calling out to our
> Lord Jesus, asking like the blind man in the Gospel,
> *Domine, ut videam!*—"Lord, let me see!" (Lk 18:41). And at
> other times, in not very elegant Latin, *Domine, ut sit!*—"Let
> it be, this thing that you want, this I don't know what!"
> And the same to the Blessed Virgin: *Domina, ut sit!* ["My
> Lady, let it be!"].[169]

And yet he insisted that he had carried out his apostolate
with real effort and conviction, "always without vacillating,
although I *did not want to!*"[170] He could not explain that apparent contradiction, that interior resistance. The problem
was not that he was unwilling to fulfill his mission, but
rather that, while entirely dedicated, he constantly aimed at
still more generous goals.

He had received a "clear general idea" of what the Work
would be, but no clue as to how to carry it out. After the inspirations stopped coming, he remained for some time in semi-
darkness, with the nucleus of the divine plan clear, but with
no specific, practical ideas on how to give it tangible shape.
There was a cessation of "that spiritual flow of divine inspiration" which had been "outlining and delineating what God
wanted."[171] He felt a lack of courage to undertake this crushing
divine task , and it was for this that he reproached himself: "I
was a coward—I feared the cross that our Lord was putting on
my shoulders."[172]

(The idea that they have been cowardly is, in saints, an offshoot of humility. It comes from recognizing that, compared with the greatness of the divine invitations they have received, they have responded—so it appears to them—tepidly and feebly.)

But does even the fear or cowardice he thought he saw in himself account for his anxieties? Are there not causes having more to do with his own makeup—in which, certainly, there was not much room for indecision, fear, or discouragement? From early childhood, as we have seen, he felt repugnance for ceremony and ostentation. That natural tendency became deeply, supernaturally rooted in him. "I have felt in my soul, from the time that I decided to listen to the voice of God—to those hints of the love of Jesus—a desire to hide myself and disappear; a desire to live out the program of John the Baptist: *Illum oportet crescere, me autem minui* ['He must increase, and I must decrease'] (Jn 3:30). It was right that our Lord's glory should grow, and that I should not be seen."[173]

His misgivings thus stemmed from the idea that "beginning a new foundation might be motivated by pride, by a desire to be immortalized."[174] He had always been mistrustful of the extraordinary and of showy novelties. In 1932 he wrote to the members of Opus Dei:

> You know the aversion I have always had to that ambition of some people to make new foundations—when it is not based on very supernatural reasons, which the Church has to judge. It seemed to me, and it still seems to me, that there are too many foundations and founders. I saw the danger of a kind of "foundation psychosis" that was causing people to create unnecessary things for reasons I found ridiculous. I thought, perhaps uncharitably, that sometimes the purported motive was the least important thing—that the essential thing was just to create something new and get to be called a founder.[175]

The most logical explanation of these contradictory senti-ments—acceptance of a mission, resistance to founding some-thing new—is God's intervention. This appears from the ces-sation of those practical inspirations he had received up to October 1928. With it came confirmation of the supernatural origin of the Work, since its founding, besides being beyond his natural capabilities, also conflicted with his personal tastes. Seeing him tacking between resistance and enthusi-asm, God decided to take a hand.

> The Lord . . . , seeing my resistance and my simulta-neously enthusiastic and feeble efforts, gave me the ap-parent humility of thinking that there might already be in the world some things which were no different from what he was asking of me. This was hardly a rational cow-ardice; it was the cowardice of love of comfort, but also proof that I was not interested in being the founder of anything.[176]

In the midst of that uncertainty, without halting his efforts to get the Work under way, he nursed a secret hope of not having to found it after all—of finding it ready-made, some-where else.

> With a false humility, while I worked on finding the first souls, the first vocations, and forming them, I said to myself, "There are too many foundations. Why more? Isn't it possible that I can find somewhere in the world, al-ready constructed, this one that our Lord wants? If so, it would be better for me to go there and become a soldier in its ranks, and not to found anything, because that would be pride."[177]

He sought information about institutions in Spain and else-where. But as soon as he took a close look at them, he saw that they were not what he was looking for. "There came into my hands," he wrote in his journal, "reports of many modern institutions (in Hungary, Poland, France, etc.) which were doing *unusual things*. . . . But Jesus was asking of us, in his Work, as an absolutely essential virtue, naturalness!"[178]

He did not specify what those "unusual things" were. From the very start, however, the spirituality of the Work was characterized by "simplicity, not attracting attention, not showing off, not being secretive"—in short, by "avoidance of any kind of spectacle."[179]

In November 1929, while Father Josemaría was still involved in that fruitless search, the inspirations began again.[180] That "resumption of the spiritual current of divine inspiration," following more than a year of drought, brought with it practical lights for his work as founder. Here was palpable proof that it was God who was managing the enterprise.

> The silence of the Lord from October 2, 1928, feast of the Holy Angels and vigil of the feast of Saint Thérèse, until November 1929, says many things. . . . It is indubitable evidence that the Work is of God, for had it not been a divine inspiration, it stands to reason that after finishing that retreat in October 1928, this poor priest would have immediately—with more enthusiasm than ever, since the enterprise was now sketched out—continued writing notes on and planning the design of the Work. But this was not the case. More than a year went by without Jesus speaking. That happened, among other reasons, for this purpose: to prove, with hard evidence, that his donkey was only an instrument—and a poor instrument at that![181]

* * *

He had already forgotten about his requests for information when one day he received some brochures about apostolic organizations.[182] Looking back, in 1948, he wrote: "Finally I received some information about Cardinal Ferrari's Company of Saint Paul. Could this be it? I tried to find out (this would have been toward the end of 1929)."[183]

(In another of these magazines, *The Seraphic Messenger*, which he sometimes distributed to the sick, some articles also appeared about the foundations established in Poland by Father Honorato.)[184]

But, continuing what he had to say about the Company of St. Paul:

> I tried to find out (this would have been toward the end of 1929) and, when I learned that the Company of Saint Paul had in it not just men but also women, I wrote in my Catherines (if I didn't burn them, they will be found among the packets in the archive, and one can read there the same thing I am writing now) that even if there were no difference between Opus Dei and the Company of Saint Paul other than the fact that we do not admit women in any capacity whatsoever, that by itself is a huge difference.[185]

The journal entry he refers to was probably in the notebook that was destroyed. Nevertheless, in anything he said on this matter at that time, women were always categorically excluded. "I wrote," he said on another occasion, "that 'never—no way—will there be women in Opus Dei.' "[186]

Evidently, what he "saw" on October 2, 1928, was not events or historic details, but only the essential element of the divine message. Considering the circumstances—his distaste for founding anything new, and the absence of practical directives from God—it is hardly surprising that he was not bent on including women in the enterprise.* He had, as a personal opinion, an idea that was specific, clear, and definitive: women were not called to form part of the organization.[187]

But God did not wait long to correct that view.

---

*At this time, under canon law, organizations in the Church that required of their members full, all-embracing dedication to God were either of men or of women, not of both.

A short time later, on February 14, 1930, I was celebrating Mass in the little chapel of the elderly Marchioness of Onteiro, Luz Casanova's mother, whom I
took care of spiritually while I was chaplain of the Foundation. During the Mass, right after Communion, the
whole women's branch of the Work! I cannot say that I
saw it, but *intellectually,* in detail, I grasped what the
women's branch of Opus Dei was to be. (Later I added
other elements, developing this *intellectual vision.*) I gave
thanks, and, at the usual time, I went to the confessional
of Father Sánchez. He listened to me and then said, "This
is just as much from God as the rest."[188]

The participation of women in Opus Dei had been something already implicit in the general vision of October 2.
Now his hesitations and investigations into similar institutions came to an end.

I noted down, in my Catherines, the event and its date:
February 14, 1930. Later I forgot the date, and I let some
time go by, but never again did it occur to me to think, with
my false humility (that is, love of comfort, fear of struggle),
of becoming a little soldier in the ranks. It was, beyond any
doubt, necessary to do some founding.[189]

The events of both October 2 and February 14 caught him
unprepared, but especially the latter, which flew in the face
of his conviction that there was no room in Opus Dei for
women. As he saw it, this made the Work's divine origin all
the more clear.

I always believed, and I still believe, that our Lord, as
on other occasions, "managed" me in such a way that there
would be a clear, external, objective proof that the Work
was his. I said, "I don't want women in Opus Dei!" and
God said, "Well, I do."[190]

That was not the end of the surprises. Speaking about the paradoxes of the founding, he would say one day:

> The foundation of Opus Dei happened without me; the women's branch, against my personal opinion; and the Priestly Society of the Holy Cross,* when I was seeking it but unable to find it.[191]

---

* The Priestly Society of the Holy Cross, which originated on February 14, 1943, made it possible for Opus Dei to have priests of its own.

6

Personal Notes

1. Why "Work of God"?

The Escrivás had been living in the apartment on Fernando el Católico Street for less than two years when, in September 1929, Doña Dolores and her children had to move to José Marañón Street. Their new home was an annex to the Foundation for the Sick with a separate entrance from the street. They made the move not out of a desire to improve their living conditions, but simply because the apartment came with the chaplaincy. For one person it would have been comfortable, but for a family it was very cramped. Still, it did have the advantage of being directly connected with the main building, so that the chaplain could enter the church without having to go outside.[1]

Doña Dolores may have seen her priest-son more often now, but then again she may not, considering how busy he was. Besides his duties as chaplain and his treks through the poorer neighborhoods of Madrid to visit the sick and the poor, new tasks were also piling up. He had to maintain his mother and siblings in a dignified fashion, and he had to complete his studies for the doctorate in law—his reason for coming to Madrid. A person with less spirit and optimism than Father Josemaría would have had the disheartening sense of being trapped in a net of commitments that tightened every day.

What money he had came from his chaplain's pay (insufficient for the needs of a family), his income from the Cicuéndez

Academy, and whatever he could make giving private lessons.[2] It did not add up to enough to raise his family out of the poverty they had been bearing, albeit nobly, since their years in Logroño. Many schemes for improving their lot occurred to him, but these were passing fancies that quickly left his mind, displaced by the demanding, inescapable mission of giving birth to the Work.[3]

Given the pressure of that divine mission and the instability of his family situation, something had to give; and that something was his legal studies. Father Josemaría did what he could under the circumstances. On December 15, 1929, he submitted to the dean of the law school a formal request for permission to take two examinations in the January 1930 session: History of Juridical Literature and Social Politics. But, as usual, his desires exceeded his possibilities. He was able to take only the History of Juridical Literature exam, and in it he obtained only the middling grade of "Notable."[4]

Now he began to look for an appropriate research topic for his doctoral dissertation. On March 7, 1930, he wrote to Father Pou de Foxá, in Saragossa, asking his advice:

> You must have already received, several days ago, a long letter from me. Well, today I am writing to send you the sheets on which I copied down the list of canon law papers which the National Library has in its manuscript section, to see if you can help me find a way I could use one or another of those manuscripts for my dissertation—perhaps, for example, by doing a commentary or critique, with introduction and bibliography. If you see that no such thing will do, then—imposing, as always, on your affection and kindness—I would appreciate it if you could suggest a specific topic and some sources.[5]

Eventually he selected a topic in canon law history concerning the ordination of mestizos and mulattos in Spanish America during the colonial era.[6] Two years later, he had collected enough material to be able to give Father Pou de Foxá this update:

> I was thinking of sending you a big stack of sheets, but it is impossible for me to write more.
>
> We'll get to talk later, if, finally, I can't keep from making a trip to the city on the Ebro.* . . . But if we don't see each other, I'll send you in June a ton of paper—arm yourself with patience, for reading it.[7]

Obviously he did not lack either tenacity or good will. But he did lack some other things indispensable to finishing the job. In his journal he writes, "I have no money. Since I have to work—sometimes too much—to support my family, I have neither the time nor the inclination to work on the next steps toward the doctorate."[8]

Those few calm words reveal the material burdens that weighed him down. Lack of money meant he had to work extra hours at the Academy to maintain his family, without omitting any of his interminable obligations as chaplain. How could he possibly devote himself to doctoral research and study?

And then, of course, there also was his most joyful and weighty burden. Making the Work a reality was a serious task. No matter how many hours were dedicated to it, they were always too few, since obviously the founding of the Work was going to require a great deal of prayer, much sacrifice, and a lot of apostolate. Father Josemaría tried by all available means to extend the range of his apostolate. He asked the Apostolic Ladies, and their auxiliaries at the Foundation for the Sick, for the names and addresses of young relatives and acquaintances, and insistently begged them to pray for his spiritual intentions. Thus, in his comings and goings, in his intense apostolic activity, the chaplain constantly proclaimed with deeds if not with

---

* The city he is referring to is Saragossa.

words the novelty of the Work. He wondered if the Ladies suspected from their chaplain's hustle and bustle that he had in hand some project unknown to them.

"But didn't you realize," he asked them many years later, "when I was at the Foundation, when I was going around with those young men, that something was afoot?" Josefina Santos confesses, "I didn't realize anything."[9]

The apostolate he was doing among young men and priests at the Academy, the Larra Street residence, and the Foundation soon began to grow. In 1930 he began among blue-collar workers and craftsmen a work similar to the one he was carrying out among students. It may have had its origin in a mission organized by the Foundation for the Sick for men of various occupations. As part of the mission, the chaplain was asked to give a talk and hear confessions. It was the first time he preached officially in Madrid before a congregation of blue-collar workers.

The exercises took place in what was called the Bishop's Chapel, which was next to the church of San Andrés. Father Josemaría spoke in simple words straight from the heart, free of the rhetorical frills and pompous gestures of traditional oratory. To overcome his nervousness and keep his hands still, he held tight to the sanctuary railing. It was June 13, 1930. In his journal he reports "I was there, in the Bishop's Chapel, when a young lawyer"—he is speaking of himself—"gave a talk about religion to several hundred laborers. The talk was well received. I was very happy. We will do this sort of thing, though not in a sacred place, and something more. . . ."[10]

He spent time on the personal formation of those people, hearing confessions at their meeting places, talking with them wherever he could.[11] In practically no time he had a group of workers following him. "By now, in the Work, there are also some lower-level employees and craftsmen," he writes in December 1930.[12] The universal call to sanctity was for people of all occupations. "Members of the mechanical trades and other manual workers," he continues, "have to understand well the beauty of their work in the eyes of God." When a painter joined the group later on, the founder observed: "His vocation is to prayer and art."[13]

* * *

The Work was beginning to develop a history. In its first months it led a "life of gestation—unborn, but very active."[14] The founder writes: "The Work was growing within, not yet born, in gestation: there was only personal apostolate."[15] Although he had no examples to follow or methods to adopt, he found that, little by little, the features of a new spirituality were emerging from his personal experience. By divine inspiration, ideas and plans for what would be the internal organization of the Work were being translated into notes and more notes, which he would later incorporate into his *Apuntes.*

One day in June 1930, upon rereading what he had just written, the founder marveled at the grandeur of what was developing. "As I consider what I have written," he says, "I am immediately convinced that it would take the imagination of a novelist who is a raving lunatic, or who has a fever of 105°, to come up with on one's own the idea of a work like this. If it was not of God, it would have to be a plan concocted by someone drunk with pride."[16]

From the point of view of canon law, of course, the Work had not yet even been baptized. For the moment, though, he did not care that it lacked even a name of its own. It was known by the generic name of "the Work," but could just as well have been called "the Mission"—anything indicating a task, dedication, a project of apostolic work, or evoking the idea of prayer raised to God for the praise of his name. What mattered for Father Josemaría was that he was putting into practice the central message of the Work. People of all classes and professions were gathering by his side. Or, rather, he was going out to meet them and gradually making the good news known. No matter that he was dealing with just a handful of souls, for from that small group would grow, in time, a vigorous worldwide enterprise. In that seed was contained the future tree.

The silence he kept is not surprising, considering the repugnance he had always felt toward anything smacking of ostentation. It was quite in keeping with his desire to "hide and disappear." He himself explains it thus: "I did not give the Work any name. I would have preferred, had it been possible (it wasn't), for the Work not to have had a name, nor any juridical identity. . . . For the time being, we were simply calling our work 'the Work.' "[17]

The founder expected that the Lord, in due time, would give it a suitable name, but meanwhile his humility was satisfied by that generic term. His thinking about a name was that it should have two specific characteristics. First, it should have no reference to himself, no mention of or link to the name "Escrivá." And second, it should be something not allowing of a derivative name for members, since they were and should always be ordinary Christian faithful. The solution, then, would be to find some abstract name.[18] The Work went for a long time without having an actual name.

Although Father Josemaría had earlier poured out his soul to several confessors, he was now without a spiritual director.[19] Thus he did not have "anyone to whom I could open my soul and communicate from my heart of hearts that which Jesus had asked of me."[20] Hearing at the Foundation that a certain Father Sánchez took very good care of his penitents, he went one morning, near the beginning of July 1930, to the residence on De La Flor Street to ask the Jesuit to be his spiritual director.

> Then, slowly, I revealed to him my soul and told him all about the Work. Both of us saw in all of it the hand of God. We agreed that I would bring him some sheets of paper—a packet of note-sized sheets, it was—where I had written out the details of the whole endeavor. I brought them to him. Father Sánchez went to Chamartín for a few weeks. When he returned, he told me that the enterprise was from God

and that he would have no problem being my confessor. A few years ago I burned the packet of papers. I regret that.[21]

Starting then (at the end of July 1930), Father Josemaría periodically met with his new spiritual director to discuss, not things having to do with the founding of the Work, but matters pertaining to his soul. . . . "But getting back to the name of our Work," he recalls, "one day I went to talk with Father Sánchez, in a parlor in the De La Flor residence. I talked to him about my personal things (I would only mention the Work insofar as it related to my soul), and the good Father Sánchez asked me at the end, 'How is that work of God going?' When I was already back on the street, I began to think, "Work of God. *Opus Dei! Opus, operatio* . . . work of God. This is the name I've been looking for!' And from then on it has always been called Opus Dei."[22]

That name fit the Work admirably, since one of its essential features is sanctification of work. The name encapsulates the theology of sanctification of work with all that it entails: the dignity of the vocation of the Christian who lives and works in the world; the possibility of a personal encounter with Christ in one's daily tasks; work as an instrument of apostolate and participation in redemption; the conversion of human efforts and activities into prayer and sacrifice offered to the Creator (all glory to God) . . . or, to put it in a word, the divinization of work which transforms children of God into contemplative souls.

Father Josemaría had found the name he was looking for. Along with its significance, it had the advantage of being "abstract, so that there could not be derived from it a common appellation for the members of the Work."[23]

Was Father Sánchez perhaps just repeating something he had read in the papers Father Josemaría had handed over to him in July? This seems entirely possible, since in one of the notes about the foundation—written probably around the end of March, but in any case before June 1930—one reads, "This is not a question of a work of my own, but of the Work of God."[24]

The above-related concerning the question asked him by his confessor was written in 1948, when Father Josemaría was trying to reconstruct historical records that he had burned. On this occasion he evidently did not consult the journal entries that had been preserved—those written after March 1930. If he had, he would have come across this note of his, dated December 9, 1930:

> *The Work of God:* today I asked myself, why do we call it that? And now I'll answer myself in writing. . . . Father Sánchez, in the course of conversation, referring to the unborn family of the Work, called it "the Work of God."
>
> Then, and only then, I noticed that in my notes I had called it that. That name—the Work of God!!—which seemed like an impertinence, something presumptuous, almost an impropriety, was something that our Lord had me write the first time without knowing what I was writing. He put it on the lips of the good Father Sánchez so that there could be no doubt that the Lord himself was directing that his work bear that name: the Work of God.[25]

It was not his confessor who gave him the name, but God acting through his confessor. In fact, as he clearly states in this note, he had written it before he started showing his notes to Father Sánchez although he had not fully grasped the significance of what he was writing.

In its deepest meaning it was a bold and ambitious name, so much so that it sounded presumptuous to Father Josemaría, who wanted to "hide and disappear." Perhaps he was waiting for a sign; if so, it came when our Lord, by way of Father Sánchez, gave it his stamp of approval. Yet more evidence that the Work was something of God and not an invention of his own! The founder saw himself as an instrument that God humiliated from time to time so that he would never forget that his foundational ideas had come by inspiration, not by his own thought processes.[26]

The name Opus Dei unites the Work's essence—sanctification of human work—with its divine origin.

*　*　*

Toward the end of 1930, Father Josemaría began to sense that God was asking of him a greater dedication to his foundational task. That would require making some time in a day already entirely filled with work. The chaplaincy and visiting the sick of the Foundation were what took up most of his time. If he left the Foundation for the Sick, he would have time; but this would present him with other problems. He would have to give up the apartment and find a way to increase his income. Worst of all would be the problems resulting from the rules concerning priests from outside the diocese, especially the rigorous norms regarding the granting of priestly faculties. It was practically impossible for a priest to reside in Madrid without a justifying ecclesiastical reason. He remembered what had happened to Father Antonio Pensado, that companion of his at the Larra Street residence who had ended up having to leave Madrid.

Around Christmas of 1930, therefore, he set out in search of a pastoral position that would be compatible with his divine mission. Through the good offices of a lady of the palace who worked with the Foundation, he was introduced to some officials of the royal household.[27] They arranged for him an interview with Father Pedro Poveda, secretary of the Patriarch for the Indies.[28]

When he went to visit Father Pedro on February 4, 1931, he found him to be a very gracious man in his late fifties. Father Josemaría briefly explained what he wanted, and Father Pedro promised to try to help him obtain a position as Chaplain of Honor to His Majesty.

"What is that?" he asked. Father Pedro explained that it was an honorary position involving no pastoral duties of any kind, but involving certain privileges with regard to dress and . . .

"But with that appointment," interrupted the chaplain, "can I solve the problem of my incardination in Madrid?"

No. It was a purely honorary appointment carrying with it no right at all to incardination in the capital. It would do nothing to resolve his situation or pull him out of his financial difficulties.

"Then I have no interest in it," he said.[29]

Father Pedro was enormously surprised to hear the young priest reject such a prestigious position, a position so sought after by other clerics simply because he wanted to be incardinated in Madrid in order to serve souls. Father Josemaría, for his part, felt that for this spiritual service he did not need privileges or titles. Nor money, for that matter. If God had so obviously deprived him of material means, would he not also take charge of the expenses of the apostolate?

A few weeks after turning down this offer, he entered into negotiations with another official. Some other ladies who worked with the Foundation for the Sick introduced him to the undersecretary of the Ministry of Justice and Ecclesiastical Affairs, Señor Martínez de Velasco, who had a position to offer that would have fit Father Josemaría like a glove and was perfectly in line with his desires.[30] Señor Martínez promised to send for him soon. That was on April 10, 1931. The interview never took place because four days later the Republic was proclaimed.

Father Josemaría wrote in his *Apuntes íntimos*: "God did not want it. It doesn't bother me a bit. May he be blessed!"[31]

2. *The "Catherines"*

These notes (*Apuntes íntimos*) to which we have been referring are writings of a confidential nature that the founder specified were not to be read until after his death.[32] They started at an early date and included the loose notes Father Josemaría brought with him to read and meditate on during his retreat of October 1928. But, as has been mentioned, neither the first notebook nor those early loose notes have come down to us, since their author destroyed them. What we have of the *Apuntes* begins with the second notebook, which he started in March 1930.

The entries are generally brief considerations, on all kinds of topics, which in the beginning he wrote for his own

spiritual benefit, so that he could think them over in prayer.
He called them "Catherines" (*Catalinas* in Spanish), because
they were, like Saint Catherine of Siena in her day, a means of
maintaining and stoking up a restlessness of spirit—in his
case, the restlessness produced by the extraordinary graces he
had been receiving since his first call, in Logroño.[33] As he
himself expresses it, "These are candid notes—Catherines, I
called them, in honor of the saint of Siena—which for a long
time I wrote kneeling down, and which served me as reminders and wake-up calls. I think that, as a rule, when I was
writing with that childlike simplicity, I was praying."[34]

The *Apuntes,* all of them handwritten, took up eight notebooks, not counting the fourteen appendices, which were written
on loose sheets of paper. They are not complete, and on more
than one occasion came near to perishing. "I burned one of the
books of my personal notes years ago," confesses their author,
"and would have burned them all if someone with authority,
and later my own conscience, hadn't forbidden me to."[35]

When Father Sánchez agreed to be his spiritual director,
Father Josemaría started using these personal notebooks also
as a way to open his soul to him more fully. The third notebook contains the following entry, written at the end of February 1931:

> When I write these Catherines (that's what I always
> call these notes), I do so because I feel urged to preserve
> not only the inspirations of God—I very firmly believe
> they are divine inspirations—but also other things in my
> life that have served, and could serve, for my spiritual
> benefit and help my father confessor get to know me bet-
> ter. Otherwise I would have torn up and burned these
> sheets and notebooks a thousand times, out of self-love
> (the child of my pride).[36]

By that time the founder already had a small group of
followers, among them some students, to whom he was

communicating the spirit of the Work by means of commentaries on some of his notes. Pedro Rocamora, the law student who at times served his Mass at the Foundation for the Sick, recalls that some Sunday evenings he would get together with a few young men and read them a page or two from a notebook, or just comment on two or three brief points.[37]

Because the things he recorded in those notebooks included inspirations from God and personal thoughts concerning the state of his soul, he saw himself exposed to possible indiscretion on the part of anyone reading them. This worry eventually led him to decide to separate the material for discussion with his confessor from the material referring to the Work and its apostolates. On May 10, 1932, he wrote:

> I am losing the freedom to write my personal things in these notebooks. Since I have not made a separate copy of the things referring to the Work, I can't show them to people to introduce the Work without the risk of their reading those other things as well. Therefore, with the help of God, I will try to do that job this summer: separating out my personal stuff, the things I write just for my spiritual director and myself.[38]

More than once he seriously considered burning all those notebooks. But his confessor forbade him to do so, and he realized that keeping these records would be a way of living in humility and simplicity, although God only knew what it cost him. "There are times, and plenty of them," he says, "when it bothers me to have written or to write the Catherines. I would burn them if I weren't forbidden to. I have to continue: it is the path of simplicity. But now I try to make everything as impersonal as possible."[39]

Following the path of simplicity meant having to let the interested party—Father Sánchez—see even his remarks on discourtesies that now and then came to him from his confessor. "I have written this out in detail," he observes in one of his journal entries, with regard to one put-down, "because, surely, Father Sánchez will have to read it and will see that these little things, which occur fairly often, hurt my feelings—and therefore are, I believe, very good for me."[40]

Once he starts censoring details of his interior life, where will it end? "The Catherines no longer have any intimacy to them. There are so many things I don't write down!" he complains on one occasion.[41] But it is useless to lament what has been lost. In spite of everything, his journal entries are still quite generous and spontaneous, even when the author is being cautious. In the entry for December 3, 1931, for example, he writes:

> This morning I backtracked and became a little boy, to greet our Lady before her statue on Atocha Street, at the top of the house the Congregation of Saint Philip has there. I had forgotten to greet her. What little boy misses a chance to tell his mother he loves her? My Lady, may I never become an ex-child.
>
> I won't relate any more details of this sort, lest by airing them I should lose those graces.[42]

Where possible states of mystical contemplation and other supernatural events are concerned, the author of the journal resorts to silence, to depersonalization, or to leaving things half said. In one journal entry he says: "I renewed my resolution of not writing anything about prayer except when I am ordered or feel forced to. If I do write something about that, because it might profit me or others, I'll have to leave out anything personal."[43]

The end result of such precautions is that the reader is left in a kind of haze with respect to supernatural phenomena and experiences. An example is the journal entry for the day after his resolution not to give details about his prayer life: "12 Dec 1931: Today, during the praying of the Divine Office, Jesus opened up to me its meaning as he has seldom done before. At moments it was ecstasy."[44] With this he considers the matter closed.

The recourse to depersonalization, which from now on will be his preferred mode for journal entries, amounts to presenting things dryly and baldly, without their marrow or juice, or perhaps by way of toned-down words and descriptions, or with the distancing that comes from speaking in the third person. For example, he writes on April 10, 1932: "Yesterday, in a place where people were talking and music was being played, I was given prayer with an inexplicable consolation." Later he reports on preparing some little girls at Santa Isabel School for First Communion, and then, with no transition, ends the entry thus: "Right after the ecstasy of Love: my usual stupidities!"[45]

What was this "ecstasy of Love," and what were those "usual stupidities"? The author of the *Apuntes* does not explain.

To be sure there are rare instances in which he lifts the veil and expresses what he feels: for instance, "I don't want to leave this out, although I have for some time been depersonalizing these Catherines: Often, when I am a little tired of the struggle (God will forgive me), I envy the scabby patients in the hospital, abandoned by everyone—I feel sure they win heaven very comfortably."[46]

Does this truncated account suffice? We must once again recall that the author wrote these personal notes only to unburden his conscience and to record graces and events in order to bring them to his prayer. We readers are intruders spying out the secrets of a soul. It should, therefore, not surprise us that he takes refuge in reticence and silence.

In some instances, however, he is making no attempt to depersonalize anything, but is simply concerned with something other than what the reader is curious about. Thus, for example, he writes at the end of February 1932:

> Last Saturday I was in Retiro Park from 12:30 to 1:30 (it was the first time since my arrival in Madrid that I've allowed myself that luxury) and I tried to read a newspaper. Prayer came upon me with such force that, against my will, I had to stop reading. And then how many acts of love and abandonment Jesus put in my heart and on my lips![47]

Is the reader to understand from this that Father Josemaría seldom allowed himself the luxury of taking walks in public parks? Is he perhaps trying to describe his feeling of being carried away in prayer? Actually, in this case his focus is something more down-to-earth: he was trying to read a newspaper and couldn't do it. For in the last line of the previous entry, he mentions waves of prayer that came over him at such times. "I would like to note," he says, "because it is rather odd, that Jesus tends to give me prayer when I start to read the newspaper."[48]

(Observe too, that, in his preoccupation with recording this anecdote, he forgets his earlier resolution not to make entries, especially not descriptive ones, about prayer-related phenomena.)

In general, all the entries that probably refer to extraordinary supernatural events would require a similar exegesis to compensate for the depersonalization imposed by the author. For example, when he speaks of tears, what should probably be understood is the gift of tears. Often when he speaks of prayer, the context indicates a high level of contemplative prayer. And when, as often happens, he declares himself to be full of wretchedness and sin, as he often does, it is surely because he is seeing himself in the light of those divine graces that God, in his mercy, usually grants to saints. Their self-knowledge convinces them that they are great sinners.

There are moments, too, when his simplicity leads him to give himself away, as when he announces: "One of these days I will try to write Catherines with memories of my life in which real miracles can be seen."[49] (Of course it never occurred to him to carry out this impromptu promise.)

* * *

"These Catherines," the founder sums up in one of them, "are for the Work and my soul."[50] The ones about the Work had to do with flashes of foundational insight regarding its supernatural essence, features of its spirit, and principles of its government and organization. The inspirations that the founder received about the Work as a whole were basic ideas from which he deduced ways, means, and other practical points. Here, for example, is the entry for October 7, 1931, written exactly one month after the Lord, in a locution, assured him of the Work's universality and perpetuity: "I believe that the characteristics of the Work of God will be unity, universality, order, and organization."[51]

From those general lines the founder later moved to praxis, to detail, to practical realization. Such apostolic ideas or initiatives sometimes were simply carried out, without further ado, when the time came. Others were touched up or amended, as the founder saw fit. For example, he says in an entry made in 1931: "It would be good for each of the members to read every day, in private, a chapter of the New Testament (everyone reading the same one, each day)."[52] Reading part of the New Testament did become a daily norm of piety, but with no stipulation as to which or how long a part.

On very rare occasions the Lord himself expressly fixed some detail. An entry from December 1931 says: "When we come together to speak about the Work as such, before beginning the talk we will say, *In nomine Patris, et Filii, et Spiritus Sancti. Amen. Sancta Maria, sedes sapientiae, ora pro nobis.* This morning, at the basilica on Atocha Street, Jesus asked me to do this."[53]

The journal notebooks contain a large number of suggestions which, if not exactly foundational, have to do with the life of piety, ways of dressing, liturgical services, and apostolate.[54]

Also reflected in the vocabulary employed by the founder is the essential novelty that the Work represented in relation to ascetical and pastoral theology. Finding the right terminology was hard—he constantly had to struggle with words in defense of a correct concept of what he wanted to express. The author of the *Apuntes* was trying to communicate something essential to the nature of the message he had received (sanctification in the midst of the world), but the standard ascetical language did not adapt itself to that idea.

In fact, its traditional meanings tended to distort what the founder was trying to say.

His continual effort to achieve greater clarity of expression in the *Apuntes* is on many occasions focused on the organization of the Work and its members. He speaks, for example, of "classes" and "members" to distinguish the lay nature or spirit of the Work from that proper to religious. At times he likens Opus Dei to a military order in the midst of the world. At first he called its members White Knights and Ladies—names he soon abandoned.

Sometimes this effort to come up with the exact word was doomed to failure because there was no term denoting a radical dedication of a Christian to the service of the Lord without any change in the person's social, familial, or professional situation. "I would like to find," he says, "a Spanish word other than 'vocation' which would have a similar meaning. Will I have to refer to it as a 'calling'?"[55]

In these terminological details and in many other aspects of the history of the founding, there is a clear gap between what pertains to the Work's essence—what the founder received by divine illumination on October 2, 1928—and subsequent human efforts to figure out how to put it into practice. As early as March 1930, when the first notes that still exist were written, the author of these journal notebooks realized that all their entries would be "a seed that will perhaps compare to the complete entity pretty much as an egg compares to the strutting chicken that emerges from its shell."[56]

* * *

The rest of the notes have to do with the founder's soul. They deal with his interior life—matters of conscience, and so forth—and external circumstances in which his apostolate and ministry unfold.

The basis of his self-knowledge, the humility of the founder, starts with an axiom: "Pure mathematics: José María = mangy donkey."[57]

This definition is used so frequently in the journal that in notes intended for his spiritual director he often abbreviates "mangy donkey." In an entry dated October 9, 1931, he describes the prayer of that day:

> Today, in my prayer, I renewed my resolution of becoming a saint. I know I will accomplish this—not because I am sure of myself, Jesus, but because I am sure of you. Then I thought about the fact that I am a mangy donkey. And I asked—and ask—our Lord to cure the manginess of my miseries with the sweet ointment of his Love, that his Love might be the cauterizing agent that will burn away all the scabs and clean out all the manginess of my soul, that I may vomit out the pile of garbage there is within me. I then decided to be a donkey, but not a mangy one.
>
> I am your donkey, Jesus, but no longer mangy. I'm saying it like this so that you'll clean me, not wanting to make a liar out of me. . . . And with your donkey, Child Jesus, do whatever you please. Like the mischievous children of earth, pull my ears, give this stupid donkey a good whack, make him run the way you want. . . . I want to be your donkey. I want to be patient, hardworking, faithful. . . . May your donkey, Jesus, get such control over his poor asinine sensuality that he doesn't respond to the spurs with kicks, that he carries his load with delight, and that his thoughts and his braying and his work are saturated with your Love. All for Love![58]

With that same frankness, he exposes from time to time that layer of sensibility that can tell us so much about a person's character. When, for example, he writes, "Death—the Bald Lady—will be for you a good friend," he is not cracking a tasteless, macabre joke, but, rather, giving free rein to cheerful familiarity with life's end.[59] Contrasting with this good-humored philosophizing is the dramatic rhythm of a rich and passionate interior life.

Lord! Grant me the virtue of order! (I believe it is a virtue, and a basic one: that's why I'm asking for it.)

Lord!! Let me be so much yours that even the holiest affections don't enter my heart except through your pierced heart.

Lord!!! Lord! Let me learn how to keep quiet (because I have never had to repent of keeping quiet, whereas of talking I often have).

Lord!! Grant that I may never knowingly offend you, not even venially.

Lord! Grant me every day a greater love of holy purity, every day a greater zeal for souls, every day a greater conformity with your most blessed will.[60]

The notebooks also record the echoes and the dissonances of the daily events of those times, together with the family affairs of the house of Doña Dolores. The journal is really a trawl net, through whose pages run, all mixed together, impulsive explosions of love for God and mundane statements. For instance, this entry from March 1934: "Fresh news: I have gotten a very close haircut. How it humiliates me to be so fat!"[61]

Announced in this laconic way, his haircut doesn't tell us much. But for him it was a mortification because it accentuated the fact that despite all his fasting and other corporal penances, he was gaining weight.

Properly speaking, the *Apuntes* is not a diary, both because of the contents and because of the discontinuity of its entries, which cover, basically, the years 1930 to 1940. However, it does constitute an authentic and abundant autobiographical source. On the whole, there is great spiritual richness in these pages, with divine graces constantly percolating in them. The author shows himself without disguise, transparently, with the simplicity of a child, even when partly hiding behind the reserve with which some notes are written. Sometimes in a low voice, as though apologetically, he tells us miniscule and delightful details which perhaps could have gone unnoted, but which reveal a magnificent depth of virtue and greatness of spirit. Other times we find complaints and rejoicings, cries of pain and of enthusiasm. "I think," he confesses, "that these Catherines have become . . . a mishmash: wonderful things that are God's, and the childish remarks and alleluias of a simple nun, or of a foolish little monk, that are the expressions of my poor little soul."[62]

This variety by itself makes the journal a stimulating and delightful read. But in addition, it has an invisible autobiographical cohesion. The author's style gives the entries life and appeal, regardless of their subject; all give immediate evidence of a heart on fire with love. Take, for example, this expression of annoyance at carelessness in the liturgy and with regard to sacred objects and places:

It is painful to see how the altars and sanctuaries are prepared for the celebration of feasts. Today, at a rich school, the altarpiece was filled with ridiculous artificial flowers set on steps of half-painted crate board. The tabernacle is usually set up in such a way that the priest, even if he is fairly tall, always has to get up on a footstool to open and close it to take out our Lord. The altar cards* are in unstable equilibrium . . . and so is the priest, because he has to do Charleston-like pirouettes to avoid hitting his head on a hideous gilded brass lamp, which hangs very low over the sanctuary, and to avoid falling flat on his face on the floor from tripping on the carpet, which has been folded over several times to make it fit the steps of the altar. Probably it was discarded as too worn out for the living room of one of those pietistic women, made up like a parrot, who come in, first thing in the morning, looking ready to be put in their casket, powdered white and splotched with red, to the Lord of simplicity, Jesus. And the songs! They are such that one could say the Mass was not sung . . . but could have been danced to!

---

* Prior to the liturgical reforms that followed the Second Vatican Council, certain fixed prayers of the Mass were written on cards that stood on the altar.

And let's just hope that behind the altarpiece, besides a ladder of poor unpainted wood, by means of which our Lord passes daily from the priest's hands into the monstrance, there isn't also a dust-covered pile of odds and ends, converting the holy place into a storeroom for Madrid's flea markets. All this I have seen.[63]

The style is reminiscent of Saint Teresa of Avila, in its informality, spontaneous simplicity, and frankness of expression. Nevertheless, there is one big difference between her autobiography and the *Apuntes*. Despite his general frankness, when it comes time to speak of personal mystical experiences, Father Josemaría slips away. That fidelity to the motto "hide and disappear" is the seal which the founder, by God's will, left imprinted on the Work as a sign of God's favor. "Other institutions have," he says, "as a blessed proof of divine predilection, contempt or persecution, etc. The Work of God will have this one: to go unnoticed."[64]

3. *Spain's Second Republic*

On March 14, 1931, Father Josemaría jotted down this thought: "How little is a life, to offer to God! And if the life is that of a donkey . . . a mangy donkey!! . . . But in spite of everything, I expect great things in this year of 1931."[65]

Just a month later, on April 14, Spain's Second Republic was proclaimed. This of course was not one of those "great things" Father Josemaría was expecting. The truly great things remain forever in the divine present, whereas the arrival of a new regime or revolution soon becomes just one more dead link in the chain of past events.

As a consequence of the municipal elections on April 12, King Alfonso XIII voluntarily gave up the throne and went into exile to avert bloodshed. In the midst of street demonstrations and riots, a provisional government was set up, formed by the various republican parties. The vacuum left by the disappearance of the old regime would quickly be filled by an impassioned wave of populist sentiment. Almost all the politicians raised to power were avowed enemies of the Church who hastily sought to create a secularist state.[66] Many Catholics, in protest, boycotted the general elections of June 28, 1931, which determined the constitutional assembly that would formulate the new Constitution. Most of its members were Socialists, Freemasons, and Radicals with aggressively anti-Catholic sentiments and ideologies.[67]

Meanwhile, terrible events were taking place. On May 11, all over Madrid, monasteries and convents and churches and secondary schools run by religious orders were burned, with the passive complicity of the police and other authorities.[68] The first building to go up in flames was the Jesuits' house of formation on De La Flor Street. Considering the tolerant attitude taken toward this arson, by the authorities in the nation's capital, the provincial capitals felt they could do no less. Incendiary vandalism spread immediately to many other cities: Seville, Málaga, Valencia, Murcia, Alicante, Cádiz . . .[69] In three days, May 11–13, 107 religious buildings, almost all of them churches, monasteries, and convents, were burned.

In the heat of summer, losing no time, the assembly moved to debate a proposed constitution which was the product of a rabid secularism. It is hard to comprehend how such a document could have come about in a democratic country with an overwhelmingly Catholic majority, but many Spaniards lacked a religious formation in civic matters and there was much anticlerical hatred. The founder would later describe the situation in this way:

At that time, in 1928, . . . despite the religious atmosphere, the basic Catholicism, of my homeland, the men were rather distant from God. No one was attending to them. The women generally had a certain piety, but almost always one with not much doctrinal foundation. Men were ashamed to be pious. They breathed the air of the *Encyclopédie,** and the sorry influence of the nineteenth century was still felt.[70]

The parliamentary debates on the religious question centered on article 24 of the draft, which eventually became, with some modifications, article 26 of the Constitution. The draft decreed the Church subject to civil law and imposed all kinds of prohibitions and restraints, especially on religious orders. Religious were forbidden to teach. The dissolution of all religious orders and the nationalization of their property were authorized and specific provisions were made for the dissolution of any religious order whose members took "a special vow of obedience to an authority other than the legitimate one of the state."[71] (This last was a clear reference to the Jesuits.) The Catholic minority in the constitutional assembly could do little to prevent the approval of this article.

On December 9 a constitution was promulgated which was an insult to Catholic sensibilities and an assault on the rights of the Church. In the face of so brazen an assault, the bishops were not slow in issuing a collective statement. On December 12, they declared in a "public and clear manner the Episcopate's firm protest and collective reprobation of the juridical attack on the Church that the promulgated constitution means."[72]

Unilaterally, and in violation of the existing concordat, the state set itself against the Church. The attack was shaped by legislation complementing the articles of the Constitution. On January 22, 1932, the Society of Jesus was dissolved. Next the cemeteries were secularized. After that divorce was legalized. But it was in the following year that relations became most strained. On May 17, 1933, the Spanish parliament approved, as an implementation of article 26 of the Constitution, the Law of

---

* This 28-volume encyclopedia published under the editorship of Denis Diderot between 1751 and 1772 included articles written by many of the most prominent French Enlightenment philosophers, including Voltaire and Rousseau. Many of the articles were strongly anti-Catholic in tone.

Religious Confessions and Congregations. By this law, Catholic worship was put in the hands of the civil authorities; all ecclesiastical goods were declared national public property; religious orders and congregations were forbidden to engage in teaching; and, finally, the state conferred on itself the right to nullify ecclesiastical appointments.[73]

The bishops replied with another collective letter, dated June 25,[74] while the Holy See weighed in even earlier, on June 3, with the encyclical *Dilectissima nobis,* in which Pope Pius XI stated:

> We have not ceased to give the present rulers of Spain frequent reminders . . . of how false is the path that they are following, and of the fact that wounding the soul of the people in its deepest and dearest sentiments is not the way to attain that concord of spirit which is indispensable for the prosperity of a nation. . . . But now We can do no less than raise Our voice still louder against the recently approved law regarding religious congregations and confessions, since this law constitutes a new and graver offense, not only against religion and the Church, but also against the proclaimed principles of civil liberty on which the new Spanish government declares itself to be based.[75]

Secularist politicians and intellectuals had both power and propaganda at their disposal. Guided exclusively by hatred for the Church, they fed grievances and stirred up hostility in the masses of blue-collar workers against religious institutions and their members.[76]

This, then, is the setting in which the founder was operating starting in 1931, and these are historic events that we must take into consideration to appreciate the full significance of his words and attitudes.

The most densely packed pages of his *Apuntes* correspond precisely to the years of the Republic (1931–1936).

Even though written solely for the benefit of the Work and his soul, the notebooks naturally reflect the historic circumstances; personal references are interspersed with references to what was happening in the streets.

* * *

The coming of the Republic on April 14, 1931, was a shock that resounded painfully in the priest's life. In one journal entry we read:

> May the Immaculate Virgin defend this poor Spain! God confound the enemies of our Mother the Church! The Spanish Republic: Madrid, for twenty-four hours, was one huge madhouse. . . . Things seem to have calmed down. But the Freemasons are not sleeping. . . . The Heart of Jesus is also awake! That is my hope. How many times these days have I understood, have I heard, the powerful cries of our Lord that he loves his Work![77]

Father Josemaría's concern was not a political one. He took events as they came, with serenity, not getting involved in partisan concerns. When it came to judging events of a political or social nature, the founder always put ahead of everything else their supernatural ramifications: What effect they would have on souls. From that perspective, the kind of government mattered less to him than the consequences of the rulers' policies on the citizens' spiritual lives. He recommended this outlook to his followers, asking them to stay focused on God. In May 1931 he wrote, "My dear Isidoro: I was very happy to receive your letter, which all of us were impatiently awaiting. . . . About the news: Don't get worked up over political changes; all that should matter to you is that they not offend God. Make reparation."[78]

As events immediately showed, his deeply mistrustful view of the Republic was not ungrounded. The very next week mobs began burning monasteries and convents in Madrid. The Jesuits' house was afire, and thick columns of smoke were billowing skyward, when the chaplain, fearing an assault on the church of the Foundation for the Sick and the sacrileges that might follow, decided to remove the Blessed Sacrament as soon as possible. He told Manuel Romeo, an army colonel (from a family the Escrivás had met in Saragossa) who lived fairly close by, that he would like to bring the Blessed Sacrament to his house. Then, wearing a suit borrowed from a son of the colonel, and accompanied by his brother Santiago and a student from the Cicuéndez Academy, he went to the church.[79]

"The persecution has begun," he says in a journal entry. "On Monday the 11th, accompanied by Don Manuel Romeo, after dressing up as a layman in one of Colo's suits, I consumed the large host for the monstrance, and then, with a ciborium filled with consecrated hosts and wrapped in a cassock and paper, we left the Foundation, through a back door, like thieves."[80]

Silently, looking just like everyone else, the group went up Santa Engracia Street toward Cuatro Caminos. With tears in his eyes, "alone with Jesus in the ciborium" and burning with expiatory sorrow for so much sacrilege, the priest said from the depths of his soul, "Jesus, may each sacrilegious fire increase my fire of love and reparation."[81]

He left the ciborium in the Romeo house. It was not the only time he would have to quickly remove our Lord from a tabernacle.[82] Anticipating history's judgment regarding what the Church in Spain was about to suffer, he summarized the events of those days in these few words: "Hell was unleashed on Madrid."[83]

His family had to flee to a new home. "On the 13th," he says, "we learned that they were planning to burn the Foundation. So at four o'clock that afternoon we went, with our belongings, to 22 Viriato Street, to a run-down apartment—one with no windows facing the street—that by God's providence I found."[84]

A full-scale campaign against the Church began. The anti-clerical press incited the masses to harass God's ministers.[85] Indeed, even on the eve of the Republic things unimaginable a few years earlier had begun happening. "Yesterday," says Father Josemaría on November 21, 1930, "at the barbershop, I gave some people a talking-to. I was tired of hearing them take as infallible the opinions of those obscene pieces of trash *El Sol* and *La Voz*. Well, today I was coming back from Chamartín. Father Sánchez had just told me, with regard to what I just mentioned, that since it's for the good of my neighbor, I should not keep quiet but should speak in a pleasant way, without harshness or anger."[86] Then, walking toward the Foundation, not far from the barbershop, "I was on Fernández de la Hoz Street, near Cisne, when I came across a group of bricklayers. One of them, in a mocking tone of voice, shouted, 'Black Spain!' The instant I heard that, I resolutely turned around and faced them. I remembered what Father had said, and I spoke calmly, without anger. They all agreed that I was right, including the one who had done the shouting. He, and also another of them, shook hands with me. Now these men will not, I feel sure, insult another priest."[87]

His natural spiritedness made it hard for him to ignore taunts and obscenities aimed at a priest. It was good that Father Sánchez toned down his temperament. But that temperament was not the source of the trouble. After the arrival of the Republic, such incidents were an almost daily occurrence.

In 1931, in late July and early August, he made a novena at the grave of Mercedes Reyna, the Apostolic Lady who had died with a reputation for sanctity. She was buried in Este Cemetery, also known as La Almudena. By now it was no longer a matter of isolated incidents. "On one of those days," he tells us, "a group of children was next to one of the two fountains on the road that leads from Aragón Road to Este. They were with some women who were standing in line, waiting to fill their pitchers, jars, cans. . . . From the group of children arose a shout: 'A priest! Let's throw stones at him!' Without even thinking about it, I shut the breviary that I was reading, looked straight at them, and said, 'You brats! Is that what your mothers are teaching you?' I also added some other words."[88]

It would have been something to hear those other words! But judging by what he says about another visit to the cemetery, the problem was more than the mischievousness or impudence of children.

> Another scene: Lista Street, at the end. This poor priest was coming back, tired, from his novena. A bricklayer turned aside from his work and said, insultingly, "A cockroach! It should be stepped on!" Often I turn a deaf ear to such insults, but this time I could not. "How courageous of you," I said to him, "to pick on a gentleman who walks by you doing nothing to offend you! That's freedom?" The others made him shut up, indicating, without openly saying so, that I was right. A few steps further on, another bricklayer tried to give me a reason for his colleague's conduct. "It's not right," he said, "but you have to understand, he hates priests." And he said it so matter-of-factly.[89]

Political demagoguery had opened wide the floodgates of hatred. This was a sad thing for a priest, especially one who was constantly walking from one neighborhood of the capital to another, and running into it everywhere. He did not have to strain his memory to find anecdotes for his journal. Here is another from the days of that same novena.

> More? Even more. Except for the last day—on all eight of the rest, I think—when I left the cemetery, I found waiting for me a devil in the guise of a boy of about twelve to fourteen. When I got a few steps past the cemetery gate, he would start singing, in a bugle-like voice that pierced one to the marrow, the nastiest verses of the Riego hymn. And what looks I then got from a laborer who was working,

with some others, in that little plaza in front of the cemetery! If looks could kill, I would not now be writing my Catherines. I remember being looked at that way one day when I was making my rounds. My God! Why this hatred for those who are yours?[90]

Things got even worse. Throwing stones soon became as popular a pastime as setting fires. The chaplain suffered more than one hit, although he gives no details. The women of the Foundation for the Sick needed plenty of courage to go on carrying out their charitable works. Leaving the Tetuán quarter one day, some of them were badly injured. "They were dragged along the street," says one of their auxiliaries, "and jabbed in the head with a shoemaker's awl. One of them, Amparo de Miguel, heroically tried to defend the others, and they tore off part of her scalp and beat her to the point of leaving her disfigured."[91]

The priest totally took to heart his own advice: "Don't get worked up over political changes; all that should matter to you is that they not offend God."[92] But his spirit was still in rebellion—if not against the political disasters, then against the offenses to our Lord. He made a firm resolve not to display his zeal for the house of God so vehemently. To gain self-control and make reparation, he imposed on himself the hard penance of not reading newspapers.

It was an epic ascetical battle, and not always did he emerge victorious. Sometimes the parliamentary debates on religious issues won out over his good resolutions.

Reading: Apart from spiritual and study-related readings . . . , lately I've prohibited myself even *El Siglo Futuro*. This last, not reading newspapers, is for me no small mortification. Nevertheless, with God's grace, I stayed faithful to it until the end of the parliamentary debate on the so-called law against the religious congregations. What battles these struggles of mine were! These *epics* can be understood only by those who have gone through similar ones. Sometimes conquering; more often, being conquered.

Having told the story of this little part of my everyday life, I consider this business before our Lord God, and I see that, given the apostolate he has put me in, I need to keep up with what is going on in the world. And so, to accommodate both this necessity and my wish to do mortification in reading, I come to the following conclusions. . . .[93]

Here he lays out a disciplined reading plan, with specifics of what and when.

Even so, he remained filled with a vehement zeal for God's glory. Consider his reaction to the approval of article 26 of the Constitution:

> Feast of Saint Teresa of Jesus, 1931: Yesterday, when I learned of the expulsion of the Jesuits and the other anti-Catholic resolutions of Parliament, I suffered. My head ached. I felt ill until evening. In the evening, dressed as a layman, I went up to Chamartín with Adolfo. Father Sánchez and all the other Jesuits are delighted to be suffering persecution on account of their vow of obedience to the Holy Father. What serenely beautiful things he said to us![94]

More than wound him, the insults that the young priest received in the streets spurred him on. He burned with holy indignation. In the beginning he could not silently pass them over, but later he would make spiritual amends for the taunts and crude jokes and, without losing his serenity, redouble his prayers for those who insulted him. At the beginning of August 1931 he wrote:

> The barrage of insults against priests continues. . . . I made the resolution—I am renewing it—of keeping quiet when they insult me, even if they spit on me. One night, in Cham-

berí Plaza, when I was going to the Mirasol building, someone threw at my head a fistful of mud that almost plugged up
my ear. I didn't say a word.

Even more: the resolution that I am talking about
includes pelting those poor haters with Hail Mary's. I
thought that my resolve was very strong, but the day before yesterday I failed twice, kicking up a fuss instead of
being meek.[95]

The effort to tolerate insults and respond with Hail Mary's
established in his ardent nature a new habit. A few weeks later
he wrote:

September 18, 1931: I have to thank my God for a remarkable change. Until recently, the insults and taunts
directed at me, as a priest, since the coming of the Republic (before that, they were very rare), made me furi-
ous. I decided that when I heard such vulgarities and obscenities, I would say to the Blessed Virgin a Hail Mary
for whoever uttered them. I have done that. It has cost
me. But now, when I hear those ignoble words, they only
make me feel, as a rule, deeply sorry for those poor, un-
fortunate people. For when they act in this way, they
think they are doing something noble, since others, ex-
ploiting their ignorance and passions, have made them
believe that, besides being a lazy parasite, the priest is an
enemy—an accomplice of the bourgeoisie which is ex-
ploiting them. Your Work, O Lord, will open their eyes![96]

He did not always succeed in maintaining that attitude.
Sometimes his inner fuming erupted. One such explosion hap-
pened in connection with the dissolution of the Society of
Jesus. In his *Apuntes* he writes:

The outrage to which the Jesuits have fallen victim
has made me physically exhausted and, of course, infuriated. I had another quarrel about this in a streetcar.

Now I will shut up. The cowardly society in which we are living is a web of egoisms. Your Work, Jesus, your Work![97]

The Work was still a creature "in gestation," a divine seed taking root in the founder's soul.

In a short space of time, from 1931 to 1932, a radical change took place in Spanish life. Religious hatred soured relations among citizens. The intellectual sectors exuded rancor against religious activities, against piety, and against doctrine. Meanwhile, under the banner of *Regnare Christum volumus* ["We want Christ to reign"], Father Josemaría was trying to bring forth the Work that God was asking of him. "What God wants is very beautiful," he mused. "On the other hand, I don't understand or see why, it being so needed, a work like this was not started before."[98]

4. *The move to Santa Isabel*

From the two foundational dates (October 2, 1928, and February 14, 1930) Father Josemaría had emerged firmly disposed to fulfill the will of God and seek holiness, since this was the message he would have to preach to everyone from then on. In April 1930 he entered in his journal a powerful expression of that desire: "I want, O Lord, to truly want, once and for all, to have an immeasurable abhorrence of anything that smacks of sin, even venial sin."[99]

In that early stage of its gestation, he understood that before the Work became known publicly it would have to mature interiorly. In April 1930 he says, "My hour has not come. First I must learn to suffer, I must have prayer, I need seclusion and tears."[100]

He understood that the Work's future soundness would depend on his embedding himself in its foundation, by means of much prayer and expiation. In October 1930 he wrote:

I've been thinking—and I'm putting it here so that later on, when I read it, it can go deeper in me and do me good—that the construction of material buildings is very similar to that of spiritual ones. For example, that gilded weather vane on a big building, however much it may glitter and however high it may be, does nothing for the solidity of the building, whereas, on the other hand, an old hewn stone hidden in the foundation, underground, where nobody sees it, is of capital importance to keeping the building from collapsing . . . even though it doesn't shine like that poor gilded brass thing up there on top. And so, for that grand building that is called "the Work of God" and that is going to fill the whole world, the gleaming weather vane should be a matter of no concern. It will come! The foundations: on them depend the solidity of the whole thing. Deep foundations, very deep and strong. The stones of such foundations are of *prayer*; and the mortar holding those stones together has but one name: *expiation*. Working and suffering, with joy. Going deep, since for a gigantic building there must also be a gigantic foundation.[101]

In the next month, he drew up this plan of priorities for his interior life: "First, *prayer*; then, *expiation*; and in third place—in a distant third place—*action*."[102] And in line with that plan, he composed some prayers to be recited daily by the members of Opus Dei—the name which he had given to the Work a short time before. (As we shall see, Father Josemaría then had only three followers.) He tells us about this in his journal entry for December 10, 1930:

These days we are making copies of the "Prayers to Be Recited by Members of Opus Dei." They have been approved by my confessor. It is obvious that our Lord—because this is the way it has to be in the Work—has wanted us to begin with prayer. Praying is going to be the first official act of members of the W. of G. The work, for now, is personal; we will be getting together only for prayer.[103]

As we have seen, Father Josemaría begged prayers from people on the street. He also asked the sick people in his care to offer up their sufferings on the altar of expiation, because he had an indestructible faith that the sufferings of the innocent can obtain graces from the Lord and make up for our wretchedness. Armed with that trust, he expected the prayer of the poor to draw down miracles of heaven. And it did not surprise him that his supplications never failed to be granted.

For him it was a proven fact. "Of this I have a fortunate experience," he confesses. "Whenever, not with emotionalism but with real faith, I have asked our Lord or our Lady for something spiritual (or even something material) for me or for others, it has been granted."[104]

Take the sudden demise of the anticlerical newspapers *El Sol* and *Crisol*. One of the people assisted by the Foundation for the Sick was a poor, somewhat retarded woman named Enriqueta who, having a speech defect, would often say to him, "Pade, le quero mucho" ("Fada, I lub you a lot"). The chaplain asked her to offer her Communions for an intention of his. It was that *Crisol* would go under.

Later he wrote in his journal, "The pride of the wise is confounded by the humility of a poor little retarded woman. It's happened—*Crisol* is defunct. They're going to bring out another paper—*Luz*—but undoubtedly if 'Dumb Enriqueta' keeps praying, that candle too will soon have no wick."[105]

He never stopped asking for prayers. He begged everywhere for spiritual alms, to the point where, as he would say, it became second nature to him.[106]

"I am absolutely certain," he says, "of the limitless power of prayer. . . . Prayer will speed up the hour (*the hour* of completed gestation) of the Work of God. Because prayer is omnipotent."[107] For him it was something like oxygen; never did he cease to breathe it, as the panacea for every ill. When burdens and worries come, he writes, a period of prayer "is the *solace* of those of us who love Jesus."[108]

* * *

Meanwhile, the terrible political events that shook the whole of Spain had created a general atmosphere of anxiety. This is reflected in a gap of nearly two months between journal entries. When the founder resumes these writings on July 15, 1931, his first comment is: "How many thoughts and feelings I could have noted down since the horrendous sacrilegious burning of religious houses! Well, later I'll write something about all that."[109]

What with his family's change of residence, the catechetical instruction and preparation for First Communion that he was giving in the schools run by the Apostolic Ladies, and his house calls to the sick, it is safe to assume that his workload was enormous. And it is certain that the thoughts and feelings he failed to note in his *Apuntes* during the spring of 1931 were only marginally connected with the political events of those days. In saying "later I'll write something about all that," he is referring not to those matters, but to the state of his soul, which he sketches in a beautiful entry dated August 31. Four years of struggle in Madrid; later, an influx of foundational graces; and always docility, abandonment in the arms of the Lord—that of a little boy who abandons himself to the security of his father's arms. God had brought him to a high prayer of union, giving him a sublimity and breadth of horizon, drawing him very close.

I see myself as being like a poor little bird who, accustomed to just flitting from tree to tree, or, at best, to a third-floor balcony, one day in his life felt he could fly up to the roof of a certain modest building, not exactly a skyscraper . . . But lo and behold, an eagle snatches up our bird—mistakenly taking it for a fledgling of its own kind—and in those powerful claws the little bird soars, soars very high, above the mountains of earth and the snow-capped peaks, above the white and blue and rosy clouds, and higher yet, until he is looking directly at the sun. . . . And then the eagle, letting go of the bird, tells him, "Go on—fly!"

Lord, may I never again fly close to earth! May I always be illuminated by the rays of the divine Sun—Christ, Eucharist! May my flight never stop until I find repose in your heart![110]

For many months God had been suggesting to him that he leave the Foundation for the Sick in order to dedicate himself more intensely to the Work. A few days before the arrival of the Republic the problem seemed almost resolved, but then came that abrupt change of political regime and the persecution of the Church. Father Josemaría's foundational and apostolic terrain was Madrid. It was there that he needed to exercise his priestly ministry and find time to dedicate to the specific apostolate of the Work; but as a priest from outside the diocese he was also facing problems getting residential permits and getting his ministerial faculties renewed.

At this point, however, he was not worried about any of those things. He was sure that in one way or another, God would advance his Work. His concern was different.

To save a soul, Father Josemaría was willing to expose himself to grave dangers, including the risk of contracting a fatal illness and the possibility of not having his faculties renewed. One day, when visiting the sick on the list given him at the Foundation, he was told that a young tuberculosis victim was awaiting death in a bordello because his sister, one of the prostitutes, lived there. Deeply concerned that this man's soul might be lost, he got permission from the vicar general to go to the bordello to hear his confession and give him the last sacraments. He went—accompanied by Don Alejandro Guzman, an elderly and very respectable Catholic gentleman sporting a short beard and a Madrid-style cape—to visit the sick man. During that first visit, he obtained a promise from the owner of the place that throughout the day when he brought the Viaticum, our Lord would not be offended in that bordello. On the appointed day, with Don Alejandro serving as acolyte, he brought the Blessed Sacrament to the dying man.[111]

It was not easy for the priest to break away from the Foundation for the Sick, despite the many supernatural reasons he could think of for doing so. His heart had put down roots in that work among children, the sick, and the impoverished. In June 1931 he writes in his journal:

> I am leaving the Foundation. I am leaving with pain and with joy. With pain, because after four long years of working in this apostolate, and of putting my soul into it each day, I know very well that I have a good part of my heart invested in this apostolic center, . . . and one's heart is not a worthless scrap of meat to be thrown around any which way. With pain, too, because another priest in my situation during these years would have become a saint, whereas I, on the other hand. . . . With joy, because I'm exhausted! I am convinced that God does not want me involved with the Foundation anymore; there I am getting destroyed, wiped out. I mean physically—at that pace I would end up getting sick, and, of course, incapable of intellectual work.[112]

But he could not see how to leave the Foundation, and so our Lord had to provide a way.

> I can't finish this part without noting that it was our Lord who put in that final period. I was asking at Holy Mass that he arrange things in such a way that I could leave the Foundation. I think it was on my fifth day of this petition that the Lord heard me. It was his doing. Of this I have no doubt, because he answered my request in full. The concession, in other words, was accompanied by humiliation, injustice, and contempt. May he be blessed! . . . On the feast of Saint Ephrem, our Lord allowed me to leave the Apostolic Ladies.[113]

We do not know in what that humiliation consisted. But his decision evidently became public knowledge right away, for a Holy Family priest, Father Luis Tallada, writes to him at the end of June: "I learned through a letter from the Fathers that you're going to leave the Foundation. The news surprised me to some extent, as I'm sure you'll understand. I predict that Doña Luz will have a hard time finding a substitute who can fill the vacuum caused by your leaving that good work. There are not too many people with a spirit of sacrifice and self-denial."[114]

The feast of Saint Ephrem was June 18. The ex-chaplain, however, continued to offer his services at the Foundation until the Ladies could find a substitute; and in the midst of that turbulent social instability the vacancy was not easily filled. For four months, from June to October, he remained at the helm of the chaplaincy and continued to visit the sick. It was hard to tear himself away from that place into which he had put so much of his heart—from that opportunity to alleviate his neighbor's sufferings and have those sufferings offered up so as to move our Lord's heart. "I think," he said to himself, "that some of those sick people whom I assisted before their death, during my apostolic years, have a lot of influence with the heart of Jesus."[115]

As for the Ladies, it was not so easy for them to accept the idea of no longer having a chaplain always there in a pinch. On the day of his final leave-taking, October 28, Father Josemaría experienced some little unpleasantness that really hurt his feelings. It may have had to do with an unfair comment made behind his back, that he learned about during a visit to the marquises of Miravalles.[116]

Did the move from the Foundation for the Sick to the Foundation of Santa Isabel—to which Father Josemaría found himself committed at the last minute—make any real sense? Certainly it was no remedy for the precarious financial situation of his family. He was leaving a stable position, albeit a demanding and poorly paid one, to become interim chaplain of a convent, without any kind of official appointment and "without receiving any pay at all."[117]

The transfer was not his decision alone, nor, by any means, one that was thought out. It was, rather, a consequence of political circumstances and of the extreme generosity of the young priest. After officially resigning from the Foundation for the Sick, but before ending his services there, he found out about the pitiful situation of the Augustinian sisters at Santa Isabel. For some time their chaplain, Father José Cicuéndez, had been ill. Augustinian Recollect priests had been filling in for him, and everything was fine, until the Republic came. Then the life of those priests became complicated. To tend to the nuns, they had to walk all the way through Retiro Park, or else cross empty lots and go down alongside the wall of the botanical garden to Atocha Street and then climb up to Santa Isabel. This was a lonely and deserted area not to be recommended for people wearing cassocks.[118]

The land occupied by the convent of Santa Isabel had been part of a country estate once owned by King Philip II's noted secretary, Antonio Pérez. After the goods of the estate were confiscated by the Crown, a school for boys and girls who were poor, orphaned, or abandoned was established there in 1595. In honor of Princess Isabel Clara Eugenia, it was named after Saint Elizabeth [Isabel], queen of Hungary.

The convent of the Augustinian Recollect Sisters of the Visitation of Our Lady was moved to this property in 1610. This was an order founded in Madrid in 1589 by a friar, Blessed Alonso de Orozco. The Augustinian nuns were to occupy part of the school and take charge of the girls. Centuries went by, and after more than a few historic vicissitudes, Assumption nuns took over the girls' school in 1876 and ran it from then on.[119]

In 1931 those two institutions, the school of the Assumption nuns and the convent of the Augustinian Recollect nuns, became the Royal Foundation of Santa Isabel. When the Republic came, a government commission was set up to administer all the former royal foundations. The civil authorities, bypassing the ecclesiastical ones, arrogated to themselves the right to make appointments to positions in the foundations.[120] On another front, the old ecclesiastical palace jurisdiction, of which Father Gabriel Palmer was vicar general, continued to function until 1933, when the Holy See suppressed it, transferring its powers to the bishop of Madrid-Alcalá.[121]

This is, in broad outline, the administrative history of the foundations formerly dependent on the royal chapel. Internally, however, the Augustinian convent and the Assumption school in that era of the Republic ran into worse difficulties than the merely legal ones. For a very long time, the Foundation of Santa Isabel had had a rector and two chaplains to take care of the spiritual needs of the nuns, but these appointments, which through the centuries had never caused any problems, were now clearly in a grave situation that left the nuns without spiritual assistance. On June 16, 1931, the rector, Father Buenaventura Gutiérrez y Sanjuán, gave up his position, having been eliminated from the staff list by government decree.[122] The head chaplain, Father José Cicuéndez, had been away on sick leave since December 1930.[123] And as for the assistant chaplain, Father Juan Causapié, some time earlier he had gone over to another of the royal foundations, Nuestra Señora del Buen Suceso. On July 9, 1931, he was named its interim rector-administrator.[124]

In these distressing circumstances, after Father Josemaría had taken care of the convent for a couple of weeks, the nuns of Santa Isabel tried to secure for themselves what they saw as this help dropped down from heaven. They decided to have Father Josemaría officially appointed chaplain as quickly as possible. On August 13, 1931, he reports:

> These days the little nuns of Santa Isabel, which used to be a royal foundation, are trying to get me appointed chaplain of that holy house. Humanly speaking, even in relation to the Work, I think it would be good for me. But

I am not doing anything about it. I am not even seeking a recommendation. If my heavenly Father sees that it will all be for his glory, he will take care of the business.[125]

The chaplaincy would give him the right to continue residing in Madrid, which would be a great advantage for him as founder and for his apostolates. Nevertheless, it seemed to him more perfect not to go seeking recommendations. But then his spiritual director, Father Sánchez Ruiz, advised him to give up this attitude of passive abandonment in the hands of God and to get actively involved in the negotiations. From what can be gathered from his journal entries for these months, his hopes of obtaining the position appeared and disappeared like the bed of a meandering river.

On September 21 the outcome of his negotiations with the civil authorities was still pending, but Father Josemaría could finally write with joy and consolation, "Feast of Saint Matthew, 1931: I have for the first time celebrated Mass at Santa Isabel. All for the glory of God."[126]

He was in fact already the chaplain of Santa Isabel. But this only partly solved his problems as a priest from outside the diocese, for obtaining an official appointment from the civil authorities was a very different kettle of fish. During the fall, therefore, he continued these efforts.

Father Sánchez insisted that he use every possible means to obtain the chaplaincy definitively, and Father Josemaría docilely went along with his confessor's view. At times he saw the turn of events as providential—when, for example, someone offered him a helping hand. At other times he felt things were getting more complicated every day. "It seems," he writes on November 12, "like the devil is interfering with this Santa Isabel thing. It must bother him a lot."[127]

What really was providential was something he learned the next week—that he had been saved in the nick of time from expulsion from the diocese. By becoming chaplain of Santa Isabel, a position at a former royal foundation, he had been transferred to the ecclesiastical palace jurisdiction, precisely at the time the bishop of Madrid was sending priests back to their dioceses of origin. In his journal the chaplain writes:

> Another caress from Jesus for his donkey: In these Catherines it is mentioned that I now belong to the jurisdiction of the Patriarch of the Indies. Well, now it turns out that the bishop of Madrid is making all the priests in the capital sign some papers which, he has publicly stated, have no other purpose than to send back to their respective dioceses all the priests who are not from this one, of Madrid-Alcalá. Of course, such is the way God has taken care of things, this does not affect me at all.[128]

Overnight, with no effort on his part, Father Josemaría had had his stay in Madrid guaranteed. As for obtaining from the government an official appointment to the chaplaincy (which would make it a paid position), this was his prayer to the Lord: "If it will benefit the Work, please let me have it. But if it would deflect me from it by so much as a millimeter, I don't want or ask for it."[129]

5. *New foundational insights*

God was arranging things for the founder to come closer to the cross. But at the same time that God was tempering his soul with sorrow, he also was refining this instrument that was to carry out his plans for Opus Dei. During the summer of 1931, in the midst of great tribulations, Father Josemaría received new lights about the core elements of the doctrine and spirit of Opus Dei. These illuminations displayed before his mind aspects already implicit in the essence of the Work. God thus helped him in his foundational task, guiding him toward its realization, even down to details.

When his sister and brother went to Fonz for summer vacation, he and his mother remained in the apartment on

Viarato Street where they had moved after leaving the Foundation for the Sick. It was then that the Lord began to do those "great things" of which he had had presentiments months before. One event took place on August 7, 1931, and is described in a letter written in 1947.

"I am embarrassed about this," he confesses before beginning the story, "but am writing it to you in response to indications I have received. I will not, however, tell you many of these things." He then continues:

> That day of the Transfiguration, while celebrating Holy Mass at the Foundation for the Sick (on a side altar), when I raised the host there was *another voice,* without the sound of speech.
>
> A voice, perfectly clear as always, said, *Et ego, si exaltatus fuero a terra, omnia traham ad me ipsum!* ["And I, when I am lifted up from the earth, will draw all things to myself!" (Jn 12:32)]. "And here is what I mean by this: I am not saying it in the sense in which it is said in Scripture. I say it to you meaning that you should put me at the pinnacle of all human activities, so that in every place in the world there will be Christians with a dedication that is personal and totally free—Christians who will be other Christs."[130]

Were there no journal entry about the event, it would be difficult to gauge its supernatural dimension, since modesty prevents the priest from telling the whole story in this letter of 1947. Here, though, is the journal entry for that day:

> August 7, 1931: Today this diocese celebrates the feast of the Transfiguration of Our Lord Jesus Christ. When making my Mass intentions, I noted the interior change that God has made in me during these years of residence in the ex-Court. . . . And that the change has come about in spite of myself—without my cooperation, I might say. I think I

then renewed my resolve to dedicate my entire life to the fulfillment of God's will: the Work of God. (A resolve that, right now, I again renew with all my soul.) The time for the Consecration arrived. At the very moment when I elevated the Sacred Host, without my losing the necessary recollection, without my becoming distracted (for I had just made, mentally, the Offering to the Merciful Love), there came to my mind, with extraordinary force and clarity, that passage of Scripture, *Et ego, si exaltatus fuero a terra, omnia traham ad me ipsum* [Jn 12:32]. (Ordinarily, before the supernatural, I feel afraid. Later comes the "Do not be afraid, it is I.") And I understood that there will be men and women of God who will lift the cross, with the teachings of Christ, to the pinnacle of all human activities. . . . And I saw our Lord triumph, attracting to himself all things.

In spite of feeling myself devoid of virtue and knowledge (humility is truth . . . without exaggeration), I would like to write books of fire—books that will race across the world like burning flames and set people ablaze with their light and heat, turning poor hearts into red-hot coals to be offered to Jesus as rubies for his royal crown.[131]

This new light was a specific grace that confirmed the message of October 2, 1928, by accentuating the importance that professional work has within the spirit of Opus Dei as a source of sanctification and apostolate.[132] At the same time, in its echoing of what Saint Paul said to the Ephesians about uniting all things in Christ, it called attention to the value and function of work in the economy of the Redemption.[133]

Christ's raised high on the cross so that all could fix their gaze on him is the sign of salvation and the redeeming cure for the damage inflicted by the sin of our first parents. It was prefigured by the bronze serpent Moses ordered to be raised as a cure for all who had been bitten by the serpents in the desert.

For many, Christ's being nailed to the cross, exposed to the scorn of his enemies and the sorrow of his friends, is a sign of contradiction. But it is not the vision of the Savior, as one condemned to death and offered as a victim on Calvary, that is the source of the locution. Rather, it is his great desire that the reign of his love be established by means of all human activities. Again the founder pronounces his *Regnare Christum volumus*, a phrase that brings all activities of human beings, including the products of their efforts and the creativity of their intelligence, to Christ's feet in praise (*Deo omnis gloria!*), so that he might reign over human wills and govern all creation.

The human being's creative power—a participation in the creative power of God—is manifested in one's human and professional vocation. When industriousness, the pursuit of perfect work to offer to God, leads us to pour ourselves into our work, it converts what is done into means of sanctification and apostolate. By consecrating to God the works of our hands and intelligence, we elevate the human vocation to the supernatural order, and this, through grace, has a sanctifying effect. Thus the reconciliation of all things with God becomes a reality: all of creation is drawn upward by the cross, to be offered by Christ to the Father.

The work of a Christian is not just an obligation owed to family or society. Work fully inserts us in the economy of redemption and is an apostolic instrument for participating in the salvific mission of the Church. The founder explains:

> Considering the magnitude of our apostolic task in the midst of human activities, I try to keep in my memory, united to the scenes of the death—the triumph, the victory—of Jesus on the cross, those words of his, *et ego, si exaltatus fuero a terra, omnia traham ad me ipsum* [Jn 12:32]; "and I, when I am lifted up from the earth, will draw all things to myself."

> United with Christ through prayer and mortification in our daily work, in the thousand human circumstances of our simple life as ordinary Christians, we will work that

miracle of placing all things at the feet of the Lord lifted up on the cross, on which he has allowed himself to be nailed because he so loves the world and us human beings.

Thus simply by doing with love the tasks proper to our profession or job, the same ones we were engaged in when he came looking for us, we fulfill that apostolic task of placing Christ at the summit and in the heart of all human activities, since no upright activity is excluded from the sphere of work that can be made a manifestation of the redemptive love of Christ.

Similarly, work is for us not only our natural means of meeting financial needs and maintaining ourselves in a reasonable and simple community of life with other people, but also—and above all—the specific means of personal sanctification that God our Father has indicated to us, and the great apostolic and sanctifying instrument that God has put in our hands to make the order that he wants shine forth in all of creation.

Work, which must accompany the life of human beings on earth (see Gen 2:15), is for us at the same time— and to the utmost degree, because to the natural exigencies are united others that are clearly of a supernatural order—the point of encounter of our will with the salvific will of our heavenly Father.[134]

* * *

From the beginning, our Lord showed the founder of Opus Dei a design of a universal scope, a catholic nature. Because of this, in the journal entry for October 2, 1930, he states with absolute faith that the Work of God "will fill the whole world."[135]

During the summer of 1931, as we will later see, great tribulations engulfed him. Our Lord used historic circumstances, calamitous in themselves, to purify his affections and bring him to a total abandonment to Divine Providence. But he did not hang back and wait for a more propitious time. The mission entrusted to him urged him on. Looking back later on those years when the Lord had put pressure on him to live exclusively by faith, he testified to the Lord's assistance:

> The first steps, to tell the truth, were not at all easy. But the Lord, as often as necessary—and I'm not talking about miracles, but about the ordinary way that our Father in heaven deals with his children, when they are contemplative souls—in every instance came to our rescue and gave us a supernatural fortitude. . . . Around the year 1930 he made this locution clearly heard, not just once but a number of times: *Et fui tecum in omnibus ubicumque ambulasti* [2 Sam 7:9]—I have been and will be with you wherever you go.[136]

That locution was entered in his journal on September 8, 1931, the feast of the Birth of the Virgin Mary:

> Yesterday, at three in the afternoon, I went to the sanctuary of the church of the Foundation to pray for a little while in front of the Blessed Sacrament. I didn't feel like it, but I stayed there, feeling like a nincompoop. Sometimes, coming to, I thought, "Now you see, good Jesus, that if I am here, it is for you, to please you." Nothing. My imagination ran wild, far from my body and my will, just like a faithful dog, stretched out at the feet of his master, sleeps dreaming of running around and of hunting and of friends (dogs like himself), and gets fidgety and barks softly . . . but without leaving his master. That's how I was, exactly like that dog, when I noticed that, without meaning to, I was repeating some Latin words which I had never paid any attention to and had no reason to recall. Even now, to remember them, I have to read them off of the sheet of paper I always carry in my pocket for writing down whatever God wants. (Right

there in the sanctuary, I jotted down that phrase instinctively on that sheet of paper, out of habit, without attaching any importance to it.) The words of Scripture that I *found* on my lips were, *Et fui tecum in omnibus ubicumque ambulasti, firmans regnum tuum in aeternum* ["And I have been with you everywhere, wherever you went . . . ; your throne shall be established forever" (2 Sam 7:9,16)]. Repeating them slowly, I applied my mind to their meaning. And later, yesterday evening and again today, when I read them again (for—I repeat—as if God was taking pains to prove to me that they were his, I can't recall them from one moment to the next), I well understood that Christ Jesus was telling me, for our consolation, "The Work of God will be with him everywhere, affirming the reign of Jesus Christ forever."[137]

These divine words confirmed the Work's universal and perennial character, in the service of the Church—the uninterrupted continuity of its mission. Strengthened by this locution, the founder wrote on January 9, 1932, to all members of Opus Dei (the few there were then and the immense multitude he expected later), with absolute supernatural faith in that divine enterprise: "Have complete confidence, then, that the Work will always fulfill with divine efficacy its mission; that it will always serve the purpose for which the Lord has wished it to exist on earth. By God's grace, it will be, for all centuries to come, a marvelous instrument for the glory of God. *Sit gloria Domini in aeternum!* [May the glory of the Lord endure forever!]."[138]

In the face of the almost revolutionary upheaval all around him, the founder stressed to his followers the Work's supernatural origin, helping them see that this was no temporary institution or apostolic organization brought about as a response to the religious persecution in Spain. The Work had not come to answer the need of a moment and then disappear once political and social peace was restored.

In the nineteenth and twentieth centuries many institutions had come into existence in response to religious persecution.

They had been created to fill a vacuum, to continue pastoral activities initiated by congregations and orders later expelled from certain countries. The life of those associations was intended to be ephemeral. Once having met the needs of the moment, they were meant to disappear. But that was not how it was and would be with the Work. "While we will see the fall of grandiose, noisy 'apostolates' which now arouse human fervor and enthusiasm," the founder writes in his journal, "the W. of G., growing ever more effective and strong, will last until the end."[139]

The echo of the locution of September 7 was still reverberating in his soul when, on the fourteenth of that same month, our Lord showed him the path that the Work's perpetuity would take: that of an identification of its members with Jesus in humiliation and on the cross. The entry for that date reads: "Feast of the Exaltation of the Holy Cross, 1931: How much today's epistle cheered me up! In it the Holy Spirit, through Saint Paul, teaches us the secret of immortality and glory. . . . This is the sure path: through humiliation, to the cross; and from the cross, with Christ, to the immortal glory of the Father."[140]

* * *

On September 21, Carmen and Santiago returned from Fonz, looking good and healthy. That same day, the feast of Saint Matthew, Father Josemaría celebrated his first Mass at Santa Isabel, with the approval of the Patriarch of the Indies, the ecclesiastical authority to whom the convent was subject.

On September 22, perhaps as he was leaving Santa Isabel, he suddenly found himself completely carried away by a joyful, clear realization of being a son of God. For a long time as he walked through the streets, he was absorbed in a prayer of union and gratitude. In the journal entry for that day, he says: "I was thinking of God's goodness to me, and I got so filled with joy inside that I wanted to shout out along the street, so that everyone would know of my filial gratitude, Father, Father! And, if not shouting, at least in a whisper, I walked along calling him that (Father!) many times, sure that I was pleasing him."[141]

For a long while it was very hard for him to keep from blurting out his filial feelings toward God. His whole day was saturated with affection, and prayer went on from morning to night. On one occasion he remarks, "I find that I pray very little and at the wrong times." But on October 13, just two days after making that remark, he clarifies it: "I said the other day that I do little praying. I need to correct, or, better, to explain, that statement. I have no order in my prayer life (I resolve to have some, starting today); I don't usually do a meditation (starting today, I will do this for one hour each day); but many days I do a prayer of affection from morning to night—sometimes, of course, in a special way."[142]

October 16 was a memorable day, a day bursting with prayer, one of those days when he could hardly read a few lines of the newspaper without being carried off into contemplative union.

> Feast of Saint Hedwig, 1931: I wanted to pray, after Mass, in the quiet of my church. I didn't succeed. On Atocha Street I bought a newspaper (*ABC*) and got on the streetcar. Up to this moment, when I'm writing this, I have not been able to read more than one paragraph of the paper. I have felt flowing through me a prayer of copious and ardent feelings of affection. That's the way it was in the streetcar and all the way home. What I am doing now, this note, is really a continuation. I only interrupt this prayer to exchange a few words with my family (and all they know how to talk about is the religious question) and to kiss my Blessed Virgin of the Kisses,* and our Child Jesus.[143]

Later on, when he had to give details about his prayer of that day (the "most sublime prayer" he ever experienced), he tried to describe the extraordinary grace of union with God

---

* This was his name for a statue of the Blessed Virgin that he used to kiss whenever he left or returned home.

that he had received while riding the streetcar and while roaming the streets. He saw a lesson here. The Lord made him see that divine filiation had to be at the very heart of Opus Dei.

> I felt the action of the Lord. He was making spring forth in my heart and on my lips, with the force of something imperatively necessary, this tender invocation: *Abba! Pater!* I was out on the street, in a streetcar. . . . Probably I made that prayer out loud.
>
> And I walked the streets of Madrid for maybe an hour, maybe two, I can't say; time passed without my being aware of it. They must have thought I was crazy. I was contemplating, with lights that were not mine, that amazing truth. It was like a lighted coal burning in my soul, never to be extinguished.[144]

The message of October 2, 1928, the call to holiness in the midst of the world, was a reiteration of that old but ever new teaching of the Gospel, *Estote ergo vos perfecti, sicut et Pater vester caelestis perfectus est.* "Be perfect, as your heavenly Father is perfect."[145] Now, plunged in the mysterious depths of divine filiation, he saw that astonishing reality not in relation to his success in living up to it, but in relation to his specific mission as founder.

> I can tell you when, to the very moment, and where my first prayer as a son of God took place.
>
> I had learned to call God Father, as in the Our Father, from my childhood. But feeling, seeing, being amazed at that desire of God that we be his children . . . that was on the street and in a streetcar. For an hour or an hour and a half, I don't know, I had to shout, *Abba, Pater!*
>
> There are in the Gospel some marvelous words—all of them are—"No one knows the Father except the Son, and anyone to whom the Son chooses to reveal him" [Mt 11:27]. That day, that day, he wanted that you, with me, would

always feel, in an explicit, clear, definitive way, the reality of being children of God, of this Father who is in heaven and who will give us what we ask for in the name of his Son. . . .[146]

For him the wonderful memory of that day was a confirmation not only of the ineffable quality of being a child of God, but also of the reality that the Work was, truly, Opus Dei. "I thank you, Lord," he said in a meditation in 1971, "for your continual protection and for the fact that you have chosen to intervene, occasionally in a very obvious way (I didn't ask for it—I don't deserve it!), so that there could be no doubt that the Work is yours. There comes to my memory that marvelous experience of divine filiation. On a very sunny day, in the middle of the street, in a streetcar: *Abba, Pater! Abba, Pater!* . . ."[147]

By that new foundational insight, our Lord gave him to understand that even though consciousness of divine filiation already existed in the Work, it had to be the very basis of its spirituality. The founder expresses it this way:

> I understood that divine filiation had to be a fundamental characteristic of our spirituality: Abba, Father! And that by living from within their divine filiation, my children would find themselves filled with joy and peace, protected by an impregnable wall; and would know how to be apostles of this joy, and how to communicate their peace, even in the face of their own or another's suffering. Just because of that: because we are convinced that God is our Father. . . .[148]

His soul was so enriched by this special consciousness of divine filiation that he incorporated it into all aspects of the spirituality of the Work. It is a basic Christian truth and mystery, of course, that, redeemed from sin, we have been elevated to the supernatural order, made adopted children of God, deified by grace, called to intimacy with the Blessed Trinity; but from then on, divine filiation received such special emphasis in the meditation and interior life of Father

Josemaría that it came to inform the whole spirit of Opus Dei and the devotional lives of its members. It empowers them to live in the authentic freedom of children of God, and to work not like employees but like heirs of glory. It induces them to make a special effort to speak to God with the intimacy of a child who is conscious of being loved. In their apostolate it makes them feel the reality of being coredeemers with Christ, in the sense that they are helping him bring souls back to the Father. And it moves them to take joy or suffering, sickness or death as coming from the loving hands of God our Father.

* * *

A few days after that high tide of filial affection in the streetcar, the Lord sent him more illuminations. One night he went to bed reciting one of the aspirations with which he calmed his soul in times of tribulation: "May the most righteous and most lovable will of God be done, accomplished, praised, and eternally exalted above all things. Amen. Amen." And on the next day he wrote:

> Like a response from heaven, to that cry of mine last night, given ahead of time and *who knows why*, this morning at nine, when I went to catch the streetcar to Chamartín, I found myself reciting a verse, which also by chance or by habit (thinking of course that it was something from God) I jotted it down on my sheet of notepaper. *Timor Domini sanctus, permanens in saeculum saeculi; iustitia Domini vera iustificata in semetipsa* ["The fear of the Lord is holy, enduring forever. The ordinances of the Lord are true, and righteous altogether" (Ps 19:9)]. Well, Lord, true indeed and altogether righteous are your ordinances, and holy is the fear of the Lord. But, my Jesus, revering your ordinances with all my soul, I ask you to lead me by paths of Love.[149]

For the rest of the day he found himself without a right understanding of the "fear of the Lord." What distress and anguish he suffered because of the clash he was experiencing between "fear of the Lord" and the aftertaste of that recent *Abba, Pater! Abba, Pater!* [150] Even when night came he remained distressed. In the morning he went to see his confessor, who explained to him the meaning of *timor Domini*: that it should be understood as a fear of offending God, who is the Supreme Goodness, or as a fear of separating ourselves from him, our Father. Father Josemaría, of course, knew this very well but at that moment he felt as if our Lord had lifted a veil from his eyes.

> October 30, 1931: Today I feel somewhat tired, undoubtedly as a result of the spiritual commotion of these last two days, yesterday especially. I don't understand my blindness in the translating of *timor*, since in other instances, e.g., in the phrase *initium sapientiae timor Domini* ["the fear of the Lord is the beginning of wisdom"(Ps 111:10)], I've always understood fear to mean reverence, respect. Jesus, I confidently put myself in your arms, burying my head in your loving breast, my heart united to yours. I want, in everything, whatever you want.[151]

So often was he swallowed up in contemplative prayer that other times, to spare himself explanations, he said only that he was "not doing prayer." On Saturday, December 12, while he was eating lunch at the home of some friends and "not doing prayer," the Lord placed a new light in his mind and on his lips:

> Yesterday I had lunch at the Guevaras' house. While I was there, not doing prayer, I found myself (as at other times) saying: *Inter medium montium pertransibunt aquae* ["Between the mountains the waters flow" (Ps 104:10)]. I think that I have, for some reason, several times had those words on my lips these days, but until this occasion I didn't pay any attention to them. Yesterday I said them with such emphasis that I felt compelled to write them down. I understood them: they are a promise that the W. of G. will overcome the obstacles; that the waters of its

apostolate will flow through all the obstacles that present themselves.[152]

The Lord was telling him that his apostolic action, the development of the Work, would make way for itself like a torrent carving gorges between rocky hills. But perhaps also that his path would not be an easy one? Our Lord was supplying him in advance with strength, optimism, and patience, but without letting him see all at once what the obstacles would consist of, because, as the founder expressed it in 1968, "if at that moment I had seen what was awaiting me, I would have died, so great is the weight of what I have had to suffer and enjoy!"[153]

6. *A cross without Cyreneans**

Father Josemaría was still avidly soliciting prayers from all quarters. Two letters have survived from his correspondence in the fall of 1931. The first, from Father Pou de Foxá, is headed Saragossa, November 20.

My dear, unforgettable José María:

I received your letter, and it made me laugh, with its witticisms. Your resolutions sound good to me. Carry them out vigorously and without flinching. A good Aragonese does not turn back—and as you say, if the Work is great, so is the one forming it, with you being just the material from which God will make what he wants, if the material, which is, to be sure, just mud, doesn't rebel against the Sculptor. Be assured that I am enthusiastically praying for you, and will continue to pray that your work goes forward. After all, I know I stand to gain from this, since it will get me some little place in your prayers, which

* The Spanish word "cirineo" means a helper or assistant. Father Josemaría writes it with a capital letter to make clearer the reference to Simon of Cyrene, who helped carry Jesus' cross.

undoubtedly will bring me graces for rising above the pettiness and baseness of this world. . . .

Regards to your mama and sister and brother, and for you a big hug from your friend,

José Pou de Foxá*[154]

Evidently the chaplain of Santa Isabel had written his friend asking for prayers and bewailing his inadequacy as an instrument for laying the foundation of such a great supernatural enterprise.

The second letter is from Father Ambrosio Sanz, a canon of Barbastro.

Barbastro, December 17, 1931

My very dear friend:

I received your letter of the 26th of last month, and also your telephone message of congratulations.

What is going on, that you speak to me about "beautiful crosses" and ask with such urgency for prayers? Is some kind of tribulation weighing you down, or are you charitably trying like Simon of Cyrene to help someone else bear one? You know I share all your joys, and with all the more reason your sorrows, so if there is anything I can do, just let me know. You will not lack my prayers—poor as they are, much poorer than you suppose. I have, by the way, spoken to some of the chaplains of cloistered convents and made the request you asked me to.

Take good care of yourself, and don't live so dependent on heaven that you forget to keep at least your feet on the ground.

---

*In Spain it was common for men who were close friends to give each other an "abrazo," a hug, rather than shake hands. Letters sent to a friend often closed "with a hug."

Affectionate greetings to your mama and sister and brother. Love and a hug,

A. Sanz[155]

Father Josemaría had, no doubt, written to Father Ambrosio to congratulate him on the occasion of Saint Ambrose's feast day (December 7), and, in passing, opened his heart a little, asking his prayers. Evidently he had worried the canon.

Taking up his cross and his pains, Father Josemaría kept walking a path sown with great graces and far from ordinary sufferings. Along with mystical exultation came a load of tribulation. In September there appeared the first symptoms of a painful trial that would last throughout that autumn.

"I am in great tribulation and distress," he records in his journal. "The reasons? Really, the same as always. But there is also something very personal which, without taking away my trust in my God, makes me suffer, because I don't see any possible *human* way out of my situation. Temptations to rebel arise, but I say *Serviam!* ['I will serve!']."[156]

Three weeks later, on September 30, 1931, he writes: "I find myself in a more difficult financial situation than ever before. But I haven't lost my peace. I have absolute trust, real confidence, that God my Father will soon resolve this matter once and for all. If only I were alone! Then, I realize, poverty would be a delight. A priest and poor, lacking even what is necessary—great!"[157]

The autobiographical entries in the journal exhibit very clearly the states and movements of his soul. "Everything having to do with my soul," he says in one entry, "I have communicated and always will communicate to my spiritual director, not holding anything back."[158]

But in leaving these notes to his spiritual children as a legacy, he asks them not to publish them. "May you have the decency not to exhibit my soul," he says.[159] He did not want his family's poverty and sacrifices publicly exposed.

Early on he had learned how our Lord typically dealt with
him: that in order to shape him, he "landed one blow on the nail
and a hundred on the horseshoe." He decided, therefore, to deal
with this matter head-on. "I confronted him," he writes on
October 2, 1931, referring to our Lord, "and told him that since
Father Sánchez has forbidden me to ask him for *that*, I was asking not for it, but that (I said it this bluntly) he set things right for
my family and bother only me."[160]

(What his confessor had forbidden him to ask for was a
serious illness.)

As one way of remedying the sufferings of his mother and
siblings, he decided to take greater pains in how he treated
them at home. "In my mother," he says, "I will see the Blessed
Virgin; in my sister Carmen, Saint Teresa or Saint Thérèse;
and in Guitín, the adolescent Jesus."[161] (He did not expect his
dealings with Santiago to be very pleasant, because, as he
puts it, "the little guy has, like me, an atrocious temper.")

Something he says a little later (October 26, 1931) may well
explain what he wrote to Father Ambrosio about "beautiful
crosses":

> My lack of formation must be the cause of many of my
> periods of discouragement, of my hours and even days of
> being upset and in a bad mood. Generally, Jesus gives me a
> cross with joy, *cum gaudio et pace* [with joy and peace]; and
> a cross with joy . . . is not a cross. Given my optimistic na-
> ture, I have habitually a joy that we might call physiologi-
> cal—that of a healthy animal. It is not to that joy that I am
> referring, but to another, a supernatural kind which comes
> from abandoning oneself and everything else into the lov-
> ing arms of God our Father.[162]

Following this, he explains what he means by that mysterious phrase, "a cross without Cyreneans," that the canon of Barbastro had asked about:

Lord, what makes my cross heavy is that others are having to share it. Give me, Jesus, a cross without Cyreneans. I am speaking badly: your grace, your help, I am going to need, as always. But as long as you, my God, are with me, there is no trial that can frighten me. I think of a serious illness, joined, for example, with total blindness. That could be my cross, mine alone. I am quite confident that I would have the joy to cry out with faith and with peace of heart, from within my darkness and suffering, *Dominus, illuminatio mea et salus mea!* ["Lord, my light and my strength!"]. But what if the cross were tediousness, or sadness? I tell you, Lord, that with you there with me, I would be happily sad.[163]

As he continued to meditate, he found that he could not tell whether his family's sharing in his burden would be a relief or an additional burden.

I don't now even know, Jesus, if my desire for a cross without a Cyrenean might not show too much or too little generosity. Too much, because what is making me suffer so much is the cross of the others. . . . Or too little, because there seems to be a lack of conformity with what you want; because it seems that what I want is not your cross, but a cross to my liking.[164]

His sensibility and imagination caused him to suffer as he realized how heavily the cross weighed on his family. "Jesus today has pressed the cross, the holy cross, down hard on the poor shoulders of the Cyreneans," he says, "and how it pains me!"[165]

He wrote these words kneeling, in his dingy little room—not out of special devotion, but because of a lack of space. "For quite a few days," he explains, "I have been making these journal entries kneeling down, out of necessity, because I have to write in my room and I can't easily make a chair fit in it. But it occurs to me that since they are a sort of confession, it will be pleasing to Jesus if I always write them this way, kneeling down. I'll try to keep this resolution."[166] In that tight squeeze, he clearly saw that he needed, on the one hand, to find a solution to the problem of his canonical situation, and, on the other hand, to achieve financial security for his family. How long could his family go on under these conditions? "I don't know how we'll be able to live," he said.[167] But the truth is they had been living that way since they left Barbastro, although things had gotten alarmingly worse in Saragossa. Now, in Madrid, life was for them almost a daily miracle. To keep his mother and siblings from worrying, Father Josemaría nurtured their hopes, suggesting that things would get better. "So far," he says in the journal, "I am hiding from my mother and siblings our true situation. I've done that at other times, too. Lord, my Jesus, it's not that I don't want Cyreneans—I want however many you want for me—but that I would like, with true generosity and for love of you, to spare them these afflictions."[168]

At the end of November the situation got worse.[169] It got so bad, in fact, that he made up his mind to ask loans from friends—who, if they did not give him money, gave him good reasons why not. Finally the Lord moved him to go to a bank, where he obtained a loan of three hundred pesetas. On that same day, November 26, he came to understand new things about poverty and detachment while attending Benediction at the church of Jesús de Medinaceli. "Then," he wrote upon arriving home, "I caught on to many things: I am not less happy because of being in need than I would be if I had more than enough; I should, indeed, not ask Jesus for anything; I will content myself with pleasing him in everything and with telling him things as if he did not know them, as a little boy does with his father."[170]

That was the day he wrote to Father Ambrosio asking his prayers. What would the canon have thought if he had read this other journal entry, of November 29?

Now that the cross is really solid and weighty, Jesus will arrange things in a way that will fill us with peace. Lord, what cross is this? A cross without a cross. With your help, knowing the formula of abandonment, this is how my crosses will always be.[171]

And, as a matter of fact, the Lord did give him back his peace all at once by calling to his attention the surprising and, humanly speaking, inexplicable behavior of his mother and sister. They were now "admirably disposed for whatever God wanted."[172] A few days later (December 10, 1931), he wrote: "Our Lord God is flooding my family with grace. . . . Now it is no longer conformity but joy. Clearly, in this house we're all crazy."[173]

* * *

Not long before Christmas, Carmen fell ill, and then so did Doña Dolores, and the evening after that, Santiago had to take to his bed. The place was like a hospital. Father Josemaría saw here an opportunity to fast without anyone knowing about it. But Doña Dolores knew her son well. In a somewhat disjointed way, and with understandable reserve, he relates what happened on the evening of December 20:

> Poor Mama got a little nervous—something perfectly natural. She said, "This cannot continue," and got mad at me because I didn't eat supper or even a snack. "That just makes you empty-headed," she told me. In their name I offered up to Jesus these bad times we're having. Afterward we prayed the holy Rosary, as usual. Until 11:00 I kept trying to pray.[174]

That testimony is, of course, one-sided. To get a balanced picture, one would have to hear his mother describe the mortifications and fasting of her son, who did at times get light-headed from not eating either lunch or supper. But evidently Doña Dolores got over her annoyance by the next morning, for her son entered in his journal this mild comment: "Today (I just got back from Santa Isabel) I find my mother very peaceful, as usual, and doing the housework, also as usual."[175]

In those days Father Josemaría was under constant pressure. His confessor was pushing him. Doña Dolores was pushing him. Things could not go on like this. His mother lamented that Madrid was becoming a purgatory for them, and he had to acknowledge that the family was indeed suffering passive purifications in the capital.[176]

Yet Doña Dolores was at peace and saw the approaching troubles without becoming upset. "This is my last time to jot down things of this kind," her son wrote on December 30. "I am amazed to see with what tranquillity, as though she were talking about the weather, my poor mother said last night, 'Never have we had it so bad as now,' and then how we went on to talk about other things, without losing our joy and peace. How good you are, Jesus, how good! You will know how to reward them generously."[177]

However, just two weeks after having made this resolution not to write any more about family stresses, he let slip another journal entry of that sort.[178]

The devil, the father of anxiety, also was a presence in that time of hard testing. Having found the Achilles' heel of the priest, he persistently attacked him by way of his family.[179] In the face of diabolical suggestions, Father Josemaría prayed for patience and strength: "Jesus, since I am your donkey, give me the stubbornness and fortitude of a donkey, so that I can fulfill your lovable will."[180]

Meanwhile, still not aware of the supernatural enterprise that her son had in hand, Doña Dolores was taking some steps of her own. Probably at the beginning of February 1932, she wrote to the bishop of Cuenca—Bishop Cruz Laplana, to whom she was distantly related—explaining Josemaría's situation and asking his advice.[181] Through a certain canon who had to make a trip to Madrid—Father Joaquín María de Ayala (the priest who in the summer of 1927 had written to Father Josemaría asking him to pick up his cassock and buy him some lighter flints)—the prelate sent his reply, the gist of which was a generous invitation. "Lola," the prelate said to her, "why not have your son come see me? I have a canonry* for him."[182]

Here was a new opportunity for the devil to tempt him. Father Josemaría discussed the offer with Father Norberto, the assistant chaplain of the Foundation for the Sick. Here is his journal entry for February 15, 1932:**

> What I am going to record is something I told Father Norberto about, both when I got the news about the position in Cuenca and afterward, when I felt the suggestion of the enemy. The devil reminded me that the doctoral canon of Cuenca had told Mama I should go apply for a canonry they have open at the cathedral. . . . But my spiritual director told me the Work must begin in Madrid, and I should at all costs stay here. . . . In short, Satan is clever, evil, and contemptible. But he made me see that I could lose my joy and peace (although I didn't actually do so) and be caused a lot of grief! Father Norbert had told me— laughing!—that this could happen, when it seemed to me it never could.[183]

From that temptation he emerged victorious and disposed to "pressure Jesus" to give to the members of his family, the "Cyreneans," "along with the spiritual peace that they now have, material well-being also."[184]

---

* Canons, as we have seen, were priests attached to the cathedral of the diocese. The position of a canon was prestigious and relatively well paid.

**The following is a very free rendering of a passage that is quite complex and obscure in Spanish. Evidently Father Josemaria felt tempted to follow up on the position in Cuenca as a way of resolving his family's economic difficulties, but Father Sánchez advised him to remain in Madrid.

It would be some time before his family attained a modicum of financial well-being. Jesus made him pray for a couple of years, in which things went from bad to worse. But as he bore the cross he happily exclaimed, "Well, Lord, I am the lucky man who didn't even have a shirt."[185]

7. *The path of spiritual childhood*

In September and October of 1931, when feelings of love were springing up so abundantly in that young priest's heart, the Lord confirmed him on the path of true filial abandonment. From that torrent of graces burst forth another stream: an inner life of spiritual childhood. In 1949 he recalled:

> I often had the custom, when I was young, of not using any book when making a meditation. I would recite, savoring them, the words of the Our Father, and, I would pause, relishing the thought, when I considered that God is *Father,* my Father, and that this makes me a brother of Jesus Christ and a brother to all people.
>
> I never got over my astonishment, contemplating that I was a son of God! After each reflection I found myself firmer in faith, more secure in hope, more on fire with love. And there was born in my soul the need, since I was a child of God, to be a small child, a needy child. That was the beginning, in my interior life, of my living whenever I could—whenever I can—the life of childhood. I have always recommended this to my sons and daughters, while, of course, respecting their freedom.[186]

On October 2—the feast of the Guardian Angels, the third anniversary of the founding of Opus Dei, and the vigil of the feast of Saint Thérèse of Lisieux—he fervently invoked the heavenly spirits, and in a special way his guardian angel. His journal entry for that day reads:

I paid him compliments and asked him to teach me to love Jesus at least—at least!—as much as he loves him. Undoubtedly Saint Thérèse . . . wanted to give me something in anticipation of her feast day, for she succeeded in having my guardian angel teach me today how to make a prayer of childhood. What very childish things I said to my Lord! With the trustful confidence of a boy talking to his Grownup Friend, of whose love he is certain, I said, "Let me live only for your Work. Let me live only for your glory. Let me live only for your love. . . ." I duly recalled and acknowledged that I do everything badly, and said, "That, my Jesus, should not surprise you—it is impossible for me to do anything right. You help me, you do it for me, and you will see how well it turns out. So, then, boldly and without straying from the truth, I say to you: Saturate me, get me drunk, with your Spirit, and thus I will do your will. I want to do it. If I don't do it, it's because . . . you're not helping me."

And I had feelings of love for my Mother and Lady, and right now I feel myself very much a child of God my Father.[187]

This journal entry is the first fruit of the new path undertaken. He spent the next several days in interior recollection, in affective and fervent prayer, while alarming rumors of new burnings of churches and religious houses swept through the city. On October 14 he learned that the infamous article 26 of the Constitution had been approved. It would mean the expulsion of the Society of Jesus. That very afternoon, he went to see his confessor at Chamartín.

But the Jesuits were not the only ones in danger. All monasteries, convents, and other residences of religious were at risk. Catholic students mounted guard at night to protect them.

On October 15, the feast of Saint Teresa of Avila, the chaplain came into the cloistered area of Santa Isabel. The nuns were very frightened by the rumors. He reassured them as best he could, speaking words full of warmth and optimism.

Today I went into the cloister of Santa Isabel. I encouraged the nuns. I spoke to them about love, about the cross, and about joy . . . and about victory. Away with anxiety! We are at the beginning of the end. Saint Teresa has obtained for me, from our Jesus, the Joy—with a capital *J*—that I have today . . . , when it would seem, humanly speaking, that I should be sad, both for the Church and about my own situation (which, truth to tell, is not good). We just need much faith and expiation, and above faith and expiation, much Love. Besides, this morning, when purifying two ciboriums, so as not to leave the Blessed Sacrament in the church I received almost half a ciboriumful of hosts, even though I gave several to each sister.[188]

The sisters rewarded him for that sowing of joy.

On my way out of the cloister they showed me, in the vestibule, a Christ Child which was a darling. I have never seen a better-looking Child Jesus! Totally captivating. They uncovered it. He has his little arms crossed on his breast and his eyes half open. Beautiful. I ate him up with kisses and . . . would have loved to kidnap him.[189]

For a long time thereafter he would go every week to the convent's revolving window, and the sister on duty would let him hold "the little one." In those days when his soul was crisscrossed by joys and afflictions—feelings of ardent affection in prayer and difficult trials in which he asked for a cross without "Cyreneans"—his devotion to the Child Jesus was beginning to shape his interior life.

The Child Jesus: how this devotion has taken hold of me since I first laid eyes on that *consummate Thief* that my nuns keep in the vestibule of their cloister! Child Jesus, adolescent Jesus—I like to see you that way, Lord, because . . . it makes

me more daring. I like to see you as a little boy, a helpless
child, because it makes me feel like you need me.[190]

As a solid devotion to the childhood of Christ took root in
his soul, Father Josemaría came to realize the paradoxical nature of this spiritual route: that it requires, simultaneously, both
strength and exquisite sensitivity.

> I recognize, my Love, my clumsiness—that it is such
> . . . such that when I want to caress, I cause harm. Soften
> the manners of my soul. Give me, I want you to give me,
> within the strength and energy of the life of childhood, that
> softness and tenderness that children have that allows
> them to relate to their parents with an intimate outpouring
> of love.[191]

By no means was this attitude one of mawkish infantilism.
On the contrary, by it the Lord strengthened the soul of the
founder, as he observes in his journal entry for November 30, 1931:

> The way of childhood. Abandonment. Spiritual child-
> hood. All this that God is asking of me and that I am trying to
> have is not foolishness, but a strong and solid Christian life.[192]

With the confidence of a little boy before his Father God, he
adjusted his old habits of prayer—not without effort—to that
new path of childhood. He became more and more convinced
of "how beautiful and pleasant is this path, because it allows
sinners to feel as the saints have felt."[193]

Most of the journal entries in which he records ideas about
the life of spiritual childhood, or expresses personal feelings of
this kind, were written in or near December 1931 and January
1932. For example, on November 30, the first day of the Immaculate Conception novena, he observes that "when praying
the Rosary or doing—like now in Advent—other devotions, I
contemplate the mysteries of the life, passion, and death of our

Lord Jesus Christ, taking active part in the actions and events as a witness and servant and companion of Jesus, Mary, and Joseph."[194]

He had already gotten used to praying the Rosary by contemplating the mysteries of the life of our Lord as a small child transported to the scene and present as a witness. To judge by some of the parenthetical observations he makes—for instance, "I am sorry to note down these details, because they might make one think well, or less badly, of me: I am full of miseries"[195]—we have reason to suppose that this way of praying the Rosary put him in an elevated state of contemplative prayer.

On the second day of the novena, December 1, he expected—without asking for it—to receive a favor, a gift connected with the novena: a sign of progress on the path of spiritual childhood.

> Immaculate Mother, Holy Mary: You will give me something, my Lady, in this novena honoring your unspotted conception. Now, I don't ask for anything—since I haven't been given permission to—but I want to set before you my desire to reach perfect spiritual childhood.[196]

One morning during this novena, after saying Mass and finishing his prayer of thanksgiving, he wrote the book *Holy Rosary* in one sitting, in the sacristy of Santa Isabel, close to the sanctuary. We don't know with certainty which day it was, but we do know that on December 7, vigil of the feast of the Immaculate Conception, he read to two young people at Santa Isabel "the way to pray the Rosary." That was why he wrote this little book: to help others pray the Rosary.[197]

In his introduction to the book, he discloses the secret of spiritual childhood:

> My friend: if you want to be great, become little.
> To be little you have to believe as children believe, to love as children love, to abandon yourself as children do . . . , to pray as children pray. . . .

Become little. Come with me and—this is the essence of what I want to tell you—we shall live the life of Jesus, Mary, and Joseph.

Gently, he introduces the reader to the scene:

> Don't forget, my friend, that we are children. The Lady of the sweet name, Mary, is absorbed in prayer.
> You, in that house, can be whatever you wish: a friend, a servant, an onlooker, a neighbor. . . . For the moment I don't dare to be anything. I hide behind you and, full of awe, I watch what's happening:
> The Archangel delivers his message . . .[198]

Also in the introduction, he tells us: "*The beginning of the way,* at the end of which you will find yourself completely carried away by love for Jesus, is a trusting love for Mary."

At home he had a small wooden statue of our Lady, which he had a habit of kissing when leaving or entering the apartment. ("My Lady of the Kisses—I will end up eating her up!" he exclaims in one of his journal entries.[199]) Not just that one, but all images of our Lady moved him. This was especially true of those he found thrown out on the street and covered with grime, or those he caught sight of in his travels through Madrid, such as a picture in glazed tile that attracted his attention every day as he was leaving Santa Isabel. This image, which was on the terrace of a house on Atocha Street, looked down upon a strange event that took place a few days after he wrote *Holy Rosary.*

> Octave of the Immaculate Conception, 1931: Yesterday afternoon, at three, when I was going to the school of Santa Isabel to hear the confessions of the girls, on Atocha Street (on the side near San Carlos, almost at the corner of Santa Ines) three young men, all of them probably thirty-something, crossed paths with me. When they got close to me, one of them rushed forward, shouted "I'm going to get him!" and

raised his arm in such a way that I thought for sure I would be struck. But before he could carry out his intended aggression, one of the other two said to him in an authoritative tone of voice, "No, don't hit him." And then immediately, in a mocking tone of voice, bending toward me, this same man added, "Little donkey, little donkey!"

I crossed Santa Isabel's corner at a calm pace, and am sure that I in no way showed on the outside the trepidation I was feeling inside. To hear myself called—by that defender!—by this name, "little donkey," that I use when speaking to Jesus: this really got to me. Immediately I said three Hail Mary's to the Blessed Virgin, who witnessed that little event from her image on the house of the Congregation of Saint Philip.[200]

The name "little donkey" (*burrito*) is one that, as earlier mentioned, he used privately and only his confessor knew about.

On the next day he recorded some more impressions of that event:

December 16, 1931: Yesterday I felt kind of tired, undoubtedly as a result of that *assault* I suffered on Atocha Street. I am convinced that it was from the devil. Father Norberto thinks so too. The one who tried to attack me had the ferocious face of a madman. About the looks of the other two, I can't remember a thing. Then, and also afterward, I did not lose my peace. There was a physiological fear that made my heart beat faster, but I could tell that it did not show on the outside, not even on my face. I was amazed, as I say, at the tone of sarcasm, of mockery, in which that one man called me, twice, "little donkey." Instinctively I lifted my heart and said three Hail Mary's to our Lady. Afterward, on my notepaper, I jotted down exactly what those people had said.[201]

One of the most beautiful and sublime pages in his journal is inspired by his mystical connection with the Lady of the

Kisses. It is not a literary flight of fancy, as at first glance might appear, but an intense interior experience: the kind of mystical experience in which the audacity of desire becomes a mandate, and with which children open up the kingdom of heaven.

It was December 28, the feast of the Holy Innocents, a day on which people in Spain traditionally play jokes on one another.[202] The chaplain went to Santa Isabel and found that, for twenty-four hours, a novice was acting as prioress and the youngest nun as subprioress. It was great fun to see the oldest and most serious nuns carrying out tasks imposed by the prioress of the day. When he got home, Father Josemaría kissed his statue of our Lady, began his meditation, and lost himself in contemplation. Immersed in prayer, he took up his pen and made the following entry in his journal:

A little boy visited a certain convent. . . .

Little boy, you are the last donkey, the least among those who love Jesus. It's your turn, you have the right, to rule in heaven. Let loose your imagination, and let your heart run wild too. . . .

I want Jesus to forgive me . . . everything. I want all the blessed souls in purgatory purified in less than a second and going up to enjoy our God . . . because today I am taking his place. I want . . . to scold some guardian angels that I know—in fun, right? but also a little bit for real—and command them to obey like this: to obey Jesus' donkey in things that are all for the glory of Christ our King. And after giving lots and lots of orders, I would say to my Mother, holy Mary: "My Lady, not even for fun do I want you to stop being Mistress and Empress of all creation." Then she would kiss me on the forehead and leave me, as a sign of that favor, a bright star above my eyes. And with this new light I would see all the children of God down to the end of the world, fighting our Lord's battles, always victorious with him, . . . and I would hear a voice more than heavenly, like the murmur of many waters and the explosion of a mighty thunderclap, gentle despite its intensity, like the sound of many zithers played in harmony by an infinite number of musicians, saying, "We want him to reign! All glory to God! All, with Peter, to Jesus through Mary!"

And before this wondrous day comes to an end, O Jesus (I will tell him), I want to be a bonfire of madly passionate love! I want my mere presence to be enough to set the world on fire, for many miles around, with an inextinguishable flame. I want to know that I am yours. Afterward, let the cross come: never will I be afraid of expiation. . . . To suffer and to love. To love and to suffer. What a magnificent path! To love, to suffer, and to believe: faith and love. The faith of Peter, the love of John, the zeal of Paul.

The little donkey still has three minutes of divinization, good Jesus, and so he commands . . . that you give him more zeal than Paul, more love than John, more faith than Peter. The last wish, Jesus: may I never lack the holy cross.[203]

Two days later, the convent having returned to normal, the nuns let him take home with him the statue of the Child Jesus. The priest wrapped "the little one" in his cloak and brought him with him to celebrate Christmas with the outside world. Taking advantage of having that Christ Child outside the convent, he had a photo taken of it.

Today I brought home with me the "Christ Child of Saint Teresa." The Augustinian nuns lent him to me. *We* went to see Father Gabriel, at the Carmelites, to wish him a merry Christmas. The little friar was happy and gave me a holy card and a medal. Afterward I saw Father Norberto's spiritual director, Father Joaquín. We talked about the W. of G. From there I went to visit another convent. I spent a good amount of time with Mother Pilar. Then to the house of Pepe R., where we took a photo of the Child. Before going home, I went up to see Father Norberto, so that he could see the

Child. At home, Mama prayed out loud an Our Father and a Hail Mary. I get to keep him here until tomorrow.[204]

In a couple of journal entries written in January 1932, he relates when and how he learned the life of spiritual childhood:

> I did not learn the path of childhood from books until after Jesus had made me start along this way.[205]
>
> Yesterday, for the first time, I began to page through a book which I will have to read slowly many times: *Caminito de infancia espiritual* [The little way of spiritual childhood], by Father Martín. I see how Jesus, with that reading, made me experience—even with the same images—the way of Saint Thérèse. I have written things in these Catherines that show this. I will also read slowly *Story of a Soul*.[206]

By now his soul was becoming so filled with graces that despite his repeated resolves not to relate extraordinary events, some inevitably crept into his journal entries. That was the case with two locutions he received in 1932. On January 4 he wrote:

> This morning, as usual, as I was leaving the convent of Santa Isabel, I went to the tabernacle for a moment to say good-bye to Jesus. I said to him, "Jesus, here is your donkey. . . . See what you can do with your donkey." And immediately I understood, without hearing any words: "A donkey was my throne in Jerusalem." This concept I grasped, with full clarity.[207]

But at that moment a doubt assailed him. His attention was fixed on the female donkey mentioned by Saint Matthew, and so he thought the locution (since it referred to a male donkey) was a mistaken, perhaps even diabolical, interpretation of the Gospel. As soon as he got home he consulted the Gospels, and was reassured. Jesus had entered Jerusalem mounted on a young male donkey.[208]

For some time, upon seeing a community of religious praying, he had been putting the way of spiritual childhood into practice, by saying, "Jesus, I don't know how much they love you, but I love you more than all of them put together."[209] Well, shortly after the locution about the donkey, in putting on record his lack of generosity toward our Lord, he lets slip another of the many locutions he had.

> February 16, 1932: For the last several days I have had a rather bad cold, and it has been an occasion for my lack of generosity toward my God to show itself. I slacked off in the thousand little things that a child—especially a child donkey—can offer his Lord each day. I started noticing this, and that I was postponing the fulfillment of certain resolutions about putting more time and effort into devotional practices, but I calmed myself with the thought, "Later, when you're well, when your family's financial situation is in better shape . . . then!" Well, today, after giving the nuns Holy Communion . . . I told Jesus what I tell him so many, many times both day and night: . . . "I love you more than these." And immediately I understood, without hearing any words: "Love is deeds, not sweet words and excuses." At that moment I saw clearly how little generosity I have. Suddenly there came to my memory many details which I hadn't been paying attention to, which made me see with crystal clarity my lack of generosity. O Jesus, help me, so that your donkey will be fully generous. Deeds, deeds![210]

*   *   *

"I expect great things in this year of 1931," he had written in his journal in March of that year. His expectations had been exceeded. Twelve months later, he found himself brimming over with divine graces like a person inebriated by wine: so filled with God that he felt like calling for a truce. "I am inundated, drunk with the grace of God," he says on March 11, 1932. "What a terrible sin if I do not respond! There are times—like right now—when I feel like shouting, Enough, Lord, enough!"[211]

The divine eagle had caught that little bird and lifted it to dizzying heights. The Lord had definitively impressed on him such a consciousness, such a strong feeling, of his divine filiation that he was moved to loving acceptance of whatever happened. As he had expressed it on November 29, 1931, "Because it comes from our Father's hands, the blow of the chisel, regardless of whether it is—as the world sees it—favorable or unfavorable, and even though it wounds the flesh, is always also a proof of Love, which smooths out our rough edges to bring us closer to perfection."[212]

His courage in traveling the way of pain and expiation was rewarded with the triumph of love, which from then on took precedence in his soul over any other feeling.

> Jesus, I feel great desires for reparation. My path is to love and to suffer. But love makes me rejoice in suffering, to the point where it now seems to me impossible for me ever to suffer. I already told you: there is no longer anyone who upsets me. And I even added: there is no one who can make me suffer, because suffering gives me joy and peace.[213]

From then on, the customary pattern of his life was a serene and harmonious combination of great sufferings with great joys: bittersweet sufferings that did not take away his peace, and joys that were not totally satisfying.

Looking at his personal writings, one can see and appreciate how much God had accomplished in him in a year, in terms of simplifying his prayer and attracting his affections. "Now," he says on April 7, 1932, "between Mary and myself, between Jesus and myself . . . nobody! Before, I would seek out intermediary saints."[214] And on February 26, 1932: "Now I go directly to the Father, to Jesus, to the Holy Spirit, to Mary. This doesn't mean I don't have devotions (to Saint Joseph, the angels, the souls in purgatory, Dominic, Joseph Calasanz, Don Bosco, Teresa, Ignatius, Xavier, Thérèse, Mercedes, etc.), but my soul definitely is getting simpler. R. Ch. V. [*Regnare Christum volumus*: We want Christ to reign]."[215]

As he pursues the life of spiritual childhood, his prayer becomes very assertive. "My way of saying, in prayer, 'I want,' " he notes on January 14, 1932, "is a childlike way of asking. So I'm not going off track."[216]

The founder also came out of 1931 with the rather odd habit, already mentioned, that as soon as he began to read the newspaper, his mind would run off to God. This happened quite a few times that year, and at first it seemed strange to him.[217] But soon he noticed that frequently and inexplicably, periods of dryness and of favors were taking him by surprise, with no regard for time or place, inopportunely and often in a breathtaking way. "It is incomprehensible," he says on March 26, 1932. "I know someone who feels cold (despite his faith, which is limitless) near the divine fire of the tabernacle, and then later, in the middle of the street, amid the noise of automobiles and streetcars and people—when reading a newspaper!—is seized with mad raptures of love for God."[218]

Was he getting practical lessons on how to lead a contemplative life in the midst of traffic, the hustle and bustle of crowds, or while reading?

Meanwhile, the devil was not inactive. First he insinuated the suggestion that he had no right to condemn his family to a life of poverty for the "folly" of the Work. Later he tried to rob him of his peace of mind by causing trouble concerning his official appointment to the Foundation of Santa Isabel. Finally, seeing how little progress he was making, with the Lord's permission he resorted to physical assault.

At first Father Josemaría did not realize that he was dealing with the rage of "Old Scratch," as he called the devil.[219] He caught on to this only when he fell victim to a peculiar series of violent acts. On his way to a tutoring appointment one Sunday in March, at noon, he was peacefully reading his breviary when suddenly he was hit hard by a ball. He kept his composure, not even turning around "to see if this was an accident or an act of malice."[220]

Ten days later, on Ash Wednesday, he went to hear the confessions of the girls residing at the school of Santa Isabel. Returning by Duque de Medinaceli Street, he saw some boys playing on the sidewalk in front of Hotel Palace. Already burned by similar encounters, he quickly crossed over to the other side of the street, but he could not avoid the unavoidable:

> A really hard kick and . . . pow! on the right-hand lens of my glasses, driving them into my nose. I didn't even turn my head. I got out my handkerchief and, calmly, kept on walking, while cleaning my glasses. . . . At that moment I perceived the devil's rage (it is too much of a coincidence) and the goodness of God, who lets him bark but not bite. One would have expected at least that the lens would have been broken, since there was nothing moderate about that blow I received. My right eye might also have been injured. Even just a broken lens would have been quite a setback, since I already have a hard time paying for the few streetcar rides I have to take. . . . The bottom line: God is my Father.[221]

But misfortune comes in threes. Here is the next entry:

> Monday, April 11: Yesterday, as I was walking on Alvarez de Castro Street, on the sidewalk, reading my breviary, on my way to catch the 48 to the hospital, they again hit me hard with a ball! I laughed. It upset him.[222]

Father Josemaría's lively sense of humor let him see that God was permitting the devil to "bark but not bite."[223] On another occasion at that time, he very clearly sensed that hell was raging against the Work of God. This incident happened "at noon on a sunny day, on Martínez Campos Avenue, near La

Castellana."[224] He says nothing more about it, since by now he was depersonalizing journal entries about supernatural events having to do with himself. But possibly it was connected with this entry made some weeks earlier:

> Hell is roaring, howling, bellowing, because Satan has an inkling about the souls that the W. of G. is going to bring to Jesus, and about the whole of its operation in the world: the effective reign of Christ in all of society. *Regnare Christum volumus.*[225]

7

The Gestation of the Work

1. Among the sick: "a beautiful work"

At the end of the sixteenth century there were in Madrid as many as fourteen small hospitals, scattered all over the city. It was a captain of the Flanders infantry regiment, Bernardino de Obregón, later known as "the Apostle of Madrid," who convinced King Philip II that he should merge them into one.[1] For this purpose a hospital committee was created, and the planning of the new building was entrusted to Juan de Herrera, the architect of El Escorial.* The site chosen was a plot of land near the property of the King's notorious secretary, Antonio Pérez. On the same plot stood the convent of Santa Isabel, as well as the Hospital de la Pasión, for women.

But the start of construction brought with it a filing of lawsuits. This was not surprising. With the unlinking of the foundations, chapels, and churches that had been dependent on the various hospitals, a multiplication of appeals to Church authorities was only to be expected. Construction was held up for nearly a century and was not completed until the time of Carlos III.** The old Hospital of the Passion was demolished in 1831, and on that lot on Atocha Street was built the San Carlos School of Medicine.[2]

Whenever Father Josemaría walked out of Santa Isabel, he found himself facing the imposing walls of the General Hospital

---

* The palace built by Philip II outside Madrid.
** Carlos III reigned from 1759 to 1788.

(also called the Provincial Hospital), in one of whose wings was the clinic run by the School of Medicine. In the summer of 1931, having not yet totally given up his involvement with the Foundation for the Sick, the sight of that immense building made him think of the sick people whom he was leaving. That thought was so disturbing to him that as soon as he said his good-byes to the Apostolic Ladies, he felt a terrible emptiness in his soul. "It was at the Foundation for the Sick," he confesses, "that the Lord wanted me to find my priestly heart."[3] Work in the hospitals, living with suffering, the patients' tearful offering of sufferings and prayers—these were roots from which the founder drew supernatural vitality at the beginning of the Work.

Time went by, and on October 28, 1931, he definitively took leave of the Santa Engracia Foundation for the Sick. And on that very day the Lord put an end to his worries by bestowing upon him a huge number of sick people to care for. "Another favor from our Lord," he writes. "Yesterday I had to definitively leave the Foundation, and therefore all those patients. But my Jesus does not want me to leave him. He reminded me that he is nailed to a hospital bed. . . ."[4]

It was through Santa Isabel's sacristan, Antonio Díaz, that God gave continuity to Father Josemaría's works of mercy with the sick. Antonio mentioned to him the Congregation of St. Philip Neri. Popularly known as "Philippians," these men tended to the sick at the General Hospital.[5] Father Josemaría looked them up, consulted with his confessor, and joyfully wrote in his journal, "Beginning next Sunday, I will start taking part in that beautiful work."[6] On November 8 he participated for the first time in the religious exercises of the Congregation. According to its constitutions, the number of brothers (all of whom were laymen) could not be more than seventy, and one of them was to be elected "Eldest Brother." Although at this time (1931) their number was down to only a little over a dozen, they were still abiding by the old customs and formalities prescribed by the constitutions. On Sunday afternoon at four o'-clock sharp, the brothers would show up, put on a black gown, and go to the Congregation's chapel, for prayer. Then, after getting their assignments, they would go in pairs, or in groups of three or four, down the halls assigned to them, first picking up items from the supply room: towels, washbowls, soap, bandages, scissors . . .[7]

The constitutions specified the manner in which the Philippians were to carry out their services with the sick: "with great humility and respect, seeing in each the living image of Christ." Also specified were the tasks of the brothers: "that they make the beds of the poor," "that they take special care of the very weak," "that they wash the feet, and cut the hair and nails, of the poor," "that when necessary they clean the bedpans," etc.[8]

In the long hours he had been spending each day at the bedsides of the sick, united to their sufferings, witnessing their miseries, consoling them with his presence, and erasing their spiritual miseries in the sacrament of Penance, Father Josemaría had come to see shining forth in them the lovable and suffering figure of Christ: Christ merciful, Christ patiently enduring, Christ loaded down with the weight and ugliness of sin, Christ bearing with us our sorrows and sufferings. And as a priest, an "other Christ," he identified with the sick in sorrow and compassion. His yearning to see and help Christ in the sick carried Father Josemaría's heart to the hospital. In his journal entry for March 11, 1932, one reads: "Children and the sick: When I write these words—'Child,' 'Sick'—I am tempted to capitalize them, because, for a soul in love, they are Christ."[9]

The Congregation was shuffling along in a listless manner, due to the small number of brothers, their lack of health care training, and the many obstacles that were being put in the way of their spiritual work. Since the coming of the Republic, the atmosphere in the wards had become hostile and even offensively so. The rancors of the street, loaded with hatred, reached even that refuge for the suffering. As a companion of Father Josemaría's describes it, "It was a very hard and very thankless job. Anti-Catholic sentiment was everywhere, and many of the patients insulted us. Here we were, fixing up their hair, shaving them, trimming their nails, bathing them, cleaning the spittoons. . . . It was horribly disgusting. We went there on Sundays, in the afternoon, and left nauseated."[10]

Due to lack of space, sick people were crowded into the wards and the corridors were strewn with thin mattresses.[11] The Philippians passed through like a merciful caress, relieving the discouragement or despair of the patients. One of the old brothers remembers "the spiritual wake" that Father Josemaría left as he passed, "lifting the spirits of the sick and the dying."[12]

Among the brothers of the Congregation who helped out at the hospital in 1931 and 1932 were Luis Gordon, Jenaro Lázaro, and Antonio Medialdea. Luis was a young, financially well-off industrial engineer who ran a factory in Cienpozuelos, near Madrid. Jenaro was a professional sculptor, about thirty years old. Antonio was a salesclerk.[13] There were also some older brothers, such as the little old man who headed the group that Father Josemaría went with one Sunday. The priest was surprised to hear the old man, upon finishing his work in one of the wards, innocently say good-bye with this "pious barbarity": "My brothers, may God give you health of body . . ."—followed by a long pause, and then, all in one breath—"and of soul, if need be."[14]

In that "beautiful work," in contact with suffering, Father Josemaría matured and was enriched. After the first Sunday he spent with the Philippians, he summed up his impression of them in these few words: "I was very edified." Three Sundays later, when he happened to have as companion that funny old man, he said the same thing: "And I was edified."[15] The physical help they could give to those many sick persons, with grooming or with personal hygiene, was certainly very little. Quite considerable, on the other hand, was the good they did to souls, sometimes with just a simple charitable gesture or a few words of Christian consolation.

One moving example was that of a Gypsy who, after generously forgiving his enemies, was disposed to reconcile himself with Christ, because "there had gone to his heart something he had heard a St. Philip brother say while helping out some other patients."[16] On a Sunday in February 1932, one of the brothers went to let Father Josemaría know that there was a dying man who did not want to receive the sacraments. The priest tells us:

> It was a Gypsy who had been stabbed repeatedly in a fight. Right away he agreed to make his confession. He did not want to let go of my hand, and, not being able to do this himself, he asked me to put it up to his mouth so that he could kiss it. He was in a pitiful condition—excretions were oozing out of his mouth. It was really painful to see him. In a loud voice he swore that he would do no more thieving. He asked me for a crucifix. I didn't have one, so I gave him a rosary. I wrapped it around his wrist and he kissed it, saying words of profound sorrow for having offended our Lord.[17]

After tending to him, the chaplain left to give Benediction. On the following Tuesday he heard that the man had died. In his journal he wrote:

> A young man, a St. Philip brother, came to tell me that the Gypsy had died in a most edifying way, saying, among other things, as he kissed the crucifix of the rosary, "My lips are putrid, not worthy of kissing you." And he called out for his daughters to look at him and to know that their father was good. That, no doubt, was why he had said to me, "Put the rosary on me, so it can be seen, so it can be seen." Jesus, I've already offered that soul to you, but now I do it again. Right now I'm going to pray for him the prayer for the dead.[18]

Father Josemaría brought with him on these Sunday visits to the hospital some of the young men to whom he was giving spiritual direction, including José Romeo and Adolfo Gómez Ruiz, and also some of their friends and associates, such as Adolfo's brother Pedro and a law student named José Manuel Doménech.[19] At about six-thirty in the evening they would finish their rounds in the wards and, priest included, go for a walk in downtown Madrid. Those young men were not people used to hospital work. They would leave with upset stomachs, with foul odors clinging to their clothes, and with vivid memories of repulsive sights—pus, ulcers, all kinds of disgusting things. Scarcely had they set foot on the street when more than one of them would throw up. There was a lot of merit in their overcoming of that natural repugnance, because their homes, in contrast, were very clean and comfortable. Luis Gordon even went to the hospital in a car of his own.

Luis had probably read what is said in the Philippians' constitutions, that the purpose of the Congregation is to practice the virtues "in a way that leads to the consolation and the spiritual and physical well-being of the poor; not omitting anything, no matter how lowly or repugnant; volunteering, when necessary, to clean the bedpans, sweep and scrub between the beds, and do whatever other things good care requires."[20] One Sunday it was his turn to accompany Father Josemaría as his assistant. While the priest was tending to a patient with tuberculosis, he asked Luis to clean the bedpan. When he saw that it was full of bloody spit, a grimace of revulsion escaped Luis, but he got control of himself and, without saying a word, took it to a bathroom at the back of the ward. As soon as he could, Father Josemaría went to help him, and found him hard at work. He had put the bedpan in the sink and filled it with water, and, with his sleeves rolled up to the elbows, was cleaning it with his hands while saying under his breath, with a look of contentment, "Jesus, may I put on a happy face!"[21]

The political changes broke the rhythm of the activities carried on by the brothers at the General Hospital. After the summer of 1932 there was a gap in their charitable exercises. Undoubtedly the official regulations regarding services that members of religious orders could carry out in the public hospitals were applied also to the Philippians. The government tried to replace the Daughters of Charity with professional, lay nurses and other lay personnel. It blatantly attempted to do away with the charitable activities of Catholic associations, such as the Congregation of St. Philip Neri. And it suspended the work of all hospital chaplains.[22]

The visits of the Philippians came to a halt in 1933, but later they started up again, and Father Josemaría, who in April of 1932 had joined the Philippians, asked its governing board to reactivate his membership. "This Council of Elders," he was notified, "has agreed in a meeting held today, June 10, by absolutely unanimous vote, to consider you a brother of our beloved congregation in accord with your good wishes. Madrid, June 10, 1934. The Brother Secretary, Tomás Mínguez."[23]

The most likely explanation is that Father Josemaría, in order to help the sick, wanted to avail himself of the rights that the Congregation had enjoyed from time immemorial. By all indications, once the hospitals no longer had chaplains (these positions having been suppressed by the government), he sought the shelter of an appointment, even if only a practically worthless scrap of paper, in order to be able to assist the patients at the General Hospital.[24]

2. *King's Hospital*

By virtue of the new, republican Constitution, churches and religious associations and institutes were henceforth to be deprived of economic help from the national and local governments. Worse still, it was planned that there be a "total abolition, within two years, of the budget for the clergy."[25] The idea was to finish off the Church, if not by armed violence, by a starving off of its ministers.

One of the clerics affected by those measures was Father José María Somoano. Ordained in 1927 by the bishop of

Madrid, this young priest in 1931 held the position of chaplain at King's Hospital [Hospital del Rey].[26] This hospital was in the far northern reaches of Madrid, about four miles from downtown, out in the country and effectively isolated. Its actual name, Hospital Nacional de Enfermedades Infecciosas [National Hospital for Infectious Diseases] explains its isolation. It had been inaugurated in 1925. (The name King's Hospital came, of course, from the previous regime.)[27] In it were treated epidemic and other contagious diseases, including the dreaded tuberculosis, at that time the sickness that filled the most beds and resulted in the most deaths.

On January 2, 1932, the portress of Santa Isabel, at the express request of the chaplain, offered prayer and mortification for the good outcome of a matter he had in hand. He, meanwhile, accompanied by Father Lino, another young priest, went to King's Hospital to speak with its chaplain, Father Somoano, who turned out to be very eager to hear about the Work. "Her prayer and penance was not in vain," he would write in his journal two days later, "for this friend now belongs to the Work."[28] (It was at this time that Father Josemaría, as we shall soon see, was getting his first priest followers.) In the eyes of the founder this priest was an excellent acquisition, a first-rate vocation, a real treasure for his apostolic work—in short, a lever for moving the heavens. In his journal he wrote: "With José María Somoano we have obtained, as they say around here, a wonderful 'connection,' because our brother knows, admirably, how to channel the suffering of the patients in his hospital so that the heart of our Jesus, moved by such beautiful expiation, will accelerate the hour of his Work."[29]

So highly did Father Josemaría value this kind of prayer, the prayer of suffering, for the development of the Work that he considered this great contribution to be more than adequate grounds for admitting a soul to the Work. "Yesterday," he says, "Father Lino told us about a sick woman at King's Hospital, a soul, very pleasing to God, who could be the first vocation of expiation. By unanimous common consent, Lino will tell her *our secret.* She may die before beginning officially—most likely she will, because she's in very bad shape—but then her sufferings will be worth all the more."[30]

The founder felt interiorly moved by the Lord to work among the sick, and thus to lay the foundation of expiatory pain needed to support the Work. When, on March 7, 1932, Father Lino proposed to him that he accept "the chaplaincy of the hospital for incurables, which is near King's Hospital," he would have done so had it not been for the opposition of Doña Dolores.[31]

*   *   *

On January 29, 1925, soon after the first pavilion of King's Hospital was completed, its first patients were admitted: two persons suffering from tuberculosis. Before that, and three months before the hospital's chief of staff showed up, the Daughters of Charity had already moved in. At the head of these religious nurses was Sister Engracia Echevarría: she worked at the hospital without interruption until 1936. Other members of the community included Sister Isabel Martín, who worked as a nurse, ran the pharmacy, and was sacristan of the chapel, and Sister María Jesús Sanz, who was in charge of the kitchen and the supply room. It was those three religious who really got to know and work with Father Josemaría, and in particular the superior, Sister Engracia, who, fortunately, has left a good amount of testimony about that period of upheaval. With the assurance appropriate to her age of ninety-nine, Sister Engracia makes a strong statement: "I preserve with full lucidity my memories of that period, not only with regard to dates, but with regard to the hue and caliber of the people and events that traversed it."[32] She was, no doubt about it, a born leader and a woman of great perspicacity. She immediately realized that the young priest who began showing up at the hospital in the early months of 1932 was Father Somoano's spiritual director. Nor did she fail to notice that his visits, besides being works of mercy, were motivated also by apostolic zeal. And so, on more than one occasion, she sent him people she thought he might be interested in working with.[33]

At first Father Josemaría visited the hospital sporadically, but soon he was coming regularly. Within a few weeks he came to realize the refinement of soul of Father Somoano, for whom "just the thought that there were priests who went up to the altar without the proper dispositions was enough to make him shed tears of love and reparation."[34] So many were the profanations, assaults, and sacrileges perpetrated by the revolutionary masses in the spring of 1931 that Father Somoano was moved to offer his life for the Church in Spain. One of the sisters heard him make that offering in the chapel—he did not know she was there.[35] Father Josemaría, who knew nothing of this, was surprised to hear Father Somoano say, on several occasions, things like "I am going to die soon; you will see."[36] Somewhat intrigued, he wanted to ask him in private why he was saying such things, but for one reason or another the right occasion for this never presented itself.

Father Somoano died on the night of Saturday, July 16, 1932, after two days of agony. He had been poisoned. On Monday he was buried. Father Josemaría, who had placed such high hopes in this vocation, offered it up to the Lord. Father Somoano had died a martyr, poisoned out of hatred for the priesthood. Upon his return from the burial, Father Josemaría wrote in his journal:

> July 18, 1932: The Lord has taken one of us: José María Somoano, an admirable priest. He died, as a victim of charity, at King's Hospital (where he had been chaplain to the end, despite all the laicist fury), on the night of the feast of Our Lady of Mount Carmel, to whom he was very devoted. He was wearing her holy scapular, and since this feast fell on a Saturday, it is certain that he entered the joy of God that same night.* A beautiful soul. . . . His life of zeal

---

* He is referring to the pious belief that our Lady promised to free from purgatory on the Saturday following their death those who die wearing the scapular.

had won him the affection of everyone who associated with him. He was buried this morning. . . . Today, willingly, I *gave* to Jesus that member. He is with him and will be a great help. I had put so much hope in his upright and energetic character. God wanted him for himself: blessed be God.[37]

Father Josemaría felt impelled to fill the void left by the death of the chaplain. "We were left without a chaplain," says Sister Engracia, "and in those circumstances, Father Josemaría Escrivá de Balaguer, who was then a young priest scarcely thirty years old, came to me and said I should not worry about the fact that we no longer had an official chaplain. Night or day, at no matter what hour, on my own initiative, I should call him, depending on how gravely ill the person was who was asking for the last sacraments."[38] The chaplain of Santa Isabel had to make room in his schedule, which was already over-crowded. He crossed the whole of Madrid, from south to north, from Atocha to Fuencarral, and came cross-country to the hospital. He showed up there every Tuesday to hear patients' confessions. But as the number of penitents increased and the visits became more prolonged, he found it necessary to hear confessions on Saturdays also.[39]

The patients waited for the young priest with real eagerness, hoping for a word of encouragement, a gesture, a simple smile that would light them up inside. "When he came to hear confessions and to help our patients with his assurances and words of advice," says Sister María Jesús, "I saw them waiting for him with joy and hope. And I saw them accept pain and death with a fervor and a self-giving that enkindled devotion in those around them."[40] "The patients who died in the hospital had no fear of death," says Sister Isabel. "They looked it in the eye and even accepted it with joy." This nun recalls the case of a young lady whose sole consolation had been to look again and again at the photo of her fiancé that she kept on her nightstand. Father Josemaría spoke to her and filled her with such consolation that she ceased to be preoccupied with the relief that the picture gave her and "died in a very holy way."[41]

On almost every Sunday and holy day he celebrated Mass for the whole hospital, and gave the homily. If the weather was good, he said Mass in the garden, out in the open, although the political situation was not favorable to public celebrations of the liturgy. The young priest was not intimidated by the dangers. "When I knew him," says the superior, Sister Engracia, on this point, "he was young but already very prudent, very serious, and very courageous."[42] Both his demeanor and his attire bore witness to his state in life. He always wore a cassock. Nevertheless, how constantly threatening the atmosphere was to the priest can be gleaned from the way that Father Somoano died and from these clear and pithy words of Sister Engracia: "Our hospital was then some distance from the city. There was opposition to the clergy on the part of most of the people who worked there. And Father Josemaría always had a serene but energetic attitude. One could see, even back then, that he would make a great leader. He was a man who could very calmly deal with anything."[43]

To go to King's Hospital in religious or priestly attire, through open country, was to expose oneself to insults and stonings. "We often had stones thrown at us," Sister María Jesús says in passing.[44] Father Josemaría was treated with no greater affection. And then, once inside the hospital, the priest was exposed to whatever contagious diseases the patients might have. To hear confessions in those communal wards, it was necessary to put one's ear close to the pillow, suffering the loud death rattle of the dying, and the spitting and coughing of the tuberculosis patients.

The story of the García Escobar sisters illustrates what tuberculosis meant in that era. In Hornachuelos, in the province of Córdoba, there was a family with three daughters: Braulia, Benilde, and María Ignacia. When Braulia was studying at the teachers' college in Córdoba, she caught tuberculosis from another girl who lived in the dorm. The family immediately tried to have her admitted to King's Hospital. Some time passed, and during the wait for a free bed, María Ignacia caught the disease from her sister. Because of the seriousness of her condition, she took, in 1930, the place reserved for Braulia. But by that time her illness was already incurable. Slowly and inexorably, disease and suffering consumed her body.[45]

María Ignacia was the patient Father Josemaría had characterized as "a soul, very pleasing to God, who could be the first vocation of expiation." In the spring of 1932 she was admitted to the Work, because Father Josemaría knew that she was offering up her sufferings to the Lord to accelerate the spiritual maturing of the apostolic enterprise in which Father Somoano was working. Soon her sisters learned that she belonged to Opus Dei. After a few months, since her end was quickly approaching, they moved to Madrid to be with her. On several occasions they were surprised by a visit of Father Josemaría to the wards. "What caught my attention," says Benilde, "was the joy and serenity of all those women, mothers of families, poor, separated from their children because of the contagiousness of the disease. As soon as they saw Father Josemaría come in, they were filled with a profound happiness."[46]

The founder tenderly nurtured that priceless vocation, encouraging her in her work of expiation and, with her, offering to the Lord the cruel pains she was suffering. On the days when the priest visited her, she could not contain her joy. The happiness of María Ignacia, says her sister Braulia, was then written all over her face, and she could hardly wait to give her the good news: "Father Josemaría has been here. I am very happy."[47]

She had spent one year in the Work, remaining faithful to her vocation, when the final phase of her Calvary began. "I stayed with her day and night," says Braulia. "She was in terrible pain, hurting from head to foot. Her last vertebra had become deformed and was sticking out something awful. She had wasted away, and had even gotten much shorter. Clarita, the nurse, could pick her up without anyone helping her."[48]

In May began a most intense expiatory holocaust, and a few days later, as he relates in his journal, Father Josemaría gave her viaticum.

> Feast of Saint Isidore, May 15, 1933: Yesterday I administered holy viaticum to my daughter María García. Hers is a vocation of expiation. Ill with tuberculosis, she was admitted to the Work, with the blessing of the Lord. A beautiful soul. She made a general confession to me before receiving Communion. I was accompanied to the national hospital (King's Hospital) by Juanito J. Vargas. That sister of ours loves the will of God. She sees in that long, painful, compounded illness (she has not a healthy bone in her body) the blessing and favor of Jesus, and, while affirming in her humility that she deserves punishment, she sees the terrible pain she is feeling in her whole system, especially on account of the abdominal adhesions, as not a punishment but a mercy.[49]

Four months she spent at death's door. Afterward came this obituary note from the founder, communicating the death of María Ignacia to his followers in the Work:

> On September 13, the vigil of the feast of the Exaltation of the Holy Cross, there fell asleep in the Lord this first sister of ours, of our house in heaven. . . . Prayer and suffering were the wheels of the chariot of triumph of this daughter of ours. We have not lost her; we have *gained* her. The realization that she has gone home should immediately turn our natural sorrow into supernatural joy, because now we are sure of an even mightier intercessor in heaven.[50]

Another sick woman, known to us only by her first name, Antonia, took the place of María Ignacia as "expiatory soul."[51]

As for Father Josemaría, how many thousands of hours he spent at the bedsides of the dying, and how many patients he tended in the crowded wards of the hospitals! He did so much tending of the dying that he even became skilled and expert in the pious art of enshrouding corpses.[52] But because he was, as Sister Isabel puts it, "not one to flaunt himself or his labors," it is hard to know how many hospitals he visited. One of the few sources of information on this point is the testimony of Archbishop Pedro Cantero, who, as a student in Madrid, occasionally accompanied Father Josemaría. He says, "He went to several hospitals: Hospital General, Hospital del Niño Jesús, Hospital de la Princesa, Hospital del Rey."[53] A journal entry mentions Hospital de la Princesa, but only by chance, in incidental fashion, simply because Father Josemaría happened to be interrupted one day when writing in his journal. Once the interruption was over and he was back from the hospital, he took up his pen again to relate what had happened.

"I had to break this off," he says, "because there came in first a priest, and then two young ladies, who gave me the name of a seriously ill young man at Hospital de la Princesa. The father of the young man—farm workers from Extremadura, the two of them were—did not want me to hear the confession of his son, who 'one time, as a child, went to confession and Communion,' because he didn't want him to be frightened. I went to the hospital. Thanks be to God, he made his confession. What ignorance! *Homines et iumenta salvabis, Domine!* [Men and beasts you will save, Lord!]"[54]

(What a reputation as a confessor to the dying he must have had if in an urgent situation first a priest and then two young ladies came to summon him! Also striking is the promptness with which he went and took care of the matter.)

Hospital de la Princesa, where (on May 8, 1933) this confession took place, was about three hundred yards from the Cicuéndez Academy—up San Bernardo Street, where it crosses Alberto Aguilera. This facility was a charity hospital, affiliated with the School of Medicine. The wards each had two hundred or more beds, which so filled up the space that there was no room even for nightstands. In December 1933 a young doctor named Tomás Canales Maeso was working at this hospital. He was an assistant to Dr. Blanc Fortacín, the same doctor who in 1927, soon after Father Josemaría's arrival in Madrid, had signed his vaccination certificate. One day Tomás found his boss speaking with a priest, whom he introduced as "a great priest, a relative of mine from my neck of the woods, from Barbastro, who is not a guerrilla."[55] ("Guerrilla" was what a priest who got involved in politics was called.) After that first meeting, Tomás came across him in the wards quite frequently. "I saw him at various hours of the morning," he says, "so I figure he must have stayed there for three or four hours at a time." Perhaps he took advantage of the hospital's proximity to the Academy and made some visits from there. In any case, he had his favorite wards—he spent the most time in the ones for contagious diseases. Repeatedly warned of the risks he was taking, he would invariably reply, calmly and with a smile, that he was "immunized against all diseases."[56]

In its service of the sick lay the solidity and hidden energy of the nascent Opus Dei. Looking back on the past, shortly before finishing his race in this world, the founder acknowledged this. "Those were intense years," he said, "in which Opus Dei was growing on the inside without us noticing it. . . . The human strength of the Work was the patients in the hospitals of Madrid, the most miserable ones; the sick who were living in their homes, having lost even the last human hope; the most ignorant in those poorest neighborhoods."[57]

Truly, his soul was strengthened in the school of suffering, in those long agonies, in fortitude in the face of pain. How many considerations and inspiring anecdotes come from his visits to the sick, and how many heroic acts will forever remain hidden! His journal entry for January 14, 1932, is like a triumphal ode to pain: "Blessed be pain. Loved be pain. Sanctified be pain, . . . pain will be glorified!"[58]

During a catechetical trip in 1974 through South America, he told the story behind that entry:

> There was this poor woman, a prostitute who had belonged to one of the most aristocratic families of Spain. When I met her, she was already decomposing—decomposing in body but being healed in soul, in a hospital for incurables. She had been a "camp follower" as they say, the poor thing. She had a husband, she had children; she had abandoned everything, driven crazy by passion. But then that creature knew how to love. She reminded me of Mary Magdalene: she knew how to love.[59]

With her body ravaged by pain and her soul purified by repentance, she entered her last agony. The priest administered the last spiritual aids, and at the threshold of death he whispered in her ear that litany of pain. Her voice breaking, she repeated the phrases aloud. "She died shortly after that, and is now in heaven, and has helped us a lot," said the founder.[60]

Thanks to so much prayer, mingled sometimes with blood and other times with tears, the Work was growing.

3. *The first followers*

María Ignacia García left behind a "little sketch" of the virtues of Father José María Somoano, in which she says that he told her, "María, you must pray hard for an intention which will benefit everyone. . . . Pray tirelessly, because the objective of the intention I'm talking about is very beautiful." And, she says, he went around the wards that way, "encouraging all the patients to offer prayers, and whatever sufferings they had, for that intention."[61]

Since he was very much loved, those petitions got a wonderful response. María Ignacia tells of a woman to whom the doctors, in desperation, applied a last-resort procedure—an excruciatingly painful throat operation carried out without any anesthetic. They cut into her neck with a large, triple-edged instrument, and as soon as she felt the piercing pain, she started repeating within herself, "My God! For Father José María's intention!"[62] During painful operations, continues María Ignacia, patients "always remembered that intention."

At the beginning of 1932 María Ignacia was suffering high fevers and was in constant pain, but still did not know what intention it was that Father Somoano was so eagerly asking them to pray for, since she was not yet a member of the Work. It occurred to her to say to him, "Father José María, I think your intention must be a very worthwhile one, because ever since you started asking me to pray and offer things up for it, Jesus has been treating me really splendidly. At night, when the pains don't allow me to sleep, I entertain myself by commending your intention to our Lord over and over again."[63]

Later, when the patient was a member of the Work, the chaplain explained to her that to construct Opus Dei well, it would be necessary to lay solid foundations of sanctity. "We're not looking for numbers, . . . never that!" the chaplain said to her. "Holy souls . . . souls in intimate union with Jesus . . . souls burning with the fire of divine love . . . great souls! Do you understand me?"

In the patient's manuscript these other words of the chaplain on the same subject immediately follow those just quoted: "No, no: it must be well grounded. This requires that we make sure the foundations are blocks of granite. . . . Foundations first; the rest will come later."[64] What was needed was primarily souls aspiring to sanctity, and secondarily a certain number to start the apostolates; that is to say, quality and at least a minimum quantity of vocations.

A journal entry from February 1932 shows Father Josemaría's sense of urgency and the headway his desire was making. "Jesus," he says, "I see that your Work can begin soon."[65] This holy impatience was a drive transmitted by the founder to his followers: to Father Somoano and to María Ignacia García; to those far away, and to those living in Madrid; to these latter by spoken word, and to the others by letter. "The Work of God—God is asking for it, loud and clear. But he wants us, too, to keep asking for it, by our behavior . . . , so as not to be obstacles. The hour, although we don't see it, is undoubtedly near."[66]

That tone of urgency is echoed not only in María Ignacia's "little sketch," but also in letters from Isidoro Zorzano. At Christmas of 1931, writing from Málaga to his "good friends" in Madrid, he asks that they fortify themselves interiorly for "when God needs us," and closes with these words: "I hope from him that this Christmas season will profit us and that in this coming year he will let us get into the ring, because that will be a sign that we are complete in quality and quantity."[67] (Spontaneously, without anyone having asked his opinion on the matter, Isidoro writes in March 1932, from Málaga: "I think our signal from God to begin our mission will be when we reach a dozen."[68])

* * *

Taking a bird's eye view from above the vicissitudes of those years, the founder would later describe the great variety of his first followers. "Almost everyone was represented," he said. "There were students, workmen, small businessmen, artists. . . . I didn't know back then that almost none of them would persevere, but the Lord knew that my poor, weak, cowardly heart needed that company and that support."[69]

More than tried vocations, it was a matter of persons, mostly young men, who had come to the priest for spiritual direction. But the Lord continued to play with him as one plays with a child. A careful reading of the journal entries shows in what that playing consisted. It shows a continuous traffic of souls, many of whom quickly became enthusiastic and then just as quickly lost interest.

The first group that gathered around him consisted of Pepe Romeo, Father Norberto Rodríguez, and Isidoro Zorzano. Actually, this group was a continuation of those "disciples" who used to appear with him at the Sotanillo.

Pepe belonged to the family to whose house he had brought the Blessed Sacrament from Santa Isabel when churches were being burned in Madrid. Father Norberto, the assistant chaplain of the Foundation for the Sick, joined the Work on his own initiative, without waiting for an invitation. The founder tells the story this way: "With a certain trepidation, I told him the secret one night. I expected him to say, 'You're imagining things; you're crazy.' But what actually happened was that, when I finished reading to him my old notes, he caught that divine craziness and said to me, in the most natural tone of voice, 'The first thing that has to be done is the work with men.'"[70]

As for Isidoro, his classmate in Logroño, he had kept up a friendly correspondence with him and occasionally run into him on the street before the summer of 1930, but now they had a new and providential encounter, which he relates in his journal entry for August 25, 1930:

> Yesterday, the feast of Saint Bartholomew, I was at the Romeos' house and I felt restless—for no apparent reason—and left earlier than expected; normally I would have waited for Don Manuel and Colo to get home. Just before arriving at the Foundation, I ran into Zorzano, on Nicasio Gallego Street. When told that I was not at home, he had left Casa Apostólica with the intention of going to Puerta del Sol, but a *certainty* of running into me—that's what he told me—made him turn onto Nicasio Gallego.[71]

Isidoro was working as an engineer in Andalusia, but had been moved by a spiritual restlessness to come to Madrid. From the first words he spoke, Father Josemaría knew this was a soul sent him by the Lord on a silver platter. So he made an appointment with him to meet that evening at the Foundation for the Sick, with the intention of speaking to him about the Work. "In the evening," the entry continues, "Isidoro came over. We spoke. He is very happy. He sees, as

I do, the hand of God. 'Now I know,' he said, 'why I've come to Madrid.' "

Some months passed after that meeting with Isidoro. In April 1931, just before the Republic was proclaimed, Father Josemaría wrote with exultant optimism: "Our men and women of God, in the apostolate of action, will have as their motto 'God and daring!' "[72] And in his next entry he enumerated the human resources on hand for his enterprise: "April 5, 1931: Yesterday—Easter Sunday—Father Norberto, Isidoro, Pepe, and I said the prayers of the Work of God."[73]

That was all: a young student, an engineer, an older and ailing priest, and, at the head, Father Josemaría. "Our men and women of God," those dreamed-of vocations, were long in coming. But the Lord was making it easier for Father Josemaría to meet young people who would understand the Work. By a kind of supernatural instinct, he observed in his proselytizing a series of curious coincidences between the arrivals of vocations and the feasts of apostles. In his journal entry for May 8, 1931, he writes:

> For the history of the Work of God, it is very interesting to note these coincidences. On August 24, the feast of Saint Bartholomew, came the vocation of Isidoro. On April 25, the feast of Saint Mark, I spoke with another. . . . On the feast of Saints Philip and James [May 1], I had occasion—without looking for it—to speak with two others. With one of them I had a long interview, and he wants to join the Work.[74]

This was no mere hunch, for three days earlier, when he had to change the date of an interview with another young man, it occurred to him to think, "The Lord is setting this up for tomorrow—is it going to be the feast of an apostle?" And so "I went to the sacristy and looked at the calendar. . . . Saint John before the Latin Gate! I had no doubt about the vocation of Adolfo."[75] When he wrote those lines, what he had already

seen confirmed the validity of those "coincidences," for he
adds, "And so it was. He is already a member. May God bless
him!"

From then on he habitually expected presents to rain down
from heaven on apostles' feasts. In 1933, on the feast of Saints
Philip and James, he wrote: "I asked myself yesterday evening,
more than once, What present will the holy apostles have for
the Work tomorrow?"[76]

From early on, he also noticed a couple of other odd "coincidences": that the vocations all came suddenly, and that they
were accepted without hesitation.

> So far, a curious fact, all vocations to the W. of G.
> have been sudden. Like those of the apostles: meet Christ
> and follow his calling. Even the first one did not hesitate.
> He came with me, behind Jesus, with no set itinerary. . . .
> On the feast of Saint Bartholomew, Isidoro; Saint Philip,
> Pepe M. A.; Saint John, Adolfo; later, Sebastián Cirac; in
> that same way, all of them. Not one hesitated; meeting
> Christ and following him was all one thing. May they
> persevere, Jesus, and may you send more apostles to
> your Work.[77]

If in the first tally of his followers he noted chronological
coincidences, and in the second that they had responded to
their vocations without resistance or delay, two years later, in
1933, he noted that his stay and ministry at the Santa Isabel
Foundation had not been a chance event with respect to the
history of the Work. Was it not obvious that a whole chain of
vocations was linked with his apostolate there? "Carmen,
Hermógenes, Modesta . . . , Gordon, Saturnino, Antonio, Jenaro. . . ."[78] The first three of these were women who frequently went to confession to the chaplain of Santa Isabel
and who ended up dedicating themselves to the Work. Father
Saturnino de Dios was a friend of Father Josemaría's who belonged to the Congregation of St. Philip Neri.

Some idea of Father Josemaría's zeal for recruiting souls can be gleaned from this paragraph of a letter to Isidoro, dated May 5, 1931:

> On the feast of Saint Mark I spoke with one. . . . On the feast of Saints Philip and James, with two. . . . Tomorrow, the feast of the apostle Saint John before the Latin Gate, I'll be speaking with another. A painter, a dentist, a fledgling doctor, a fledgling lawyer. . . . Also, Doral, the young man at the Institute, sent me a most beautiful letter.[79]

There was certainly no shortage of feasts of apostles in the liturgical calendar. So what happened to that harvest of vocations?

Frequent though the feasts were, the total number of vocations did not at that time increase. It would grow, and then, as some abandoned the enterprise, be reduced like the troops of Gideon. Some turned out not to have the necessary spiritual mettle and others were derailed by distractions. Among those who left was that Adolfo whom Father Josemaría had interviewed on the feast of Saint John before the Latin Gate.

On October 31, 1933, in the course of clarifying Adolfo's situation with respect to the Work, the founder made a quick and summary inventory of forces:

> Seeing that he does not have a vocation, he has ceased to belong to the W.
> Between the dead and . . . the *dead*, there are now . . . seven, Lord![80]

Counting Adolfo, there were four who had recently decided to stop following him. The founder suffered on account of this, though of course he realized that perseverance in the Work would require not just certain personal qualities and good will, but also a divine calling.

But what about the other three losses, those members of the Work who had died within the past few months? They had been very select souls, with a crystal-clear vocation. First God took Father Somoano, and most recently María Ignacia García, who had more than fulfilled her role of expiatory soul. (Indeed, when the priest did his spiritual accounting, the loss of María Ignacia got moved, as we have seen, to the credit column. "We have not lost her; we have *gained* her," he says in the obituary notice he wrote for her.[81])

Who could have foreseen that Luis Gordon would die in the same year in which he requested admission to the Work? Young, healthy, with a brilliant career and an enviable social position, he had everything needed to help provide the material and apostolic foundations that Father Josemaría was looking for. Our Lord took him without there having been any sign suggesting an early death. The obituary notice the founder wrote on November 5, 1932, the day of Luis's death, sets out a long list of virtues: "A good model: obedient, most discreet, charitable to the point of extravagance, humble, mortified, and penitent . . . , a man of the Eucharist and of prayer, most devoted to the Blessed Virgin and to Saint Thérèse . . . , a father to the workers in his factory. They cried when they heard of his death."[82]

Meditating on the first two deaths—those of Father Somoano and Luis Gordon, in 1932, when he was most in need of helping hands in the apostolic work, and of mature souls— Father Josemaría thought about his own life history, and in light of those memories he ended his obituary notice with these words:

> Let us love the cross, the holy cross which is falling on the Work of God. Our great King Jesus Christ chose to take away the two best-prepared ones so that we would not put our trust in anything earthly, not even someone's personal virtues, but only and exclusively in his most loving Providence.[83]

As for the rest, when the priest filially complained to the Lord that now there were already seven dead, he knew by experience the "divine logic" and was not discouraged. He kept using supernatural means, turning to prayer and mortification and active apostolate, even though he knew that in his apostolic fishing many souls would wriggle through his hands. "I set to work," he was to say, with an undertone of fatigue, "and it wasn't easy. Souls slipped away like eels in the water."[84]

During the retreat he made in 1934, it occurred to the founder to list, under the title "What Our Lord God Has Given Specifically to Me," all the many graces and special favors he could remember having received from heaven. In the list there appears an attribute not easy to classify, which he describes as "this *sanctifying* I-don't-know-what which brings it about that many souls are enkindled when I talk to them, although I myself am left feeling *extinguished*."[85] This was not something new. Already for some years there had been profound changes in souls who came into contact with that priest. The sculptor Jenaro Lázaro, who often chatted for a while with Father Josemaría when leaving the General Hospital on Sunday afternoons, says in his memoirs, "Those conversations made an indelible impression on me. He was a man of God who drew toward God the people he dealt with."[86]

On January 2, 1932, when he went to King's Hospital to explain the Work to Father Somoano, he was physically worn out (or, as he puts it, extinguished). "As a result of a talk with Father Norberto that morning, I was drained of energy, and when I went to speak with Somoano in the evening, I was less articulate than usual. Now this friend belongs to the Work."[87]

We can get some understanding by its fruit of this "sanctifying I-don't-know-what" that he mentions, and even more from reading what María Ignacia García wrote in her "little sketch" about Father Somoano's state of soul after that conversation with Father Josemaría about the Work. "I remember," she says, "his telling me that something unique had happened to him the first day he belonged to it: he could not get to sleep that night, for being so happy."[88]

Archbishop Pedro Cantero also bears witness to the tremendous spiritual impact of his words. Telling how he first met Father Josemaría (in a corridor of Madrid's law school, in September 1930), he adds that after that first chat, "a friendship began that would last for the rest of our lives. . . . Josemaría, little by little, got into my soul, doing a real priest-to-priest apostolate."[89] Afterward came the Republic, with the already mentioned sacrileges and other terrible outrages. For some time the two friends did not see each other. But then, quite unexpectedly, on the evening of August 14, 1931, when "the smoke from the burning of the religious houses" still "seemed to be floating" over Madrid, Father Josemaría showed up at the home of his friend. Father Pedro was feeling very dejected and pessimistic, but the founder got him out of his depression. His words, in fact, had such power that, as Archbishop Cantero testifies, "he changed the whole perspective of my life and of my pastoral ministry."[90] What he did not know at the time was that the founder, in order to accomplish that change, had solicited prayers and mortifications from Isidoro Zorzano, Father Norberto, the nuns at Santa Isabel, the patients in the hospitals, and even his own guardian angel.[91] For it was a habitual thing for Father Josemaría to seek the "complicity" of the angels in his apostolic endeavors.

* * *

When Father Josemaría recalled the great variety that there had been among his followers even in the early days, he said it was as if the Lord had wanted to show him that in Opus Dei there would have to be all kinds of people and professions: "college students, manual workers, small businessmen, artists. . . ." Surprisingly, in this list he did not mention priests. Nevertheless, he had already started some meetings with priests, which he called "Monday conferences." These began on February 22, 1932, the Monday before the feast of Saint Matthias. "Last Monday," he says in his journal, "we five priests had our first meeting. We will continue meeting once a week, to be united. I gave everyone the first meditation of a series on our vocation."[92]

Some of these priests—Father Norberto and Father Lino Vea-Murguía, for example—had joined Father Josemaría early and more or less spontaneously.[93] Others, such as Father Somoano, had come a little later. When it came to trying to communicate to them the spirit of the Work, Father Josemaría found himself faced with a long, hard task. It turned out, in fact, to be much harder than he had anticipated, since it involved creating a both supernatural and natural bond of affection and doctrine that would unite them to himself as founder of Opus Dei. As part of the formation process, he would bring them with him on hospital visits and to teach catechism classes in parishes and schools.[94]

Something else said by María Ignacia García about Father Somoano gives us a good idea of the interest Father Josemaría took in the formation of that group of priests: "When he returned on Mondays from taking part in the spiritual meetings of our Work, one had only to look at him to see how happy and satisfied he was. His most prized possession was the little notebook in which he recorded the points of the meditations and other little things from those meetings."[95]

Father Josemaría certainly preached to the priests by example and infused his words with the vibrant warmth of his faith and optimism, giving them glimpses of glowing ideals. All this was reflected in the attitude of Father Somoano, as appears from a statement in the obituary written about him by the founder: "At our last priestly meeting, the Monday before his death, with what enthusiasm he listened to the plans for beginning our activity!"[96]

The number present at those first meetings rarely exceeded half a dozen. In the journal entry for September 28, 1932, we read: "Last Monday, with Father Norberto and in his house, Lino, J. M. Vegas, Sebastián Cirac, and I got together. We talked about the Work and prayed for the repose of the soul of José María Somoano."[97] (Half of that group died as martyrs, as victims of religious hatred; Fathers Lino Vea-Murguía and José María Vegas were among the thousands of priests assassinated in 1936.[98])

In giving formation to people, Father Josemaría also made use of correspondence, since some of those he directed lived outside Madrid. Through letters written to him by Isidoro Zorzano, who for several years resided in Málaga, we learn something of the impassioned words of Father Josemaría. A few days after that memorable chat of August 24, in Madrid, during which Isidoro discovered his vocation, he wrote the founder this letter:

> Málaga, September 5, 1930. . . . The gist of our last conversation left me very satisfied, because it suggested to me new ideas and gave me new hopes, or, better to say, restored lost hopes. . . . [But] the optimism that you injected into me is in some danger. I feel the need to get together with you so that with your help I can get definitively oriented in that new era to which you have opened my eyes, which is precisely the ideal that I had been forging for myself, but which I had thought unattainable.[99]

And a week later he wrote this:

> Málaga, September 14, 1930. . . . You say your letter is long, but to me it seems very short. I have read it several times, because it really lifts my spirits. I went to Communion today, and followed your advice to unite my spirit to the Work of God. I now find myself completely comforted, my spirit pervaded with a sense of well-being, with a peace I have never felt before. I owe it all to the Work of God.[100]

The second anniversary of the beginning of the women's branch of Opus Dei was approaching, and this apostolic field was still practically a desert. There was an obvious delay in the coming of these vocations. Within the confines of Santa Isabel's confessional the founder patiently waited—sowing his time of waiting with prayers—for our Lord to send him souls.

In his journal he writes, "Sunday, November 8, 1931: This past Friday, I believe our Lord presented me with a soul who could begin, in due time, the women's branch of the Work of God."[101] And on the following Tuesday he writes to Isidoro, "You know, I think our King has sent me a soul to begin the women's branch."[102] This soul vacillated for a while, but then one day she asked the priest for an interview, having decided to ask admission to the Work. It had been some time since Father Josemaría had made any journal entries, but when he did take up his pen to record the date and event, he noted another "coincidence." "Precisely yesterday, the fourteenth of February of 1932, was the day of the first female vocation—exactly two years after our Lord asked for this work of women. How good Jesus is!"[103]

A few weeks later, María Ignacia requested admission. Carmen Cuervo (the first female vocation) and the new "vocation of expiation" met at King's Hospital on Sunday, April 10, 1932. On the following Monday, when the priests had their meeting, Father Josemaría suggested that they pray a *Te Deum*.[104]

He had good reason. Thanks be to God, the work with women was now under way. But if he had no hesitation in approaching suffering women patients and even those with contagious diseases, Father Josemaría had quite a different stance toward healthy women. He inflexibly kept his distance, caring for them only in the confessional. Such, in fact, was his delicacy in dealing with the first women of the Work that for spiritual direction he sent them to Father Norberto or Father Lino.[105]

On the third anniversary of the founding, he could not help seeing that the women's side of the apostolate was rather weak. But the founder did not get discouraged; he kept hoping for vocations, without getting impatient. "February 14, 1933: It is now three years since our Lord asked for the women's branch. How many graces since then! But, so far, very few women."[106]

A year later, Carmen Cuervo's visit to María Ignacia at King's Hospital was reenacted, but in a different place and by different persons. Now Hermógenes was visiting Antonia at the General Hospital.

> February 14, 1934: It is four years today since the Lord inspired the women's branch. I have had Hermógenes take a present to Antonia, a patient at the hospital. Let's see when you're going to send me, my God, the woman who can head them up in the beginning, letting herself be formed![107]

The story of his first followers, whether students, priests, or women, was that of a weaving and an unraveling, a constant building up and crumbling. Father Josemaría knew very well that some of those whom God was sending to encourage him would never fit in, but he also knew that in the meantime they would improve in their interior life. He realized that, as the Latin proverb goes, "anguillam cauda tenebat"—that he was trying to catch eels by the tail. They slipped away.

In spite of that, neither the withdrawals nor the deaths caused him to lose his supernatural optimism, although those losses caused him great pain. But graver consequences resulted from his leaving the direction of the female vocations in the hands of the other priests—priests who never fully understood the spirit of Opus Dei.

In 1939 Father Josemaría added a brief note to one of his earlier journal entries, explaining, in as few words as possible, that lacking time to give to the women, he had entrusted the task of forming them to Fathers Norberto and Lino, and it was yet to be accomplished.[108]

4. *A retreat with Saint John of the Cross*

"If you could see how much I long for solitude!" Father Josemaría wrote on April 8, 1932, to Father José Pou de Foxá. "But

honey is not made for the mouth of a donkey. I have to be content with a life of noise and movement, of dancing all day long
from here to there. Blessed and beloved be the will of God."[109]

His life really was one of constant activity: Masses, other
church functions, confessions of nuns and parishioners at Santa
Isabel; confessions of nuns and the preparation of girls for First
Communion at the nearby Assumption School; visits to hospitals; chats with, and spiritual direction of, young people and
priests. . . .[110] This exhausting pastoral dedication did not benefit him financially, so to all those activities he was forced to add
the giving of classes at the Cicuéndez Academy and of private
lessons at home. None of these occupations could be eliminated.
The pastoral ones were indispensable to his soul, and the educational ones to his support, or at least to that of his family.

That desire for solitude which he expressed in the above-
quoted letter was at times a temptation, in which weariness or
the devil suggested that it would not be a bad idea for him to
dedicate himself to a life of greater spiritual tranquillity, free
of the hustle and bustle of the apostolic struggle. In his journal
we read:

> The temptation returns, whispering in my ears about
> a life of peace and virtue: not that of Father X or Brother
> So-and-so, but that of a simple little priest in the most re-
> mote rural parish, with no great struggles or great ideals
> calling for immediate action. . . .[111]

It was around April 1932 that he was assaulted by these
temptations to lead a different kind of life. To repel them,
the chaplain sought the help of the powerful prayers of innocent souls. On the days when he went to prepare the little
girls for their First Communion, he would ask that they all
pray, together with him, "a Hail Mary for the saint of the
whacks."[112] (Would those tender souls understand what he
meant by "saint of the whacks"?) But his reason for writing the
above-mentioned letter to Father Pou de Foxá was something

quite different. "If God doesn't do something to prevent it," Father Josemaría told him, "I will have to go to Saragossa next June, so that a son of the Guevaras can take an examination."[113]

His confessor urged him to buy a cassock and a priest's hat before the trip. (He must have been in a bad way as far as clothes were concerned.) He also bought "a new notebook, because I was thinking about putting my Catalinas in a journal."[114]

On June 13, when he got back to Madrid, the new notebook was still empty. He had not made a single entry. But he had sent a few short letters to his family.[115]

The summer of 1932 was rough. Never could he find the solitude he was yearning for. On August 10 some army officers and groups of monarchist students staged a disorderly uprising in Madrid. The government and the police had advance warning, so the revolt was quickly put down and peace restored. Those involved ended up in prison. José Manuel Doménech, one of those students who accompanied Father Josemaría to the General Hospital on Sundays, relates his adventures. "I had taken part," he says, "together with other students in Madrid, in the events of August 10. We had gone early in the morning, armed, to take over the post office building. Most of us were arrested and sent to Cárcel Modelo, first to the area for political prisoners and later to a high-security area with strict regulations."[116]

Also imprisoned was Adolfo Gómez—the young man who had joined Opus Dei on the feast of Saint John before the Latin Gate, and one of those who had stood guard over churches and religious houses at night to prevent them from being set on fire or otherwise attacked.

In the journal entry for that day, we read:

Feast of Saint Lawrence, August 10, 1932: At 5:00 this morning, I was awakened by shots, real volleys, and the rattle of machine guns. I went to Santa Isabel dressed as a layman. Our Adolfo is in prison. He is a great soul who understands the ideal and knows how to make sacrifices for it. May the Lord preserve him for us.[117]

That same day, August 10, he learned where Adolfo was being held, but was not allowed to see him. He spent several days in sorrowful waiting, without getting to speak with the prisoner. Finally he was able to leave a few lines of consolation for him.

Vigil of Saint Bartholomew, August 23, 1932: We have been sending Adolfo a few things. I go to the prison every day. I believe that today—I am going with his mother—I will see him. For now I'm not going to write any more on this matter.[118]

The young priest showed up at Cárcel Modelo dressed in his cassock, "even though by making such visits to those held he was calling attention to himself and risking persecution," says José Antonio Palacios, another of the jailed students.[119] Father Josemaría got acquainted with some of those activist students. He spoke with them in the political prisoners' visiting room, a large hall with a continuous grille of closely spaced bars separating visitors and prisoners. He recommended cheerfulness and good humor, speaking to them about our Lady and about working with a supernatural outlook, so that they would not fall into idleness and would continue to offer to the Lord some hours of study. Books were not, in those circumstances, a matter of great concern to those agitated students. But the priest told them things in such a persuasive way, says José Antonio, that "to make good use of the time, I set about giving a class and reviewing my French."[120]

One day, while in his cell, José Manuel Doménech heard his name called out. When he opened the grating, a prison official handed him an envelope. In it was a small copy of the Little Office of Our Lady, with the following inscription:

Blessed and undefiled Virgin Mother, glorious Queen of the World, intercede with the Lord for the Spanish people.
To José M. Doménech, with great affection
Madrid, August 1932
José M. Escrivá[121]

"The affection of the Father and his concern for my interior life," says José Manuel, "made a profound impression on me; he knew that I knew and prayed the Little Office."[122]

In September, Father Josemaría lost track of many of these youths. A good number of the political prisoners were deported to Africa. But that did not cause him to suspend his visits to inmates who remained in Cárcel Modelo.

All summer the priest had felt intense longings for solitude, for a spiritual retreat. On June 1, nearly two months after complaining about this to his friend Father Pou de Foxá, he wrote in his journal:

> I need solitude. I am yearning for a long retreat, to speak with God, far from everything. If he wants this, he will give me an opportunity. There I'll be able to settle so many things that are churning within me. And Jesus, surely, will impress on my mind some important details about his Work.[123]

Finally, in September, arrangements were made. With the authorization of the Carmelite provincial, he prepared to make a weeklong retreat in Segovia, at the monastery where the remains of Saint John of the Cross are kept. On October 2 he wrote:

> Feast of the Holy Guardian Angels, vigil of Saint Thérèse, 1932: Four years! The Lord even reminded me of this, by sending a vocation for the women's branch. . . . Tomorrow I go to Segovia for a retreat, close to Saint John of the Cross. I have asked, I have *begged*, for a lot of prayer. We shall see.[124]

He arrived at the monastery of the Discalced Carmelites of Segovia on Monday, October 3, 1932, and immediately set about preparing a plan for the retreat. He was thinking of doing it in complete isolation, as was his custom, not attending any talks or sermons. His cell had "a beautiful number"—33, which for him was a double reminder of the Persons of the Blessed Trinity—and a small plaque which read, "*Gloriatio. Et in timore Dei sit tibi gloriatio. Sir 9:16*" ["Glorying. Let your glorying be in the fear of the Lord"]. At once there came to his mind that bad time he had gone through the previous October, when, in the midst of his contemplation of his divine filiation, our Lord had veiled from his mind a right understanding of "the fear of the Lord." It seemed too much of a coincidence for the little plaque not to be a reminder from the Lord.[125]

He adjusted the plan of his retreat to the demands of the monastery schedule. Rising time was 4:45 A.M. At 5:30 there would be an hour of meditation, followed by Holy Mass. At 8:00 was breakfast; at 9:30, another hour of meditation; at 11:30, lunch. In the afternoon there would be two one-hour meditations, the Rosary, and spiritual reading. At 6:15 came supper, followed by examination of conscience and use of the discipline. At 10:00, after having said the prayers of the Work, he went to bed.[126]

There was a magnificent view from the monastery. Above the grove stretching down toward the river valley, one could see in the distance a sharp promontory with a castle perched on its ridge. Father Josemaría felt assured that our Lord would be treating him well, because of his being "in the house of the Lord's Mother, at a Carmelite monastery." And suddenly there came to him that long-ago memory of Logroño, of footprints left in the snow by a Discalced Carmelite.[127] That was how his story had begun, and here he was, in a Carmelite monastery, alone with his God.

* * *

The notes from the first days of his retreat are brief. A few lines are enough to indicate the course of his thinking.

First day. God is my Father. And I'm not departing from this consideration. . . . I am God's, . . . and God is mine.

Second day, Wednesday. O Domine! Tuus sum ego, salvum me fac! Et a te nunquam separari permittas! [Lord, I am yours—save me! And never let me be parted from you!] Lord, it's not that easy to become a saint! I can very well believe that Saint Teresa said to you, "that's why you have so few friends."

Third day, Thursday. Neither the consideration of the gravity of sin nor the thought of the eternal punishments that it merited, and does merit, moves me. . . . I am so cold. At most, I come out of all this crying out to my God, "I love you, because you are good. I am a wretch. . . . Punish me, but make me love you more each day."[128]

For that third day, October 6, there is also this entry:

Today, in the chapel of Saint John of the Cross (I spend some periods of accompanied solitude there each day), I saw that when beginning the priests' meetings and all other meetings having to do with the W. of G., we should say the following prayers . . . : (1) *Veni, Sancte Spiritus.* (2) *Sancte Michaël, ora pro nobis. Sancte Gabriel, ora pro nobis. Sancte Raphaël, ora pro nobis.* (3) *In nomine Patris, et Filii, et Spiritus Sancti. Amen.* (4) *Sancta Maria, Sedes Sapientiae, ora pro nobis.*[129]

The special significance of those words would have gone unnoticed had there not been other autobiographical testimonies corresponding to and complementing them, such as this one written in 1941:

I spent long periods of prayer in the chapel where the remains of Saint John of the Cross are kept; and there, in that chapel, I was for the first time inwardly moved to invoke the three archangels and the three apostles whose intercession we members of Opus Dei ask for in our prayers.

From that moment they were taken as the patrons of the three works that make up Opus Dei.[130]

As will be explained later, that supernatural impulse came to determine the structure and apostolic organization of Opus Dei. From Friday, the fourth day of the retreat, come the following considerations:

> The reign of Jesus Christ: that's what I'm about! . . . The donkey! No longer is it a mangy donkey. . . . From its poor remains they can make drums—war drums, and the tambourines and rustic flutes of a shepherd. That's what the remains of Jesus' donkey can be used for: to sound the call to the great battle for God's glory and for the universal and effective reign of Christ, my Lord, and to sing passionate songs, songs of the shepherds of Bethlehem, to the Child born to die for me! . . .
>
> I felt as though within me voices were saying to me, "Get out of here, you hypocrite. You're wasting time, devoting yourself . . . to concocting flowery phrases." And at that moment, as if to confirm that thought, I had an idiotic notion, which I'm going to record. Seeing the Alcázar of Segovia, I thought that that castle, jagged against the sky, looking like cardboard, is asking out loud for some little tin soldiers, to be played with by a boy who is the son of giants. I wondered: Have I before now also been concocting phrases without substance? And I clearly perceived: No, I have been praying.[131]

In his retreat he was following a personal plan, on his own, but not just as he pleased. Father Sánchez had given him some guidelines to go by. Afterward, moreover, his confessor would read all that the retreatant wrote during those days. "I am adding this sentence," he expressly states in one place, "so that when my Father Sánchez reads my notes, he will see how I'm doing: I haven't gotten out of the coldness, except for a few flashes of fervor."[132]

On Sunday he meditated on purity—"holy purity, humility of the flesh"—and decided to renew before the Blessed Virgin, when he finished the retreat, his priestly commitment of faithful love.[133] From there he went on to examine his level of detachment, and resolved to be more generous and leave everything in the hands of the Lord.[134] Next he made this declaration of submission of his will: "I am determined always to obey my spiritual father. The same goes for my superiors in the hierarchy."[135]

Since July 1930 he had been going to confession to Father Valentín Sánchez Ruiz, with the exception of the weeks in which the good Jesuit had been in hiding because of the decree dissolving the Society of Jesus. From the start they had had an understanding that the foundational mission and the governing of the Work lay outside the scope of the spiritual direction he expected from his confessor. His confessor was director not of the Work of God but of the priest. About the spiritual direction of Father Sánchez, the founder would later write: "He had nothing to do with the Work, in that I never let him control or have a say in it."[136]

With this proviso, and with absolute simplicity, he declares: "Everything having to do with my soul, I have communicated and always will communicate to my spiritual director, keeping nothing back."[137]

Even so, behind this steadfast behavior one can see how much it cost him to bare his soul when that might tend to raise him in the eyes of the other person.

> Feast of Saint Mark, April 25, 1932: This morning I was with my Father Sánchez. I had decided to tell him what happened on the 20th. I felt a kind of reluctance or shame. It cost me, but I told him.[138]

This event was no small thing. A few nights earlier, upon going to bed, he had asked Saint Joseph and the souls in purgatory, to whom he had a special devotion, to do him the favor of waking him up at a quarter to six. (He had to appeal to them because his sleepiness was mixed with exhaustion.) This is his journal entry about what happened:

> As always happens when I've asked this with humility, regardless of what time I've gone to bed, this morning I woke out of a deep sleep as if I had been called, totally sure it was time for me to get up. And sure enough, it was a quarter to six. Last night, also as usual, I had asked the Lord to give me strength to overcome my laziness at wake-up time, because—I confess this to my shame—something so small is enormously hard for me and there are plenty of days when, in spite of that supernatural call, I stay in bed a while longer. Today, when I saw what time it was, I prayed, I struggled . . . and I stayed in bed. Finally, at six-fifteen according to my alarm clock (which has been broken for some time), I got up. Full of humiliation, I prostrated myself on the floor, acknowledging my fault, and then—with a *Serviam!* ["I will serve!"]—got dressed and started my meditation. And then, somewhere between six-thirty and a quarter to seven, I saw, for quite some time, that the face of my Virgin of the Kisses was filled with happiness, with joy. I looked very carefully. I believed she was smiling, because it had that effect on me, even though her lips hadn't moved. Very calmly, I said to my Mother a lot of sweet things.[139]

It was not the first time something like that had happened. He tried not to attach too much importance to such things. He refused to "easily admit extraordinary things." But after testing them to see if they were just products of sensory suggestion, he had to submit to the evidence. "I went so far as to set up some tests," he writes, "to see if this was just coming from my imagination, because I don't easily admit extraordinary things. But it was all to no avail. The face of my Virgin of the Kisses, when I did my absolute best to get myself to see her smiling, kept that hieratic seriousness that the poor statue has."[140]

The little statue of the Holy Virgin of the Kisses, "Sancta Os-
culorum Virgo," had actually done an amazing thing. "Well,
then, my Lady Holy Mary . . . has given her little boy a caress."[141]

Father Sánchez's spiritual directee kept quiet about many
little humiliations by which he was advancing on the road of patience. It really hurt him, to the point of bringing tears to his eyes,
to have to go very hurriedly, after giving classes or visiting the
sick, practically running to Chamartín, where the Jesuit priest
lived after the burning of the order's residence on De La Flor
Street, and then, when he asked for him, often to be told by the
porter to come back another day. Didn't his confessor realize that
it was not easy for him to find the time to travel there, outside
Madrid? Nor did he feel it appropriate to disclose that he had to
get there on foot, taking a tiring trek through the boondocks,
since he did not have the few cents needed to take the streetcar.[142]

Father Sánchez was a good director of souls, and Father
Josemaría was very grateful to him, because even the annoyance
of the waits in Chamartín did him "some real good."[143] In his
journal and in his correspondence there are occasional discreet
words of praise for his confessor. There are also some observations, on such matters as those long waits and wasted trips, that
could not have been much to his confessor's liking, but he jotted
them down anyway, aware as he was that they would be read by
the interested party. However, this particular aspect of his relationship with his confessor was secondary and incidental. The
essential thing, the founder insisted, was for him "to fulfill the
very clearly manifested will of God regarding his Work."[144]

During the last days of his retreat in Segovia, he meditated
on the passion and resurrection of our Lord—but not without
the devil, "Old Scratch," giving him a bad time all through
Sunday night with his dirty tricks.

> Last night, the devil was at large in my cell and again
> stirred up things from the past. He gave me a hard time. This
> morning, too. I offer it up to you, my God, as expiation. But
> I am weak. I can't do anything, I'm not worth anything—

don't leave me. Grieved by all this, I had a talk with my father John of the Cross: "This is the way you treat me in your house? How can you allow Old Scratch to torment your guests? I thought you were more hospitable. . . ."[145]

*   *   *

To the retreat he brought some questions of conscience that he needed to resolve as soon as possible, since they affected his dedication to the Work. The first had to do with his studies: "Should I get doctorates in civil law and sacred theology?"[146] For greater clarity in his examining of this question, he adopted the system of setting out, in written and numbered form, all the pros and cons. The result was that he resolved to present his law dissertation and obtain the doctorate in sacred theology in 1933.[147]

Now he went to the second question: "Would it be a good idea for me to take some competitive examinations, for a university professorship, for instance?" He must have debated the matter fairly thoroughly with himself when he wrote, "Arguments in favor: I can honestly say that I don't see any." He did not see any because he was firmly convinced that God did not need any such thing to bring about the Work. "For me to seek a secular occupation, after considering what lies ahead, would be to doubt the divine origin of the Work—of that which is my reason for being on this earth."[148]

Besides, everything seemed to militate against a professorship. Although he had an aptitude for canon law, a subject he had delved into during his last years of teaching in Saragossa and Madrid, it would take many years and a lot of study to prepare for a career in it. And that's to say nothing of the financial aspect, for how would he support his family in the meantime?

Also against it were some serious supernatural considerations. To dedicate himself to a professorship would be to steal time from the Work of God. His vocation demanded a total availability. He must be "only and exclusively—and always—this: a priest, a father director of souls, hidden, buried alive, for Love."[149]

He saved for last the most delicate of his problems—most delicate because it involved other persons. This was the question of "the family, my family." On this matter Father Norberto had given him a note to meditate on. Father Josemaría made a visit to the Blessed Sacrament to think it over—"Let's see what Jesus says!"[150] The note from Father Norberto, says Father Josemaría, was focused "very much on the divine." That is to say, he presented only supernatural arguments—irrefutable, but in a sense dehumanized, since, in his particular case, they amounted to a demand that he shake off all affection for his blood relatives.

Putting that focus "on the divine" above every other consideration, as the basis of his analysis, Father Josemaría calmly reviewed the events and realities that had affected the development of his life and that of his family. These considerations passed before him without being retouched or softened: the sacrifices his parents had made to give him a good education despite their financial setbacks; the hopes they had placed in him, and the "indisputable financial harm" done them by his becoming a priest; and, finally, the fact that the household situation had taken a turn for the worse when, in his determination to follow a "divine whim," he refused to accept an ecclesiastical position.[151] Thus he came to the conclusion that the really practical way to protect his family was to let the Lord operate.

> Things of God must be done as God wants. I am God's, I want to be God's. When I truly am such, he will—immediately—take care of all this, rewarding my faith and my love and the quiet and not at all small sacrifices made by my mother and sister and brother. Let's let the Lord work.[152]

Before ending the retreat, he sketched out a "minimal program of spiritual life," which comprised various devotions: the Divine Office; an hour of prayer in the morning and another in the evening; a half hour of thanksgiving after Mass; praying the Rosary, bringing to life each scene; examinations of conscience at midday and in the evening; a visit to the Blessed Sacrament; praying the prayers of the Work; and reading from the New Testament and from some other spiritual book. To this program he added a page of "Resolutions" that included "not to overlook the little things," "to invoke my guardian angel," and "to acquire a grave and modest demeanor." All this was accompanied by new corporal mortifications: the daily wearing of a cilice; sleeping on the floor three times a week; and a total fast, without even bread or water, one day each week.

Finally, just before leaving Segovia, he made an explicit reaffirmation of his faith in the supernatural origin of the Work, thus strengthening his determined efforts at self-surrender:

> In conclusion: I feel that even if, by God's permission, I should remain alone in this enterprise, and even if I should find myself dishonored and poor—more so than I already am—and sick. . . . I will not have any doubt about either the divine origin of the Work or its realization! And I stand by my conviction that the sure means of carrying out the will of God, prior to moving and acting, are to pray, pray, pray, and expiate, expiate, expiate.[153]

5. *The Saint Raphael work*

During the Segovia retreat, he had written that he had only two paths open to him: "the path of the cross, fulfilling the will of God in the founding of the Work, which will lead me to sanctity . . . and the wide—and stupid!—path of perdition, fulfilling my own will."[154]

"Now, right now, what can I do for the Work?" he afterward asked himself, fully determined and eager to follow the path of the cross. Faithful to his resolve always to give priority to the use of the supernatural means of prayer and expiation before launching into apostolic activity, he made some impressive resolutions for expiation involving all his senses, both internal and external. The new list of mortifications complements the one drawn up in Segovia. Dated December 3, 1932, it consists of nine categorical and concrete declarations of intent. The first is this very brief one: "Not to look—ever!"[155]

This was his response to a consideration he had pondered on the sixth day of his retreat. "Why look," he had asked himself, "if *my world* is inside me?"[156] This was not disdain; it was a personal ascetical renunciation of an unlimited enjoyment of sight, of curiosity regarding the infinity of pleasing forms, the diversity of light and colors, the charm of created beings. That resolve never to gaze at anything is best understood in relation to its character as a holocaust. One must take into account the proclivities of his sense of sight. His eyes were quick to discover the beauties of the external world and tended to linger on them like someone caressing fine velvet. "My God!" we read in his journal entry for November 14, 1932, "I find charm and beauty in everything I see. I will guard my sight at all times, for Love."[157] The rest of the resolutions constituted a broad and substantial program of mortification of the bodily senses and inner faculties.

* * *

From the very start the Work was perfectly "sketched out," but to make it a reality it was necessary to carry out apostolate, gathering vocations and transmitting to them the spirituality proper to Opus Dei.[158] By this time Father Josemaría had a group of priests, a group of young laymen, and two or three women, all prepared to respond to the call to sanctity in the midst of the world. There also were other individuals to whom he was giving spiritual direction. For some time now he had seen a need to organize the personal apostolate he was developing with such different persons, and had been seeking a way to give it some structure. At one point he thought of perhaps creating an association for university students, under the title "the Pious Union of Our Lady of Hope."[159] But he gave up that idea on Thursday, October 6, 1932, when, while praying in the chapel of Saint John of the Cross during his retreat at the Discalced Carmelite monastery in Segovia, he was "for the first time inwardly moved to invoke the three archangels and the three apostles whose intercession we members of Opus Dei ask for in our prayers": Saints Michael, Gabriel, and Raphael, and Saints Peter, Paul, and John.[160] From that moment on he considered them the patrons of the different fields of apostolate that would make up Opus Dei.

Under the patronage of Saint Raphael would be the work of Christian formation of young people. From it would come Opus Dei's celibate vocations, which the founder would place under the patronage of Saint Michael for their formation, both spiritual and human. Married people who participated in the apostolic tasks of the Work, or who formed part of it, would have Saint Gabriel as their patron.

Ultimately the founder came to the conclusion that the apostolate with young people should not function as any type of association, but could be carried out in the setting of an "academy," a private facility offering supplemental education.[161] But first there was a change in Father Josemaría's life that, although at first sight it would seem to have little to do with the Saint Raphael work, was in fact closely connected with the beginning of the formation of university youth.

"After a lot of prayer to our Lord," we read in the entry for December 9, 1932, "I found, *providentially,* a decent little apartment in which to live with my family. *Deo gratias.* I requested a loan from the 'Corporation,' to be paid, like the other, in a year. So I'm able to move."[162]

The apartment was on the second floor, left-hand side, of a building on Martínez Campos Street. The rent was 1,380 pesetas a year, to be paid by the month, in advance.[163] This arrangement must have been quite an improvement in some way for Father Josemaría to have welcomed it with a *Deo gratias.* Once more

Doña Dolores had to move her furniture, but this time to a good-size apartment, where its quality would be more easily observed; in the apartment on Viriato Street there had not been room even for her chairs. Now, without waiting until he could have an "academy," Father Josemaría started hosting meetings with priests and students. There, at the apartment, they had their get-togethers and he gave them formational talks.

That he undertook to pay 1,380 pesetas a year should not, however, be taken to imply an improvement in the financial situation of the Escrivá family. Consider this anecdote jotted down by Father Josemaría a few days after he signed the rental agreement:

> Yesterday my pocket watch stopped. This put me in a real bind, since it's the only watch I've got and since my *capital*, at the moment, amounts to seventy-five cents. . . . I talked this over with my Lord, and suggested that he have my guardian angel, to whom he has given more talent than all the watchmakers in the world, fix my watch. He seemed not to have heard me, because I shook and fiddled with the broken watch again and again, to no avail. Then . . . I knelt down and started saying an Our Father and a Hail Mary. I think I hadn't yet finished when I picked up the watch, touched the hands . . . and it started running! I gave thanks to my good Father.[164]

It seems this was not an isolated or fortuitous incident. Evidently he was used to handing over mechanical problems to his guardian angel—"the watchmaker, I'll call him from now on," he writes.[165] The angel, in any case, now certainly had no lack of work, for it was many months before Father Josemaría was able to pay to have the watch repaired.

Poverty—"my great lady," he called it—presided over his whole life, including the start of the Saint Raphael work, the work with young people. The rental agreement was signed December 10. So what was his financial situation at the end of November?

Around this time, he found a discarded picture of the Immaculate Virgin, smudged with dirt, near the gate of one of the schools run by the Foundation for the Sick. Father Josemaría used to pick up religious pictures thrown out on the street and then, when he got home, burn them. But when he picked this one up, he got the feeling that an offense had been intended— that this was a page torn from a catechism out of hatred. "For this reason," he says in his journal, "I will not burn the poor picture, though it is badly done and the paper it's on is cheap and torn. I will save it, and put it in a nice frame when I have the money . . . and who's to tell me that there won't someday be a devotion, of love and reparation, to 'Our Lady of the Catechism'!"[166]

On December 2, a week before renting the new apartment, not having the money for a small frame, he took stock of his evangelical poverty with neither pride nor lamentation. "I am," he says, "more impoverished than ever. Our poverty (my great lady, poverty) has for years been as real as that of the people who beg in the streets. Our Father in heaven feeds and clothes us (with nothing superfluous, and even without some things normally considered necessities), just as he feeds and clothes the birds, as the Gospel says. This financial situation doesn't bother me the least little bit. We're used to living on miracles."[167]

He got a loan for the apartment, and managed to get a frame for the picture. In exchange for that favor and homage, he asked our Lady to provide him a place where he could teach catechism. Our Lady did not have to be asked twice.

Father Josemaría was very familiar with the poor neighborhoods between Tetuán de las Victorias and King's Hospital. Groups of shacks, with miserable hovels here and there, made up "La Ventilla," or "Barriada de los Pinos."[168] In 1927 the Missionaries of Christian Doctrine built in Los Pinos the School of the Divine Redeemer, for the children of those poor families. The school was at the bottom of a valley; when it rained, water from the surrounding areas poured down there in torrents.

One of the nuns, Sister San Pablo, tells us this:

> One morning—I remember this very well, because there had been a heavy snowfall and everything was white—we saw from our community's recreation hall, which was on the floor above the school, two priests coming, in cassocks and cloaks. It must have been early, because everything was still white and clean; later it all turned into a mire. Father Josemaría, accompanied by a priest named Father Lino, had come to ask us to let him set up a catechetical program in the school.[169]

Tuesday, January 17, 1933, was the day they made this visit, as we can tell from Father Josemaría's journal entry for January 19:

> Last Sunday I went to Pinos Altos, or Los Pinos, where there is a school run by nuns. In that school, starting on the 22nd, we will teach catechism. On Tuesday, despite the heavy snowfall, Lino and I went to see the place and to greet the sisters and their chaplain. Those sisters have a very good spirit. They were surprised to see us come in the snow. With such a small thing we've gained something for the Lord.[170]

Father Josemaría's group of followers was at that time very much reduced. Some had left Madrid. Others were suffering "illnesses and other tribulations," and still others had grown tired of following him because "their hearts were not entirely in it."[171] In those circumstances the appearance of a medical student by the name of Juan Jiménez Vargas turned out to be especially providential. Father Josemaría spoke with him a couple of times. In their second interview, on January 4, 1933, he laid out before the student the supernatural panorama of the Work. And along with this vocation came a few of Juan's friends as well.

These friends were passionately patriotic young men heavily involved in political activities, which generally took place on Sunday—precisely the day set for the catechism classes. Something from within must have calmed those agitated students to make them decide they were more needed to teach catechism than to take part in political rallies. The first visit to Los Pinos was set for Sunday, January 22, 1933.

Meanwhile, Father Josemaría had already begun to work on the souls of those students. On Saturday, January 21, Juan showed up with two friends so that Father Josemaría could give them a class of religious formation. The meeting took place in the Porta Caeli shelter, in a room made available by the nuns who ran the shelter.

> Last Saturday, thanks be to God, I began the work which is under the patronage of Saint Raphael and Saint John with three boys at Porta Caeli. After the talk we had a short time of exposition of the Blessed Sacrament, and I gave them Benediction. We will get together each Wednesday.[172]

Juan was impressed by the faith and devotion that shone through the liturgical gestures and prayers, and especially by "the way he held the monstrance in his hands and gave the blessing."[173] Years later Father Josemaría explained what had been going through his mind when he gave that blessing with the Blessed Sacrament:

> When class was over, I went to the chapel with those boys, and I took our Lord sacramentally present in the monstrance, raised him, and blessed those three, . . . and I saw three hundred, three hundred thousand, thirty million, three billion . . . , white, black, yellow, of all the colors, all the combinations, that human love can produce. And I fell short, because this has become a reality after not even half a century. I fell short, because our Lord has been generous beyond my wildest dream.[174]

*   *   *

Father Gabriel, the chaplain of the nearby El Arroyo School, used to say Mass at eleven for all who took part in the catechetical program. Students came in groups from the neighborhood of Tetuán to meet there with Fathers Josemaría and Lino, who took turns presenting the doctrine. Classes began after Mass.[175]

Coming to El Arroyo was in itself an act of heroism, because of the overt hostility of the neighborhood. Sister San Pablo tells the story of one savage attack. "On May 4, 1933," she says, "the school was attacked by a group of men. They splashed gasoline on some of the buildings, intending to set them on fire, while a group of women shouted, 'Don't leave any of them alive! There are eight of them—kill them all!' The police arrived just in time to prevent the fire."[176]

Father Josemaría also took on other catechetical responsibilities. On a regular basis he went to hear confessions of, and to teach catechism to, the youngsters living at Porta Caeli, the shelter where the nuns let him use a room to get together with college students. He invited some of those students to the Wednesday meetings, partly in the hope of getting more vocations, whether for the Saint Gabriel work (fathers of families) or for the Saint Michael work (vocations to apostolic celibacy).[177]

At this time Father Josemaría was also giving private classes of religious instruction to the children in a certain household. Two widowed brothers, named Sevilla, were remedying their sad situation by raising their children together, in a single household presided over by their sister María Pilar, who had never married. Fourteen people, domestic staff included, lived in the house. Doña Pilar helped the priest put together a religion class for four or five Sevilla children and the young servant girls. These classes took place in 1932 and 1933 "twice a week, on Wednesday and Saturday, from five to six in the evening."[178] The classes were delightful. The little ones sat in a circle and Father Josemaría put a textbook on a low table. Whenever he referred to one of the illustrations, the children, in curiosity, would put their little heads together around that picture. Sometimes he told them about the infancy of the Child Jesus, or told them stories about when he himself was a little boy. His audience was not happy about how soon class was over. "'Don't go, Father Josemaría!' was something we would say every day, over and over again," recalls one member of that audience—Severina Casado, who grew up to become a nun, taking the name Sister Benita. "We would say, 'What's the hurry? Why do you have to go so soon?' "[179]

The above-mentioned attack on El Arroyo School above was not an isolated incident. The year of 1933 had started out rife with violent acts provoked by demagoguery. A revolutionary anarchist uprising, preceded by strikes and acts of terrorism, was set for the eighth of January. On that day there was an ostentatious display of the most elementary things in the revolutionary's repertoire. Bombs exploded. There were gunfights with the police. Attempts were made to attack some barracks. And there was no lack of torchings, murders, and disturbances of all kinds in many of Spain's cities and villages. A good number of anarcho-syndicalists ended up at Cárcel Modelo. They were put in quarters separate from those of José Antonio Palacios and his companions, but all the prisoners went on walks and did exercises in the same courtyard.

When Father Josemaría went to visit his young friends imprisoned for the revolt of the previous summer, he found that they did not want to have anything to do with those terribly antireligious people. He advised them to show respect for them. The best thing, he said, would be to point out their errors to them with affection and treat them in a friendly way. "Go over your catechism," he would keep telling them. "The teaching of Christ is clear: you must love those men as you do yourselves."[180] He even brought some catechisms to the prison, so that they could reread them. After a few days of managing just a simple peaceful coexistence, they really put the priest's advice into practice. In the words of José Antonio, "We set up soccer teams with the two groups mixed together. I remember that I was playing goalie and my two defenders were both anarcho-syndicalists. I never played soccer with more style and less violence."[181]

6. *An organized disorganization*

February 16, 1933, was the anniversary of the locution he had received just after giving Communion to the nuns at Santa Isabel. "My God," Father Josemaría exclaimed at the recollection, "how much that 'Love is deeds, not sweet words and excuses' hurts me!"[182] He knew and felt himself to be in the Lord's hands in a privileged way: in prayer that went on day and night (a gift that lasted the rest of his life), except when our Lord momentarily interrupted that grace. Then he felt the dead weight of his will.

"There are moments," he had written on November 24, 1932, "when, deprived of that union with God that gives me continual prayer even when I'm asleep, I feel like I am fighting the will of God. It's just weakness, my Lord and Father, as well you know. I love the cross, the lack of so many things everyone in the world considers necessary, the obstacles in undertaking the Work . . . , my own littleness and spiritual wretchedness."[183]

Was it not a divine madness to set out to conquer the whole world with no material means? While writing this entry, he looked around at his unpleasant, dingy quarters on Viriato Street, and the place where *Don Quixote* had come into being came to his mind: "a prison," Cervantes had said, "where every discomfort has its seat and every sad noise makes itself at home." Because what, in the eyes of the Lord, did it matter?

Nothing, in comparison with the wonder implied by this reality: a terribly poor instrument and sinner, planning, with your inspiration, a conquest of the whole world for his God, from the spectacular observation post of an interior room of a poor house where every material discomfort finds its place. Fiat, adimpleatur. [Let it be, let it be accomplished.] I love your will. . . . I am sure—because I am your son—that the Work will soon come forth and will conform to your inspirations. Amen. Amen.[184]

Realizing that he had been gratuitously chosen for an enterprise of divine dimensions, he wrote during his Segovia retreat: "God doesn't need me. It is a most loving mercy of his heart. Without me the Work would still go forward, because it is his; he would raise up another person or persons, the same as he found substitutes for Eli's sons, for Saul, for Judas. . . ."[185]

Soon he was presented with another very specific opportunity to show his absolute fidelity to God's plans. After two years of enduring abuses and outright persecution of the Church, Spanish Catholics began to react. Future cardinal Angel Herrera, who at that time, as a layman, was editor of *El Debate*, the most influential Catholic newspaper, came up with a proposal to create a center of formation for priests from which would come the spiritual advisors for Catholic Action in Spain. Don Angel was the president of Catholic Action, and he wanted for the spiritual direction of its members priests with some prestige. Father Pedro Cantero (the future archbishop) mentioned Father Josemaría to him. Herrera met with Father Josemaría and explained his plans for a directors' center. To give him time to think the matter over, they scheduled another meeting, for February 11.

Father Josemaría made the following summary of that second conversation:

Señor Herrera has offered me the position of giving spiritual formation to the priests chosen by Spain's bishops to live in community in Madrid (in the parish in Vallecas) in order to receive that formation and also social formation, which will be given them by a Jesuit priest (he told me the name, but I don't remember it). I told him that position is not for me, because that would not be to hide and disappear. But how good God is, to have put such a position in my hands! In my hands, which have never received, I can honestly say, even the lowest ecclesiastical appointment![186]

Herrera tried to change his mind, but Father Josemaría refused to perform services that were incompatible with a total dedication to the Work.

He asked me to give a retreat to a group of young men (members of the National Association of Catholic Propagandists), but I refused, stating that I don't have the necessary training and am too involved in other things to be able to take on that one. . . . He kept insisting that we must speak again.[187]

On his return home, he gave a very superficial report of the interview, mentioning the possibility of getting some position in the future. "Let's hope they give you something that will do souls a lot of good, but that will also pay well," said his brother Santiago.[188]

Don Angel's surprise was probably even greater than Father Pedro Poveda's had been on the day that Father Josemaría rejected the offer of the honorary chaplaincy of the royal house. That position with Catholic Action was not a merely honorary one. It would have put in his hands the spiritual direction of a group of select souls, and would have brought with it a recognition of his personal gifts by the Spanish hierarchy.[189]

* * *

After the abortive monarchist uprising of August 1932, police surveillance and control of all kinds of gatherings became tighter and tighter. Now that Father Josemaría had a stable group of young men following him, he needed to find some legally recognized entity that could serve as a setting for his apostolic and formational activities. The best would be some kind of educational facility. He came to this conclusion after discarding, as we have said, the idea of an association of the faithful for students.[190]

For the moment, the Work as such did not need a juridical structure. Its apostolic dynamism reflected the reality of life itself. And so its founder came to define it as "an organized disorganization."[191]

Its apostolates were made up of people of different social classes, professions, ages, and other personal circumstances. Between those persons and the Work there was no juridical bond, but simply obligations of service and fidelity undertaken freely and willingly within the framework of a generous response to a divine vocation. In that "disorganization" apostolic tasks were organized under the patronage of the three archangels and given the internal cohesion proper to the spirituality of the Work, whose essence consists in the sanctification of work and in apostolate carried out through the exercise of one's profession.

Its most recent vocations were proof of the diversity of Father Josemaría's enterprise. Juan Jiménez Vargas, who asked admission on January 4, 1933, was a student. Jenaro Lázaro, who entered in February 1933, on the eve of Father Josemaría's interview with the president of Catholic Action, was a sculptor, "a mature man, an artist employed by a railroad company." The third vocation of this period came on February 11. His story goes back to the time when Father Josemaría was chaplain at the Foundation for the Sick.

Back then the chaplain, from his confessional, saw a certain young man come into the church every morning.* They would greet each other, and sometimes see each other on the street, but did not get to the point of having an actual conversation.

---

* In Spain confessionals were typically open in front. A priest sitting in the confessional could, therefore, see what was going on in the church.

Finally the priest decided to take the initiative. In his journal entry for March 25, 1931, he tells the story:

> Today, the 25th, the feast of the Annunciation of our Lady, with my *apostolic* audacity (daring!) I went up to a young man who, with great piety and recollection, receives Communion every day in my church. He, in fact, had just received our Lord when I said to him, "Listen, would you be so good as to pray a little for a special intention that's for the glory of God?" "Yes, Father," he answered—and he even thanked me! The intention was that he, being so devout, be chosen by God to be an apostle in his Work. On other occasions, when I have seen him from my confessional, I have made this same request of his guardian angel.[192]

The young man was at that time a student. Two years later, when he was a professor at the Institute of Linares (a town in Andalusia), his guardian angel came through. "On the feast of Our Lady of Lourdes," the founder wrote, "the Lord, through that guardian angel, brought us this young man. He is José María González Barredo. 1933."[193]

*   *   *

"The Work was growing within, not yet born, in gestation."[194] While waiting for the time to come for it to take on visible, external form, Father Josemaría dedicated himself to fostering fraternity among the members and to giving them apostolic training. And above that obscure and quiet labor, his supernatural optimism opened up horizons for the future as if they were already solidly established elements of the Work. "In all our houses, in a very visible place," he wrote on August 23, 1932, "we will put up this verse from chapter 15 of Saint John: *Hoc est praeceptum meum, ut diligatis invicem sicut dilexi vos* ['This is my commandment, that you love one another as I have loved you']."[195] He had no idea when those houses would be in operation, but in the meantime he felt the need to be able to get together with his people in a private, intimate setting. The "organized disorganization" was crying out for a family kind of life.

Father Josemaría rented the apartment on Martínez Campos with the idea of not having to go to someone else's place for the gatherings with students and priests. While he awaited the dreamed-of "academy," the home of Doña Dolores was more or less the headquarters of the Work. On the afternoon of March 19, 1933, the Escrivás waited, with some eagerness, for Father Josemaría's young people to take possession of the apartment. They celebrated its blessing with a family meal which included some pastries sent by Father Norberto's mother.[196]

There, in the apartment on Martínez Campos, an intense apostolate was carried out, even though the Escrivá family did not always have the financial resources to offer hospitality to all the young people invited by Father Josemaría. In Doña Dolores' home there were formation classes, study circles, and then lively get-togethers presided over by Father Josemaría. Finally, before saying good-bye, he would get out a large missal, read the Gospel of the day, and, in a few words, give an incisive commentary that came from deep in his heart. "The Father," says Juan Jiménez Vargas, who was one of those present, "knew the Gospel in great depth and used it as a springboard for a lot of prayer."[197]

Those gatherings had a homey atmosphere. By his actions Father Josemaría did all he could to make everyone understand what family life in the Work meant. "His mother, his sister, and his brother," says Jenaro Lázaro, "gladly collaborated in that task." Often the Escrivás offered the young men something to eat. The tone of elegance in the house, the courtesy and graciousness with which Carmen and Doña Dolores offered those snacks, "kept us from realizing at first what those invitations meant in the way of real sacrifice," says Juan Jiménez Vargas.[198] (This is, however, a later reflection. Juan, like the rest of those young men, satisfied his appetite at the expense of Doña Dolores' pantry. A visitor, José Ramón Herrero Fontana, once heard little Santiago rather discreetly but quite audibly voice his concern. "Josemaría's boys," he said, "eat up everything."[199])

The founder received many visitors at the Martínez Campos apartment. At Pepe Romeo's house he had met Ricardo Fernández Vallespín, a young man a year away from getting his degree in architecture, who was tutoring other students to help himself financially. Father Josemaría had set up an appointment with him for a visit at the Martínez Campos apartment. Ricardo showed up there at the agreed-upon time, feeling a little apprehensive, suspecting that the visit was going to have "a big influence" on his life. "He spoke to me about things of the soul," he recalls, giving no elaboration. When they parted, the priest gave him a book on the Passion of Christ. On its first blank page he had written this inscription:

+ Madrid, 29 May 1933
May you seek Christ.
May you find Christ.
May you love Christ.[200]

It was around that time that the project of the dreamed-of "academy" for developing the apostolate with students began to take shape. This appears from the account that another of those young students gives of an interview Father Josemaría had with him on June 14, 1933. "At about seven-thirty," says Manolo Sainz de los Terreros, "I very calmly went to 4 Martínez Campos Street to see that priest who wanted to talk to me 'about the academy.' How far I was from expecting all that was going to happen!" The first effect the priest had on him was "an inclination, a special pull, a compulsion like nothing I had ever felt with anyone else, to open up to him," says Manolo.[201] And so, "not leaving out a single thing," he bared his soul to the priest.

*   *   *

What there is of "organization" in the Work consists partly in the observance of certain practices of Christian life.

Through spiritual direction, Father Josemaría sketched out a daily program of basic norms to foster a life of prayer throughout the day. These included a period of mental prayer, Holy Mass, examinations of conscience, reading from the Gospel, and a visit to the Blessed Sacrament. To these norms were later added some other prayers and customs, such as reciting together the prayers of the Work: a set of invocations from the liturgy of the Church and from Sacred Scripture, offered for the needs of Opus Dei and its members. Reciting the prayers of the Work together was that "first official act" which took place in December 1930.[202]

This plan of life does not consist in a simple list of pious practices, but is fused in a unity of life with the asceticism proper to a Christian in the exercise of his or her profession. For, in virtue of the spirit proper to Opus Dei, one's professional activity is another way of praying and readily becomes apostolate, and apostolate requires the support of an intense prayer life. And so the plan of life includes not only ascetical practices that must be carried out at a set time, like participating in the Mass, but also others (examinations of conscience, aspirations, acts of attentiveness to God's presence, of reparation, of consideration of our divine filiation) that can be woven into the fabric of the day to help keep the contemplative life always active.

In February 1933 the founder judged that the time had come to establish a unified plan. "I want to set up a plan of life to which all of us in the Work will submit ourselves," he wrote on February 14. "I'd like for us to be able to officially oblige ourselves to carry it out starting on this year's feast of our father and lord Saint Joseph."[203]

By the end of the next month he had worked up some "provisional norms" which he soon distributed to his followers, after testing their adaptability and suitability to the kind of life lived by the people in the Work. Some of those norms, such as getting together for a commentary on the Gospel before going to bed at night, were practices observed from the time Father Josemaría started gathering young people at his mother's home on Martínez Campos Street.[204]

It is not the novelty of such norms that makes this step important, but the way the members of the Work took them on. They resolved to live them in a stable way, harmoniously integrating them with persevering work throughout the day; maintaining, that is, the unity of a contemplative life in the midst of all types of activities, thus facilitating the practice of the virtues, from the theological to the so-called natural or human ones: sincerity, optimism, loyalty, cheerfulness, and so forth.

8

1. A "cruel test"

From the moment they started meeting at Martínez Campos, Father Josemaría realized that the apartment was going to be too small. For their Saint Raphael and Saint Gabriel activities, they would need to set up an academy.*[1] This would take people and money, so they began looking for both. In March 1933 they hired the first teachers. When the second was hired, Father Josemaría wrote with exuberant optimism, "With him and with Rocamora and with all the others whom I'm sure the Lord will send me, we'll be able to start up the part of the Work entrusted to Saint Gabriel and to Saint Paul."[2]

On June 1 the two members of the Work living in Andalusia, Isidoro Zorzano and José María González Barredo, showed up in Madrid, and became available to help: "We talked about the academy. They've even started looking for apartments already. Everything is being worked out. By some time this summer, the academy will be an accomplished fact, ready to start in October." But along with those words, there are others hinting at how much energy Father Josemaría had already spent and how much physical exhaustion lay ahead: "The work wears out your body and you can't pray. . . . You are always in the pres-

---

* The type of "academy" referred to here would probably be similar to the institutes in which Father Josemaría had taught. These were small private schools that prepared students for taking examinations. They often consisted of only a few teachers working in an apartment or a small office suite.

ence of your Father. If you can't say much to him, do what very small children do: just look at him from time to time, and he will smile at you."[3]

His eagerness to start up the academy made him throw himself into this work so intensely that even time spent reading the morning paper made him feel remorseful. "I've suffered some really painful, intensely sorrowful moments upon seeing, on the one hand, my own wretchedness, and, on the other hand, the need and urgency of the Work. I've had to cut short my reading. . . . I get so angry with myself when I think of all the time I have wasted, and continue to waste—time that belongs to my Father God!"[4]

He was wasting time? "It's getting late. It's twenty minutes till midnight, and I've still got things to write. For today, the last entry: Yesterday I ran off copies of a sheet of paper requesting prayer and expiation for the purpose of getting guidance from the Lord, so that I can find time to put in order quickly and well everything having to do with the organization of the Work, just as God wants it."[5]

Having to give private lessons was something he wanted to avoid as much as possible. How would he ever recoup those hours? Why didn't God give his family security and financial independence, so that he could devote himself exclusively to the Work? Still, it was a definite, well-verified fact that the Lord would always come to the aid of the household of Doña Dolores. Those interventions always occurred, remarkably, at the last minute and in such a way that although the family was taken care of, and given a renewed spirit of peace, it was not freed from financial hardships. In the Escrivá home poverty was handled with such a virtuous spirit that it was nearly impossible to guess their suffering. "God, my Father and Lord, usually gives me joy in the midst of the total poverty in which we live. To everyone else in the house, except for a little while every now and then, he also gives that joy and peace."[6]

The founder was used to unexpected providential interventions in cases of extreme financial difficulty. But as head of the family, he had to be concerned not only with the mission he had received from God, but also with supporting his mother, sister, and brother.[7]

*   *   *

Not seven months after his stay in Segovia he once again felt a need for solitude. "Every day I feel more the need to get away for a while and live exclusively a life of contemplation—God and the Work and my soul."[8] Having made all the necessary arrangements with the Redemptorists on Manuel Silvela Street, he went on June 19, 1933, to their monastery to make a private retreat. Everything went along quite peacefully until one day a ferocious uproar broke out on the street. A group of young men armed with a can full of gasoline came up to the grille and threatened to set fire to the monastery. The retreatant leaned out the window to hear what was being shouted, but then withdrew to recollect himself in silence upon seeing that the brother on duty as doorkeeper was on the alert and armed with a good-sized club.[9]

Actually, this anecdote, related in such detail, was nothing more than a digression that partly concealed what had happened to Father Josemaría the day before—that is, on June 22, a Thursday, the vigil of the feast of the Sacred Heart. Then he had written, "I felt the cruel test that Father Postius warned me about some time ago."[10]

Father Postius, the Claretian who was Father Josemaría's confessor during the months when Father Sánchez had to stay in hiding, had indeed told him that he would undergo a severe trial. There is a journal entry specifically about this: "Father Postius, to whom I have been going to confession since Father Sánchez went into hiding (when the decree on the dissolution of the Jesuits went into effect), also told me there would come a time when the test would consist in my not being able to feel this supernatural enthusiasm and love for the Work."[11]

That painful trial was the result of being unable to sense the divine origin of the Work. But it would come a year and a half after Father Postius' prediction of it, and it is possible that Father Josemaría's recollection of the warning was a little off.[12]

On Thursday afternoon, the vigil of the feast of the Sacred Heart, Father Josemaría was meditating on death. If it came to him at that instant, how prepared would he be? What could be taken from him? He examined himself and found that he was detached from everything, or almost everything. "Today I don't think I am attached to anything. If I am—it just now occurs to me—it's just to the affection that I have for the youngsters and for all my brothers and sisters in the Work." He prayed that when death did come to take him into God's presence, he would be found "not attached to any earthly thing."[13]

That afternoon, he was given the ultimate test of his detachment. It was as if, for a few short moments, the Lord snatched away from him the clear light he had been given on October 2, 1928, and left him staggering among the contrary thoughts assaulting his mind. "I was all by myself, in a pew in the church of Our Lady of Perpetual Help, trying to pray to Jesus, who was sacramentally exposed in the monstrance. Suddenly and for no reason that I could see—really, there isn't any—this terrible thought came to my mind: 'What if it's all a lie, an illusion of yours, and you've been wasting all this time? And, worse yet, what if you've led all these others astray?' "[14]

A sudden emptiness and an overwhelming anguish flooded him with grief. "It was just a matter of seconds," he says, "but what a suffering it was!" Then, in an outburst of generosity, he made a radical offering to the Lord—to give up the Work if it was an obstacle. "If it is not yours," he said, "destroy it. But if it is, give me a confirmation of this."

Like Abraham, he surrendered in sacrifice the child he had nurtured since October 2, 1928. He surrendered too the hopes he had had for ten years before that, from the time he had begun praying in Logroño, *Domine, ut sit!* And then, says

Father Josemaría, "I felt a confirmation of the truth concerning God's will about his Work."[15]

* * *

During one of the meditations he made on this retreat, he drew up a list of what he called his "actual sins": "Disorderliness. Gluttony. Sight. Sluggishness."[16]

According to a note headed "Immediate Action," written at the end of the retreat, the remedy for his disorderliness would be to cease doing anything not directly of service to the Work. "I need to give up every activity, no matter how truly apostolic, that isn't directly connected with fulfilling the will of God, which in my case means the Work. Intention: On a weekly basis I have been hearing confessions in seven different places. I will give up hearing those confessions, except for those two little groups of college girls."[17]

Those seven places where he regularly heard confessions every week were the Porta Caeli shelter, Colegio del Arroyo, La Ventilla, the Teresian Institute on Alameda Street, La Academia Veritas on O'Donnell Street, Colegio de la Asunción, and the church of Santa Isabel. In most of these places he was taking care of young people; he does not mention all the sick and dying whom he was also visiting in the hospitals.[18]

At Santa Isabel he got into the confessional first thing in the morning. And every morning, while hearing a confession or reading his breviary, he would hear the church door banged open and a clattering and clanking coming up one of the aisles. Curious to know what it was, one day he stationed himself at the church entrance. When the door banged open, there was a milkman, loaded with his milk cans. The priest asked him what he was doing. "Father," he said, "I come here every morning . . . and I greet him saying, 'Jesus, here is Juan the milkman.'"

He felt humbled. "Lord," he spent the rest of that day repeating, "here is this wretched person who doesn't know how to love you like Juan the milkman."[19]

As for gluttony, what did he mean by that? To improve the fare and lift the spirits of his family, he would on rare occasions bring home a dessert. "My gluttony is involved," he says, because he liked sweets.[20] Then there was the hunger that drove him to eat "too much bread, to the point where I think I commit the sin of gluttony by eating bread, since it not only makes me put on weight but also gives me indigestion."[21]

Obviously, with his never-satisfied desire for mortification, his conscience was working in an area beyond the boundaries of hunger and gluttony. During the retreat he wrote to his confessor this note: "The Lord is definitely asking me, Father, to intensify my practice of penance. It seems that when I am faithful to him in this matter, the Work gains momentum."[22] And so the apostolic vigor of the Work was renewed by its founder's redoubled penances.

His capacity and eagerness for work carried him to the point of exhaustion, and so he devised some strategies to ward off the early-morning attractions of sleep. "I find myself so inclined toward laziness," he wrote in a note to his confessor, "that instead of being motivated to get myself up on time in the morning just by the desire to please Jesus—now, don't laugh—I have to trick myself, by saying, 'Later on in the day you can go back to bed for a little while.' And then when I'm walking to Santa Isabel, just before six, I dash those hopes of this deadweight that I'm carrying. I say to him, 'Donkey of mine, you'll just have to put up with it: until night comes, you're not going back to bed."[23]

And finally, as for his reference to "Sight," his striking resolution "Not to look—ever!" undoubtedly arose from a demanding delicacy of conscience which insisted on continual renunciations of sense pleasures.

*   *   *

A few months before, in the "Official Bulletin of the Bishopric of Madrid-Alcalá," there appeared a circular letter from

Bishop Leopoldo Eijo y Garay announcing that as of April 1, 1933, the separate ecclesiastical jurisdictions for the military and for the royal court would be abolished. All persons, places, and things formerly under those jurisdictions would henceforth "be solely the responsibility of the respective diocesan ordinaries, in accord with the norms of canon law."[24]

The chaplain of Santa Isabel first heard of this on March 23, as he records in his journal. "The palace jurisdiction is going to disappear. This morning I was with Father Pedro Poveda, and he told me that he will speak with Monsignor Morán and that I will be able to continue on at Santa Isabel, the same as now. Well, it's all the same to me. I am a child of God. He takes care of me. Maybe I've already completed my mission in this place."[25]

Most likely the news first reached him from Father Pedro Poveda, secretary to the Patriarch of the Indies, since it was he who had advised him to meet with the vicar general of Madrid, Monsignor Francisco Morán, to explain his situation at the Santa Isabel Foundation.[26]

Monsignor Morán was Bishop Leopoldo's right-hand man. He had heard mention of Father Josemaría from the time of his obtaining for him, at Doña Luz Casanova's request, his first permits to work in Madrid. They had become acquainted when they happened to be sitting side by side in the subway one day, probably in January 1931. On that occasion they had agreed to get together at the vicar's office the next day for a chat, and there Father Josemaría received all kinds of help in renewing his ministerial permits.

Something that happened at an April 29, 1933, meeting indicates the esteem in which Monsignor Morán held Father Josemaría. "I went to see Father Poveda, who is so good, always so much a brother to me. He told me that yesterday there was a meeting of the rectors of all the foundations that have been transferred to the jurisdiction of the diocese. And it happened that, as they were discussing their personnel, the vicar general of Madrid (Monsignor Morán), who was presiding, gave this poor donkey a eulogy that delighted Father Poveda. When I left the Teresian Institute and caught the 48, what embarrassment, what deep pain our Lord made me feel on account of the vicar's words of praise!"[27]

*   *   *

By the time Father Josemaría finished his eight-day retreat at the Redemptorist monastery, the university students had taken their final exams and were getting ready to leave for their summer vacations. Before they went their separate ways, he got together with them one more time to give them some guidelines and suggestions. By mid-summer, with all of them far from Madrid, he felt very much alone. "How lonely I feel sometimes!" he wrote on August 12. "But it's still necessary to open the academy, no matter what happens, in spite of everyone and everything."[28]

After August 15 the entries are interrupted. But a letter written in Fonz on August 29, to Juan Jiménez Vargas, makes clear what was going on. It begins, "Just two lines—it's the night of the 29th, going into the 30th, and I'm watching over my uncle. He's still in serious condition, but putting up quite a resistance with that iron constitution of his."[29]

In connection with this illness of his paternal uncle, Father Teodoro Escrivá, Father Josemaría made two trips to Fonz, accompanied by the rest of the family. The emergency put a sudden stop to the plans for the academy. When he returned to Madrid and celebrated the fifth anniversary of the founding of the Work, he felt a strong sense of apostolic urgency—as is evident from the entries of those days. "1 Oct 1933: Tomorrow, five years since I saw the Work. My God, what an account you're going to ask of me! What a lack of responsiveness to grace!"[30] "6 Oct 1933: I don't lose peace, but there are times when it feels like my head is going to explode with all the ideas I have bubbling inside me for glorifying God with this Work of his. It hurts me to see that they haven't yet begun to be crystallized into something tangible."[31] "18 Oct 1933: I've got a headache. I suffer from my lack of responsiveness and because I'm not seeing the Work *get moving*."[32]

On October 26 he wrote a note to his confessor briefly examining the causes of his impatience. There is here a strong streak of self-reproach and discouragement at the slow progress of the Work. "I am tormented," he says, "to the point of getting a headache, by the thought that I am failing to carry out God's will (1) because of the disorder in my interior life . . . [and] (2) because I don't take care of—I can't get to it, I can't do any more—the youngsters who are coming to us, brought to us by God."[33]

November came, and the members of the Work still had not found a place suitable for the academy. "These days— again!—we're running around looking for a place. So many stairs to climb, and so much impatience! God forgive me!"[34]

On November 4, Ricardo Fernández Vallespín—the architecture student to whom he had given a copy of *Story of the Holy Passion* inscribed with an exhortation to seek, find, and love Christ—visited him at the Martínez Campos apartment. Father Josemaría spoke about the Work, affirming that God wanted this plan from heaven to be realized on earth, that it had a universal character—that it was to be for the whole world and for all times—and that it could be carried out only by a group of lovers of Christ who would sanctify their work in the midst of the world and be nailed to his cross. Enthusiastically, Ricardo says, "I told him simply, 'I want to be that,' because I didn't even know the name of 'that,' which was the Work of God."[35] From that moment, the priest had another helper in the setting up of the academy. "November 13, 1933: . . . These days we're trying to get furniture for the center. I've put Ricardo Fernández Vallespín in charge of buying it. Isidoro came by, because the contract is in his name, but—always I end up alone—even though he came by, I have to make all the arrangements myself."[36]

2. *The DYA Academy*

In December, Father Josemaría began a new journal note-book with this entry: "The first thing is that the Guardian Angel House has been blessed. On the feast of the Immaculate Conception, in an impromptu way, we did it as a gift to our Lady. . . . With what enthusiasm our young men are fixing up the house!"[37] On December 30 he noted with a deep joy, "This is the first entry I'm writing in the director's office of the DYA Academy, at our Guardian Angel House."[38]

At last he had his long-dreamed-of academy. He called it "DYA" for "Dios y Audacia" (God and Daring). For some time this name had been reserved for the first publishing company they would start; but the Academy got there first. "DYA" could also stand for "Derecho y Arquitectura" (Law and Architecture), the two courses of study offered there. Father Josemaría made a drawing of the metal plate for the front door. Isidoro had it cast at a workshop in Málaga.[39]

The apartment occupied by the Academy, at 33 Luchana Street, had very few rooms, but even so, it was a cultural center where students attended classes or conferences. It was, in fact, something more than an academic center: it was a Christian formation center where university students could talk with the priest and get spiritual direction from him. Father Josemaría wanted it to function like a home. "For those of Saint Raphael, he wrote, the Academy is not an academy; it's their home."[40]

He had also written, before the fact, "Every Saint Raphael academy will have to have a library and a good, very comfortable study room."[41] But although he meant it when he said "very comfortable," those words had little or no connection with the Luchana Street apartment. The study room was a rather small, bare-bones room with no decoration other than the framed picture of "Our Lady of the Catechism." The office in which the priest received visitors was even smaller. The impression was one of severe austerity. On his desk he kept a skull, and on the wall a bare black wooden cross, not a crucifix. If someone became curious and asked its meaning, he said, "It is waiting for the crucified figure that it lacks; and that crucified figure has to be you."[42]

Returning late in the afternoon from hearing confessions or visiting the sick or giving classes, he would find his office and the other rooms filled with students. Though exhausted, he would rise to the occasion. Taking refuge in the apartment kitchen, he received the young men in private and heard their confessions. So many came to him there that he used to joke that the kitchen had turned into a veritable cathedral.[43]

No sooner did they get out of one financial bind than they fell into another. With the small donations given by those who frequented the Academy, as Lázaro (the sculptor) recalls, they barely managed to pay the monthly rent. Even the acquisition of a simple wall clock was preceded by a long string of little frustrations. Three times they were at the point of getting one, and each time some more urgent need intervened. Finally the Countess of Humanes gave them a clock—warning them "not to eat it." [She had learned that previous "clock funds" had been used to buy food.][44] They had drawn up a budget, but what good was it without income? The small sum they saved at the start for any contingencies went to legal fees for the license needed for an educational center.[45] For Father Josemaría the important thing was that he now had a means for his apostolate and a home in which to develop a "family life" for the members of the Work. He had a place where they could meet for get-togethers and where his sons would have access to the means of formation: classes, talks, and informal conversations with him.

The first month after they rented the apartment something happened which astonished all those present. It was January 5, 1934, the vigil of the Epiphany. "The Father suggested to us, to the small group of his sons gathered around him there," says Ricardo Fernández Vallespín, "that by the beginning of the 1934–1935 school year, in October 1934, we ought to have a larger place with a residence. Some of us could live there and thus make it possible to have an oratory with our Lord present in the tabernacle."[46] That way they could get to know and assimilate the spirit of Opus Dei by living with the Father, hearing explanations from his own lips, and taking his example as their pattern.

Apparently, however, not everyone shared the optimism implied by the house motto, "God and Daring." The founder reports, "We had just opened the Guardian Angel House when one of my brother priests came up to me and, full of anxiety, advised me to shut it down, because it was a failure. To make a long story short, I did not shut it down, and it has been, beyond all expectation, an unqualified success."[47]

Even though the Academy had just gotten started and still had difficulties to work out, Father Josemaría was already impatient for a new and bigger place. Properly speaking though, this was not impatience, but docility to God's urging. "Haste. It's not haste. It's that Jesus is spurring us on."[48] The Lord seemed to be encouraging the enterprise. Not three days had passed when a charitable soul offered a very substantial donation, which the founder set aside for the new center he was thinking of opening. He wrote about this on his birthday, January 9.[49]

* * *

Every time he gave Communion at Santa Isabel, he was stung by the memory of that divine locution, "Love is deeds, not sweet words and excuses." He would sorrowfully say to himself, "What a lukewarm life I lead! What a wretched person I am! How long, O Lord, how long?"[50] That locution was a spur to his apostolic pursuits. Having taken him from Martínez Campos to Luchana, it was what made him start making much more far-ranging plans as soon as the DYA Academy had begun.

When "Josemaría's boys," as Santiago called the young men whom his brother brought to the Martínez Campos center, moved to the DYA Academy, the Escrivá family could see that the priest now had a place of his own. Simply and without any bad will, his brother often reminded him of it. "Every day," wrote Father Josemaría many years later, "when I went to my mother's place, my brother Santiago came over, put his hands in my pockets, and asked me, 'What are you taking to your nest?'"[51]

Doña Dolores' home had furniture, household goods, and objects of quality that had survived the long journey from Barbastro to Madrid, but financially it was no better off than the Guardian Angel House. It was a miracle that either of them made it.[52] Having studied education in Logroño, Carmen, Father Josemaría's sister, now began teaching.[53] The Escrivás handled their difficulties well, with great confidence in Divine Providence.[54]

Determined to relieve the burdens on his family, Father Josemaría thought of eliminating the expense of renting the Martínez Campos apartment by moving into the house provided for the chaplain of Santa Isabel. He consulted the vicar general of the diocese, and the vicar gave him permission to put in a request at the Ministry of the Interior, supported by a letter from Sister María del Sagrario, the prioress of the convent. In his application, Father Josemaría explained that he was carrying out the office of chaplain with no official recompense, and was simply asking to be allowed to occupy the house provided by the convent for whoever served in this capacity.[55] Before sending it, and after considering this matter in the presence of God, he decided it would be a good thing to do as a step toward obtaining an official appointment and thus stabilizing his canonical situation in Madrid.[56]

Five days later he received notification that "regarding your petition requesting that you be granted residence in the house: because you are temporarily serving as chaplain to the Augustinian Recollect Sisters of the Convent of Santa Isabel, and because of the favorable reference given you by said community, this board has decided to grant your request. . . ." The response says nothing about an official appointment.[57] Later he found out that the rector of Santa Isabel, whose views had not been taken into account, favored neither the initiative he and the nuns had taken nor the subsequent decision of the civil authorities. Because of this, and also to spare himself any unpleasantness, Father Josemaría decided not to move into the house at that time. But besides what the rector thought about this matter, he had other reasons for his decision, which he recorded promptly and in very orderly fashion in his journal: "My reasons? (1) My family couldn't live there without me living there too. (2) It wouldn't be good for me to live at the convent, because I would be more tied to my family, when I'm trying to become freer. (3) Jesus wants, for the next school year, a student residence—and I have to live in it."[58]

By then Santiago had visited the Luchana Street "nest," and Doña Dolores and Carmen had no trouble guessing what was going on behind the facade of the Academy—that is, the apostolic activity of Father Josemaría. He had no choice but to keep the family in suspense after informing them of the favorable response from the Ministry of the Interior.[59] They were all getting ready for the transfer, asking him when they would be moving into the house at Santa Isabel. But the priest kept putting them off, offering vague excuses, changing the subject. He would not say a word.

Tired of evasions, the family came straight to the point on February 10. "Why are we still in Madrid, where we are having such a hard time?" they asked him. Fending off the question and silently riding out the storm, the priest said within himself to the Lord, "You already know why I'm here."[60]

And he thought about the reasons which, in orderly and meticulous fashion, he had entered in his journal a few days before.

*   *   *

In his meetings with the vicar general, Father Josemaría gave him detailed information on the work of Christian formation being done at the DYA Academy: conferences, religion classes, Latin lessons, a course in apologetics, study groups, confessions, formation talks.[61] In March, having persuaded the

Redemptorists to let him use a chapel of theirs, he started giving monthly days of recollection. These were always held on a Sunday, from morning to midafternoon; the average attendance was twenty or thirty boys.[62]

Opus Dei members and students at the Academy continued to give the Sunday catechism classes of the "Colegio del Arroyo" and to visit the sick. Some helped out in catechetical programs already organized in other places. These works of mercy continued to have their risks, as appears from what happened to Manolo Sainz de los Terreros and his companions. One Sunday, catechism class over, he and four or five fellow students went to visit some poor people in Vallecas. Suddenly they were attacked by about twenty individuals. Manolo was hit and kicked in the head so many times that his assailants left him for dead. The others fared no better. One of them, Alvaro del Portillo, escaped while bleeding from a terrible gash in his head.[63]

Word of the apostolate and activities of the DYA Academy spread quickly among students and clergy. Little by little, the zeal of the chaplain of Santa Isabel and his new approach to Christian life and spirituality, with its insistence on sanctity for everyone, were gaining ground. Father Josemaría also happily noted that in their conversations the vicar general was already repeating, as if they were his own, ideas which came from the spirit of the Work. "Last Monday," he says, "I was with the vicar general of Madrid—I went there to discuss with him a matter concerning the convent of Santa Isabel. We talked about a lot of things—our apostolates, the boys. . . . Monsignor Morán had a good time and has really changed a lot. Before, he was urging me to teach at a university. Now he says that what is lacking is not priest-teachers or priest-professors, but priests who can form teachers and professors."[64]

On March 1, a few days after this visit, he had an opportunity to speak with Bishop Cruz Laplana (of Cuenca), who had promised Doña Dolores a benefice for her son, and explain why he had turned down the bishop's generous offer. He spoke to him in broad outlines about the Work.[65] Once the bishop understood the direction of Father Josemaría's apostolic efforts, he offered to have booklets of spiritual considerations printed very inexpensively in Cuenca to help the young men at the Academy to make their meditations. Father Josemaría speaks of this in his letter of April 26 to the vicar general. "In this Redemptorist house," he says, "I'll be giving another day of recollection on the first Sunday of May. I expect it to be, with the help of God, very fruitful, since the college fellows who have taken part in the previous days of recollection have responded so well. I'm convinced that the Lord is blessing these young men who run the Academy, because in so many ways we are finding it easy to conduct our *priestly* apostolate among intellectuals, while fulfilling the clear will of God in my regard, which is to hide and disappear. . . . For economic reasons, with the approval of the bishop of Cuenca, a booklet is being printed by the 'Modern Press,' previously known as the 'Seminary Press,' of that capital (Cuenca). Later we will print others."[66]

But confused and distorted accounts of what was going on at the Academy also were circulating. The priest discovered this one day in May, upon going to see the vicar general to get his ministerial permits renewed. Monsignor Morán very accommodatingly phoned the relevant office and directed that this be done. But as Father Josemaría approached the office window, he heard one diocesan official say to another, "He's the one running that fundamentalist sect." He calmly drew near and said to the man, "Listen, it won't make you mad if I say something to you?" The man stared at him, obviously a bit disconcerted, so Father Josemaría said with a smile, "Really, now, it won't make you mad?" "No, why?" "Well, look—it's not a sect, and it's not fundamentalist." And the man at the window said, "How do you know I was talking about you?" "No question, I do know it." "Well, if the shoe fits, wear it," the man replied. Then, wrote Father Josemaría in his journal, "staying friendly and keeping a smile on my face, I told him that everything I do is very well

known to the vicar general. Later I was told by the good G. C.*
(who let it slip out because he was taken aback) that accusations
had several times been leveled against me on account of the
Work. He spoke of a letter, and of some ridiculous fabrications
having to do with the skull and the cross in my office."⁶⁷

Not long after, on Monday, May 28, a note from the chancery office arrived, requesting that Father Josemaría report to
the vicar general. It did not take much imagination to guess
what was behind that summons. He went to the vicar's office
the next day. When he got home, he recorded the substance of
the meeting: "The vicar general welcomed me very warmly.
He had me sit down (those who frequent the vicariate know
well what a distinction this detail implies!), and he said to me,
'Tell me about the DYA Academy.' I told him absolutely everything. Monsignor Morán, with his eyes half closed, listened
and often nodded in approval. Basically, I told him (1) that I
was very happy that he was asking me about this; that in my
letters (I write him often) I purposely told him things so that
he could ask me whatever he wanted about them; (2) the
whole external history of the Work from October 2, 1928, to
the present; (3) that we had gone to Luchana knowing that a
great friend of his was living there; that we had done this
because we had nothing to hide; and (4) about my priest-sons;
I praised especially the ones he knew, as any father would do.
He, in turn, (1) told me not to stop giving those days of recollection during the summer; (2) let me know that I now had his
permission to publish *Holy Rosary*; and (3)—here comes the
good part—asked me (as if there were no theologians or theological associations at hand in Madrid) to work up a plan of
religious studies for university students."⁶⁸

When leaving the vicar's office, he blessed all the angels in
heaven for having allowed him the opportunity to say everything he had wanted to. On the advice of his confessor, however, he had recounted only the external history of the Work.

---

* The official he spoke with in the office, who later became friendly.

The internal history, the gestation of the spiritual creature, was a private matter of his soul. Reflecting on all this, he continued: "Now, two words: *we're clandestine?* In no way. What would people say about a pregnant woman who wanted to register her unborn child at city hall and in the parish records? What if she tried to enroll this child in a university? 'Señora,' she would be told, 'wait. Let your child come into the light of day, grow, and develop. . . .' Well, then, in the womb of the Catholic Church there is an unborn child with a life and activities all its own, like a child in the womb of its mother. . . . Be patient: soon the time will come for registering it, for seeking the appropriate approvals for it. In the meantime, I will always give an accounting to the Church authorities of all our external works (as I've been doing till now), without trying to rush the paperwork, which will come in due time. This is the advice of Father Sánchez and Father Poveda—and, I might add, the dictate of common sense."[69]

Then, with much common and supernatural sense, he says, "They see us. They take notice. All right, that's fine. Where there is fire, can smoke, heat, and light be avoided? Well, neither can we have the Work and avoid the smoke of calumny or of murmuring, or the heat of our works of apostolate, or the light of the love for God that shines forth in our example and in our words."[70]

He was beginning to have an idea of what it meant to "hide and disappear," and what the cost would be for the applying of this divine motto to the Work.

3. *The rector of Santa Isabel*

In May 1934, he again felt a longing to be alone with God. "How much good it would do me," he wrote, "to have two or three months of solitude just for prayer and penance!"[71] And yet, as he began his retreat at the Redemptorist house on July 16, he felt "very little desire to do it."[72]

So first of all, to awaken in himself a sense of compunction, he drew up a long list of favors granted to him. It was astonishing. "Countless favors, some of them quite extraordinary—the Work of God!!"[73] Then he meditated on his priestly vocation, on the urgency with which the Lord had charged him with the Work, and on the resistance he was getting from some priests who did not share his zeal.[74] He reflected on the work accomplished through the Academy . . . and felt totally unsatisfied with his efforts and the results obtained thus far. "I can see at a glance that we certainly are not running. In fact, we're going so slow that some might say there is no Work. Well, then? Let us look at what the saints have done!"[75]

As a yardstick for his own desire he took the "exquisite prudence" of Saint Ignatius, who undertook such wonderfully daring works. He thought about the holy decisions made by Saint Teresa of Avila, who likewise "was not one to hold back." Finally he took a long, hard look at what he himself had done. What decisions had he made? What had he done about expanding the DYA Academy? What use had he made of the generous fistful of money that the Lord, like a good father, had sent him at the beginning of the year? Then it occurred to him that just as six thousand pesetas had come into his hands then, so now all the money he needed for the student residence might suddenly turn up in the same way. Emboldened by this thought, he turned to prayer. "Come on, Lord," he said, "why not give us the whole amount all at once? I'm still *waiting. . . .*"[76] (The money took a lot of praying for.)

One of the frustrations of Father Josemaría's apostolate was that as soon as the school year ended and the young people went on vacation, many of them vanished like water on a sandy beach. He completely lost track of them. Every autumn he had to make a new start, with just a very few old hands. Thinking about this in the summer of 1934, before the students left Madrid, he came up with an idea: he would get their summer addresses and send them a monthly newsletter to encourage them in the interior life and foster continuity. With the help of those who remained in Madrid, he duplicated these newsletters (which he titled *Noticias*) and got them in the mail before beginning his retreat. Upon his return two weeks later, he found on his desk about fifty letters. He cheerfully answered them all, offering the vacationers some words of advice.[77]

In the first few days of August, the hottest part of summer, Father Josemaría and his friends walked all over Madrid in search of suitable houses or apartments. Finally they found a place, in a good location, large enough to accommodate both the Academy and a student residence. But before they could begin to come to an agreement with the landlord, they needed twenty-five thousand pesetas. At once, the priest launched a prayer campaign, writing to anyone and everyone who might participate. Three of these letters are dated August 5, 1934, and they all sing the same song. To one person he writes, "Make a triduum to our Immaculate Mother, asking for the twenty-five thousand pesetas that we need immediately. We here are relying on the principle that 'God helps those who help themselves,' but we also need the prayers of everyone else."[78] To another he writes, "Look, one small favor: make a triduum to our Immaculate Mother, asking her, if such is the will of God, to send us the twenty-five thousand pesetas we need for the Guardian Angel's House."[79] And to a third, "A student residence is essential. We are doing what we can, but we have not yet come up with the money we need. Help us: do some asking yourselves, and get others to ask too. We must make our Father-God *dizzy* with our pleading. However, even if he seems to be asleep and not paying attention, the Blessed Virgin will help us. . . . We shall see the Guardian Angel's House completed! Never doubt it for a moment. . . . Listen, Manolo, make yourself like a child before the tabernacle and pray this prayer to Jesus with simplicity, confidence, and boldness . . . and perseverance: 'Lord, we want—for you—twenty-five thousand pesetas in cold, hard cash.'"[80]

On August 30, in the company of Juan Jiménez Vargas and Ricardo Fernández Vallespín, Father Josemaría celebrated Mass at the shrine of El Cerro de los Angeles, not far from the capital. During his thanksgiving after Mass, he felt that characteristic spiritual instinct of his, to always turn to Mary. Then and there he dedicated the Work to the Blessed Virgin.[81]

August was a hard month, as he noted that same day: "So many tears shed, at this time, for my sins and for the Guardian Angel's House! Visits, refusals, storm clouds on the human horizon. . . . But with you helping us, Jesus, in spite of my wretchedness, we shall surely pull through!"[82]

They made detailed calculations of the expenses and income of the academy-residence complex. Then both Isidoro Zorzano and José María González emptied their bank accounts and together managed, just barely, to make the deposit and first payment on some apartments at 50 Ferraz Street: two on the second floor and one on the third. "We moved in at the beginning of September," recalls Ricardo Fernández Vallespín. "Construction workers did what was needed to convert two apartments into one and install showers in one of the bathrooms for the future residents, and we started furnishing it all."[83]

Before the construction work began, they found themselves with a perilous shortfall of fifteen thousand pesetas. Once again Father Josemaría had to write letters asking for help. All those dated September 6 carry basically the same message. "We are so worried," he writes to Father Eliodoro Gil, a good friend of his. "We have rented a new property at 50 Ferraz Street. We have wonderful projects in mind that are perfectly viable and could become realities right away, except that when we put all our money together, we found ourselves fifteen thousand pesetas short, and we don't know where we're going to get that money. Please earnestly keep this intention in your Masses and in your private prayers."[84] In another letter he writes, "We are so worried about this wretched money. . . . I can't lie: humanly speaking, I see no possible solution. Yet there must be a solution. We can't turn back now. Prayer, prayer, and more prayer!"[85]

Only in his letter to the vicar general, also dated September 6, was he silent on the subject of his financial problems. The words flow smoothly, showing no hint of concern: "My dear and most venerable Vicar General: Once again I must take up some of your valuable time to inform you, in the first place, of the new address of the DYA Academy. It is now at 50 Ferraz Street. We are renting three apartments there, one for the Academy and the other two as a residence. The house looks really good. The move will be made about the middle of the month."[86]

Clearly he meant to burn his bridges. There was no way for him to turn back after having officially notified the vicar general of the new address. God would have the final say.

*   *   *

Around this time there is a gap of several weeks in the *Personal Notes*. It ends with these words: "Poor journal! How many things I have failed to jot down!"[87] His notes do not start up again until late November, when the silence is broken by this puzzling entry: "November 20, 1934: At the Guardian Angel's House now—on Ferraz Street—I'm finally able today to write in this journal. But I am writing just for the sake of writing. There are so many things I should note down that I am not going to say anything!"[88]

They were now settled at Ferraz Street, with the financial problem that had given them such headaches a few weeks earlier now solved. It happened like this. On September 16 Father Josemaría left Madrid for Fonz, to join his mother, sister, and brother and make arrangements with them to sell properties they had inherited upon the death of Father Teodoro the previous year. It was a curious journey, for on the train he shared a compartment with a Madrid family that had brought along a monkey for entertainment. Ignoring his traveling companions, the priest made good use of his time looking for churches. "From the moment we left Madrid," he wrote, "I kept myself occupied with a heavenly game. I kept scanning the horizon so that I could say something to Jesus every time we passed a tabernacle."[89]

He spent the night in Monzón. When he arrived in Fonz the next day, he decided the time had finally come for him to discuss his financial problem with the family and tell them about the Work. Afterward he wrote to those in Madrid with the jubilation of someone who is finally rid of a burden borne for many years. "Fonz, September 17, 1934. May Jesus keep you safe. I arrived this afternoon, at five. I have spoken with Mama and with my sister and brother—I had earnestly commended the matter to Saint Raphael, . . . and he heard us. My mother will write you a few lines. Tomorrow I'm going to Barbastro with my sister, Carmen, to set the whole business in motion."[90]

Three days later he explained to them in great detail what had happened in that discussion. "Going in chronological order, I want to give you a brief account of all that has happened to me. Just wait till you see! About fifteen minutes after I arrived in this town (I'm writing from Fonz, though I'll mail this tomorrow in Barbastro), I spoke with my mother and sister and brother, in broad outlines, about the Work. How persistently I had called on our friends in heaven to help me at that vital moment! Jesus made sure it went over very well. I'll tell you word for word how they responded. My mother: 'That's fine, son. But don't beat yourself or put on a long face.' My sister: 'I figured it was something like that, and even said so to Mama.' And the little one: 'If you have sons, . . . then they better treat me with lots of respect, those boys of yours, because I'm their uncle!' Without a moment's hesitation, all three saw it as the most natural thing in the world that their money should be used for the Work. And—praise God!—such was their generosity that even if they'd had millions, they would have given it to me just the same.

"We are going to discuss this devil's filth called money. My mother thinks she might be able to come up with thirty-five or forty thousand pesetas. . . . So, to sum up: tomorrow I'm going down to Barbastro with Guitín; from there I'll go to Monzón to discuss this with you, because in Barbastro everybody knows everybody else's business. The judge has promised me that all the paperwork will be completed by the first of October, thanks be to God.

"I'll try, of course, to arrange for the sale to take place next Tuesday or Wednesday—any earlier is impossible—and we'll send whatever we get. . . .

"Meanwhile, why not try to buy furniture as one usually can from factories, where you have thirty days or more to pay?

"Needless to say, I won't budge from here without the money, no matter what!

"Another thing: they agree that I should sleep at the Academy and take with me all the stuff in my room. That way they can take with them the maid they have here. Otherwise they couldn't, since they wouldn't have a room for her."[91]

The young men in Madrid enthusiastically started shopping for furniture and other household goods while waiting for Father Josemaría to return. He kept his promise not to come back without the money. Very soon they got another letter from Fonz announcing that "on Wednesday—or maybe even tomorrow—I'll be able to send you the first bit of the twenty thousand we need."[92]

When he returned, they went ahead with the final preparations. Ricardo Fernández Vallespín, the architect who was to be the director of the academy-residence, says "it was furnished with the bare necessities." They bought kitchen utensils and dishes, and got the bed linen on credit. Unfortunately, having only enough money to furnish one of the bedrooms with two beds, they had to pile most of the mattresses, blankets, sheets, towels, and pillows on the floor of one of the empty rooms.[93]

Father Josemaría decided to bless the house as soon as possible. The ceremony took place one evening. By the dim light of a few candle stubs—the house had been plunged into darkness by a power failure—he moved from room to room, generously sprinkling each one with holy water. "We had bed linen, which one of the big department stores let us have on credit, with the understanding that we would pay for it when we could. But we had no cabinets to keep it in. So, with great care, we had covered the floor with newspapers and laid the linen on top. There was an enormous amount of it. . . . Well, I brought with me from Santa Isabel a holy water bucket and a sprinkler. My sister Carmen had made me a splendid surplice. . . . I also brought from Santa Isabel a stole and a book of rites and ceremonies. And I went through the empty house blessing it, with great solemnity and joy—and with a great sense of assurance!"[94]

On October 30 he sent the vicar general a letter informing him that the new center was in operation. "School has started at the DYA, and I expect much supernatural fruit, fruit of Catholic formation and culture, from this house. I feel very confident in this hope because our work is founded on prayer and sacrifice. I can tell you with no exaggeration that these boys of *ours* are heroic. If only you could see how they go about their tasks here at the house—young university professors down on their hands and knees; engineers painting walls; young lawyers, medical interns, and students (who actually study) doing the work of carpenters—and how they put their own savings into this apostolate!"[95]

He was not exaggerating. One of the apprentice carpenters was a student named José María Hernández Garnica, known to his friends as Chiqui. He was introduced to Father Josemaría in the midst of all this chaos, and the priest, without further ado, invited him to pitch in. saying: "Hi, Chiqui, good to meet you! Here, take this hammer and some nails and get going! Hammer them in up there. . . ."[96]

Shortly after the Academy opened on Ferraz Street, the founder entered upon a time of "big tribulations, both interior and external." The Lord was leading him "by means of countless adversities." Yet he never lost his serenity. "So many worries, and so many nights of not much sleep!" says one of his journal entries. "However, I generally do sleep well, because my peace, thank God, is deep and strong."[97]

*   *   *

The changes made to what had been the palace jurisdiction of the Church meant that Father Josemaría's canonical situation was for a long time uncertain. He spent three years serving the Augustinian nuns, who appreciated the robust interior life of their chaplain; he was, in the words of Sister María del Buen Consejo, "a priest who lived by faith and was filled with God." His love for the Eucharist became almost tangible when he gave Communion to the sick nuns. With great reverence, love, and concentration he would cover the pyx with his stole and, holding the Blessed Sacrament tightly to his chest, walk carefully along the convent corridors. "Father Josemaría always reminded me of pictures I have seen of Saint Christopher carrying the Christ Child on his shoulders, bent down under his load," says Sister María.[98]

One day the community heard that Father José Huertas Lancho, rector of the Santa Isabel Foundation, was thinking of resigning. The nuns thought the time had come to get Father Josemaría appointed rector. When they told him so, he refused to apply for the position, on the grounds that it was not yet open. But the prioress, Sister María del Sagrario, was not about to let anyone else beat him to it. On July 4, 1934, after consulting the rest of the community and the vicar general, she wrote to the director general of the Social Services head office on behalf of the interim chaplain. "I am sending you this letter before the rector proffers his resignation," she said, "because everyone knows he is leaving, and I am sure there will be priests applying for the position. Although I believe you will not take the step of offering it to any of them, knowing that there is someone already here who deserves the appointment, I am nonetheless taking the liberty of calling him to your attention once more, asking your forgiveness if I offend your delicate sensibilities. Trustfully and affectionately yours, Sister María del Sagrario, Prioress."[99]

The rector soon left Madrid, but did not submit his formal resignation until the first of October. The administrative machinery was then set in motion. Father Josemaría, who until then had taken no part in the process, wrote to the vicar general to let him know that the prioress had, on her own initiative, put before the Foundations Board a request that he be appointed rector. "I myself have not submitted an application," he said, "nor do I intend to do so. I am totally open to whatever God wants and ready to carry out whatever orders you give."[100]

On December 11 the president of the Republic signed the decree of appointment. It reads as follows: "As proposed by the Secretary of Labor, Health, and Welfare, and in accordance with the rules laid down in the Decree of February 17, 1934, I hereby appoint to the position of Rector of the Santa Isabel Foundation Don José María Escrivá Albás, Licentiate in Civil Law. Approved in Madrid on the eleventh day of December in the year nineteen hundred and thirty-four. —NICETO ALCALÁ-ZAMORA Y TORRES. —Secretary of Labor, Health, and Welfare, ORIOL ANGUERA DE SOJO."[101]

The publication of this news left Father Josemaría unmoved. "As an affirmation of our spirit, of our desire to hide and disappear," he says, "our Lord saw to it that my two surnames were not recognized—they were given incorrectly in all the newspapers and in all the radio broadcasts."[102] Going to the Ministry of the Interior to pick up his official letter of appointment, he found that some civil servant, without consulting or even informing him, had already drawn up the document confirming his acceptance of the post, and had given December 19 as the effective date.[103]

Father Josemaría knew very well that before accepting any civil appointment to an ecclesiastical post, he would need authorization from the bishop. He therefore went straight from the Ministry to the chancery office to tell the vicar general what had happened. Monsignor Morán congratulated him, promised to settle the matter with the bishop, and, upon learning that his ministerial permits were about to expire, immediately renewed them until June 1936.[104]

At first he could not understand why the vicar general was showing him such kindness. But the following week, he got a letter from the bishop of Cuenca telling him that the bishop of Madrid had a high opinion of him, based largely on what he had heard from his vicar general. Now he once again saw how God was bringing good out of evil—in this case, the evil of the slanderous accusations being made against him. He notes in his journal, "The bishop of Cuenca writes and tells me that on the day when I spoke with Monsignor Morán in such detail— after those insinuations—the vicar general then gave the bishop a report about me which, in his view, explains why the bishop is so favorably disposed toward us. Praise God, who writes straight with crooked lines!"[105]

When, on January 23, he again went to visit the vicar general, Monsignor Morán told him that he could now legitimately consider himself the rector. He had the bishop's approval, though it was a matter of policy with Bishop Leopoldo never to give written confirmation of any ecclesiastical appointment made by the civil authorities, in view of their generally hostile attitude toward the Church since 1931. In passing, Monsignor Morán advised him to inform the archbishop of Saragossa of his appointment. He did so without delay, and received from Archbishop Rigoberto Doménech this unofficial response: "My dear friend: Please accept my warmest congratulations on your appointment as Rector-Administrator of the Santa Isabel Foundation. I wish you every satisfaction, and I pray that God will afford you his aid so that you may carry out this office to the benefit of all. At this time I would also like to thank you for your sincere and generous offerings, whose value I know well."[106]

Courteous though it is, the letter seems to have a tone of studied ambiguity, perhaps signaling disapproval. In those years of persecution against the Church, accepting an ecclesiastical post from the hands of the civil authorities was often considered tantamount to collaborating with the enemy.[107]

Father Josemaría's suspicion that chancery office gossip lurked behind this seemingly friendly letter proved correct, despite all the explanations he had given concerning the appointment, and despite Father Pou de Foxá's acceptance of those explanations. Only later did he find out, from a letter written him by this good friend, what a certain sector of Saragossa's clergy really thought. "When the chancery office secretary arrived," Father Pou de Foxá informed him, "and started talking about you—which I coaxed him to do, simply because I wanted to know what his judgment was based on—he told me that for a priest to have dealings with the Republic did not look good, since it suggested an agreement with its policies."[108]

Meanwhile, unaware of all such political and ecclesiastical problems, the community of Augustinian Recollect nuns at Santa Isabel continued to live a holy life. They were just happy to have gotten what they wanted.

4. *The academy-residence on Ferraz Street*

The aggressively hostile religious policy adopted by Spain's Second Republic culminated in the "Law on Confessions and Religious Associations" of June 1933. This law so irritated the sensibilities of a predominantly Catholic nation that huge masses of believing citizens mobilized in protest. As a result of popular reaction in the 1933 general election, a more moderate government took office. The socialists and the Marxist and anarchist groups then adopted a provocatively belligerent stance. In October 1934 an armed insurrection broke out in Asturias which led to an all-out civil war against the legally constituted government. The government had to send in troops to subdue the revolutionaries, and that "Red October" campaign was a long and bloody one. The "Asturias Revolution" left in its wake a host of martyrs, both diocesan priests and religious, while many churches were burned or otherwise destroyed.[109]

Disruptions of the 1934–1935 school year were one inevitable result of the politically volatile situation. What with the October Revolution, the general strikes in Madrid, and the postponement by universities of the start of their school year, no one applied for admission to the Ferraz Street residence. Ads in the newspapers produced no results.[110] The calculations on which their budget was based were irrelevant because they had no income. By Christmas they were in serious financial trouble.

*   *   *

The difficulties that faced Father Josemaría at the start of his apostolate were many and varied. Students showed an initial enthusiasm that often did not go very deep; they tended to shy away from any commitment to a regimen of sacrifice and surrender. With the women, because of a lack of time, his careful explanations of the Work and its spirit did not go beyond the confines of spiritual direction in the confessional. As for priests, he found himself dealing, for the most part, with older men already set in their ways. For over three years he did everything he could to instill the youthful, supernatural spirit of Opus Dei in a group of them, but apparently they could not quite understand him, and as a result, some of them kept a certain distance from him.[111] He realized that this was caused not by a lack of affection, but by the lack of a determined effort on their part to make this divine endeavor their own. Only one—Father José María Somoano, the chaplain of King's Hospital—had really identified with it, and God had taken him very soon afterward.

With an eye to promoting solidarity, Father Josemaría sought to establish formal ties with the priests who worked most closely with him. Of the priests among his first followers, five had promised to practice and foster a "complete adherence to the authority of the Work," through a "Commitment" entered into on February 2, 1934.[112] But their living out of that commitment left much to be desired. God plainly had so arranged things that, although "very saintly," they left it to the founder to do the apostolic work. All his physical energies and good will went into nurturing the impulse that the Lord had imparted to the Work.[113]

Setting up the DYA Academy-Residence on Ferraz Street was a trial for his followers. The motto DYA (*Dios y Audacia:* God and Daring) was the banner raised by the founder. Full of faith and supernatural confidence, he threw himself whole-heartedly into an enterprise far beyond his natural capabilities. Some of the priests who worked with him thought what he was doing was colossally imprudent: to press ahead an academy-residence lacking the material means for viability was, in their view, just plain crazy—in business terms, suicidal. One of them said it was like "jumping from a great height without a parachute and saying, 'God will save me.'"[114] Why rush things? Why not wait a year and open the academy-residence after more preparation?

Those priests may have lacked apostolic daring, but they also lacked a grasp of the supernatural criteria that guided the founder. He knew the time had come for a residence where he could live with his sons and help give them formation. In prayer he explained it this way: "Lord, the setback for the Work would not be a matter of just one year. . . . Don't you see, my God, what a different kind of formation we could give to our young men if we had a place where they could live? And the potential that this would give us for getting new vocations? . . . A year? Let us not be men of narrow vision, immature and shortsighted, without supernatural horizons. . . . Am I working for my own benefit? Well, then! . . ."[115]

"God and Daring" distinguished those priests disposed to follow Father Josemaría from those who considered what he was doing imprudent. Bishop Pedro Cantero says of the latter, "I don't know, though, if they were really capable of doing what the Father asked of them. The horizons that Josemaría opened up were so vast that they could be understood only by those who truly had the virtue of magnanimity. It seems to me that the young men, with their natural daring, were better able to grasp what Josemaría needed to accomplish."[116]

The founder soon realized that for priests to understand the spirit of Opus Dei in its entirety, they would have to come from the ranks of lay members already formed in that spirit.[117] Meanwhile, it seemed that the Lord was using this episode to purify his soul. A journal entry of January 1935 reads: "It is not that they don't love either the Work or me—they do love me. But the Lord does allow many things to happen, doubtless to increase the weight of the cross."[118]

Despite many problems, both internal and external, Father Josemaría remained firm and unflinching in his resolve, sure that God would see him through. "For it is not stubbornness," he says, "but the light of God which makes me hold firm, as though grounded in rock."[119] He turned eagerly to prayer and penance—with a drive that his spiritual director had to slow down. "He will not let me undertake any heavy penances," he writes. "He will only let me do what I was doing before, no more, and two fasts (on Wednesdays and Saturdays), and six and a half hours of sleep, because he says that if I do any more, I'll be of no use to anyone in two years' time."[120]

Already, the previous December, on the feast of Saint Nicholas, he had chosen that holy bishop to be the patron saint of the Work's financial affairs.[121] He also celebrated a votive Mass in honor of Saint Joseph, in thanksgiving for the many gifts he had received from him in the past . . . and in hopes of more to come, for the sake of the future of the Academy.[122]

* * *

Once the Escrivás had left the Martínez Campos apartment and settled into the house at Santa Isabel, Father Josemaría found himself with one foot in the Foundation and the other in the Ferraz Street complex. He had to devote most of his time to the DYA residence, which was continually plagued by staff and housekeeping problems. By the end of the month there was usually not enough money left to pay the rent or the bills at the butcher shop, the bakery, and the grocery store. They lived partly on credit where food was concerned, and as for the rent, the priest would go see the landlord, Don Javier Bordiú, and beg him to be patient. "How I suffered," says Ricardo Fernández Vallespín, the center's director. "Sometimes I even wept, and my tears fell on the account book."[123]

If Ricardo had to go out in the evening, Father Josemaría would fill in for him, and often it was very late when he left the residence and set out for Santa Isabel. On dark winter nights, thinking about the dangers a solitary priest might encounter in the streets and alleyways of Madrid, his family waited anxiously for his return, looking out the window until they saw his cloaked figure emerge from a side street. In time they became more accustomed to the situation, but Doña Dolores was always anxious until he got home.[124]

Thinking about all the adversities of those last few months, Father Josemaría felt like Jonah; he became convinced that he himself was a hindrance to the progress of the Work. "It is my sins—my ingratitude!—that must bear the blame for the tribulations we are enduring," he said. And then, "Lord, punish me, and carry the Work forward!"[125]

He found a remedy in penance. Although his spiritual director, to keep him from becoming "of no use to anyone within two years' time," had ruled out any "heavy penances," we know that he was allowed fasting and use of the cilice, and use of the discipline on Mondays, Wednesdays, and Fridays.[126] Father Sánchez gave his approval to the frequency of these bodily mortifications, but how could he gauge their intensity? Doña Dolores, on the other hand, was well aware of their severity; she made this clear in that family meeting in Fonz, when her son first spoke to her about the Work. Even his brother knew he was using a cilice. The Escrivás offered to give the Work their entire inheritance from Father Teodoro. But his mother asked of him this one thing: "Don't beat yourself or put on a long face."[127] The sound of the discipline was a martyrdom for her, and in the Martínez Campos apartment, and later at Santa Isabel, there was no way to avoid hearing it, even though he turned on all the bathroom faucets full force to drown it out.

And although he carefully cleaned up the bathroom afterward, his sharp-eyed mother could hardly fail to notice the little spots of blood accidentally left on the floor or walls.[128]

As soon as he could, he resumed his use of the discipline at the Ferraz Street residence. Then it was Ricardo's turn to hear the sounds of the lash. As he tells it, "The Father—I don't know how often—would shut himself up in the bathroom and start hitting himself with the discipline. One time I noticed, because the Father got careless for a moment, that his discipline was not like the ones we used, which consisted only of rope. His had bits of metal attached. I can't recall if they were nails or nuts or what exactly, but I am sure that they were pieces of metal. The Father didn't know that I could hear the sound of the lashes, but they used to bother me a lot. I would plug up my ears for a long time, but still the sound of the lashes would go on and on, whack, whack, whack. . . . I thought it would never stop. I never dared to say anything about it to the Father, but when he had left, if I went into the bathroom, I could see that the discipline had drawn blood. Despite his careful attempts to clean up, I would find a stretch of the tiled wall spotted with blood. . . . I would have given anything not to have seen or heard these proofs of his penances."[129]

Meanwhile, alarmist criticisms continued to be heard from some of the priests who worked with Father Josemaría. As they saw it, he said, "the Academy was a failure, and why should I expect God to work a miracle for me? It was a disaster! We were so much in debt!"[130] But he never lost his serenity. When he consulted Father Sánchez and Father Poveda, about whether he had committed a serious error of judgment, both encouraged him to go ahead. What was happening, they said, was undoubtedly a trial from the Lord.[131]

On February 21, without consulting the other priests, he met with three of his sons and laid out a possible temporary solution to their financial difficulties: give up the apartment occupied by the DYA Academy and move the Academy down to the same floor as the Residence, where there was plenty of room. In the next school year, he said, they could expand like a tightly wound spring, quickly making up the ground they had lost.[132] The decision was then made known to those away from Madrid at the time, and all reacted with great faith and optimism. "We'll keep ourselves tightly in check now, at this embryonic stage of our development," Isidoro Zorzano wrote from Málaga, "so that we can acquire, like a spring, the elasticity needed to make the great leap of a tiger at the appropriate time."[133]

For Father Josemaría, giving up the apartment amounted to "an apparent strategic withdrawal."[134] For some of his fellow priests, however, it was a clear proof of failure. In view of this, and of his recent experiences with them, he decided on how to deal with them in the future: "I shall try to get them to contribute what they can, until I can see if they are growing in the spirit of the Work." It was a tactic of "wait and see." Yet he knew perfectly well why they were not responding: "They have little supernatural vision, and not much love for the Work, which to them is like a stepchild, whereas for me it's the soul of my soul."[135]

For months the vacillation of that group of priests was a constant source of worry for Father Josemaría. Priests whom he had invited to the Work to be his collaborators and brothers had instead become a burden to him. Only a few weeks earlier, several had promised obedience for the purpose of reinforcing the authority and leadership of the founder. But their conduct was far different from his expectations. Weighed down by this bitter anxiety, he sometimes referred to them as his "crown of thorns." Some of them took a negative attitude that led them further and further from the spirit of the Work. As a result, on March 10, 1936, he had to record: "For some time now, it has been *impossible* to hold the priestly conferences that we had had every week since 1931."[136]

From then on, his relations with the priests who had made a commitment in 1934 became virtually unsustainable, and he had to carry the cross of their criticism. Friends advised him to dissociate himself from them entirely, but he preferred that they continue to collaborate with their priestly ministry, but without taking any direct part in the apostolates of the Work. Such was the course of action he outlined in 1935: "Rather than follow the advice of Father Sánchez and Father Poveda (implicit in the case of the former, and very clearly stated by the latter) to *throw out* those priests (for reasons which charity forbade me to mention in my entries of that time), I chose instead—because I saw the virtuousness of all of them, and their undeniable good faith—the middle course of *putting up with them*, keeping them outside the activities specific to the Work but always, when need be, making use of their priestly ministry."[137]

Father Josemaría could not go against the dictates of his heart. Not only did he feel a special affection for those diocesan priests, but soon they would be a cause of admiration and holy envy, for several died as martyrs a few months later. He felt a lifelong deep concern for diocesan priests, that they not find themselves isolated or lacking spiritual attention. It was a source of great joy for him when at last he saw that diocesan priests could, in time, become united to the Work by becoming members of the Priestly Society of the Holy Cross.

*   *   *

The feast of Saint Joseph in 1935 was a very great day. On that March 19, all the sufferings of the previous months seemed to converge in the founder's heart: the material difficulties, the apparent failure of his apostolic efforts, the critical attitudes and the rebelliousness of those priests. "May you be blessed, Jesus, for having ensured that this foundation would not lack the royal seal of your holy cross!" In this journal entry, dated March 20, he set aside the sorrows of the previous day and focused instead on something of which he had become convinced years before: "Jesus has always wanted me for himself—I'll explain that later, on another day—and that's why he put a damper on all my celebrations, tempered my joys with bitterness, and made me feel the thorns in all the roses along my path. . . . And me, I was blind. I didn't see, until now, this predilection of the King, who throughout my entire life has stamped my body and my soul with the royal seal of his holy cross!"[138]

March 19, 1935 brought the first definitive incorporation into the Work of persons with proven vocations. Wishing to avoid any misunderstandings and make it clear that there was no question of taking vows or making promises as religious do, the founder explained exactly what this step meant. "It means that without a vow or any kind of promise, you are dedicating your life to the Work forever." This definitive incorporation, enacted before the plain wooden cross of the future oratory at the DYA Residence, was at first called "Slavery," and later "Fidelity."[139] Symbolically, the ceremony was marked by the putting on of rings engraved, inside, with the date and with the word *Serviam* ("I will serve"). To underline how far the responsibilities of that self-surrender extended, Father Josemaría asked each of them, one by one, after their declaring of fidelity: "If the Lord calls me home before the Work gets all the canonical approvals it needs for stability, will you keep working to carry forward Opus Dei, even if it costs you your property, your reputation, and your career? Will you, in other words, put your whole life at the service of God in his Work?"[140]

The days that followed were full of expectation. For some time now everyone had been preparing for the arrival of Jesus in the Blessed Sacrament—the "Resident par excellence," as Father Josemaría said. His desire to have a tabernacle in his home was the main reason he had moved out of the Luchana Street building. But the devil, faced with the prospect of such a great event, certainly did his best to obstruct it. "The devil," reads one journal entry, "keeps putting difficulties in our way to delay Jesus' coming to the tabernacle here in the house."[141] For example, just when they were on the point of requesting the necessary approval for setting up the oratory, the vicar general fell ill. But on March 2, in a letter telling the vicar general—

now recovered—about the monthly days of recollection and the catechism classes they were giving at Colonia Popular, Father Josemaría closed with this strong hint: "I think Jesus would be very happy if right here, in the midst of this band of young folk of his, we had *a real oratory and tabernacle*."[142] On March 13 he put in a formal request at the chancery office.

For the oratory they reserved the best room in the apartment. They obtained an altar with a portable altar stone, and for an altarpiece, a painting of the supper at Emmaus. The tabernacle, altar cloths, and candlesticks came as gifts or loans. Father Josemaría could hardly wait. "Jesus, are you coming soon to your Guardian Angel's House? We so much want you here!"[143] But by the vigil of the feast of Saint Joseph, he still had not received a reply to his request for permission to set up a semi-public oratory.[144] And a number of items, such as the cruets, Sanctus bell, vigil light, and paten, were still to be acquired. Father Josemaría made a list of the things they needed, and then put it away, commending to Saint Joseph the task of finding a charitable soul to donate them. That same day, March 18, the porter delivered a parcel that a gentleman had dropped off. In it, the priest found everything they needed—exactly the items on his list. They tried to find out who the donor was, but all the porter could tell them was that it was a man with a beard. Deeply grateful for this favor that brought so much closer the day when Jesus would be sacramentally present in the center, the founder decreed that in all the future centers of the Work, the key to the tabernacle should have attached to it a medallion engraved with the words "Ite ad Ioseph" ("Go to Joseph").[145]

"At last! Jesus is coming to live with us. *Et omnia bona pariter cum eo*—and all good things will come with him," the priest joyfully announced in a letter dated March 30, to José María Barredo.[146] On March 31, in an oratory full of young men, Father Josemaría celebrated Mass in a white chasuble. The altar was adorned with flowers; rows of candles of graded length sloped up toward the crucifix above the tabernacle. Before giving Communion, Father Josemaría spoke a few words of thanks to the new "Resident." Afterward he wrote to the vicar general, "Holy Mass has been celebrated in the oratory of this house, and His Divine Majesty has remained with us in the Blessed Sacrament, at last fulfilling the desires we have had for so many years (since 1928!)."[147]

After that date the atmosphere in the Residence seemed different, more homey. Saturday afternoons at 50 Ferraz Street were full of activity. The priest would lead a meditation for the students, and then they would have Benediction. Afterward a collection was taken up for "our Lady's flowers."[148] With some of this money they would buy flowers for the altar, and some would go as alms to the poor and destitute of the slum districts. They also helped those that they called "our Lady's poor"—people who had come down in the world and, ashamed of their poverty, were trying to hide their hunger and other sufferings under a cloak of dignity. To these people they would bring (besides the consolation of a visit) some kind of present, such as a delicious treat, or perhaps a book they could not afford to buy for themselves.

The Sunday catechism classes multiplied; it became necessary to hold two monthly days of recollection; a class was started up for workmen in Carabanchel. Father Josemaría said, "Since we have had Jesus in the tabernacle of this house, it's been phenomenally noticeable: he came, and our work increased in both range and intensity."[149]

*   *   *

The previous year, Ricardo Vallespín had suffered a rheumatic attack so severe that, had it lasted any longer, he could not have taken his final exams at the School of Architecture. Having a great love for the Blessed Virgin, he had made her a promise when he appealed to her for a prompt recovery; and he did, indeed, take his exams. However when he told Father Josemaría about all this, he was by then a member of the Work, and the founder dispensed him from fulfilling his promise, which included going from Madrid to Avila on foot. But with the end of the school year at hand, and having at the Ferraz Street center a good supply of young people from whom he hoped to get vocations and residents for the following year, Father Josemaría decided to adopt Ricardo's idea. He had been looking for some special way to thank our Lady for the favors he had received from her that year. So on May 2, accompanied by Ricardo and by José María Barredo, he set out for the shrine of Our Lady of Sonsoles (near Avila).

Having decided to go to Sonsoles, I wanted to celebrate Holy Mass at the DYA before setting out toward Avila. During this Mass, in the Memento of the Living, with a determination that was particularly strong (more than just my own), I asked our Lord Jesus to increase in us—in the Work—our love for Mary, and I asked that this love might be expressed in deeds. When we were on the train, my thoughts kept spontaneously returning to the same idea: that our Lady is no doubt pleased with our affection, crystallized as it is in substantial Marian devotions: her image always kept before us; the tender greetings we give her as we enter and leave the room; our Lady's poor; the Saturday collection; *omnes . . . ad Jesum per Mariam* [all . . . for Jesus through Mary]; Christ, Mary, the Pope. . . . But in the month of May, something more was needed. Then I thought of the "May Pilgrimage" as a custom that must be incorporated— and it has been incorporated—into the Work.[150]

Without going into the walled area of Avila, they headed straight for the road leading to the shrine. From far off they could see the shrine on the top of a hill. They prayed the joyful mysteries of the Rosary walking up, the sorrowful mysteries inside, standing before the image of the Virgin, which was surrounded by votive candles and other offerings, and the glorious mysteries on the way back to the train station. Their experiences on this pilgrimage provided Father Josemaría with material for considerations on perseverance:

As we walked from Avila, we kept our eyes fixed on the shrine, and, naturally, when we reached the foot of the hill, Mary's house disappeared from view. We talked about how this is what God often does with us. He gives us a clear sight of the end of our journey, and allows us to fix our gaze upon it, in order to set our feet firmly on the path of his most lovable will. And then, when we get near him, he leaves us in darkness, seemingly abandoning us. This is the time of temptation: doubts, struggles, obscurity, weariness, the desire to lie down along the way. . . . But no: forward! The time of temptation is also the time of faith and of trusting surrender to our Father-God. Away with doubts, vacillations, and indecision! I have seen the way, I set out on it, and I am following it, up the hill—Come on, hurry up!—panting, out of breath with the effort, but not stopping to pick the flowers which, to the right and to the left, offer me a moment's rest and the enchantment of their scent and color . . . and of possession of them. For I know very well, from bitter experience, that if I were to pick them they would instantly start shriveling up and fading, and so there is nothing in them for me—neither color nor scent nor peace.[151]

In memory of that pilgrimage, Father Josemaría kept a handful of ears of wheat in a small chest. It was a symbol of his hope for great apostolic productiveness in the month of May.[152]

* * *

The DYA Academy-Residence was just beginning to thrive again when reports of slander and backbiting started coming their way once more. One day the son of the landlord of 50 Ferraz Street told them that someone had asked his father, "Why have you rented apartments to the DYA, when it's run by the Masons?" His father's reply was, "Oh, really! I wasn't aware that the Masons pray the Rosary every day with such devotion!"[153] (From his own apartment, Señor Bordiú could hear the residents praying the Rosary together.)

Then they learned that a friend of a student who came regularly to the Residence refused to visit the house because he had heard that "that Father José María is nuts."[154] Such slander spread rapidly among the clergy of Madrid. On March 7 the founder wrote in his journal, "The run of insinuations against the Work is continuing." This was because of a conversation he had had a few days earlier with a priest he barely knew. "How's that work going?" asked the priest. "What work?" asked Father Josemaría. "The academy you're running," replied the priest. "The academy where I work is run by an architect—a professor at the School of Architecture," explained Father Josemaría. "Well, what about that clandestine Freemasonry?" "That is a total slander. We have nothing there that's clandestine—no secrets, no whispering, just a group of young men who are studying hard and trying to live a good Christian life . . . and who therefore don't deserve to be insulted with such malicious insinuations."[155]

But the gossip abounded. As Father Josemaría noted in his journal, one "saintly but talkative priest" was scandalized by the fact that the wooden cross in the oratory had on it no figure of the Crucified.[156] Masons, madmen, heretics . . . Thus, as early as 1935, the seeds of slander against the Work had been sown.

5. *"A father, a teacher and guide of saints"*

The summer of 1935 was for Father Josemaría one long, continuous workday. With the help of those who stayed in Madrid, he prepared the "Noticias" newsletter and sent it out to the ones who were away on vacation. He started up two spiritual formation courses, and the monthly days of recollection he had been giving for the students continued.

July brought an unexpected gift: vocations that, in time, would provide the Work with two of its first three priests. One of these was Alvaro del Portillo, the student who in Vallecas had sustained that terrible head injury and had made his escape on the subway. Having met Father Josemaría at the Ferraz Street center in March, he thought it would be rude to go on vacation without saying good-bye, so on Saturday, July 6, he showed up at the Residence. Father Josemaría invited him to take part in the day of recollection to be held the following day. That Sunday, for the first time, the Work was explained to him, and on that same day he asked to be admitted.[157] The other was José María Hernández Garnica, the young man nicknamed Chiqui—the one whose introduction to the founder had led straight to hammering in nails from the top of a ladder.

Father Josemaría was exhausted by the physical and moral wear and tear of the past year, but the prospect of new vocations revived him. He had high hopes for the next school year and wanted to avoid being caught unprepared, as he had been in 1934. At the end of August he told the vicar general, "The Work is going well. Here *we see God.*"[158] However, the long months of tension and fatigue were wearing down the health of all involved in running the Residence. The first to succumb was Ricardo, the director: he had to spend much of the month of August in bed.[159] Father Josemaría, tougher and more resilient than the others (though also more tired), kept going as best he could until September, when he made a retreat at the Redemptorist house on Manuel Silvela Street. Monsignor Morán, noting his exhaustion some months before, had offered him a few days' rest at a property he owned in Salamanca, but Father Josemaría had been unable to accept.[160]

He went to the Redemptorist house the afternoon of Sunday, September 15, so worn out that his body would no longer do what he wanted. Judging from what he wrote the next day, it had in all likelihood been over a year since he had slept seven hours at a stretch:

> *Monday:* It's a quarter past nine in the morning, and I still can't say that I have started my spiritual exercises. Last night

I was really worn out—I slept from eleven till six-thirty! . . .
I threw up part of my dinner. I am so weak. . . . I haven't
done a thing—today I haven't even used the discipline yet,
but I will before I go to bed—and still I'm as wiped out as if
someone had beaten me up. Perhaps I'm doing wrong in jotting down these physical details. But the fact is that right
now I could lie down anywhere—even in the middle of the
street, like a vagrant—and not get up again for two weeks![161]

Then he made his first resolutions: to sleep on the floor, and
for no more than six hours. Next day he wrote:

Tuesday: I slept soundly on the floor. . . . Since I have to
say everything, I accuse myself of laziness. So much for
yesterday's resolutions! The clock struck five in the morning, and cathedral bells rang out that could have awakened
a deaf person. . . . At six, strong as a long-haired Samson—
but weak as a babe when it came to serving my God—I
arose from my soft bed. I feel amazingly well. Ergo . . . , for
the donkey, no coddling; only the stick![162]

Though physically far away, he kept close in his heart to all
those in the Residence, supporting them with prayer and mortification. "How constantly I think of those sons of mine!" he
wrote. "Tonight, at eight, they will hold their *emendatio*, or 'Brief
Circle' [a short gathering for instruction and prayer], as usual. So
at eight on the dot, I will use the discipline for their sake."[163]

On Thursday, Ricardo brought a letter to him at the Redemptorist house. The priest was struck by the realization that
his heart was bursting with joy, and that he loved his boys with
all his soul.

*   *   *

Almost all the members of the Work were students who
had never seen Father Josemaría before his ordination. The one

exception was Isidoro. They were the same age and had been classmates at the school in Logroño. In 1930, when Isidoro was admitted to the Work, a new bond developed between them. But the basic equality already established in their relationship, while it did lead to a deeper than usual human affection, coexisted with an indefinable spiritual distance that changed the relationship in a way that neither would have predicted. The change is reflected in their letters to one another, especially the salutations and closings.

From 1930 to 1932, Isidoro's greeting was usually "My dear friend José María," and his closing was "With a hug from your good friend."[164] At a second stage, in 1933, the formulas become fraternal: "My dear brother José María," or "My dear friend and brother"; "With a hug from your old friend and brother," or "With a brotherly hug."[165] But from May 1934 on, there is a very different salutation: "My dear Father José María."[166]

In contrast, the salutations and closings of the priest's letters follow no clear pattern, though they are always affectionate: "Madrid, March 1, 1931. Dearest Isidoro: . . . Entrusting you to the Master and giving you a brotherly hug, José María"; "Madrid, March 3, 1931. Dearest Isidoro: . . . My blessing as a priest and as Father, with a big hug, in the name of this whole insane asylum, José María."[167] But three years later, the notion of fraternity has completely disappeared, replaced by an ever stronger sense of paternity. In June 1934, in a letter to all members of the Work, he says, "Upon all of you, the blessing of your Father, who thinks of you constantly and asks for your prayers. José María."[168] That sense of spiritual and familial paternity, which starts to grow in the spring of 1934, comes through very clearly in this journal entry: "Sunday, March 11, 1934. . . . In the Work of God we don't go in for titles. The Father, President of the Work, will simply be called 'Father'—not 'Reverend,' or 'Your Excellency,' or anything else."[169]

He had felt this vocation to paternity from the very beginning. In a journal entry in 1931 he wrote, "Jesus doesn't want me to be learned in human knowledge. He wants me to be a saint. A saint with a father's heart."[170] In 1933, when asking his confessor for permission to step up his penitential practices, he makes his appeal in these words: "Look, God is asking this of me, and besides, it's necessary that I should be a saint and a father, a teacher and guide of saints."[171]

It did not come easy to him to call the members of the Work his sons. Given his personal motto, "Hide and Disappear," it embarrassed him a bit. So at first he took the easy way out, as he himself confesses, and simply called them brothers: "Until 1933 I was embarrassed at the thought of referring to myself as 'Father' of all these associates of mine. For this reason I almost always called them brothers, instead of sons."[172]

His youthfulness was part of the problem. He was not yet thirty; how could he claim to be head of a family whose members—both priests and lay people—were the same age he was, or even older? Often he prayed, "Lord, give me the gravity of an eighty-year-old!"[173] After a while he noticed himself becoming rather more serious. He still enjoyed a good joke, a hearty laugh, a healthy amount of fun. But even that legitimate pleasure, with its hint of frivolity and foolishness, occasionally turned sour, leaving a bad taste in his mouth. "It's Jesus' doing," he would tell himself. "He's putting eighty years' worth of gravity into my poor heart, because it's too young."[174] He kept a careful watch on his conversation, and tried, especially in public, to say and do everything with good taste and good manners. He even tried to walk in a more sedate manner. But he was not about to give up the life of spiritual childhood for an old man's gravity. So he sought a formula to unite them. "Jesus," he prayed, "I want to be a two-year-old child with eighty winters' worth of gravity and seven locks on my heart."[175]

By 1934, gravity was becoming less of an issue. In his journal he wrote, "*Gravity:* Jesus was thirty-three when he died on the cross. I can't use youthfulness as an excuse for anything. And besides, I soon won't be a young man anymore."[176]

As for the "seven locks," that was something he had been thinking about for a long time, ever since his stay at the monastery of Saint John of the Cross. One of his retreat meditations was this: "Holy purity: humility of the flesh. Lord: seven locks, for my heart! Seven locks and eighty years' worth of gravity. This isn't the first time you've heard me make this request. . . . My poor heart yearns for tenderness."[177]

His emotional life was too rich and full of joy to adapt well to "eighty winters' worth of gravity." He tried to contain his feelings, just as he tried to comport himself in a sedate and dignified way, but all to no avail. His heart would break loose—he could not hold it back—and beat with an intensity that frightened him. Until, that is, the Lord showed him that this overwhelming tenderness was directed to God, and, through him, to his children.

He became aware of this fatherly vein in him on September 19, when Ricardo came to the Redemptorist house to bring him a letter: "Ricardo came over, as I said, and I was very happy to see him. I love my boys with all my heart. And my will is always to have this affection for them, for the sake of Christ. And yet, several times this afternoon, I felt qualms of conscience about it. I wondered whether this affection—which, naturally, I feel more strongly toward those sons of mine whom I see as being more dedicated to the Work—might be displeasing to Jesus. A moment ago, Jesus made me see and feel that he is not displeased, because I love them for his sake, and because, much as I love my boys, I love him millions of times more."[178]

In conjunction with the role of Father—which he had taken on "with a full consciousness of being on earth solely for this purpose"[179]—he felt called to be "a teacher and guide of saints." Did this mean trying to excel in his studies and become a professor, or did it mean sacrificing that noble aim? After thinking it over, he gave his reply to his spiritual director: "My way is the second one: God wants me to be a saint, and he wants me for his Work."[180]

* * *

The 1935–1936 school year began with a recovery of the ground lost by their "strategic withdrawal" of moving the DYA Academy to the downstairs apartment. At the beginning of September they wrote to the best-known high schools outside the capital and placed ads in the national newspapers. Many requests for admission followed—so many, in fact, that there were not enough beds at 50 Ferraz Street to accommodate them all. Since they were unable to re-rent that other apartment, they set up an annex next door at 48 Ferraz Street. To fix up the new apartment, Father Josemaría again had to turn to Doña Dolores. She put 45,000 pesetas at his disposal.[181]

Seven years after the foundation of the Work, Father Josemaría wrote in his journal, "Since that October 2 of 1928, how many mercies from the Lord! Today I cried a lot. Now, when everything is going very well, is when I find myself weak, without strength. How clearly I see that everything has been done, and is done, by you, my God!"[182]

Running the Residence in the previous year had truly been a daily miracle. They had begun with a good household staff: two menservants, and a chef—whom they had to dismiss immediately (with due compensation), for want of residents. Now more cautious, they took on a smaller staff of just a cook and a young man who had previously worked as a bellboy in the Residence; he was to run errands, answer the door, and serve the meals.

The cook was a woman with a lot of professional experience and expertise, but the young man was not exactly a gem.[183] When the residents were out, the priest and the director did household chores: making beds and sweeping the floor, washing dishes and setting tables. . . . They had gotten plenty of practice the year before. There were about twenty residents; but the housekeeping chores were done with a good spirit. In one journal entry we read, "The feast of Saint Charles, November 4, was the second anniversary of Ricardo's vocation. He celebrated it by washing all the dishes for the whole house that evening. I dried everything and put it away. We got done at about twelve, with a holy joy."[184]

During November 1935 two architecture students—friends who both came from the Levante region of Spain—asked to be admitted to the Work. One of them, Pedro Casciaro, had met Father Josemaría in January 1935 and, from then on had attended formation classes at the Residence. The other knew nothing at all about the Work until October. His name was Francisco Botella. At Christmas they both went to live at 48 Ferraz Street.[185]

The atmosphere there was a lively blend of "piety, study, and apostolate," says Aurelio Torres-Dulce, a medical student who often visited the Residence. It was very clear that "the basic objective of the entire enterprise was a supernatural one: namely, improvement in Christian conduct."[186] Students came to the apartment precisely because it was not a recreation center. They were asked to study, "because studying is a serious obligation." They were expected to treat the house as "their own"—which included sharing in the work and expense of running it. They were not allowed to be mediocre or "just one of the crowd." They were constantly encouraged to raise their sights and to entertain the noblest ambitions.[187]

In the midst of the oppressive and tense political situation in the country, the residence was a haven of joy and peace. Knowing well the tendency of the young to adopt extreme positions, and the devastation wrought in Spanish history by the unleashing of such impulses, Father Josemaría noted in his journal both what needed to be corrected and what needed to be instilled in the young men:

> For the spirit of the Saint Raphael work: the boys should not be allowed to argue about political matters at our house. We should make them see that God is the same as he's always been, that he doesn't have his hands tied; remind them that the apostolate we do with them is of a

supernatural kind; keep calling to their attention the presence of God, in private conversations, in communal talks, all the time; make them *Catholic* both in heart and in understanding.[188]

José Luis Múzquiz, an engineering student, met Father Josemaría at the beginning of 1935. "He gave me a brief explanation," he says, "of what was going on at the DYA Academy—of how, without setting up a new association of any kind, it was attempting to form good Christians by teaching and encouraging people first to live in a way that was consistent with the name of 'Christian,' and then, little by little, to get involved in giving this formation to other young people who wanted it. He told me that there were, at the talks and in the study circles, young people from all over Spain who were studying in Madrid, and that they were of all political persuasions and parties, but that, in these gatherings, nobody asked anybody what party they belonged to."[189]

Ricardo Vallespín depicts the spiritual atmosphere of the Residence as one "of joy, of peace, of love for God, and of serenity amidst the adverse circumstances consequent upon the political and social situation."[190] Such was the state of mind of the Father. He had discovered earlier the secret of staying serene in the midst of turmoil. "I believe that the Lord has put in my soul another characteristic: peace—the ability to have peace and to give peace—judging by what I see in the people whom I deal with or whom I direct."[191]

6. *The apostolate with women*

Father Josemaría was concerned to be objective and dispassionate in everything he wrote, especially regarding the Work, its apostolic endeavors, and the interior events of his own life. In May 1935, he expressed calm satisfaction with the progress of the Work: "And I see that *everything* is up and running: Saint Raphael, Saint Gabriel, and Saint Michael, the three branches of the Work; the entire apostolate with men. The dedication of everyone is beyond doubt."[192]

As far as the Work was concerned, he had totally given up on those priests of whom he had said a few months earlier, "So far, unfortunately—no offense to anyone, they're all very saintly men—I haven't found one priest who is willing to help me by becoming dedicated, like me, *exclusively* to the Work."[193] His hopes that they would relieve him of some of the work had faded. "If only those priests, those brothers of mine, would help me. . . ."[194] But they had left him alone with his burden.

This lack of collaborators had negative consequences for his work with women. His concern is already evident in a note to his confessor in October 1933. He was disturbed that "very little" was being done "for our women" and that in this respect God's will was not being carried out. "If they have persevered till now," he said to himself, "it's by a special favor from God."[195] (He was extremely upset by the thought that he was leaving God's will undone, and this led him to express himself with a certain inaccuracy. The problem really had to do with limitations of time and physical energy. He could see this where the apostolate with young men was concerned. He says, for example, "I'm not taking good enough care of the boys who have come to us—because I can't, because there's only so much I can do.")

At Christmas, 1933, the young men of the Work, led by the founder, made a triduum to the Holy Spirit in petition for vocations, and in particular, as he says in his journal, "for a woman to be the head of the women's branch (or, better, the heart)."[196]

Although he was father also to the women of the Work, Father Josemaría continued to be very careful about keeping a certain respectful distance when dealing with them. He had no relationship with them "outside the confessional, and avoided doing anything that might arouse suspicion," says Natividad González Fortún.[197] Not yet having "eighty years' worth of gravity," he preferred to leave them in the care of other priests, Fathers Norberto and Lino. But he did not feel entirely confident about the results of this arrangement. How could those admittedly fine priests give the women a formation in Opus Dei's unique spirit when they themselves had not acquired it? Several vocations won by him with great effort in the confessional were lost in a short time.[198]

On April 28, 1934, he held the first meeting ever with some women members of the Work—there were not yet even half a dozen—in the parlor of the Santa Isabel Convent. Afterward, on Saturdays, they were able to use a room at the "Students' House," thanks to Father Pedro Poveda.[199] For the time being, the founder's plans for an apostolate with women did not seem urgent. He would say to himself, optimistically, "As soon as my daughters are a little more organized. . . ." But it was obvious that they were hardly organized at all. Considering the circumstances, he did what he could. But the opening of the Ferraz Street residence, the tense situation created by the critical attitudes of fellow priests, and insurmountable financial problems kept him from regularly attending to the needs of those souls, and they lacked both direction and government. Once the Blessed Sacrament was reserved in the oratory of the Ferraz Street complex, however, things changed dramatically. From time to time, at an hour when the residents were out, the priest would preach a meditation for the women and then give Benediction. He spoke to them about sanctification of work and about apostolate. They listened enthusiastically to everything he said, though he always wondered how much they really understood.[200] "The truth is that we had plenty of good will," Felisa Alcolea candidly comments, "but no more than that."[201]

Lacking help, Father Josemaría found it physically impossible to get really involved in the apostolate with women. His duties as rector, hospital visits, and, above all, spiritual direction of an increasing number of students at the Residence took all his time and energy. On several occasions, in fact, Father Josemaría found himself on the verge of total exhaustion. The end result was that those women, having received so little formation in the spirit of Opus Dei, soon disbanded once war broke out in Spain in 1936.

*   *   *

The founder was enormously proud of his children. "My lay children—all of them—are heroic," he stated with entire conviction.[202] In them he found the help he needed to get the Work launched. Certain that they were the long-awaited instruments needed to set the supernatural enterprise in motion, he made this request of God at the start of the 1935–1936 school year: "Lord, please fix everything so that we can work well—in a manner that is pleasing to you—in this year that has just begun. Jesus, may your poor little donkey know how to form, according to your most lovable will, these apostles of yours, our Saint Michael boys, so that they may accomplish the Work."[203]

Anyone setting foot in the Residence encountered a human warmth that, as one witness testified, "seemed to permeate everything—not only the people who were there, but even inanimate material objects."[204] After going into the oratory and greeting our Lord, the first-time visitor was introduced to the Father. He received visitors in the director's room, since his own, besides being small and dimly lit, was almost entirely occupied by a cabinet containing files and items needed for Mass. The director's room measured about ten feet by thirteen. It had in it a bed without a headboard, a small chest of drawers, a desk, and three or four chairs.[205]

Father Josemaría's style was direct, informal, and affable. In a few minutes the visitor was talking about the most personal matters, opening up to the priest as if they had known each other all their lives. Some left this first meeting having already begun a radical change in their lives, with new plans and ideals, with souls made restless by the sight of unsuspected horizons.[206]

The priest was of medium height, or perhaps a little taller than average, and stocky. He had a round face with a broad, square forehead; he wore glasses, and his hair, which was very dark was cut very short. Most of the time he wore a slight smile, and only now and then looked serious. His fine bearing, cheerful demeanor, and affectionate manner of speaking gave many people a mistaken impression of a man who led an easy life of tranquil priestly routines. But behind his rather dark complexion was an ascetic pallor reflecting the fatigue produced by long vigils and harsh penances; there were disciplines and fasts behind his cheerfulness. Many nights he would arrive at the Residence without having eaten a bite of food all day, and would invite a student to talk with him while he ate an omelet of just one egg for his supper. And sometimes if the boy looked longingly at his plate, he would give it to him, pretending he had lost his appetite. Then his fast would continue into the next day.[207]

His spotless cassock and well-shined shoes belied any suggestion of poverty. When kneeling in the oratory, he was careful to hide the worn soles under the expansive spread of his cassock. The shoes were not new; they were ones the residents had discarded.[208]

Giving meditations, he would often pray aloud. His listeners were moved at sharing in the priest's thoughts and feelings. Moved, too, were those who attended his Masses. Stirred by the devotion of a celebrant so obviously immersed in the divine mysteries, they would say to one another outside the oratory, "That priest is a saint."[209]

7. *Formational writings*

The Father strenuously devoted himself to being "a teacher and guide of saints." In his sons—then scarcely a dozen—he saw souls called to sanctity, diamonds in the rough that it was his task to cut, one by one, to bring out their greatest possible brilliance, according to their individual gifts and characteristics. "Our members," he says in his journal, "should not all be put in one mold. Instead, *without detriment to unity or discipline, we* must make sure that each man of God develops his own personality, his own character."[210]

From time to time he had a private talk with each one in which he provided guidance for their interior life. In spiritual direction he was demanding; he was convinced that "it is a colossal blunder for a director to allow a soul to give four when it is capable of giving twelve."[211] Consistent with the message he constantly preached, he was never satisfied that his children be anything less than "canonizable saints." In these calculations, of course, the women were included. Felisa Alcolea says, "He used to tell us very emphatically, 'You must be saints, and I mean canonizable saints. I won't settle for anything less.'"[212]

From the beginning, as we have seen, he used both loose notes and the notebooks of his journal to make the Work and its spirit known. But besides his *Personal Notes*, he wrote other documents as well. Among these are his general letters, which could be called foundational, since in them he develops essential points about the Work and its spirituality, putting together some "mother ideas" and principles that are always valid and valuable, regardless of historical circumstances.[213]

As early as 1931, he established as his governing principle for the formation of members of Opus Dei a cultivating of both unity and diversity: "The members should be as varied as are the saints in heaven, each of whom has their own very individual personal traits—and as alike as are the saints, none of whom would be a saint if they had not become totally identified with Christ."[214] In his periodic private talks with them he focused more on their individual characteristics, while in his general letters he focused more on forming in them a spirit of unity.

In the first of these foundational letters, dated March 24, 1930, he talks about the universal call to holiness and how his children must put into practice the virtues leading to Christian perfection, since "sanctity is not something for just a privileged few."[215]

The following year, on the same date, he finished the second of these letters. Some fifty pages long, it offers spiritual advice for navigating safely "on a sea agitated by human passions and errors."[216] With the solicitude of a father and teacher, he points to obstacles along the way and stresses the need to keep struggling and to use human and supernatural means to overcome discouragement and weakness: fidelity to one's vocation, joy in the fight, humility, sincerity, piety, hope, taking comfort in the knowledge of being a child of God, recourse to the Blessed Virgin . . .

"The Work has not come to change, much less reform, anything in the Church," he declares in a third letter, dated January 9, 1932. This one concludes with "an old piece of news: After all these centuries, the Lord wants to use us so that all Christians may discover, at last, the potential of ordinary life—of professional work—for being sanctified and for sanctifying, and the effectiveness of evangelizing by example, friendship, and a building up of trust. Our Lord Jesus wants us to proclaim today in a thousand languages, in every part of the world, that message as old and as new as the Gospel. He wants us to do it with the gift of tongues, so all will know how to apply it to their own lives."[217]

But how were they to "bring this doctrine to every part of the world, in order to open up *the divine paths of the earth*"?[218] This is the theme of another of his general letters, dated July 16, 1933. He answers that question thus: You will do this by carrying out an apostolate based on friendship and trust—by forgiving, by understanding, by drowning evil in a sea of goodness, by having a holy acceptance of people and a holy intransigence toward evil, by being sowers of peace and joy, and by fostering liberty, solidarity, and dialogue with those who do not share our ideas.

*   *   *

On October 30, 1931, Father Josemaría had been assailed by a doubt concerning his journal entries. He confided it to the fourth notebook, by then nearly full: "The writing of these entries—is it not pride, or at least a waste of time?"[219] It was not a frivolous question. In 1930 he had been assailed by a similar doubt, with the result that he burned the first notebook of his journal to avoid being thought a saint. But in 1931, every trace of what he had written around the two foundational dates (October 2, 1928, and February 14, 1930) having disappeared, he answered that question as follows: "Of course, for the Work of God many of these notes will be useful. Besides, I firmly believe that they are inspired by God. And they're useful for my soul, too."[220] In other words, he was to keep his journal—out of humility, to avoid thinking himself a saint; and because he realized that it was part of the common property of the Work.

He continues: "Pride? No. From a spiritual point of view, it is obvious that these notes will cause me only humiliation, since they make so clearly visible the goodness of God and my own resistance to grace. And from a literary standpoint—I have said this many times—these disjointed notes are also for me the greatest humiliation."[221] In fact, the temptation to polish his literary skills—much as he repressed it—did plague him in those days. The week before, he had observed, "Each day my writing gets worse. Well, just keep going—this isn't intended to win any literary prize."[222] His apostolic imperatives did not permit an indulging of his literary inclinations. He had little time for writing, and sometimes no desire or energy for it.[223]

Certainly he could see the usefulness of his *Apuntes*. Those notes—first jotted down on scraps of paper, wherever he was when inspiration struck, then written out neatly on sheets of paper, and finally transcribed into the notebooks—were obviously a rich spiritual vein waiting to be mined. In them he had recorded sweet outpourings of love, harsh ascetic thoughts, practical initiatives, foundational inspirations, and "mother ideas" pregnant with solutions to various problems. But for the time being, as he remarked in a journal entry, those ideas bore "about as much resemblance to the completed being, perhaps, as an egg does to the strutting chicken that will hatch from its shell."[224]

In December 1932, Father Josemaría selected 246 thoughts from his *Apuntes* which he typed and then duplicated in the

form of booklets to provide a method and themes for meditation to his children and others who came to him for spiritual
direction. This first compilation of *Consideraciones espirituales*
was also known as *Consejos* ("Words of Advice").[225]

Later, in 1934, he decided to put the *Consideraciones* in print,
adding new thoughts from his *Apuntes,* for a total of 438
points.[226] From a letter from Father Sebastián Cirac, a canon of
Cuenca, we know that by April he had taken steps to have
them published. Father Sebastián, who had attended one of Father Josemaría's Monday meetings with priests in Madrid, was
delighted to undertake to obtain an estimate from the Imprenta
Moderna [Modern Press]. (They asked 310 pesetas for five
hundred copies.) It was convenient, too, that Father Sebastián
had been appointed diocesan censor of books.[227] Everything
was going very smoothly.

But then he hit a snag. "I sent the *Consideraciones* to
Cuenca," he says in a journal entry dated May 18, 1934, "and it
appears that they are scandalized—no, that's not right—they
are frightened by certain words which, needless to say, have
nothing in them of error or disrespect: for instance, the phrase
'holy shamelessness.' Yesterday I said this in a letter to Cirac,
and, having given in on all the rest, I'm hoping the booklet will
be printed *with 'shamelessness.'* But the important thing is that
it be published, even if this means collaboration (!). The time
will come when it can be published without alterations."[228]

By return mail the canon replied: "Having received and read
your letter, I read it also to the bishop, and he does not like your
position on the word 'shamelessness.' He says he cannot give his
stamp of approval to a book in which a word is recommended
which sounds bad and has an objectionable meaning in everyday language. He recommends that you use another word instead: 'resolution,' 'decision,' 'boldness.' . . . I would ask you to
consider carefully His Excellency's advice, for here and in his
diocese he speaks with the authority of a divine oracle."[229]

In the opinion of Bishop Cruz Laplana, "shamelessness"
was an ill-sounding word for a priest to use, however much

Father Josemaría might try to sanctify it by placing it in the context of spiritual childhood. With the dispute threatening to turn into hairsplitting, Father Josemaría gave in. The argument did not seem worth winning against the wishes of the bishop, who was a good friend and a relative of the Escrivás—and who, furthermore, had to ratify the censor's decisions and controlled the Imprenta Moderna (previously known as the Imprenta del Seminario). But although Father Josemaría gave in, he put his disagreement on record by writing in the margin of the letter from Father Sebastián, "Well, so much for *my* shamelessness! Or, shall we say (for now), daring."[230]

At stake in this curious incident was more than a question of semantics. The argument was apparently not so much about a word as about ecclesiastical propriety and social convention. Preachers generally took certain precautions—for example, avoiding the vulgar-sounding word "pigs," in favor of "beasts with a low perspective" or "filthy beasts"; or, if they did utter such a common word, immediately begging the congregation's pardon.* Father Josemaría had no use for such childishness. An entry of August 1931, reads, *"Margaritas ad porcos!* [Pearls before swine!] The choicest morsel, if eaten by a pig (for that is, minus the euphemisms, what it's actually called), either emerges from the filthy beast as revolting excrement or, at best, is turned into pig flesh! Let us be angels, so as to dignify the ideas we assimilate. Or let us at least be human beings, so as to convert our food into strong, fine muscles or perhaps into a powerful brain, capable of understanding and adoring God. But let us not be beasts, like so many, so very many!"[231]

Another circumstance in this episode deserves mention. The author of the *Apuntes* wrote down maxims and considerations as and when he was so inspired. His notes on "holy shamelessness" are scattered over the pages of Notebook 5, which covers the first half of 1932.[232] When the time came

---

* In Spain at this time, the word for "pig" was considered vulgar by some, perhaps because of its frequent use as an insult.

(in December of that year) to put together some of these considerations for publication, he organized them by subject matter, placing like with like. Thus all his considerations on this subject ended up on the same page, numbered consecutively (starting with 90). When he sent the expanded edition of *Consideraciones espirituales* to Cuenca in 1934, he kept the layout of some of those pages from 1932, so that under the heading "Your Blueprint for Holiness," the bishop would have read this:

> The plane of the sanctity our Lord asks of us is determined by these three points: holy steadfastness, holy forcefulness, and holy shamelessness.
>
> Holy shamelessness is one thing, and worldly boldness quite another.
>
> Holy shamelessness is characteristic of the *life of childhood*. . . . Shamelessness, carried to the supernatural life . . .[233]

On this one page, "holy shamelessness" appears a total of six times. Perhaps one can see why the bishop was alarmed.

In any event, Father Josemaría's acquiescence took a load off the bishop's shoulders. He was completely satisfied, as Father Sebastián makes clear in a letter dated May 28: "Dear José María: Your last letter gave me great joy because of the trust you put in the bishop. He is also very pleased with your conduct and submission to his point of view."[234]

The booklet was printed in June.[235] In it the expression "holy daring" appeared repeatedly. Faithful to his inspiration, the author let some time go by, and when he could publish it "without alterations"—when, that is, he published *The Way*—he put "holy shamelessness" back in all the original places.[236] It was not the only time in his life, and in the history of Opus Dei, when he would exercise holy stubbornness, "giving in without giving up, with every intention of regaining what was lost."[237]

The introduction to this booklet states that these "spiritual considerations" were offered in response "to the needs of young lay university students being directed by the au-

thor," and "are notes that I use to help me in the direction and formation of these young people."[238] Among the themes included is the practice of mental prayer, which for a university student was like the discovery of a whole new world. "You say you don't know how to pray? Put yourself in the presence of God, and once you have said 'Lord, I don't know how to pray,' rest assured that you have begun to do so."[239] In a thousand different ways, Father Josemaría emphasized to the university students that the road of apostolate passes first through the sanctification of one's professional duties. "An hour of study, for a modern apostle, is an hour of apostolate."[240]

* * *

Sometimes on Sunday afternoons, says Francisco Botella, "the Father called us into his room, and we sat facing him, around his desk, and, taking phrases from his 'Instruction on the Supernatural Spirit of the Work,' or from the 'Saint Raphael Instruction,' he would tell us more about the Work."[241]

These books of instructions by the founder set out and explained essential points relating to the history, spirit, and apostolate of Opus Dei.[242] In the "Instruction on the Supernatural Spirit of the Work of God," for example, he emphasized to the members that the apostolic plan they were putting into effect was not a human enterprise but "a great *supernatural enterprise*"—divine in origin and nature—because "*the Work of God was not dreamed up by a man, to remedy the sad situation of the Church in Spain since 1931.*"[243] His clear intention was to impress indelibly upon their minds and hearts these three considerations:

1) *The Work of God comes to fulfill the will of God.* Have, therefore, a deep conviction that Heaven is committed to seeing it accomplished.

2) When our Lord God plans some work for the benefit of human beings, he first thinks of those he will use as
his instruments . . . and *gives them the necessary graces.*

3) This supernatural conviction of the divine nature of
the enterprise will eventually give you *such an intense enthusiasm and love for the Work* that you will feel *delighted to
sacrifice yourselves to bring it to fulfillment.*[244]

These are powerful, incisive ideas which "fill the mind and
heart to overflowing," in the words of Francisco Botella. Reading them, Ricardo Fernández Vallespín says on behalf of all
those young men, "did our souls an enormous amount of good
and increased our desire for sanctification to the point where
we were prepared to give our lives to see the Work accomplished, and thus carry out the will of God."[245]

But to spread the Work of God everywhere, "affirming the
reign of Jesus Christ forever" [see Rev 11:15], they would
need to attract others. That is the main theme of another book
of instructions.[246] There the founder points out the human
and divine means that they must use; some obstacles they
may encounter; and some typical human traits, good and
bad. He also speaks of those who have the right qualities for
belonging to Opus Dei, and of those who do not: "There is no
room in the Work for those who are selfish, cowardly, indis-
creet, pessimistic, indifferent, foolish, aimless, timid, or frivolous. There is room for the sick (God's favorites!) and for all
those who have a big heart, even if they have had greater
weaknesses."[247]

The third of these books—the one "for the Saint Raphael
work"—is dated January 1, 1935, but probably was written
in the autumn of 1934, in the wake of the revolution in Asturias, when the house was empty and many critical and pessimistic comments were coming from some of his fellow
priests. Despite all this, from the first lines of the introduction, the tone is one of peace and optimism and assurance of
a bright future:

Dearest ones: For some time now there has been an evident need for a book of instructions outlining the *general norms to be followed by those in charge of formation*, so that the new souls whom the Lord sends us may find their rightful place in the Work.

I cannot do everything.[248]

8. *Preparations for expansion: Madrid, Valencia, Paris*

After the revolution in Asturias in 1934, political coexistence among Spaniards became extremely problematic. A general election was set for February 1936. On the one side was the Popular Front, Marxist in inspiration; on the other, an unstable coalition of right-wing parties. The weeks leading up to the election were tense.

The house where the Escrivás lived was near the entrance to the church of Santa Isabel. There they were particularly vulnerable to assault or fire, so they decided it would be wise to move elsewhere until it was clear what was going to happen. Father Josemaría took this opportunity—he had been waiting for one for so long!—to move into the Ferraz Street residence. In his journal he writes, "January 31, 1936: It is almost midnight. I'm at our Guardian Angel House. Jesus has been so kind as to arrange things such that I get to spend a whole month here, with my sons. My mother, sister, and brother, meanwhile, will stay in a boarding house on Calle Mayor."[249]

The Popular Front won the February 16 elections. The victory, though by no means a landslide, excited revolutionary spirits and intensified the antireligious sentiment already poisoning civic life. To return to the apartment at the Santa Isabel Foundation would have been highly imprudent. So, for the seventh time, Doña Dolores moved to a new home. Meanwhile, with his usual optimism, her son could see a positive side even to what seemed like an impending disaster for the cause of religion: namely, the appointment of Don Manuel

Azaña as president of the new government.* "My mother, sister, and brother are living at 3 Rey Francisco Street—now renamed Dr. Cárceles. I took the opportunity to tell them that I am now going to live permanently with my sons. There is no evil that does not work to the good. Azaña is my opportunity, and I don't want to miss it. Mama is taking it well, though it's not at all easy for her."[250]

A storm of street riots, crimes, strikes, and all kinds of violence soon broke out all over Spain. On March 11 Father Josemaría recorded in his journal, "Fires continue to rage, both in the provinces and in Madrid. . . . This morning, while I was celebrating Holy Mass at Santa Isabel, the government ordered that the guards be disarmed. . . . I, with the consent of the nuns, took a ciborium that was almost full of consecrated hosts and consumed them all. I don't know if anything will happen. Lord: enough of these sacrileges!"[251]

What he had feared took place two days later: "On the thirteenth they started to attack Santa Isabel. They broke down some doors. Providentially, though, the mob had run out of gasoline and could only set on fire the outer door of the church before they were chased away by a couple of guards. . . . People around here are very pessimistic. I cannot lose my faith and my hope, which are a consequence of my love. . . . At Santa Isabel there's nothing but trouble. I can't understand why the nuns haven't all had heart attacks! Today [March 25, 1936], when I heard everyone talking about priests and nuns being assassinated, and about fires and assaults and all kinds of horrors . . . , I shuddered and—this shows how contagious terror is!—for a moment I was afraid. I won't stand for having pessimists at my side; we must serve God with joy and without fear!"[252]

In this atmosphere charged with hatred and the threat of death, amid the most alarming news, the journal entries do not

---

*Manuel Azaña was a leading leftist, Republican politician. He was not a Marxist, but was anticlerical in the tradition of the Enlightenment.

deviate from their apostolic focus. "I see the necessity, even the urgency, of opening houses outside Madrid and outside Spain," he writes on February 13, 1936. And, around that time: "I sense that Jesus wants us to go to Valencia and to Paris. . . . A campaign of prayer and sacrifices is already under way that will be a solid foundation for those two houses."[253]

Central to the plan for expansion of the Work in Spain and beyond was the universality of God's design. Father Josemaría had discussed it with the vicar general in 1934 and, more recently, had told him in a letter dated March 10, 1936, "It's quite possible that during this coming summer the Work will open a house somewhere in the provinces—perhaps in Valencia—and I'm laying the groundwork for sending a little group to Paris. . . ."[254]

At this time he had only a handful of vocations. As always, the Lord was driving him on. There was a trick—a clever human and supernatural tactic—that he often used in those days. He would announce his plans to the Church authorities, in a sense burning his bridges and leaving himself no possibility of turning back. It was an excellent tactic in another way, too: it was a surefire way of getting the prayer and mortification needed to give his projects a firm foundation, as he confesses to himself in his journal. Referring to the letter he is writing to the vicar general about Valencia and Paris, he says, "On purpose, I'm speaking about those two houses: on the one hand, to ensure that there will be much prayer and sacrifice, and on the other hand, to burn my boats, as did Cortés."[255]

As he did with Madrid's vicar general, so too he made every effort to explain the apostolates of Opus Dei to bishops passing through Madrid. He would invite them to celebrate Mass or dine at the DYA Residence so that he could talk with them afterward. "It is comforting," he wrote on November 2, 1935, "to see how the hierarchy has only to know the Work in order to love it."[256]

He wrote to the bishop of Pamplona, Bishop Marcelino Olaechea, about the expansion of the apostolate and about the

Lord's wish that they open a house in Valencia and another in Paris.[257] When he wrote to the auxiliary bishop of Valencia, Bishop Francisco Javier Lauzurica, he promised to visit him, and set an approximate date. "In the second half of April," he said, "I'm planning to go to Valencia, because never under any circumstances will we open up an academy or a residence without the blessing of the local bishop."[258]

He never forgot the need for supernatural foundations. "Our houses in Valencia and Paris must be built on foundations of suffering," he said in a journal entry dated March 11. "Blessed be the cross! Problems? Barely a day goes by without them."[259]

It is impossible to know what problems he was referring to, since from the beginning of November 1935 until the spring of 1936 he made fewer than twenty entries in his journal.[260] His last entry for 1935 reads: "Thursday, December 12, 1935: A few days ago I was saying to Jesus, as I celebrated Holy Mass, 'Say something to me, Jesus, say something to me.' And then, as his response, I saw clearly a dream I had had the night before, in which Jesus was a seed, buried and rotting—apparently—only later to become a ripe, fertile ear of wheat. And I understood that this, and no other, is the way for me. Good answer!"[261]

*   *   *

In those early years, the founder felt that he lacked the experience needed to determine the exact steps he should take. He was at the helm of an enterprise which, though well defined in terms of its supernatural origin, ends, and means, did not have the material support needed for its various apostolates. He had yet to determine its characteristic modes of operation and much to do to form its members. For him it was largely a matter of trial and error, like a child taking its first steps. In fact, that was the image he used for it. "The Work of God," he said, "will not be born fully realized. It will be born like a baby. It will be weak at first. Later it will begin to walk, and then talk, and then act on its own. All its faculties will develop. The Work of God will have an adolescence, young adulthood, maturity . . . , but never decrepitude. Always it will be virile in its impulses and prudent—daringly prudent. United with Jesus, whose apostolate must be carried out until the very last day, it will forever be in its prime."[262]

This vision of an organization always in its prime had its roots in the spirit of the Work, which includes a distinctive and positive approach of valuing and "divinizing" temporal structures in order to offer them to God. Seeing historical realities as wonderful opportunities for encountering Christ is far removed from the *contemptus mundi* that was prevalent in the religious thought of that era, in which a total detachment from temporal activities was considered a prerequisite for the pursuit of sanctity. Opus Dei sees work as a *means* of sanctification. Members respond to God's call while remaining in the world. They continue to have a secular mentality and do not change their professions; the professions instead become instruments of apostolate.

The result is a lifestyle by which Christians accomplish their coredemptive mission from within their individual situations, at the heart of the society to which they belong. They are a kind of apostolic yeast, acting from within, constantly adapting to social and historical circumstances.

In the 1930s, apostolic enterprises were created or promoted by the Church hierarchy or by religious orders or institutes, and were carried out as activities superimposed on society, or performed outside its regular workings. Lay people usually did not direct them. The kind of apostolic work Father Josemaría proposed in accord with the secular spirit of Opus Dei—an apostolate carried out by lay people within the context of their professional environment—had no precedent.

From as early as 1930, he had sought a practical way of making it clear that members of Opus Dei are lay people— ordinary believers, ordinary citizens. For this reason he also looked for a way of making "a sharp distinction between the

Work of God as a spiritual association and the diverse activities of its various apostolic enterprises."[263] On the feast of Saint John the Evangelist (December 27) in 1930, he found a solution to the problem of "how to avoid confusion between the spiritual element and the material enterprises."[264]

Hence the various corporate works of an apostolic nature. The DYA Academy was the first. It was a cultural center of a secular nature, registered as such, which paid the corresponding taxes to the government. It offered courses in law and architecture. And lay people ran it. As the founder had written in a journal entry, the priests would be "only—though this is nothing small—directors of souls."[265] At the same time, the Academy was a center of the Work giving both spiritual and secular formation. With this first enterprise, the lay character of the apostolic activities of the members of Opus Dei was firmly established. Father Josemaría, though he was the initiator and driving force of the enterprise, stayed discreetly in the background. This was to highlight the Academy's identity as a secular enterprise and avoid any hint of clericalism, especially in the eyes of the ecclesiastical authorities. This concern is reflected, for example, in his petition of March 13, 1935, for permission to set up a semipublic oratory. It begins with this clarification: "José María Escrivá y Albás, priest and spiritual director at the DYA Academy (50 Ferraz Street), whose managing director is Don Ricardo Fernández Vallespín, an architect and an instructor in the Graduate School of Architecture, to Your Excellency: Respectfully explaining. . . ."[266]

The creation of the DYA Academy also marked the beginning of an apostolate with young professionals, some of them married. And when the Academy moved to 50 Ferraz Street, says Miguel Deán, who by then had already earned a degree in pharmacology, "the Father spent a great deal of time giving spiritual direction and formation to all the people he encountered there."[267]

During those years of civil unrest, when the right to hold meetings was frequently suspended and there was heavy police surveillance, the Work had no juridical identity of any kind—indeed, it did not even have any legal status. In 1933 the founder had decided to start a "Sociedad de Colaboración Intelectual" (abbreviated as "So-Co-In")—a group of university professionals seen as a nucleus for the Saint Gabriel work. He drew up its bylaws at that time, but he did not submit them for approval by the civil authorities (specifically, the Head Office of Security) until after the general elections of February 1936. In a letter dated March 3, he informed Bishop Olaechea that "a 'Society for Intellectual Collaboration' (Saint Gabriel work) was founded, together with a 'Foundation for Higher Studies' which will handle all the finances of the Work."[268]

Because this was a cultural association, these professionals could come together to receive formational classes without running the risk of being in violation of the law every time the government suspended the right to assemble. As a civil society, with cultural objectives and capital furnished by elected members, it could acquire the material means—the academies, residences, libraries, schools, and so forth—needed to realize its objectives.

* * *

As their activities grew—and they grew rapidly—they experienced what happens to children: things became too small for them. This happened first with the four rooms of the DYA Academy on Luchana Street. Then it was the turn of the Saint Gabriel work. On October 14, 1935, the founder wrote, "Thank God, we are growing. Our clothes are getting too small for us. . . . It's time to set up the 'So-Co-In' and the 'Foundation for Higher Studies.' The latter is for financial matters; the former is the Saint Gabriel work."[269] Then it was the house: in February 1936 the founder wrote to the vicar general, "Even now that we've rented another apartment, at 48 Ferraz Street, we're finding the house too small for us."[270] The next growth spurt was Valencia and Paris.

What was happening convinced him for good that it would make no sense to lock the Work irrevocably into particular situations or patterns. "What I have said on so many occasions is now obvious to all: it is useless to make rules, because it must be the very life of our apostolate that sets the pattern, in its own good time."[271]

He kept his promise to go visit Bishop Lauzurica in the second half of April. As he had written him, he was keeping his plan for a house in Valencia under supernatural protection: "How many prayers and sacrifices, how many sanctified hours of study, how many visits to the poor, how many hours of vigil before the Blessed Sacrament, and how many disciplines and other mortifications have been offered to the Lord in petition for the graces needed to carry out his most lovable will in this regard!"[272]

On Monday April 20, accompanied by Ricardo Fernández Vallespín, Father Josemaría arrived in Valencia. That afternoon he met with Bishop Lauzurica, and he left with him copies of his books of instructions and other writings about the Work. On Tuesday the bishop invited the visitors from Madrid to dine with him. He was warm and enthusiastic, and promised to speak with the archbishop about their having a semipublic oratory at the center they would soon establish. "And so it is," wrote Ricardo, "that in August, or at the end of July, we'll be coming and setting up in Valencia the Saint Raphael House."[273] In Valencia, the Father also spoke with a young student named Rafael Calvo Serer; after a long walk with him through the streets, Rafael asked for admission to the Work.

Starting at this time, the pages of the *Personal Notes* are suddenly full of groaning and sadness. His Communions are cold; he cannot "even pray properly one Hail Mary"; it "seems as if Jesus has gone out for a walk," leaving him all alone. He feels unhappy with himself, "with no desire for anything," unable to organize his ideas, "somewhat lame and arthritic, despite the heat," with no energy for mortifications, hungry for "a few days of peace" because the Lord seems to be hitting him "like a ball—up in the air one moment, and down to the ground the next, and always hard. Ut iumentum! [Like a donkey!]"[274] These spiritual trials and tribulations caught him at a moment when he was physically run-down and eroded his resistance still further, to the point of terrible weakness. In a letter to the vicar general at the beginning of May, he wrote: "I feel I must be very straightforward with you, Father. I'm fat and flabby, and very tired."[275]

Two days later he had a heart-to-heart talk with Father Pedro Poveda, who had once had a similar experience. Father Pedro recommended what Monsignor Francisco Morán had recommended to him: rest, preferably in bed. He took this advice, and a little later he wrote, "I went to my mother's house and spent the whole day in bed, without speaking to or even seeing anyone, and for a while I felt a little better. It's physical exhaustion. Over the past eight months, I've given—counting sermons, meditations, and Saint Raphael conferences—about three hundred forty talks, most of them at least half an hour long. On top of that there is also the directing of the Work—the directing of souls, the visiting, etc. That explains why I have these terrible moments when I'm sick of everything, even of what I love most. And the devil sees to it that my times of physical weakness coincide with a thousand little vexations."[276]

But the things then troubling him were not really all that small. He had just been informed that the church and convent of Santa Isabel had been confiscated by the state, and that the nuns would have to move out; he was becoming aware of a lot of criticism, gossip, and backbiting; he could not find money to buy the new residence; his ministerial faculties were about to expire; he was suffering from a bad attack of arthritis.[277]

Having gotten through May 1936, he summed up his situation in words that reflect great suffering:

I'm weak, weak in every way, in body and in soul, despite the great front I put on. This is making me act strangely. I don't want to be this way. Help me, dearest Mother.

Dying is a good thing. How can it be that there are people who are afraid of death? ... But for me, dying would be an act of cowardice. Live—live and suffer and work for Love—that's what I must do.[278]

He was being not childish but childlike, taking refuge in the life of spiritual childhood and pouring out his sufferings to the Lord:

Lord, will you let me complain just a tiny little bit? There are times (because of my wretchedness, mea culpa) when I feel I can do no more. Now I've made my complaint. Forgive me.

My heavenly Mother has been very patient with me over this last month of May. I behaved like a bad son.[279]

Then there is an isolated note of rejoicing, like the sun breaking through clouds: "May 30, 1936: Last night I slept very well. I did not wake up until a quarter past six. It's been a long time since I got that much sleep all at one stretch. I also feel an inner joy and peace that I wouldn't trade for anything. God is here: the best thing I can do is to tell him my troubles, because then they cease to be troubles."[280]

The respite lasted two days—just enough time for him to finish writing his *Instrucción para los directores*, in preparation for the new centers about to be opened. "Today," he says, "on account of the imminent foundations in Valencia and Paris, I am addressing these instructions to those sons of mine who share the burden of government at the houses or centers of the Work."[281] He then gives future directors all kinds of advice, sharing his experiences as a director of souls and outlining the principles they should follow in their work of governing.[282]

Then the clouds closed in again.

June 5, 1936: I feel I need to make a retreat, in solitude and silence. I don't think I can get any days like that. What a shame! *Fiat.* [Your will be done.][283]

Two weeks later he was still longing for a retreat. However, he was so worn out physically that he did not consider it wise to go into seclusion. Also, at that time they were looking for two new houses, one in Madrid and one in Valencia.

At last, on Wednesday June 17, he was able to make this entry: "This afternoon the papers were signed for the purchase of the house [in Madrid]. I have not been frustrated in my hopes, although over these past few days I have given Jesus plenty of good reason to abandon us. It's one more proof of the divine origin of the Work: it is from him, so he does not abandon it. If it were mine, he would long ago have given it up as a lost cause."[284]

He could hardly wait to share the good news. On the very next day he told the vicar general. "In Valencia," he wrote, "we are looking for a house and will soon be opening up a center. . . . Here we also have good news: Yesterday the papers were signed for the purchase of the house at 16 Ferraz Street, which used to belong to Count del Real."[285]

It was, however, a time of uncertainty. The streets were charged with tension and the threat of violence. In the midst of it all, the founder set down in his *Personal Notes* the apostolic goals they were determined to pursue, regardless of the chaos into which the nation was plunged: "Madrid? Valencia? Paris? The world!"[286]

A few days went by, and Father Josemaría again started feeling strange—in fact, "nothing less than desolate, depressed, crushed." There seemed to be no explanation for the disappearance of his customary joy—that joy so "alive with bells and tambourines."[287] In the last days of June, he felt an indefinable restlessness of spirit. He was tense, constantly on the alert, in a state of suspense, full of "yearnings for the cross and for suffering and for Love and for souls."[288]

Two days after he wrote those words—that is to say, on June 30, 1936—this intuition that Christ was waiting for him on the cross gradually crystallized into a certainty. There came to his mind a matter between himself and our Lord that up to now had remained unresolved. "August 1929 and August 1936: I don't know—yes, I do know—why these two dates come together in my mind," he wrote in his journal on the last day of June or early in July 1936.[289]

The incident had occurred on August 11, 1929. While giving Benediction at the church of the Foundation for the Sick, as he was giving the blessing with the Blessed Sacrament, he had been moved to ask the Lord to send him "a serious, painful illness, for expiation."[290] And now here it was: his request was being granted. He writes, "Without thinking, in an instinctive movement—which is Love—I stretch out my arms and open my palms so that he can fasten me to his blessed cross: to be his slave—*serviam!* [I will serve!]—which is to reign."[291]

He felt a burning desire for a definitive conversion, a radical cleansing of all his affections, "even those that are by nature holy."[292] From time to time he felt that the time for the illness promised him by God was near, no more than a month away. "Sometimes," he wrote, "I think that my Father-God is going to accept in this coming August the offering I made in August 1929."[293] He could not foresee the kind of sufferings reserved for him, nor where they would come from, but he was filled with the thought of offering himself as an expiatory victim on whatever cross was coming his way. At the same time he struggled to reject this idea, which he considered show-offish and conducive to vanity or pride. He sought to put it aside "because in the prose of the thousand little details of everyday life there is more than enough poetry for feeling that one is on the cross. Even on the days when all the hours seem wasted—a victim, on an unspectacular cross!"[294] But when at last the time came for him to draw close to the Lord on the cross, he spurred himself on: "Josemaría, onto the cross!"[295]

The cross reserved for him was an unsuspected holocaust of love and pain, to be made in atonement for the horrors of the Spanish Civil War, which was now at hand.

*   *   *

His carefully nurtured plans for apostolic expansion were becoming a reality. With what joy they made the move to the new house! In the first few days of July they moved their furnishings from 50 Ferraz to 16 Ferraz. When they got finished, the house was in chaos; they spent the next week putting things in order. By July 15 they were settled, and began making some minor repairs.[296]

The moving and repair team was not very large. Most members of the Work who did not live in Madrid had gone home to their parents' houses in the provinces. Pedro Casciaro and Francisco Botella had left for Valencia on July 3, to enjoy a few days' rest after their intense final weeks of study, and also with the assignment of finding a house for the new center. In this search they were helped by Rafael Calvo.

Everything happened very quickly. On July 16 they sent a telegram saying they had found a suitable house. On July 17 Ricardo set out for Valencia. On the morning of July 18, they were all gathered in the office of the real estate agent, finishing up the closing of the contract, when the agent's family, clearly alarmed, called him with news: The Spanish army in Africa had revolted, and in Barcelona artillery was being set up in the streets.[297]

In that instant the dreams of expansion came to a screeching halt.

Appendix 1   Escrivá de Balaguer–Albás Family Tree

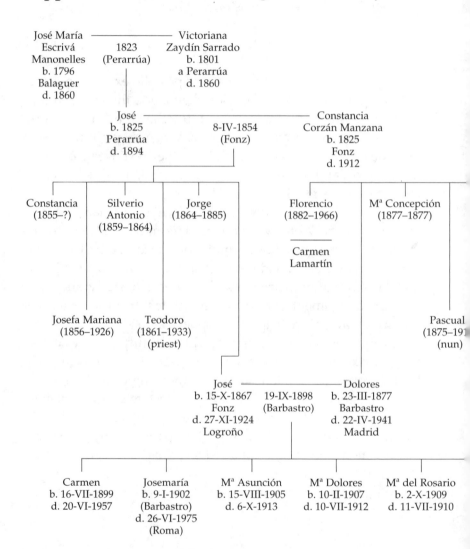

José María
Escrivá
Manonelles
b. 1796
Balaguer
d. 1860

1823
(Perarrúa)

Victoriana
Zaydín Sarrado
b. 1801
a Perarrúa
d. 1860

José
b. 1825
Perarrúa
d. 1894

8-IV-1854
(Fonz)

Constancia
Corzán Manzana
b. 1825
Fonz
d. 1912

Constancia
(1855–?)

Silverio
Antonio
(1859–1864)

Jorge
(1864–1885)

Florencio
(1882–1966)

Mª Concepción
(1877–1877)

Carmen
Lamartín

Josefa Mariana
(1856–1926)

Teodoro
(1861–1933)
(priest)

Pascual
(1875–19?)
(nun)

José
b. 15-X-1867
Fonz
d. 27-XI-1924
Logroño

19-IX-1898
(Barbastro)

Dolores
b. 23-III-1877
Barbastro
d. 22-IV-1941
Madrid

Carmen
b. 16-VII-1899
d. 20-VI-1957

Josemaría
b. 9-I-1902
(Barbastro)
d. 26-VI-1975
(Roma)

Mª Asunción
b. 15-VIII-1905
d. 6-X-1913

Mª Dolores
b. 10-II-1907
d. 10-VII-1912

Mª del Rosario
b. 2-X-1909
d. 11-VII-1910

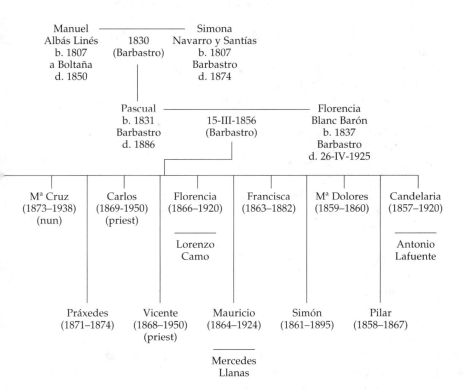

Manuel
Albás Linés
b. 1807
a Boltaña
d. 1850
— 1830
(Barbastro) —
Simona
Navarro y Santías
b. 1807
Barbastro
d. 1874

Pascual
b. 1831
Barbastro
d. 1886
— 15-III-1856
(Barbastro) —
Florencia
Blanc Barón
b. 1837
Barbastro
d. 26-IV-1925

Mª Cruz
(1873–1938)
(nun)

Carlos
(1869-1950)
(priest)

Florencia
(1866–1920)
_____
Lorenzo
Camo

Francisca
(1863–1882)

Mª Dolores
(1859–1860)

Candelaria
(1857–1920)
_____
Antonio
Lafuente

Práxedes
(1871–1874)

Vicente
(1868–1950)
(priest)

Mauricio
(1864–1924)
_____
Mercedes
Llanas

Simón
(1861–1895)

Pilar
(1858–1867)

Santiago
b. 28-II-1919
d. 25-XII-1994
— 7-IV-1958 —
Gloria
García-Herrero
b. 5-VIII-1933

Mariajosé (1959)
Santiago (1960)
Luis Joaquín (1961)
Pilar (1962)
Carmen (1963)
Gloria (1964)
Isabel (1965)
Josemaría (1968)
Alvaro (1974)

Appendix 2

Baptismal Certificate of Josemaría's Father

The original baptismal certificate is in the archive of the parish of Our Lady of the Assumption in Fonz (Huesca), in Book of Baptisms no. 9, fol. 271. It has some errors: e.g., "Escribá," "Zaidin," and "Perarruga," in place of "Escrivá," "Zaydín," and "Perarrúa." Of the location and text of this certificate we have the following testimony:

I, Father Antonio Buil Salinas, Administrator of the Parish of Our Lady of the Assumption and person in charge of the parish archive in Fonz, Diocese of Barbastro, Province of Huesca,

DO HEREBY CERTIFY that on folio 271 of Book of Baptisms no. 9 of the archive of this parish, there is inscribed an entry which, copied verbatim, says:

(On the side) "José Escribá"

(In the center) "On the fifteenth of October of eighteen hundred sixty-seven, I, Antonio Comet, pastor of this village of Fonz, solemnly baptized a boy born at twelve o'clock noon of this same day: the legitimate son of José Escribá y Zaydin, a native of Perarrúa, and of Constancia Corzan Manzana, of Fonz. Paternal grandparents: Don José, of Balaguer, and Doña Vitoriana Zaidin, of Perarruga; maternal, Don Antonio Corzan and Doña Nicolasa Manzana, both of Fonz. He was given the name José. His godmother is his sister Constancia; I explained to her the relationship and obligations. Signed: Antonio Comet Quintana."

The above is an exact copy of the original to which it refers. I certify it to be such, signing this and sealing it with the parish seal, in Fonz, on January 21, 1985.

Signed and sealed: Antonio Buil

Appendix 3

Baptismal Certificate of Josemaría's Mother

The original baptismal certificate is in the archive of the parish of Our Lady of the Assumption in Barbastro, Book of Baptisms no. 37, fol. 121. The girl was baptized together with her twin sister, María Concepción, who died two days later. The certificate contains an error: her maternal grandmother's name was Isidora Barón Solsona, not Isidora Blanc.

I, Father Lino Rodríguez Peláez, person in charge of the archive of the parish of Our Lady of the Assumption (cathedral) of the diocese of Barbastro,

DO HEREBY CERTIFY that on folio 121 of Book of Baptisms no. 37 of the archive of this parish, there is inscribed an entry which, copied verbatim, says:

(On the side) "María de los Dolores Albás, the firstborn of twins (the other of whom died)"

(In the center) "In Barbastro on the twenty-third of March of eighteen hundred seventy-seven, I, Father Teodoro Valdovinos, pastor of same, solemnly baptized a girl born at two o'clock in the afternoon of this same day: the legitimate daughter of Don Pascual Albás and Doña Florencia Blanc, natives and residents of this place, confectioners. Paternal grandparents: the deceased Don Manuel, of Boltaña, and Doña Simona Navarro, of this place; maternal, Don Joaquín and Doña Isidora Blanc, deceased, of this place. She was given the name María de los Dolores. Her godmother is her aunt Doña Dolores Blanc, a married woman, of this place, informed of her responsibilities. Signed: Teodoro Valdovinos."

The above is an exact copy of the original to which it refers. In witness whereof I sign this in Barbastro on January 21, 1985.

Signed and sealed: Lino Rodríguez

461

Appendix 4

Marriage Certificate of Josemaría's Parents

The original is in the archive of the parish of Our Lady of the Assumption in Barbastro, Book of Sacraments (Marriages) no. 42, fols. 51v–52. The appended note refers to the change in the family name. Although the certificate gives Don José Escrivá's age as twenty-nine, he was in fact thirty.

I, Father Lino Rodríguez Peláez, acting pastor of the parish of Our Lady of the Assumption (cathedral) of the diocese of Barbastro,

DO HEREBY CERTIFY that in folios 51v and 52 of Book of Sacraments (Marriages) no. 42, there is inscribed the marriage certificate of Don José Escrivá and Doña Dolores Albás, which, copied verbatim, says:

"In Barbastro on the nineteenth of September of eighteen hundred ninety-eight, I, Father Maximino Lafita, priest in charge of this city, authorized the illustrious Father Alfredo Sevil, Vicar General of the Archdiocese of Valladolid, Canon and Archdeacon-elect of the same, who, in the presence of Señor Francisco Armisén, substitute municipal judge, assisted at the marriage which here, with the legitimate formulas, was contracted in the eyes of the Church by Don José Escrivá, a bachelor, native of Fonz, resident of Barbastro, merchant, twenty-nine years of age, legitimate son of Don José, of Perarrua, and Doña Constancia Corzán, of Fonz; and Doña Dolores Albás, a single woman, native and resident of Barbastro, twenty-one years of age, legitimate daughter of the deceased Don Pascual, of Barbastro, and Doña Florencia Blanc, native and resident of this city. All the necessary prerequisites for the validity and legitimacy of this sacramental contract were fulfilled. The witnesses were Don Mariano Romero and Don Luís Sambeat, married men, proprietors, and residents of this city. The contracting parties respectively obtained favorable legal counsel and consent, and had a nuptial Mass. Signed: Alfredo Sevil. Maximino Lafita."

In witness whereof I sign this in Barbastro on March 19, 1981.

Signed and sealed: Lino Rodríguez

Verification of signature and authentication
Barbastro, March 20, 1981
Signed and sealed: Raimundo Martín, Vicar General

Note:

Don José Escrivá and Doña Dolores Albás, single persons, 29 and 21 respectively. By order of the Episcopal Delegate of this Diocese of Barbastro, given on May 27, 1943, on this certificate the surname "Escrivá" is changed to "Escrivá de Balaguer." From now on there should be read and written "Don José Escrivá de Balaguer Corzán," legitimate son of Don José Escrivá de Balaguer and of Doña Constancia Corzán. —Barbastro, June 20, 1943. — José Palacio.

Appendix 5

Baptismal Certificate of Josemaría's Sister Carmen

The original is in the archive of the parish of Our Lady of the Assumption in Barbastro, Book of Baptisms no. 43, fol. 22. There are errors in the spelling of the name "Escrivá."

I, Father José Palacio, canon, priest in charge of the parish of the city of Barbastro,

DO HEREBY CERTIFY that on folio 22 of volume 43 of the books of this parish is a record which states:

(In the margin) "María del Carmen Constancia Florencia Escribá"

(In the center) "In Barbastro on the eighteenth of July of eighteen hundred ninety-nine, I, Father Maximino Lafita, parish priest of this city, solemnly baptized a girl born day before yesterday at seven-fifteen in the evening: the legitimate daughter of Don José Escribá, of Fonz, and of Doña Dolores Albás, of Barbastro, residents and merchants here. Paternal grandparents: Don José and Doña Constancia Corzán, of Fonz; maternal, Don Pascual and Doña Florencia Blanc, of Barbastro. She was given the names María del Carmen, Constancia, and Florencia. Her godparents are her uncle Don Mariano Albás, a married man, and her maternal grandmother (a widow), residents and natives of this city, informed of their responsibilities. Signed: Maximino Lafita."

In witness whereof I sign this in Barbastro on March 24, 1941.

Signed and sealed: José Palacio

Note:

The Central Office of Registration and Notarization has authorized the adding of "de Balaguer" to that first surname, to form the composite "Escrivá de Balaguer." It will be used as a single first surname, leaving as a second surname the one presently there.

Appendix 6

Josemaría's Birth Certificate

Of the birth certificate there is no original in Barbastro's city register, due to the destruction of the archives during the Spanish Civil War, in 1936. There does exist, however, a birth certificate made out on April 26, 1912, by Don Joaquín Salcedo, the municipal judge in charge of Barbastro's city register, for inclusion in Josemaría's student records. This certificate is in the archive of the General and Technical Institute of Huesca, in the student files section. The birth certificate currently in Barbastro's city register is an authenticated copy made after the death of Monsignor Josemaría Escrivá de Balaguer.

Don Joaquín Salcedo y Tormo, Municipal Judge in charge of the City Register of Barbastro,

CERTIFIES that in the City Register in my charge, section for births, volume 25, folio 81, is found the following:

Record of Birth: Number 9
Don José Maria Julian, Mariano Escrivá y Albás

In the City of Barbastro, province of Huesca, at nine in the morning of the tenth day of January of nineteen hundred two, before Don Francisco Armisen, Municipal Judge, and Don Victoriano Claver, Secretary, there appeared Don Manuel Clavería, a native of Barbastro (municipal district of same, province of Huesca), of age, a widower, a constable by profession, living in this city, at 7 Encomienda Street. He came for the purpose of having a boy inscribed in the City Register, having been asked to do this by the parents of same, and declared in writing:
That said boy was born at 10:00 P.M. yesterday in the home of his parents, at 26 Mayor Street.
That he is the legitimate son of Don José Escrivá, merchant, 33 years old, and of Doña Dolores Albás, 23 years old, of Fonz and Barbastro respectively.
That he is the grandson, on his father's side, of Don José Escrivá, deceased, and of Doña Constancia Cerzán [sic], natives of Peralta de la Sal and Fonz respectively.

And on his mother's side, of Don Pascual Albás, deceased, and of Doña Florencia Blanc, natives of Barbastro.

And that said boy has been registered with the names of José María, Julián, and Mariano.

Present as witnesses to all of this were Don Ramón Meliz, a retired military man, and Don Amado Beltran, a barber, both married, of age, residents of this neighborhood.

Having read this entire document and invited those persons who are to sign it to read it for themselves, if they so desire, His Honor the Judge had it stamped with the seal of the municipal court. It is signed by him, by the declarant, and by witnesses, whom I vouch for. Signed: Francisco Armisen. Manuel Clavería. Ramón Meliz. Amado Beltran. Victoriano Claver.

This is completely faithful to the original that I have. In witness whereof I issue the present document in Barbastro on the twenty-sixth of April of nineteen hundred twelve.

Signed and sealed: Municipal Judge, Joaquín Salcedo /
Secretary, Victoriano Claver

Appendix 7

Josemaría's Baptismal Certificate

The original is in the archive of the parish of Our Lady of the Assumption in Barbastro, Book of Baptisms no. 43, fol. 115. It has a later appended note about the change of the surname Escrivá to "Escrivá de Balaguer." The certificate contains one error. Josemaría's paternal grandfather was born in Perarrúa, not Peralta de la Sal.

I, Father Lino Rodríguez Peláez, acting pastor of the parish of Our Lady of the Assumption (cathedral) of the diocese of Barbastro,

DO HEREBY CERTIFY that in folio 115 of Book of Baptisms no. 43 of the archive of this parish, there is inscribed the record for Monsignor Josemaría Escrivá de Balaguer y Albás, which, copied verbatim, says:

"In Barbastro on the thirteenth of January of nineteen hundred two, I, Father Angel Malo, Cathedral Vicariate Regent, solemnly baptized a boy born at 10:00 P.M. on the ninth: the legitimate son of Don José Escrivá, a native of Fonz, and Doña Dolores Albás, a native of Barbastro, who were married and reside and do business in this city. Paternal grandparents: Don José, of Peralta de la Sal, deceased, and Doña Constancia Corzán, of Fonz; maternal, Don Pascual, deceased, and Doña Florencia Blanc, of Barbastro. He was given the names José, María, Julián, and Mariano. His godparents are his uncle Don Mariano Albás, a widower, and his aunt Doña Florencia Albás, a married woman residing in Huesca and represented by Doña Florencia Blanc. I informed them of their responsibilities. Signed: Angel Malo, Regent."

In witness whereof I issue the present document in Barbastro on March 19, 1981.

Signed and sealed: Lino Rodríguez
Verification of signature and authentication
Barbastro, March 20, 1981

Signed and sealed: Raimundo Martín, Vicar General

Note:

I, Father Lino Rodríguez Peláez, acting pastor of the parish of Our Lady of the Assumption (cathedral) of the diocese of Barbastro,

DO HEREBY CERTIFY that on folio 115 of Book of Baptisms no. 43 of the archive of this parish, there is inscribed the record for Monsignor Josemaría Escrivá de Balaguer y Albás, with a marginal note which reads exactly as follows:

"By order of the Episcopal Delegate of this Diocese of Barbastro, given on May 27, 1943, on this certificate the surname 'Escrivá' is changed to 'Escrivá de Balaguer.' From now on there should be read and written 'José María Julián Mariano Escrivá de Balaguer y Albás,' legitimate son of Don José Escrivá de Balaguer and of Doña Dolores Albás. Barbastro, June 20, 1943. Signed: José Palacio."

In witness whereof I issue this document in Barbastro on March 19, 1981.

Signed and sealed: Lino Rodríguez

Appendix 8

Secondary School Studies (1912–1918)

The original files are archived in the offices of the Institutes of Huesca and Lérida. In the Práxedes Mateo Sagasta Institute in Logroño, where Josemaría finished his secondary school studies, can be found the complete file: protocol no. 265/6935.

I, Don Pedro García Santamaría, Secretary of the Secondary School Institute Práxedes Mateo Sagasta, of Logroño,

DO HEREBY CERTIFY that Don José María Escrivá y Albás, native of Barbastro (Huesca), took and passed the following studies:

June 11, 1912 (Huesca)
Primary Education: Passed

1912–1913 (Lérida) — Private School
Latin I: Outstanding
Spanish: Outstanding
Geography of Spain: Outstanding
Principles of Arithmetic and Geometry: Outstanding (First Place)
Religion I: Outstanding
Penmanship: Notable

1913–1914 (Lérida) — Private School
Latin I: Outstanding
Geography of Spain: Notable
Arithmetic: Outstanding (First Place)
Religion II: Outstanding
Physical Education I: Passed

1914–1915 (Lérida) — Private School
Latin II: Passed
French I: Notable
Spanish History: Notable
Geometry: Outstanding (First Place)
Physical Education II: Passed

469

1915–1916 (Logroño) — Private School
Grammar and Composition: Outstanding (First Place)
French II: Outstanding
World History: Notable
Algebra and Trigonometry: Outstanding
Drawing I: Outstanding

1916–1917 (Logroño) — Public School
Psychology and Logic: Notable
History of Literature: Outstanding
Physics: Notable
Physiology and Hygiene: Outstanding
Drawing II: Outstanding

1917–1918 (Logroño) — Public School
Ethics and Law: Outstanding (First Place)
Natural History: Outstanding
Chemistry: Notable
Agriculture: Outstanding

He was awarded the degree of "Bachiller Superior" by the rector of the University of Saragossa, on August 6, 1923.

In witness whereof, for whomever it may concern, this document is signed and sealed by the Director of this Center on the tenth of January of nineteen hundred eighty-four.

Signed and sealed: The Director
The Secretary
The Assistant Secretary

[The signatures are illegible.]

Appendix 9

Ecclesiastical Studies in the Seminaries of Logroño (1919–1920) and Saragossa (1920–1924)

I, Don Julio Fleta Plou, priest, professor, and Secretary of Studies at Saragossa's Metropolitan Seminary,

DO HEREBY CERTIFY that Don José María Escrivá Albás, native of Barbastro, Diocese of Barbastro, Province of Huesca, took and passed in this Metropolitan Seminary of Saragossa—having taken the humanities, philosophy, and first-year theology courses in Logroño—the courses which, with the respective marks, are listed below.

Academic year 1920–1921
SECOND-YEAR THEOLOGY
De Incarnato et Gratia: Meritissimus
De Actibus et Virtutibus: Benemeritus
Homiletics: Meritissimus
Patristics: Meritissimus
Liturgy: Meritissimus

FROM FIRST-YEAR THEOLOGY
Introductio in S. Scriptura: Meritissimus
Exegesis Novi Testamenti: Meritissimus

FROM FOURTH-YEAR LATIN
Lingua Graeca: Meritus
Lingua Hebraica: Meritus

Academic year 1921–1922
THIRD-YEAR THEOLOGY
De Deo Creante: Meritissimus
Theologia Moralis (Praecep.): Meritissimus
De Re Sacramentaria: Benemeritus
Theologia Pastoralis: Meritissimus

Academic year 1922–1923
FOURTH-YEAR THEOLOGY
Exegesis Veteris Testam.: Meritissimus
De Deo Uno et Trino: Meritissimus
Theol. Moralis Sacramentalis: Meritissimus
Paedagogia Catechetica: Meritissimus

Academic year 1923–1924
FIFTH-YEAR THEOLOGY
Disquisitiones Theologicae: Meritissimus
Institutiones Canonicae: Meritissimus
Casus Conscientiae: Meritissimus

Note: In the first volume of the Book of School Records, folio 348, no. 693, one reads the following about his previous studies:

"In his four years of Latin and three of philosophy at the General and Technical Institute of Logroño, which were incorporated by said seminary of Logroño with the mark of 'Meritus,' he took and passed the following subjects:

Academic year 1919–1920
FIRST-YEAR THEOLOGY
Theological Topics: Meritissimus
Church History: Meritissimus
Archaeology: Meritissimus
Sociology: Meritissimus
Pastoral Theology: Benemeritus
Spanish Law: Meritissimus
French: Meritissimus"

That is what the documents in my office show. In witness whereof I give the present certification, signed by the Prefect of Studies and given the seal of this seminary, in Saragossa, on the twelfth of November of nineteen hundred seventy-five.

Signed: The Prefect of Studies [signature illegible]
Signed and sealed: Julio Fleta Plou, Secretary

Appendix 10(a)

Data referring to the seminarian José María Escrivá in the book
"De vita et moribus" [Of the Life and Customs] *of the Students of the Seminary of San Francisco de Paula,* **1920–1925**

The original of this book is in the archive of the diocese of Saragossa. Previously it was in the archive of the Royal Seminary of San Carlos; it was kept there until a few years ago. In the certified copy an error in the original is left uncorrected: the naming of the father of the seminarian as "José María," rather than "José."

I, Don Agustín Pina Lancís, Canon-Archpriest of the Metropolitan Cathedral Chapter of Holy Savior, Episcopal Vicar of the Chancery, and President of the Royal Priestly Seminary of San Carlos,

DO HEREBY CERTIFY:

I. That among the documents in the archive of the Royal Priestly Seminary of San Carlos there is a book entitled *"De vita et moribus"* of *the Students of the Seminary of San Francisco de Paula,* which begins in February 1913. It is known that the Seminary of San Francisco de Paula was located on the upper floors of this building of San Carlos, from 1866 until 1945.

II. That page 111 of said book, *De vita et moribus,* contains facts pertaining to the seminarian José María Escrivá for the five years that he was in this seminary: September 1920 to March 1925. Here is a literal transcription:

1. At the top of the page, under the preprinted title of "Seminary of San Francisco de Paula," is this personal information:
"Don José María Escrivá Albás, 18 years of age, native of Barbastro, Diocese of same, legitimate son of José María and María Dolores, residents of Logroño. He was recommended by Father Carlos Albás Blanc, who lives at 9 Espoz y Mina Street, on the third floor.
"He entered this seminary on September 28, 1920. He has a half scholarship. Prefect."
2. The sheet then has seven preprinted columns: "Academic

Courses," "Piety," "Application," "Discipline," "Character," "Vocation," and "General Observations."

3. In the first column are listed the courses for 1920–1921,
1921–1922, 1922–1923, 1923–1924, and 1924–1925. Then, in the space
supposed to be reserved for the next five columns, there are transcribed the marks received in each subject. I am not transcribing these
marks, because they can be found in his student file at the Seminary of
San Valero and San Braulio, where the seminarians took these subjects
and the exams for them. I only point out that he received a "Meritissimus" in all theology courses except two—one in his second year and
one in his third—in both of which he received a "Benemeritus."

4. Under columns 2 to 5 appear the evaluations given him in his
first four years. (For 1924–1925 there is no notation.)
"PIETY: Good. / Ditto. / Ditto. / Ditto.
"APPLICATION: Average. / Good. / Ditto. / Ditto.
"DISCIPLINE: Average. / Good. / Ditto. / Ditto.
"CHARACTER: Inconstant and haughty, but well-mannered and
courteous. / Ditto. / Ditto. / Ditto.
"VOCATION: He seems to have one. / Ditto. / Ditto. / He has
one."

5. In the column "General Observations" appear the following
notations:
"1920–1921: Comes from the Seminary of Logroño, where he did
his prior studies.
"1922–1923: Was named prefect in September 1922 and given the
tonsure on the 28th of same.
"1923–1924: Ordained to the subdiaconate in June 1924.
"He had a fight with Julio Cortés, and I gave him the appropriate punishment. But the acceptance and carrying out of it was really
a glory for him, since in my judgment it was his adversary who had
struck first and most, and he had spoken to him in gross language
improper for a cleric, and, in my presence, he had insulted him in the
Cathedral of La Seo."

6. At the end of the document, it says:
"Ordained to the diaconate at Christmas 1924, and to the priesthood on March 29, 1925. He ceased to belong to the Seminary as of
the last-mentioned date." (Illegible signature.)

I must note that this last annotation contains an error which could lead to confusion. His ordination as a priest actually took place on March 28, though it was on the 29th that he ceased to belong to the Seminary.

III. In witness whereof, for whatever purposes it may serve, I sign and seal this document in Saragossa on the twenty-eighth of March of nineteen hundred eighty-four.

Signed and sealed: Agustín Pina

Appendix 10(b)

Testimony of Father José López Sierra,
Rector of the Seminary of San Francisco de Paula, given in
Saragossa on January 26, 1948
(AGP, RHF, D–03306)

Father José María Escrivá de Balaguer. It is a difficult task to detail his life as a seminarian. He started his studies in sacred theology as a boarding student—coming from the Institute of Logroño, the cradle of his formal education—at the Seminary of San Francisco de Paula, an adjunct of that of San Carlos, of Saragossa, whose archbishop was His Eminence Cardinal Soldevila, and whose rector, the one who is writing these lines. However, it is not so difficult to describe some of his outstanding characteristics, among which predominates his inclination toward apostolate, his predilection for young people. His little book *The Way* is proof of this, for to whom is it directed if not to them?

First as a seminarian, he is distinguished among his classmates by his polished manners, his friendly and simple manner, his obvious modesty, his respectfulness toward his superiors, and his friendliness and kindness toward his companions; he was highly esteemed by the former, and admired by the latter. Eminent qualities, harbingers of his fruitful apostolate.

Later he becomes director of seminarians, a distinction conferred on him by the cardinal, even before his reception of Holy Orders, in consideration of his exemplary conduct and, no less, his application. For he is simultaneously pursuing an ecclesiastical career and a career in law. Little by little is being revealed that incipient apostle for whose ministry Heaven is preparing him with sweet blessings.

It was not surprising that this molder of aspirants to the priesthood later became a molder of young lay people. He knew them well, having spent a lot of time with them in the halls of the Institute and of the university, and having, nonetheless, observed a vacuum in the religious formation of these young intellectuals. The existing institutions cannot adequately accommodate the needs of the youth of modern times; a new institution is needed for them. On several occasions he spoke to me about this matter, because of an anonymous set of rules which came into our hands by chance and, I can say today, providentially, for Providence *disponit omnia suaviter* [works all things sweetly].

It is in the seminary, then, that there begins this great work of his which is amazing not only Catholic Spain but even the very center of Catholicism, Rome itself, where the institution now has some centers. Yes, in our seminary in Saragossa is found in germinal form Opus Dei, that great work of God destined to produce such choice fruits for consumption outside of the seminary.

His motto was to win all for Christ, that all might be one in Christ, and he did indeed achieve this, with his right way of acting. He did not go in for punishments; he was always gentle and compassionate; his mere presence, which was always attractive and likable, was enough to keep in line the most undisciplined; a simple, friendly smile would appear on his lips whenever he observed some edifying act on the part of his seminarians, while a discreet look—penetrating, sometimes sad, but always very compassionate—was enough to keep in check the most willful. With this simplicity and charming gentleness he gave formation to his young seminarians.

He is ordained a priest, and he prepares himself to celebrate his first Mass, in the way in which the sun, as the day progresses, gives more and more light and warmth. So, too, the impetus that he felt toward the apostolate with youth is on the increase. When the day arrives—no invitations having been sent, because of the recent death in the family—he celebrates his first Mass in the Holy and Angelic Chapel of Our Lady of the Pillar, in Saragossa. Two priests, friends of his parents, assisted him at the altar. For the new priest the first choice would have been his rector; but how could his rector have left alone that mother who was dissolved in a sea of tears and at times seemed close to fainting, and those two young ones, the little brother and the sister, who accompanied her? I declined the honor; and the four of us, on our knees, without even blinking, remained immobile through the whole Mass, contemplating the sacred gestures of that angel on earth, who, for this first time, offered his Mass for that good father whom he had lost on earth and who was watching from heaven.

He is a priest devoured by thirst for apostolate. The field of the parishes contained in this archdiocese of Saragossa is much too small for his Work. Providence—not without first having him suffer great tribulations—brings him to a broader field, to the populous Madrid, where it seems more necessary to establish it because of the corruption of so many young people. In this field there seems to ring in his ears the saying of our Divine Master, "The harvest is great, the laborers are few." The molder of seminarians is eager to be a molder of young lay people. It is his favorite ministry. He hears confessions, gives retreats and days of recollections, prays, publishes various writings, always with his sights set on the young, who are the apple of his eye. I am sorry to say that, for reasons beyond my control, I cannot give dates—a new tribulation for me. To supply details about his efforts in Madrid is the responsibility of the children of such a good father.

José López Sierra
Saragossa, January 26, 1948

Appendix 11

Certification of Holy Orders Received: 1922–1925

The original records are preserved in the Book of Holy Orders (the volume for May 27, 1889, to 1947) in the archive of the diocese of Saragossa.

I, Don Fernando Pérez Aysa, priest, canon of this holy metropolitan church, and chief notary of the Archdiocese of Saragossa,

DO HEREBY CERTIFY that in the Book of Holy Orders which is kept in the archive of the chief notary, in my care, are the records for the holy orders received by the person later to be known as Monsignor Josemaría Escrivá de Balaguer y Albás. He received all of the orders, including the presbyterate, between the years of nineteen hundred twenty-two and nineteen hundred twenty-five, while residing, as a seminarian, in the old seminary of San Francisco de Paula.

The details of these ordinations, as shown in the abovementioned book of records, are as follows.

1. **First Clerical Tonsure**, conferred by His Eminence Juan Soldevila y Romero, Cardinal-Archbishop of Saragossa, on the twenty-eighth of September of nineteen hundred twenty-two, in the oratory of his residence as archbishop of Saragossa. Reg. fol. 327, no. 4,410.

2. **Porter and Lector**, conferred by His Eminence Juan Soldevila y Romero, Cardinal-Archbishop of Saragossa, on the seventeenth of December of nineteen hundred twenty-two, in the oratory of his residence as archbishop of Saragossa. Reg. fol. 329, no. 4,423.

3. **Exorcist and Acolyte**, conferred by His Eminence Juan Soldevila y Romero, Cardinal-Archbishop of Saragossa, on the twenty-first of December of nineteen hundred twenty-two, in the oratory of his residence as archbishop of Saragossa. Reg. fol. 329, no. 4,426.

4. **Subdiaconate,** conferred by the Most Reverend Miguel de los Santos y Díaz de Gómara, Titular Bishop of Tagora, with the permission of the illustrious Vicar Capitular of the Archdiocese of Saragossa, on the fourteenth of June of nineteen hundred twenty-four, in the church of the Priestly Seminary of San Carlos Borromeo, of Saragossa, and for service to this diocese. Reg. fol. 350, no. 4,580.

5. **Holy Order of the Diaconate**, conferred by the Most Reverend Miguel de los Santos y Díaz de Gómara, Titular Bishop of Tagora, with the permission of the illustrious Vicar Capitular of the Archdiocese of Saragossa, on the twentieth of December of nineteen hundred twenty-four, in the church of the Priestly Seminary of San Carlos Borromeo, of Saragossa. Reg. fol. 358, no. 4,644.

6. **Holy Order of the Priesthood**, conferred by the Most Reverend Miguel de los Santos y Díaz de Gómara, Titular Bishop of Tagora, with the permission of the illustrious Vicar Capitular of the Archdiocese of Saragossa, on the twenty-eighth of March of nineteen hundred twenty-five, in the church of the Priestly Seminary of San Carlos Borromeo, of Saragossa. He had received a pontifical dispensation for the ten months by which he was short of the canonical age. Reg. fol. 363, no. 4685.

In witness whereof I issue the present document, and seal it with the seal of the Archdiocese, in Saragossa on the twenty-sixth of March of nineteen hundred eighty-one.

Signed and sealed: Fernando Pérez Aysa

Saragossa, March 27, 1981
Verification of signature and authentication:
Agustín Pina / Episcopal Vicar of the Chancery

Appendix 12

Data from Josemaría's Student File in the Archive of the Law School of the University of Saragossa

UNIVERSITY OF SARAGOSSA
SCHOOL OF LAW
No. 886

I, Don José Antonio Izuel Vera, Associate Professor and Secretary of the Law School of the University of Saragossa,

DO HEREBY CERTIFY that Don José María Escrivá Albás, native of Barbastro, Province of Huesca, has taken and passed the courses required for the Licentiate in Law, with the marks shown below.

PREPARATORY STUDIES

Spanish Language and Literature	1922–1923	Notable
Fundamental Logic	1922–1923	Outstanding
Spanish History	1923–1924	Passed

PERIOD OF THE LICENTIATE

FIRST GROUP

Elements of Natural Law	1923–1924	Notable
Principles of Roman Law	1923–1924	Special Honors
Political Economy	1923–1924	Outstanding

SECOND GROUP

General History of Spanish Law	1923–1924	Passed
Principles of Canon Law	1923–1924	Special Honors
Spanish Political Law	1925–1926	Notable

THIRD GROUP
Spanish Civil Law: Common and

Statutory (First Year)	1923–1924	Passed
Administrative Law	1925–1926	Passed
Penal Law	1925–1926	Passed

FOURTH GROUP
Spanish Civil Law: Common and

Statutory (Second Year)	1924–1925	Notable
Judicial Procedure	1925–1926	Passed
Public International Law	1925–1926	Special Honors
Elements of Public Finance	1925–1926	Passed

FIFTH GROUP
Business Law of Spain and of
the Principal Nations of

Europe and the Americas	1925–1926	Notable
Legal Methods and the Wording of Legal Documents	1926–1927	Passed
Private International Law	1925–1926	Notable

Forwarded to Madrid on the thirtieth of March of nineteen hundred twenty-seven, with all courses passed and the degree of Licentiate granted, for pursual of the doctorate.

Degree of Licentiate in Law issued by the authorities on the twelfth of June of nineteen hundred thirty-four.

In witness whereof, at the request of an interested party, I issue the present certification, with the approval of the Dean of this School and with the seal of the same, on the thirtieth of April of nineteen hundred eighty-one.

Signed and sealed: José A. Izuel
Approved by: The Dean
[Signature illegible.]

Data from Josemaría's Student File in the Archive of the Law School of Universidad Complutense, in Madrid

Personal Academic Certification
Vol. 1, no. 03873

I, Don Juan Vivancos Gallego, Adjunct Professor and Secretary of said School,

DO HEREBY CERTIFY that Don José María Escrivá Albás, native of Barbastro, Province of Huesca, has taken and passed all of the subjects required for the Licentiate in Law at the University of Saragossa, having obtained the marks indicated. . . .

PERIOD OF THE DOCTORATE: At the University of Madrid, year 1927–1928: "History of International Law," Passed; "Philosophy of Law," Notable. Year 1929–1930: "History of Juridical Literature," Notable.

In witness whereof, for the purposes of and at the request of an interested party, I issue the present certification at the order of and with the approval of the Dean of this School and with the seal of the same.

Madrid, twenty-first of May of nineteen hundred eighty-one.

Approved by: Fernando Sequeira de Fuentes, Vice Dean
Signed and sealed: Juan Vivancos, Secretary
C. Caballero, Chief of the Secretariat

Appendix 13

Obituary notice for Father José María Somoano: original in AGP, RHF, AVF–0098

+

IN THE NAME OF THE FATHER AND OF THE SON AND OF
THE HOLY SPIRIT, AND OF BLESSED MARY.

JOSE MARIA SOMOANO, Priest (+ 16 July 1932)

On Saturday, July 16, 1932, the feast of Our Lady of Mount
Carmel (to whom he was very devoted), at eleven o'clock at night,
our brother José María died, a victim of charity, and perhaps of sec-
tarian hatred.

The life of this admirable priest was short but productive, a mature fruit that our Lord wanted for heaven.

The thought that there were priests who dared to go up to the
altar without the proper dispositions was enough to make him shed
tears of reparation.

Before being introduced to the Work of God, after the sacrilegious torchings of May, at the beginning of the officially decreed persecution, he was overheard in the chapel of the hospital (where he
was chaplain and an apostle to the end, despite all the laicist fury), offering himself to Jesus—out loud (since he thought he was alone),
spurred by the momentum of his prayer—as a victim for this poor
Spain.

Our Lord Jesus accepted the holocaust and, with a double
predilection, predilection for the Work of God and for José María,
sent him to us, so that our brother might round out his spiritual life,
his heart burning hotter and hotter with the fires of Faith and Love,
and so that the Work might have someone up there with the Blessed
Trinity and with Mary Immaculate who would continue to be concerned about us.

At our last priestly meeting, the Monday before his death, with
what enthusiasm he listened to the plans for beginning our activity!

I know that his prayers will have a lot of influence with the merciful Heart of Jesus, when he intercedes for us crazy ones—crazy like

him . . . and like Him!—that we may obtain the abundant graces that we will need to fulfill God's will.

It is right that we should weep. And even though his holy life and the circumstances that surrounded his death make us feel sure that he is enjoying the eternal rest of those who live and die in the Lord, it is also right that we offer suffrages for the soul of our brother.

J. M.

Appendix 14

Obituary notice for Luis Gordon y Picardo; original in AGP, RHF, AVF–0098

LUIS GORDON Y PICARDO (+ 5 November 1932)

He went to his eternal rest in the Lord on the morning of November 5, 1932. Another one!

Our Lady took him, too, on a Saturday. Now we have two saints: a priest and a layman.

Incidentally, José María Somoano left a written statement of the good impression made on him by the character of our brother Luis.

A good model: obedient, most discreet, charitable to the point of extravagance, humble, mortified, and penitent . . . , a man of the Eucharist and of prayer, most devoted to the Blessed Virgin and to Saint Thérèse . . . , a father to the workers in his factory. They cried when they heard of his death.

The Lord, when we, including Luis, were consoling one another about the death of our José María, had us say, "If God called you or me, what would we do, from heaven or from purgatory, except cry out again and again, many times and always: 'My God! Help them— my brothers who are fighting on earth—that they may do your will. Smooth out the path, hasten the hour, remove the obstacles . . . sanctify them!'?"

Our brother Luis concurred in that idea, because it is a necessary consequence of the real and very strong spiritual fraternity that unites us, a fraternity that he knew how to live in such a practical way.

With what enthusiasm will he now be fulfilling his *obligation* as our brother!

Let this certainty serve to console us, and let us love the cross, the holy cross which is falling on the Work of God. Our great King Jesus Christ chose to take away the two best-prepared ones so that we would not put our trust in anything earthly, not even someone's personal virtues, but only and exclusively in his most loving Providence.

The Merciful Love has cast another seed in the furrow, . . . and how much we expect from its fertility!

J. M.

Appendix 15

Obituary notice for María Ignacia García Escobar: original in AGP, RHF, AVF–0098

MARIA GARCIA ESCOBAR (+ 13 September 1933)

On September 13, the vigil of the feast of the Exaltation of the Holy Cross, there fell asleep in the Lord this first sister of ours, of our house in heaven. Some time before, at her request, and considering the seriousness of her condition, we gave her holy viaticum.

What peace she had! How she spoke, with what naturalness, of going soon to her Father-God, . . . and how she received the commissions we gave her for the Homeland—the prayers for the Work!

A priest brother of ours was the instrument of the Lord by which María came to the Work, as a vocation of expiation, offering herself as a voluntary victim for the sanctification of others. Even before hearing about the Work of God, María was already offering up for us the terrible sufferings of her sickness. And Jesus received those sufferings as a sweet scent, urging the victim on, placing more of his cross upon her, to the point where the sick woman had to say to that holy priest, our brother Father José María Somoano, "Father José María, I think your intention must be a very worthwhile one, because ever since you started asking me to pray and offer things up for it, Jesus has been treating me really splendidly."

Prayer and suffering were the wheels of the chariot of triumph of this daughter of ours. We have not lost her; we have *gained* her. The realization that she has gone home should immediately turn our natural sorrow into supernatural joy, because now we are sure of an even mightier intercessor in heaven.

J. M.

Notes

Notes to Chapter 1

[1] *Mons. Josemaría Escrivá de Balaguer y El Opus Dei. En el 50 Aniversario de su Fundación* (Pamplona: Eunsa, 1982), pp. 21–27 (under the heading "De la mano de Dios"). See also AGP, P01 1975, p. 357.

[2] *Meditation* of 14 Feb 1964. For more on the influence of his parents' virtues on Josemaría's early formation, see Javier Echevarría, *Sum.* 1775 and 1798; Santiago Escrivá de Balaguer y Albás, PM, folio 1297; and Martín Sambeat, *Sum.* 5678.

[3] This remark confirms what was noted a few lines above: that in nearly every autobiographical statement by the founder, one finds some reference, either overt or implied, to his calling of October 2, 1928. See Alvaro del Portillo, *Sum.* 3, and Javier Echevarría, *Sum.* 1760.

[4] See Appendix 6.

[5] See Appendix 7.

[6] See Javier Echevarría, *Sum.* 1763, and Joaquín Alonso, PR, p. 1649. Concerning his gratitude toward his godparents, see Alvaro del Portillo, PR, p. 19, and Angel Camo, AGP, RHF, T–02846, p. 1.

[7] See the cathedral chapter's *Liber de Gestis,* year 1635, fol. 38v.

[8] *C 2828* (21 Apr 1959). The remnants of the baptismal font arrived in Rome in 1959. The founder, after the necessary reconstruction, had it placed as a holy water font at the entrance of the oratory of Our Lady of Peace (now the prelatic church of Opus Dei), together with a commemorative plaque inscribed with the following text:

HVNC SACRVM BAPTISMATIS FONTEM SANCTAE ECCLESIAE CATHEDRALIS BARBASTRENSIS + IN QVO CONDITOR NOSTER EIVSQVE MATER ET SOROR AQVAS REGENERATIONIS ACCEPE-RVNT + HISPANICO BELLO FLAGRANTE ANNO MCMXXXVI IN ODIVM RELIGIONIS DIRVPTVM + OPERI DEI AB EPISCOPO ET CAPITVLO ANNO MCMLVII DONO DATVM + CONSILIVM ATQVE ASSESORATVS CENTRALIS AD PRISTINAM FORMAM ANNO MCMLIX RESTITVERE FECERVNT.

[9] See Appendix 6.

[10] This particular error in transcribing his family name occurred often enough that it was bound to be upsetting to Don José. In fact, on his own birth certificate, in Fonz, he himself appears as the "legitimate son of José Escribá y Zaydin" (see Appendix 2). Later the error was repeated and multiplied at the baptisms of one of his sons and three of his daughters. Of the eldest daughter it is recorded that "María del Carmen Constancia Florencia Escribá" is the daughter of "Don José Escribá"; of "María Asunción Escribá," that her father is "Don José Escribá" and her godfather is "Don Teodoro Escribá"; and of "María Dolores Escribá," that her father and grandfather are named "José Escribá." And on the death certificate for this last girl, the name "Escribá" reappears. It is by way of exception that the baptismal and death certificates of María del Rosario Escrivá do not contain any errors. See the archive of the parish of Our Lady of the Assumption in Barbastro: Books of Baptism no. 43 (fol. 22) and no. 44 (fols. 35 and 64v), and Book of the Dead no. 45 (fol. 14v).

Regarding Josemaría, we find his name written as "Escribá" in several places: for example, in the 20 Feb 1925 document of papal dispensation from the age requirement for ordination as a priest, which begins, "Most Blessed Father, Diac. Joseph M. Escribá . . ." (Sacred Congregation for the Sacraments, Prot. N. 871/25; AGP, RHF, D–03263); in the 19 Dec 1925 letter from the archbishop of Saragossa to Antonio Lasierra, president of the city council (AGP, RHF, D–05188); in the 12 Dec 1937 safe-conduct pass from the military headquarters of Fuenterrabía (AGP, RHF, D–15073); and on the envelope of the 8 Oct 1952 letter from Julio M. Cortés Zuazo (AGP, RHF, D–15282).

[11] See Alvaro del Portillo, *Sum.* 57.

[12] *Apuntes,* no. 1273. Rereading in 1939 what he had written in 1935 about his campaign to defend the *v* in "Escrivá," his thoughts went back to his childhood years, when his father, with the honorable pride of a person of noble birth, in order to show his son that this concern about one letter was neither capricious nor fanatic, but appropriate because the name had been forged through many generations of history, spoke to Josemaría about his family, about "our heritage . . .." But those suspension points in the note of 1939 conceal an ongoing concern. If we look back at the notebooks of his *Apuntes íntimos* (Personal Notes), in the first week of June 1933 (with an explanatory note inserted in December 1934) he writes this: "Cast far from you that despair caused by recognition of your misery. It's true: in terms of financial prestige, you are a zero; in terms of social prestige" (inserted note: "My parents have told me things that indicate that this is not so; but with respect to me personally, it was so"), "another zero; and

another for your virtues, and another for your talents. . . . But to the left of those negations stands Christ, . . . and what an incalculable number results!" (*Apuntes*, no. 1017).

Among the well-known names in his ancestry are Saint Joseph Calasanz and Michael Servetus. Monsignor Escrivá referred to them publicly on a few occasions.

Once he said, "An ancestor of mine, Michael Servetus, was burned by the Protestant inquisition of Calvin. Although we're only distantly related, my brother and sister and I are the only remaining relatives of the family" (see AGP, P04 1972, p. 655). For more about the trial of Servetus, see *Registres de la Compagnie des Pasteurs de Genève au temps de Calvin*, vol. 2, R. M. Kingdon, 1553–1564, and *Accusation et procès de Michel Servet, 1553* (Geneva: E. Droz, 1962).

On another occasion he said, "There is a saint, a distant relative of mine, whom I love very much. Don't get any illusions—I don't have the makings of a saint! Another ancestor of mine was burned by the Protestant inquisition. Come on! I don't have the makings of a heretic, either! Everyone is what they are, regardless of their ancestry. The saint, Joseph Calasanz, said, 'If you want to be holy, be humble; if you want to be holier, be more humble; if you want to be very holy, be very humble'" (see AGP, P04 1972, p. 353). Concerning the life and spirit of Saint Joseph Calasanz, see *Epistolario de San Giuseppe Calasanzio*, edited with commentary by Leodegario Picanyol (Rome, 1950–1951). (See also *Apuntes*, no. 1017.)

[13] C 3022 (26 Nov 1960).

[14] Among the documents of the chancery of Jaime I the Conquistador (in the archive of the Crown of Aragon), in the section on Valencia and in the correspondence regarding the division of the kingdom, appears the name of a Guillem Escrivà, notary of Jaime I (1227–1251). See M. Batllori, "El cronista Bernat Desclot i la familia Escrivà," in *Storiografia e Storia. Studi in onore di Eugenio Duprè Theseider*, Università degli Studi di Roma (Rome: Bulzoni Editore, 1974), pp. 123–50; A. Huici, *Colección diplomática de Jaime I, el Conquistador*, I, 1 (Valencia, 1916); and J. Miret i Sans, *Itinerari de Jaume I (el Conqueridor)* (Barcelona, 1918).

[15] The Ministry of Justice, through the Registry Office, granted permission to add the words "de Balaguer" to form the compound name of "Escrivá de Balaguer." Authorization to use this name was given to Josemaría and Carmen on October 18, 1940, and to their brother, Santiago, on November 12, 1940. On October 18, 1940, this decision of the Ministry of Justice was communicated by the Registry Office to the relevant authorities in Madrid.

[16] For more information on the Escrivá side of Josemaría's family, see AGP, RHF, D–12131, and Appendix 1.

¹⁷ When he was in a mood to share confidences, Don José would tell his
son about some of the adventures and misadventures of his youth. There
was, for example, the time he was given a bicycle with wheels of solid
rubber. He rode around at great speed through the village, to the amazement of the neighbors, until, in a spectacular fall, he broke his arm. His
father (Josemaría's grandfather), after giving someone else the bicycle,
sternly warned him, "I never want to see you on that infernal machine
again." (See AGP, P04 1972, p. 809.)

¹⁸ For many years, Don José's mother and two of his siblings, Father
Teodoro and Josefa, lived in Fonz. See María del Carmen de Otal Martí,
Baroness of Valdeolivos, *Sum.* 5986, and Esperanza Corrales, AGP, RHF,
T–08203, p. 1.

¹⁹ See Martín Sambeat, AGP, RHF, T–03242, p. 2.

The name José Escrivá appears twice during this period in the record
books of the parish of Our Lady of the Assumption where the making of
their Easter duty by parishioners was recorded in compliance with
norms laid down by the Council of Trent. Some of the volumes with
these yearly updates have been lost. Pertinent to this biography is the
fact that in the volume for 1882 there appears for the first time the name
of Doña Dolores, Josemaría's mother, who at that time was four years old
and living in her parents' home at 20 Romero Street. The volumes for
1892 and 1893 attest to her fulfillment of the Easter duty (noting that she
is 15, and then 16) and, for the first time, also to that of Don José, whose
home address is 8 Rio Ancho Street. It is, however, quite possible that
Don José was living in Barbastro before 1892, since the volumes for the
years between 1882 and 1892 have been lost.

²⁰ See AGP, RHF, D–12131, and Appendix 1.

²¹ See Martín Sambeat, AGP, RHF, T–03242, p. 2; Sixta Cermeño, AGP,
RHF, T–02856, p. 3; and Angel Camo, AGP, RHF, T–02846, p. 1.

²² *Meditation* of 6 Jan 1970.

²³ See Appendices 2 and 3.

²⁴ See Santiago Escrivá de Balaguer y Albás, *Sum.* 7320. Teodoro Escrivá
Corzán was the priest beneficiary of Moner House, a chaplaincy founded
in Fonz in 1889 by Joaquín Moner y Siscar. The main duty of the chaplain
was to celebrate Mass daily in its semipublic oratory, which was located
on Cerbuna Street and known as Bardaxi House. In 1901 a new chaplaincy was established in the older house of the Moner family.

Vicente Albás was ordained in 1892, after studying at the seminaries
in Teruel and Barbastro. He served as ecclesiastical administrator of Ra-
mastué and Coscojuela de Sobrarbe, and then as pastor at Olvena, between 1900 and 1918, and from 1918 to 1925 he held a benefice at the
cathedral of Burgos. He went blind, and lived in Saragossa until his
death in 1950.

Carlos Albás was ordained in 1894, was named coadjutor of Laspuña, and in 1897 was appointed to the staff of Cardinal Cascajares. Later he became canon archdeacon of the cathedral chapter of Saragossa. (See Carmen Lamartín, AGP, RHF, T–04813, p. 1.) He died on February 1, 1950.

María Cruz became a Carmelite nun, at the Convent of the Incarnation in Huesca. Her name as a religious was María de Jesús. She died on February 27, 1938.

Pascuala became a Daughter of Charity. She died in Bilbao on March 7, 1910.

Mariano Albás Blanc, Josemaría's godfather, was a cousin of Doña Dolores. Born in 1866, he married Carmen Mora in 1896, and when his wife died in 1899, he entered the seminary. Ordained a priest in 1902, he held a benefice in Barbastro and served as chaplain for the Servants of Mary. In 1915 he lived at 26 Argensola Street, where the Escrivás also lived before they left Barbastro. During the Spanish Civil War he was administrator of the diocese, and was assassinated because of hatred for the Church.

Monsignor Escrivá was also related, on his mother's side, to Bishop Cruz Laplana Laguna, who served as bishop of Cuenca from 1921 to 1936, when he was assassinated. See *Apuntes*, nos. 598, 1146, and 1739, and *Letter 15 Oct 1948*, no. 200.

25 Father Carlos was the brother of Doña Dolores whom we have already mentioned; Father Alfredo Sevil was an uncle of hers; and the Most Reverend José Blanc Barón, bishop of Avila, was another uncle—a brother of Doña Florencia (see Carmen Lamartín, AGP, RHF, T–04813, p. 1).

26 See *Apuntes*, no. 1476. A corroboration of what he says here is the fact that the first anecdote concerning his reentry into Spain after his crossing of the Pyrenees in December 1937 involves friends of Doña Dolores.

27 See Appendix 4, a transcription of the marriage certificate. For more about the chapel where the wedding was celebrated, see *Apuntes*, no. 229, note 248. The Albás family belonged to the parish of Our Lady of the Assumption, whose church was the cathedral. In the parish books are recorded the following facts: in 1877, when Doña Dolores was baptized, the pastor was Father Teodoro Valdovinos; in 1898 and 1899, when she married and had her first daughter, there was no pastor but a priest administrator, Father Máximino Lafita; and in 1902, when Josemaría was baptized, the regent was Father Angel Malo Arias.

28 See F. Fita, *Cortes y Usajes de Barcelona en 1064. Textos inéditos*, BAH, vol. 17 (1890), pp. 385–428; R. Menéndez Pidal, *La España del Cid*, vol. 1 (Madrid: Espasa-Calpe, 1969), pp. 147–51; and *Kitab Ar-Rawd Al-Mitar* (Valencia, 1963), pp. 86–89. For the history of Barbastro, see E. Bernad Royo, "Aragón de 1902 a 1923," in *Aragón en su Historia*, by various

authors (Saragossa, 1980); E. Fernández Clemente, *Aragón contemporáneo (1833–1936)* (Madrid, 1975); R. del Arco, *Historia de Barbastro* (unpublished; written in 1950); S. López Novoa, *Historia de Barbastro*, 2 vols. (Barcelona, 1861; reprinted in 1981); S. Lalueza, "Barbastro," in *Diccionario de Historia Eclesiástica de España* (Madrid, 1972), vol. 1, pp. 183–87; E. Gros Bitria, *Los límites diocesanos en el Aragón oriental* (Saragossa); and R. Martí Ibarz,"Visión retrospectiva de Barbastro en las primeras décadas de este siglo," in *Realizaciones* 26 (1981), p. 10.

29 *Le siège de Barbastre* was published for the first time in 1926, in Paris, by J. L. Perrier. A condensed version of this chanson de geste can be found in A. Becker's "Der Siège de Barbastre," in *Beiträge zur Romanischen Philologie* (Halle a. S.: Max Niemeyer, 1899), pp. 252–66.

30 See Jerónimo Zurita, *Anales de la Corona de Aragón*, book 1, *Rey don Sancho Ramírez.*

31 See S. López Novoa, op. cit., vol. 1, p. 233.

32 See S. Lalueza, op. cit., pp. 183–87, and E. Gros Bitria, op. cit. The first apostolic administrator of the diocese was Bishop Juan Antonio Ruano y Martín (1898–1905).

33 See Appendix 5.

34 See María del Carmen de Otal Martí, *Sum.* 5986.

35 That is how his contemporaries remember him. Esperanza Corrales says, "Don José was from Fonz, a nearby village; it is somewhat to the north, on the left bank of the Cinca River, just a few miles from Barbastro. He belonged to a family of landholders who came from Balaguer, in Lérida. He was a merchant; he settled here after establishing, with some partners, a textile business, Heirs of Cirilo de Latorre, later called Juncosa & Escrivá. It was on General Ricardos Street, near the road that goes from Tarragona to San Sebastián. They also made chocolate there. It became, in other words, a store with various functions, as stores so often do in cities like Barbastro. By the time Don José married Doña Lola—that's what we called Dolores Albás—he was already very well known and had business connections throughout the region" (Esperanza Corrales, AGP, RHF, T–08203, p. 1).

Adriana Corrales, Esperanza's sister, tells us that "Don José was not much of a talker, but was noted for his serene and affectionate smile. . . . He also had a lot of dignity. He was a man of elegant bearing. . . . He lived a robust life of piety, which manifested itself in his practice of the traditional devotions: the family Rosary, Mass, frequent Communion, etc." (Adriana Corrales, AGP, RHF, T–08202, p. 4). See also Martín Sambeat, AGP, RHF, T–03242, p. 1, and Pascual Albás, AGP, RHF, T–02848, p. 1.

[36] See Appendices 6 and 7, and Alvaro del Portillo, *Sum.* 7. When as a little boy he was asked his name, he answered, "José," which was also the name of his father. Years later he commented, "How I could have been so stupid, I cannot understand! For Mary cannot be separated from Joseph, or vice versa." See also AGP, P03 1974, p. 1125.

Following the trail of the deeply felt exclamations of the founder in his interior dialogues with himself, one finds the moment when he put this change of name into effect indicated in a note written at the end of June 1936—the one in which he quotes himself as saying, "Josemaría, on the cross!" (see *Apuntes*, nos. 1282 and 1371). In his correspondence he signed his name "Josemaría" starting with *C 136* (28 Nov 1935).

[37] See Adriana Corrales, AGP, RHF, T–08202, p. 4, and Martín Sambeat, AGP, RHF, T–03242, p. 2.

[38] In the High Middle Ages it was customary for Confirmation to be administered right after Baptism, even though after the Council of Cologne in 1280, the Western churches began to set the requirement of the age of discretion. The Catechism of the Council of Trent, while acknowledging that the sacrament of Confirmation could be conferred on baptized babies, recommended deferring it until they attained the use of reason. In Spain and Portugal, however, and in the lands evangelized by these countries, the practice continued of having bishops confirm children of any age during their pastoral visits. This custom was neither outlawed nor discouraged by the 1917 Code of Canon Law. On June 22, 1897, Pope Leo XIII wrote to the bishop of Marseilles earnestly recommending that children be confirmed before making their First Communion.

[39] The original record of the Confirmation is found in the archive of the parish of Our Lady of the Assumption. An extract from the document bears the annotation "Escrivá de Balaguer" and reads as follows: "On pages 1 and 2 of Book 43 of Sacraments (Confirmations) it is stated that Josemaría Escrivá de Balaguer y Albás, together with other boys and girls, received Confirmation in the cathedral of this city on the twenty-third day of April in 1902. The holy sacrament of Confirmation was administered by His Excellency the Most Reverend Juan Antonio Ruano y Martín, Bishop of Barbastro; the sponsors were Don Ignacio Camps and Doña Juliana Erruz."

[40] See María Dolores Fisac, AGP, RHF, T–04956, p. 28.

[41] "Among my memories of Josemaría," relates Pascual Albás, "what stands out from those years of early childhood is something I heard my father mention several times: namely, the pilgrimage that Josemaría's parents made to Our Lady of Torreciudad. When he was two years old, they went to her, carrying him in their arms, to give thanks because he had been cured of a life-threatening illness through her mediation. The doctors had given up any hope of a cure" (Pascual Albás, AGP, RHF, T–02848, p. 1).

Esperanza Corrales gives this account: "The Escrivás, and with them many who shared their life in Barbastro, were forever convinced that they owed to the intercession of the Blessed Virgin the fact that Josemaría survived the serious illness that he contracted when he was two years old. The doctors had already predicted a fatal outcome, inevitable and imminent. There was nothing left but his mother's prayer, along with a promise to make a pilgrimage to Torreciudad with the child once he was cured. And that is what happened. The illness took an unexpected turn and little Josemaría came out of it, despite the grim predictions of the doctors. When he was well again, the Escrivá couple, with the child in their arms, fulfilled their promise to go as pilgrims to give thanks to Our Lady of Torreciudad" (Esperanza Corrales, AGP, RHF, T–08203, p. 5). See also Martín Sambeat, *Sum.* 5678, and Santiago Escrivá de Balaguer, *Sum.* 7320.

[42] See Alvaro del Portillo, *Sum.* 13; Javier Echevarría, *Sum.* 1767-68; Francisco Botella, *Sum.* 5608; and José Luis Múzquiz, *Sum.* 5792.

[43] Bishop Alvaro del Portillo adds, "I heard this directly from the mother of our founder" (Alvaro del Portillo, PR, p. 32). Another version goes, "My son, you were already more dead than alive; if God has kept you on earth, it must be for something great" (AGP, P01 1977, p. 121). See also Javier Echevarría, *Sum.* 1767.

[44] *Apuntes*, no. 122. In 1934, during a retreat, he wrote a long list of favors he had received, and the first of them was precisely this, his cure. This is how the list begins:

Meditation. What our Lord God has done for me in particular:
1) By means of his Mother—my Mother—when I was a child, he restored me to health.

(See *Apuntes*, no. 1756. See also Silvestre Sancho, *Sum.* 5393.)

[45] See Alvaro del Portillo, *Sum.* 56. For more about this sudden and complete cure, see Martín Sambeat, *Sum.* 5678; Santiago Escrivá de Balaguer, *Sum.* 7320; and Pascual Albás, AGP, RHF, T–02848, p. 1.

[46] See "Lista de oraciones que el Siervo de Dios aprendió de sus padres; oídas directamente del Siervo de Dios y fielmente trascritas" (List of prayers that the Servant of God learned from his parents; heard directly from the Servant of God and faithfully transcribed), Joaquín Alonso, PR, p. 1651 (document 41). Two other examples: "Sacred Heart of Jesus, I trust in you," and "Sweet Heart of Mary, be my salvation." See also Alvaro del Portillo, *Sum.* 22; Javier Echevarría, *Sum.* 1796; and Javier de Ayala, *Sum.* 7623.

[47] Another of these prayers is, "Twelve o'clock has sounded, and Jesus delays. Who is the lucky one with whom he stays?" See Alvaro del Portillo, PR, p. 43; Javier Echevarría, *Sum.* 1777; and Jesús Alvarez Gazapo, PR, p. 1272.

[48] See the above-mentioned "Lista de oraciones."

[49] See *Conversations with Monsignor Escrivá de Balaguer* (Princeton, N.J.: Scepter, 1993), no. 103; AGP, P04 1972, p. 748; and AGP, P04 1974, p. 114.

[50] See Alvaro del Portillo, *Sum.* 45; Encarnación Ortega, PM, fol. 27v; and María del Carmen de Otal Martí, *Sum.* 5995.

[51] See AGP, P01 12/1957, p. 47, and Alvaro del Portillo, *Sum.* 24.

[52] See Alvaro del Portillo, *Sum.* 10.

[53] For the anecdote about the splotch on the wallpaper, see Javier Echevarría, *Sum.* 1794.

[54] For these anecdotes, see *Letter 29 Dec 1947/14 Feb 1966*, no. 8. See also Alvaro del Portillo, PR, p. 55.

[55] These three paragraphs come, respectively, from *Letter 24 Mar 1931*, no. 39; *Meditation* of 14 Feb 1964; and *Letter 9 Jan 1932*, no. 39. See also *Letter 6 May 1945*, no. 44; Alvaro del Portillo, *Sum.* 10; Javier Echevarría, *Sum.* 1793; and Francisco Botella, *Sum.* 5608.

[56] See AGP, P04 1974, p. 433.

[57] See Alvaro del Portillo, *Sum.* 55. Don José had such a high regard for his servants that he said to his son, "Josemaría, you have to respect the people who work in service of our household just as you do everyone else, and as if they're part of the family, because that's what they are" (Javier Echevarría, *Sum.* 1789). See also *Letter 29 Jul 1965*, no. 26.

[58] For these anecdotes, see Alvaro del Portillo, *Sum.* 27, 28, and 29.

[59] See Alvaro del Portillo, *Sum.* 10.

[60] See Alvaro del Portillo, *Sum.* 27, and Javier Echevarría, *Sum.* 1794.

[61] Pascual Albás, AGP, RHF, T–02848, p. 2. See also Esperanza Corrales, AGP, RHF, T–08203, p. 2.

[62] See Javier Echevarría, *Sum.* 1771.

[63] Even as a very small child he loved going to "the Rooster Mass"— Christmas Midnight Mass—and to the three Masses on All Souls' Day, so awed was he by the solemnity of the liturgy. See Javier Echevarría, *Sum.* 1770 and 1776.

[64] *Apuntes*, nos. 228 and 229. Concerning the images of the Christ of the Miracles and of the Dormition of our Lady, see S. López Novoa, op. cit., vol. 1, pp. 255–60. Concerning the devotion of the founder to that first image, the crucifix, see Alvaro del Portillo, *Sum.* 23. Both images were destroyed in 1936 by the revolutionaries.

[65] See *Meditation* of 14 Feb 1964, and Francisco Botella, *Sum.* 5609.

Santiago Escrivá de Balaguer sketches in a few words the formation that his brother received as a child: "The people who played the decisive roles in the moral and religious formation of the Servant of God were, in the first place, our parents, and especially our mother. His formal intellectual education was received first in a preschool and kindergarten run by the Daughters of Charity, and then, when he was a little older, in a school run by the Piarist Fathers of Barbastro" (see Santiago Escrivá de Balaguer, PM, fol. 1297). The school run by the Daughters of Charity was the first children's school started in Spain by that congregation, which was founded in 1633 by Saints Vincent de Paul and Louise de Marillac.

Near the end of the eighteenth century a canon of Barbastro's cathedral, Father Antonio Jiménez, left his entire estate to the Daughters of Charity for the founding of a school for girls. In 1782 the Vincentian priests in Spain sent six young ladies to Paris to be trained in the spirit and work of that congregation so that they could then start it up in Spain. Of these young ladies, four were Catalonian and two were Aragonese. One of them, María Blanc, was from Barbastro; her surname was, coincidentally, one of those of the Servant of God. In 1790 the six returned to Spain, and in 1792 they founded the school in Barbastro. (See S. López Novoa, op. cit., vol. 1, pp. 320–24.)

The Law of Instruction of 1857, also known as the Moyano Law, regulated education in Spain—with many modifications by decrees, administrative rulings, etc.—for over a century.

[66] See Alvaro del Portillo, *Sum.* 33. The pupil would forever be thankful to the Daughters of Charity for all that they taught him. When, many years later, he heard that one of them (a nun who had also been a good friend of Doña Dolores) had been assassinated during the Spanish Civil War, he could not hold back his tears.

[67] See Alvaro del Portillo, *Sum.* 19, and Javier Echevarría, *Sum.* 1774.

[68] See *Boletín Eclesiástico Oficial del Obispado de Barbastro*, year 55, no. 18 (24 Nov 1908), which includes circulars from the previous year, criteria for the contests, results, prizes, and so forth.

[69] Ibid.

[70] Officially authorized by the Holy See in 1617, these schools (also known as Pious Schools) have spread, along with this religious congregation, throughout Europe and America. Already in 1677 the city of Barbastro requested the superior general of the Piarists that they open a school there. The foundation was approved in 1679, both by the pope and by King Carlos II, but because of certain difficulties and injustices, its teachers backed out. Later, some relatives of Saint Joseph Calasanz made a donation of their property, and in 1721 the Piarist Fathers were able to open an elementary school that taught, among other things, Latin grammar (see S. López Novoa, op. cit., vol. 1, pp. 307–14). The school was built in the Entremuro district, together with a magnificent church.

[71] For more on this pastoral visitation, see "Observaciones sobre la S. Visita Pastoral," in *B.E.O. de Barbastro*, year 1908, p. 180. For more on

the preparation given Josemaría by his mother, see Florencio Sánchez Bella, *Sum.* 7539, and Javier de Ayala, AGP, RHF, T–15712, p. 4. See also AGP, RHF, D–04311–7.

Father Enrique Labrador de Santa Lucía was born in Codoñera (Teruel) in 1855. He was stationed in Barbastro from October 1902 until August 1909; he was about fifty-two when little Josemaría made his First Confession. He died a few years later, in 1912, in Daroca.

[72] See Javier Echevarría, *Sum.* 1780, and Alvaro del Portillo, *Sum.* 40.

During his catechetical journey through the Iberian peninsula in 1972, Monsignor Escrivá said this:

> There are many people who don't like the sacrament of Penance, or who see no value in it. They even go so far as to say that to hear confessions of children is a waste of time, and that it frightens the children.
>
> My mother took me to her confessor when I was six or seven, and it made me feel wonderful. It's always made me very happy to remember it. You know what he gave me for my penance? I'll tell you, and you'll die laughing. I can still hear the hearty laughter of my father, who was very pious, but not pietistic. The good priest—he was a very nice little friar—couldn't come up with anything but this: "Tell your mama to give you a fried egg." When I told this to my mother, she said, "My son, that priest might have told you to eat a piece of candy; but a fried egg?"
>
> Obviously he himself loved fried eggs! Isn't that delightful? Just imagine what came into the heart of this little boy, who as yet knew nothing about life, upon being told by his mother's confessor that he should be given a fried egg. It's magnificent! That man was worth his weight in gold!

(See AGP, P04 1972, p. 312.)

[73] Their baptismal certificates are in the archive of the parish of Our Lady of the Assumption in Barbastro, in Book of Baptisms no. 44, fols. 35, 64, and 115v.

[74] "My older sister, Esperanza," says Adriana Corrales, "became close friends with Carmen, Josemaría's older sister, because they were practically the same age. . . . I spent many an hour of my childhood in that apartment that the Escrivás had on Argensola Street, the main balconies of which looked out on the plaza. . . . Sometimes we stayed in a room that was reserved for us children. We used to call it 'the lions' den,' because Doña Lola liked us to play in her house" (Adriana Corrales, AGP, RHF, T–08202, p. 1).

[75] See Alvaro del Portillo, PR, p. 28, and *Letter 29 Jul 1965,* no. 49.

[76] See Javier Echevarría, PR, p. 1921, and Jesús Alvarez Gazapo, *Sum.* 4464.

[77] "Doña Dolores," she adds, "liked to take part in our games and other activities. Sometimes she gave us some old clothes—the kind you find in

any home—to use as costumes" (Esperanza Corrales, AGP, RHF, T–08203, p. 3).

[78] María del Carmen de Otal Martí, AGP, RHF, T–05080, p. 1.

[79] Adriana Corrales, AGP, RHF, T–08202, p. 8.

[80] In primary school, Josemaría took the following subjects: Christian Doctrine and Introduction to Bible History; Reading, Writing, and Spanish Grammar; History and Geography; Rudiments of Law; Basic Ideas of Geometry; Basic Ideas of Physics, Chemistry, and Other Natural Sciences; Elementary Hygiene and Human Physiology; Drawing; Singing; Handicrafts; and Physical Exercise.

The revolutionary storm of 1936 carried off with it most of the documents in the archive of the Piarist Fathers' school. However, both the standard attendance record books (the *Libros de Registro de Asistencia*) and the so-called *Cuadernos del Padre Manuel* (Notebooks of Father Manuel) survived.

Most of the attendance records are loose sheets of paper now bound up in books. The sheets are not in very good condition. References to Josemaría have been found in the *Libro de Registro de la Escuela Completa de niños o Escuela de Escribir* (1904–1912) and in the *Libro de Registro de la Escuela de Ampliación o Escuela Nueva*.

Father Manuel Laborda kept track of his students' attendance in notebooks. Some still exist—stitched together, though not in perfect order—dating from 1872 to 1915, when he stopped giving classes.

There are also mentions of little Josemaría in the *Boletín Oficial del Obispado* (Official Diocesan Bulletin), year 55, p. 284 (no. 18: 18–24 Nov 1908), and in the 13 Mar 1914 and 12 Jun 1914 issues of the weekly diocesan paper *Juventud*. These documents show that during the 1908–1909 school year he was in the "Escuela de párvulos" (little ones' school), and in 1910–1911, in the "Escuela elemental completa." Though we have no documentation for this, it is safe to assume that during the 1909–1910 school year he was in the "Escuela elemental incompleta." For 1911–1912 he shows up as enrolled in the "Escuela de ampliación." He graduated from primary school on June 11, 1912, and then entered a secondary school run by Piarist priests with state exams taken first at Huesca and later at Lérida.

There are also documents showing that in 1912–1913 and 1913–1914 he completed the first and second years of secondary school, and that *Juventud* mentioned him as one of the most outstanding students of the Piarist Fathers. There are no records of his attendance for 1914–1915, his third year of secondary school. See, however, the certificate issued by Father Vicente Moreno, principal of the school in Barbastro, on February 14, 1984: AGP, RHF, D–04311–8.

[81] See J. Lecea Pellicer, *Las Escuelas Pías de Aragón en el siglo XVIII* (Madrid, 1972), pp. 48ff. and 264ff.

[82] See Alvaro del Portillo, "Monseñor Escrivá de Balaguer, instrumento de Dios," in *En Memoria de Mons. Josemaría Escrivá de Balaguer* (Pamplona: Eunsa, 1976), p. 34. In *The Way,* no. 882, we find another school image, also autobiographical, used for a spiritual reality: "Take pity on your child: You see, I want to write a big page each day in the book of my life. But I'm so clumsy that if the Master doesn't guide my hand, instead of graceful strokes my pen leaves behind blots and scratches, that can't be shown to anyone. From now on, Jesus, the writing will always be done by both of us together."

[83] See Encarnación Ortega, AGP, RHF, T–05074, p. 90. Carmen's friend Esperanza Corrales says: "Josemaría had many friends—children of families with whom his parents were acquainted, and also classmates. They sometimes gathered at the house of the Estebans. Those kids' father, a notary public, was the owner of the building in which the Juncosa & Escrivá business was established. The Estebans lived on the first floor of that same building on General Ricardos Street. There the Cagigós, the Sambeats, the Lacaus, and the Fantobas would get together with Josemaría and the Esteban brothers" (Esperanza Corrales, AGP, RHF, T–08203, p. 10).

[84] Martín Sambeat, *Sum.* 5681. Sambeat adds that "he was a good companion to everyone and played all the games that kids usually played in those days, such as top spinning, marbles, handball, basketball, and pretend bullfighting." Josemaría's cousin Pascual Albás says, "He got terrific grades; he was very intelligent. At home they were always setting before us as an example the good grades he got. But he was also very good-natured. He was very cheerful, faithful to his obligations, devout. His great personality was already in evidence" (Pascual Albás, AGP, RHF, T–02848, p. 1).

[85] See Alvaro del Portillo, PR, p. 88, and Javier Echevarría, *Sum.* 1774 and 1775.

[86] See Alvaro del Portillo, *Sum.* 62, and Javier Echevarría, *Sum.* 1775.

[87] See Alvaro del Portillo, *Sum.* 18, and Javier Echevarría, *Sum.* 1774.

[88] See Javier Echevarría, *Sum.* 1793.

[89] See Alvaro del Portillo, *Sum.* 31.

[90] In 1898, the year in which Josemaría's parents were married, an era in the history of Spain came to a close. On December 10, with the Treaty of Paris, the colonial empire of Spain ended. The loss of Cuba, Puerto Rico, and the Philippines had disastrous effects on the morale of the whole nation. At the same time, however, it brought about a critical resurrection of the spirits and ideas of certain intellectuals, known as "the generation of '98."

Just as in the rest of Europe, the "problem of the working class," latent for the previous twenty years, now became acute. With the restoration of the monarchy in 1874 and the flexible Constitution of 1876, a long period of peace and order had been attained, in which conservatives and liberals took turns in power. But the tensions in Spanish life were of a deeper order, involving questions of social reform, economic exigencies, and workers' rights.

[91] *La Cruz del Sobrarbe* (The Cross of the Sobrarbe [region]) was of Carlist (monarchist) inspiration and was founded in about 1889. *La Epoca* (The Times) was conservative; *El País* (The Nation) was liberal. *El Eco del Vero* (The Echo of the Vero [river]) was republican (antimonarchist), while *El Cruzado Aragonés* (The Aragon Crusader), founded in 1903, was a Catholic paper. The weekly paper *Juventud*, mentioned earlier, was a diocesan publication founded in 1914. For more information about Barbastro at the end of the nineteenth century, see P. Riera y Sans, *Diccionario Geográfico, Estadístico, Histórico . . . de España*, vol. 2 (Barcelona, 1882), pp. 48ff.

[92] An effort of this type was the apostolic social enterprise spearheaded by Cardinal Cascajares, Archbishop of Valladolid. This political initiative had very little success. It lacked the necessary experience and ended up causing a strong anticlerical reaction. See G. Redondo, "La Iglesia en la Edad Contemporánea," in *Historia de la Iglesia* (by various authors), vol. 3 (Madrid, 1985), p. 173.

Pope Leo XIII, with his encyclical *Graves de Communi* (18 Jan 1901), renewed the call he had made in *Rerum Novarum* for joint action by Catholics; and he named the cardinal primate of Toledo and his successors as directors of this initiative. Of particular importance was the letter sent by the cardinal primate to the bishops on October 16, 1909. Its indications were taken up by Bishop Isidro Badia y Sarradell of Barbastro and relayed to the faithful of his diocese in a pastoral letter published on February 9, 1910.

[93] See *Boletín Eclesiástico Oficial del Obispado de Barbastro*, year 57, pp. 96–105 (no. 5: 22 Mar 1910). The bylaws of the Centro Católico Barbastrense were presented to Barbastro's apostolic administrator, and he approved them in a decree dated December 8, 1908. A few days later, on December 16, they were also presented to the civil authorities of Huesca. The document was signed by fourteen persons, including José Escrivá, the father of Josemaría. Also among the founders of the Center were Juan Juncosa, business partner of José at Juncosa & Escrivá, and José's brother-in-law Mauricio Albás.

From the very beginning, the Barbastro Catholic Center had a markedly social character. A year after its foundation, in fulfillment of what was prescribed in article 7 of its bylaws, it created the Mutualidad Católica, which consisted of a mutual relief fund (Caja de Socorros Mutuos), a credit union (Caja de Ahorros), and a [nonprofit] pawnshop (Monte de Piedad). See *Boletín Eclesiástico Oficial del Obispado de Barbastro*,

year 57, pp. 104–30 (no. 6: 1 Apr 1910), in which the bylaws of the Mutualidad Católica were published with the approval of both the apostolic
administrator and the civil authorities.

In 1910 the bishop set up the Consejo Diocesano de las Asociaciones
Católico-Obreras (Diocesan Council of Catholic Worker Associations) to
coordinate social initiatives in the diocese, and appointed to it the same
people who made up the board of directors of the Barbastro Catholic
Center.

[94] See Javier Echevarría, *Sum.* 1761; Joaquín Alonso, PR, p. 1648; and José
Ramón Madurga, PM, fol. 269.

[95] "Aetas discretionis tum ad Confessionem tum ad S. Communionem ea
est, in qua puer incipit ratiocinari, hoc est circa septimum annum . . ."
(*Acta Apostolicae Sedis*, II, no. 15, p. 582).

[96] See Alvaro del Portillo, *Sum.* 42. Also relevant is this excerpt from
Javier Echevarría, *Sum.* 1778: "He always remembered with a special affection the old Piarist who taught him the prayer for making a spiritual
communion. From back when he was a boy, from when he was preparing for First Communion, he constantly repeated that formula. I heard
him preach many meditations in which he used that prayer, repeating it
word for word. He said that it filled his soul with peace and serenity,
even in moments of dryness or scruples, to see itself, so poor and so
loaded down with miseries, faced with this marvel of a God who unreservedly gives himself to us." See also Jesús Alvarez Gazapo, *Sum.* 4278.

For more about Father Manuel Laborda, see AGP, RHF, D–04311–7.
Born in Borja (Saragossa) in 1848, Father Laborda was sixty-four at the
time of Josemaría's First Communion. He was a teacher of religion, history, Latin, and handwriting; he was the one who recorded data about
his students in notebooks, some of which have been preserved. He died
in Barbastro in 1929.

[97] See Alvaro del Portillo, *Sum.* 18; Javier Echevarría, *Sum.* 1781; and Encarnación Ortega, AGP, RHF, T–05074, pp. 45 and 140.

[98] On March 28, 1950, his silver jubilee as a priest, he said to some of his
daughters, "Today has been a totally happy day—something I hardly
ever get for the big dates in my life. On such days our Lord has almost
always chosen to send me some kind of mishap. Even on the day of my
First Communion, when they were getting me ready, fixing up my hair,
trying to make it curly, they burned me with the curling iron. It wasn't
anything serious, but for a child of that age it was something." See Encarnación Ortega, AGP, RHF, T–05074, pp. 45 and 140.

[99] See Alvaro del Portillo, *Sum.* 42; see also AGP, P01 1969, p. 116. Here
are some entries from his journal:

"April 23, 1931: Saint George. It is nineteen years ago that I
made my First Communion" (no. 194).

"Feast of Saint George, 1932: Today it is twenty years since I received Holy Communion for the first time. Saint George, pray for me" (no. 707).

"Vigil of Saint Mark, 1933: Yesterday it was twenty-two years since my First Communion. My God!" (no. 989).

"April 23—Saint George! Let me not forget that today is the anniversary of my First Communion. How many things I forget to write down!" (no. 1180).

"April 30, 1936: . . . In Valencia, on the feast of Saint George, the anniversary of my First Communion, I acted like a drone. Or, rather, like a perfect donkey, braying, and even. . . . I can honestly say that I don't know how to pray well even one Hail Mary. Mother, Mama in heaven!" (no. 1332).

See also *C 209* (29 Apr 1937).

[100] See Appendix 8. Despite the freedom of education provided by the 1857 Law of Instruction, the state always reserved to itself the right to give examinations and award any kind of diploma. It granted the freedom to establish private secondary schools, but these not only had to use state-authorized programs and texts, but also had to have their students take exams at the public centers authorized to give diplomas. When religious schools were recognized, they were given discretionary rights only with regard to religion classes. However, although their students were not "official" students, their studies were generally more highly regarded than those of the "independent" students. This was the case with the Piarists' school in Barbastro.

[101] The death certificates of María del Rosario and María de los Dolores can be found in the archive of the parish of Our Lady of the Assumption in Barbastro, in Book of the Dead no. 44, fols. 14v and 72, respectively.

[102] *Letter 24 Mar 1930*, no. 5.

[103] *Friends of God* (Scepter, 1986), no. 151.

[104] *Meditation* of 8 Jun 1964.

[105] *Letter 29 Sep 1957*, no. 22.

[106] See Alvaro del Portillo, PR, p. 43; Javier Echevarría, *Sum.* 1777; and Jesús Alvarez Gazapo, PR, p. 1272.

[107] "Outstanding" in all those subjects, and "First Place" for Arithmetic and Geometry. See Appendix 8.

[108] María del Carmen de Otal Martí, AGP, RHF, T–05080, p. 2. See also Alvaro del Portillo, *Sum.* 67.

[109] María del Carmen de Otal Martí, *Sum.* 5988. María Asunción's death certificate is in the archive of the parish of Our Lady of the Assumption in Barbastro, in Book of the Dead no. 45, fol. 31v.

[110] See Alvaro del Portillo, PR, p. 78; Javier Echevarría, PR, p. 52; and María del Carmen de Otal Martí, *Sum.* 5986.

[111] See Alvaro del Portillo, PR, p. 78. Other testimonies include the following. "More than once he commented to his mother, 'Now it's my turn,' or else, 'Next year it's my turn'" (Javier Echevarría, *Sum.* 1785). "He said at one of those times, 'Next it's my turn,' to which his mother replied, 'No, because you are consecrated to our Lady'" (Francisco Botella, *Sum.* 5609). "He thought that next it would be his turn, because it had gone from youngest to oldest. I know that the Servant of God suffered a lot, and that it was just to keep his mother from suffering that he stopped repeating that he would be the next to die" (Encarnación Ortega, PM, fol. 28).

[112] See Javier Echevarría, *Sum.* 1791, and Joaquín Alonso, PR, p. 1659.

[113] See Alvaro del Portillo, *Sum.* 19.

[114] See AGP, P01 1978, p. 390.

[115] See Alvaro del Portillo, *Sum.* 36; Javier Echevarría, *Sum.* 1800; Encarnación Ortega, PM, fol. 28v; and José Ramón Madurga, PM, fol. 270.

[116] See the 13 Mar 1914 and 12 Jun 1914 issues of *Juventud* (Barbastro), and Appendix 8.

[117] Adriana Corrales, AGP, RHF, T–08202, p. 9.

[118] *Meditation* of 14 Feb 1964. See also *Letter 29 Dec 1947/14 Feb 1966*, no. 6; Alvaro del Portillo, *Sum.* 47; Javier Echevarría, *Sum.* 1788; and Esperanza Corrales, AGP, RHF, T–08203, p. 6.

[119] The Baroness of Valdeolivos says that its ruin was caused by a business associate. See María del Carmen de Otal Martí, *Sum.* 5988.

[120] Martín Sambeat, *Sum.* 5680, and Adriana Corrales, AGP, RHF, T–08202, p. 11.

[121] Esperanza Corrales, AGP, RHF, T–08203, p. 3.

[122] Cited by Alvaro del Portillo, *Sum.* 49.

[123] *Meditation* of 14 Feb 1964. See also Martín Sambeat, AGP, RHF, T–03242, p. 3.

[124] Concerning his conduct toward those who caused the ruin, see Alvaro del Portillo, *Sum.* 50, and Esperanza Corrales, AGP, RHF, T–08203, p. 5. Bishop Alvaro del Portillo states that he heard from the founder himself that Don José sought advice, specifically from one of the Claretian priests at Immaculate Heart of Mary Church in Barbastro. This priest confirmed what Don José had already heard from others: namely, that he was not obliged to compensate the creditors from his personal funds. (See Alvaro del Portillo, *Sum.* 48.)

[125] Pascual Albás, AGP, RHF, T–02848, p. 2.

[126] María del Carmen de Otal Martí, AGP, RHF, T–05080, p. 2. See also María del Carmen de Otal Martí, *Sum.* 5988.

[127] Pascual Albás, AGP, RHF, T–02848, p. 2.

[128] Told by Monsignor Escrivá de Balaguer and his sister Carmen to Alvaro del Portillo: PR, p. 79.

[129] AGP, P01 1970, p. 1071; also cited by Alvaro del Portillo, *Sum.* 50. See also Pascual Albás, AGP, RHF, T–02848, p. 2; Esperanza Corrales, AGP, RHF, T–08203, p. 5; and Adriana Corrales, AGP, RHF, T–08202, p. 11.

[130] *Meditation* of 14 Feb 1964, and AGP, P01 1975, p. 219. See also Encarnación Ortega, PM, fol. 28.

[131] See Alvaro del Portillo, *Sum.* 69 and 70; Javier Echevarría, *Sum.* 1802; Francisco Botella, *Sum.* 5610; and Esperanza Corrales, AGP, RHF, T–08203, p. 3.

[132] See Martín Sambeat, *Sum.* 5681; Encarnación Ortega, PM, fol. 28v; and José Romeo, AGP, RHF, T–03809, p. 3.

[133] Adriana Corrales, AGP, RHF, T–08202, p. 11. See also Esperanza Corrales, AGP, RHF, T–08203, p. 6.

Notes to Chapter 2

[1] Martín Sambeat, *Sum.* 5679. Josemaría, now thirteen, was "a rather tall, husky boy who wore long socks, up to the knees, and short pants, like all boys of his age in those days. . . . He was quiet, likable, intelligent," says María del Carmen de Otal Martí (AGP, RHF, T–05080, p. 1).

[2] In the private-school system, as has been pointed out, classes were taken outside the official state schools, but at the end of the year the students had to be tested by teachers at those schools. It was customary for those teachers to be presented with a list of the students' names and the grades that their own teachers believed they deserved. On the list presented by the Piarists, Josemaría appears as head of the class. See Alvaro del Portillo, *Sum.* 37, and also Appendix 8.

[3] See Francisco Botella, *Sum.* 5608; Pedro Casciaro, *Sum.* 6331; and Santiago Escrivá de Balaguer y Albás, PM, fol. 1297.

[4] See Alvaro del Portillo, *Sum.* 64.

[5] "The family was very bad off," says the Baroness of Valdeolivos, "so my grandmother helped them out and bought the house from them, even though the family continued to live there until they moved to Logroño" (María del Carmen de Otal Martí, *Sum.* 5988).

[6] Esperanza Corrales, AGP, RHF, T–08203, p. 6. See also Alvaro del Portillo, *Sum.* 69.

[7] See S. Lalueza, *Martirio de la Iglesia en Barbastro,* ed. Obispado de Barbastro (Barbastro, 1989), p. 172; G. Campo Villegas, C.M.F., *Esta es nuestra sangre (51 claretianos mártires, Barbastro 1936)* (Madrid: Claretian Fathers, 1990), p. 380; Vicente Cárcel Orti, *La persecución religiosa en España durante la segunda república (1931–1939)* (Madrid: Rialp, 1990); Antonio Montero, *Historia de la persecución religiosa en España, 1936–1939* (Madrid,

1961), pp. 209–23 and 763ff.; and *Diccionario de Historia Eclesiástica de España* (Madrid, 1972), vol. 1, p. 185.

[8] Article 5 of the Concordat of 1851, as has been mentioned, called for the elimination of Barbastro as a separate diocese and for its incorporation into the diocese of Huesca. But the history of that concordat between Spain and the Holy See was very uneven; a great number of its articles never were implemented. For long periods it was completely suspended. Relations with the Holy See were broken off during the first Spanish Republic (1873–1874), and the juridical basis of the concordat was destroyed by the second Republic (1931–1936). However, it was never formally abrogated. With the treaties of 1946 the Spanish government tried to reactivate some of its provisions, up until the negotiation of the Concordat of 1953. See S. López Novoa, *Historia de Barbastro* (Barcelona, 1861; reprint, Barbastro, 1981), vol. 1, pp. 233ff., and *Diccionario de Historia Eclesiástica de España*, vol. 1, pp. 581–95.

Martín Sambeat testifies, "The relations of the founder and of Opus Dei with the nuncio in Spain were, I believe, very good. So when attempts were made to suppress the diocese of Barbastro, we thought about who might both have some influence with the nuncio and be interested in warding off the blow of that suppression, and we agreed that Father Escrivá de Balaguer would be one of those people" (Martín Sambeat, *Sum.* 5682). See also Florencio Sánchez Bella, *Sum.* 7495.

The founder followed a general practice of not making endorsements except when it came to a question of the welfare of his hometown, as in the case of the attempts to suppress the diocese of Barbastro, when he interceded with the nuncio in 1945, and later with the Holy See, and even with Pope Paul VI himself (see Alvaro del Portillo, *Sum.* 1448).

In November 1970 the founder wrote to the mayor of Barbastro as follows: "Because the task that our Lord has entrusted to me is a strictly spiritual one, my rule of conduct has always been never to make any endorsement, except when the matter concerns my beloved city of Barbastro or that general vicinity. I am convinced that by acting in this way, I am fulfilling my obligations as a priest and as a Barbastran." See *C 4721* (13 Nov 1970).

As for the documentation concerning these steps and the progress of the official negotiations with the Holy See, I have not done any research on those subjects, because I consider them to lie outside the framework of this story. For information on them, see Manuel Garrido, *Barbastro y el beato Josemaría Escrivá* (Ayuntamiento de Barbastro, 1995), pp. 111–23.

[9] *C 5793* (29 Jan 1966), *Appunto* II, pp. 305–306.

[10] *C 4882* (28 Jun 1971); see also *C 4721* (13 Nov 1970).

[11] *C 4826* (28 Mar 1971).

[12] Paula Royo, AGP, RHF, T–05379, p. 1, and *Sum.* 6296.

[13] See *Anuario de la Vida Oficial, el Comercio y la Industria, de la Provincia de Logroño—1915,* edited by Hijos de Alesón (Logroño, 1915). For all kinds of information on this period (1915–1920) in Logroño, see the doctoral dissertation of Jaime Toldrá, *Fuentes para una biografía del beato Josemaría Escrivá, Fundador del Opus Dei* (Pamplona: University of Navarre, 1994).

[14] Paula Royo, AGP, RHF, T–05379, p. 1.

[15] See Paula Royo, AGP, RHF, T–05379, p. 2, and *Sum.* 6298. For a number of years, following the civil war, Portales Street was renamed "General Mola"; in some documents it appears as such.

[16] See Santiago Escrivá de Balaguer y Albás, PM, fol. 1297v, §9, and José Romeo, *Sum.* 7847.

[17] Paula Royo, AGP, RHF, T–05379, p. 2, and *Sum.* 6298.

[18] Francisco Moreno Monforte, AGP, RHF, T–02865, p. 9.

[19] *C 2806* (14 Jan 1959).

[20] Paula Royo, AGP, RHF, T–05379, p. 2.

[21] Francisco Moreno Monforte, AGP, RHF, T–02865, p. 9.

[22] Ibid.

[23] See Appendix 8.

[24] See articles in the 12 Aug 1907 issue of *Rioja Ilustrada,* and also advertisements in *Anuario.. . . de la Provincia de Logroño.*

[25] The teachers at Saint Anthony's all had "science or liberal arts degrees," which apparently was not the case with Saint Joseph's. In 1917 the principal of Saint Anthony's was Bernabé López Merino, an associate professor at the Institute.

As for academic results, Don José could not have helped seeing in the local newspaper, in the summer of 1915, in large headlines, the results of the secondary-school examinations: "Saint Anthony's: Graduating with High Honors, 61; Outstanding, 128; Notable, 123. Saint Joseph's: Graduating with High Honors, 37; Outstanding, 98; Notable, 88; Passing, 136; Failing, 2." (See the July 3, 6, and 8 editions of *La Rioja.*)

As for Saint Anthony's classification as a "secular" school, newspaper reports indicate that it did have a resident chaplain, who "in a beautiful oratory celebrated the Holy Sacrifice of the Mass daily": see the article "Primary and Secondary School of Saint Anthony in Logroño" in the 12 Aug 1907 edition of *Rioja Ilustrada* (Logroño). But perhaps the school had changed with the years. In a personal note written on November 17, 1930, Father Josemaría said, "I remember that for a time I went to a school, run by laymen, which called itself Saint Anthony's, and they only remembered Saint Anthony once a year, on his feast day, with a religious ceremony which basically amounted to just an advertisement or a pitch for the school" (*Apuntes,* no. 105).

26 Javier Echevarría, *Sum.* 1804.

27 See Paula Royo, *Sum.* 6298.

28 A well-known Carmelite historian said of the old convent in Logroño, "This was one of the buildings which suffered the most from the secularization of the religious, for it was torn down for construction of the Institute of Secondary Studies and for conversion of the rest of the old holdings into public gardens" (Father Silverio de Santa Teresa, *Historia del Carmen Descalzo,* vol. 13 [Burgos, 1946], p. 832).

29 See Appendix 8. In June 1916 Josemaría took his fourth-year exams, and no other "nonofficial" student got marks as high as his. His subjects and grades for that fourth year were as follows:
Grammar and Composition: Outstanding (First Place)
French II: Outstanding
World History: Notable
Algebra and Trigonometry: Outstanding
Drawing I: Outstanding

30 See Appendix 8. The subjects and marks for the 1916–1917 school year were the following:
Psychology and Logic: Notable
History of Literature: Outstanding
Physics: Notable
Physiology and Hygiene: Outstanding
Drawing II: Outstanding
(See also Alvaro del Portillo, PR, p. 147.)
Father Calixto, principal of the Institute of Logroño, signed a "Certificación Académica Personal" for Father Josemaría on September 26, 1941. (See archive of the Instituto Práxedes Mateo Sagasta de Logroño.)

31 See Javier Echevarría, *Sum.* 1819, and Francisco Botella, *Sum.* 5612. Bishop Alvaro del Portillo states that he once had a long private conversation with Father Calixto in which this priest extolled the natural and supernatural virtues of his former student and said he considered him an ideal example for the whole Institute (see Alvaro del Portillo, PR, p. 147).

32 See the *Memorias Anuales del Instituto,* later published by, and now kept in the principal's office of, Logroño's Instituto Práxedes Mateo Sagasta. See also Alvaro del Portillo, *Sum.* 99.

33 See Alvaro del Portillo, PR, p. 149, and Javier Echevarría, *Sum.* 1822.

34 See Alvaro del Portillo, *Sum.* 74.

35 Paula Royo, AGP, RHF, T–05379, p. 2.

36 Encarnación Ortega, PM, fol. 29v.

[37] See Alvaro del Portillo, *Sum.* 96, and Javier Echevarría, *Sum.* 1795.

[38] See Javier Echevarría, PR, p. 79.

[39] *C 4889* (19 Aug 1971).

[40] See Francisco Botella, *Sum.* 5611, and Juan Jiménez Vargas, PM, fol. 909v.

[41] This response, dated 8 Nov 1918, is in the archive of the diocese of Calahorra.

[42] Cited by Alvaro del Portillo in *Sum.* 67; see also *Meditation* of 4 Feb 1962. Josemaría had not yet discovered the deep meaning of suffering, which in *The Way* (no. 699) he would express thus: "Cross, toil, tribulation: such will be your lot as long as you live. That was the way Christ followed, and the disciple is not above his Master."

[43] See the interview with Manuel Ceniceros on p. 3 of the 28 Jun 1975 issue of Logroño's *La Gaceta del Norte*.

[44] See AGP, P06, V, p. 267.

[45] *C 4919* (14 Oct 1971).

[46] Javier Echevarría, *Sum.* 1814. (He heard this directly from the lips of the founder.)

[47] *Letter 24 Oct 1965,* no. 29. Earlier, on September 2, 1931, Father Josemaría noted in his journal, "All this reminds me of a certain interesting Japanese picture in which the practical man (the apostolic man, we would say here) places his one and only lamp at a low height, so that it lights up the night for his family, who are amusing themselves and chatting in the light of the humble flame, while the pretentious man (the pseudo-apostle) puts the lamp on top of a sixty-foot pole, so that from far away they will think, 'What a beautiful light they have up there!'—but it neither gives light to those strangers nor warms his own family, who are also left in the dark" (*Apuntes,* no. 259).

[48] See AGP, P01 1975, pp. 357–58.

[49] See Francisco Botella, *Sum.* 5612.

[50] *Meditation* of 14 Feb 1964. His parents contributed in a special way to the change and maturation of his character. He never forgot their example or the debt that he owed them. In one letter he says, "I have had good models who were very close to my heart, who limited themselves to accepting misfortunes with a noble cheerfulness, not exaggerating the weight of the holy cross and not neglecting the duties of their state" (*Letter 8 Dec 1949,* no. 202).

On May 27, 1970, in a get-together in Mexico, Monsignor Escrivá summed up that chapter of his life in this way (see AGP, P01 1970, p. 913):

> For my father, nothing ever went right when it came to business. And I thank God for this, because as a result I know what poverty is; had it been otherwise, I would not. You see how good this is? Now I

love my father all the more. He was so marvelous that he knew how to have a magnificent serenity and endure adversity with the peace of a Christian and a gentleman.

[51] See Appendix 8.

[52] The letter followed the formal style of the period. It goes like this: ". . . Having obtained, in the examinations taken this past June, the evaluation of 'Outstanding, with Prize' for the subject of Literature and Composition, and having, in accord with current regulations, the right to a scholarship for one subject, I ask that you deign to grant this to me and apply it to the subject of General History of Literature. It being a fair thing to ask, this petitioner has no doubt of obtaining it thanks to the right judgment of yourself, whose life may God safeguard for many years. / Logroño: September 1, 1916." (This is in the school records of the Instituto Práxedes Mateo Sagasta; it is protocol no. 265/6935.)

[53] For more information about the faculty, see in the archive of Logroño's Instituto Práxedes Mateo Sagasta the file titled "Faculty personnel of this Institute for the school year of 1916 to 1917, with the dates on which the full-time teachers were hired and their rankings on the salary scale as of January 1, 1915—approved by Royal Decree of February 9, 1916."

[54] See Alvaro del Portillo, *Sum.* 64 and 65; Pedro Casciaro, *Sum.* 6331; and Javier Echevarría, *Sum.* 1812.

[55] AGP, P01 1970, pp. 487–88; AGP, P06, V, p. 275; cited by Alvaro del Portillo in *Sum.* 65.

Here is an excerpt from poem no. 103, "Como Maria feze estar o monge trezentos anos ao canto de passarya . . .":

"... fez-lo entrar en hua orta / en que muitas vezes ja
Entrara; mais aquel día / fez que hua font'achou
mui crara e mui fremosa / e cab'ela s'assentou.
... A tan gran sabor avia / daquel cant'e daquel lais,
que grandes trezentos anos / esteveo assi, ou mays. . . ."

(*Cantigas de Santa María*, ed. Walter Mettmann, in Acta Universitatis Conimbrigensis, vol. 2 [Coimbra, 1961], pp. 6–7.)

[56] *C 3647* (7 Jun 1965). For the literary passages quoted in this letter, see Gonzalo de Berceo, *Vida de Santo Domingo de Silos*, verse 757, in *Poetas Castellanos anteriores al siglo XV*, BAE, vol. 57 (Madrid, 1952), p. 63, and R. Menéndez Pidal, *Cantar del mío Cid*, 3 vols. (Madrid, 1908–1911), especially pp. 518, 910, and 1027, where he discusses verses 54–55.

That second cited verse describes the departure of El Cid for exile: his entrance into Burgos, his prayer in the cathedral, and his leaving from there to cross the Arlanzón River. The full verse is, "La oración fecha, / luego cavalgava; / salió por la puerta / e Arlançon passava" (The prayer made, he then rode; he went out the door and crossed the Arlanzón).

Josemaría retained the poem's spiritual flavor but not the historical circumstances behind it, and so in his memory the passionate outbursts merged with a pious glorification. The reading of this poem still arouses in young readers a torrent of idealistic visions inspired by the strength, nobility, loyalty, and courtliness of the hero. Beyond any doubt, his reflections on these themes left a deep imprint on the sentiments of the young Josemaría.

"El Cid," says one historian about this hero, "has always been of great human interest, because of all the obstacles and failures that run through the story of his great deeds . . . ; he will always be a powerful inspiration for young people" (R. Menéndez Pidal, *La España del Cid* [Madrid: Espasa-Calpe, 1947], vol. 1, prologue to the first edition).

57 See Alvaro del Portillo, *Sum.* 75.

58 See Alvaro del Portillo, *Sum.* 87.

59 See Alvaro del Portillo, *Sum.* 87. In Spanish the expression is "ni tan guapa que encante, ni tan fea que espante."

60 See Alvaro del Portillo, *Sum.* 96.

61 The founder himself would admit that he had a forceful character— "un caratteraccio," he would say in Italian—and would comment that "'our Lord, with his grace, wanted to make use also of that defect, to teach me not to give in when the defense of God's rights demanded not giving in'" (Alvaro del Portillo, *Sum.* 96). But, adds Bishop del Portillo, "to tell the truth, it seemed to us to be not a defect but, rather, even from a human point of view, one of the gifts that God had given to our founder and that he always put at the service of the supernatural virtue of fortitude."

62 From the time that England became Protestant under Henry VIII and Elizabeth I and the terrible suppression by Cromwell (1649), there was an unjust repression of Irish Catholics by their British rulers. During the eighteenth and nineteenth centuries, the civil and penal legislation that had excluded Catholics from political and social life was very slowly revised. But religious discrimination continued; and when, at the beginning of the twentieth century, strong movements for autonomy gained strength in Ireland as elsewhere, there was still a flavor of the old antipapist feeling in a saying of the Protestants in Ulster, "Home rule is Rome rule."

Taking advantage of Britain's involvement in the First World War, the independence activists engineered an armed uprising with some minor help in the way of arms from Germany. The uprising, set for April 23, 1916, did take place that Easter week. It was soon suppressed by British troops. On May 3 began the executions of the rebels, or patriots, which caused a strong public reaction and helped lead to Irish self-rule in 1921 and eventual independence.

These events were covered by the Spanish press with emphasis on the religious aspects of the conflict. See *The Times—History of the War*, vol. 8 (London, 1916), pp. 414ff.

[63] Cited by Alvaro del Portillo, in *Sum.* 76. See also Javier Echevarría, *Sum.* 1816. The pictorial services of *Blanco y Negro* covered the events of the war.

[64] See Javier Echevarría, *Sum.* 1825; Alvaro del Portillo, *Sum.* 101; and Paula Royo, *Sum.* 6300. The founder mentioned this near the end of his life. In 1974, during his trip to Brazil, he had to consecrate some altars. Energetically wielding the pallet to set one of the altar stones in its niche, and then sealing it, he said to a professional construction worker who was at his side, "How badly I am doing this! Isn't it true, my son? I, who wanted to be an architect—you wouldn't hire me as the least of your bricklayers!" (AGP, P04 1974, I, p. 42).

[65] *Apuntes*, no. 1688.

[66] *Apuntes*, no. 1748.

[67] *Meditation* of 14 Feb 1964.

[68] See Alvaro del Portillo, *Sum.* 73, 79, and 81, and Paula Royo, AGP, RHF, T–05379, p. 2.

[69] The authority of the abbot over the other pastors in Logroño was demonstrated by the fact that later on, when the superiors of the seminary of Saragossa asked for official information on the conduct of the seminarian Josemaría during the summer of 1921, they asked this from Father Antolín himself, even though the family belonged to the parish of Santiago el Real. (See Alvaro del Portillo, *Sum.* 79.)

[70] The ancient diocese of Calahorra, which in Roman times belonged to the occupied province of Tarraconensis, suffered various vicissitudes in the course of its history. When Nájera was reconquered from the Mohammedans in the tenth century, the seat of the old diocese of Calahorra was transferred to that city. The bishops resided in Nájera for over a century, despite the fact that Calahorra became Christian territory in 1046. These frontier lands between Castile and Navarre suffered political tensions because of battles between those Christian kingdoms, whose kings established the episcopal seat sometimes in Calahorra and sometimes in Santo Domingo de La Calzada. During the early Middle Ages, however, the bishops resided in Logroño, even though the diocese was called "Calahorra and La Calzada." In the seventeenth and eighteenth centuries the diocese lost importance, and when, via the Concordat of 1851, a restructuring of church districts was undertaken, a new diocese—that of Vitoria—was set up at the expense of the territories of Calahorra and La Calzada. This breakup of territories and creation of another diocese took effect in 1862. But only that one part of this provision of the Concordat

was carried out, because the episcopal see of Calahorra was not moved to Logroño. See F. de Coello and P. Madoz, *Mapa de Logroño con límites de obispados* (Madrid, 1851); F. Bujanda, *La diócesis de Calahorra y La Calzada* (Logroño, 1944); E. Hinojosa, "Calahorra and La Calzada," in *The Catholic Encyclopedia*, vol. 3 (New York, 1908); and *Diccionario de Historia Eclesiástica de España*, vol. 1, pp. 305ff.

All kinds of data on the diocese—on church officials, their duties, and diocesan statistics—can be found in the *Anuario Eclesiástico* published yearly by E. Subirana in Barcelona (see "Diócesis de Calahorra y Santo Domingo de La Calzada").

[71] During the years that Josemaría spent in Logroño, the canons at the cathedral included Father Valeriano-Cruz Ordóñez, the rector of the seminary; Father Francisco Xavier de Lauzurica, who later on, as auxiliary bishop of Valencia and then apostolic administrator of Vitoria and archbishop of Oviedo, would be a close friend of the founder; and Father Ciriaco Garrido Lázaro, who for some time was Josemaría's confessor (see *Anuario Eclesiástico*, years 1915 to 1920).

[72] The Carmelite nuns had a guest house right next to the convent church. The bishop of Calahorra, the Most Reverend Juan Plaza y García, was happy to have the Carmelite priests come to Logroño. He simply included in his written permission this proviso: "For the time being, the two Carmelite fathers who will establish a new residence may stay in the guest house of said convent of the Carmelite mothers, paying them whatever is appropriate for this and endeavoring to establish as soon as possible a separate residence of their own." It was to this proposal that the nuns in Logroño gave their approval on October 23, 1917. See Silverio de Santa Teresa, *Historia del Carmen Descalzo*, vol. 13 (Burgos, 1946), p. 832.

[73] Silverio de Santa Teresa, *Historia del Carmen Descalzo*, p. 833.

[74] According to the national weather service (Servicio Meteorológico Nacional), Logroño had nine days of snowfall in December 1917 and three in January 1918. Reporters for the local paper (*La Rioja*) measured the ice and snow in terms of consequences, and for that purpose described citizens' lives in minute detail. A few examples: it was ordered that straw be strewn through the streets to help pedestrians keep from falling (29 Dec 1917); on December 30, 1917, it was -8 °C (18 °F); on the following day temperatures fell as low as -16 °C (3 °F), and stores selling meat and fish had to close because these items were freezing; on the last day of the year three people died of the cold; on January 2, 1918, it snowed heavily for several hours, and pipes burst; on the following day the wine in the canteens of the night watchmen froze, and one of them said he had seen a wolf near the artillery barracks.... (See sections "Hace 25 años" and "Hace 50 años" of those issues of *La Nueva Rioja* which correspond to these dates.)

The founder never gave a date for the sudden change of his life, or for the external sign which prompted it, that we are now about to mention. What he did say and write is a little vague: "I was fourteen or fifteen. . . ." (*Meditation* of 19 Mar 1975); ". . . from the age of fifteen" (*Letter 29 Dec 1947/14 Feb 1966*, no. 19); "From when I was fifteen or sixteen. . . . " (*Letter 29 Dec 1947/14 Feb 1966*, no. 16); "Since I was fifteen years old. . . ." (*Letter 25 May 1962*, no. 41); "I was almost sixteen" (*Apuntes*, no. 1637).

However, this seeming lack of precision (fourteen or fifteen? fifteen or sixteen?) may mean he is simply thinking in terms of some kind of change of years, marked perhaps by New Year's Day, or his birthday (January 9), or possibly both. So taking some dates that we do know (concerning the heavy snow which closed out the year 1917 and the fact that by January 9 the streets were cleared), it seems logical to assume that the date in question must be situated between New Year's Eve and Josemaría's birthday.

[75] Cited by Alvaro del Portillo, in *Sum.* 77.

The founder's thoughts about the origin of his vocation are communicated in other testimonies as well. A few examples:

"In 1964, speaking to me about his vocation to the priesthood, Monsignor Escrivá said to me, but more as a question addressed to himself, 'What was the origin of my priestly vocation? Something apparently trivial: prints left in the snow by the bare feet of a Carmelite.' He then explained to me how, thinking about the sacrifice made by that religious for the love of God, he had asked himself what he himself was doing for our Lord. He had thought that perhaps God was calling him right then and there, on the street, and that if this was the case, then because of his love for the Eucharist, he would be called Brother Amador de Jesús Sacramentado [Lover of Jesus in the Blessed Sacrament]" (Jesús Alvarez Gazapo, *Sum.* 4279).

"The founder told us that it made a profound impression on him to see in the snow the footprints of a Discalced Carmelite, that it made him think about how little he himself was doing for the Lord, and that he realized then and there that our Lord wanted something specific from him" (Encarnación Ortega, PM, fol. 30).

"The Father, as he himself confessed to me, began to experience desires for a more perfect and committed Christian life when, during the winter of 1917–1918, he contemplated tracks left in the snow by the bare feet of a Carmelite religious. . . . He told me he had felt the call to the priesthood right after seeing those footprints in the snow" (José Luis Múzquiz, PM, fol. 350v).

For more on this episode of the footprints in the snow, see Francisco Botella, *Sum.* 5610, and Pedro Casciaro, *Sum.* 6337.

76 See *Meditation* of 14 Feb 1964.

"It was a matter of a change dictated," says Bishop Alvaro del Portillo, "by a disposition to do something great, heroic if need be, for our Lord—a disposition which actively seeks to follow the will of God" (Alvaro del Portillo, *Sum.* 80). See also Alvaro del Portillo, *Sum.* 94.

"It was in December 1917 or in January 1918," says Bishop Javier Echevarría, "that he realized for the first time that our Lord was calling him to his service, but he did not then know in what or how. From that moment, he started making good use of the means for acquiring a much more intense and intimate relationship with God. With true generosity he dedicated himself to prayer and to a life of piety and penance" (Javier Echevarría, *Sum.* 1831). See also José Luis Múzquiz, PM, fol. 349v.

77 *Letter 25 Jan 1961,* no. 3.

78 *Meditation* of 19 Mar 1975. See also *Apuntes,* no. 179, note 193.

79 Witnesses use different expressions, but say basically the same thing: "he suggested to him that he become a Discalced Carmelite" (Alvaro del Portillo, *Sum.* 84); "he proposed that he become a Carmelite" (Javier Echevarría, *Sum.* 1808); "this priest tried to determine whether he had within him the seed of a Carmelite vocation" (José Ramón Madurga, PM, fol. 270v).

80 "Our Lady of Mount Carmel was pushing me to become a priest. Up until I was sixteen years old, dear Mother, I would have laughed at anyone who said I would one day be wearing a cassock. It happened all of a sudden, when I saw that some Carmelite friar had walked barefoot in the snow. . . . How obligated you are, sweet Virgin of the Kisses, to lead me by the hand like a little child of yours!" (*Apuntes,* no. 1637). (The "Virgin of the Kisses," as we will see later, was a little statue of his that was especially dear to him.)

81 As he says in his journal, "Jesus undoubtedly wanted me to cry out from within my darkness, like the blind man in the Gospel. And I cried out for years, without knowing what I was asking for. And I shouted many times the prayer 'Ut sit!' [Let it be!], which seemed to be a request for a new being" (*Apuntes,* no. 290).

82 See Alvaro del Portillo, *Sum.* 84; Javier Echevarría, *Sum.* 1808 and PR, p. 131; Jesús Alvarez Gazapo, *Sum.* 4280; and Pedro Casciaro, *Sum.* 6337.

The ecclesiastical status he would have as a diocesan priest would leave him with a freedom of choice and movement that would allow him (a) to take care of the needs of his family, which he considered only right; (b) to have a secular career that was compatible with the priesthood, as did some of the teachers at the Institute; and (c) to be more available to respond to the requests of our Lord, since he would not be bound by a vow of obedience.

Throughout his life, however, Monsignor Escrivá would remember with great gratitude that Carmelite priest. In 1938 he encountered him again in Burgos (see *Apuntes*, no. 1484). Father José Miguel died on September 23, 1942. For more information on him, see the obituary articles in the 15 Dec 1942 edition of *Ecos del Carmelo y Praga* (Burgos), pp. 212–14, and *El Monte Carmelo*, 44 (Burgos, 1943), p. 58.

[83] *Apuntes*, no. 289. See also Alvaro del Portillo, PR, p. 159; Pedro Casciaro, *Sum.* 6337; and José Romeo, AGP, RHF, T–03809, p. 2.

From the seminary in Logroño, he wrote on several occasions to his Carmelite aunt. Those letters were destroyed, in accord with Carmelite custom, as soon as they had been read. But there is also a reference to that convent in *Apuntes*, no. 98: "Maybe it would be good to get in touch especially with those who are dedicated to praying and suffering for those who work. The little nuns at the convent of San Miguel of Huesca (my favorites) and the lepers at Fontilles would do very nicely for us. We will send them a monthly alms in exchange for their prayers and sufferings. The more we tell them, the better off we will be."

[84] See AGP, P04 1974, p. 398. The cited text is also picked up by Alvaro del Portillo, in *Sum.* 105.

The father "was mistaken" in that he could not imagine the kind of life the founder of Opus Dei would have—one filled with natural and supernatural affection, coming from his thousands of spiritual children—and also inasmuch as he did not realize that a priest who is in love with God never feels lonely, because he is always accompanied by his Love, as Monsignor Escrivá so often used to put it.

[85] "I heard him say more than once," reports Bishop Alvaro del Portillo, "that having made to the Lord this very precise request, having asked specifically for a boy, he did not worry about this any more" (Alvaro del Portillo, *Sum.* 111). See also Jesús Alvarez Gazapo, *Sum.* 4281; José Romeo, AGP, RHF, T–03809, p. 3; and Javier de Ayala, AGP, RHF, T–15712, p. 4.

A reflective note written years later, during his retreat in Segovia in 1932, shows what his interior dispositions were back then and how disposed he already was toward fulfilling his filial obligations to his family before he decided to become a priest: "Had I remained a layman—I am perfectly sure of this—either I would never have gotten married or I would have done it only when I was able to comfortably support two households: my mother's and my own" (*Apuntes*, no. 1688).

[86] Father Antolín Oñate was abbot of the collegiate church from February 1905 until January 1943, when he retired. As abbot, he was at the same time a pastor, because the collegiate church had a parish assigned to it. Years later he had to send in a report to the archbishop of Saragossa so that Josemaría could receive the minor orders. Today the position of

abbot no longer exists in Logroño. It has been replaced by that of the
dean, and the chapter reassigned accordingly, since the collegiate church
has become a co-cathedral of what is now the diocese of Calahorra, La
Calzada, and Logroño. See *Anuario Eclesiástico,* and also *Diccionario de
Historia Eclesiástica de España,* vol. 1, pp. 305ff.

[87] Father Albino Pajares was a military chaplain. In 1913, after coming
out number one in the competitive examinations, he entered the Army
Chaplains Corps. He was assigned to Logroño, as part of Cantabria Infantry Regiment no. 39, from February 1917 until May 1920.

For the rest of his life Josemaría was very grateful to these priests
who helped him at the onset of his priestly vocation. See Alvaro del Portillo, *Sum.* 110, and Javier Echevarría, *Sum.* 1809.

[88] Paula Royo, AGP, RHF, T–05379, p. 2. One of Doña Dolores' sisters-in-
law recalls a trip that she and her husband made. "We also went to
Logroño," she says, "and visited the home of José and Lola—a nice
apartment, with lovely furnishings. They spoke to us about Josemaría's
decision to become a priest. I don't remember any details, but I do recall
that Josemaría was in contact with a Carmelite, and at first even thought
of becoming a Carmelite, but almost immediately saw that this was not
his path—that his calling was to the diocesan priesthood" (Carmen
Lamartín, AGP, RHF, T–04813, p. 2). Other witnesses say, on the contrary,
that he never considered becoming a Carmelite.

See also Javier Echevarría, *Sum.* 1829, and Santiago Escrivá de Balaguer y Albás, PM, fol. 1298.

[89] See *Apuntes,* no. 959, where he mentions Don Ciriaquito as being one
of his confessors. Father Ciriaco Garrido Lázaro was named coadjutor of
Santa María de La Redonda in 1899, and in October 1916 he was named
its "quasi-penitentiary" (part-time confessor) canon. His main pastoral
activity was, in fact, the hearing of confessions. He died in Logroño in
1949. For a brief biographical sketch, see F. Abad's booklet *Las Adoratri-
ces de Logroño. Un siglo al servicio de la Rioja* (Logroño, 1984), pp. 40–42.

For more on Josemaría's visits to La Redonda, see Javier Echevarría,
Sum. 1810, 1846, and 2798.

[90] See Appendix 8. He had finished his studies, and a diploma from the
school was enough to prove this. But for certain administrative purposes, the law required that one have a degree as well. So his secondary-school records show that on August 6, 1923, "he was awarded
the degree of 'Bachiller Superior' by the rector of the University of
Saragossa."

Concerning his father's recommendation that he study law, see
Javier Echevarría, *Sum.* 1829; Alvaro del Portillo, *Sum.* 102; and Jesús Alvarez Gazapo, *Sum.* 4280. This last witness adds that "it was good advice" because, as the founder himself would later remark, the Lord

would make good use of this too, by thus making him acquire a juridical mentality which would later come in very handy.

[91] Father Albino Pajares himself gave Josemaría private lessons in Latin that summer: see Joaquín Alonso, PR, p. 1696, and Alvaro del Portillo, PR, p. 162.

[92] Diocese of Calahorra and La Calzada, *Boletín Eclesiástico*, year 59, p. 300 (no. 15: 4 Sep 1918).

[93] See ibid., p. 294.

[94] See F. Bujanda, *Historia del viejo Seminario de Logroño*, Instituto de Estudios Riojanos, Logroño, 1948.

On September 30, 1914, Bishop Juan Plaza y García reformed the seminary's program of studies, specifying the courses, professors, and textbooks for the philosophy and theology departments. See Bujanda, op. cit., p. 179, and *Boletín Eclesiástico*, year 55, pp. 382–87 (no. 25: 29 Oct 1914).

[95] A certified copy of this letter can be found in AGP, RHF, D–03385; the original is in the archive of the diocese of Calahorra.

[96] *Boletín Eclesiástico*, year 59, p. 368 (no. 20: 20 Nov 1918). See also year 59, p. 382 (no. 21: 5 Dec 1918).

[97] A certified copy of this letter can be found in AGP, RHF, D–03385; the original is in the archive of the seminary of the diocese of Calahorra, La Calzada, and Logroño, protocol no. 1138. The applicant's letter of request (Logroño, 6 Nov 1918) was accompanied by copies of his Baptism and Confirmation certificates (Barbastro, 29 Jun 1918 and 11 Nov 1918).

[98] See *Estadística del Obispado de Calahorra y La Calzada* (Logroño, 1946), pp. 36–38: the section on the silver anniversary of Bishop Fidel García Martínez's consecration as a bishop in 1921.

Bishop Fidel García Martínez initiated a reconstruction of the seminary that would merge what used to be the seminaries of Logroño and Calahorra. The new seminary opened in 1929, and in 1934 the old one was demolished. See Bujanda, op. cit., pp. 160–61, and the 30 Apr 1978 issue of *La Gaceta del Norte* (Rioja edition, published in Bilbao).

[99] See *Seminario Conciliar del Obispado de Calahorra y La Calzada, establecido en Logroño. Disciplina interior que deben observar los Señores collegiales que pertenecen al mismo* (Logroño, 1909). The titles of the code's sections are "Distribution of Time," "Way of Using Time," "Principal Duties," and "Special Prohibitions." An attentive reading makes it clear that the seminary had a problem getting the young men to "carefully observe the rules of good manners in the dining hall, at recreation, and especially when dealing with outsiders."

[100] "All the seminarians I knew whose families lived in Logroño were day students," says Paula Royo (*Sum.* 6301). The bishop dispensed them

from the obligation of living in the seminary. See *Prevención*, no. 16, and *Boletín Eclesiástico*, year 59, p. 298 (no. 15: 4 Sep 1918).

Nonresident students made up over 20 percent of the seminarians in Spain. See *Anuario Eclesiástico*, year 1925; Alvaro del Portillo, *Sum.* 116; and Javier Echevarría, *Sum.* 1835.

[101] Máximo Rubio, *Sum.* 6283. See also Javier Echevarría, *Sum.* 1840.

[102] See the interview with Amadeo Blanco in AGP, RHF, D–05390, and also *Boletín Eclesiástico*, year 55, p. 387 (no. 25: 29 Oct 1914), where the catechism classes are shown as starting at ten in the morning. See also Alvaro del Portillo, PR, p. 179; Javier Echevarría, *Sum.* 1844; and José Ramón Madurga, PM, fol. 272v.

[103] The change of domicile is documented in several places, including the records of the parish of Santiago el Real, within whose boundaries Canalejas Street was located. Houses on this street were at that time identified not by number but by letter. The Escrivás' address was "L" Canalejas.

[104] See Alvaro del Portillo, *Sum.* 111; Encarnación Ortega, PM, fol. 32; and José Romeo, AGP, RHF, T–03809, p. 3.

[105] *Apuntes*, no. 1688. One of the witnesses recalls something that the founder said about the birth of his brother: "'Santiago was born because of a prayer that I made to our Lord. This is obvious because he was born ten months later [on February 28, 1919]. My mother had not had any children for ten years. My parents were physically worn out by their many hardships and were also well on in years'" (Jesús Alvarez Gazapo, *Sum.* 4281).

The gynecologist who attended Doña Dolores was a Dr. Suils. One of his sons had been a classmate of Josemaría's at the Institute and would later help him in Madrid during the religious persecution. (See Juan Jiménez Vargas, AGP, RHF, T–04152–1, p. 100.)

[106] The original baptismal certificate is in the archive of the parish of Santiago el Real, Book of Baptisms 25, fol. 370, no. 579. It reads as follows: "*Santiago Justo Escrivá Albás.* In the City of Logroño, capital of the province of that name, Diocese of Calahorra and La Calzada, on the second of March of nineteen hundred nineteen, I, Father Hilario Loza, Pastor of the parish of Santiago el Real of the same place, solemnly baptized a boy, to whom I gave the names Santiago and Justo and, as patron saint, Saint Joseph. He was born, according to his birth certificate, on the twenty-eighth of this past February at eight o'clock in the morning, at 'L' Canalejas Street. He is the legitimate son of José Escrivá, native of Fonz (Huesca), and María Dolores Albás, native of Barbastro. His paternal grandparents are José Escrivá and Constancia Corzán, natives of Fonz; his maternal grandparents are Pascual Albás and Florencia Blanc, natives of Barbastro. The godparents were José María Escrivá and Carmen Escrivá, natives of Logroño; I explained to them the spiritual parenthood and obligations they were contracting. The witnesses were Mar-

cos López and José Ruiz, of this neighborhood. To which I give my signature, written above. Hilario Loza. Signed and sealed." Appended is this marginal note: "By disposition of the Vicar General, I attest that the family name 'Escrivá' of Santiago is hereby amended to read 'Escrivá de Balaguer.' The pastor, J. Santamaría. Signed and sealed."

There are a few mistakes on that certificate, such as the statements that Santiago's paternal grandfather was a native of Fonz and that Josemaría and Carmen were natives of Logroño.

[107] For the curriculum, titles of the textbooks, and descriptions of the courses, see *Boletín Eclesiástico*, year 55, p. 382 (no. 25: 29 Oct 1914). The grades earned by Josemaría in the school years 1918–1919 and 1919–1920 are recorded in various places: for example, *Boletín Eclesiástico*, year 60, p. 230 (no. 14: 14 Jul 1919), and year 61, p. 190 (no. 12: 10 Jul 1920); and AGP, RHF, D–15020. In the *Libro de Certificados de Estudios* (in the administrative office of the Metropolitan Seminary of Saragossa), vol. 1 (which starts with 1912), fol. 348, no. 693, the records of Josemaría's two years at Logroño are combined into one: 1919–1920. See Appendix 9.

[108] Josemaría was officially too young for the fast track [*carrera breve*]. Article 3 of the instructions issued for the 1918–1919 school year reads, "No one who has not reached the age of twenty-one may be admitted to the first-year theology fast track"; see *Boletín Eclesiástico*, year 59, p. 294 (no. 15: 4 Sep 1918). Since this was his case, he did the five years of theology.

[109] Amadeo Blanco, AGP, RHF, D–05390, and Luis Alonso Balmaseda, AGP, RHF, D–05391.

[110] Pedro Baldomero Larios, AGP, RHF, D–05392, and Amadeo Blanco, AGP, RHF, D–05390.

[111] Máximo Rubio, *Sum.* 6279. One of the day students with whom Josemaría forged a close friendship was José María Millán. Their closeness shows up very clearly in a letter dated September 6, 1933, in which Millán asks advice from the founder. "What do you think?" he says. "You've always given me very good advice. I am most interested in hearing your ideas (for which I've always had the highest respect)" (AGP, RHF, D–04833; also in Alvaro del Portillo, PR, p. 179). It shows just as clearly in a letter from the founder to Father José María Millán on November 25, 1940. "Dear Pepe," it begins, "So we have actually *found each other*, after twenty years. For both of us it will be good. . . . When we see each other, we can resume our confidences. We mustn't let too much time go by." See *C 903* (25 Nov 1940).

[112] The original is in the archive of the diocese of Calahorra. A certified copy can be found in AGP, RHF, D–09678.

[113] From 1915 to 1921 the rector of the seminary was Father Valeriano-Cruz Ordóñez Bujanda, the secretary was Father Gregorio Lanz, and the school principal was Father Gregorio Fernández Anguiano.

Father Gregorio Fernández taught physics, chemistry, geology, physiology, and natural history. When in 1921 the new apostolic administrator, Bishop Fidel García Martínez, named himself rector of the seminary, he delegated the actual running of it to the new vice-rector, Father Gregorio Fernández Anguiano.

Father Gregorio was mentioned by the founder as one of those who fostered his vocation. In his journal he wrote, "Jesus, I am aware and very grateful that I've never been able to say 'Non habeo hominem!' [I don't have anyone!]" (*Apuntes,* no. 959). See also Alvaro del Portillo, *Sum.* 118.

After he stopped going to Father José Miguel for spiritual direction, Josemaría went to Father Ciriaco Garrido Lázaro, the "part-time confessor" canon of the collegiate church. Later he also went to the vice-rector of the seminary, Father Gregorio Fernández. (See Alvaro del Portillo, *Sum.* 85, and Javier Echevarría, *Sum.* 1809.)

[114] Juan Cruz Moreno, AGP, RHF, T–07331. This former classmate, a day student of the seminary, adds, "One has to take into account that our schedule included a communal Rosary prayed in midafternoon, which means he was praying at least two sets of mysteries."

[115] Bishop Javier Echevarría mentions, in this regard, that when the two of them visited the collegiate church of Logroño in 1972, old memories moved him to exclaim, "I spent a lot of time here adoring Jesus in the Blessed Sacrament!" and keep repeating with devout joy, "How many hours I spent here!" (see Javier Echevarría, *Sum.* 1846 and 1810).

[116] Máximo Rubio, *Sum.* 6278.

[117] Paula Royo, *Sum.* 6297 and 6304.

[118] Máximo Rubio, *Sum.* 6291.

[119] Cited by Alvaro del Portillo, in *Sum.* 95.

[120] *Apuntes,* no. 53.

[121] The social standing of the priest—apart from religious deference—depended on the post or position that he held. In the villages he was one of the "powers that be," as they said in those days, together with the mayor, the doctor, the pharmacist, and the teacher. But there were very few diocesan priests who had access, via personal prestige, to the higher levels of society. In some documents from this period one catches an undertone of admiration for the fact that Josemaría had a secondary-school degree, as, for example, when the rector of the seminary writes that "he comes from the secondary school of the Institute and is a Bachelor of Arts" (AGP, RHF, D–09678).

In Spain, the confiscation of ecclesiastical goods and the consequent lack of material means contributed to a deficient formation of the clergy. Many dioceses did not even have seminaries, or lacked the funds necessary for them to function as they should. The Concordat of 1851 tried to remedy this situation by stipulating that each diocese must have "at least a seminary sufficient for the instruction of the clergy" (article 28).

An attempt was made, also in compliance with the Concordat, to improve the financial situation by determining an amount that the state would pay in support of religion and the clergy, as compensation for the ecclesiastical goods that had been confiscated. But the instability of the government, the financial crises that plagued the state throughout the nineteenth century, and the lack of organization in civil administration ended by reducing the clergy to poverty. The recompense from the state dwindled as the decades went by. And this situation, indirectly, was reflected in the average social level of the people who entered the seminaries.

[122] AGP, P04 1974, II, p. 398.

[123] *Meditation* of 14 Feb 1964.

[124] See Alvaro del Portillo, *Sum.* 109.

[125] AGP, P03 1975, p. 218; cited by Alvaro del Portillo in *Sum.* 104. See also Javier Echevarría, *Sum.* 1834, and Encarnación Ortega, PM, fol. 30v.

[126] *Apuntes,* no. 179, note 193.

[127] *Apuntes,* no. 127; see also *The Forge,* no. 582. The testimony of Archbishop Pedro Cantero shows how Josemaría was preserving the priestly vocation in all its purity twelve years after his entry into the seminary: "I could see [in 1930] that Josemaría was a priest with a great spirit of prayer and love of God, and with a great dedication. What edified me the most, without question, was that dedication to God. Here he was, a man with outstanding natural gifts that would have enabled him to excel in many activities, and I saw him detached from all that. He had totally left all things, including those legitimate things that pertained to what we used to call, back in those days, 'carving out an ecclesiastical career.' He had no desire to shine, humanly speaking. He was not moved by any thought other than that of full dedication to the service of the Church, wherever and in whatever way God called him" (Pedro Cantero, AGP, RHF, T–04391, p. 5).

[128] See *Meditation* of 14 Feb 1964.

[129] *Apuntes,* no. 1594.

[130] María del Carmen de Otal Martí, AGP, RHF, T–05080, p. 3. See also Joaquín Alonzo, PR, p. 1690.

[131] AGP, RHF, D–09678. The original document is in the archive of the diocese of Calahorra. On the handwritten page of the petition to the bishop is included, also in handwriting, the bishop's request for information from the rector of the seminary, and the rector's response.

[132] Ibid.

[133] See AGP, RHF, D–09678. The original annotation is in the *Libro de Decretos Arzobispales* (a records book begun in 1919), in fol. 156, no.

1489. This book was at first archived in the office of the chief notary of the archdiocese, but was later transferred, together with all the other documents in that office, to Saragossa's diocesan archive.

[134] See AGP, RHF, D–03296–3. Father Carlos, at the request of his sister Doña Dolores, facilitated the acceptance of his nephew by the seminary (see Alvaro del Portillo, *Sum.* 126). Before leaving for Saragossa, Josemaría had obtained a half-tuition scholarship, which "must have been requested by Uncle Carlos, the archdeacon" (see *Apuntes*, no. 1748).

Notes to Chapter 3

[1] See Josemaría Escrivá de Balaguer, "Huellas de Aragón en la Iglesia Universal," in *Universidad* 3–4 (Saragossa, 1960), p. 6.

[2] See Appendix 10 (a).

[3] If we read the commentary of the famous author of *Viaje de España*, we see how much artistic tastes vary. "Think about the fact," wrote Antonio Ponz at the end of the eighteenth century, "that the church which back then belonged to the Jesuits and today is the Royal Seminary of San Carlos became for a while a mirror shop—particularly the Communion chapel. It was all because of this very good stucco work which, imitating marble, served as a frieze or molding for the whole church, including its chapels. The best example that I found was the altar of San Lupercio. . . . The entrance to this church is in as bad taste as anything else in it. I don't know what Father Norbert Caimo o Vago Italiano was thinking of when, in his letter of July 7, 1755, he said of this church that it was the *più vaga*—the most esthetically pleasing—in Saragossa, as well as the richest in gold and jewels. Surely he must have been dazzled by the gilding and by the stucco which he took for marble" (A. Ponz, *Viaje de España*, ed. M. Aguilar [Madrid, 1947], vol. 15, p. 1318 [letter 2, no. 33]; originally published in 1788). It is, of course, a well-known fact that Ponz was systematically scornful of baroque art.

[4] See E. Subirana, *Anuario Eclesiástico* (Barcelona), the section for the archdiocese of Saragossa, where for each year the names of the priests at the Royal Seminary of San Carlos are listed.

[5] The diocesan bulletin printed a convocation notice, dated September 6, 1886, for an examination on the basis of which fifty full-tuition scholarships would be awarded.

In the archive of books belonging to the seminary (now transferred to the archive of the diocese of Saragossa) there is a manuscript in the form of originally blank pages bound as a book, eighty-three of which have been written on. This is the *Historia de la fundación del Seminario de pobres de San Francisco de Paula.* It describes events and customs from the beginnings of the seminary in 1886 up until the 1905–1906 school year. In the 1897–1898 school year there were two major events. First, the conciliar seminary was elevated to a pontifical university, with three departments: philosophy, theology, and canon law. And second, the Seminary of San Francisco de Paula began to admit paying seminarians (pp. 77–79).

6 *Reglamento para el régimen y buen gobierno del Seminario de Pobres de San Francisco de Paula de la Ciudad de Zaragoza, dispuesto por el Eminentísimo y Reverendísimo Sr. D. Francisco de Paula, Cardenal Benavides, Arzobispo de Zaragoza, etc.,* Saragossa, 1887. With the exception of the daily schedule and a few other points, the *Reglamento* was still in force during the years that Josemaría spent in this seminary.

7 During the 1920–1921 school year there were three students taking Latin, eleven taking philosophy, and twenty-three taking theology: a total of thirty-seven seminarians (see *Hojas de inscripción y Actas de exámenes*). "The two seminaries were basically the same," says Hugo Cubero, a classmate of Josemaría's. "The one was simply an extension of the other. There was no privilege or distinction attached to belonging to the one or the other" (Hugo Cubero Berne, AGP, RHF, T–02859, p. 1).

During the 1897–1898 school year, when the archbishop gave orders to admit paying seminarians, the charge for room and board was set at 1.25 pesetas a day—an amount that did not change for over twenty-five years. See *Historia de la fundación,* pp. 78–79, and *Hojas de Cuentas de los cursos 1920 a 1925 del Seminario de San Francisco de Paula, vistas y examinadas por la Junta de Hacienda del Real Seminario Sacerdotal de San Carlos.* (These manuscripts, with the rest of the documents of San Francisco de Paula Seminary, were recently transferred to the archive of the diocese of Saragossa.)

As for the students at the conciliar seminary, their regulations distinguished between "students from this diocese and students from outside this diocese." For the former, the charge for room and board was "1.50 pesetas a day," and for the latter, "2.50 pesetas." Additionally, "there will be a charge of 20 pesetas for the use of the iron bed with the spring mattress, the table, nightstand, washstand, water jug, coatrack, chair, candlestick, etc." (See *Reglamento disciplinar del Seminario General Pontificio de San Valero y San Braulio de Zaragoza,* year 1925, articles 222 and 223.)

As one can see from the charge for extradiocesan students, both seminaries functioned with the help of subsidies.

[8] When the seminary was established it was decided that the seminarians would wear this uniform. It was given them by the cardinal himself in a solemn ceremony on December 5, 1886. (See *Historia de la fundación,* school year of 1886–1887.)

[9] It seems that by the end of the twenties all the bedrooms had electric light. For more information on the seminaries of Saragossa, see F. Torralba, *Real Seminario de San Carlos Borromeo de Zaragoza,* Saragossa, 1974, and J. Cruz, *El Seminario de Zaragoza. Notas históricas,* Saragossa, 1945.

[10] The meditation was based on some points read out loud from a book by Father Francisco Garzón: *Meditaciones espirituales, sacadas en parte de las del V. P. Luis de la Puente,* Madrid, 1900.

[11] The conciliar seminary originated in this way: The College of the Eternal Father, which had belonged to the Jesuits, was designated by King Carlos III for use as a seminary. But during the first siege of Saragossa by Napoleon's troops it was used as a powder magazine, and was destroyed by an explosion in 1808. Ten years later its upper stories were fitted out as a seminary for young men, and in 1848 everyone there moved to the building fronting on La Seo Plaza.

For more on the reorganization of ecclesiastical studies and the creation of new pontifical universities in Spain, see *Diccionario de Historia Eclesiástica de España* (Madrid, 1972), vol. 4, pp. 2427–28.

The code of conduct for the pontifical seminary included these statements: "The students of the seminary are classified into resident students, of the conciliar seminary or of San Francisco, and nonresident students" (*Reglamento disciplinar,* art. 49) and, further on, "The students of the Seminary of San Francisco shall adapt themselves in all things to the Plan of Instruction of the Pontifical University. The hours of class and the courses that they must take shall be, for the duration of their stay in this seminary, subject to the regulations of same" (art. 51).

[12] Among the books read in the dining room was one by Juan María Solá, S.J.: *La Profecía de Daniel,* Barcelona, 1919. This is shown by an entry in the *Hoja de Cuentas del Curso de 1921–1922* (Book of Accounts for the School Year of 1921–1922): "*Profecía de Daniel,* 'Ley de expiación,' by Father Solá, for reading in the dining room: receipt no. 4, 16.50 pesetas."

[13] For spiritual reading they used the book *Ejercicio de Perfección,* by Father Alonso Rodríguez, S.J.

[14] From 1920 to 1922 the prefects were Santiago Lucus, who was a subdeacon, and Luis Torrijo, who had received the minor orders. See *Boletín Oficial de la Diócesis* (Saragossa, 1922), pp. 5–15.

[15] See Appendix 10 (a).

[16] Another uncle and aunt, Florencio and Carmen, came fairly often to the seminary to visit Josemaría. "We used to go on Sunday afternoons

and chat as we strolled along some of those large walkways" (Carmen Lamartín, AGP, RHF, T–04813, p. 3). See also Javier Echevarría, *Sum.* 1895, and Francisco Moreno Monforte, AGP, RHF, T–02865, p. 6.

[17] See Francisco Moreno Monforte, AGP, RHF, T–02865, p. 5. See also the *Libro de Sesiones de la Asociación del Apostolado de la Oración del Sagrado Corazón de Jesús* of the Seminary of San Francisco de Paula (1902–1934); entries for 1920–1925 are found on manuscript pages 92 to 103. During those years the Association was sometimes simply called the Apostolate of Prayer (see AGP, RHF, D–03454). The director and the assistant directors of the association were the superiors of the seminary (the rector and the prefects).

See also E. Subirana, op. cit., 1924, p. 45, for information on the ends, exercises, and activities of this association in which "all members of the faithful" could participate.

[18] Jesús López Bello, *Sum.* 6005.

[19] Aurelio Navarro, AGP, RHF, T–02863, p. 2.

[20] Arsenio Górriz, AGP, RHF, T–02867, p. 2.

[21] See *Meditation* of 14 Feb 1964. Another of his personal devotional practices was the praying of the Stations of the Cross, which is usually done only during Lent. Josemaría "had this so much incorporated into his life that he made the Stations quite often, even outside of Lent" (Javier Echevarría, *Sum.* 1861). He was known for his "devotion to the Passion of our Lord, which he encouraged among the seminarians" (Jesús López Bello, *Sum.* 6011).

[22] What would later be called the entrée was then called the main dish. The conciliar seminary's list of rules gives an idea of the meals provided for the students: "In the morning, coffee with milk; at midday, soup, stew, beef and bacon, dessert; for the afternoon snack, bread and fruit; at supper, salad, vegetables, and main dish. At both meals they will be given a glass of wine. On Sundays and second-class feasts, a main dish will be added to the lunch. On first-class feasts, lunch [which was the main meal] will consist of paella, two main dishes, fine biscuits, cake, and sweet wine. On feast days of the seminary's patron saints (the feasts of the Immaculate Conception, of Saint Valerius, and of Saint Braulius), they will have soup, three main dishes, a glass and a half of red wine, fine biscuits, rice with milk, coffee, and a small glass of liqueur" (*Reglamento disciplinar*, art. 227).

[23] See Alvaro del Portillo, *Sum.* 145, and Pedro Casciaro, *Sum.* 6319.

[24] See Agustín Callejas, AGP, RHF, T–02861, p. 3.

[25] "In the seminary there was no heating anywhere, despite the harshness of Saragossa's winters" (Jesús López Bello, *Sum.* 6015). See also Alvaro del Portillo, *Sum.* 138, and Javier Echevarría, *Sum.* 1857.

[26] Sixta Cermeño, wife of José María Albás (another nephew of the

archdeacon), speaks of the good disposition of Father Carlos toward Josemaría. "That attentiveness of Uncle Carlos," she says, "even extended to material details. It was, for example, in his house that Josemaría's clothes were washed and ironed; an employee of mine is a niece of the woman who went to the seminary every Saturday to collect his laundry. Uncle Carlos also took an interest in how Josemaría was doing. He could speak with the seminary superiors and professors because he had a lot of connections, on account of his position in the diocese as a canon and because of the kind of person he was" (Sixta Cermeño, AGP, RHF, T–02856, p. 1).

[27] "Every day, as soon as they get up in the morning, they will fold up their beds very carefully, wash up, comb their hair, and brush their clothes—no excuses" (*Reglamento disciplinar*, art. 51).

[28] Francisco Moreno Monforte, AGP, RHF, T–02865, p. 4.

[29] José María Román, AGP, RHF, T–02864.

[30] *Letter 14 Sep 1951*, no. 75.

[31] "There were no sinks in the rooms," Monsignor Escrivá said, "so in order to wash myself from head to toe I had to get three or four pitchers of water; that may be what scandalized some of them" (AGP, P03 1976, p. 180). "The fact is," says Bishop Alvaro del Portillo, "that it was for this reason that they started to call him 'pijaito'—an Aragonese expression meaning 'señorito' in a pejorative sense" (Alvaro del Portillo, *Sum.* 138). Bishop Javier Echevarría concurs: "He washed from head to foot every day, with cold water. His conduct attracted the attention of some of his classmates, and they began to give him the nickname of 'el pijaito'—an Aragonese expression meaning 'el señorito,' an affected, overly fastidious person" (Javier Echevarría, *Sum.* 1857).

Francisco Artal, a student at the conciliar seminary, says, "The seminarians in Saragossa, in those days, mostly came from rural areas and had the cultural level of average country families in Aragon's small towns. . . . I remember that in Belchite, where we did our studies in the humanities, they gave us a course in etiquette, and I'll never forget that the teacher told us that we must become well-mannered, and that to do this we must learn some etiquette, but that we should also not forget that a person who tries to be a saint acquires good manners in that way too. 'Try to be saints,' he used to say, 'because then good manners will be given to you as a bonus'" (Francisco Artal, AGP, RHF, T–02858, p. 1).

[32] See Alvaro del Portillo, PR, p. 222, and Javier Echevarría, *Sum.* 1865. Francisco Moreno Monforte says he heard him comment on that occasion, "I don't think dirtiness is a virtue" (AGP, RHF, T–02865, p. 5).

[33] See Alvaro del Portillo, *Sum.* 139, and Javier Echevarría, *Sum.* 1858.

[34] See Alvaro del Portillo, *Sum.* 139. Encarnación Ortega says, "He had

from a very early age a burning zeal for the salvation of souls. I remember hearing someone tell his sister Carmen that in the seminary they called him 'the dreamer' on account of that zeal" (Encarnación Ortega, *Sum.* 5366).

[35] See Javier de Ayala, AGP, RHF, T–15712, p. 2.

[36] *Apuntes,* nos. 53 and 54.

[37] See *Meditation* of 14 Feb 1964.

[38] Alvaro del Portillo, *Sum.* 158. The founder knew how to see the positive side of those crude little annoyances at San Carlos which he called trifles.

His sister Carmen, too, used to mention that she had often heard him say he "remembered from the seminary nothing but good things." (See Encarnación Ortega, PM, fol. 31, and Javier de Ayala, AGP, RHF, T–15712, p. 2.)

[39] *Apuntes,* no. 1748. This is one of the notes he wrote during his July 1934 retreat.

[40] José María Román, AGP, RHF, T–02864.

[41] Agustín Callejas, AGP, RHF, T–02861, p. 5.

[42] See Appendix 10 (a).

[43] One classmate, for example, says of Josemaría, "He was very simple, not at all pretentious, when he was in the seminary" (Aurelio Navarro, AGP, RHF, T–02863, p. 3).

On the same page of the book *De vita et moribus,* right next to the personal evaluations, the rector would write in the results of the examinations, subject by subject.

[44] See AGP, RHF, D–07056. The pages that the prefects had to fill out and hand in monthly were put together and printed as the "Report on the Conduct of the Seminarians of San Francisco de Paula." The names of all the students were listed there, next to four columns entitled "Piety," "Application," "Discipline," and "Conduct," which were filled in with a "Good," "Average," "Below average," or "Bad." On the reverse side were recorded the punishments imposed by the prefects and by the rector.

As an exception to the usual practice, in October 1920 the prefect Santiago Lucus retitled the "Conduct" column as "Vocation," and for this he gave twenty-six seminarians a "Good" and nine an "Average."

[45] AGP, P04 1974, II, pp. 398–99.

[46] AGP, RHF, D–15016. The rector of San Francisco de Paula Seminary wrote to the rector of the conciliar seminary of Logroño, but it was the vice-rector, Father Gregorio Fernández Anguiano, who had been Josemaría's Prefect of Discipline, who answered him, since the new bishop of the diocese, Bishop Fidel García Martínez, had assumed the rectorship and was directing the seminary with the assistance of the vice-rectors.

(See E. Subirana, op. cit., 1922, "Diocese of Calahorra and Santo Domingo de La Calzada.")

47 E. Subirana, op. cit., "Diocesan archive: Documents of the Royal Priestly Seminary of San Carlos," file no. 7: "Documentation on Seminarians, 1921–1925."

48 *Apuntes,* no. 959.

49 AGP, RHF, D–03306.

50 Article 60 of *Reglamento para el régimen* reads, "Smoking is forbidden. So also are eating and drinking outside the dining room." See also the reverse sides of the prefects' reports, on which the reasons for, and the circumstances of, the punishments imposed are spelled out (AGP, RHF, D–15022).

51 See *Reglamento para el régimen,* art. 56.

52 Psalm 120:6 (in the Vulgate version). He would never forget this. In 1930 he wrote, "Old buildings without light ('Per diem sol non uret te, neque luna per noctem,' I saw in the room of a seminarian, written on the window)," and ten years later, "I'm writing to you from the seminary, which is a big old ugly, unpleasant, dirty building. It's no wonder some seminarian wrote on his window, 'Per diem sol non uret te, neque luna per noctem.'" (See *Apuntes,* no. 55, and *C 869,* 4 Jul 1940.)

53 Article 63 of *Reglamento para el régimen* begins, "They will always address one another as 'usted,' and in someone's absence refer to him as 'Señor' so-and-so, by the last name. No use of epithets or nicknames of any kind will be allowed."

54 See *Reglamento para el régimen,* art. 49.

55 Augustus Caesar founded a colony made up of veterans of the Roman legions who had fought against the mountain tribes in northern Spain during the so-called Cantabrian wars. The colony, called Caesaraugusta (Saragossa), was in the province of Tarraconensis, one of the three provinces into which the Romans had divided the Iberian peninsula.

When Saragossa was reconquered from the Moors, King Alfonso I ("the Warrior") restored the Church hierarchy and named as bishop Pedro de Liébana. The bishop made the church of Our Lady of the Pillar his headquarters at first, it had been a Christian church for centuries. Then he relocated to what had been the great mosque of Saragossa—a building which, after being gutted by a fire, had been converted into the cathedral of La Seo. The canons of both episcopal sees (El Pilar and La Seo) kept vying for the primacy of their respective cathedrals until in 1675, by an apostolic letter, Pope Clement X brought peace to the two chapters by combining them and ordering that the bishop's place of residence alternate yearly between the two sites.

For more on the ecclesiastical history of Saragossa, see *Diccionario de Historia Eclesiástica de España,* vol. 4, pp. 2806ff. See also E. Subirana, op. cit., 1925, p. 314.

[56] Juan Soldevila Romero was born in Fuentelapeña, Zamora, in 1843. He studied in Valladolid and was ordained to the priesthood in 1867. In 1875 he became a canon of the diocese of Orense and secretary to the bishop. When Queen Mercedes died, in 1878, he gave a funeral oration which led King Alfonso XIII to name him as royal preacher. He was bishop of the diocese of Tarazona and Tudela from 1889 until December 16, 1901, when he was promoted to the see of Saragossa. He very actively involved himself in the concerns of his diocese (the Basilica of Our Lady of the Pillar, the material situation of his priests, of primary schools and charitable organizations, etc.) and in various social projects in Aragon. As a Senator of the Realm he defended the interests of the Church both by spoken word and in writing. (See *Diccionario de Historia Eclesiástica de España,* vol. 4, p. 2499.)

[57] At the beginning of the century, as a result of Spain's having lost its two sugar-producing colonies, Cuba and Puerto Rico, a sugar beet industry sprang up in Saragossa , and with it the industries of distilling alcohol, molasses, and beet pulp.

The population of workers without stable roots in the area increased considerably, and with this increase came socialist movements and agitation of the masses. But the most serious tension arose from the appearance of the anarchist-socialist movement known as the Confederación Nacional de Trabajadores (National Workers' Confederation), which had close ties with the "sindicatos," or labor unions, in Saragossa and Barcelona.

Between 1917 and 1923 twenty-three people in Saragossa were shot to death by gangsters.

[58] In the archive of the administration office of the Metropolitan Seminary of Saragossa can be found the following books in which students' grades are recorded.

In the *Libro de Matrículas,* references to Josemaría are found on folio pages 89, 96, 104, and 113. Grades first noted in the examination records book are copied into the *Libro de notas de exámenes;* Josemaría's are recorded on folio pages 129, 139, 151, and 164. Finally, in the *Libro de certificados de estudio,* which gives a summary of the grades of each student, the summary for Josemaría is in vol. 1 (which begins in 1912), fol. 348, no. 693. The notes in *De vita et moribus,* the records book of the rector of San Francisco de Paula, are incomplete. See AGP, RHF, D–15020.

For more on the curriculum of the pontifical university of Saragossa, see *Estatutos de la Universidad,* nos. 33–36 and 39, and the *Reglamento Académico,* art. 31 and 33.

[59] "But once I rectified my intention," he continued, "I did become very serene." (Cited by Javier Echevarría, in *Sum.* 1881.)

60 See Appendix 9.

61 Francisco Moreno Monforte, AGP, RHF, T–02865, p. 4.

62 See Alvaro del Portillo, *Sum.* 163. A list of Josemaría's professors at the pontifical university of Saragossa is provided by Joaquín Alonso, in *Sum.* 4595.

63 Cited by Alvaro del Portillo, PR, p. 250. See also Javier Echevarría, *Sum.* 1880.

64 Agustín Callejas, AGP, RHF, T–02861, p. 2.

65 See *Reglamento académico,* articles 67–74, which have to do with "academics" versus "other literary activities." The "academics" were more or less formal public events, which the students were obliged to attend. Someone would speak for twenty or thirty minutes defending a thesis, either in Latin or Spanish, and then students would propose arguments against that thesis. Given the circumstances, the event to which reference is made here was probably, instead, a "literary evening."

66 Bishop Miguel de los Santos y Díaz de Gómara was born in Fitero (Navarre) on July 7, 1885. In 1909, having completed his seminary studies in Pamplona and Saragossa, he was ordained to the priesthood. In 1912 he won (by taking the competitive examination) a canonry at the cathedral of Saragossa. On July 8, 1920, he was named auxiliary bishop of Saragossa; on December 19, 1920, he was consecrated at the Basilica of Our Lady of the Pillar (see E. Subirana, op. cit., 1925). In 1924 he became bishop of Osma-Soria, and in 1935, bishop of Cartagena-Murcia. In 1939 he was named apostolic administrator of Barcelona. He died as bishop of Cartagena-Murcia, in 1949. It is possible that this special event was held in honor of his consecration as a bishop.

67 See Alvaro del Portillo, *Sum.* 131, and Javier Echevarría, *Sum.* 1853.

68 See Alvaro del Portillo, *Sum.* 167.

69 See Francisco Artal, AGP, RHF, T–02858, p. 3.

70 See *Hojas de Cuentas.* That school year went from June 5, 1920, to June 7, 1921. The income total was 2,474 pesetas and 60 centimos; the expense total, 619 pesetas and 60 centimos.

On the last of the accounts sheets for the 1920–1921 school year, we see that the cardinal, once he had looked over and approved all the entries for that year, decided that of the 1,855 pesetas remaining in favor of San Francisco de Paula Seminary (the difference between income and expenses), "1,000 pesetas should be put into the funds of the Priestly Seminary of San Carlos and the other 855 pesetas can be carried over for next year's expenses."

71 "As for the time frame for residence of students in the seminary, the general and ordinary norm is that they will arrive on the evening before the start of the school year and will not leave until the examinations are over" (*Reglamento disciplinar,* art. 168).

In the 1921–1922 school year, Josemaría paid the one-half of room and board expenses for 261 days, and checking in the same way as for the previous year, we can see that he did not leave Saragossa at any time in that whole school year.

72 "Madre, en la puerta hay un Niño, más hermoso que el sol bello, diciendo que tiene frío . . ."; see Alvaro del Portillo, *Sum.* 24.

73 "One day he was looking very serious," a friend relates, "so I asked him what was the matter, and he said something like this: 'I just received a letter from my father, and he tells me . . . —the poor man doesn't deserve this!'" (Francisco Moreno Monforte, AGP, RHF, T–02865, p. 3).

74 Father Hilario Loza, when asked for a certificate of good conduct for his former parishioner, wrote this about Josemaría's summer vacations in Logroño: "Throughout the months that he has spent at home with his parents, I have seen him conduct himself in an irreproachable manner . . . as befits a young man who aspires to the priestly state, receiving the holy sacraments of Penance and Communion frequently and attending all the regular religious services. Logroño, March 6, 1924." (See the file for the subdiaconate: starting in 1975 it was kept in the archive of the chief notary of the archdiocese of Saragossa, but in 1985 it was transferred, with the rest of the files in that archive, to the archive of the diocese of Saragossa.) For more on Josemaría's relations with his pastor in Logroño, see Alvaro del Portillo, *Sum.* 180.

75 Francisco Moreno Monforte, AGP, RHF, T–02865, p. 10.

76 Ibid., p. 9.

77 Ibid., p. 7.

78 Ibid., p. 8. See also Alvaro del Portillo, *Sum.* 149, and Javier Echevarría, *Sum.* 1867.

79 Carmen Noailles, AGP, RHF, T–02855, p. 2.

80 See Antonio Navarro, AGP, RHF, T–05369, p. 2. The notebook was lost during the civil war.

81 Ibid.

82 See Alvaro del Portillo, "Monseñor Escrivá de Balaguer, instrumento de Dios," in *En Memoria de Mons. Josemaría Escrivá de Balaguer* (Pamplona: Eunsa, 1976), p. 29.

83 See Francisco Moreno Monforte, AGP, RHF, T–02865, p. 6, and Javier Echevarría, *Sum.* 1852.

84 See Alvaro del Portillo, *Sum.* 151. The rector says that "later on he was a director of seminarians, a distinction that His Eminence the Cardinal bestowed on him before he had even received Holy Orders, because of his exemplary conduct no less than his industriousness" (AGP, RHF, D–03306).

Regarding his early reception of the tonsure, see Francisco Botella, PM, fol. 209v, and José Luis Múzquiz, PM, fol. 351.

[85] On Josemaría's page in *De vita et moribus* (fol. 111), under the heading of "General Observations," is written, "Was named prefect in September 1922 and given the tonsure on the 28th of same." See also AGP, RHF, D–03235, and Appendix 10 (a).

In article 1 of the Regulations, there is mention of the "rector" and of the "director"; in article 27 they are referred to together as "superiors," and so forth (see *Reglamento para el régimen*). The custom of referring to the directors as "inspectores" (prefects) was introduced during the 1889–1890 school year. See *Historia de la fundación*, pp. 31–38.

In the personal file for Monsignor Escrivá de Balaguer in the archive of the general secretary of the archdiocese of Madrid, there is a note handwritten by him at the end of the civil war which includes the following datum: "Director of the Seminary of San Francisco of Saragossa, September 1922—March 1925" (AGP, RHF, D–08074–5). See also Javier Echevarría, *Sum.* 1868.

As one might expect, the date of his leaving this position appears in the seminary's accounts book, near the end of the section for the school year of 1924–1925, in reference to the termination of his reimbursement for this service: "Prefect Escrivá, who ceased to serve in this capacity on March 28. . . ."

[86] See Josemaría Escrivá de Balaguer, "Huellas de Aragón en la Iglesia Universal," in *Universidad* 3–4 (Saragossa, 1960), p. 6. See also "*Libro de Sagradas Ordenes*" *del arzobispado de Zaragoza* (May 27, 1889, to 1947), fol. 327, no. 4.410. There is mentioned the place in which that "first clerical tonsure" was conferred: "in hujus nostr. archiep. sacell. particulares."

Bishop Alvaro del Portillo tells us that he twice accompanied the founder to Saragossa to visit the archbishop (first Archbishop Morcillo and later Archbishop Cantero), and that on both occasions Monsignor Escrivá sought out the chapel in the archbishop's residence where he had received the tonsure, got down on his knees, and, moved to tears, recited the prayer for the ceremony of tonsure: "Dominus pars haereditatis meae, et calicis mei, tu es qui restitues haereditatem meam mihi" ["The Lord is my chosen portion and my cup; thou holdest my lot"] (Ps 16:5). See Alvaro del Portillo, *Sum.* 189.

[87] The previous prefects were a subdeacon and a man with minor orders only, and those after Josemaría and Juan were a deacon and another man with minor orders only.

The rector of the conciliar seminary governed with the help of prefects and "disciplinary assistants." The latter were "chosen from among the most outstanding students." (See *Reglamento disciplinar*, art. 23, and also Jesús Val, AGP, RHF, T–06889, p. 1.)

[88] If one carefully examines the seminary's accounts book, one sees noted for each year, in the expense column, a sum of 100 pesetas for

remuneration of the prefects and another amount, a variable one, for payment of the examination fees. In the section for the school year 1922–1923, for example, one reads, "Examination fees for Prefects José M. Escrivá and Juan José Jimeno; receipts nos. 2 and 3 . . . 20 pesetas," and, further down, "Remuneration of Prefects Escrivá and Jimeno . . . 100 pesetas."

[89] José María Román, AGP, RHF, T–02864. For more on the relations of Prefect Escrivá with his assistant, see Jesús López Bello, *Sum.* 6009, and Javier Echevarría, *Sum.* 1873.

[90] "He became very close friends with Don Miguel de los Santos y Díaz de Gómara," says Bishop Javier Echevarría. "The bishop held in profound esteem this subject of his, the seminarian Josemaría Escrivá, and after a while he considered him a very dear friend. Don Miguel saved for a very long time their correspondence and some notes from conversations that he had had with Josemaría back when he was a seminarian and when he first started working as a priest. Unfortunately, this file was lost, because the person who looked after the bishop in his old age carried out his order to destroy all such material after his death" (Javier Echevarría, *Sum.* 1853).

[91] See Antonio Navarro, AGP, RHF, T–05369, p. 2.

[92] See *Historia de la fundación*, pp. 52–59; Alvaro del Portillo, *Sum.* 132; and Javier Echevarría, *Sum.* 1853.

[93] See Alvaro del Portillo, PR, pp. 244–45. Father Antonio Moreno died on January 14, 1925, and was succeeded as vice president of San Carlos by Father Luis Latre Jorro. (See E. Subirana, op. cit.: 1925, p. 314, and 1926, p. 395.)

[94] See Hugo Cubero Berne, AGP, RHF, T–02859, p. 2.

[95] In a barbershop in Logroño, Don José heard that some women were chasing his son in Saragossa. As soon as he got a chance to take up this matter with Josemaría, he told him it would be better for him to be a good father of a family than a bad priest. With a clear and easy conscience, his son then explained what had happened. A couple of women had indeed tried to allure him, but he had immediately informed the rector about it and had let him know that priesthood meant more to him than life itself. (See Alvaro del Portillo, *Sum.* 162, and Javier Echevarría, *Sum.* 1877.)

[96] The request is in the file entitled "Expediente de Ordenaciones de las Témporas de Adviento de 1922," in the archive of the diocese of Saragossa.

The power of the Catholic priesthood—the power to offer the Eucharistic Sacrifice, administer the sacraments, and preach the Word of God—was given in its fullness to the Catholic Church as such, by our Lord. The Church is able to communicate this power, with more fullness or less, to the individuals who receive it. This implies different degrees, which constitute the particular orders. Only the priestly ministry properly speaking (in its two grades: the episcopacy and the priesthood) and the diaconate are of divine institution. Through the centuries, there came to be made a distinction between major orders (episcopate, priesthood, diaconate, and subdiaconate) and minor orders (porter, lector, exorcist, and acolyte). The subdiaconate and all the minor orders were not of divine institution; they were instituted by the Church. [Translator's note: In 1972 they were abolished as orders and reclassified as ministries.]

[97] Ibid.

[98] Ibid. See also Appendix 11.

[99] Jesús López Bello, AGP, RHF, T–02862, p. 3.

[100] See Jesús Val, AGP, RHF, T–06889, p. 2.

[101] Cited by Javier Echevarría, in *Sum.* 1871.

[102] See Jesús Val, AGP, RHF, T–06889, p. 3.

[103] See Jesús López Bello, *Sum.* 6010.

[104] See AGP, RHF, D–03306.

[105] Cited by Alvaro del Portillo, in *Sum.* 153.

[106] These manuscripts were later transferred, together with all of San Francisco de Paula's other documents, to the archive of the diocese of Saragossa. See AGP, RHF, D–15022, pp. 573ff.

[107] This is written on the back of the report for March 1923, with the list of "Punishments Imposed by the Prefect."

[108] Report for November 1922.

[109] Report for February 1923.

[110] Report for April 1923.

[111] Report for February 1924.

[112] Jesús Val, AGP, RHF, T–06889, p. 5.

[113] Cited by Javier Echevarría, in *Sum.* 1874.

[114] Report for November 1924.

[115] See Javier Echevarría, *Sum.* 1795.

[116] *C 653* (4 Sep 1938).

[117] *Letter 7 Oct 1950*, no. 34.

[118] A. Ponz, op. cit., p. 1318. Of Manuel de Roda, Charles III's right-hand man, who had much to do with the expulsion of the Jesuits from Spain, it was said that being the good, stubborn Aragonese that he was, he bequeathed his library to the Royal Seminary of San Carlos to make everyone see that he was neither anti-Church nor antireligious. (It was already well known that he was anti-Jesuit.)

[119] See Agustín Callejas, AGP, RHF, T–02861, p. 4; Aurelio Navarro, AGP, RHF, T–02863, p. 1; and Francisco Moreno Monforte, AGP, RHF, T–02865, p. 3.

[120] See Appendix 9; *Libro de notas de exámenes*, fol. 151; and *Libro de certificados de estudios*, vol. 1, fol. 348, no. 693. For the licentiate in the different schools of the pontifical university it was required that one have passed three courses in philosophy, two in canon law, and four in theology (see *Estatutos de la Universidad*, nos. 39–42, and *Reglamento académico*, art. 37). There was also what was called the "carrera breva" (fast track), which some seminarians took, and which required only two years of theology.

[121] *Boletín Eclesiástico Oficial del Arzobispado de Zaragoza*, year 59, pp. 134–35 (no. 5: 11 Mar 1920). See also Pope Leo XIII's instruction "Perspectum est Romanos Pontifices" (July 21, 1896) and Pope Saint Pius X's motu proprio "Sacrorum Antistitum" (September 1, 1910).

[122] Bishop Peralta, of the diocese of Vitoria, says, "At that time anyone who combined his ecclesiastical studies with secular studies in law at the University of Saragossa was still considered something of an oddball. It did not often happen, because permission was granted only by way of exception. Monsignor Escrivá de Balaguer had obtained that permission from Cardinal Soldevila" (Francisco Peralta, AGP, RHF, T–06887, p. 2). See also José López Ortiz, *Sum.* 5264. Javier de Ayala adds, "I once heard him comment about how grateful he was to Cardinal Soldevila for giving him permission to study law and theology simultaneously" (AGP, RHF, T–15712, p. 3).

[123] See AGP, RHF, D–05194, p. 1.

[124] See ibid., p. 2.

[125] See Carlos Sánchez del Río, AGP, RHF, T–02853, p. 1, and Miguel Sancho Izquierdo, PM, fol. 141.

[126] See Luis Palos, AGP, RHF, T–07063, p. 2. The other three courses that he took in the school year of 1923–1924 were Political Economy, General History of Spanish Law, and Spanish Civil Law: Common and Statutory (First Year). See Appendix 12.

[127] See Alvaro del Portillo, *Sum.* 173, and Javier Echevarría, *Sum.* 1884.

[128] See Joaquín Alonso, *Sum.* 4598.

[129] See José Luis Soria Saiz, AGP, RHF, T–07920, appendix 2. See also AGP, RHF, D–15249.

[130] See José López Ortiz, *Sum.* 5303; Alvaro del Portillo, *Sum.* 176; and Javier Echevarría, *Sum.* 1885 and 1886.

[131] See Josemaría Escrivá de Balaguer, "Huellas de Aragón en la Iglesia Universal," in *Universidad* 3–4 (Saragossa, 1960), p. 6.

[132] Cited by Alvaro del Portillo, in PR, p. 221. See also Javier Echevarría, PR, p. 176.

[133] The allusion itself is a bit vague, but better understood in the context of the entire quote. "When I was very young," Father Jose-

maría said, "and living in the seminary in Saragossa, one day I suffered a major unpleasantness. Soon after, the canon law professor told us this story: Once there was a merchant who bought cinnamon in its raw state. . . . Those words did me a lot of good. Indeed, none of us is going to achieve sanctity by dealing with Prester John of the Indies, but rather through our dealings with those persons that we have right here beside us." (See Alvaro del Portillo, PR, p. 221, and Javier Echevarría, PR, p. 176.)

[134] See Jesús López Bello, *Sum.* 6013.

[135] Francisco Artal, AGP, RHF, T–02858, p. 4.

[136] Handwritten note by the rector, Father José López Sierra. See Appendix 10 (a) and Alvaro del Portillo, *Sum.* 147.

Julio Cortés Zuazo was forty-three years old and was a student at the conciliar seminary—one of those who had taken the fast-track route for their studies. (This was done by those who were much older than average upon entering the seminary or who had difficulties in their studies.)

[137] Letter of Father Gregorio Fernández Anguiano, 26 Oct 1923, in AGP, RHF, D–15449.

[138] Javier Echevarría, *Sum.* 1865. On the card is printed, "Julio María Cortés / Chaplain of the Tuberculosis Hospital / 'El Neveral' / Jaén." It is dated October 8, 1952. (The original is in AGP, RHF, D–15282.)

[139] This comes from "La Virgen del Pilar," an article published in *Libro de Aragón* (Saragossa, 1976), pp. 97ff. There are also references in other writings: for example, "During the time that I spent in Saragossa studying for the priesthood . . . I made a visit to the Pillar at least once every day" ("Recuerdos del Pilar," an article published in the 11 Oct 1970 edition of the Saragossan newspaper *El Noticiero*). See also Alvaro del Portillo, *Sum.* 142.

The architectural history of the shrine of Our Lady of the Pillar is truly complex, there having been many vicissitudes in all its stages: planning, construction, expansion, and restoration. The work was not completed until the twentieth century. For more on the history of this shrine, see R. del Arco, "El templo de Nuestra Señora del Pilar en la Edad Media," in *Estudios de la Edad Media de la Corona de Aragón*, vol. 1, Saragossa, 1945, and F. Fita, "El templo del Pilar y San Braulio de Zaragoza. Documentos anteriores al siglo XVI," in *Boletín de la Real Academia de la Historia*, 44 (1904).

[140] See *Meditation* of 14 Feb 1964.

[141] See Alvaro del Portillo, *Sum.* 144, and Javier Echevarría, *Sum.* 1862. Article 52 of the *Reglamento para el régimen* says, "Do not enter anyone else's room at any time, for any reason." Nevertheless, an eyewitness

reports: "The seminarians used to talk about his mortifications. I remember that one day someone told me he had been in his room and had seen a cilice. ["Cilice" here refers to a wire band, smooth on the outside and with little points on the inside, that would usually be worn on the leg.] I immediately mentioned this to Josemaría, a bit indiscreetly, and he got very serious and told me flat out, 'It is bad taste to talk about this: such things shouldn't be mentioned.' I also remember his saying to me, on another occasion, 'Paco, the flesh is weak: that's the reason for cilices." (See Francisco Moreno Monforte, AGP, RHF, T–02865, p. 6.)

142 *Letter 25 May 1962*, no. 41.

143 Saint Teresa of Avila, *The Way of Perfection*, chapter 34. [In the Doubleday Image Book edition of 1964, p. 227.]

144 See A. Ansón and B. Boloqui, "Zaragoza barroca," in *Guía histórico-artística de Zaragoza* (Saragossa, 1983), pp. 248–55.

On a trip to Saragossa in 1960, the founder visited the church of San Carlos. One of those with him recalls that, going toward the main altar and "pointing to a balcony covered by a screen, at the upper right-hand side of the sanctuary, he told us: 'I spent many hours praying there at night'" (Florencio Sánchez Bella, AGP, RHF, T–08250, p. 2).

145 *The Way*, no. 104.

146 File for the subdiaconate, included in the "Expediente de Ordenaciones de las Témporas de Pentecostés de 1924," in the archive of the diocese of Saragossa. This file contains the following documents as well.

Also dated May 14, 1924, there is another request made by Josemaría to the chapter vicar, which says, "I request of Your Excellency that you deign to grant me ordination for service to the diocese."

Also bearing the same date is this declaration: "Certified: that I am exempt from military duty. This certification is being made for the purposes indicated on May 14, 1924. — José María Escrivá y Albás."

A few days later, in the report sent by the rector of the Seminary of San Francisco de Paula to the archbishop's secretary on May 18, he notes that Josemaría has been declared "totally" exempt from military service "because of defective eyesight."

147 "Expediente de Ordenaciones de las Témporas de Pentecostés de 1924."

148 See Appendix 11.

149 See Appendix 9.

150 "He told us with joy and exactitude what the functions of the subdeacon were in the liturgical ceremonies. He knew them perfectly because he had carried them all out and had really put himself into them" (Javier Echevarría, *Sum.* 1899).

[151] Francisco Moreno Monforte, AGP, RHF, T–02865, p. 2.

[152] Sixta Cermeño, AGP, RHF, T–02856, p. 1.

[153] Francisco Moreno Monforte, AGP, RHF, T–02865, p. 3.

[154] Carlos Sánchez del Río, AGP, RHF, T–02853, p. 1. See also Javier Echevarría, *Sum.* 1886.

[155] *Letter 29 Dec 1947/14 Feb 1966*, no. 19.

In January 1924 the seminarians of San Francisco de Paula put out an issue of a magazine entitled *La Verdad* (The Truth), undoubtedly with the knowledge of their prefect, according to what Agustín Callejas says: "We made a big effort to produce a seminary magazine so that the people in the conciliar seminary would realize that we existed. It took a lot of work to bring to light the first issue—which turned out also to be the last issue, since they didn't let us publish any more. It was called *La Verdad*. Josemaría wrote an article on culture and literature, and I wrote another one on some aspects of the public life of Spain at that time" (Agustín Callejas, AGP, RHF, T–02861, p. 5).

From those vague descriptions it is not easy to tell which articles are referred to, since all were signed with pseudonyms. But it is interesting to note that there is a long poem, entitled "The Coming of Our Lady of the Pillar," signed "The Troubador," and that in the publisher's presentation of the magazine we read: "Most Holy Virgin of the Pillar, . . . bless our humble magazine, and may you, we pray, be not only the honorary but the real publisher of *La Verdad*." (See copy of *La Verdad* in AGP, RHF, D–15488.)

[156] "Recuerdos del Pilar," *El Noticiero* (Saragossa, 11 Oct 1970). See also AGP, P03 1978, pp. 21–22.

[157] Josemaría Escrivá de Balaguer, "La Virgen del Pilar," in *Libro de Aragón* (Saragossa, 1976), p. 97.

[158] AGP, P03 1975, pp. 222–23. See also Alvaro del Portillo, *Sum.* 141; Javier Echevarría, *Sum.* 2556; and Jesús Alvarez Gazapo, *Sum.* 4281.

Pascual Albás Llanas, the cousin married to Sixta Cermeño, testifies that "that statue came from the house of Father Carlos Albás, and Manolita, his niece, gave it to my wife" (Pascual Albás, AGP, RHF, T–02848, p. 2).

Among other accounts of the same event is that of Encarnación Ortega (AGP, RHF, T–05074, p. 169):

Taking advantage of a trip from Rome to Spain . . . , Mercedes Morado, at that time secretary of the Central Advisory of the women's branch of the Work, picked up in Saragossa, from some relatives of our Father, a plaster statue of Our Lady of the Pillar that had belonged to our founder.

As soon as it arrived in Rome we went to give it to the Father.

"Father," we said to him, "there has arrived here this statue of

Our Lady of the Pillar which you had in Saragossa."

Our Father answered that he did not remember any such statue, but I insisted, "Yes, look at it—there's something written on it by you."

I showed him the base of the statue where the aspiration "Domina, ut sit!" and a date, "24-5-924, had been written with a nail." The Latin words were followed by an exclamation point, which our Father always used for any aspiration he wrote in Latin.

The Father then recognized the statue and his own writing and was deeply moved.

(The date inscribed in the base is not, by the way, September 24, as was erroneously reported in some publications, but May 24. The "5" was mistaken for a "9.")

[159] See the interview with Manuel Ceniceros published on p. 3 of the 28 Jun 1975 edition of Logroño's *La Gaceta del Norte.*

[160] For more on the death of Don José Escrivá, see Alvaro del Portillo, *Sum.* 182; Javier Echevarría, *Sum.* 1891; and Paula Royo, AGP, RHF, T–05379, p. 3. The death certificate is in the *Registro Civil de Logroño,* section 3a, p. 586.

[161] Manuel Ceniceros says of Don José, "That day he didn't show up on time, so the boss asked me to go to his house, at 18 Sagasta Street (today the house number is 12), at the corner of Sagasta and Rúa Vieja. When I saw him he was already looking very bad. He died a short time later." (See the above-mentioned interview. This article does, however, contain a few errors.)

[162] Santiago Escrivá de Balaguer, *Sum.* 7321.

[163] For more on this incident and Josemaría's profound sense of justice, see Ernesto Juliá, *Sum.* 4206; Alvaro del Portillo, *Sum.* 183; and Francisco Botella, *Sum.* 5616.

[164] See *Apuntes,* no. 583.

[165] Cited by Alvaro del Portillo, in *Sum.* 183, and by Javier Echevarría, in *Sum.* 1893.

[166] See, in the records of the City of Logroño, the municipal census of December 1, 1924 (taken in accordance with the municipal statute of March 8, 1924), registration page no. 1579. The form shows that the Escrivás had left their home on Canalejas Street and had returned to Sagasta Street, but were now living in a second-floor apartment instead of a fourth-floor one.

[167] The seventeen-year age difference between the brothers obliged Father Josemaría to look after and involve himself in Santiago's support and education, see to his human and spiritual formation, and, years later, provide counsel to his family. See Alvaro del Portillo, PR, p. 22.

[168] "He accepted the death of his father with great trust in our Lord and strength of spirit, and did not let it change his decision to be a priest," says one of the witnesses (Francisco Botella, in *Sum.* 5616). "The death of his father reaffirmed his vocation," says another (Encarnación Ortega, in PM, fol. 32). In explanation of this case and its circumstances, Bishop Javier Echevarría comments, "What is more, he understood as a clear manifestation of Divine Providence the fact that he had already received the subdiaconate. He saw the commitment he had undertaken to dedicate his whole life to our Lord in celibacy as an obligation that he could not back out of even at that extraordinary moment, although he was not unaware that he could obtain a dispensation with relative ease if there were urgent reasons justifying this" (Javier Echevarría, PR, p. 216).

[169] *Meditation* of 14 Feb 1964. See also *Letter 29 Dec 1947/14 Feb 1966*, no. 6; Alvaro del Portillo, *Sum.* 47 and 506; and Esperanza Corrales, AGP, RHF, T–08203, p. 6.

The meaning of that famous expression used by the founder is that for every blow of the hammer given him by our Lord in order to forge him spiritually, those around him, especially his family, received many more—and that this was an indirect but also very painful way of forming him.

Bishop Javier Echevarría says, "When he touched on the subject of these trials and others that he had to deal with, the Servant of God—filled with gratitude to our Lord—expressed himself by saying that 'they were axe blows that our Father God was giving to the trunk of my life to shape me into the image of Christ that he wanted me to be.' Or he would comment that our Lord, to prepare him, would 'hit the nail once and the horseshoe a hundred times, because that's where it would hurt me the most.' And whenever he would say this, either in the one form or the other, he would always add, 'Thank you, Lord, for having treated me that way; and forgive me my hardheadedness in not having known how to respond with due sensibility to the calls you were making to me at that time'" (Javier Echevarría, PR, p. 1316).

[170] *Meditation* of 14 Feb 1964. On September 28, 1932, he wrote, "As of yesterday I have a small crucifix, with the image very worn down, which my father (may he rest in peace) always carried with him, and which was given him on the death of his mother, who used it all the time. Since it is very poor and worn out, I don't dare give it to anyone, and so the holy memory of my grandmother (a great devotee of the Most Blessed Virgin) and that of my father will increase my love for the cross" (*Apuntes*, no. 829).

Two months later, on November 27, 1932, he added (in *Apuntes*, no.

880), "Today it is eight years (!) since my father died. Eight years which have been, in spite of my sins, a continual paternal providence of God with us. Thus we keep going, day by day, always in poverty, without my being able to earn enough to support us. Fiat, adimpleatur, laudetur et in aeternum superexaltetur iustissima atque amabilissima Voluntas Dei super omnia. [May the most righteous and most lovable will of God be done, accomplished, praised, and eternally exalted above all things.] Amen. Amen."

[171] *C 572* (9 May 1938).

[172] Josemaría's request to the vicar general of Saragossa reads as follows: "Desiring to receive the holy order of the diaconate during the coming ember days, since I have fulfilled the necessary requirements and I believe I am called to the priestly state, I entreat Your Excellency to deign to grant me the requisite dimissory letters. . . . Saragossa, November 11, 1924" (in "Expediente de Ordenaciones de las Témporas de Adviento de 1924," a file in the archive of the diocese of Saragossa).

Attached, and also dated November 11, 1924, is a certificate signed by the rector of the seminary, Father José López Sierra, which reads as follows: "I affirm that the subdeacon José María Escrivá y Albás has exercised the office of subdeacon various times in the church of San Carlos Seminary." In this same file, among the declarations of witnesses with regard to the conduct of the ordinand, is that of "Don Daniel Alfaro, priest, who after offering to tell the truth under oath" was questioned and said "that he knows Don José María Escrivá y Albás very well, from having associated with him in Logroño during the vacations that he spent at home with his parents."

[173] See Appendix 11.

[174] She says it was probably "at the beginning of 1925" that the Escrivás moved out, since it seems to her that they were still in Logroño for the Christmas of 1924 (Paula Royo, AGP, RHF, T–05379, p. 3).

[175] See José Romeo, AGP, RHF, T–03809, p. 3, and Sixta Cermeño, AGP, RHF, T–02856, p. 2.

[176] Sixta Cermeño, AGP, RHF, T–02856, p. 1.

A first cousin of the founder writes, "My uncle died leaving practically nothing, since he was living on the salary he made at Señor Garrigosa's store in Logroño. I understood that my Albás uncles Carlos (a canon of Saragossa), Mariano (also a priest, shot in Barbastro during the war), Vicente (who held a benefice in Burgos), and Florencio were thinking of giving her a sum of money if she would remain in Logroño— I don't know why. . . . Anyway, it seemed to bother the uncles when the Escrivás decided to come to Saragossa to be with Josemaría, and they did not help them at all" (Angel Camo, AGP, RHF, T–02848, p. 2). Another first cousin says that "some of the uncles purposely distanced themselves so that they would not have to help" (Pascual Albás, AGP, RHF, T–02848, p. 2). Josemaría, nevertheless, "always had feelings of understanding and Christian charity toward his uncle Father Carlos Albás" (Francisco Botella, _Sum._ 5617).

Bishop Javier Echevarría explains that "Father Carlos, a domineering person, tried to get his nephew to fall in with the plans he had devised for him, but he didn't succeed" (Javier Echevarría, _Sum._ 1897).

[177] See Santiago Escrivá de Balaguer y Albás, _Sum._ 7322.

Francisco Moreno says of Josemaría that "in his uncle's house he met with an attitude of blunt indifference and coldness toward him and his family which was encouraged in a particular way by the niece, his cousin" (Francisco Moreno Monforte, AGP, RHF, T–02865, p. 6).

It is possible that this niece, Manolita, feared a loss of her influence over her uncle. The most probable opinion, however, is that it was a matter of malicious gossip pure and simple. (See Alvaro del Portillo, _Sum._ 188).

[178] See Alvaro del Portillo, _Sum._ 187, and Javier Echevarría, _Sum._ 1897.

[179] Javier de Ayala, AGP, RHF, T–15712, p. 4. When the danger was imminent that the state would do away with the tax for religion and the clergy, Father Josemaría wrote this note, dated October 17, 1931: "I have told Mama and my sister and brother that if the canon-archdeacon of Saragossa and his brother stop receiving those payments, I will lovingly write to them, sincerely offering my help. We have to return good for evil" (_Apuntes,_ no. 336). See also Alvaro del Portillo, _Sum._ 188, and Santiago Escrivá de Balaguer, _Sum._ 7322.

[180] _C 1325_ (6 Jan 1948); see also Alvaro del Portillo, _Sum._ 188. Father Carlos Albás actually died two years later, on February 1, 1950: see AGP, RHF, D–15243.

[181] See Angel Camo, AGP, RHF, T–02846, p. 2.

[182] In November 1970 the founder related how one day at Mass, during the Washing of the Hands, his hands had trembled at the thought that they would soon be touching the consecrated host. He remembered the first time he had touched our Lord at a Benediction, and from deep within came these words of a person in love: "Lord, let me never get used to being close to you. Let me always love you as I did that time, when I touched you trembling for faith and love." (See _Articles of the Postulator,_ no. 355, and Umberto Farri, _Sum._ 3337. See also Ernesto Juliá, _Sum._ 4184, and Joaquín Alonzo, _Sum._ 4597.)

[183] See Florencio Sánchez Bella, AGP, RHF, T–08250, p. 2.

[184] See the 20 Feb 1925 document of the Sacred Congregation for Sacraments, protocol no. 871. (There is also a copy in the file for the priesthood: see AGP, RHF, D–03263.)

The requested dispensation was for ten months. In its response, the

Congregation left its granting to the discretion of the ordinary ("ut pro suo arbitrio et conscientia dispensationem largiatur").

185 See the file "Expediente para el Presbiterado, Témporas de Cuaresma, 1925," in the archive of the diocese of Saragossa.

The dimissory letters were requested from the vicar general because the archdiocese was still *sede vacante*.

In the file are also the following two items, both dated March 4, 1925: a certificate signed by the rector, Father José López Sierra, declaring that "the deacon Don José María Escrivá y Albás has solemnly exercised his ministry in the church of San Carlos," and another certificate, signed by the ordinand, attesting that "ever since I received the holy order of the diaconate on December 20, 1924, I have resided only at the Seminary of San Francisco de Paula in Saragossa."

Also in this file is another certificate, dated March 5, written by the ordinand but signed by Father José López Sierra, noting that the prefect, "since his last ordination, has received the holy sacraments with due frequency and Holy Communion daily, as is proper for an aspirant to the priesthood."

186 See the above-mentioned file for the priesthood.

187 See Appendix 11.

188 See Javier Echevarría, *Sum*. 1903; Francisco Botella, PM, fol. 211; and José Luis Múzquiz, PM, fol. 351v.

For the rest of his life he would pray for those men who received the priesthood with him: see Javier Echevarría, *Sum*. 1904. Another witness says, "He had a special affection for his classmates at the seminary of San Francisco de Paula. In 1975 they celebrated their golden anniversary as priests, and they remembered him with great affection. The Servant of God asked me to take part in the ceremony on his behalf and to do something special for them" (Florencio Sánchez Bella, *Sum*. 7480).

Upon being asked, on one occasion, about his memories of the day of his ordination, he answered the questioner, "Listen, my son, I don't remember anything that I could tell you all now. But I would not be telling the truth if I said that I don't remember much about those moments. I think I remember everything." (Cited by Alvaro del Portillo, PR, p. 283.)

189 See AGP, RHF, D–15285.

On the family nature of that celebration, see José López Sierra, AGP, RHF, D–03306, and Martín Sambeat, AGP, RHF, T–03242, p. 3.

["A.M.D.G." stands for "Ad majorem Dei gloriam," or "To the greater glory of God."]

190 "Recuerdos del Pilar," *El Noticiero* (Saragossa, 11 Oct 1970), p. 67.

191 Santiago Escrivá de Balaguer y Albás, *Sum*. 7322, and Sixta Cermeño, AGP, RHF, T–02856, p. 1. Also present were Professor Moneva and his family: see Alvaro del Portillo, *Sum*. 194.

192 Amparo Castillón, AGP, RHF, D–15285, p. 1.
193 José López Sierra, AGP, RHF, D–03306.
194 Sixta Cermeño, AGP, RHF, T–02856, p. 2.
195 See Alvaro del Portillo, *Sum.* 194; Javier Echevarría, *Sum.* 1905; and Umberto Farri, PR, p. 29.
196 See Encarnación Ortega, PM, fol. 32v.
197 See Sixta Cermeño, AGP, RHF, T–02856, p. 2.
198 See Manuel Botas Cuervo, AGP, RHF, T–08253, p. 59.

Chapter 4

1 The earliest record of this appointment is in the *Libro de Register de Documentos Arzobispales* (1922–1942), fol. 278, no. 2.697 (30 Mar 1925).
2 The archdiocese of Saragossa covered an area of about 7,880 square miles, and the number of souls was about 475,600. There were 380 parishes, 852 diocesan priests, and 334 male religious, many of whom were also priests. See E. Subirana, *Anuario Eclesiástico* (Barcelona), 1924, p. 196.
   "For the whole month of March 1925," says Teodoro Murillo, "the pastor, Father Jesús Martínez Pirrón, was absent from Perdiguera on account of illness" (AGP, RHF, T–02849, p. 1).
3 Although the parish of Perdiguera was classified as "entry level" (*entrada*), meaning one of the least important parishes, it did have a rectory. But probably it was still filled with the furniture and personal belongings of the pastor, so Father Josemaría would not have felt comfortable staying there. (See, in the diocesan archive, the internal file on pastoral positions, and also AGP, RHF, D–03296–4.)
4 See Alvaro del Portillo, *Sum.* 206. In the village this boardinghouse was known as Casa de las Mangas. See Teodoro Murillo, AGP, RHF, T–02849, p. 1.
5 The relations between the new priest and the Arruga family were extremely affectionate, and, as Bishop Javier Echevarría testifies, "they prepared his room with affection and respect, putting in it the best bed they had in the house" (Javier Echevarría, *Sum.* 1915).
6 Teodoro Murillo, AGP, RHF, T–02849, p. 2. The men worked away from home a great part of the day, and Father Josemaría "made his visits only when the men were present" (Javier Echevarría, *Sum.* 1909).
7 See Teodoro Murillo, AGP, RHF, T–02849, p. 2. See also Umberto Farri, PR, p. 31, and Francisco Botella, PM, fol. 211v.
8 Teodoro Murillo, AGP, RHF, T–02849, p. 2.
9 Ibid., p. 1.

[10] Bishop Alvaro del Portillo recalled that when he requested admission to the Work, the founder suggested that he recite aspirations, make spiritual communions, and offer up small mortifications, and then explained that although some ascetical authors recommend keeping track of the number, this involves a danger of pride or vainglory, so it is best to let one's guardian angel do the counting. (See Alvaro del Portillo, *Sum.* 204, and also Javier Echevarría, *Sum.* 1913.)

[11] See Alvaro del Portillo, *Sum.* 200, and Javier Echevarría, *Sum.* 1911. The new priest had authorization "to celebrate Mass and to give absolution" from the very day of his ordination, March 28, 1925. He was at that time granted these faculties by Father José Pellicer Guíu, vicar general of the archdiocese, for a period of six months. See *Libro de concesión de "Licencias Ministeriales" del Arzobispado,* years 1902–1952, fol. 227, no. 5980, and also AGP, RHF, D–03296–2.

[12] The original is in AGP, RHF, D–11694.

Father Carlos' trip to Burgos (the trip mentioned in the first sentence of this letter) may have had to do with the sickness of his mother, Doña Florencia Blanc Barón (Father Josemaría's grandmother), who died two days later, on April 26. Doña Florencia lived in Burgos with another son, Father Vicente, a canon of the cathedral. See Carmen Lamartín, AGP, RHF, T–04813, p. 1.

[13] See Santiago Escrivá de Balaguer, *Sum.* 7323.

[14] See Alvaro del Portillo, *Sum.* 202; Javier Echevarría, *Sum.* 1910; AGP, P01 1977, p. 264; and AGP, P01 1975, p. 225.

[15] Of this projected book nothing has come down to us except a couple of anecdotes. See Alvaro del Portillo, *Sum.* 205, and Javier Echevarría, *Sum.* 1908.

[16] See Alvaro del Portillo, PR, p. 299. In a more condensed fashion, Father Julián Herranz also relates this meditation, and gives as its date February 24, 1958. (See Julián Herranz, PR, p. 889.)

[17] See the parish archive of Our Lady of the Assumption Church in Perdiguera, Book of Deaths, vol. 7, p. 22, and Book of Baptisms, vol. 7, fol. 44–44v.

[18] See AGP, RHF, D–03296–4.

[19] Teodoro Murillo, AGP, RHF, T–02849, p. 1.

[20] See Alvaro del Portillo, PR, p. 302.

[21] Sixta Cermeño, AGP, RHF, T–02856, p. 2. Another witness recalls that when the family came to Saragossa from Logroño after the death of Don José, "they went through some major hardships. They lived in a small apartment on Rufas Street, which was in a poorer area of town. There were all sorts of difficulties. They suffered a real scarcity of food, sometimes hunger. They could furnish their home only in an extremely modest fashion, and they had to pay the closest attention to the most minor

expenses and to the care of clothes." And he adds a comment made, though not as a complaint, by Father Josemaría's sister: "Carmen said that the people who associated with the family in those days never seemed to notice that they lacked so much." (See Javier de Ayala, AGP, RHF, T–15712, p. 58.)

22 See Alvaro del Portillo, *Sum.* 265, and Javier Echevarría, *Sum.* 1930.

23 Santiago Escrivá de Balaguer, *Sum.* 7322. Father Carlos Albás, from that day on, had nothing more to do with his sister and her children.

24 The original request is in his personal file in the archive of the law school of the University of Saragossa. There is a certified copy in the archive of the law department of Madrid's Complutense University; see AGP, RHF, D–15047.

The official response, which bears the registration number 14 and a summons for June, is dated April 30, 1925. It mentions that the student is a native of Barbastro and is twenty-two years of age, but this last is an erroneous transcription from the request; he was in fact twenty-three.

25 See the file for him entitled "Expediente académico personal y Registro de Identidad Escolar," in the archive of the law department of the Universities of Madrid and Saragossa. See also Appendix 12.

26 Ibid.

27 Ibid.

28 The course in Spanish history was part of a program called Preparatory Studies and was taught in a different school of the university: that of Philosophy and Literature. Following Preparatory Studies came the Licentiate Period, which consisted of explicitly juridical courses that were taught in the law school.

29 For more on this incident of the Spanish history examination, see Javier de Ayala, AGP, RHF, T–15712, p. 43. The founder saw an important rule of conduct at work in the professor's effort to set things right: When you have made a mistake, never be ashamed or afraid to rectify it. (See Alvaro del Portillo, *Sum.* 171.)

30 See David Mainar, *Sum.* 6142.

31 Juan Antonio Iranzo, AGP, RHF, T–02850, p. 1.

32 José López Ortiz, AGP, RHF, T–03870, p. 1.

33 Ibid., p. 2.

34 Luis Palos, AGP, RHF, T–07063, p. 1.

35 Juan Antonio Iranzo, AGP, RHF, T–02850, p. 1. See also Domingo Fumanal, AGP, RHF, T–02852, p. 2.

36 *The Way,* no. 72.

37 "The founder mentioned to us," says Bishop Echevarría, "that in his days at the university only a few women were taking those courses. With the ones who came to talk with him, the founder of the Work maintained a moderate friendliness in a natural way, not doing anything pe-

culiar. He greeted them politely, and if they had any question he answered it politely, but he tried—then as always—to limit his association with women to what was necessary. This behavior did not go unnoticed by his companions, since they never saw him speaking alone with a woman, either in the university halls or anywhere else" (Javier Echevarría, *Sum.* 1887).

[38] Domingo Fumanal, AGP, RHF, T–02852, p. 2.

[39] José Romeo, AGP, RHF, T–03809, p. 3.

[40] Juan Jiménez Vargas, AGP, RHF, T–04152–1, p. 20.

[41] Florencio Sánchez Bella, *Sum.* 7550.

[42] About his priestly zeal for the recovery of straying souls, it is also known that when he lived in Madrid he learned of a young priest from another diocese who had abandoned his ministry and was working in a store specializing in herbs. He found out where the store was, went up to the young man, and said in a low voice, "Good morning, my brother." The young man asked who he was and how he knew him.

Father Josemaría said he would like to talk with him, and they made an appointment. After praying and doing penance for that man, he met him at the agreed-upon place and brought about his complete conversion. The young man was not able to return to his former diocese; the bishop did not consider it prudent, since the situation he had gotten into was already known and was the only scandal among the thousand or so priests in the diocese, all the rest having remained faithful to their vocation. So, after a period of probation in the Madrid diocese, and after Father Josemaría bought some cassocks for him, he was sent to a small outlying village. (See Alvaro del Portillo, *Sum.* 405, and Javier Echevarría, *Sum.* 1976.)

[43] See "Expediente académico personal" and Appendix 12.

[44] See Appendix 12.

[45] As mentioned earlier, the faculties granted to the newly ordained were those of celebrating Mass and giving absolution: "valeat etiam ad mulierum confessiones audiendas."

On September 22, 1925, Father Josemaría had his faculties renewed "until the October synod," and on October 5, 1925, they were extended for another six months (see *Libro de Licencias Ministeriales* [1902–1952], fol. 230, no. 6.094, and fol. 231, no. 6.108). On July 3, 1926, they were granted for a full year (see *Libro de Licencias Ministeriales* [1902–1952], fol. 235, no. 6.244). For the period of March 5–July 3, 1926, see *Boletín Oficial de la Archidiócesis de Zaragoza*, year 65, no. 1 (January 1926), p. 9, circular no. 2, in virtue of which, in accord with the standard practice in all of the dioceses, he, together with the other priests ordained on March 28, 1925, had his ministerial authorization extended to the time of the June examinations three years from then. (See "Impreso acreditativo y autenticado de

las licencias concedidas a don Josemaría," in AGP, RHF, D–03296–2 and
D–03296–5.)

⁴⁶ Bishop Rigoberto Doménech y Valls (1870–1955) had studied at Valencia's
Seminario Central and had doctorates in both theology and canon law.
After serving as bishop of Mallorca, he was appointed to the metropolitan
see of Saragossa on November 13, 1924, but was not installed until May
1925. (See E. Subirana, op. cit., 1926, p. 390.)

⁴⁷ "Among the recollections that now come back to my mind most
vividly," wrote Father Josemaría in 1945, "is one from back when I was a
young priest. From that time, with no small frequency, I have received
two unanimous pieces of advice on how to get ahead: first of all, don't
work, don't do a lot of apostolic work, because this causes envy and cre-
ates enemies; and second, don't write, because anything written—no
matter with how much precision and clarity it is written—can be misin-
terpreted. . . . I thank our Lord God that I never followed these counsels,
and I am content, because I did not become a priest to get ahead" (*Letter
2 Feb 1945*, no. 15).

⁴⁸ The original document is in AGP, RHF, D–03876. A certified copy,
dated March 11, 1931, is in Saragossa; Father Josemaría needed it in order
to get the testimonial letters that the archbishop of Saragossa wrote for
him on March 28, 1931.

⁴⁹ The original document is in AGP, RHF, D–03876.

⁵⁰ In AGP, RHF, D–15264, there is this original memo:

　　October — Fr. José Escrivá
　　　　31 Masses, at 4 ptas.　　　124 ptas.
　　　　Apostolate　　　　　　　　_ 31_
　　　　Total　　　　　　　　　　 155

In Father Josemaría's handwriting is added, "Saint Peter Nolasco,
Saragossa."

　　"The Father," says José Romeo, "said weekday Mass at Saint Peter
Nolasco Church, which was staffed by Jesuit priests, and I used to go and
serve for him on my days off from school. He said Mass slowly and with
great care. It seemed like nothing ever distracted him. Just being at his
Mass taught one what he later explained to me: that the Holy Sacrifice is
the center of all interior life. At the end he would spend several minutes
in thanksgiving, remaining very recollected the whole time" (José
Romeo, AGP, RHF, T–03809, p. 1).

⁵¹ For more about these activities on feast days and other special days,
see the "Crónica religiosa" section of the Saragossan newspaper *El
Noticiero*. (Saint Peter Nolasco Church sometimes appears there as
"Church of the Sacred Heart.") See also Alvaro del Portillo, *Sum.* 217, and
Javier Echevarría, *Sum.* 1924.

There are testimonies about the apostolate that Father Josemaría carried out among his friends in those days. José Romeo, for example, says, "I met him when I was thirteen or fourteen. I hadn't yet finished high school; it may have been in the school year of 1924–1925. The Father often came to my family's house because my brother Manuel, who later died in the Spanish Civil War, was a classmate of his at the law school of the University of Saragossa. Many afternoons the Father got together with Manuel and other friends to compare notes or to study. In this way he became acquainted with the whole family" (José Romeo, AGP, RHF, T–03809, p. 1).

[52] See Alvaro del Portillo, *Sum.* 171; Francisco Botella, PM, fol. 211v; and Juan Jiménez Vargas, AGP, RHF, T–04152–1, p. 22.

[53] See AGP, P04 1972, p. 760. This is also cited by Alvaro del Portillo, in PR, p. 312.

[54] To this anecdote, which he related at a get-together with priests during his catechetical trip to Spain in 1972, he added, "You should not do that kind of thing, even with your fellow priests. They already pray. . . . Give them a short penance."

On another occasion, referring to Don Alvaro del Portillo, who was his confessor from the day after his ordination in 1944, he said, "Alvaro usually gives me one Hail Mary for my penance. Then he tells me, 'I will do your penance for you.' And I've certainly done the same kind of thing, my children. I've never given big penances" (AGP, P01 1970, p. 995).

Additional testimony on this subject: "He would give very light penances and then make up the difference by taking on himself severe penances, such as wearing cilices that he made himself, using nails, and so forth. He would also pray and mortify himself for the conversion of the unrepentant" (Pedro Casciaro, *Sum.* 6391). "He advised his priest-sons to give easy penances and then supplement them with their personal penance" (Fernando Valenciano, *Sum.* 7138).

[55] See Domingo Fumanal, AGP, RHF, T–02852, p. 3.

[56] Luis Palos, AGP, RHF, T–07063, p. 1.

[57] Domingo Fumanal, AGP, RHF, T–02852, p. 1.

[58] See Juan Antonio Iranzo, AGP, RHF, T–02850, p. 1, and Domingo Fumanal, AGP, RHF, T–02852, p. 1.

[59] David Mainar, *Sum.* 6141.

[60] Domingo Fumanal, AGP, RHF, T–02852, p. 2.

[61] See Fernando Vivanco, AGP, RHF, T–03713, p. 2.

[62] "I liked to go to confession to him, once he became a priest. And I did it quite often," says Fernando Vivanco. (See ibid.)

[63] Domingo Fumanal, AGP, RHF, T–02852, p. 2.

[64] Francisco Moreno Monforte, AGP, RHF, T–02865, p. 7.

[65] See Javier de Ayala, AGP, RHF, T–15712, p. 3.

66 Don Miguel describes him as having been, as he saw him in class, "an intelligent, very gifted, and hardworking student" (Miguel Sancho Izquierdo, *Sum.* 5504). With regard to this friendship, Bishop Javier Echevarría states, "I saw the kindness and real affection with which they treated one another. Don Miguel showed a great veneration for him, despite their difference in age. For his part, whenever he saw this professor, Father Josemaría always greeted him with great affection, calling him 'Don Miguel, my master'—an epithet that Don Miguel did not like to accept, because he was convinced that the one who called himself his student surpassed him in every respect, both spiritual and human" (Javier Echevarría, *Sum.* 1885).

67 See *Apuntes*, no. 1554. His friendship with Professor Inocencio Jiménez was very long-lasting, and he turned it into an opportunity for apostolic service that included the professor's whole family. Luis Palos remembers this well. "Josemaría had a warm friendship with Don Inocencio and with his family," he says. "I'm sure that his children, José Antonio and María, must remember him very well. José Antonio Jiménez Salas is now a professor of geotechnology at the School of Highway Engineering. María is a very intelligent woman, a good intellectual, who was a librarian but is now nearly blind. Don Inocencio was a great Christian sociologist. Together with Severino Aznar and Salvador Minguijón, he was the soul of the National Forecasting Institute" (Luis Palos, AGP, RHF, T–07063, p. 3). See also Alvaro del Portillo, PR, p. 338.

For information about Father Josemaría's dealings and friendships with other professors at Saragossa's law school, see Carlos Sánchez del Río, AGP, RHF, T–02853, pp. 1–4; Alvaro del Portillo, *Sum.* 175 and 176; Francisco Botella, *Sum.* 5616; and Javier de Ayala, *Sum.* 7577.

68 See *Apuntes*, nos. 231, 407, 751, 959, 1344, and 1357.

69 See Alvaro del Portillo, *Sum.* 1447, and Juan Jiménez Vargas, PM, fol. 917. See also *C 362* (20 Oct 1937), in which he tells his mother about his visit in Barcelona with Father José Pou de Foxá.

70 See Juan Jiménez Vargas, AGP, RHF, T–04152–1, pp. 199–201, and Pedro Casciaro, AGP, RHF, T–04197, pp. 5–7.

71 See Juan Antonio Cremades, AGP, RHF, T–05846, p. 1; Francisco Botella, PM, fol. 211v; and José Ramón Madurga, PM, fol. 274v. Another testimonial includes this recollection: "One day in 1941 we were walking along Canal Street, and when we got to where it crosses the old highway to Valencia, in the Casablanca neighborhood, he told us how he had organized catechism classes there and brought in students to teach them." (Javier de Ayala, AGP, RHF, T–15712, p. 2).

72 *Apuntes*, no. 441.

73 *Apuntes*, no. 387.

74 *Letter 7 Oct 1950*, no. 47. According to eyewitness accounts, almsgiv-

ing, as a work of mercy, was a practice deeply rooted in the entire family. See, for example, José López Ortiz, *Sum.* 5267.

[75] Father Josemaría had been ordained a priest *ad titulum servitii dioecesis* [for service of the diocese].

[76] See AGP, RHF, D–05188.

[77] Ibid.

[78] See Javier Echevarría, *Sum.* 1917.

[79] See Alvaro del Portillo, *Sum.* 235.

[80] "I remember that Father José Pou de Foxá, a man with a great memory and a detailed knowledge of the ecclesiastical life of the city, told me in 1942 that he himself had advised the Father to go to Madrid. 'In those conditions'—these are the words of Father Pou de Foxá—'Josemaría had no future here'" (Javier de Ayala, AGP, RHF, T–15712, p. 2).

[81] *Apuntes*, no. 193. These testimonials were the good-conduct references that a priest transferring from one diocese to another needed from the one bishop for presentation to the other.

[82] This was the founder's spontaneous answer when Don Alvaro del Portillo asked him what had happened to his testimonials in the Saragossa chancery office (see *Apuntes*, no. 193, note 209).

[83] About this trip by the founder, Bishop Javier Echevarría says, "On many occasions I heard him comment that he went to Madrid in 1926; however, we have not found any document that tells us the time of year when he made that trip" (Javier Echevarría, *Sum.* 1945).

The University of Madrid had graduate schools and departments of every type. In those days it was the only place in Spain in which one could earn a doctorate, in any field.

[84] See *Alfa-Beta*, the Institute's monthly magazine, the first issue of which came out in January 1927. See also AGP, RHF, D–04357–8.

[85] This letter of 26 May 1927 from Nicolás Tena Tejero can be found in AGP, RHF, D–04743.

[86] Students who needed to pass only one or two more subjects to obtain their degree were permitted by that royal ordinance to take their exams in January, rather than having to wait until June, the regular time. Father Josemaría's petition, which he signed on January 10, 1927, boils down to this: ". . . finding myself in the conditions specified by the royal ordinance of December 26, 1926, since I only need to pass the subject of Forensic Practice to obtain my degree . . ." (see "Expediente académico personal").

[87] See the February 1927 issue of *Alfa-Beta*, p. 16.

[88] See the March 1927 issue of *Alfa-Beta*, pp. 10–12. The other studies included in this issue are "Inheritance and Prior Right of Purchase, or the Law of Sales," by "Pedro de la Fuente, District Attorney"; "Meaning of the term 'Ius ad rem,'" by "Ramón Serrano Suñer, Public Prosecutor"; and "Comments on Mortgage Law," by "J. M. Franco Espés, Lawyer."

[89] Letter of Father Prudencio Cancer, C.M.F., in AGP, RHF, D–15003–6. The letter is written on paper imprinted with the heading "The College of the Missionary Sons of the Immaculate Heart of Mary / Segovia" and is addressed to "Reverend José María Escrivá / Saragossa."

[90] In a letter dated December 9, 1927, Father Prudencio tells Father Josemaría that in Madrid, "at 12 Orfila Street, lives my cousin from Fonz, Antonia Santaliestra." The familiarity and affection with which he asks about Father Josemaría's mother and siblings indicate a previous close acquaintance with them.

See T. L. Pujadas, C.M.F., *El Padre Postius: un hombre para la Iglesia* (Barcelona, 1981), p. 327. With regard to facts and ideas about the founder of Opus Dei, this work contains some major errors, but this is understandable because the book is based on oral testimony which has been blurred by time. The main error is that it situates these events a year and a half after they actually occurred, which significantly distorts the truth of what happened. Specifically, the book claims that the founder attended a retreat given by Father Cancer at the seminary in Madrid in October 1928, and places the offers made by Father Cancer after that retreat.

A look at the documentation shows that Father Cancer's collaboration in the founder's move to Madrid centers on the months of February and March of 1927. It is also a documented fact that in October 1928 the founder was attending a retreat conducted at the headquarters of the Congregation of the Missions (Vincentian priests) on García de Paredes Street in Madrid (see the 1 Dec 1928 issue of *Boletín Oficial del Obispado de Madrid-Alcalá*, p. 384).

[91] Letter of 7 Feb 1927, previously cited.

[92] Letter of 28 Feb 1927 (original in AGP, RHF, D–15003–5).

[93] Nevertheless, Father Cancer does not seem to have understood what Father Josemaría was really trying to do: get himself established in Madrid, with his family, so that he could complete his studies for a doctorate in law.

[94] *Circular de la Nunciatura Apostólica de Madrid, a los Rmos. Prelados de España*, November 30, 1887, in the archive of the secretarial office of the archdiocese of Madrid. At that time Spain's nuncio was Bishop Angelo di Pietro.

[95] *Circular de la Nunciatura Apostólica de Madrid, a los Rmos. Prelados de España*, May 5, 1898. The nuncio at that time was Bishop Giuseppe Francesco Nava di Bontifé.

[96] See "Primer Sínodo Diocesano de Madrid-Alcalá. Convocado y presidido por el Excmo. y Rvmo. Sr. D. José María Salvador y Barrera, y celebrado en la Santa Iglesia Catedral de esta Corte en los días 10, 11 y 12 de febrero de 1909," *Sinodales Diocesanas*, book 4, section 4.5 (Madrid, 1909), pp. 369–70.

Bishop José María Salvador y Barrera, the bishop of Madrid-Alcalá, published in the 10 Jun 1914 issue of *Boletín Oficial del Obispado de Madrid-Alcalá* a circular restating the above-mentioned dispositions about extra-diocesan priests and adding to the list an instruction dated 15 Nov 1910 and numerous circulars previously published in the diocesan bulletin. In the very next year he had to give another reminder of all these dispositions (see the 20 Dec 1915 bulletin, pp. 727–29). And this time, to cut down on abuses, he announced that "from now on, priests will not be allowed to say Mass here, not even on one day, who show up without having previously asked and obtained the written permission repeatedly stipulated by the papal nuncio, unless the urgency of their trip has rendered this impossible, in which case it will be sufficient to present a letter or memo from the vicar general, or from his secretary, stating that this person is not attempting to establish residence in Madrid, but intends only to spend a few days here to take care of the business that is the purpose of his trip" ("Circular de Mons. José María Salvador y Barrera a los Obispos de España," p. 2, in AGP, RHF, D–08068).

[97] Letter of 9 Mar 1927; the original (which is handwritten on a sheet of paper with a letterhead) is in AGP, RHF, D–15003-5. As stated in this letter, the Mass stipend will be 5 pesetas and 50 centimos.

[98] Letter of Father A. Santiago, C.SS.R., to Father Prudencio Cancer, Madrid, 7 Mar 1927 (original in AGP, RHF, D–15003–6).

[99] The family had such confidence in Josemaría that they always felt certain that his decisions were, as his brother puts it, "the best." See Santiago Escrivá de Balaguer, *Sum.* 7325.

[100] See, in Saragossa's diocesan archive, *Libro de Registro de Documentos Arzobispales* (1922–1942), year 1927, fol. 120, no. 1813 (17 Mar 1927: "Permiso para dos años, para Madrid, con motivo de estudios"), and fol. 121, no. 1820 (22 Mar 1927: "Comendaticias para Madrid, por dos años").

In regard to this, Bishop Echevarría says: "In his explanation to the archbishop of Saragossa, he emphasized—because this was his plan—that while doing his studies he would continue to dedicate most of his time to pastoral activity, thus continuing to nurture his love for that ministry for which he had received ordination. He would subordinate to his priestly work the work of doing research for the doctorate and of writing his dissertation" (Javier Echevarría, *Sum.* 1945).

[101] By virtue of a royal decree of 10 Mar 1917 (see the March 15 edition of *Gaceta de Madrid*), the Minister of Public Education and Fine Arts declared that once all of the courses required for a degree were passed, "no further revalidation or exam" was to be required.

The fees charged by the Ministry of Finance for rights to the licentiate diploma, etc., which Father Josemaría paid on March 15, 1927, amounted to 37.50 pesetas: see his file in the archive of the law school of the University of Saragossa. As noted in this file, this amount was transmitted to Madrid on March 30, 1927.

[102] See Domingo Fumanal, AGP, RHF, T–02852, p. 1.

[103] In the archives of the diocese of Saragossa and of the parishes of Fombuena and Badules, there is no reference to Father Josemaría's stay at the parish of Fombuena.

In the *Libro de Registro de Documentos Arzobispales* (1922–1942) of the archdiocese of Saragossa, fol. 300, no. 3.190 (28 Mar 1931), in connection with some testimonial letters that were being drawn up in the chancery office, is some information on the ecclesiastical studies and pastoral responsibilities of the founder. A memo handwritten and signed by him (in Madrid, on 2 Mar 1931), entitled "Things I Would Like Mentioned in the Testimonials," includes this item: "6. In April 1927 I was in charge of the parish of Fombuena; I was there until after Easter that year." (The original is in AGP, RHF, D–15334.)

[104] Letter of 20 Mar 1927 from Father A. Santiago (in Madrid) to Father Prudencio Cancer; original in AGP, RHF, D–15003–6. Given that the letter was probably sent to Segovia and then sent on to Father Josemaría by Father Cancer, it would have arrived in Saragossa around March 24.

[105] *Apuntes,* no. 640. See also Javier Echevarría, *Sum.* 1917.

Father Cancer, in the above-mentioned letter of 28 Feb 1927 to Father Josemaría, speaks of "a couple of very prominent individuals in Saragossa" and then says, further down, "They will be able to give you the help you need, but this needs to be at just the right moment. Actually, you may need that help sooner than you think, for other steps that you'll have to take." One prerequisite for residence in Madrid was permission to leave the diocese of Saragossa. How did he get this so easily?

In this whole matter of his move to Madrid and the negotiations conducted in Saragossa's chancery office, it seems that several of his friends were involved, but especially Fathers José Pou de Foxá and Luis Latre Jorro, with both of whom he resumed contact by letter shortly after arriving in Madrid (see AGP, RHF, D–04355).

Father Luis Latre Jorro was the secretary who accompanied Cardinal Juan Soldevila on his pastoral visits. On the infamous day on which the cardinal was assassinated, Father Luis was with him in the car and was injured. In 1925 he taught philosophy at the Pontifical University of Saragossa: see "Estadística del Arzobispado de Zaragoza," in the 1 Apr 1925 issue of *Boletín Eclesiástico Oficial del Arzobispado de Zaragoza,* pp. 16–17. Also in 1925 he succeeded Father Antonio Moreno Sánchez as vice president of the Royal Priestly Seminary of San Carlos: see E. Subirana, op. cit., year 1925, p. 314, and year 1926, p. 395. He was a friend of Father José Pou de Foxá: see letter of 9 May 1927 from Father Luis Latre to Father Josemaría, in AGP, RHF, D–15003–8.

106 The original of this undated letter from Father A. Santiago to Father Josemaría is in AGP, RHF, D–15003–8. It is written on stationery imprinted with the letterhead "Rector of the Redemptorist Fathers / 2 Plaza Conde de Miranda." The beginning of the letter ("I received several days ago your very welcome letter, which I have not yet answered") suggests that it was written very near the end of March. Easter Sunday fell on April 17 that year. Father Josemaría was expected to arrive in Madrid, therefore, around April 20.

107 The original of this letter is in AGP, RHF, D–15334.

108 "This crucifix," he later wrote, "accompanied me everywhere I went. With me it went to Fombuena, and with me it came to Madrid" (*Apuntes*, no. 583).

109 See AGP, P04 1972, p. 99.

110 See Javier Echevarría, *Sum.* 3212 and 3213. This is also cited by Alvaro del Portillo, in *Sum.* 1562.

111 The bill is in AGP, RHF, D–15247–2.

112 *Meditation* of 14 Feb 1964.

113 See *Apuntes*, no. 704.

114 *Apuntes*, no. 414.

115 *Meditation* of 14 Feb 1964.

116 *Apuntes*, no. 1090.

Notes to Chapter 5

1 See AGP, RHF, D–15247–2. Probably he was not able to say Mass in Madrid until the following day, since celebration of an evening Mass was not permitted at that time, but he may have already said Mass in Saragossa before boarding the train. (See Alvaro del Portillo, *Sum.* 332, and Javier Echevarría, *Sum.* 1947.)

2 At the time of Father Josemaría's arrival in Madrid, the Pontifical Church of Saint Michael was run by a community of Redemptorist priests, as earlier mentioned. Today it is in the care of priests of the Prelature of the Holy Cross and Opus Dei. See *Diccionario de Historia Eclesiástica de España* (Madrid, 1972), vol. 2, p. 1381.

3 The diocese of Madrid was created on March 7, 1885, by virtue of Pope Leo XIII's papal bull *Romani Pontifices Praedecessores*. Two days later a royal decree appeared announcing the appointment of the first bishop of Madrid. By virtue of Pope Paul VI's papal bull *Romanorum Pontificum Semper*, dated March 25, 1964, the diocese of Madrid was elevated to an archdiocese directly dependent on the Holy See.

4 See his student file in the archive of the law school of Madrid's Complutense University. See also AGP, RHF, D–03365.

[5] See AGP, RHF, D–15155. The vaccination certificate may have been presented together with the request, despite their different dates, although it may be that when he turned in his request he was then asked for a vaccination certificate.

[6] See the letter of 7 Mar 1927 from Father A. Santiago to Father Josemaría (AGP, RHF, D–15003–6) and the letter of 9 Mar 1927 from Father Prudencio Cancer to Father Josemaría (AGP, RHF, D–15003–5).

[7] There is a receipt, on paper without a letterhead, signed April 30, 1927, for 78 pesetas for "10 days of room and board, plus other items." On the back of the receipt is an itemization showing that the cost of room and board is 7 pesetas per day. Added in a different handwriting is the word "Farmacia." (See AGP, RHF, D–15247–2.)

[8] *Boletín Trimestral de la Obra Apostólica Patronato de Enfermos*, no. 72 (Madrid, January 1928), pp. 12–13.

[9] Letter of 9 Mar 1927 from Father Cancer to Father Josemaría (AGP, RHF, D–15003–5).

[10] Letter of 9 May 1927 from Father Luis Latre to Father Josemaría, sent from Saragossa (AGP, RHF, D–15003–8). Note how this "place yourself at the disposition of our prelate, who is so much in need of personnel" relates to the "providential injustices" discussed in the previous chapter.

[11] See Appendix 12.

[12] Father Fidel Gómez Colomo studied at the seminary in Toledo and was ordained to the priesthood in 1925. Assigned to the military vicariate general, he rose to become lieutenant vicar of the navy. He died in Madrid in 1980.

Father Justo Villameriel Meneses became a military chaplain in 1927.

Monsignor Avelino Gómez Ledo was ordained in Madrid in 1918. He served as assistant priest at Immaculate Conception in Madrid, and later at Our Lady of the Angels. In 1940 he became pastor of Saint Augustine's, also in Madrid. He died in 1977.

Born in 1897, Father Antonio Pensado Rey was ordained in 1920, in Santiago de Compostela.

[13] This monastery of the Augustinian Recollects was founded by King Philip III and his wife, Lady Margarita of Austria. Its church became that of the parish of the royal palace, and from early times the Chief Chaplain of His Majesty, who traditionally was the archbishop of Santiago, had exclusive jurisdiction over these premises. The bishop of Madrid, in other words, did not have jurisdiction over that church, and neither did the Royal Ordinary, or Pro-Chaplain of His Majesty, who had jurisdiction over all other royal foundations. (See *Diccionario de Historia Eclesiástica de España*: vol. 1, pp. 338–39; vol. 2, pp. 1382–83; vol. 3, p. 1887; and vol. 4, pp. 2743–46.)

[14] The letter from the vicar general of Madrid to the archdiocese of Santiago (27 Jan 1927) is very strongly worded. In response a notice was sent from Santiago (1 Feb 1927) stating that Father Antonio's faculties for his own diocese were suspended until such time as he returned there. The following week he stopped saying Mass at Incarnation. Judging by the tenor of his letter of 30 Jul 1927, Father Antonio must have remained in Madrid for the whole month of June 1927. There is no mention of the possibility of his being incardinated in the diocese of Madrid. (The abovementioned data can be found in the archive of the general secretariat of the archdiocese of Madrid-Alcalá and in the archive of the major seminary in Santiago de Compostela.)

[15] The request is addressed to "Your Excellency the Vicar General of the Diocese of Madrid-Alcalá" (see AGP, RHF, D–15147).

No information has come to light as to how and why Doña Luz Rodríguez Casanova took such an interest in Father Josemaría so early on.

[16] *Apuntes*, no. 178.

[17] Doña Luz was born in 1873, to Don Florentino Rodríguez Casanova and Doña Leónides García de San Miguel. The title of Marchioness of Onteiro was granted to her mother, for herself and her descendants, by a royal decree of 15 Jul 1891, in recognition of the public services rendered by her late husband.

Doña Luz founded the Congregation of Apostolic Ladies on 24 May 1924, in Madrid. In 1950 Pope Pius XII granted the congregation its definitive approval. Doña Luz died on 8 Jan 1949, with a reputation for sanctity. On 25 Jan 1958 the cause for her beatification was opened. (See E. Itúrbide, *El Amor dijo sí. Luz R. Casanova,* Pamplona, 1962.)

[18] In 1927 he was a doctor of sacred theology and of canon law (as of 1900 and 1902, respectively), a knight of the Great Cross of the Civil Order of Benefactors, a public education consultant, a member of the Roman Pontifical Academy of Saint Thomas Aquinas, and a member of the Royal Academy of the Spanish Language (as of 1926). Previously he had been a professor of Hebrew at the seminary in Seville, a canon in Jaén (starting in 1904), a theology instructor in Santiago de Compostela (starting in 1908), bishop of Tuy (starting in 1914), and bishop of Vitoria (starting in 1917). See E. Subirana, *Anuario Eclesiástico* (Barcelona), 1927, p. 249.

[19] This memorandum is in the archive of the general secretariat of the archdiocese of Madrid-Alcalá.

[20] See, in the archive of the general secretariat of the archdiocese of Madrid-Alcalá, *Libro de Licencias Ministeriales,* no. 8, fols. 53 and 55. Note that Father Josemaría's request of 10 Jun 1927 matches up with the entry for 8 Jun 1927. The only possible explanation is that he was first granted his faculties at the request of Doña Luz, two days before his own request was turned in.

21 See E. Subirana, op. cit., 1927, p. 247.

22 Canon 130 of the 1917 Code of Canon Law reads as follows: "Expleto studiorum curriculo, sacerdotes omnes, . . . examen singulis annis saltem per integrum triennium in diversis sacrarum scientiarum disciplinis, antea opportune designatis, subeant secundum modum ab eodem Ordinario determinandum."

23 The answer to his request to be given the examination by the rector of Saint Michael's reads, "Dear brother in the Lord: His Excellency has determined that for the renewal of your ministerial faculties, since you fall into the category to which canon 130 applies, you may take the examination at Saint Michael's." The original of this letter (dated 17 Jun 1927) is in AGP, RHF, D–15003–10.

24 See Alvaro del Portillo, *Sum.* 487. Bishop Echevarría notes that the rector gave him "the evaluation in an open envelope, so that he himself could put it in the mail," and that, after sealing the envelope, he tossed it into the first mailbox that he came across after leaving Saint Michael's (see Javier Echevarría, *Sum.* 1947).

25 After 8 Jul 1927 he was on three occasions granted faculties for one year, and on 10 Jun 1931, for five years. (See archive of the diocese of Saragossa, *Libro de concesión de licencias ministeriales,* years 1902–1952: fols. 242, 250, 258, 268, 273, and 311.)

About the granting of faculties in 1936 he wrote: "May 31, 1936: Our Lord, by means of the bishop of Pamplona and Father José Pou, has just taken care of my faculties for Saragossa: the archbishop has granted them generally and in perpetuity" (*Apuntes,* no. 1344).

As for the dimissory and commendatory letters, he had to have these renewed annually from 1929 to 1931, at which time he was granted permission to reside in Madrid until 1936. (See, in the archive of the diocese of Saragossa, *Libros de Registro de Documentos Arzobispales*: 1929, fol. 406; 1930, fol. 191; 1931, fol. 300; and 1931, fol. 318, no. 3.367, which reads, "Faculties for Madrid, plus commendatory letters, for five years.")

26 Asunción Muñoz, AGP, RHF, T–04393, p. 1. Asunción Muñoz González (1894–1984) was one of the first Apostolic Ladies. She met Father Josemaría in 1927, and when, in 1929, she became mistress of novices for the novitiate of Chamartín de la Rosa (in Madrid), the founder helped her with his counsel.

27 Father Joaquín María de Ayala Astor was born in Novelda, in Alicante, and was ordained to the priesthood in 1901. In 1911 he was named a doctoral canon of Cuenca, and in 1922, rector of the seminary there. In 1936 he was assassinated. See S. Cirac, *Crónica Diocesana Conquense de la Epoca Roja,* vol. 2, *Martirologio de Cuenca* (Barcelona, 1947), pp. 178–81.

Father Joaquín was at the Larra Street residence on the occasion of a national Franciscan congress celebrated in Madrid from June 15 to 19 of

1927: see S. Eijan, O.F.M., *Crónica de fiestas cívico-religiosas y especialmente el IV Congreso Nacional de Terciarios Franciscanos que con carácter iberoamericano se celebró en Madrid los días 15, 16, 17, 18 y 19 de junio de 1927, en conmemoración del VII Centenario de la muerte de San Francisco de Asís,* Barcelona and Madrid, 1930.

[28] Letter of 30 Jun 1927 from Father Joaquín María de Ayala to Father Josemaría: original in AGP, RHF, D–06929.

[29] Letter of 30 Jul 1927 from Father Antonio Pensado to Father Josemaría: original in AGP, RHF, D–05186. Doña Aurora Balenzátegui was a lay auxiliary of the Apostolic Ladies.
   Two receipts signed by Doña Aurora for Father Josemaría's room and board still exist. One is dated 5 Aug 1927 and is for July 30 to August 5; the other is dated 19 Aug 1927 and is for August 13–19. Both are in AGP, RHF, D–15246.

[30] Letter of 19 Jul 1927 from Father Prudencio Cancer to Father Josemaría, sent from Segovia: original in AGP, RHF, D–15003–5.

[31] See Santiago Escrivá de Balaguer y Albás, AGP, RHF, T–07921, p. 7, and Javier Echevarría, PR, p. 70.

[32] Avelino Gómez Ledo, AGP, RHF, T–03714, p. 1.

[33] Fidel Gómez Colomo, AGP, RHF, T–01364, p. 1.

[34] Avelino Gómez Ledo, AGP, RHF, T–03714, p. 2.

[35] Ibid., p. 1.

[36] Fidel Gómez Colomo, AGP, RHF, T–01364, p. 1.

[37] Avelino Gómez Ledo, AGP, RHF, T–03714, p. 1.

[38] *Letter 29 Dec 1947/14 Feb 1966,* no. 16.

[39] Letter of 9 Dec 1927 from Father Cancer to Father Josemaría, sent from Segovia: original in AGP, RHF, D–15003–5.

[40] On 14 Jun 1964 the founder, who had lived through and suffered the hazardous ordeals of the dictatorship and the Second Spanish Republic, wrote His Holiness Pope Paul VI a letter briefly but very well summarizing that historic situation insofar as it had affected the Church. Here are a couple of paragraphs (C 5753):

> In 1923 General Primo de Rivera carried out a coup d'état and, with the consent of King Alfonso XIII, set up a dictatorship that lasted until 1930. Although on the whole the action of Primo de Rivera was rather beneficial to Spain, in many respects it wounded the liberty of Spaniards, as any other dictatorship would. The fact that such a lack of freedom was sanctioned or at least tolerated by the king provoked a strong reaction against the monarchy: a movement led by some noted anti-Catholic intellectuals, some members of the National Association of Catholic Propagandists (directed by a

journalist by the name of Herrera), and the leaders of anarchist and Marxist unions. Thus began a pendulum swing that swept the masses from one extreme, a lack of freedom, to the opposite, license. This kind of swing of the pendulum is always potentially dangerous, but in a passionate people it is extremely so, and it continues to hang menacingly over Spain.

On April 14, 1931, as a result of the state of tension created especially in Madrid by the republican victory in the administrative elections in some of the most important cities of Spain, and fearing a possible civil war, Alfonso XIII decided it was best for him to leave the country, and thus the Republic was proclaimed.

41 Santiago Escrivá de Balaguer y Albás, AGP, RHF, T–07921, p. 8.

42 See the 19 Sep 1918 issue of *ABC*, p. 27, and also Alvaro del Portillo, *Sum.* 490.

There is no record of how Father Josemaría established contact with the Academy, but one motivation may have been the fact that several priests worked there. Among its professors were Fathers Salvador Pérez, Angel Ayllón, and Isidoro Arquero. Father Arquero was the one in charge of the Academy's residence.

43 A printed summary of the Academy's bylaws is in AGP, RHF, D–03395. Father José Cicuéndez Aparicio was, beginning in July 1920, chaplain of the Royal Foundation of Santa Isabel, first for the church and then for the school. On 2 Feb 1931 he sent a letter to the General Intendant of the Royal House and Estate informing him of his health problems (exhaustion and acute neurasthenia) and requesting a three months' sick leave. This was granted on the ninth of that month. On May 12 he asked for an extension of the leave, and on July 4 he received an answer from the Ministry of the Interior granting the extension but stating that it would be without pay. (See the Patrimonio Nacional archive, section "Expedientes personales," file 182/17: "Expediente del Capellán José Cicuéndez Aparicio.") In November 1932, at the age of fifty-eight, he died at Villa de Don Fadrique (in Toledo), after a long illness that deprived him of his mental faculties a few months before his death (see Alvaro del Portillo, *Sum.* 271).

When Father Cicuéndez had to leave Madrid in 1931 on account of his illness, the position of director fell to Professor Florián Ruiz Egea, who had a doctorate in philosophy and literature and also was the librarian of the Municipal Library of Chamberí. He was married but had no children. During the civil war he was assassinated. (See Manuel Gómez-Alonso, AGP, RHF, T–03771, p. 1.)

44 Mariano Trueba, AGP, RHF, T–03277.

45 See Alvaro del Portillo, *Sum.* 496, and Javier Echevarría, PR, p. 473, for quotes from Julián Cortés Cavanillas, a former student of Father Jose-

maría's at the Cicuéndez Academy who became a well-known journalist. By the fifties he was already the Rome correspondent for *ABC*. During his years in Rome he frequently visited the founder and also spoke with Bishops Alvaro del Portillo and Javier Echevarría; they have included in their declarations some of the recollections he shared with them.

[46] See AGP, RHF, T–03771, p. 1. Manuel Gómez-Alonso was a student at the Academy in 1930–1931.

[47] See Javier Echevarría, *Sum.* 2105.

[48] Letter of 27 Jun 1928 (handwritten) from Father José Pou de Foxá to Father Josemaría: original in AGP, RHF, D–15309–1.

[49] See Alvaro del Portillo, *Sum.* 498.

[50] Original in AGP, RHF, D–03395–8.

[51] Original also in AGP, RHF, D–03395–8.

[52] There is a letter from Father Angel Ayllón to Father Josemaría, dated July 27, 1928, written on Academy stationery, which bears the notation "Presente," meaning that the addressee was present in Madrid. The letter reads: "Dear José María: I just received from the director a letter with instructions that he wants me to relay to you about the classes starting in August. I therefore ask you to do me the favor of stopping by the Academy for a nice long chat, some evening around 7:00. I send my kindest regards to your mother, and to you an embrace from your best friend and colleague." (Original in AGP, RHF, D–03395–7.)

Father Josemaría's last journal entry concerning the Cicuéndez Academy is dated 28 Jan 1932: see *Apuntes*, no. 591, and also Alvaro del Portillo, *Sum.* 490. About the founder's apostolate with his students and fellow professors, there are later references: see *Apuntes*, nos. 362, 420, 492, and 591, and Javier Echevarría, *Sum.* 2109.

[53] See AGP, RHF, T–03277. Mariano Trueba was taught by Father Josemaría during the school year of 1928–1929. He was enrolled in the law school as an unofficial student, and he attended the Academy to accelerate the pace of his studies. He became a judge, in Vizcaya.

[54] See Alvaro del Portillo, *Sum.* 494. This incident was recalled by José Manuel Sanchiz Granero; he was taught by Father Josemaría in 1927–1928. He became a lawyer and a member of the High Council for the Protection of Minors.

[55] See AGP, RHF, T–03277. During the sixties, someone who had heard this story from Mariano Trueba wrote it down and sent it to Father Josemaría. Upon reading it he wrote this note at the end: "I remember this. 12 Feb 1966." (See Joaquín Alonso, PR, p. 1742.)

[56] See AGP, RHF, T–03277.

[57] Recollection of Julián Cortés Cavanillas, cited in Alvaro del Portillo, *Sum.* 496, and Javier Echevarría, *Sum.* 2105.

[58] The building was designed by Luis Ferrero, finished in 1924, and inaugurated by King Alfonso XIII. See *Guía de Arquitectura y Urbanismo de Madrid*, vol. 2, *Ensanche y Crecimiento* (Madrid: Colegio Oficial de Arquitectos de Madrid, 1984), chapter entitled "Ensanche Chamberí: Patronato de Enfermos de Santa Engracia."

[59] See issues no. 72 (January 1928) and no. 78 (January 1930) of the Apostolic Ladies' publication *Boletín Trimestral de la Obra Apostólica Patronato de Enfermos.*

The umbrella term "Apostolic Work" (Obra Apostólica) included the Foundation for the Sick, the Work of Preservation of the Faith in Spain (schools for children), the Charity Dining Halls, the Priests' House, the Work of the Holy Family (for rectifying irregular marriage situations), the Protection Society (for help in paying medical, pharmaceutical, and funeral bills), the Saint Joseph Clothes Distribution Center, the Work of Perseverance (catechesis and formation of young girls), the Poor Souls Association (offering suffrages for the dead), etc. (See issue no. 78 of *Boletín Trimestral*, pp. 2–10.)

[60] See Aniceta Alvarez Sánchez de León, AGP, RHF, T–04865, p. 3. Born in Daimiel (in Ciudad Real) in 1910, Aniceta Alvarez had contact with Father Josemaría from 1927 to 1931 as a lay auxiliary of the Apostolic Ladies at the Foundation.

[61] María Vicenta Reyero, *Sum.* 5970. This Apostolic Lady notes also that Father Josemaría "used to celebrate Holy Mass on Sundays, and on some other days, in the private oratory of the Marchioness of Onteiro."

[62] Pedro Rocamora, AGP, RHF, T–05829, p. 6. Another witness tells us that Don Julián Cortés Cavanillas and Don José María González Barredo "described to me the emotion they felt when assisting him at Holy Mass: an emotion ending in tears" (Florencio Sánchez Bella, *Sum.* 7481).

[63] Emilio Caramazana, AGP, RHF, T–05335, p. 3.

[64] José María González Barredo, AGP, RHF, T–04202, p. 1. He also mentions a recollection of the chaplain of the Foundation shared with him by his sister in a letter. "My attention was caught in an extraordinary way," she said, "by this priest who said the Rosary with such great devotion. He prayed and enunciated it so well that I never could get over my surprise."

[65] María Vicenta Reyero, *Sum.* 5969.

[66] Asunción Muñoz, AGP, RHF, T–04393, p. 2. This religious of the Congregation of Apostolic Ladies lived from 1894 to 1984. She met Father Josemaría in 1927 at the Foundation and associated with him during the time that he was chaplain there.

[67] Josefina Santos, AGP, RHF, T–05255, p. 2. Born in Segovia in 1895, Josefina Santos, as an assistant to the sisters at the Foundation, had contact

with Father Josemaría from 1927 to 1931.

[68] See *Boletín Trimestral,* issue no. 72, p. 14, and issue no. 78, p. 12. The statistics for 1927 are similar: 4,396 sick persons attended to; 3,225 confessions; 486 anointings of the sick; 1,192 weddings; 161 baptisms.

[69] "Also, at the Foundation, there were other activities in which I suppose Father Josemaría also took part, such as marriage preparation and religion classes for workers," says Margarita Alvarado Coghem, who, as a lay auxiliary at the Foundation, worked with Father Josemaría when he was chaplain there. Years later she became a Discalced Carmelite, taking the name of Mother Milagros [Miracles] of the Most Blessed Sacrament. (See Margarita Alvarado Coghem, AGP, RHF, T–04676, p. 1.)

Her supposition was correct, since among the preserved papers of the founder there is this notice from the Work of the Holy Family, which is dated 18 Mar 1928 (the vigil of the feast of Saint Joseph): "Rev. Fr. José Ma.: While wishing you a happy feast day, I would also like to ask you to give a talk next Friday, at the Foundation, to married people, about the faith—a one-hour talk, starting at about 8:15 P.M." (original in AGP, RHF, D–03283).

[70] See *Boletín Trimestral,* issue no. 72, p. 7.

[71] See *Boletín Trimestral,* issue no. 72, p. 7, and issue no. 78, p. 5.

Josefina Santos (AGP, RHF, T–05255, p. 2) mentions that "on Sundays all of the children attending the schools that the Apostolic Ladies had in the different neighborhoods gathered at the Foundation, and Father Josemaría heard their confessions."

From another angle, María Vicenta Reyero (*Sum.* 5969) speaks of how he instilled Christian life into these children "with the preparations, including explanations of the catechism and of the Gospel, that he gave them for the three days before their First Communion."

[72] See *Boletín Trimestral,* issue no. 78, p. 10.

"Father Josemaría also went to the schools that we had in the suburbs of Madrid," says Asunción Muñoz. "About four thousand children made their First Communion each year. He gave them talks and spoke in a friendly way with each one, using all his personal charm and apostolic energy to bring the hearts of those little ones to the knowledge and love of Jesus" (Asunción Muñoz, AGP, RHF, T–04393, p. 3). María Vicenta Reyero (*Sum.* 5969) tells us that Father Josemaría, "with other priests, heard the confessions of the children who were about to make their First Communion, and these children were very often the ones who came to our church for confession." At the Foundation for the Sick, Father Josemaría was assisted in these and other tasks, by another chaplain, Father Norberto Rodríguez García (see Asunción Muñoz, AGP, RHF, T–04393, p. 4).

[73] Margarita Alvarado Coghem, AGP, RHF, T–04676, p. 1.

[74] *Meditation* of 19 Mar 1975.

[75] "At that time," says Josefina Santos (AGP, RHF, T–05255, p. 2), "it was not customary for the parish priests to bring our Lord, except in cases of imminent danger of death. Luz Casanova asked permission from the chancery office, and it was granted, and so Father Josemaría brought Communion to all the sick who requested it."

"Except in special cases," says Margarita Alvarado (AGP, RHF, T–04676, p. 1), "he brought Holy Communion to the sick on Thursdays, in a car lent him by Doña Luz Casanova. On the other days he went by streetcar, or on foot—whatever way he could get there. Sometimes he did this in really bad weather, because he tended to the sick in winter as well as in summer."

[76] Josefina Santos, AGP, RHF, T–05255, p. 2.

[77] Asunción Muñoz, AGP, RHF, T–04393, p. 2. As the founder himself pointed out, all of these activities were carried out with the consent of the parish priests, as stipulated by canon law (see Alvaro del Portillo, *Sum.* 255).

[78] Asunción Muñoz, AGP, RHF, T–04393, p. 2, and María Vicenta Reyero, *Sum.* 5979.

[79] *Apuntes*, nos. 119 and 120.

[80] Margarita Alvarado Coghem, AGP, RHF, T–04676, p. 2, and Asunción Muñoz, AGP, RHF, T–04393, p. 1.

[81] *Apuntes*, no. 178.

[82] Asunción Muñoz, AGP, RHF, T–04393, p. 1. From Mercedes Sagüés, who was present at many of these events, Bishop Alvaro del Portillo received the following testimony: that in the entire time that Father Josemaría was tending to the sick, not one of them died without receiving the last sacraments. (See Alvaro del Portillo, *Sum.* 257.)

[83] See Ernesto Juliá, PR, p. 1074. "There certainly are a lot of kind and just acts of God that I could tell about," says Father Josemaría, "that I saw in my visits to the sick" (*Apuntes*, no. 121).

[84] In AGP, RHF, D–03283 are preserved a good number of these sheets from the Apostolic Work, and of notes sent to the chaplain about his visits to the sick, from the years 1927, 1928, and 1929.

[85] María Vicenta Reyero, *Sum.* 5976. In a note on the sheet for 25 Nov 1927, for example, we read, "The sick man at 8 Artistas wants Father José to come again. The Ladies who give the catechism classes say he has gotten worse" (AGP, RHF, D–03283).

[86] See AGP, RHF, D–03283.

[87] See Ernesto Juliá, PR, p. 1074.

[88] Heard from the founder by Bishop Javier Echevarría (*Sum.* 1958).

[89] See Josefina Santos, AGP, RHF, T–05255, p. 1, and also Javier Echevarría, *Sum.* 1958.

[90] See AGP, RHF, D–03283.

[91] "There was at that time," explains Bishop del Portillo, "no lack of extraordinary favors, of divine locutions which burned themselves into his soul and left indelible imprints on his mind" (see *Sum.* 532).

[92] *Meditation* of 2 Oct 1962.

[93] See Alvaro del Portillo, "Monseñor Escrivá de Balaguer, instrumento de Dios," in *En Memoria de Mons. Josemaría Escrivá de Balaguer* (Pamplona: Eunsa, 1976), p. 30.

[94] *Letter 6 May 1945,* no. 41.

[95] *Letter 29 Dec 1947/14 Feb 1966,* no. 17.

[96] María Vicenta Reyero, *Sum.* 5972. A note has been preserved from the director of the Academy, signed by Father José Cicuéndez himself and dated 30 Jun 1930, in which "is enclosed the monthly payment for June," but there is no mention of the amount. (See AGP, RHF, D–03395.)

[97] The 150 pesetas was for the government fee (127 pesetas), the fee for putting together his student file (7 pesetas), the fee to be paid to the university's board of trustees (15 pesetas), and a tax stamp. The three courses were History of International Law, History of Spanish Juridical Literature, and Philosophy of Law.

[98] Father Josemaría had no savings. Nor had he time to prepare for the exams. He must have foreseen that he would not be able to take the one in History of Spanish Juridical Literature, since the exams were coming up in two weeks. This is all the more reason to assume that it was Father José Cicuéndez who paid the fees, especially since we know he did so on at least one other occasion (see Alvaro del Portillo, *Sum.* 271).

As for the two exams that Father Josemaría did take, he evidently had done most of his preparations for the Philosophy of Law exam a year earlier, since on August 29, 1927, he requested permission to take it and paid the required fees, though he then either was not able or chose not to take it in September 1927; and for the History of International Law exam he also obviously had a good head start, since he had earned the second highest grade at Saragossa in the Public International Law exam.

[99] In August 1928 the chancery office published a "Circular on Retreats" which said, "In conformity with the practice established in this diocese in previous years, several retreats for priests will be given this fall. It should be kept in mind, in this regard, that all priests who have not made a retreat within the last three years are required by canon law to do so this year." (See *Boletín Oficial del Obispado de Madrid-Alcalá,* no. 1469 [16 Aug 1928], p. 249.)

The Vincentians had organized three retreats, the second of which would run from September 30 to October 6. (See *Boletín Oficial*, no. 1469, p. 250.)

100 *Guía de Arquitectura y Urbanismo de Madrid*, vol. 2, p. 10. See also *Anales de la Congregación de la Misión y de las Hijas de la Caridad*, vol. 9 (Madrid, 1901), pp. 254–301, and M. Horcajada, *Reseña Histórica de las Casas de la Misión fundadas en España desde 1704 hasta nuestros días* (Madrid, 1915), pp. 481–509. In the forties this building underwent a substantial transformation, and a good part of the old construction is now a hospital. The rest, rebuilt and enlarged, is now the residence of the Vincentian community that staffs the Basilica of La Milagrosa.

101 On October 2, 1928, he received the definitive supernatural illumination about the Work "while reading those papers" (*Apuntes*, no. 306).

102 *Apuntes*, no. 414.

103 About this notebook Bishop del Portillo says, "Our Father told me on several occasions that the reason he destroyed it was that he had mentioned there many things of a supernatural nature and many extraordinary graces that our Lord had granted him. Some years later, he decided to burn that document because he did not want us to consider him a saint on account of those extraordinary gifts, 'when,' as our Father would say with complete conviction, 'I am nothing more than a sinner.'" (See *Apuntes*, introduction, p. 4.)

104 At the previous Vincentian retreat (September 16–22) there were twenty-five priests, and at the following one (October 14–20) there were thirty-nine (see *Boletín Eclesiástico del Obispado de Madrid-Alcalá*, no. 1476 [1 Dec 1928], p. 384). The director of this retreat was Father Laredo (see *Anales de la Congregación de la Misión*, vol. 36 [Madrid, 1928], p. 609).

As prescribed by the schedule, Holy Mass was celebrated between 7:00 and 8:00 A.M. Then came breakfast, an examination of conscience, and, at 9:00, the praying of the minor hours, followed by a reading from the New Testament. The time between this reading and the next talk, which started at 11:00, was a free period. It was during this free time for meditation—sometime between 10:00 and 11:00 in the morning, in other words—that the event now to be related took place. (See AGP, RHF, D–03610: "Daily Schedule for Those Making the Retreat.")

105 Whenever he had to speak about this extraordinary moment of grace, the founder, out of humility, was very evasive. But there was also another reason why he did not give details: so that his children in Opus Dei would see that the Work is not based "on miraculous occurrences," as he put it. "I have firmly taught you never to desire extraordinary interior paths." (See *Letter 6 May 1945*, no. 4.)

106 Later he added, "I compiled into some kind of unity the separate notes that I'd been taking up to that time" (*Apuntes*, no. 306).

[107] Commenting on those separate notes, José Luis Illanes says: "All those realities, which up to then had been like the individual pieces of a mosaic not yet assembled, suddenly acquired their finished meaning under a higher light that God now communicated to him" (J. L. Illanes, "Dos de octubre de 1928: alcance y significado de una fecha," in *Mons. Josemaría Escrivá de Balaguer y el Opus Dei,* by various authors [Pamplona, 1982], p. 78). Different interpretations are possible, provided it is acknowledged that the mosaic was incomplete, that this illumination gave a new dimension to the previous inspirations, and that the foundation (as we will see later on) would need new divine lights, which would underline the supernatural origin of the Work.

[108] *Letter 6 May 1945,* nos. 4–5. The founder is relating his own experiences, although he is speaking in third person plural. About this, see also *Meditation* of 14 Feb 1964.

[109] He repeated once more his "Here I am, for you called me" (see *Meditation* of 2 Oct 1962), keeping alive that call and that response made in Logroño in 1918, when, like the blind man of Jericho, he had asked for light. Jesus, "with that authoritative act, established himself in my soul," he says. He gave thanks to the Lord for having given him this clear call "to labor in his Work, with a well-defined vocation" (see *Letter 9 Jan 1932,* no. 9, and *Letter 11 Mar 1940,* no. 32).

[110] *Meditation* of 14 Feb 1964. In 1974 he spoke of the joy and "wakefulness of spirit still left in my soul—after almost half a century—by those bells of Our Lady of the Angels" (*Letter 14 Feb 1974,* no. 1).

[111] *Meditation* of 14 Feb 1964.

[112] *Meditation* of 2 Oct 1962.

[113] *Apuntes,* no. 306, and *Letter 14 Feb 1950,* no. 3. Bishop Javier Echevarría (*Sum.* 2139) expresses it in this way: "The founder did not originate the idea of founding Opus Dei. Our Lord showed him the Work on October 2, 1928, during a retreat that he was making at the Vincentian house on García de Paredes Street in Madrid. . . . It was an inspiration that our Lord gave exclusively to the Servant of God. It was not, in other words, an idea that he came up with on his own, nor a project started with the cooperation of other people."

[114] *Meditation* of 19 Mar 1975.

[115] *Instruction* of 19 Mar 1934, nos. 6–7.

[116] One of his journal entries begins, "Vigil of the feast of the Guardian Angels, 1 Oct 33: Tomorrow, five years since I saw the Work" (*Apuntes,* no. 1055). Rereading that entry years later, he commented to Bishop Alvaro del Portillo, "For me that is the clearest way to say it: since I saw the Work!" (*Apuntes,* no. 1055, note 808). Our Lord, then, had founded, and Father Josemaría had "seen."

Bishop del Portillo explains: "In the mind of the Father—in what God had engraved in his soul—there was no associative phenomenon, because in that case Opus Dei would not have been founded yet, when there were not even two members, the Father and the first of his sons. On the contrary, this repeated affirmation of our Father that Opus Dei was founded on October 2, 1928, clearly shows that our Father saw the Work as a work of God, and himself only as an instrument for God's accomplishing of that work. At the very moment in which our Lord God took this instrument into his hands and let him see what it was he wanted, so that he could set to work, Opus Dei was founded" (*Apuntes*, no. 306, note 300).

[117] *Meditation* of 2 Oct 1962.

[118] Bishop del Portillo transcribes some comments made by the founder in 1968 about that moment: "I had presentiments from the beginning of 1918. Later I kept on *seeing*, but without being able to determine what it was that our Lord wanted of me. I was *seeing* that our Lord wanted something of me. I asked, and kept on asking. On October 2, 1928, comes a *clear general idea* of my mission. After that 2nd of October in 1928, I stopped getting those inspirations that the Lord had been giving me" (*Apuntes*, no. 179, note 193).

[119] *Apuntes*, no. 179, note 193.

[120] Alvaro del Portillo, *Sum.* 532.

[121] *Letter 24 Mar 1930*, no. 1.

[122] Ibid., no. 2.

[123] Ibid.

[124] Ibid., no. 12.

[125] Ibid., no. 14.

[126] *Apuntes*, no. 154.

[127] *Apuntes*, no. 306.

[128] *Letter 9 Jan 1932*, no. 9.

[129] *Apuntes*, no. 290.

[130] *Letter 25 May 1962*, no. 41.

[131] *Letter 9 Jan 1932*, no. 92.

[132] *Letter 14 Feb 1944*, no. 1.

[133] *Letter 9 Jan 1932*, no. 5.

[134] *Apuntes*, no. 240.

[135] *Letter 14 Feb 1974*, no. 10.

[136] *Apuntes*, no. 215.

[137] *Apuntes*, no. 171.

[138] *Apuntes*, no. 93.

[139] *Apuntes*, no. 993.

[140] *Letter 11 Mar 1940*, no. 32.

[141] *Letter 29 Dec 1947/14 Feb 1966*, no. 11.

[142] He was conscious of having made "a great divine and human commitment" (*Meditation* of 3 Mar 1963).

[143] See Pedro Rocamora, AGP, RHF, T–05829, p. 1; Alvaro del Portillo, *Sum.* 679; and José Romeo, AGP, RHF, T–03809, p. 1.

[144] Pedro Rocamora, AGP, RHF, T–05829, pp. 2–3.

[145] See *Apuntes*, no. 410, note 359, and no. 469, note 393.

[146] He says, "Tell me what you're up to. Are you finally going to pursue a career in the consular corps?" (AGP, IZL, D–1213, letter no. 3). According to the testimony given by Father Josemaría for the cause of beatification of Isidoro Zorzano, the founder first met him in about 1927, in Madrid, and that brief meeting was followed by two others at La Castellana, and then one in August 1930. (See *Copia Publica Transumpti Processum . . .Servi Dei Isidoro Zorzano Ledesma*, year 1968, vol. 4, fol. 1074. See also the biography of Zorzano by José Miguel Pero-Sanz: *Isidoro Zorzano Ledesma*, Madrid, Ediciones Palabra, 1996.)

[147] See Alvaro del Portillo, *Sum.* 240.

[148] Father Norberto Rodríguez García was born in Astorga (in León) in 1880, and was ordained to the priesthood in 1905. By October 1910 he was already living in Madrid, with his parents, and serving as chaplain of the general hospital. In 1914 he had a nervous breakdown. He recovered, but then had a relapse which for quite a while made it impossible for him to hold any ecclesiastical position. From September 1924 to October 1931 he was assistant chaplain at the Foundation for the Sick. Afterward he held various chaplaincies for orders of nuns and worked as an assistant priest in a parish in Madrid. He died on 8 May 1968.

[149] Asunción Muñoz, AGP, RHF, T–04393, p. 4.

[150] Letter of 4 Mar 1929 from Father José Pou de Foxá to Father Josemaría, sent from Avila: original in AGP, RHF, D–15309.

[151] Carlos Sánchez del Río, AGP, RHF, T–02853, p. 1. Sánchez notes that "the Work had already been born, but he did not speak to us about it at that time."

[152] *Apuntes*, no. 1476. In 1938, when the founder was in Burgos, Father Manuel was the secretary of that city's seminary, which until 1931 had been a pontifical university.

[153] See his article in the 24 Oct 1973 issue of San Salvador's *La prensa gráfica*. Father Rafael Fernández Claros was canon-theologian of the Metropolitan Cathedral of San Salvador.

[154] See AGP, RHF, D–15511.

[155] See AGP, RHF, D–15511. Also for apostolic purposes, Father Josemaría, along with some other priests, had enrolled in a pious union, as he himself relates in his journal: "On March 12, 1929, *feast of Saint Gregory*

the Great, Father Norberto and I enrolled in the priests' union of Lisieux, the union of spiritual brothers of Saint Thérèse" (*Apuntes,* no. 536).

[156] *Letter 29 Dec 1947/14 Feb 1966,* no. 6. Within a little while, as he wrote in 1931, he began to feel an urgent need to ask prayers from everyone under the sun. "I have a real obsession," he said, "with requesting prayers. From nuns and priests, from pious lay people, from the sick people I take care of, from everyone, I ask an alms of prayer for my intentions, which are, naturally, the Work of God and vocations for it" (*Apuntes,* no. 302).

In 1932 he wrote, "I continue to ask prayers even from strangers—nuns, for example, whom I come across on the street—asking them to give me, out of their goodness, the spiritual alms of an Our Father" (*Apuntes,* no. 569).

[157] See *Apuntes,* no. 569, note 472.

[158] See AGP, RHF, T–03714, p. 2.

[159] *Apuntes,* no. 195.

[160] See Josefina Santos, AGP, RHF, T–05255, p. 1.

[161] *Apuntes,* no. 70; see also *Apuntes,* no. 1594. Entry no. 70 is from one of the first days of July 1930. Mercedes Reyna O'Farril, a sister who worked at the Foundation for the Sick, died on January 23, 1929, with a reputation for sanctity. Upon her death the founder felt, as he put it, "inclined to entrust myself to her protection," since he had attended her in her last days, up to the very moment of her death (see *Apuntes,* nos. 174 and 178).

[162] He started the novena on July 31, 1929. "On all nine days," he says, "I went to the cemetery on foot and returned the same way, after praying the Rosary on my knees at her tomb" (*Apuntes,* no. 178). On the second day he wrote in a letter to her sister Rosario Reyna, "I am making a novena to little Mercedes (I started it on the feast of Saint Ignatius), going every day to visit her grave. There are two very essential things I am asking her for. I will very much appreciate it, Señora, if you help me pester your sister" (*C 3,* 1 Aug 1929).

[163] *Apuntes,* no. 432; see also *Apuntes,* no. 1732, note 1014. Regarding the "victim soul" idea, the founder says, "The idea of being or considering myself a victim never appealed to me" (*Apuntes,* no. 413, note 362). And several times he says, "I never had any liking for either the term or the concept of 'victim soul'" (see *Apuntes,* nos. 1372, 1380, and 1014).

[164] *Letter 29 Dec 1947/14 Feb 1966,* no. 90.

[165] *Apuntes,* no. 839.

[166] *Meditation* of 19 Mar 1975.

[167] *Letter 8 Dec 1949,* no. 5.

[168] See *Letter 24 Dec 1951,* no. 249.

[169] *Letter 29 Dec 1947/14 Feb 1966*, no. 19.

[170] *Apuntes*, no. 306.

[171] *Apuntes*, no. 179. "After that 2nd of October of 1928, I stopped getting those inspirations that the Lord had been giving me" (*Apuntes*, no. 179, note 193).

[172] *Apuntes*, no. 1870. Many years later he still would recall what he considered his failures in duly responding to his foundational graces. Just a few months before his death he asked himself, "What means did I use? I did not conduct myself well. I have even been a coward . . ." (*Meditation of 19 Mar 1975*).

[173] *Letter 29 Dec 1947/14 Feb 1966*, no. 16.

[174] Ibid., no. 17.

[175] *Letter 9 Jan 1932*, no. 84. This same idea is found in *Apuntes*, no. 373, dated 3 Nov 1931. And it goes back still further, since in that entry the founder says he has already written on this subject. No such text is found in the earlier entries, so we must assume that he is referring to something in the first book of his *Apuntes*, which he burned. It must have been written, therefore, no later than March 1930.

[176] *Meditation of 14 Feb 1964*. He expressed this same thought in *Letter 14 Sep 1951*, no. 3.

[177] *Apuntes*, no. 1870. Father José Luis Múzquiz remembers hearing him say that in the months following October 2, 1928, he "had no desire to be a founder," and if he could have found some organization similar to the Work, he "would gladly have gone there as a rank-and-file soldier" (see José Luis Múzquiz, AGP, RHF, T–04678/1, p. 118).

[178] *Apuntes*, no. 1870. The expression "unusual things" (*cosas raras*) implies no criticism, but simply a contrast to the kind of naturalness proper to members of Opus Dei, who are supposed to be ordinary Christians and citizens (see *Letter 29 Dec 1947/14 Feb 1966*, no. 17).

[179] *Meditation of 14 Feb 1964*. Father Josemaría soon realized, says Bishop del Portillo, that there were no institutions of this type in Spain, but he was hearing news of new foundations in other countries: Italy, Switzerland, Germany, Poland, etc. (see *Sum.* 536).

[180] As he himself put it, "There started up again that special, very specific help from the Lord" (*Apuntes*, no. 179, note 193).

[181] *Apuntes*, no. 475. A little later he wrote to the members of the Work: "Although I am not fond of dramatic gestures, I have often had the temptation, the desire, to get down on my knees and beg your pardon, my children, because with this aversion to foundations, despite having plenty of reasons for certainty about founding the Work, I resisted as much as I could. I would use as an excuse, before our Lord God, the real fact that since October 2, 1928, in the midst of that internal struggle of

mine, I have worked to fulfill the holy will of God, going ahead and starting the apostolic activity of the Work. Three years have passed, and now I see that perhaps our Lord wanted me to suffer then, and to still feel that complete repugnance now, so that I will always have a tangible proof that *everything is his and nothing mine"* (*Letter 9 Jan 1932*, no. 84).

[182] In addition to material he had received in response to his requests, he often found information in Spanish religious magazines. In his journal entry for 25 Aug 1930, he spoke of something he had already been doing for several years: "For quite some time, besides bringing religious magazines (*El Mensajero, Iris de Paz*, mission magazines, and others from various congregations) to the sick, I have been calmly and brazenly handing them out in the streets. There have been times when I couldn't walk down some streets in the poor neighborhoods without people asking me for magazines" (*Apuntes*, no. 86).

"If I remember correctly," says Father Múzquiz, "he said he was given them by a friend of his, Don Alejandro Guzmán" (José Luis Múzquiz, AGP, RHF, T–04678/1, p. 20).

[183] *Apuntes*, no. 1870. Bishop del Portillo mentions in his note to this entry that the founder often spoke to him about an old friend and classmate at the law school in Saragossa, Enrique Luño Peña, who on one occasion visited the Foundation for the Sick and spoke to him about the Company of Saint Paul. This friend also wrote an article, "Pan y Catecismo," for the Saragossan magazine *La Acción Social*. (See issue no. 4:73 [January 1928], p. 7.)

In addition, the 1928 edition of the official Church directory (which at that time was widely distributed in Spain) carried a long article about Cardinal Ferrari's foundation. (See P. Voltas, C.M.F., "Hombres y hechos de la Iglesia Contemporánea. El Cardenal Ferrari. Su Obra. La Compañía de San Pablo," in E. Subirana, op. cit., 1928, pp. 105–128.)

[184] In *El Mensajero Seráfico*, which he sometimes distributed to the sick, there was a series of articles about the foundations set up in Poland by Father Honorato Kozminski of Biala Podlaska. (See L. Martínez de Muñecas, "Un gran Apóstol de la Acción Católica," in *El Mensajero Seráfico*, 1 Jan 1930, pp. 15–16; 16 Jan 1930, pp. 50–51; and 1 Feb 1930, pp. 81–83.) In these articles we read that in reaction to the decree of the czarist government suppressing the religious orders in Poland, Father Honorato fostered religious vocations, secretly organizing a group whose members took vows but lived in the world without a religious habit and without any regular community life. Starting in 1892 he had founded several religious congregations, men's and women's, for different social groups.

Father Laureano Martínez de Muñecas was a Spanish Capuchin who was then living in Krakow and working with Father Honorato's foundations. He later returned to Spain and, in 1950, founded the Congregación de las Misioneras Franciscanas del Suburbio.

[185] Father Josemaría did burn all the journal entries written before 1930, as we mentioned earlier.

José Luis Múzquiz testifies that the founder once told him that after reading those magazines, "'I felt very much at peace. I wrote that those associations were completely different from the foundation that our Lord wanted of me, and that, in addition, there was this other fundamental difference: that in those groups there were women, whereas in Opus Dei there would be no women'" (José Luis Múzquiz, AGP, RHF, T–04678/1, p. 20).

[186] *Meditation* of 14 Feb 1964. Father Pedro Casciaro (*Sum.* 6338) testifies that "he went so far as to write, 'In Opus Dei there will be no women, no way,'" and Blanca Fontán Suanzes (PM, fol. 1061) says that "in the beginning the Servant of God stated clearly that he would not work with women, 'no way.'"

[187] On October 2, 1928, says Bishop del Portillo (*Sum.* 537), the founder saw the Work as it was to be and to continue to be until the end of time: priests and lay people seeking sanctity through the fulfillment of their familial and social duties. At that moment he just did not see the specific, rightful places that women and the Priestly Society of the Holy Cross would have in Opus Dei.

The light he received on October 2 was about "the Work as a whole"—its spiritual focus and message of sanctity, but not any details of its composition and structure. That is why he saw no place in the Work for women, or, to put it in his own words, "I did not think there would be women in Opus Dei" (*Letter 29 Jul 1965*, no. 2), or, "it will never have women." On October 2, 1928, he received "the light about the Work as a whole." On February 14, 1930, the date of the foundation of the women's branch of Opus Dei, he "grasped," through a new grace of God, another aspect of that panorama.

[188] *Apuntes*, no. 1871. On one February 14, in a meditation he was giving, the founder said, "I went to the home of an eighty-year-old lady whose confession I used to hear, to celebrate Mass in the small oratory that she had. And it was there, after Communion, in the Mass, that the women's branch came into the world. Later, at the regular time, I went running to my confessor, and he told me, 'This is just as much from God as the rest'" (*Meditation* of 14 Feb 1964). Note that his words, "Later, at the regular time," are written from the vantage point of 1964.

[189] *Apuntes*, no. 1872. Among the documents kept in the General Archive of the Prelature is a letter from an "A. Slatri," dated Milan, July 21, 1930, informing the founder about "the Company of Saint Paul and the Work of Cardinal Ferrari," as well as two letters sent from Krakow by Father Laureano Martínez de las Muñecas, dated 4 Feb 1932 and 1 Apr 1932,

about the foundations of Father Honorato in Poland (see AGP, RHF, D–15059 and D–03293).

Given their dates, these letters evidently have nothing to do with the search for an institution similar to the Work, such as the founder saw it on October 2, 1928, but are about questions of an organizational and juridical nature. In those years, and especially in 1932, he consulted the constitutions and regulations of other institutions (see *Apuntes*, no. 716, which is dated 10 May 1932). He also checked out some practical points with other persons, such as Father Sánchez (see *Apuntes*, no. 769, dated 7 Jul 1932, and no. 808, dated 12 Aug 1932).

[190] *Apuntes,* no. 1871. "That there might be no doubt that it was he who wanted the Work brought into being, our Lord provided external proofs. I had written, '*Never*—no way—will there be women in Opus Dei.' And a few days later. . . . February 14. This makes it obvious that the Work was not my doing, but something going against my inclination and will" (*Meditation* of 14 Feb 1964).

[191] Cited by Alvaro del Portillo, in *Sum.* 537.

Notes to Chapter 6

[1] See Santiago Escrivá de Balaguer y Albás, *Sum.* 7325; Alvaro del Portillo, *Sum.* 249; and Joaquín Alonso, PR, p. 1738.

[2] See *Apuntes,* nos. 620 and 656. There were times when many students wanted private lessons, but other times when Father Josemaría urgently needed money for immediate necessities, he found himself without students. At one of those stressful moments when he saw no way out of this predicament, a special class was offered to him. After accepting it he wrote in his journal, "This will allow me to pay the rent (this month I haven't yet been able to make it) and Guitín's tuition at the Institute. Thanks be to God" (*Apuntes,* no. 620).

Tutoring positions sometimes involved obtaining notes, taking care of transferrals of academic records, and even accompanying students to other cities for exams. In a letter to Father Pou de Foxá, dated 8 Apr 1932, Father Josemaría speaks of one of those trips.

[3] See letter of 9 Dec 1928 from Isidoro Zorzano to Father Josemaría, in AGP, IZL, D–1213, no. 3.

[4] See Appendix 12, and also his student file in the archive of the law school of Madrid's Complutense University.

[5] C 7 (7 Mar 1930). What with the accumulation of jobs and other activities, finding the time to work on his dissertation was becoming more and more difficult.

[6] See Alvaro del Portillo, *Sum.* 485.

7 *C 28* (9 Apr 1932).

8 *Apuntes*, no. 1676.

9 Josefina Santos, AGP, RHF, T–05255, p. 2.

10 *Apuntes*, no. 39. See also *Apuntes*, no. 39, note 52. The so-called Bishop's Chapel was founded in 1520, in Madrid, by Francisco Vargas y Carvajal, who served as secretary-councilor to Ferdinand and Isabella (and later to Charles V), and by his son Gutierre, the bishop of Plasencia.

11 See *Apuntes*, no. 163. One such person was a salesclerk whom he mentions in his journal (see *Apuntes*, no. 444).

12 *Apuntes*, no. 137.

13 *Apuntes*, no. 200.

14 *Apuntes*, no. 179, note 193.

15 *Apuntes*, no. 164. This entry is dated 27 Jun 1932. On other occasions the founder speaks of "the secret of gestation" (see *Apuntes*, no. 205, note 225) and of "the unborn Work" (see *Apuntes*, no. 89).

16 *Apuntes*, no. 67.

17 *Apuntes*, no. 1867.

18 See *Apuntes*, no. 1310, and Alvaro del Portillo, *Sum.* 542.

19 The priests he remembered having spoken with earlier included Father Norberto (the assistant chaplain of the Foundation) and "a canon of Tarazona who later went to Toledo"—probably Father Angel del Barrio, a canon of Tarazona (see E. Subirana, *Anuario Eclesiástico* [Barcelona], 1928, p. 453) who later served as chaplain at La Capilla de los Reyes. There still exists a letter to Father Josemaría, dated Toledo, 18 Aug 1944, in which Father Angel reminds him of their conversations and of the "restlessness" that had filled him in about 1928: see original in AGP, RHF, D–12807. Father Josemaría also mentions "a Valencian parish priest" and "a young religious of the Congregation of the Holy Family": see *Apuntes*, no. 1864, and Alvaro del Portillo, *Sum.* 327.

20 *Apuntes*, no. 1864.

21 *Apuntes*, no. 1866. He wrote this in 1948, without consulting entry no. 73 of his *Apuntes*. Written on about 26 Jul 1930, this entry reads as follows: "On Sunday, July 6, I gave Father Sánchez those sheets of paper, at the Foundation, when he came for the Preservation of the Faith examinations. On Monday the 21st of the same month, in Chamartín, Father returned the notes to me and promised to be our director. *Laus Deo!*"

22 *Apuntes*, no. 1868.

23 *Apuntes*, no. 1867.

24 *Apuntes*, no. 21; see also *Apuntes*, no. 73. Prior to 6 Jul 1930 he speaks in various places in his *Apuntes* about "Works of God" (see nos. 32 and 38) or the "Work of God" (see nos. 4 and 72).

25 *Apuntes*, no. 126. Bishop del Portillo comments: "On other occasions

the Father explained to us that when he heard Father Sánchez speak of the 'Work of God,' he associated this name with the essence of the Work (sanctification of work, conversion of it into prayer); that with this new interpretation, the name 'Work of God' no longer sounded presumptuous to him, but, rather, seemed perfectly appropriate; and that, in addition, he considered it a command from God (as he wrote here) that the name be this: Work of God, Opus Dei" (*Apuntes*, no. 126, note 146).

[26] See *Apuntes*, no. 66.

[27] The lady was Doña Carolina Carvajal, sister of the Count of Aguilar de Inestrillas. These efforts made in the palace are referred to in a letter to the founder from one of his followers, Isidoro Zorzano. In this letter, dated Málaga, 26 Jan 1931, we read: "Now you must tell me how things are going at the palace." (See AGP, IZL, D–1213, no. 13.)

[28] Father Pedro Poveda Castroverde was the founder of the Teresians. Born in Linares (Andalusia) in 1874, he was ordained to the priesthood in 1897 and became a professor at the seminary in Guadix (Granada). In 1906 he was transferred to Asturias, where he became intensely involved in teaching; there he founded, in 1911, two teachers' colleges, in Gijón and in Oviedo. In 1921 he was assigned to the Royal Chapel in Madrid, and in 1931 was named secretary of the ecclesiastical palace jurisdiction. On July 28, 1936, he was assassinated because of antireligious hatred. In 1955 his cause for canonization was opened; in 1958 the process on the diocesan level was completed; and in 1980 the Congregation for the Causes of the Saints issued the decree of introduction of the cause. (See A. Serrano, *La estela de un Apóstol*, Madrid, 1942; S. De Santa Teresa, O.C.D., *Vida de D. Pedro Poveda Castroverde*, Madrid, 1942; and Flavia Paz Velázquez, *Cuadernos Biográficos*, Narcea, 1986 and 1987.) On October 10, 1993, Pedro Poveda was beatified by Pope John Paul II.

[29] See Alvaro del Portillo, *Sum*. 240, and Javier Echevarría, *Sum*. 3250. "This appointment was one to which many aspired," explains Bishop Echevarría. "As a result of that conversation, a deep friendship developed between the two priests and, despite their difference in age, Father Pedro Poveda often visited Father Josemaría to fraternally confide in him and to ask his advice and help on matters related to priestly ministry."

[30] In his journal he tells us that after he turned down that honorary royal chaplaincy, "the Marchioness of Los Alamos and María Luisa Guzmán and María Machimbarrena and her niece Maruja (daughter of the first of these)—the four of them—accompanied me to the Ministry of Justice and Ecclesiastical Affairs to introduce me to the undersecretary, Don José Martínez de Velasco. Four days later, the Republic. . . . Last Friday [17 Apr 1931], in the home of Aguilar de Inestrillas, I was introduced to Señora de Martínez de Velasco, who hastened to tell me—and one could see that she was telling the truth—that her husband was sorry that he

had not had time to find positions for a relative of his and for me" (*Apuntes*, no. 192).

31 *Apuntes*, no. 192.

32 The packet containing the *Apuntes íntimos* was found in the archive of the Prelature, together with other packets and an envelope on which the founder had written: "After my death, these papers—as well as the notebooks which make up my *Apuntes íntimos*—are to be put in the hands of Don Alvaro, without anyone else reading them first, so that he can write the appropriate notes. That son of mine is the one person who is in a position to make whatever commentaries and clarifications are necessary, since I have discussed these writings with him often and in detail. Mariano, Rome, September 2, 1968."

33 "The saints," he wrote in 1932, "were necessarily some disconcerting people. They were men and women—like my Saint Catherine of Siena!—who by word and example were a continual cause of uneasiness for consciences compromised by sin" (*Letter 9 Jan 1932*, no. 73).

34 *Apuntes*, no. 1862 (Rome, June 14, 1948).

35 *Apuntes*, no. 1862. "I burned notebook no. 1," he wrote on the first page of notebook no. 2. The reason was his fear that upon reading the accounts given there of extraordinary events of a supernatural nature, someone might take him for a saint, when he himself was firmly convinced that he was nothing but a sinner (see *Apuntes*, introductory note).

36 *Apuntes*, no. 167.

37 See Pedro Rocamora, AGP, RHF, T–05829, p. 2.

38 *Apuntes*, no. 713. In the entry for 24 May 1932 one reads: "Resolution: Barring some real necessity, I will never talk about the personal things" (*Apuntes*, no. 735). Probably he burned the first notebook by the end of that summer, since he wrote in another place—as he had planned to do— his notes for the retreat he made in October of that year. (Upon returning to Madrid, after having made that retreat in Segovia, he writes in his journal, "October 14, 1932: I will keep the retreat notes separate"; see *Apuntes*, nos. 839 and 1701.) The last entry in his journal indicating that the first notebook still exists is that of 11 Dec 1931 (*Apuntes*, no. 470), in which he says he has read one of the entries "in the first notebook" to Father Lino, to give him "a more detailed understanding of the Work." In the entry for the previous day he comments that upon rereading "a certain entry in the first notebook of Catherines," he came to understand for the first time a certain aspect of his spiritual life (see *Apuntes*, no. 474).

39 *Apuntes*, no. 996.

40 *Apuntes*, no. 379.

41 *Apuntes*, no. 1040.

42 *Apuntes*, no. 446.

[43] *Apuntes,* no. 472; see also *Apuntes,* no. 477.

[44] *Apuntes,* no. 475.

[45] *Apuntes,* no. 691.

[46] *Apuntes,* no. 1115. Another of these rare instances is what he wrote on 26 Nov 1931: "After Holy Mass today, during my thanksgiving and later in the church of the Capuchins of Medinaceli, the Lord flooded me with graces. I experienced what the psalm says: 'Inebriabuntur ab ubertate domus tuae: et torrente voluptatis tuae potabis eos' ['They feast ("become inebriated" in the Vulgate version) on the abundance of thy house, and thou givest them drink from the river of thy delights' (Ps 36:8)]. Full of joy in the will of God, I feel that I told him with Saint Peter, 'Ecce, reliqui omnia et secutus sum te' ['Lo, I have left everything and followed you' (see Mk 10:28)]. And my heart felt the 'centuplum recipies' ['you will receive a hundredfold']. . . . I truly lived the Gospel of the day" (*Apuntes,* no. 415).

[47] *Apuntes,* no. 619. Most likely he occasionally had to take a shortcut by crossing Retiro Park, and did not do this simply for recreational purposes (see *Apuntes,* no 473).

[48] *Apuntes,* no. 618.

[49] *Apuntes,* no. 349. "Luckily," he commented years later, on rereading that note, "despite the path of childhood that I was on, I did not write those notes. At least I don't recall having written them" (see *Apuntes,* note 334).

[50] *Apuntes,* no. 263.

[51] *Apuntes,* no. 311.

[52] *Apuntes,* no. 343.

[53] *Apuntes,* no. 471. [The Latin means, "In the name of the Father, and of the Son, and of the Holy Spirit. Amen. Holy Mary, seat of wisdom, pray for us."]

[54] See, for example, *Apuntes,* no. 342.

[55] *Apuntes,* no. 13.

[56] *Apuntes,* no. 14.

[57] *Apuntes,* no. 116.

[58] *Apuntes,* no. 313.

[59] See *Apuntes,* no. 875.

[60] *Apuntes,* no. 15.

[61] *Apuntes,* no. 1166.

[62] *Apuntes,* no. 423.

[63] *Apuntes,* nos. 458 and 459. He wrote all this not only to vent his righteous indignation, but also with an eye to the oratories that the Work would have in the future, so that, as the entry ends, "we may avoid falling into similar discourtesies toward Christ our King."

64 *Apuntes*, no. 581. See also *Letter 24 Mar 1930*, no. 21.

65 *Apuntes*, no. 173.

66 At its inception on April 14, the provisional government, in which there were two Catholics and five Freemasons, established itself as "a government of full powers" and granted itself a juridical statute whose third article presented freedom of belief and of worship as the basis of its policies. (See the 15 Apr 1931 edition of *Gaceta de Madrid*: no. 105, p. 195.)

Catholics, clergy and faithful alike, took these events and the new political order calmly, although they were worried about the anticlerical character of the republican forces. On April 24 the papal nuncio, Monsignor Tedeschini, sent to all the bishops a letter giving some indications about the posture they should adopt. "It is," said the letter, "the desire of the Holy See that Your Excellency recommend to the priests, religious, and faithful of your diocese that they respect the constituted powers and obey them for the maintenance of order and of the common good." (See F. de Meer, *La Cuestión religiosa en las Cortes Constituyentes de la II República Española* [Pamplona, 1975], pp. 30–31.)

The Holy See trusted that the government would respect the rights of the Church and the existing concordat.

67 The parties with the greatest numbers of representatives in the constitutional assembly, or Cortes, were the Socialists (117), the Radicals (93), the Radical Socialists (59), and the Republican Left of Catalonia (43). The rest of it was made up of small factions from nine parties. (See *República Española. Cortes Constituyentes* [Madrid, 1932], p. 124.) In all, there were 406 representatives.

During the election the Right could not organize itself, or did not know how to. As a result, the representation in the assembly did not correspond to the reality of Spanish society.

68 The police did nothing to restrain the mobs, even though they were notified of the riots the day before they began. Police in Madrid witnessed the burning of the Jesuit building on De La Flor Street, for example, without intervening. This passivity enabled the incendiaries to repeat such actions in many other major cities of Spain without the public authorities intervening.

Everything seemed to be set up and arranged so that the mobs could act with impunity. On the evening before the riots, a circular was distributed in all police stations of Madrid, signed by the police chief himself, prohibiting the use of anything but verbal persuasion against the rioters. (See J. Arrarás, *Historia de la Segunda República Española*, vol. 1 [Madrid, 1956], pp. 73–100, and F. Narbona, *La quema de conventos*, Madrid, 1954.)

69 The burning of churches and religious houses was not confined to May 1931. It happened numerous times during the era of the Spanish

Republic: in January 1932, in Saragossa, Córdoba, and Cádiz; in April 1932, in Seville; in July 1932, in Granada; in October 1932, in Cádiz, Marchena, and Loja. . . . In December 1933 ten churches and religious houses were burned in Saragossa, and six churches in Granada. All this was before the beginning of the revolutionary outbreak in Asturias in 1934 and the burnings all over Spain during the months of the Popular Front government in 1936, just prior to the Spanish Civil War. (See Antonio Montero, *Historia de la persecución religiosa en España, 1936–1939* (Madrid, 1961), pp. 26–27.)

[70] *Letter 29 Dec 1947/14 Feb 1966*, no. 28.

The proposed constitution appeared officially on August 18. The articles pertaining to religious issues were no. 3, "There is no state religion"; no. 24, by which religious organizations were subjected to the general laws of the country and which declares that "the state shall dissolve all religious orders and nationalize their goods"; no. 25, on freedom of conscience and limitations on the exercise of religion; no. 41, by which divorce was legalized; and nos. 46 and 47, on education.

These articles prompted the appearance of two important documents on the relations between church and state: a pastoral letter by Cardinal Segura (dated 15 Aug 1931) and a message from the Ecclesiastical Province of Tarragona. In accord with the teachings of Pope Leo XIII, these documents condemned the doctrine of separation of church and state and that of laicism, or secularism. "Cardinal Segura's pastoral letter and the message from the bishops of Tarragona came to be viewed, in principle, as declarations of an absolute incompatibility between the Church and the constitution which was proposed for the Republic" (F. de Meer, op. cit., pp. 84–85).

[71] On the parliamentary debate with regard to article 26 (no. 24 of the draft) of the constitution approved by the Cortes on October 14, see F. de Meer, op. cit., pp. 129ff.

As soon as the definitive version and the approval of that article became public knowledge, Pope Pius XI sent to the hierarchy and "faithful children of the Church in Spain" a telegram, dated October 16, protesting the offense against "the sacrosanct rights of the Church, which are the rights of God and of souls," and inviting all Catholics in Spain to unite themselves to his intentions "at the celebration of the Holy Sacrifice on the Sunday of Christ the King, that this great tribulation afflicting the Church and the Spanish nation might cease." (See *Boletín Oficial del Obispado de Madrid-Alcalá*, no. 1546 [year 1931], pp. 405–406.)

[72] The pastoral letter from the Spanish episcopate is dated 20 Dec 1931, but was not published in the dioceses until 1 Jan 1932.

[73] See the 3 Jun 1933 edition of *Gaceta de Madrid*. This law was approved by the Spanish parliament on May 17, but also had to be endorsed and

signed by the president of the Republic, Alcalá Zamora, who remained undecided for a couple of weeks. He signed it on June 2.

[74] The bishops' document begins with a reminder that the Spanish hierarchy, in its pastoral letter of December 1931, has already "expressed the deep feeling of the Church concerning those excesses of the state that violate the Christian conscience and religious rights" without the state's being able to accuse the Church authorities of inciting their faithful to any unlawful behavior. The faithful have, on the contrary, conducted themselves peacefully, always promoting public order. Later it analyzes "the terribly harsh treatment that is being given to the Church in Spain," pointing out that the Church "is being treated not as a moral and juridical entity duly recognized and respected within the established law, but rather as a danger," and that "attempts are being made to suppress it with regulations and political measures." (See "Declaración del Episcopado con motivo de la ley de Confesiones y Congregaciones religiosas," in *Boletín Oficial del Obispado de Madrid-Alcalá,* no. 1585 [year 1933].)

[75] AAS, 25 (1933), pp. 275–76. The archbishop of Toledo published a pastoral letter (*Horas Graves,* dated 12 Jul 1933) in which he minced no words. "The tentacles of state power have reached everywhere," he said, "and have been able to penetrate everything, rapidly obeying the single thought that tells it to crush the Church." (See A. Montero, op. cit., p. 32.)

[76] On the basis of the legal foundations laid in the Constitution and inspired by its secularistic spirit, legislation was adopted which not only was contrary to the declaration of human liberty contained in the Constitution but was inspired by a whipped-up fratricidal hatred. This orientation, in fact, is what led to the civil war of 1936–1939.

As the first president of the Republic, Niceto Alcalá Zamora, would say in the year the civil war broke out, the Constitution invited it. "A constitution has been created," he said, "which is an invitation to civil war, both from the dogmatic viewpoint, in which passion rules over a calm fairmindedness, and from the organic point of view, in which improvisation and an unstable equilibrium are substituted for experience and a solid construction of powers" (N. Alcalá Zamora, *Los defectos de la Constitución de 1931* [Madrid, 1936], p. 51).

The attitude of the hierarchy and of Spanish Catholics in general had from the very first been one of obedient and respectful acceptance of the constituted powers. Instructions to this effect were given by the bishop of each diocese. Those for the diocese of Madrid-Alcalá were given in Circular no. 93, "Sobre el respeto y obediencia a los Poderes constituidos," in compliance with the norms received from His Holiness by way of the papal nuncio (see *Boletín Oficial del Obispado de Madrid-Alcalá,* no. 1534 [1 May 1931], pp. 173–75).

[77] *Apuntes,* no. 191. The entry is dated April 20, 1931.

For more on the activities and influence of Freemasons in the secularistic politics of the Second Spanish Republic, see Joaquín Arrarás, op. cit., pp. 107–11.

78 *C 18* (5 May 1931).

79 On April 26, 1931, the bishop of Madrid, to prevent sacrileges, decreed that in view of the turmoil caused by the events of April 14 and their antiecclesiastical character, the clergy could under certain circumstances wear secular clothes. (See the circular "Ad clerum sive saecularem sive regularem circa usum vestis talaris," in *Boletín Oficial del Obispado de Madrid-Alcalá,* no. 1534 [1 May 1931], pp. 176–77.)

Santiago Escrivá de Balaguer, who was then twelve, says, "I accompanied Josemaría when he took the Blessed Sacrament from the Foundation's chapel on Nicasio Gallego Street to Pepe Romeo's house, which was right there at Santa Engracia, corner of Maudes, near Cuatro Caminos. It's possible that Cortés Cavanillas also went with us, but I don't remember. I know we went on foot, because I remember the surroundings, the people on the street, etc. Josemaría went dressed as a layman, in one of Pepe Romeo's suits and a beret that covered the big tonsure he had at the time. The streets were relatively safe because even though the atmosphere was one of revolution, the agitation was centered around monasteries and convents" (Santiago Escrivá de Balaguer y Albás, AGP, RHF, T–07921, p. 12). See also Alvaro del Portillo, PR, p. 1353, and Mario Lantini, *Sum.* 3562.

80 *Apuntes,* no. 202.

81 *Apuntes,* nos. 573 and 724.

82 On the nights of May 11, 12, and 16 (this last time because of a false alarm), he took the Blessed Sacrament to the Romeo house. See *Apuntes,* no. 202.

83 *Apuntes,* no. 424.

84 *Apuntes,* no. 202. See also Santiago Escrivá de Balaguer, *Sum.* 7325, and Joaquín Alonso, PR, p. 1738.

85 "In this campaign that has been and is being waged against religious orders, priests, and the Church, I have been confirmed in the opinion— already expressed in these notes—that there is a secret organization that is moving the people (always a child) via the press, pamphlets, cartoons, calumnies, spoken propaganda. Later they will lead it where they wish: to hell itself" (*Apuntes,* no. 331).

86 *Apuntes,* no. 114.

87 *Apuntes,* no. 114.

88 *Apuntes,* no. 210.

89 *Apuntes,* no. 211.

90 *Apuntes,* no. 212. One verse of the Riego hymn goes like this: "If the

priests and friars knew / the beating they are going to get, / they would join the chorus singing / Freedom, freedom, freedom." This is probably one of those "nastiest verses" to which he refers.
[91] Margarita Alvarado Coghem, AGP, RHF, T–04676, p. 1.
[92] *C 18* (5 May 1931).
[93] *Apuntes*, no. 1726. His conclusions are these:
   a) I should read one newspaper: *El Siglo*, since I am a subscriber.
   b) If, without my buying it (since I must always practice poverty), some Catholic magazine or other comes into my hands and there is something pertinent in it, I will read it.
   c) In no publication will I read any article that is purely literary or recreational.
   d) I will not read any pictorial magazines, or even leaf through them, . . . except for scientific magazines and—naturally—those having to do with Catholic missions.
   e) I will read *El Siglo* the morning after it comes out.

El Siglo Futuro was a traditionalist newspaper for which Father Antonio Sanz Cerrada, a friend of Father Josemaría's, worked, writing under the pseudonym of "Brother Juniper." It had a Catholic orientation, and Father Josemaría read it out of friendship for this priest, although he did not agree with some of the ideas that it promoted. (See *Apuntes*, no. 1691.)
[94] *Apuntes*, no. 327. The date of this entry is 15 Oct 1931.
[95] *Apuntes*, no. 222.
[96] *Apuntes*, no. 291. A month later the insults were not disturbing even his exterior peace. He wrote on 26 Oct 1931: "I'm going to note down a curious process that I have observed in myself. I've already said something about this. The insults used to make me mad. Later they gave me joy. And now the laughter and mockery and insults leave me as calm as if they were directed at a wall of concrete" (*Apuntes*, no. 348).
[97] *Apuntes*, no. 590.
[98] *Apuntes*, no. 164.
[99] *Apuntes*, no. 23.
[100] *Apuntes*, no. 28.
[101] *Apuntes*, no. 92.
[102] *Apuntes*, no. 111. In various ways he incorporates this trilogy in the practices and resolutions of his interior life. For example, he makes these three elements the three points of his daily examination of conscience (see *Apuntes*, no. 75); he considers apostolate to consist of prayer, expiation, and action (see *Apuntes*, no. 129); and he says, "Pray, pray, pray. Expiate, expiate, expiate. Then . . . off to work, all for his glory!" (*Apuntes*, no. 154).

[103] _Apuntes_, no. 128. The insistence of the founder on unceasing prayer and mortification took root in those who followed him. "I am more and more convinced," wrote Isidoro Zorzano, "that only with God's help can we attain our goal, and that only with prayer, action, and expiation can we attain that singular grace" (Letter of Isidoro Zorzano to Father Josemaría, dated La Roda, 27 Oct 1931: original in AGP, IZL, D–1213, no. 18).

As can be seen from letters of the founder to Isidoro Zorzano, these ideas are repetitions of received teachings. The founder had said to him, for example, "We must firmly base ourselves, before anything else, on _prayer_ and _expiation_ (sacrifice)" (_C 12_, 23 Nov 1930), and "I trust that things will soon be arranged . . . such that action can accompany the hidden apostolate of prayer and sacrifice" (_C 21_, 3 Sep 1931).

[104] _Apuntes_, no. 160 (10 Feb 1931). His faith in the merits of the suffering of innocent persons is very movingly expressed in another journal entry: "Feast of Saint John the Evangelist, 1930: Today, from morning on, I have offered my work to that most lovable 'disciple whom Jesus loved'. . . . Our Lord chose to compensate the miserable poverty of my merits by providing me with a sick boy of sixteen, a boy with tuberculosis. When I left after visiting him (at 11 Canarias Street), I offered the soul of that suffering young man to this holy apostle. And Saint John repaid me immediately" (_Apuntes_, no. 140 [27 Dec 1930]).

[105] _Apuntes_, no. 522. The founder also attributed the earlier collapse of _El Sol_, another antireligious paper, to the efficacy of the innocent prayer of "Dumb Enriqueta": see _Apuntes_, no. 522, note 431, and Alvaro del Portillo, _Sum._ 1189.

Even in his journal entries, the founder often avoided use of the word "I" or of first person. In one narration of this event, he tries to depersonalize it by presenting it as the idea of Father Norberto, the assistant chaplain of the Foundation (who surely was aware of what happened), but the syntax makes it clear that it was the founder himself who encouraged Enriqueta. In another place (Letter 7 Oct 1950, no. 12) he says:

> Around the years 1927 to 1931 a priest was giving spiritual direction to a poor, mentally retarded, ignorant, uneducated woman who nevertheless had an exquisite fineness of soul. People called her Dumb Enriqueta. Back then there was a very prestigious and rabidly anti-Catholic newspaper, run by a group of intellectuals, that was causing great harm to souls and to the Church. One day that priest—firm in the faith and having no other weapon—said to that poor little woman, "From today on, until I tell you otherwise, I want you to pray for an intention of mine." The intention was that that newspaper cease to be published. Well, within a short time the saying of

Scripture was fulfilled: "quae stulta sunt mundi elegit Deus ut confundat sapientes" (1 Cor 1:27); "God chose what is foolish in the world to shame the wise." That newspaper went under because of the prayer of a poor "dumb" woman. She went on praying for the same intention, and a second newspaper, and then a third one, succeeding the first and likewise doing great harm to souls, also went under (*Letter 7 Oct 1950*, no. 12).

The founder of *El Sol*, *Crisol*, and *Luz* was José Ortega y Gasset. See *Apuntes*, no. 522; for more on the history and the fall of these newspapers, see Gonzalo Redondo, *Las empresas políticas de José Ortega y Gasset.* *"El Sol," "Crisol" y "Luz" (1917–1934)*, Madrid, 1970.

[106] See *Apuntes*, no. 302.

[107] *Apuntes*, no. 390.

[108] *Apuntes*, no. 430.

[109] *Apuntes*, no. 205.

[110] *Apuntes*, no. 244.

[111] See Alvaro del Portillo, *Sum.* 257 and *Sum.* 258.

[112] *Apuntes*, no. 207.

[113] *Apuntes*, nos. 208 and 209. The feast of Saint Ephrem was at that time June 18 [it is now June 9], but, as it turned out, Father Josemaría did not stop working at the Foundation until October 28 (see *Apuntes*, no. 209, note 236). He did not leave his position until the nuns found someone to take his place. See Alvaro del Portillo, *Sum.* 257. The date of his leaving is corroborated in the 23 Jun 1931 entry for him in the ministerial faculties records book, which mentions the church of Santa Barbara and not the Foundation.

[114] Letter of 30 Jun 1931 from Father Luis Tallada to Father Josemaría: original in AGP, RHF, D–15399.

Beginning in 1929 the Apostolic Ladies had a novitiate in Chamartín. Its chaplain was the father superior of the Holy Family community in Madrid. In those early years the mistress of novices was Asunción Muñoz, and she testifies that they were also often visited by the chaplain of the Foundation. See E. Itúrbide, *El Amor dijo sí* (Pamplona, 1962), pp. 175–77, and Asunción Muñoz, AGP, RHF, T–04393, p. 4.

From what can be deduced from his correspondence with Father Luis Tallada, Father Josemaría also was acquainted with other Holy Family priests in Madrid.

[115] *Apuntes*, no. 689.

[116] See *Apuntes*, no. 356. (The "Miravalles," or "marquises of Miravalles," were counts of Aguilar de Inestrillas.) Of this incident Bishop Alvaro del Portillo comments, "It was a small thing, of no actual importance,

our Father assured me, but the Lord allowed it to really hurt him" (*Apuntes*, no. 356, note 338). Afterward, when he went to say good-bye to the nuns, Father Josemaría not only forgot what had pained him so much, but asked their pardon for whatever it was. "The affairs of the Foundation . . . I took care of them as Father S. had told me to: very affectionately. I went back to them to ask pardon for whatever I might have done to disedify them with my temper, etc." (*Apuntes*, no. 363). ("Father S." is Father Valentín Sánchez Ruiz, his confessor.) On the admiration and appreciation that he would always have for the Apostolic Ladies and their activities, see Alvaro del Portillo, *Sum.* 447, and Javier Echevarría, *Sum.* 2077.

[117] See the application submitted by Father Josemaría to the Ministry of Labor on 26 Jan 1934, in the Patrimonio Nacional archive, "Patronatos Reales," "Patronato de Santa Isabel," file 182/21.

[118] It was in July that Father Josemaría first heard about the state of neglect that the chaplaincy of Santa Isabel was in. It was mentioned to him by Catalina García del Rey, a lay auxiliary of the Apostolic Ladies (see *Apuntes*, no. 354).

Sister Cecilia Gómez Jiménez, relaying the tradition handed down in the convent, says, "According to what I've heard the sisters say, coming here to celebrate Mass meant risking one's life; so no one wanted to come, and so they were left without a chaplain" (Cecilia Gómez Jiménez, *Sum.* 6515).

[119] See José Luis Sáenz Ruiz-Olalde, O.A.R., *Las Agustinas Recoletas de Santa Isabel la Real, de Madrid*, Madrid: Real Monasterio de Santa Isabel, 1990. See also Leticia Sánchez Hernández, "El convento de Santa Isabel: Madrid 1589-1989," in *Real Fundación del Convento de Santa Isabel de Madrid*: Patrimonio Nacional, 1990.

[120] See, in the 21 Apr 1931 and 22 Apr 1931 editions of *Gaceta de Madrid*, "Decreto del 20–IV–1931 sobre Bienes del Patrimonio de la Corona." See also, in the 24 Apr 1931 edition, the decree of 22 Apr 1931 by which a committee was set up in the Ministry of the Interior to direct the foundations of the defunct Royal House, and in the 26 Nov 1931 edition, "Decreto del 20–XI–1931 sobre Provisión de vacantes en Patronatos de la Corona." Whatever vacancies exist or arise, says this last decree, "will be filled by the president of the Republic, or the president of the government, in accord with the suggestions of the Secretary of the Interior."

[121] On the palace jurisdiction depended the royal foundations, and Father Palmer's offices were in one of these: the Patronato de Nuestra Señora del Buen Suceso. See the Patrimonio Nacional archive, "Patronatos Reales," file 2756/22. See also, in the same file, the 2 Feb 1933 letter from the Council for the Administration of the Patrimony of the Republic to Bishop Ramón Pérez Rodríguez, Patriarch of the Indies,

announcing its takeover of the archive and office (at 2 Quintana) of the abolished Pro-Chaplaincy Major of the Palace—which at that point was *still* exercising the palace jurisdiction.

[122] For more on the responsibilities of the chaplains, see Joaquín Alonso, PR, p. 1738; Cecilia Gómez Jiménez, *Sum.* 6510; Juan Jiménez Vargas, *Sum.* 6703; and Santiago Escrivá de Balaguer, *Sum.* 7328.

Father Buenaventura Gutiérrez y Sanjuán was ordained in Toledo in 1904, became Honorary Chaplain of His Majesty on January 29, 1909, and was named rector of the Royal Foundation of Santa Isabel on December 1, 1919. He held the latter position until "on June 16, 1931, he was dropped by virtue of a government order that eliminated from the roster of active service employees all persons who had been assigned to the chapel of what had been the royal palace" (Patrimonio Nacional archive, "Patronatos Reales," "Patronato de Santa Isabel," file 182/20). See also E. Subirana, op. cit., 1931, p. 430.

[123] Father José Cicuéndez Aparicio, the director of the Cicuéndez Academy, had been named chaplain of Santa Isabel in July 1910. He died at Villa de Don Fadrique (in Toledo) in November 1932. (See the Patrimonio Nacional archive, "Patronatos Reales," "Patronato de Santa Isabel," file 182/17, and also E. Subirana, op. cit., 1931, p. 430.)

[124] See letter dated Madrid, 9 Jul 1931, from a "Dr. Cifuentes" of the Ministry of the Interior to Father Juan Causapié, "Majordomo of the Foundation, Hospital, and Church of Buen Suceso," notifying him of his appointment as interim rector-administrator: in the Patrimonio Nacional archive, "Patronatos Reales," "Patronato de Santa Isabel," file 178/73. See also E. Subirana, op. cit., 1931, p. 430.

[125] *Apuntes*, no. 225.

[126] *Apuntes*, no. 294.

[127] *Apuntes*, no. 387.

[128] *Apuntes*, no. 403.

[129] *Apuntes*, no. 497.

[130] *Letter 29 Dec 1947/14 Feb 1966*, no. 89.

[131] *Apuntes*, nos. 217 and 218. In the diocese of Madrid-Alcalá the feast of the Transfiguration of the Lord was celebrated on August 7 because August 6 was also the feast of Saints Justo and Pastor, the principal patron saints of the diocese.

The capital of Spain had always been called the Villa of Madrid. In the era of the monarchy it was called the Villa and Court, because the royal court was there. At the time Father Josemaría was writing these entries, the Republic had been proclaimed a few months earlier; hence his use of the expression "ex-Court."

The Offering to the Merciful Love was in those days a very popular prayer. It goes like this: "Holy Father, through the Immaculate Heart of Mary I offer you Jesus your most beloved Son, and in him, through him, and with him I offer myself for all his intentions and on behalf of all creatures." (See Alvaro del Portillo, *Sum.* 337 and *Sum.* 1118.)

Later in this chapter we will say more about this Merciful Love devotion.

[132] Testifying to this grace of 7 Aug 1931, having heard of it directly from the founder himself, are Alvaro del Portillo (*Sum.* 1711), Javier Echevarría (PR, p. 1698), Mario Lantini (*Sum.* 3741), and Julián Herranz (PR, p. 982). The idea of work as a means of sanctification and apostolate was constantly present in the preaching and writings of the founder. See, for example, *Letter 11 Mar 1940*, nos. 11–13, and *Christ Is Passing By*, nos. 14, 39, 105, 156, and 183.

[133] See Eph 1:10.

[134] *Letter 11 Mar 1940*, no. 13.

[135] *Apuntes*, no. 92.

[136] *Letter 29 Dec 1947/14 Feb 1966*, no. 5.

[137] *Apuntes*, no. 273. Prior to this locution of 7 Sep 1931, he had written of Opus Dei: "It will fill the whole world, and will be spread all over the globe, . . . so that the whole earth will be one single flock with one single Shepherd" (*Apuntes*, nos. 92 and 134).

[138] *Letter 9 Jan 1932*, no. 93. The last sentence is from Psalm 104:31.

[139] *Apuntes*, no. 629.

[140] *Apuntes*, no. 284. In the *Instruction* of 19 Mar 1934, nos. 28 and 29, this idea is picked up and related to something he had said on September 10, 1931 (*Apuntes*, no. 277) with explicit reference to the Work and to each of its members. The passage in the *Instruction* reads:

> Our Lord does not want an ephemeral identity for his Work. He asks of us an immortal identity, because he wants there to be in it— in the Work—a group nailed to the cross. The holy cross will make us everlasting, always with the same spirit of the Gospel, which will bring about the apostolate of action as the savory fruit of prayer and sacrifice.
>
> In this way the Work of God and each of its members will come to live that divine secret that Saint Paul taught in Philippians 2:5–11, the surest route to immortality and glory: through humiliation, to the cross; and from the cross, with Christ, to the immortal glory of the Father.

[141] *Apuntes*, no. 296.

[142] *Apuntes*, nos. 317 and 326.

[143] *Apuntes*, no. 334. Returning, years later, to the memory of that day, he

would write: "The most sublime prayer I have ever experienced . . . was when I was riding a streetcar, and then walking through the streets of Madrid, contemplating that marvelous reality, God is my Father. I remember that, without being able to help it, I kept repeating, 'Abba, Pater!' They must have thought I was crazy" (*Instruction* of May 1935/September 1950, no. 22, note 28). Through this experience our Lord showed him that "the street does not impede our contemplative dialogue; the hubbub of the world is for us a place of prayer" (*Letter 9 Jan 1959*, no. 60).

Referring to divine filiation, which is the basis of the spirituality of Opus Dei, he wrote: "This characteristic feature of our spirit was born with the Work and took shape in 1931, in moments that were difficult, humanly speaking, but in which I nevertheless had a certainty of the impossible, of what today you see become a reality" (*Letter 9 Jan 1959*, no. 60).

[144] *Apuntes*, no. 60, and *Letter 8 Dec 1949*, no. 41. See also Alvaro del Portillo, *Sum.* 1077 and *Sum.* 1297.

[145] Mt 5:48, quoted in *Letter 24 Mar 1930*, no. 2.

[146] *Meditation* of 24 Dec 1969.

[147] *Meditation* of 2 Oct 1971.

[148] *Letter 8 Dec 1949*, no. 41.

[149] *Apuntes*, no. 357. As he himself would say, the very thought that it is possible to fear God made him suffer. See Alvaro del Portillo, *Sum.* 1030, and Javier Echevarría, *Sum.* 2517.

[150] See *Apuntes*, no. 358. Once he calmed down, there came over him one of those highly intense transports of prayer that filled him with interior joy (see *Apuntes*, nos. 358 and 359).

[151] *Apuntes*, no. 364. See also Alvaro del Portillo, *Sum.* 1030; Mario Lantini, *Sum.* 3666; and Ignacio Celaya, *Sum.* 5935.

[152] *Apuntes*, no. 476.

[153] Words of a homily of 2 Oct 1968, recorded in AGP, P02 1968.

[154] Letter of 20 Nov 1931 from Father José Pou de Foxá to Father Josemaría: original in AGP, RHF, D–15309.

[155] Letter of 17 Dec 1931 from Father Ambrosio Sanz to Father Josemaría: original in AGP, RHF, D–15241. Ordained in Santander in 1911, Father Ambrosio Sanz Lavilla had doctorates in both sacred theology and canon law. He became a canon of Barbastro in 1927 and taught at the seminary in that city until 1956, the year of his death. (See E. Subirana, op. cit., 1928, p. 103.)

In journal entry no. 423 we read, "Yesterday I wrote to the canon of Barbastro, Father Ambrosio Sanz, asking for prayers," and this is obviously written on the same day as entry no. 421, which is dated "Vigil of the Apostle Saint Andrew"—in other words, November 29.

Father Ambrosio, however, refers to "your letter of the 26th of last month." It is possible that, barring a lapse of memory, Father Josemaría dated his letter the 26th but continued writing and mailed it on the 28th.

[156] *Apuntes*, no. 274 (9 Sep 1931).

[157] *Apuntes*, no. 301.

[158] *Apuntes*, no. 560.

[159] *Apuntes*, introductory note.

[160] *Apuntes*, no. 307. See also *Meditation* of 14 Feb 1964.

[161] *Apuntes*, no. 335.

[162] *Apuntes*, no. 350.

[163] *Apuntes*, no. 351.

[164] *Apuntes*, no. 355.

[165] *Apuntes*, no. 356 (28 Oct 1931).

[166] *Apuntes*, no. 363.

[167] *Apuntes*, no. 387 (12 Nov 1931).

[168] *Apuntes*, no. 388.

[169] See *Apuntes*, no. 415.

[170] *Apuntes*, no. 416.

[171] *Apuntes*, no. 429.

[172] *Apuntes*, no. 426.

[173] *Apuntes*, no. 467.

[174] *Apuntes*, no. 493.

[175] *Apuntes*, no. 493.

[176] "In this Madrid," said Doña Dolores, "we are going through purgatory." See *Apuntes*, no. 500 (23 Dec 1931).

[177] *Apuntes*, no. 523.

[178] See *Apuntes*, no. 564 (14 Jan 1932).

[179] See *Apuntes*, no. 597 (15 Feb 1932).

[180] *Apuntes*, no. 596.

[181] For more on this prelate, see Sebastián Cirac Estopañán, *Vida de Don Cruz Laplana, Obispo de Cuenca*, Barcelona, 1943.

[182] See AGP, P01 1979, p. 251.

[183] *Apuntes*, no. 598.

[184] *Apuntes*, no. 599.

[185] *Apuntes*, no. 587.

[186] *Letter 8 Dec 1949*, no. 41.

[187] *Apuntes*, no. 307.

[188] *Apuntes*, no. 328. Article 26 of the Constitution (article 24 of the draft), which was approved on the morning of October 14, 1931, said: "Hereby dissolved are those religious orders which juridically impose, besides the

three canonical vows, a special vow of obedience to an authority other than the legitimate one of the state."

There was no doubt about the main target of this article. By a decree published on January 24, 1932, all Jesuit schools, novitiates, and residences were shut down. See Gonzalo Redondo, *Historia de la Iglesia en España (1931–1939)* (Madrid: Rialp, 1993), vol. 1, pp. 164ff.

[189] *Apuntes,* no. 328. "That statue of the Child Jesus," comments Bishop del Portillo, "gave our Father occasion for a lot of prayer and a lot of acts of love for the most holy humanity of Jesus. He used to ask the nuns for it, especially around Christmastime, and go around dancing with it and rocking it and caressing it."

[190] *Apuntes,* no. 347. He goes on to say in this entry, "You make me feel that the Work of God will not have any special devotions or images such as the religious families usually have. (The Merciful Love devotion, as well as the teaching behind it, is universal.)"

The Merciful Love devotion was one of the founder's personal devotions. From written accounts—both his own and those of witnesses—we know that he practiced it from his first years in Madrid (see *Apuntes,* nos. 432 and 1380, and Alvaro del Portillo, *Sum.* 1268), and that, every day, he made a mental offering to the Merciful Love right after the Consecration of his Mass (see *Apuntes,* no. 217; Alvaro del Portillo, *Sum.* 337, 1118, and 1119; Javier Echevarría, *Sum.* 2580; and Joaquín Alonso, *Sum.* 4751). He also propagated this devotion, handing out or sending prayer cards to people (see *Apuntes,* no. 1029, and José Ramón Herrero Fontana, AGP, RHF, T–05834, p. 1).

The Merciful Love devotion is a complement to and development of the Sacred Heart devotion. It was begun in France, in connection with Saint Thérèse of Lisieux and her path of spiritual childhood, by a Salesian religious, Marie Thérèse Desandais.

[191] *Apuntes,* no. 570.

[192] *Apuntes,* no. 435. On the following day (1 Dec 1931) he adds, "Spiritual childhood! Spiritual childhood is not spiritual silliness or *weakness;* it is a sensible and vigorous way which, due to its difficult easiness, the soul must begin and continue led by the very hand of God" (*Apuntes,* no. 438).

[193] *Apuntes,* no. 574.

[194] *Apuntes,* no. 435.

[195] *Apuntes,* no. 435.

[196] *Apuntes,* no. 437.

[197] See *Apuntes,* no. 454, note 382. He sent his confessor the original manuscript, of December 1931, along with a note saying, "I'm handing over to you these mimeographed pages for the purpose of giving *our friends* a

push along the path of contemplation" (see AGP, RHF, D–04668). And on 1 Jan 1932 he wrote, "Yesterday I was with Father Sánchez. He returned to me, with notes written in the margins, my sheets on the Holy Rosary" (*Apuntes*, no. 529).

Very modestly, and with the intention of giving the copies away, he had the text published in 1934 in Madrid, at Juan Bravo Press, with ecclesiastical approval, as "*Santo Rosario*, by José María."

The first edition after the civil war (José María Escrivá, *Santo Rosario*, Gráficas Turia de Valencia) probably was published at the beginning of October 1939, since its ecclesiastical approval was obtained on October 2, 1939. This edition has a foreword by the bishop of Vitoria and was printed as a booklet.

The first commercial edition (Josemaría Escrivá de Balaguer, *Santo Rosario*, Madrid: Minerva, 1945), unlike the previous ones, came out in a book format, of small size, and with beautiful illustrations. The author slightly amplified the text of 1934 in his commentary on some of the mysteries.

[198] *Holy Rosary* (Scepter, 1979), first joyful mystery.

His journal entry for August 15, 1931, seems to indicate that previously, at least on occasion, he had used this method of contemplation: "Feast of the Assumption of Our Lady, 1931: Yesterday and today I pestered our Lady, maybe to the point of getting tiresome, asking her protection for the W. of G. I'm going to make, starting this evening, a novena to our Mother, celebrating her assumption in body and soul to heaven. I really rejoice, feeling like I'm there . . . with the Blessed Trinity, with the angels receiving their Queen, with all the saints acclaiming their Mother and Lady" (*Apuntes*, no. 228).

[199] *Apuntes*, no. 226 (13 Aug 1931). Later entries referring to the "Lady of the Kisses" are *Apuntes*, nos. 239, 325, 488, 701, and 702.

[200] *Apuntes*, no. 484. Bishop del Portillo adds this commentary: "Our Father did not like to talk about events of a supernatural nature that had to do with just him, personally. Nevertheless, he told me this story on more than one occasion. In relating it, I must point out that the time when it took place was not one in which mistakes could easily be made, because it was a sunny day and only three in the afternoon. When the Father related to me what his defender had said to him, he told me that he had heard 'burrito, burrito,' which was what our Father used to call himself, but that no one had known this except for his confessor (Father Sánchez) and, of course, our Lord God. The Father attributed the attack to the action of the devil, and the defense to his guardian angel" (*Apuntes*, no. 484, note 397).

[201] *Apuntes*, no. 485.

[202] The feast of the Holy Innocents in Spain is equivalent to April Fools'

Day in English-speaking countries, and the jokes are like what the French call "poissons d'avril" and the Italians call "il pesce d'april" [both expressions mean "April fish"].

203 *Apuntes,* nos. 516, 517, and 518.

204 *Apuntes,* no. 528. "Mother Carmen de San José (now deceased), who was sacristan at the time when Father Josemaría was chaplain, said that the community had, and has continued to have, a small Child Jesus which is brought to the church only at Christmastime, for veneration, and that when they passed it to him via the revolving window, they could hear him speaking to the Child very familiarly and calling him sweet names as though the statue were a living child, and that sometimes the Servant of God would ask them to let him bring this Child home with him, so that he could do his prayer in its presence, and afterward would return it to the community" (Cecilia Gómez Jiménez, *Sum.* 6511).

The sisters at Santa Isabel have recently issued holy cards with a picture of the statue on the front and this text on the back:

THE CHILD JESUS OF MONSIGNOR ESCRIVA

The Royal Convent of the Augustinian Recollect Sisters of Madrid-Atocha-Santa Isabel, founded by Blessed Alonso de Orozco in 1589, has a rich history of art and sanctity. Although very many of its treasures were destroyed by flames in the civil conflict of 1936–1939, there remains a small image of the Child Jesus, carved in wood, apparently dating from the 17th century, which in former times was exhibited, and still is exhibited, during the Christmas season for the veneration of the faithful.

Monsignor Josemaría Escrivá de Balaguer, the founder of Opus Dei, was chaplain and senior rector of this monastery from 1931 to 1946. The contemplative nuns there still keep very much alive the memory of that young priest so much in love with the Eucharist and so much given to prayer. And they cherish in particular the memory of the unusual affinity of Father Escrivá for this Christ Child, by means of which they believe he received some very extraordinary graces. The priest often took the already famous statue to his home, with the permission of the prioress, and when he returned it he always seemed deeply moved and jubilant. At that time he was consumed with mystical fervor. It was then that he wrote the book *The Way* (under the title *Spiritual Considerations*), as well as his little tract *Holy Rosary.*

People come from the most distant countries to contemplate and venerate this little statue of the Christ Child of Monsignor Escrivá at the convent of the Augustinian Recollect sisters.

205 *Apuntes,* no. 560.

206 *Apuntes,* no. 562 (14 Jan 1932). He continues:

> I think I already read it once, but without giving it much impor-
> tance, and without, apparently, its leaving any trace in my spirit. It
> was Mercedes who first made me understand and admire and want
> to put into practice the synthesis of her admirable life: to hide one-
> self and disappear. But this plan of life, which was for her the con-
> sequence, the savory fruit, of an intimate and profound humility, is,
> when all is said and done, nothing other than the essence of spiritual
> childhood. So, then, little Thérèse took me and led me, with Mer-
> cedes, through Mary, my Mother and Lady, to the love of Jesus.

His approach as founder to this path of spirituality is expressed in
his journal entry for 2 Jan 1932: "When I say in these Catherines that
our Lord wants the members to know and live the life of spiritual childhood, it is not my intention to 'homogenize' the souls of 'people of
God.' On the contrary, . . . what I see is that (1) each and every one of
the members should know about the life of spiritual childhood, and (2)
no member should ever be forced to follow this path, nor any other particular spiritual path" (*Apuntes,* no. 535). As he will later write, he is not
imposing this path on his spiritual children, but he is recommending it
(see *Letter 8 Dec 1949,* no. 41).

207 *Apuntes,* no. 543.

208 "I was a little embarrassed," the entry continues, "because I only remembered the passage from chapter 21 of Saint Matthew, and so I thought
that Jesus sat on a female donkey for his entry into Jerusalem. But now I
open up the Gospels (how poor I am in exegesis!) and read in chapter 11
of Saint Mark verses 2, 4, 5, and 7, and find there, 'Et ait illis: ite in castel-
lum, quod contra vos est, et statim introeuntes illuc, invenietis *pullum* lig-
atum, . . . Et duxerunt *pullum* ad Iesum: et imponunt illi vestimenta sua, et
sedit super eum.' [See also Lk 19:30, 35; and Jn 12:14–15.] R. Ch. V.

"Good child, tell Jesus many times each day, I love you, I love you, I
love you."

["R. Ch. V." stands for "Regnare Christum volumus": "We want
Christ to reign."]

Bishop del Portillo comments: "This was a taste of honey that the Lord
gave to our Father, and that filled him with joy and peace. As for the Father's remark about 'how poor I am in exegesis,' we might note that he always got the highest possible grades in scriptural exegesis, of which he
took four courses. What happened was that our Lord blinded him for a
few moments so that he would have to make himself good and sure about
those Gospel passages, and thus not have to suffer any more doubts about

that locution: that was our Father's comment" (*Apuntes*, no. 543, note 451). See also Javier Echevarría, *Sum.* 3272; Julián Herranz, *Sum.* 4029; José Luis Múzquiz, *Sum.* 5853; and César Ortiz-Echagüe, *Sum.* 6902.

[209] *Apuntes*, no. 421.

[210] *Apuntes*, no. 606; see also *The Way*, no. 933. Concerning this intellectual locution from our Lord, Bishop del Portillo says that "our Father was very moved by it" not because he was getting lax in his prayer life, but because "the Lord was asking more from him and, with this locution, giving him light by which he was catching on to 'many unexpected details'" (*Apuntes*, no. 606, note 496). See also Javier Echevarría, *Sum.* 3272; Julián Herranz, PR, p. 982; Ernesto Juliá, *Sum.* 4245; Giovanni Udaondo, *Sum.* 5083; Cecilia Gómez Jiménez, *Sum.* 6517; and María Isabel Laporte, *Sum.* 5189.

[211] *Apuntes*, no. 653.

[212] *Apuntes*, no. 430.

[213] *Apuntes*, no. 582 (24 Jan 1932). This entry continues, "Father Norberto often tells me that I will lose this and will suffer. I don't believe it, Jesus. I can't see you taking away from me what you have so generously given me. But just in case you do want to, from this moment on, forever, I tell you this: do it."

[214] *Apuntes*, no. 690.

[215] *Apuntes*, no. 618. The founder had organized his devotions by days of the week: "Sunday I will dedicate to the Blessed Trinity; Monday, to my good friends the souls in purgatory; Tuesday, to my guardian angel and all other guardian angels, and to all the angels of heaven without distinction; Wednesday, to my father and lord Saint Joseph; Thursday, to the Blessed Eucharist; Friday, to the Passion of Jesus; Saturday, to the Blessed Virgin Mary, my Mother" (*Apuntes*, no. 568 [18 Jan 1932]).

The "Mercedes" to whom he refers is the previously mentioned religious of the Apostolic Ladies of the Sacred Heart—Mercedes Reyna O'Farril—who died in 1929 with a reputation for holiness. Father Josemaría intended to write a biography of this nun and spent some time collecting documentation from her family. Among his letters are a number to Doña Rosario Reyna de Ribas, a sister of Mercedes. See *C* 2 (21 Jul 1929); see also *C* nos. 3, 4, 5, 6, 8, 9, 11, and 13.

In a letter to Rosario Reyna dated 28 Jan 1932, written in response to her request for the return of Mercedes' letters, he asks for more time for the sake of his biographical work, which, he says, has been delayed due to "the political circumstances, first of all; then, the burning of convents, which forced me to change residence, leaving the Foundation; and finally, the hard necessity of having to make a living." Furthermore, he adds, "the fact that the present moment is not a very good one for editorial ventures has also hindered my progress on the path which I had traced out" (*C* 25,

28 Jan 1932). As is indicated in later letters, Father Josemaría ended up having to return the documents without being able to work on the biography of Mercedes Reyna: see *C 27* (5 Feb 1932), *C 29* (17 Apr 1932), and *C 37* (1 Oct 1932).

[216] *Apuntes,* no. 563.

[217] See *Apuntes,* no. 618.

[218] *Apuntes,* no. 673.

[219] See *Apuntes,* no. 556. The term he used was "grandísimo tiñoso."

[220] *Apuntes,* no. 659 (13 Mar 1932).

[221] *Apuntes,* no. 671 (23 Mar 1932).

[222] *Apuntes,* no. 693.

[223] *Apuntes,* no. 671.

[224] *Apuntes,* no. 482.

[225] *Apuntes,* no. 393.

Notes to Chapter 7

[1] This holy man, Bernardino de Obregón, had founded the Hospital de Convalecientes, on Fuencarral Street. With the hospital experience he had acquired over the years, he proposed that the king consider creating a general hospital, whose administration he thought should be entrusted to a committee of illustrious and pious persons, presided over by someone from the Tribunal of the Council of Castile, with its support coming from donations, bequests, alms, and, later on, payments from the Treasury and from Madrid's city council. This royal foundation received important donations and bequests from Kings Philip II, Philip III, Philip V, Fernando VI (who donated to it Madrid's bullring), Carlos III, and Fernando VII.

The hospital represented a real medical revolution for its time, and became one of the best hospitals of Europe.

King Philip III assisted at the funeral of Brother Bernardino de Obregón, and also in the process of his beatification.

See *Memoria de la Excma. Diputación Provincial de Madrid—La labor de seis años: 1924–1929,* Madrid, 1929, pp. 17–23; and *Como yo os amé,* published by the Hospital Brothers of St. Philip Neri in Madrid: issue no. 1 (14 May 1967), pp. 31–33.

[2] Construction of this building, which was to follow the plans drawn up by Herrera for Philip II, was held up by an appeal to the Holy See that took over eighty years to be decided. Thus it began during the reign of Fernando VI and was completed by Carlos III's architects: Hermosilla and Sabatini.

Annexed to the School of Medicine was the hospital clinic. In 1931 this occupied a wing of the General Hospital, having been ceded to the state by a settlement in accord with the Royal Decree of 24 Dec 1903 (see *Memoria*, p. 17).

The General Hospital was a huge, 242,000-square-foot building—rectangular, with spacious corridors. At one time it had a capacity of 2,000 beds. During the sixties it ceased to be used for medical purposes. Today a part of the old building has been renovated and is the Queen Sofía Cultural Center.

3 *Apuntes*, no. 731.

4 *Apuntes*, no. 360.

5 See "El R. P. José María Escrivá de Balaguer y la Congregación de Hermanos Filipenses," in *Como yo os amé*, no. 32 (1 Oct 1975), pp. 5–6. This article presents interesting recollections of the Philippians about the chaplain of the sisters at Santa Isabel, although there are some errors in dates.

One instance: "Our Brother Antonio Díaz informed him of our existence and of our prayer services for the sick." This statement is completely consistent with *Apuntes*, no. 360, and is not contradicted by the testimony of another witness that it was from a medical student, Adolfo Gómez Ruiz, that he learned of the hospital's situation, and that he then thought of collaborating with the Philippians in order to "get into the hospital to take care of the sick, and be allowed to use their chapel to do his prayer" (José Romeo, AGP, RHF, T–03809, pp. 7–8). The talk with Adolfo Gómez was evidently subsequent to the one with the sacristan, and probably prior to Father Josemaría's first visit to the hospital, which took place two Sundays later.

6 *Apuntes*, no. 360.

7 See *Apuntes*, nos. 381 and 383. The Congregation of St. Philip Neri of Lay Servants of the Sick of the Holy General Hospital of Madrid was founded in 1694. Its constitutions were first approved in 1707, by the archbishop of Toledo, and were modified and reapproved on 4 May 1745.

The Congregation was a continuation of the Obregón Hospital Brothers, and had for its use one of the hospital wards. At the end of the nineteenth century the Philippians were authorized to build a chapel, with offices attached, in the garden surrounding the hospital.

The objective of the Congregation was to reach out in charity to the sick, "seeing in each of them a living image of Christ our King, reflecting on his saying that whatever one does for them he will take as done to himself, and realizing that the reward he is offering is nothing less than his eternal glory" (*Constituciones de la Congregación de nuestro Padre y Patriarca San Felipe Neri de Seglares*, Madrid, 1899, p. 22).

The internal government of the organization was made up of an Eldest Brother and a Council of Elders. There were at the time very few brothers in the Congregation of the General Hospital of Madrid, and since all were laymen, they were to consult in certain situations with two priests, called Advisors.

In 1931 the priests of St. Philip Neri were not living in Madrid but resided in Alcalá de Henares. So, for some time, the Advisors were diocesan priests. See *Libros de Actas de Juntas de Ancianos de la Congregación, en su sede de la calle de Antonio Arias*, no. 17.

[8] *Constituciones*, p. 22. The Philippians also buried the dead and distributed food and clothing among the sick. Because of this, they were also popularly known as "the Soup Brothers."

[9] *Apuntes*, no. 647.

[10] José Romeo, AGP, RHF, T–03809, p. 8.

[11] Despite the optimism and discretion with which the abovementioned *Memoria* was written, one only need read the sections about the problems caused by a lack of beds in the hospital to get an idea of the conditions there. In the volumes of *Libros de Actas de Sesiones de la Diputación de Madrid* (in Madrid's city library) for 1930 to 1932, there is a continuation of the story of the "calamities" which one of the brothers of the Congregation, Patricio González de Canales, mentions in a letter (dated 18 Jul 1967) to the rector of the Basilica of San Miguel (see AGP, RHF, D–15312). For example, ten or twelve patients fled the hospital every day, since the doorkeepers could not keep track of "the thousands of patients in the hospital" (vol. 95 [1931], fol. 219); a war of words was underway over a proposal to replace the hospital's Daughters of Charity with lay nurses; and when some of the sick people in the wards petitioned that the brothers of the Congregation of St. Philip Neri be allowed to continue their work, the petition was rejected (see vol. 96 [1932], fol. 75).

The founder occasionally spoke of "that General Hospital of Madrid, loaded with sick, destitute people, people lying in the corridors because they did not have beds." See Gonzalo Herranz, "Sin miedo a la vida y sin miedo a la muerte," in *Memoria*, pp. 139–40.

[12] See "El R. P. José María Escrivá."

[13] See José Romeo, AGP, RHF, T–03809, p. 8; Jenaro Lázaro, AGP, RHF, T–00310, p. 1; and Alvaro del Portillo, *Sum.* 263.

[14] *Apuntes*, no. 433.

[15] *Apuntes*, nos. 383 and 433.

[16] *Apuntes*, no. 609.

[17] *Apuntes*, no. 608.

[18] *Apuntes*, no. 609. See also Alvaro del Portillo, *Sum.* 262, and Javier Echevarría, *Sum.* 1961.

[19] See José Romeo, AGP, RHF, T–03809, p. 8, and José Manuel Doménech, AGP, RHF, T–00872.

[20] *Constituciones*, p. 26.

[21] See *Letter 15 Oct 1948*, no. 192. See also Alvaro del Portillo, *Sum.* 264; Javier Echevarría, *Sum.* 1960; and *The Way*, no. 626.

[22] See vol. 96 of *Libros de Actas de Sesiones de la Diputación de Madrid*, especially fols. 75, 135, 136, 147, 147v, 160v, and 162.

In *Apuntes*, no. 685, Father Josemaría writes: "April 5, 1932: Last Sunday I made my profession in the Congregation of St. Philip. I know this pleased the Lord."

This note refers to the formal ceremony. Actually, he had been taking part in the spiritual exercises of the Congregation since 1931 (see *Apuntes*, no. 622).

We do not know with certainty how the measures taken by the directors of the General Hospital affected the Congregation of St. Philip Neri and its brothers during 1933, since this was not a congregation of religious, but, rather, a simple charitable confraternity.

[23] See letter of 10 Jun 1934 from Tomás Mínguez (the Brother Secretary) to Father Josemaría: original in AGP, RHF, D–15312. According to its constitutions, the Congregation was to have two Advisors, with neither voice nor vote in its government, and, as a rule, these were to be priests of the Congregation of the Oratory of St. Philip Neri (see *Como yo os amé*, 14 May 1967, pp. 11–12). Since in 1931 the Oratorians resided far from Madrid and traveling was hazardous, it is quite possible that Father Josemaría carried out the functions of an Advisor and led the prayers in the chapel in 1931 and 1932. This is implied by something said by Brother Patricio: "Father Escrivá made contact with us, and shortly thereafter was named Father Advisor" (see "El R. P. José María Escrivá").

Nowhere does he himself say that he was an Advisor. However, a statement in his journal entry for 21 Nov 1932, "Father Sánchez has a file on my activities in the Congregation of St. Philip; I am under obedience" (*Apuntes*, no. 871), together with what he says on 9 Dec 1934 about "the matter of the hospital" (*Apuntes*, no. 948), leads one to believe that when the priests of the Oratory of Alcalá de Henares resumed their responsibilities as Advisors (see José Romeo, AGP, RHF, T–03809, p. 8), there must have been a diversity of opinion about the policies to be followed in the hospital in light of the obstacles created by the authorities.

[24] This supposition is corroborated by two loose notes, written in 1934, saying "Sunday: Santa Isabel—Class or catechism. Afternoon, hospital" and "Sunday: morning, General Hospital" (*Apuntes*, nos. 1794 and 1796).

The spiritual exercises of the Congregation were held in the afternoon, at the General Hospital. Apparently, then, the chaplain of Santa Isabel took care of the sick independently of the schedule of visits by the Philippians.

[25] In its session of March 22, 1932, for approving the Ministry of Justice budget, the Cortes, to wipe out obligations to the Church, cut the

66.9 million pesetas allocated for it in the 1931 budget to 29.5 million. All diocesan ecclesiastical personnel depended on this budget for religion and the clergy: some 35,000 men (bishops, canons, pastors, and curates).

[26] See A. Valdés, "Quincuagésimo aniversario de la muerte de José María Somoano Berdasco," in the 15 Aug 1982 edition of *La Nueva España*.

[27] See J. Torres Gost, *Medio siglo en el hospital del Rey*, Madrid, 1975, and Alvaro del Portillo, *Sum.* 264. With the coming of the Republic, King's Hospital began to call itself the National Hospital, although people continued to call it King's Hospital.

[28] *Apuntes*, no. 541.

[29] *Apuntes*, no. 545. Thus he administered those prayers of pain: "Lino and the two José María's have been charged, each of them, with winning one vocation. I have asked them to apply to this end the expiation being done at King's Hospital" (*Apuntes*, no. 552). The priests were Fathers Lino Vea-Murguía, José María Somoano, and José María Vegas.

[30] *Apuntes*, no. 685.

[31] *Apuntes*, no. 640. "Her suggestions seem to come from God. She is always right," he adds. In that same month of March 1932—two weeks, that is, after he consulted Doña Dolores—the Ministry of Justice budget for religion and the clergy was cut by over 50 percent, and shortly afterward the chaplaincies were suppressed.

[32] Engracia Echevarría, AGP, RHF, T–04389, p. 1. See also Isabel Martín Rodríguez, *Sum.* 5774, and María Jesús Sanz Zubiría, AGP, RHF, T–05138, p. 1.

[33] See *Apuntes*, no. 1003.

[34] *Apuntes*, no. 785.

[35] See *Apuntes*, no. 789.

[36] See *Apuntes*, no. 793.

[37] *Apuntes*, no. 785. See also Alvaro del Portillo, *Sum.* 267; Joaquín Alonso, *Sum.* 4615; and J. M. Cejas, *José María Somoano en los comienzos del Opus Dei*, Madrid, Rialp, 1995.

[38] Engracia Echevarría, AGP, RHF, T–04389, p. 1. "The government budget for all establishments requiring the presence of clergy was eliminated," explains Sister Engracia. "Our hospital's chief of staff, Dr. Manuel Tapia, was a man of a high moral caliber. He was very honorable, very respectful, and very reasonable, although he was poorly informed about the duties of the Christian. . . . Always he acted with great propriety. And so, when the budget for the clergy disappeared, he called and said that from our stipend as hospital workers, which had recently been increased, we should set aside a certain amount to pay the expenses of a priest who would continue the spiritual care of the hospital's patients.

And I did so, because I knew that the patients had a right to receive the sacraments and the necessary spiritual assistance."

The decree of the Ministry of the Interior by which the Chaplains' Corps was abolished is dated 26 Mar 1932: see *Boletín Oficial del Obispado de Madrid-Alcalá*, no. 157 (15 Apr 1932), p. 149. Article 3 of this decree states that "when any sick person . . . requests a religious rite, this should be taken care of whenever possible, regardless of what religion the person professes." But in the hospitals this article could not be implemented, because the official budgets were always insufficient.

[39] See Isabel Martín Rodríguez, *Sum.* 5776, and María Jesús Sanz Zubiría, AGP, RHF, T–05138, p. 2.

[40] María Jesús Sanz Zubiría, AGP, RHF, T–05138, p. 2.

[41] See Isabel Martín Rodríguez, *Sum.* 5776 and 5777.

[42] Engracia Echevarría, AGP, RHF, T–04389, p. 2.

[43] Ibid. "It was very common for priests to stop wearing clerical clothes," says José Romeo. "The Father always wore the cassock" (AGP, RHF, T–03809, p. 9). "Many priests who felt capable of decisive and heroic action if the need arose," says Juan Jiménez Vargas, "went around in secular clothing. . . . The Father would never dress as a layman. In fact, he wore a cape which undoubtedly was more conspicuous—for want of a better word—than an overcoat" (AGP, RHF, T–04152/1, p. 4).

[44] María Jesús Sanz Zubiría, AGP, RHF, T–05138, p. 1.

[45] See Braulia García Escobar, AGP, RHF, T–04966, p. 1.

[46] Benilde García Escobar, AGP, RHF, T–04965, p. 1.

[47] See Braulia García Escobar, AGP, RHF, T–04966, p. 3.

[48] Ibid., p. 4.

[49] *Apuntes,* no. 1006. His companion, Juan Jiménez Vargas, a witness to this visit, says: "When I first met and associated with the founder, he was still making his visits and exercising his priestly apostolate in those hospitals. And one day, by chance, I accompanied him when he brought Communion to a very seriously ill woman at King's Hospital. After giving her Communion, he encouraged and exhorted her to prepare herself worthily for the hour of death" (Juan Jiménez Vargas, *Sum.* 6702).

[50] See Appendix 15.

[51] The founder mentions her in his journal entry for 14 Feb 1934 (*Apuntes,* no. 1136). See also Natividad González Fortún, *Sum.* 5874.

[52] See Alvaro del Portillo, *Sum.* 315, and Javier Echevarría, PR, p. 1590. An eyewitness states, "Another time, I myself accompanied the founder to a family's home, located near Plaza de España, in which was the corpse of a young man to whom the Servant of God had earlier administered the last sacraments. In my presence, he enshrouded the body" (Juan Jiménez Vargas, *Sum.* 6702).

[53] Pedro Cantero, AGP, RHF, T–04391, p. 9.

[54] *Apuntes*, no. 1002.

[55] Tomás Canales, AGP, RHF, T–02219.

[56] Ibid.

[57] *Meditation* of 19 Mar 1975.

[58] *Apuntes*, no. 563; see also *The Way*, no. 208.

[59] See AGP, P04 1974, II, p. 406.

[60] Ibid. This anecdote, including the cited quote, is related also by Alvaro del Portillo, in *Sum.* 269.

[61] *Pequeño bosquejo de las virtudes del celoso apóstol D. José Ma. Somoano (q.e.p.d.) por una enferma del Hospital Nacional* [A little sketch of the virtues of the zealous apostle Father José María Somoano (R.I.P.) by a patient at the National Hospital], handwritten by María Ignacia García Escobar in 1932: see AGP, RHF, D–03381.

[62] Ibid.

[63] Ibid.

[64] Ibid.

[65] *Apuntes*, no. 615.

[66] *C 20* (14 Aug 1931).

[67] Letter of 24 Dec 1931 from Isidoro Zorzano to Father Josemaría: original in AGP, IZL, D–1213 (letter no. 19).

[68] Letter of 2 Mar 1932 from Isidoro Zorzano to Father Josemaría: original in AGP, IZL, D–1213 (letter no. 21).

[69] *Meditation* of 19 Mar 1975.

[70] *Apuntes*, no. 354.

[71] *Apuntes*, no. 84.

[72] *Apuntes*, no. 186. That cry—"God and daring!"—would be repeated during the next few days: see *Apuntes*, nos. 190 and 224.

[73] *Apuntes*, no. 187.

[74] *Apuntes*, no. 197.

[75] *Apuntes*, no. 198.

[76] *Apuntes*, no. 997.

[77] *Apuntes*, no. 354.

[78] *Apuntes*, no. 963 (23 Mar 1933). Braulia García Escobar met those first women of the Work during visits to her sister at King's Hospital. "My sister María Ignacia," she says, "was marvelously cared for spiritually by the Father. Other girls also went to see her and keep her company, and some belonged to the Work. One of these was named Modesta Cabeza, and she was a simple girl. Father Lino was her spiritual director. The Father asked her to pray for specific intentions. . . .

"Carmen Cuervo Radigales also came to the hospital to keep my sister company. She lived in Asunción Hall, at the Royal Foundation of

Santa Isabel. She was a Labor Commissioner—something unheard-of in those days, when it was practically unthinkable for women to hold public office.

"The last one I remember from that group was Hermógenes. I think she worked for a bank."

(This is from AGP, RHF, T–04966, pp. 2–3. See also the testimony of Ramona Sánchez: AGP, RHF, T–05828, p. 2.)

[79] *C 18* (5 May 1931).

[80] *Apuntes*, no. 1072.

[81] See Appendix 15.

[82] See Appendix 14.

[83] See Appendix 14. "Luis Gordon's entrance into the Work had promised a big financial boost for its apostolic initiatives. The founder's comment was that his death had been providential. Opus Dei continued to grow in the most absolute poverty, without material means. It was necessary for the Work to be born poor, as was Jesus in Bethlehem" (Alvaro del Portillo, *Sum.* 1220).

[84] *Meditation* of 2 Oct 1962. See also *Letter 14 Sep 1951*, no. 4.

[85] *Apuntes*, no. 1756.

[86] Jenaro Lázaro, AGP, RHF, T–00310, p. 1.

[87] *Apuntes*, no. 541.

[88] *Pequeño bosquejo*, AGP, RHF, D–03381.

[89] Pedro Cantero, AGP, RHF, T–04391, pp. 3–4.

[90] Ibid., p. 5.

[91] On August 14, 1931, the founder wrote to Isidoro Zorzano: "Yesterday I made the decision to tell our great secret to someone else. . . . I ask you for very special prayer and some small act of expiation, a voluntary one. Look, this way we are going to carry out the 'business' just between you and me. I'm not going to ask prayer or expiation from anyone else. It will be up to us to move the heart of our King. . . . That vocation, if God grants it, will have been *engendered* by you, through your opportune and inopportune prayer. You should be toning up your spiritual life these days, and not slack off later" (*C 20*, 14 Aug 1931).

In a letter dated August 26, 1931, addressed to the members of the Work, Isidoro answered that request. "I have intensified my prayer," he said, "and since I have no lack of annoyances at any time of day, I have plenty of material to offer to God as expiation. . . . I am offering it all for a happy conclusion of our 'business'" (AGP, IZL, D–1213, no. 16). See also *Apuntes*, nos. 231, 362, 365, and 591.

[92] *Apuntes*, no. 613.

[93] Father Lino Vea-Murguía Bru was born in 1901, in Madrid, and was ordained in 1926. In 1927 he became chaplain of the Foundation for the

Sick, and from 1930 on was senior chaplain of the Slaves of the Sacred Heart. On August 15 or 16 of 1936 he was assassinated in Madrid. (See his personal file in the archive of the general secretariat of the archdiocese of Madrid-Alcalá.)

As already indicated, as soon as Father Josemaría read him a few pages of his "Catherines," Father Norberto considered himself incorporated in the Work. As for Father Lino, Father Norberto—on his own initiative, without consulting the founder—invited him to join (see *Apuntes,* nos. 354 and 412).

[94] See Pedro Cantero, AGP, RHF, T–04391, p. 9.

[95] *Pequeño bosquejo,* AGP, RHF, D–03381.

[96] See Appendix 13.

[97] *Apuntes,* no. 834. Father Sebastián Cirac Estopañán had for some time been receiving spiritual direction from Father Josemaría. Born in Caspe (near Saragossa) in 1903, he was ordained in 1928. In 1932 he became a canon of Cuenca; in 1934 he moved to Germany to continue his studies; and in 1940 he won, by competitive examination, the chair of Greek philology at the University of Barcelona. He died in 1970.

[98] Father José María Vegas Pérez was born in 1902, in Madrid, and was ordained a priest in 1927. In 1928 he was assigned to the parish of San Martín and then became chaplain of the Chapel of Santísimo Cristo de San Ginés. In 1935 he was appointed rector of Cerro de los Angeles. On November 27, 1937, in Paracuellos del Jarama, he was assassinated. (See his personal file in the archive of the general secretariat of the archdiocese of Madrid-Alcalá.)

[99] Letter of 5 Sep 1930 from Isidoro Zorzano to Father Josemaría: original in AGP, IZL, D–1213, no. 7.

[100] Letter of 14 Sep 1930 from Isidoro Zorzano to Father Josemaría: original in AGP, IZL, D–1213, no. 8.

[101] *Apuntes,* no. 381.

[102] C 22 (10 Nov 1931).

[103] *Apuntes,* no. 602. He then adds, "Carmen Cuervo—that's the name of the woman that Jesus was preparing for the W. of G." See also *Apuntes,* no. 1872.

[104] See *Apuntes,* no. 693. In this journal entry, written the morning of April 11, 1932, he says with reference to that first vocation of expiation, "Thanks be to God. Today, in our weekly meeting, I suggested to my brother priests that we pray a Te Deum."

[105] See *Apuntes,* no. 434.

[106] *Apuntes,* no. 931.

[107] *Apuntes,* no. 1136.

[108] See *Apuntes*, no. 381. "I continued to work with the boys," he says in another journal entry, "without ceasing to feel the need to seek souls among the women" (*Apuntes*, no. 1872). "Work was being done in women's circles . . . , but I was not finding people who seemed to me to be ready" (*Apuntes*, no. 381).

[109] *C 28* (8 Apr 1932).

[110] In *Apuntes*, no. 691 (10 Apr 1932), he says: "These days I am preparing girls at Santa Isabel School for First Communion."

[111] *Apuntes*, no. 402.

[112] *Apuntes*, no. 710.

[113] *C 28* (8 Apr 1932).

[114] *Apuntes*, no. 748.

[115] It is possible that the Escrivá family was going through some difficulty that worried Father Josemaría. See *C 30* (7 Jun 1932).

[116] José Manuel Doménech, AGP, RHF, T–00872. The history of the Second Spanish Republic was a very stormy one. The summer of 1932 was plagued by riots, criminal assaults on individuals and churches, and nationalistic tensions connected with the movement for Catalonian autonomy and with various separatist movements, not to mention work stoppages and the country's economic problems.

In those conditions various monarchist elements and some military personnel who were unhappy with the army reforms undertaken by the republican government forged a conspiracy.

The time set for the revolt was 4:00 A.M., August 10. It was supposed to take place both in Seville and in Madrid. But it was neither well organized nor well supported. The government, moreover, had known about the plot since some time in July.

On August 10, General Sanjurjo launched the uprising in Seville, but elsewhere the troops were disorganized. The uprising in Madrid was easily and quickly put down.

[117] *Apuntes*, no. 800.

[118] *Apuntes*, no. 814.

[119] José Antonio Palacios, AGP, RHF, T–02750, p. 1.

[120] Ibid., p. 3.

[121] José Manuel Doménech, AGP, RHF, T–00872.

[122] Ibid. Apart from penalties imposed generally on civilians and military personnel who had revolted, such as confiscation of the country homes of those who had conspired against the regime and those believed to have supported them, other sanctions were also applied. One of these was the deportation to Villa Cisneros, in the old Spanish Sahara, of 145 accomplices or suspected accomplices, among them José Manuel Doménech. Some of the prisoners were sent from Madrid to Cádiz, and

then by ship to Africa, on September 22, 1932. Other suspects or pre-
sumed accomplices were kept as political prisoners in Madrid's Cárcel
Modelo, or "model prison."

[123] *Apuntes*, no. 746.

[124] *Apuntes*, no. 838. On September 12, 1932, Father Josemaría went to the
Carmelite monastery in Madrid to request admission to the Third Order
of Discalced Carmelites. "For two purposes (besides love) I want to become a Carmelite tertiary: to put more pressure on my Immaculate
Mother, now that I see myself weaker than ever; and to provide suffrages
to my good friends the blessed souls in purgatory" (*Apuntes*, no. 823).
The date of his entrance into the Third Order was, as he requested, October 2, 1932 (see *Apuntes*, no. 838).

[125] See *Apuntes*, nos. 1635 and 1636. See also Jesús Alvarez Gazapo, *Sum.*
4347, and Giovanni Udaondo, *Sum.* 5080.

[126] See *Apuntes*, no. 1634.

[127] See *Apuntes*, no. 1637.

[128] *Apuntes*, nos. 1637–40.

[129] *Apuntes*, no. 1642.

[130] *Instruction* of 8 Dec 1941, no. 9. On the archangels as patrons of the
Work, see *Apuntes*, no. 1642, note 1211; Javier Echevarría, *Sum.* 2645;
Mario Lantini, *Sum.* 3587; Joaquín Alonso, *Sum.* 4616; and Carmen Ramos,
Sum. 7361.

[131] *Apuntes*, nos. 1644, 1646, and 1648.

[132] *Apuntes*, no. 1655.

[133] See *Apuntes*, no. 1658.

[134] See *Apuntes*, no. 1660.

[135] *Apuntes*, no. 1661.

[136] "Father Sánchez," the founder explains, "has repeatedly given me to
understand (without directly saying this) that he is the director of my
soul, not the director of the Work of God. And I understand, very clearly,
that that is how it should be" (*Apuntes*, no. 565). This idea is repeated in
another journal entry: "I have already said this several times: Father
Sánchez is the director of my soul, but not the director of the Work. Now,
his opinion is very worthy of respect. Even more, I will always find myself very much inclined to accept it. But I know I do not have an obligation to abide by it" (*Apuntes*, no. 784). About Father Sánchez he would
write in 1947: "He had nothing to do with the Work, in that I never let
him control or have a say in it. By a clear light from God I understood
that in this I could not grant or tolerate that others manage what our
Lord was asking of me" (*Letter 29 Dec 1947/14 Feb 1966*, no. 20).

[137] And he gives his reasons for acting in this way: because he feels supernaturally driven to it; because a life of spiritual childhood requires it;

and "because this way one can never be deceived" (*Apuntes*, no. 560). In moments of doubt or confusion, when he had to make a decision affecting his soul, he always consulted his spiritual director. "I immediately went to my Father Sánchez, to tell him the state of my soul," he writes on May 12, 1932 (*Apuntes*, no. 719). "I went to Father Sánchez and laid out before him the state of my soul: today I suffered, and yesterday too. My Father Sánchez was very much a father" (*Apuntes*, no. 744).

[138] *Apuntes*, no. 708.

[139] *Apuntes*, no. 701.

[140] *Apuntes*, no. 702.

[141] *Apuntes*, no. 702.

[142] In a journal entry from November 1931 he tells of one of these episodes. He had walked to Chamartín to see Father Sánchez. "After I had waited a long time, a servant boy came down and brusquely said to me, 'Father says he is very busy.' 'Then I can't see him?' I asked. 'Of course not,' the boy answered.

"I was thunderstruck. But right away I offered it to Jesus and, despite my rebellious pride, tried to think like this: 'Father S. has too much patience with me! I am a bother. Besides, even if he wasn't busy, these humiliations are very good for you, José María'" (*Apuntes*, no. 379; see also *Apuntes*, no. 1757).

On one occasion when invited to dine at the Jesuits' generalate in Rome, he started relating these recollections, and the lay brother serving at the table spontaneously interrupted the conversation with these words: "I remember this very well, because often it was I who had to tell you that Father Valentín Sánchez could not see you" (see Javier Echevarría, *Sum.* 2063).

[143] See *Apuntes*, no. 1757.

[144] *Apuntes*, no. 1661. On the gifts of his spiritual director and the kind of treatment he received from Father Sánchez, the founder wrote, "What grace the Lord has given him for directing!" (*C 20*, 14 Aug 1931), and, later, "He gave me the kind of care that any good priest should give me. Often he treated me with severity, and I praise that severity" (*Letter 29 Dec 1947/14 Feb 1966*, no. 20). In the notes that he wrote during his retreat of 1934, which he intended Father Sánchez to read, he wrote: "The interest that you have always shown in the Work of God and in my spiritual well-being fills me with gratitude. For that, my father, I love you very much in Christ Jesus. Every day I remember you in my prayer, and *twice* every day I remember you *intra missam* [in my Mass]" (*Apuntes*, no. 1791).

[145] *Apuntes*, no. 1665. Apparently the rage and the dirty tricks of the devil had recently increased. The founder does not say much on this subject, nor does he give any more details about this incident. (See also *Apuntes*,

nos. 719, 720, 721, 739, and 743.)

[146] See *Apuntes,* no. 1676. Possibly in June 1932, in Saragossa, he spoke with Father Pou de Foxá, who would have encouraged him in his studies: see *C 28* (8 Apr 1932) and *Apuntes,* no. 780.

[147] See *Apuntes,* no. 1678. The crux of the problem was his poverty, which already had prevented him from getting the doctorate in sacred theology upon completion of his academic studies at the Pontifical University of Saragossa. "I don't have the money," he says, "and this has a double consequence: (a) since I have to work, sometimes too much, in order to support my family, I don't right now have either the time or the inclination to work on those doctorates; and (b) even if I had the time, without money it is impossible to get through those academic exercises" (*Apuntes,* no. 1676).

[148] *Apuntes,* nos. 1680 and 1681.

[149] *Apuntes,* no. 1679.

[150] *Apuntes,* no. 1686.

[151] See *Apuntes,* no. 1688.

[152] *Apuntes,* no. 1689.

[153] *Apuntes,* no. 1699.

[154] *Apuntes,* no. 1695.

[155] *Apuntes,* no. 1702. The rest of this entry reads: "(2) Not to ask questions out of curiosity. (3) Not to sit down any more than necessary, and never to lean against the back of the chair. (4) Not to eat anything sweet. (5) Not to drink water, except for that of the ablution. (6) After lunch, not to eat bread. (7) Not to spend even five cents, if *a poor beggar,* in my place, could not afford it. (8) Never to complain about anything to anyone, if not for the purpose of seeking direction. (9) Not to praise, and not to criticize.

"Deo omnis gloria! I will read this note every Sunday."

[156] *Apuntes,* no. 1658.

[157] *Apuntes,* no. 870. All his life he struggled to guard his sight, mortifying himself even in licit things. This is illustrated by a curious incident around the end of 1931. Father Josemaría was friends with the Marquis of Guevara and his wife. (The Marquis, Floro Rodríguez Casanova, was a brother of Doña Luz, the foundress of the Foundation for the Sick.) One day when he was at their house, he asked them, with the intention of providing work for a young painter who needed it, if they would like to commission a portrait. The Marchioness graciously agreed. The painter showed up; she posed for him; and later she lent him a dress so that he could finish the portrait in his studio. A few days later the painter went to see Father Josemaría. He had a problem: he needed to know what color the lady's eyes were. The priest confessed his ignorance, but as-

sured him of an easy solution to the problem. That week he was to dine with the couple, and so he would find this out.

At that dinner, right there at the table, he innocently mentioned his meeting with the painter and the problem he had run into. "Well, look at me, Father," said the Marchioness, "my eyes are a beautiful green." And the priest replied, "Now I'll look at them even less, silly!" (See *Apuntes*, nos. 181, 356, 450, and 462; and AGP, P04 1974, II, 510.)

[158] On October 2, 1928, writes the founder, "the enterprise was sketched out." The task of realizing it followed, of fixing the spirituality proper to Opus Dei and carrying out its apostolates. "This poor priest," as he himself put it, would have to "continue to note down and fill in the Work" (*Apuntes*, no. 475; see also *Apuntes*, no. 475, note 391).

[159] He mentioned this "pious union or whatever" in *Apuntes*, no. 772, prior to his retreat in Segovia. With Father Juan Postius [his confessor during the time Father Sánchez was in hiding] he consulted as to whether or not it would be a good idea at that time to start an association for university students (see *Apuntes*, no. 769 [7 Jul 1932]). Very soon the idea of a pious union was discarded. On September 29, 1932, he writes: "Today I talked with Father Postius. He advises against setting up a young people's association. Working without setting up an association—opening an academy, for example—this is what I'm now thinking of" (*Apuntes*, no. 837).

[160] See *Instruction* of 8 Dec 1941, no. 9. See also *Apuntes*, no. 1642.

Two days later, on Saturday, he wrote: "I prayed the prayers of the W. of G., invoking our patrons the holy archangels: Michael, Gabriel, Raphael. And how sure I am that this triple invocation, of personages so high in the kingdom of heaven, must be—is—most agreeable to the Three and One, and will hasten the hour of the Work!" (*Apuntes*, no. 1653).

His recourse to these archangels and apostles, seeking their intercession when starting an apostolate, goes back to much earlier dates. For example, on December 27, 1930, the feast of Saint John the Evangelist, he had invoked this apostle and obtained a favor (see *Apuntes*, no. 140). On January 14, 1931, he asked himself in a journal entry, "Saint John—our patron?" (see *Apuntes*, no. 152). And in his entry for May 8, 1931, feast of "the Apparition of Saint Michael," we read: "I have entrusted the Work to Saint Michael, the great warrior, and I think he has heard me" (*Apuntes*, no. 198).

[161] During his retreat in Segovia, in 1932, he wrote that the work of apostolate with university students should be done "under the protection of Our Lady of Hope and the patronage of Saint Raphael the archangel. This—now and later—on the basis of academies, without forming any kind of association" (*Apuntes*, no. 1697). That idea is also expressed in an earlier entry: "The work of Saint Raphael and Saint John will always be done in our academies, without our forming with the students an association of any kind" (*Apuntes*, no. 921).

[162] *Apuntes,* no. 890.

[163] A copy of the lease can be found in AGP, RHF, D–15113. The lease is for "the apartment at 4 Franco Giner Street (formerly Martínez Campos), second floor, left." The monthly rent was 115 pesetas. Item no. 3 of the "Conditions of Contract" states, "A delay of four days in the payment of the rent will be considered sufficient cause to initiate eviction proceedings."

[164] *Apuntes,* no. 892.

[165] *Apuntes,* no. 893.

[166] *Apuntes,* no. 883.

[167] *Apuntes,* no. 884.

[168] In his journal entry for July 18, 1932, referring to a visit made to Father José María Somoano (who was then near death), he wrote: "The doctor in charge said we were putting him at risk, so I had to leave King's Hospital. After hearing the confessions of some children at 'La Ventilla,' I went to Father Norberto's house" (*Apuntes,* no. 787).

[169] Sister San Pablo Lemus y González de la Rivera, AGP, RHF, T–05833. See also Pilar Angela Hernando Carretero, AGP, RHF, T–05250, p. 1.

[170] *Apuntes,* no. 907.

[171] *Apuntes,* no. 863.

[172] *Apuntes,* no. 913.

[173] Juan Jiménez Vargas, AGP, RHF, T–04152/1, p. 19. Another of the students present was José María Valentín-Gamazo: see AGP, RHF, T–02710.

[174] See AGP, P04 1975, p. 278. "Our Father told us many times," comments Bishop del Portillo, "that when he gave that blessing with the Blessed Sacrament, he did not see just three boys, but three thousand, three hundred thousand, three million . . . , white, black, yellow, of all languages and from all parts of the world" (*Instruction* of 9 Jan 1935, note 25).

[175] See José Ramón Herrero Fontana, AGP, RHF, T–05834, p. 3, and Pilar Angela Hernando Carretero, AGP, RHF, T–05250, p. 1.

[176] Sister San Pablo Lemus y González de la Rivera, AGP, RHF, T–05833.

[177] As he himself expressed it, he did this "to select those who will later go into the work whose patrons are Saint Gabriel and Saint Paul, and those who will come to the *heart* of the W. of G." (*Apuntes,* no. 913 [25 Jan 1933]). Later, when the Work was more fully developed, the founder would explain that in reality all members of the Work are "heart," since there is just one, identical vocation to Opus Dei.

[178] Benita Casado, AGP, RHF, T–06242, pp. 1–2. At that time her name was Severina; she later joined the Congregation of the Slaves of Mary. Luis Sevilla, a nephew of Doña Pilar, recalls that in 1933 Father Josemaría prepared him for his First Communion, which he made on March 15, and that he gave him a little picture as a souvenir (see Luis Sevilla, AGP, RHF, T–06243, p. 2).

179 Benita Casado, AGP, RHF, T–06242, p. 3. See also Luis Sevilla, AGP, RHF, T–06243, p. 3.
180 See José Antonio Palacios, AGP, RHF, T–02750, p. 5.
181 Ibid., p. 6.
182 *Apuntes,* no. 912; see also *Apuntes,* no. 606.
183 *Apuntes,* no. 877.
184 *Apuntes,* no. 877.
185 *Apuntes,* no. 1696.
186 *Apuntes,* no. 925. See also Alvaro del Portillo, *Sum.* 241; Javier Echevarría, *Sum.* 2080; Joaquín Alonso, *Sum.* 4618; and Joaquín Mestre, AGP, RHF, T–00181, p. 34.

Angel Herrera Oria was born in Santander in 1886 and died as cardinal bishop of Málaga in 1968. He was the first president of a national Catholic Action organization (Asociación Católica Nacional de Propagandistas) founded in 1908 by Father Angel de Ayala, S.J. Herrera was also editor of *El Debate* from its inception in 1911 until 1933. Throughout those years he was noted for his promotion of social action among Catholic students. In 1933 he was named president of the Central Committee of Spanish Catholic Action. He was ordained to the priesthood in 1940, consecrated as a bishop in 1947, and made a cardinal in 1965.

For more on Angel Herrera's projects, including the creation of the Center for Advisors, see Gonzalo Redondo, "Historia de la Iglesia en España (1931–1939)," in *Historia de la Iglesia* (by various authors), vol. 3 (Madrid, 1985), pp. 202ff.
187 *Apuntes,* no. 926. For more on his refusal of Herrera's offers, see Florencio Sánchez Bella, *Sum.* 7488. Within a short period of time, the founder had at least three meetings with Angel Herrera. But at the one on February 11, their second talk, they really got into the subject of the Center for Advisors and the offer was made to Father Josemaría. He declined it then and there. (See *Apuntes,* nos. 923, 925, 926, 927, 933, and 934.)

In his journal entry for 11 Feb 1933 (*Apuntes,* no. 923), he writes: "Our Lady, no doubt, gave me two presents yesterday evening. The second was that I became lame and almost unable to sleep last night. . . . And the first, that she brought us another vocation for the Work: Jenaro Lázaro." Bishop del Portillo explains that lameness. He says that when the founder went to see Herrera, he felt no pain whatsoever, but when he left, he was limping; it was his first attack of rheumatism (see Alvaro del Portillo, *Sum.* 242).
188 See *Apuntes,* no. 927.
189 Convinced of the heroic holiness of this act, the Most Reverend Marcelino Olaechea (being by now the archbishop of Valencia but having been back then the bishop of Pamplona) entrusted the task of testifying to

it to his secretary, Father Joaquín Mestre Palacio. Father Joaquín (see AGP, RHF, T–00181, p. 34) expressed it in these words:

> President Herrera himself insisted, arguing, in a nutshell, "I want you to realize, Father Josemaría, that in that center I will be gathering, with God's help, the best priests of Spain, and that what I am offering you is this: that you be their director."
>
> But the Father, as I say, invariably and categorically responded, "No, no. I appreciate it, but I cannot accept it, because I have to follow . . . the path to which God has called me. Also I cannot accept it because of the very thing you have just told me: that in that center will be gathered the best priests of Spain. Obviously I wouldn't be suitable for directing them."

The president of Spanish Catholic Action and future cardinal was so impressed by the founder's behavior on that occasion that thirty years later he spoke of that detachment to Father Florencio Sánchez Bella (see *Sum.* 7488).

Bishop Javier Echevarría recalls the refusal of Herrera's offer as having been expressed thus: "I have thoroughly thought it over, and I cannot change my mind. Besides, if the most outstanding priests of Spain are going to be there, there are much better persons than myself who could take charge of those priests—men who tower over me. Plus, I have other tasks that I can't stop tending to, because that would be a betrayal of what God is asking of me" (Javier Echevarría, *Sum.* 2080).

Other testimonies on this subject include Alvaro del Portillo, *Sum.* 241; Joaquín Alonso, *Sum.* 4618; Julián Herranz, *Sum.* 3881; Francisco Botella, PM, fol. 221; and Pedro Casciaro, *Sum.* 6320.

[190] See *Apuntes*, nos. 768, 773, 774, and 837.

[191] "Our organization is an organized disorganization," he wrote on March 19, 1933 (in *Apuntes*, no. 956).

His attempts to get guidelines from other institutions, or to learn from their experiences, never helped the founder in any way. Information he had sought at the beginning of 1930 about modern apostolic institutions in other countries—institutions he had by now forgotten about—arrived around February 14, 1932, in a letter from Poland, from one Father Laureano de las Muñecas (see *Apuntes*, no. 603). This was an answer to a letter sent to Krakow by Father Josemaría (see *Apuntes*, no. 581). Father Lino saw Father Laureano in Santander in the middle of September 1932. But Father Josemaría did not expect him to provide a solution to the question of how the Work ought to be established, and in any case he had already decided to create a cultural center, or a residence. "I don't know," he says, "that Father Laureano will come up with any practical solution for the setting up of the Work with regard to the ecclesiastical or civil authorities. . . . The members and associates should form cultural organizations" (*Apuntes*, no. 835).

192 *Apuntes*, no. 184.

193 *Apuntes*, no. 184.

194 *Apuntes*, no. 164.

195 *Apuntes*, no. 815.

196 See *Apuntes*, no. 952. About Doña Dolores' and Carmen's offering of their home for apostolic purposes, Bishop Echevarría says: "The spirit of Opus Dei benefited from their open and complete collaboration, because, without interfering in the founding of the Work, they knew how to help provide the home atmosphere that he, in fulfillment of the will of God, wanted it to have" (Javier Echevarría, PR, p. 488).

197 Juan Jiménez Vargas, AGP, RHF, T–04152/1, p. 25. See also Jenaro Lázaro, AGP, RHF, T–00310, p. 2.

198 Juan Jiménez Vargas, AGP, RHF, T–04152/1, p. 25.

199 See José Ramón Herrero Fontana, AGP, RHF, T–05834, p. 2. See also José Ramón Madurga, PM, fol. 283v; Ignacio María de Orbegozo, *Sum.* 7274; and *Instruction* of May 1935/Sep 1950, no. 85, note 153.

200 See Ricardo Fernández Vallespín, AGP, RHF, T–00162, pp. 2–4. The book he gave him was *Historia de la Sagrada Pasión*, by Father Luis de la Palma.

201 Manuel Sainz de los Terreros, AGP, RHF, T–12082.

202 "It is obvious that our Lord—because this is the way it has to be within the Work—has wanted us to begin with prayer. Praying is going to be the first official act of the members of the W. of G." (*Apuntes*, no. 128).

203 *Apuntes*, no. 935.

204 The "provisional norms" were written by the founder on 24 Mar 1933, the feast of Saint Gabriel (see *Apuntes*, no. 966). They originated in a summary of a plan for norms of piety that he sketched out during his retreat in Segovia in 1932. See also *Apuntes*, nos. 939 and 1700.

Notes to Chapter 8

1 At that time the founder, optimistically looking to the future, jotted down in his *Apuntes íntimos* (Personal Notes) some data about the structuring and the running of the Saint Gabriel work. For example: "In the centers where there are a lot of people, we'll need to divide those involved in the Saint Gabriel work into groups, putting together those of related professions" (*Apuntes*, no. 1027). The Saint Raphael work

consisted of Christian formation activities for young single people; the Saint Gabriel work was an apostolic outreach to married people.

2 *Apuntes,* no. 957. He did not miss an opportunity to invite acquaintances who had finished their university studies to join the new academy as professors. "April 30, 1933: . . . The Lord keeps sending us professors for the academy: Rocamora, González Escudero, Luelmo, and Atanasio, plus our own. Last night they brought me Fernando Oriol" (*Apuntes,* no. 993).

3 *Apuntes,* nos. 1018 and 1016.

4 *Apuntes,* no. 1021 (13 Jun 1933). In another entry made on that date or a few days later, he says, "Today, what with the political mess we're in right now, I'm giving in to the temptation to read the papers. I'm not even able to do this [give up reading the papers]" (*Apuntes,* no. 1024).

Most probably, he was reading articles and editorials about the Law on Confessions and Religious Associations (see *Gaceta de Madrid,* 3 Jun 1933), which placed limitations on the practice of the Catholic faith and subjected the activities and administration of religious orders and congregations to inspection by the civil authorities.

5 *Apuntes,* no. 945.

6 *Apuntes,* no. 957.

7 See *Apuntes,* no. 1050. See also *Apuntes,* nos. 976, 986, and 992.

8 *Apuntes,* no. 1005 (11 May 1933).

9 See *Apuntes,* nos. 1713 and 1714.

10 *Apuntes,* no. 1729. Father Juan Postius Sala was born in 1876 in Berga (Barcelona) and died in 1952 in Solsona (Lérida). In 1894 he entered the Congregation of the Immaculate Heart of Mary (also known as the Claretian Order). In Rome he finished his doctoral studies in both canon and civil law. He was especially dedicated to spreading Marian devotion through international Marian congresses. It was he who organized the Twenty-second International Eucharistic Congress, held in Madrid in 1911. He had many writings published, notably *El Código canónico aplicado a España en forma de instituciones* (Madrid, 1926).

11 *Apuntes,* no. 599 (15 Feb 1932).

12 See *Apuntes,* no. 742. In one entry, written in April or May of 1930, we read: "Not even one time has it occurred to me to think that I've been deceived, that God doesn't love his Work. Quite the contrary" (*Apuntes,* no. 27).

13 *Apuntes,* no. 1710. Father Josemaría respected and obediently followed the instructions given him by Father Sánchez in regard to themes for meditation, as well as the schedule given him by Father Gil, a Redemptorist priest, upon his arrival at the monastery (see *Apuntes,* nos. 1704 and 1705).

14 *Apuntes,* no. 1729. See also Alvaro del Portillo, *Sum.* 464, and Joaquín Alonso, *Sum.* 4612. The founder writes that he made an additional note

of this event, besides the one included in the notes he gave to Father Sánchez at the end of his retreat, "because I want everyone to know about the little things from God that have surrounded the birth of this new army of Christ. With this knowledge, and with the knowledge of my shortcomings that they will acquire by dealing with me, they won't be able to do any less than to love the Work and to exclaim, 'This Work truly is . . . the Work of God!'" (*Apuntes*, no. 1730).

15 *Apuntes*, no. 1730. The words of his offering of the Work were put in writing by Father Josemaría "at the very instant in which it happened, right there in the church" (*Apuntes*, no. 1729).

16 *Apuntes*, no. 1709. On May 1, 1933, he had drawn up another list of his "actual sins" which basically coincides with this one made during his June retreat. The previous list reads: "Crying: I don't know if this means my soul is getting weak; I don't think so; it's that I'm a child. I have the faults and the sins of a bad boy: gluttony, laziness, sluggishness, . . . all kinds of lively sensuality. And in prayer—how am I going to get some order in my prayer?" (*Apuntes*, no. 995).

17 *Apuntes*, no. 1723.

18 See *Apuntes*, nos. 787, 938, and 955, and notes 685 and 1281. The Veritas Academy on O'Donnell Street was run by Teresians. As for the Teresian Institute on Alameda Street in Madrid, Father Josemaría heard confessions there fairly often, according to the testimonies of Father Silvestre Sancho, O.P., and Father Eliodoro Gil Ribera. "I first met the Servant of God in the Teresian house of Father Poveda, at 7 Alameda Street in Madrid. And afterward we saw each other on numerous occasions" (Silvestre Sancho, *Sum.* 5392; see also Eliodoro Gil Ribera, *Sum.* 7747).

As one can tell from a loose note written in 1934 (*Apuntes*, no. 1794), Father Josemaría only partly made good on his resolve to stop hearing confessions in some places:

Sunday: Santa Isabel—class or catechism. Afternoon, hospital.

Monday: Confessions at La Asunción, at three. Priests' meeting.

Tuesday: José María Valentín (10:30). Academy.

Wednesday: Confessions at La Asunción. Saint Raphael meeting. Jenaro Lázaro.

Thursday: Class. Afternoon, Academy. Confessions, 7 O'Donnell (5:30).

Friday: First, talk with the poor girls at Santa Isabel (and hear their confessions), and at Porta Caeli. Angel Cifuentes (8–9). Pepe Romeo. 4:30—talk with English ladies.

Saturday: Acad. Confessions: girls at Santa Isabel (9), Porta Caeli (11), and Teresians (5:30). Academy—Jaime Munárriz (8–9). Juanito J. Vargas (12). Benediction at Las Esclavas.

[19] See AGP, P04 1974, II, pp. 418–19. This happened sometime in 1932 or 1933—certainly no later. Sister Benita Casado testifies that when Father Josemaría was talking to the Sisters about how to pray, he told them "the story of Juan the milkman, who every morning would say to the Lord, 'Here is Juan the milkman'" (Sister Benita Casado, AGP, RHF, T–06242, p. 4).

[20] *Apuntes*, no. 719.

[21] *Apuntes*, no. 974.

[22] Retreat note, dated June 22, 1933. It goes on to ask approval from the confessor of the following schedule for use of the discipline, the wearing of cilices, fasting, and sleeping on the floor (*Apuntes*, no. 1724):

> Use of the discipline: Mondays, Wednesdays, and Fridays. Additionally on vigils of feasts of our Lord or of the Blessed Virgin. Also, every other week, an extra one for petition or thanksgiving.
>
> Cilices: two every day until lunch; then, until supper, one. Tuesday, the one around the waist, and Friday, the one over the shoulders, as I've been doing.
>
> Sleep: on the floor, if it is wooden, or on a bed without a mattress, Tuesdays, Thursdays, and Saturdays.
>
> Fasting: Saturdays, taking only what they give me for breakfast.

In this note he also proposes the times and types of reading he should do and confesses that "for me, not reading newspapers is ordinarily a big mortification" (*Apuntes*, no. 1726). In those times of political unrest and of persecution against the Church in Spain, it was necessary to keep up with the news and to be forewarned.

[23] *Apuntes*, no. 1727.

[24] *Boletín Oficial del Obispado Madrid-Alcalá*, no. 1580 (1 Apr 1933), p. 114. The date of circular letter no. 109, signed by Bishop Leopoldo Eijo y Garay, is March 27, 1933.

An order from the Minister of War (Manuel Azaña) to the generals, dated March 9, 1932, prohibited any act of worship in the barracks. The bishopric, as of April 1, 1933, took "immediate charge of all matters which until now have been under the ecclesiastical jurisdiction of the military" in that diocese.

The military and palace jurisdictions, though they were different, were both headed by the Patriarch of the Indies, Bishop Ramón Pérez Rodríguez, who on April 14, 1933, was named bishop of Cádiz by the pope. He took possession of the Cádiz bishopric on May 30 and made his entrance there on June 11. (See E. Subirana. *Anuario Eclesiástico* [*Barcelona*], 192, p. 73. See also "Informe de D. Leopoldo Eijo y Garay al

Director General de Beneficencia," 24 Nov 1939, in the archive of the general secretariat of the archdiocese of Madrid-Alcalá, "Patronatos," file "Buen Suceso").

[25] *Apuntes,* no. 963. He speaks of his ecclesiastical situation at Santa Isabel also in *Apuntes,* nos. 556, 636, 719, and 886.

[26] On the relationship between the founder and Father Pedro Poveda, see *Apuntes,* nos. 251, 295, 731, 745, 938, and 955. The founder also wrote a note about his friendship with Father Pedro for the purpose of correcting some inaccurate statements made, many years later, by the then nuncio of Spain (1962–1967), Monsignor Riberi. (See also *Apuntes,* note 266 and nos. 1627 and 1628; AGP, RHF, AVF–0041, pp. 47–48; and Alvaro del Portillo, *Sum.* 240.)

On January 13, 1931, he had a talk with Monsignor Francisco Morán, the vicar general of Madrid.

Previous to 1933, as has already been mentioned, the vicar general knew about the activities of the founder. He learned more and more about them in connection with the founder's appointment as chaplain of the Foundation for the Sick; when he renewed the founder's ministerial permits; when he gave him permission to celebrate Masses in the church of the Foundation; gave him permission to bring Communion to a sick man in a brothel, and got him the position of chaplain at the Santa Isabel Foundation, when Father Lino, in the name of Father Josemaría, came to see him about teaching catechism at the Colegio del Arroyo, etc., etc.

In an entry dated 19 Jun 1933, we read: "I went to renew my permits. Who would have believed it! With great kindness they gave them to me right away and waived the fee. I agreed to visit Monsignor Morán from time to time, to update him on what I'm doing" (*Apuntes,* no. 1025).

On the granting of priestly faculties in the diocese of Madrid-Alcalá in 1932–1936, see *Libro de Licencias Ministeriales,* no. 8, fol. 55v; and no. 9, fol. 58v.

[27] *Apuntes,* nos. 994 and 995.

[28] *Apuntes,* no. 1049.

[29] C 42 (29 Aug 1933). The next reference is on September 18, when he tells of the death of Father Teodoro and the whole family's trip to Fonz. "We had to make two trips to Fonz when my uncle died" (*Apuntes,* no. 1055).

[30] *Apuntes,* no. 1055.

[31] *Apuntes,* no. 1057.

[32] *Apuntes,* no. 1065. He adds, "Father Sánchez scolded me for my impatience in desiring, to the point of suffering on this account, that our apostolate of the Work will be crystallized into *something*" (*Apuntes,* no. 1067).

[33] *Apuntes,* no. 1732.

[34] *Apuntes,* no. 1072.

[35] Ricardo Fernández Vallespín, AGP, RHF, T–00162, p. 6. Ricardo had spent the whole summer of 1933 without being able to see Father Josemaría, because of a bad rheumatic attack. Shortly afterward it made him drop out of school for the year, because he could not study for tests.

[36] *Apuntes*, no. 1077.

[37] *Apuntes*, no. 1083. Except for the first two houses in Madrid and one in Burgos (set up in 1938), no house or center of the Work has been named after a saint. See *Apuntes*, no. 1106 and note 834.

[38] *Apuntes*, no. 1094.

[39] On January 13, 1934, from Málaga, Isidoro wrote to Father Josemaría, "The little plaque for the academy is already finished. They did a good job; it's very faithful to your drawing" (AGP, IZL, D–1213, no. 45).

"Our first corporate work," said the founder, "was the academy that we called DYA—Derecho y Arquitectura [Law and Architecture]—because classes were given in those two subjects. But for us the initials really stood for Dios y Audacia [God and Daring]" (*Meditation* of 19 Mar 1975). The motto "God and Daring!" appears for the first time in a journal entry of March 27, 1931: "Our men and women of God, in their apostolate of action, have as their motto: God and Daring!" (*Apuntes*, no. 186; see also *Apuntes*, nos. 190 and 224).

[40] *Apuntes*, no. 989.

[41] *Apuntes*, no. 1071.

[42] See *Apuntes*, no. 1102 (5 Jan 1934). About the wooden cross, see José Ramón Herrero Fontana, AGP, RHF, T–05834, p. 3.

[43] See Alvaro del Portillo, PR, p. 464, and Ricardo Fernández Vallespín, AGP, RHF, T–00162, p. 10.

[44] See Alvaro del Portillo, *Sum.* 304; see also AGP, P01 July 1955, p. 44, and AGP, P03 1979, p. 251.

Some months, to pay the rent on the apartment, they had to take up a collection among those who attended activities there. See Jenaro Lázaro, AGP, RHF, T–00310, p. 2.

[45] See Alvaro del Portillo, *Sum.* 302. According to the testimony of Ricardo Fernández Vallespín (AGP, RHF, T–00162, p. 14), the difficulties and hardships were sometimes relieved by happenings that clearly involved the extraordinary intervention of Divine Providence. Juan Jiménez Vargas gives a detailed account of one such instance. The electric bill came in, and they did not have the money to pay it. The next morning, Father Josemaría, while going through some old papers in his office at Santa Isabel, tore up an apparently empty envelope and threw it in the wastepaper basket. At that moment it became apparent that there was something in that envelope: a twenty-five peseta bill, enough

to pay a little more than the amount due. (See Juan Jiménez Vargas, AGP, RHF, T–04152/1, p. 26.)

46 Ricardo Fernández Vallespín, AGP, RHF, T–00162, p. 12.

47 *Apuntes*, no. 1753.

48 *Apuntes*, no. 1753.

49 See *Apuntes*, no. 1109. On January 7 of that year (1934) he had approached Saint Joseph like a lawyer. "If my father and lord Saint Joseph makes this house prosper," he said, "then the second one we open on this earth will be the Saint Joseph House" (*Apuntes*, no. 1106).

50 *Apuntes*, no. 1120.

51 *Meditation* of 19 Mar 1975.

52 See *Apuntes*, no. 1091.

53 See *Apuntes*, no. 1091.

54 See *Apuntes*, no. 1063.

55 See Father Josemaría's *Instancia al Ministro de Trabajo,* dated 26 Jan 1934, and the letter from the prioress of the convent to the Minister of Labor, dated 28 Jan 1934: originals in the Patrimonio Nacional archive, "Patronatos Reales," "Patronato de Santa Isabel, file 182/21.

Letter of the Prioress of the Convent to the Minister of Labor, of Jan 28, 1934. Original in *Archivo General del Patrimonio* (Palacio Real)—*Patronatos Reales* [Royal Foundations]—*Santa Isabel*, File of Don Josemaria, Box 182/21.

The old royal foundations were under the authority of the Head Office of Social Services. During the Second Spanish Republic, this office formed part, at different times, of the Ministries of Labor, the Interior, and Public Education.

56 See *Apuntes*, no. 1125.

57 See "Ministerio de la Gobernación," dated 31 Jan 1934: original in the Patrimonio Nacional archive, "Patronatos Reales," "Patronato de Santa Isabel," file 182/21.

58 Judging by what he says in his note of February 3 on the subject of the house, he seems to feel that he has taken a step toward "stabilizing" himself in Madrid. However, he decided not to change residence, for the above-mentioned reasons and especially the last one: his hope of living soon in a center of the Work with our Lord in the tabernacle. "It's because I am hoping," he says, "that Jesus is going to go live with his sons—for we are sons of God—at the Guardian Angel House, by Christmas of 1934. Who on earth could possibly think that with Jesus there (we're already checking out prices for a good tabernacle), I wouldn't be there?" (*Apuntes*, no. 1128).

59 See *Apuntes*, no. 1124 (27 Jan 1934).

60 *Apuntes*, no. 1133 (11 Feb 1934).

[61] About his conversation on January 26, 1934, with Monsignor Francisco Morán, he writes, "With a holy shamelessness I took advantage of this opportunity to say a few good words to Monsignor Morán about two of my priests. The most important thing at this meeting was that when I mentioned to him the 'academy of Señor Zorzano,' where I'm continuing my work with university students, he said to me, 'Why don't you people give some religion classes for intellectuals?' And he said, regretfully, that the diocese could have advertised in its official bulletin and in some separate flyers that it publishes—he gave me one—the courses being given at 33 Luchana Street. This '33 Luchana Street' sounded familiar to him; he had heard of it before I mentioned it to him. I agreed to send him a list of teachers and students, and he gave me the freedom to organize the classes as I saw fit" (*Apuntes*, no. 1126).

[62] On or about March 22 he writes with joy, "We made the Work's first day of recollection this past Sunday. I am happy" (*Apuntes*, no. 1167). These days of recollection were given in the Redemptorists' chapel on Manuel Silvela Street (see José Ramón Herrero Fontana, AGP, RHF, T–05834, p. 3). They consisted of three or four meditations given by Father Josemaría, the Stations of the Cross, a Rosary, spiritual reading, a visit to the Blessed Sacrament, and an examination of conscience (see Ricardo Fernández Vallespín, AGP, RHF, T–00162, p. 13).

In 1934 the founder wrote a list of activities of this type carried out at the DYA Academy on a monthly, weekly, or daily basis. From this list we can see that he also gave classes in Latin and not one but several formational classes for the boys in the work of Saint Raphael, and likewise more than one monthly day of recollection (see *Apuntes*, no. 1798).

[63] On this occasion, says Bishop del Portillo (who was not at that time going to the DYA Academy), he was attacked by a group of fifteen or twenty persons. His head was deeply gashed when he was brutally hit with brass knuckles, and the injury took several months to heal. Wounded and bloodied, he managed to save his life by rushing into a subway entrance and onto a train that was just about to leave. (See *Apuntes*, no. 1131 and note 851.)

[64] *Apuntes*, no. 1140.

[65] See *Apuntes*, no. 1146.

[66] *C* 48 (26 Apr 1934).

[67] See *Apuntes*, nos. 1187 and 1188.

[68] *Apuntes*, no. 1191.

[69] *Apuntes*, no. 1192.

[70] *Apuntes*, no. 1193.

[71] *Apuntes*, no. 1184.

72 *Apuntes,* no. 1738.
73 *Apuntes,* no. 1743.
74 See *Apuntes,* nos. 1753 and 1754.
75 *Apuntes,* nos. 1786 and 1787.
76 *Apuntes,* no. 1790.
77 See *C 57* (23 Jul 1934), *C 58* (23 Jul 1934), and *C 62* (24 Jul 1934).
78 *C 65* (5 Aug 1934).
79 *C 67* (5 Aug 1934).
80 *C 68* (5 Aug 1934).
81 "After Mass, during my thanksgiving, without having thought of this beforehand, I was suddenly moved to dedicate the Work to the Blessed Virgin. I believe that this impulse came from God. . . . I think that today— as simply as that—a new stage began for this Work of God" (*Apuntes,* no. 1199).
82 *Apuntes,* no. 1199.
83 Ricardo Fernández Vallespín, AGP, RHF, T–00162, pp. 17–18.
84 *C 73* (6 Sep 1934).
85 *C 76* (6 Sep 1934).
86 *C 74* (6 Sep 1934). According to Ricardo Fernández Vallespín, Father Josemaría "decided that for external matters I should serve as director of the residence, and that it would also be good that he be the one to sign the contract as leaseholder of the house" (see Ricardo Fernández Valle- spín, AGP, RHF, T–00162, p. 16).
87 *Apuntes,* no. 1202.
88 *Apuntes,* no. 1203.
89 *C 79* (17 Sep 1934).
90 *C 80* (17 Sep 1934).
91 *C 81* (20 Sep 1934).
92 *C 82* (24 Sep 1934).
93 See Ricardo Fernández Vallespín, AGP, RHF, T–00162, pp. 18–19.
94 *Meditation* of 19 Mar 1975.
95 *C 85* (30 Oct 1934).
96 See *Meditation* of 19 Mar 1975.
97 *Apuntes,* no. 1206.
98 María del Buen Consejo Fernández, AGP, RHF, T–04953.
99 The original of this letter is in the Patrimonio Nacional archive, "Pa- tronatos Reales," "Patronato de Santa Isabel," file 182/21.
100 *C 87* (22 Nov 1934).
101 See *Gaceta de Madrid,* no. 347 (13 Dec 1934), p. 2121. The decree of Feb- ruary 17, 1934, established a distinction, in the jurisdiction of adminis- trative functions, between charitable foundations and charitable teaching

foundations. The Santa Isabel Foundation was under the jurisdiction of the Ministry of Labor, Health, and Welfare, which at that time was headed by Don José Oriol Anguera de Sojo.

[102] *Apuntes,* no. 1205.

[103] On December 27 he went to the Ministry to pick up his confirmation of appointment and read there that he had already taken "possession of this office" as of December 19. The text reads, "In view of the Decree of the eleventh of the present month, by which you have been appointed to the post of Rector of the Santa Isabel Foundation, you have possession of this office as of the nineteenth day of the same month. This is communicated to you for your information and satisfaction, and for record-keeping purposes. Madrid, December 27, 1934 / The Director General / J. Sáenz de Grado." The original of this document is in the archive of the general secretariat of the archdiocese of Madrid-Alcalá. A copy of it is in the Patrimonio Nacional archive, "Patronatos Reales," "Patronato de Santa Isabel," file 182/21.

[104] See handwritten note by the founder on his 27 Dec 1934 meeting with the vicar general: original in AGP, RHF, AVF–0003.

[105] *Apuntes,* no. 1214.

[106] Letter of 2 Feb 1935 from Archbishop Rigoberto Doménech to Father Josemaría: original in AGP, RHF, D–15514/2.

[107] In a letter to Father Pou de Foxá, dated January 28, Father Josemaría says he has written to the archbishop of Saragossa (to whom he is subject), informing him of his appointment as rector and clarifying that he has been serving as a priest at Santa Isabel since 1931, "as authorized by the Patriarch of the Indies," and that his services there have been "always exclusively priestly" (*C 96,* 28 Jan 1935).

[108] As was in fact later said, was tantamount to branding him a collaborator with an anti-Catholic regime, for so the Republic had shown itself by the measures taken against the Church. Therefore, in a long postscript to a letter dated February 8, 1935, the founder asked the bishop of Cuenca to "calm down" the archbishop of Saragossa. "To me personally," he said, "this is of no importance whatsoever. But as a priest, and as the base—the foundation—of the Work which God has entrusted to me, I feel I have a duty to set the record straight and have the truth be known. And the truth is this:

1) that I never do anything without the permission of my spiritual director;
2) that I refused to put in an application for the post of rector;
3) that it was the prioress and community of Santa Isabel who, with the permission of the vicar general, Monsignor Francisco Morán, requested this position for me;

4) that if it was wrong to put in an application for the position of rector, it was not I who did this wrong thing (though I've done plenty other wrong things!), but, rather, some of the local canons—among them a dean—and several of Madrid's diocesan priests;

5) that the previous rector, who, like me, was appointed by the Republic, committed such a terrible offense by accepting the appointment that his ordinary, the bishop of Astorga, punished him by appointing him as his personal secretary—an office which he holds to this very day;

6) and, finally, that there is no cause for anyone to be upset about this, since my bishop knows full well that at the slightest indication either from himself or from my spiritual director, Father Sánchez, and without suffering in the least—because this never was, and still is not, a matter of personal ambition—I would give up the rectorship, and twenty other posts of rector or canon, were they mine, because (glory be to God!) my only motive is a burning desire to do the will of Jesus.

7) Ah! It is well to remember, too, that having had—and, indeed, having at this very moment—more than one opportunity to accept appointments or engage in activities of a civic nature, as many of my fellow priests do (without being criticized for it; rather, the contrary is true), I have always chosen to engage only in tasks that are *exclusively priestly* in nature.

8) Furthermore, it was the Patriarch of the Indies—not the government of the Republic—that had kept me at Santa Isabel from 1931 on. And it is from that year that I can date my friendship, for which I can never show enough gratitude, with the saintly Father Poveda, secretary to the Patriarch. . . .

"I believe it was only fitting that I should open my heart to Your Excellency, and I trust that Your Excellency will, in turn, reassure His Excellency the Archbishop. May Jesus repay your kindness in this matter a thousandfold" (*C 98*, 8 Feb 1935).

[109] See Antonio Montero, *Historia de la persecución religiosa en España, 1936–1939* (Madrid, 1961), pp. 41–52.

[110] See Ricardo Fernández Vallespín, AGP, RHF, T–00162, p. 19.

[111] See *Apuntes*, no. 756.

[112] See *Apuntes*, nos. 1037 and 1127.

[113] See *Apuntes*, no. 1751.

[114] *Apuntes*, no. 1210. This tactless criticism may be a distorted echo of ideas and words used by Father Josemaría in his Monday conferences. In an entry from 1930 we read, "We must not tempt God. If, with great faith in

Providence and without a parachute, I throw myself onto the street from the top of a telephone pole, I am a fool and a bad Christian. If, on the other hand, with great faith and a parachute I jump out of a plane flying half a mile above the ground, I will probably achieve my goal and deserve to be called a wise man and a good Christian. . . . We must not put our trust in human wisdom alone; for if we do, we are sure to fail. Rather, with great trust in God, we must make use of all the resources that we would for any other enterprise, plus prayer and expiation" (*Apuntes,* nos. 60 and 61).

[115] *Apuntes,* nos. 1754 and 1755.

[116] Pedro Cantero, AGP, RHF, T–04391, p. 7.

[117] See Saturnino de Dios Carrasco, AGP, RHF, T–01478, p. 3.

[118] *Apuntes,* no. 1217. In December 1937, with the serenity and objectivity that historical distance and foundational grace gave him, Father Josemaría accepted what Father Sánchez said about those events having been "one of the unmistakable proofs of the divine origin of our enterprise." In his journal he writes, "I got those saintly priests to meet with me on Mondays, for what I called 'priestly conferences,' with the intention of communicating to them the spirit of the Work so that they could become sons and coworkers of mine. In 1932 or 1933, several of those priests voluntarily, spontaneously, and totally freely made a promise of obedience at our house on Luchana Street. It was impossible to imagine at that time that—with the very best of intentions, no doubt—they would, almost immediately, completely forget about the Work" (*Apuntes,* no. 1435).

[119] *Apuntes,* no. 1232.

[120] *Apuntes,* no. 1221. In a previous note, on the subject of fasting, he says, "Lord, what a struggle fasting is for me! . . . If I'm not even up to a battle that small, how hard would a Lepanto be for me?" (*Apuntes,* no. 1219). [Lepanto was the culminating naval battle between Christian Europe and the Turkish Empire for control of the Mediterranean.].

[121] "On the feast of Saint Nicholas, as I was going up to the altar to say Mass," he wrote in his journal, "I promised the holy bishop that if he took care of our financial problems at the Guardian Angel House, I would appoint him administrator of the Work of God" (*Apuntes,* no. 1206). But right away, Bishop del Portillo comments, "it struck him that what he had said was very ungenerous. So he added, 'Even if you don't listen to me now, you will still be our patron saint for financial affairs.' And ever since that day—December 6, 1934—Saint Nicholas has been our patron saint for all financial matters" (*Apuntes,* note 913).

Actually, he had already turned to this saint for help prior to this day in 1934. As he himself explains, "In Madrid, in the Plaza de Antón Martín, there stands Saint Nicholas Church. It was there that I first went to Saint Nicholas to hit him up for some money" (AGP, P04 1975, p. 74).

[122] See *Apuntes,* no. 1222.

[123] Ricardo Fernández Vallespín, AGP, RHF, T–00162, p. 21.

[124] See *Apuntes,* no. 1220.

[125] *Apuntes,* no. 1222.

[126] See *Apuntes,* nos. 1795, 1796, 1800, 1801, and 1804. These entries correspond to a bundle of loose notes from 1934 setting out complete plans for his bodily mortification, with periodic revisions by his confessor. In no instance is his use of the discipline reduced to less than three times a week.

In an entry dated March 11, 1934, we read, "Yesterday I was brought to tears because Father Sánchez would not let me fast this week. I believe it is precisely against gluttony that I must fight hardest! But yesterday, on the bus, I got dizzy; that's why he won't let me fast" (*Apuntes,* no. 1155). The subject of fasting appears also in the above-mentioned loose notes from 1934.

[127] See *C81* (20 Sep 1934).

[128] Juan Jiménez Vargas, who lived with the founder at the Ferraz Street center, testifies that he practiced "bodily mortifications and penances, such as disciplining himself, to the point of drawing blood, and wearing cilices. Though he tried to hide these things from us, he couldn't entirely do so. I saw in his room splashes and stains of blood which obviously came from these penances, and when the Reds searched his room, they found, in a drawer of his desk, disciplines with bloodstained metal hooks. He also made use of cilices and advised us to do so too, and made them available to us. Fairly often he slept on the floor. Occasionally he would spend the whole night in prayer, not sleeping at all. And often he mortified himself in little ways, for example at mealtime, and advised us to do the same. On certain days he fasted" (Juan Jiménez Vargas, *Sum.* 6706). See also Alvaro del Portillo, *Sum.* 360.

There is also this testimony from his brother: "When he lived at our house, he would shut himself up in the bathroom and turn on all the faucets so that we could not hear him use the disciplines, but I heard it" (Santiago Escrivá de Balaguer y Albás, *Sum.* 7346).

[129] Ricardo Fernández Vallespín, AGP, RHF, T–00162, p. 22.

[130] *Apuntes,* no. 1227.

[131] See *Apuntes,* no. 1229.

[132] See *Apuntes,* no. 1234. That day—February 21, 1935—was the first occasion on which the founder gathered members of the Work to inform them officially of a decision of this sort. In this instance, the members were Ricardo Fernández Vallespín, Juan Jiménez Vargas, and Manolo Sainz de los Terreros.

[133] Letter of 27 Feb 1935 from Isidoro Zorzano to Father Josemaría: original in AGP, IZL, D–1213, no. 75.

[134] *C 101* (27 Feb 1935).

[135] *Apuntes,* nos. 1232 and 1233. In characterizing the conduct of the priests around him, the founder made an exception in two cases: that of Father Saturnino de Dios and that of Father Eliodoro Gil (see *Apuntes,* nos. 1217 and 1235).

[136] *Apuntes,* no. 1243.

[137] *Apuntes,* no. 1277.

[138] *Apuntes,* nos. 1246 and 389. Concerning the unpleasant experiences of those days, see *Apuntes,* nos. 1234, 1237, 1245, 1247, and 1266.

[139] See *Apuntes,* no. 1225. For a few details about the ceremony, see Ricardo Fernández Vallespín, AGP, RHF, T–00162, p. 25.

[140] *Apuntes,* no. 1287 and note 974; see also Juan Jiménez Vargas, AGP, RHF, T–04152/1, p. 6. Neither Isidoro Zorzano nor José María González Barredo could make their fidelity that day, since they were out of town. For this, see *C 104* (11 Mar 1935) and *C 108* (24 Mar 1935), and also Isidoro Zorzano's letter of 18 Mar 1935 (AGP, IZL, D–1213, no. 78).

[141] *Apuntes,* no. 1258.

[142] *C 102* (2 Mar 1935).

[143] *Apuntes,* no. 1237.

[144] The founder's formal request to the bishop of Madrid-Alcalá for permission to set up a semipublic oratory is dated March 13, 1935. Because of the location of the house, inspection of the room set aside for liturgical worship was the responsibility of the pastor of the parish of San Marcos. On March 27, 1935, he declared the oratory to be "in suitable condition and duly provided with all that is necessary for the liturgy" and then proceeded to give his blessing, "leaving the place ready for the celebration of Mass" (see "Relación del párroco de San Marcos," 27 Mar 1935, in the archive of the general secretariat of the archdiocese of Madrid-Alcalá, "Oratorios, 1931–1936"). The decree authorizing the setting up of the oratory is dated 10 Apr 1935; original in AGP, RHF, Sec. Jurídica 1/8066.

[145] The founder occasionally spoke about this providential donation. They never could discover the identity of their benefactor, but (we know from Bishop Alvaro del Portillo) Father Josemaría was not at all surprised by this. He was convinced that his prayers had been answered by Saint Joseph himself, to whom he had entrusted the matter. (See Alvaro del Portillo, *Sum.* 305.) "He brought up this event several times in his meditations and conversations, to encourage trust in God" (Juan Jiménez Vargas, PM, fol. 927).

As a sign of gratitude, he attached to the tabernacle key a medallion engraved with the words "Ite ad Ioseph." It was an echo of Scripture's advice to the hungry—"Go to Joseph!"—which in the Bible refers to the Joseph who was Pharaoh's prime minister (see Gn 41:39–43, 55).

Concerning the tabernacle key, see Ricardo Fernández Vallespín, AGP, RHF, T–00162, p. 24.

146 *C 109* (30 Mar 1935).

147 *C 110* (2 Apr 1935). On Friday, March 29, he got verbal permission from the vicar general to say Mass on Sunday, March 31, and to keep the Blessed Sacrament reserved (see AGP, RHF, AVF–0007, p. 8, dated 29 Mar 1935, and AVF–0009, p. 10, dated 24 Apr 1935). Isidoro, informed by telephone, wrote in his letter of April 1, "What great joy you gave me yesterday! . . . Last night I woke up several times thinking about it" (AGP, RHF, IZL, D–1213, no. 80).

148 See Ricardo Fernández Vallespín, AGP, RHF, T–00162, p. 26, and Aurelio Torres-Dulce, AGP, RHF, T–03773, p. 3.

149 *C 113* (15 May 1935).

150 About the pilgrimage to the shrine of Our Lady of Sonsoles, there is an entry, dated 7 May 1935, which says, "There, in Avila, was born a Marian custom which will forever be a part of the Work. I shall say no more about it here, for it is all recounted elsewhere" (*Apuntes*, no. 1270). Indeed, an account of this pilgrimage has been given. Begun by Ricardo Fernández Vallespín, it was continued and completed by the founder, and can be found in AGP, RHF, AVF–0010.

151 Account in AGP, RHF, AVF–0010.

152 In his account of their return from the Sonsoles pilgrimage (see AGP, RHF, AVF–0010), Father Josemaría gives a little anecdote and closes with the points on which they meditated that afternoon:

On the way back, as we were praying (in Latin!) the holy Rosary, an unusual bird flew across the road. It distracted me, and I shouted, "Look at that!" That was all; we went on praying, but I was a little ashamed of myself. How often the birds of worldly dreams try to distract us from your apostolates! With your grace, never again, Lord.

Now, one last detail: the points on which we meditated on our way home, on the train:

1) how God our Father could, with good reason, have chosen any number of other people for his Work, and not us;
2) how we should respond to the merciful love of Jesus, in choosing us for his Work (this was more or less how we put it);
3) seeing how beautiful the apostolate of the Work is, and how great an enterprise it will be in a few years—or can be right now—if only we will respond as we should to that love.

Our petition: a spirit of total sacrifice, of slavery, for Love, for the Work.

— Madrid, May 1935

[153] *Apuntes,* no. 1240; see also *Apuntes,* no. 1295.

[154] See *Apuntes,* no. 1244.

[155] See *Apuntes,* no. 1267.

[156] See *Apuntes,* no. 1285.

[157] See Alvaro del Portillo, *Sum.* 1 and 588. Obviously, he very readily assimilated what he learned in this brief contact with the Work and its founder, for in the September 1935 issue of *Noticias,* sharing some of the anecdotes and news items that he had heard from those on vacation, the Father wrote, "Alvaro del Portillo, in La Granja, dedicated himself very successfully to the fishing that Saint Mark speaks of in the first chapter of his Gospel" (AGP, RHF, D–03696).

[158] *C 126* (22 Aug 1935).

[159] In a letter dated 5 Sep 1935, Father Josemaría says to him, "My dear son Ricardo, I am very concerned about not having told you—because it did not seem necessary—to be sure to offer up to the Lord, through Mary, all the little annoyances of your illness. . . . Take care of yourself. Don't worry about anything, and don't come back to the Residence until you've regained your strength" (*C 129,* 5 Sep 1935; see also *C 130,* 6 Sep 1935).

[160] See Alvaro del Portillo, *Sum.* 452.

[161] *Apuntes,* nos. 1808, 1810, and 1811.

[162] *Apuntes,* nos. 1812 and 1813.

[163] *Apuntes,* no. 1821.

[164] Letters of 30 Oct 1930 and 27 Feb 1931 from Isidoro Zorzano to Father Josemaría: originals in AGP, IZL, D–1213, nos. 10 and 14.

[165] See letters dated 3 Feb 1933, 15 Feb 1933, 21 Mar 1933, and 24 Mar 1933 (nos. 26, 27, 30, and 31).

[166] See letters dated 8 May 1934, 21 May 1934, 8 Jun 1934, 9 Jul 1934, and 26 Jul 1934 (nos. 52, 54, 56, 57, and 59).

[167] *C 15* (1 Mar 1931) and *C 16* (3 Mar 1931). In the founder's writings and homilies such words as "insane" and "crazy" appear often, because some people stigmatized him as such on account of his call for sanctification in the world. But Father Josemaría turned these insults around and gave them a positive meaning: an affirmation of his radical love for God, which rose above all human prejudice.

Other closings for his letters to Isidoro include the following: "With a loving brotherly embrace from this other madman, José María" (*C 19,* 6 May 1931); "With a brotherly embrace, José María" (*C 20,* 14 Aug 1931);

and "Keeping you, with brotherly love, in my prayers, José María" (*C 22*, 10 Nov 1931).

168 *C 51* (1 Jun 1934).

169 *Apuntes*, no. 1152. On the use of the title "Father," see *Apuntes*, no. 1032.

170 *Apuntes*, no. 385. This entry continues, "Prayer is what he asks of me. He leads me along paths of Love so that I may be a red-hot coal and a madman. A red-hot coal which will set ablaze in an all-consuming fire many apostolic souls—making them madmen too, men mad for Christ—who will end up setting the whole world on fire."

171 *Apuntes*, no. 1725.

172 *Apuntes*, no. 1293 (28 Oct 1935). See also *Apuntes*, nos. 1199 and 1200.

173 *Apuntes*, note 357. On November 22, 1931, he wrote, "Lord God, put eighty years' worth of wisdom and experience into my heart, for it is too young" (*Apuntes*, no. 409).

174 The full quote is, "Now, if I hear such amusing things, I still enjoy them, but at the same time I also feel bad. And if I'm the one saying them, if some silly comment slips out, I am immediately left with a bitter taste in my mouth. It's Jesus' doing. He's putting eighty years' worth of gravity into my poor heart, because it's too young" (*Apuntes*, no. 465).

175 *Apuntes*, no. 506. One of the resolutions he made on his retreat in June 1933 has to do with the way he should say Mass. His, he says, should be "the Mass of a grave old priest with no affectations" (*Apuntes*, no. 1720). In an entry dated November 6, 1933, he returns to the subject, saying, "I still have a long way to go to get the gravity that we desire" (*Apuntes*, no. 1073).

176 *Apuntes*, no. 1766.

177 *Apuntes*, no. 1658.

178 *Apuntes*, no. 1832.

179 *Letter 6 May 1945*, no. 23.

180 *Apuntes*, no. 678; see also *Apuntes*, nos. 1078 and 1080.

181 See *Apuntes*, no. 1841.

182 *Apuntes*, no. 1283.

183 See Alvaro del Portillo, *Sum.* 308; Juan Jiménez Vargas, *Sum.* 6713 and 6716; *Meditation* of 19 Mar 1975; and *C 124* (12 Aug 1935).

184 *Apuntes*, no. 1298.

185 These vocations came about in different ways, but both are typical of how people come to know the Work and understand its supernatural character.

"I first met Father Josemaría," says Pedro Casciaro, "in January 1935, in Madrid, at the DYA Academy-Residence at 50 Ferraz Street. I was introduced to him by a childhood friend of mine who was then study-ing law.

"I visited him on a regular basis every week, for confession and just to talk with him. After a while I started coming to some of the formation classes he was giving for university students—I was at that time study-ing at Madrid's Graduate School of Architecture. All this was before summer vacation. . . . Because I was afraid I might be late in applying for admission, I asked for this in a letter, and sent it by mail. When I figured he must have received it, I went to see him. That's when I got my first formation session with him" (Pedro Casciaro, *Sum.* 6312 and 6313).

"I met Father Josemaría," says Francisco Botella, "on October 13, 1935, at the residence at 50 Ferraz Street, in Madrid.

"I was then studying architecture and mathematical sciences. A friend of mine, Pedro Casciaro, took me to the residence, even though up to that time I didn't even know Opus Dei existed. . . . I continued to go to the residence, to some of the talks given by Father Josemaría. On November 23, 1935, I asked to be admitted to the Work. And on January 7, 1936, I went to live at the residence" (Francisco Botella, *Sum.* 5605).

[186] Aurelio Torres-Dulce, AGP, RHF, T–03773, p. 3.

[187] See *Apuntes,* nos. 1163, 1165, and 1167.

[188] *Apuntes,* no. 1160.

[189] José Luis Múzquiz, *Sum.* 5790.

[190] Ricardo Fernández Vallespín, AGP, RHF, T–00162, p. 26.

[191] *Apuntes,* no. 1095.

[192] *Apuntes,* no. 1268.

[193] *Apuntes,* no. 1751. This was written in July 1934.

[194] *Apuntes,* no. 1789.

[195] *Apuntes,* no. 1732.

[196] *Apuntes,* no. 1093.

[197] She continues, "On this subject there is little to say. As for the women's groups, our relations with Father Josemaría were limited to re-ceiving spiritual direction from him" (Natividad González Fortún, *Sum.* 5875 and 5869).

Speaking of his dealings with some of these women penitents who come to him for confession, Father Josemaría writes, "I am so disagree-able." Bishop Alvaro del Portillo comments that "the Father tried, in the confessional, to be very firm and detached in his dealings with women." (See *Apuntes,* no. 1304 and note 987.)

[198] Felisa Alcolea, who met Father Josemaría in 1933 and asked admis-sion to the Work in the following year (in March 1934, according to *Apuntes,* no. 1169), testifies that "we had one or two more meetings with

Father Josemaría, but a little while later, since he had so much work, it was Father Lino Vea-Murguía who mainly worked with us" (Felisa Alcolea, AGP, RHF, T–05827, p. 2).

Father Lino's contribution is attested also by Ramona Sánchez, who asked admission to the Work at the same time as Felisa Alcolea (see *Apuntes*, no. 1196). Referring to the catechism classes they were giving at the parish in Tetuán, she says, "Father Lino Vea–Murguía then took part in that catechetical program as well" (Ramona Sánchez, AGP, RHF, T–05828, p. 1).

199 See *Apuntes*, no. 1181.

200 In an entry dated April 26, 1935, we read, "On the Saturday after the Friday of the Seven Sorrows of Our Lady, something very unpleasant happened—so unpleasant that I was sorry I had made that arrangement to meet with five of the women that day. But they came, and I spoke to them about the Work—specifically about their apostolate—and their response was enthusiastic" (*Apuntes*, no. 1265).

201 Felisa Alcolea, AGP, RHF, T–05827, p. 5.

202 *Apuntes*, no. 1200. This entry continues, "My Jesus, what a comfort they must be to you, with their conduct! Do not abandon these children of mine. And my Mother—my heavenly Mama—be very much a mother to my children."

203 *Apuntes*, no. 1288.

204 Eduardo Alastrué, AGP, RHF, T–04695, p. 1.

205 See Pedro Casciaro, *Sum.* 6319, and Alvaro del Portillo, *Sum.* 375.

206 "Conversation with the Father," declares José Ramón Herrero Fontana, "opened up a whole new world, with unsuspected horizons for your interior life and apostolate. He spoke about real issues—he was very realistic—but he said things that no one had ever said before. When you were with him, you had a powerfull sense of the call of God to sanctification in the midst of the world. . . . My first meeting with the Father transformed me: he revealed to me an interior world whose existence I had never suspected, and awoke in me a strong desire to bring others to meet and know our Lord Jesus Christ" (José Ramón Herrero Fontana, AGP, RHF, T–05834, p. 4).

"I still have a clear memory of his penetrating gaze, which pierced my soul, and of his joy, which stirred me deeply, filling me with happiness and peace," says another of the students about his first meeting with Father Josemaría (Francisco Botella, AGP, RHF, T–00159/1, p. 201).

207 See Alvaro del Portillo, *Sum.* 365.

208 See Pedro Casciaro, *Sum.* 6401.

209 See Alvaro del Portillo, PR, p. 397. For more on the impact of his preaching, see Eduardo Alastrué, *Sum.* 5526.

210 *Apuntes*, no. 304.

[211] *Apuntes,* no. 901.

[212] Felisa Alcolea, AGP, RHF, T–05827, p. 5. See also José Ramón Herrero Fontana, AGP, RHF, T–05834, p. 4.

[213] See *Apuntes,* Introduction, p. 9, and note 152.

[214] *Apuntes,* no. 503.

[215] *Letter 24 Mar 1930,* no. 2. Over the years this letter, like some of the other early ones, has undergone some touching up with regard to terminology, but the substance of its content has not been affected. For this reason the founder always used the date of the first edition.

[216] *Letter 24 Mar 1931,* no. 1.

[217] *Letter 9 Jan 1932,* no. 91. Some of these letters are very long. This one has eighty pages.

[218] *Letter 16 Jul 1933,* no. 1.

[219] *Apuntes,* no. 368.

[220] *Apuntes,* no. 368.

[221] *Apuntes,* no. 368.

[222] *Apuntes,* no. 352.

[223] See *Apuntes,* nos. 695 and 941.

[224] *Apuntes,* no. 527; see also *Apuntes,* no. 14.

[225] See *C 40* (24 Jul 1933). Three of the points, as noted in the text itself, are taken from *Decenario al Espíritu Santo* (English title: "About the Holy Spirit"), by Francisca Javiera del Valle. See also *Apuntes,* no. 688.

[226] Here he omitted the three points from *Decenario.* However, he kept two considerations that had originally come from his confessor, though he altered them slightly. One of these is "a very beautiful saying from Father Sánchez for members of the Work of God: 'There is no excuse for those who could be luminaries and are not'" (*Apuntes,* no. 234), which appears in *Consideraciones espirituales* (p. 24), and later in *The Way* (no. 332), as "There is no excuse for those who could be scholars and are not." The other is in *Apuntes,* no. 329, and *The Way,* no. 61.

[227] See letter of 9 Apr 1934 from Father Sebastián Cirac to Father Josemaría: original in AGP, RHF, D–15225.

[228] *Apuntes,* no. 1183.

[229] Letter of 18 May 1934 from Father Sebastián Cirac to Father Josemaría: original in AGP, RHF, D–15225.

[230] Ibid.

[231] *Apuntes,* no. 1233. This reflection appears in *The Way,* no. 367, but without the reference to "revolting excrement."

[232] See *Apuntes,* nos. 530, 580, 674, and 735, for example. The time frame for Notebook 5 is December 3, 1931, through August 12, 1932.

[233] *Consideraciones espirituales,* p. 37. On the proper use and meaning of "holy shamelessness," or "holy and apostolic shamelessness," see

Apuntes, nos. 178 and 1126.

[234] Letter of 28 May 1934 from Father Sebastián Cirac to Father Josemaría: original in AGP, RHF, D–15225. If Father Josemaría lost his battle with the bishop over "holy shamelessness," he also lost a battle "of the gerunds" with Father Sebastián, in whose opinion too many gerunds were coming from his pen. Two instances appear in the introduction to *Consideraciones espirituales,* despite Father Sebastián's instructions that they were to be eliminated. These are (1) "responding to the needs of young lay people," and (2) "not attempting to fill in undeniable gaps and omissions." See *Apuntes,* no. 1298.

[235] It was published as *Consideraciones espirituales,* by "José María," Cuenca, Imprenta Moderna, 1934; this first edition carried only the first name, not the surnames, of the author. Bishop del Portillo, after noting that this was done out of humility, tells us that "a little later, in 1939, *The Way* was published with his complete name; 'I was back,' as the Father used to say" (*Apuntes,* no. 190, note 206).

In a letter to the vicar general of Madrid, the founder wrote: "Enclosed is a copy of the little booklet published in Cuenca. The 'Holy Rosary' one has not yet been printed; when it is, I'll send you a couple of copies" (*C 55,* 6 Jul 1934).

[236] See *The Way,* nos. 387, 388, 389, 390, and 391.

[237] Alvaro del Portillo, *Sum.* 559. See also *Letter 29 Dec 1947/14 Feb 1966,* no. 84, and *Letter 14 Sep 1951,* nos. 28 and 65.

[238] See *C 48* (26 Apr 1934).

[239] *Consideraciones espirituales,* p. 14.

[240] *Consideraciones espirituales,* p. 34. In *Apuntes íntimos* we find the following notes: "An hour of study is now—and, for our young men, is always—an hour of apostolate," and "Every hour of study—for the Work, for Love—will be in God's sight an hour of prayer" (*Apuntes,* nos. 801 and 1677). *The Way* (no. 335) has a third version: "An hour of study, for a modern apostle, is an hour of prayer."

On the first page of the September 1934 issue of *Noticias* (see AGP, RHF, D–03696)—a family newsletter for all those to whom Father Josemaría gave spiritual direction, most of them students—we read:

> The plan for the next school year: Faith. Perseverance. Stubbornness! And conduct consistent with our faith.
>
> *Studying,* from the very first day, knowing that we are fulfilling a *serious obligation.*
>
> More important than study: *forming ourselves spiritually,* so as to *live the interior life* which is the duty of a Catholic gentleman . . . , with all its consequences.

[241] Francisco Botella, AGP, RHF, T–00159/1, p. 5.

[242] The instructional texts that the founder had written by that time were the following: *Instrucción acerca del espíritu sobrenatural de la Obra de Dios* (19 Mar 1934), *Instrucción sobre el modo de hacer el proselitismo* (1 Apr 1934), and *Instrucción para la Obra de San Rafael* (9 Jan 1935).

[243] *Instruction* of 19 Mar 1934, nos. 1 and 6.

[244] *Instruction* of 19 Mar 1934, nos. 47–49.

[245] Francisco Botella, AGP, RHF, T–00159/1, p. 5; Ricardo Fernández Vallespín, AGP, RHF, T–00162, p. 17.

[246] See *Instruction* of 1 Apr 1934.

[247] *Instruction* of 1 Apr 1934, no. 65.

[248] *Instruction* of 9 Jan 1935, nos. 1 and 2.

[249] *Apuntes*, no. 1312. He goes on to explain why they are making the move: "We have a double reason for leaving the convent [of Santa Isabel] for a while. On the one hand, we want to escape any riots resulting from the upcoming election. On the other hand, Mama needs some time away from that house at Santa Isabel anyway, since it's so damp and not good for her health" (*Apuntes*, no. 1313).

[250] *Apuntes*, no. 1317.

[251] *Apuntes*, no. 1320.

[252] *Apuntes*, nos. 1324 and 1325.

[253] *Apuntes*, nos. 1315 and 1318.

[254] *C 146* (10 Mar 1936). The founder wrote an account of his meeting of August 31, 1934, with the vicar general, Monsignor Francisco Morán, and in one paragraph he says, "I also mentioned to him that 'these boys' want to open academies, with residences, near major foreign universities. I don't remember what expressions he used, but he thinks this is wonderful." See AGP, RHF, AVF–0002, pp. 2–4 (31 Aug 1934).

[255] *Apuntes*, no. 1322.

[256] *Apuntes*, no. 1295. He continues, "These days, both the bishop of Pamplona and the auxiliary bishop of Valencia are showing me such affection that I don't know how to thank them. Also, Madrid's vicar general, Monsignor Francisco Morán, who came over this past Thursday to celebrate Holy Mass in our oratory, has the greatest affection for the Work." See also Alvaro del Portillo, *Sum.* 593, and Joaquín Alonso, *Sum.* 4627.

[257] See *C 145* (3 Mar 1935). Bishop Marcelino Olaechea Loizaga was born in Baracaldo (in Vizcaya) on January 1, 1889. A Salesian, he was ordained a priest in 1912. He served as provincial of Castile and Tarragona. For the academic year of 1934–1935 he was president of the Salesian college on Ronda de Atocha in Madrid, which was very close to the Santa Isabel Foundation. In 1935 he was made bishop of Pamplona, and in 1946, arch-

bishop of Valencia. He governed that diocese until 1966. He died in Valencia on October 21, 1972.

258 *C 144* (3 Mar 1936). Bishop Francisco Javier Lauzurica y Torralba was born in Yurreta (in Vizcaya) on December 3, 1890. Ordained a priest in 1917, he soon became an archivist canon at the collegiate church in Logroño and a professor of cosmology and psychology at that city's major seminary. In 1931 he was made auxiliary bishop of Valencia, and from 1931 to 1936 he served as rector of the seminary in Valencia. In 1937 Bishop Lauzurica was named apostolic administrator of Vitoria; in 1947, bishop of Palencia; and in 1949, archbishop of Oviedo, where he died on April 12, 1964.

259 *Apuntes,* no. 1321.

260 See *Apuntes,* nos. 1320 and 1323.

261 *Apuntes,* no. 1304.

262 *Apuntes,* no. 409.

263 *Apuntes,* no. 144.

264 *Apuntes,* no. 147.

265 *Apuntes,* no. 158.

266 See the archive of the general secretariat of the archdiocese of Madrid-Alcalá, "Oratorios, 1931–1936." It is also significant that when informing the vicar general of such apostolic initiatives, the founder mentions, either as his own idea or as that of "these boys," the fact that they "want to open academies, with residences, near major foreign universities" (see AGP, RHF, AVF–0002, pp. 2–4).

267 Miguel Deán Guelbenzu, AGP, RHF, T–04741/1, pp. 9–10. In the meditations he gave those young professionals, the Father often talked to them about the "vocation to marriage" to which they were called, and in which those young men of the Saint Gabriel work were to sanctify themselves, although at the time the majority of them were still single. (See Juan Jiménez Vargas, AGP, RHF, T–04152/1, p. 24, and Alvaro del Portillo, *Sum.* 1099.)

On this subject, Miguel Deán remembers a conversation that a friend of his, Angel Santos Ruiz, had with the Father. "I took Angel to Ferraz Street," he says. "He talked with the Father and went to confession to him. I know that the Father said to him, 'You have a vocation to get married, so let's see if you can find a woman who is good, beautiful, and rich.' And then, in that same playful tone of voice, he added, 'But you'll have to find her for yourself—I'm no matchmaker'" (Miguel Deán Guelbenzu, AGP, RHF, T–04741/1, p. 8).

268 *C 145* (3 Mar 1936). In June 1933, while on retreat, the founder thought about this apostolic endeavor of the Saint Gabriel work with a view to starting up a "Society for Intellectual Collaboration" ("So-Co-In") to

provide the nucleus for the future work. We know this from an entry in his journal: "In the last few days, based on what I saw on my June retreat, I have drawn up the bylaws and the ceremonial for the So-Co-In" (*Apuntes*, no. 1049).

There is also a note to his confessor, dated October 26, 1933, in which he speaks of his desire to set up weekly meetings at the DYA Academy for adults who have completed their studies: "another weekly meeting for our Saint Gabriel friends—lawyers, doctors, architects, engineers, people who have earned at least a B.A. and possibly a doctorate in philosophy, literature, history, the sciences, etc.—and all of them young, to serve in the founding of the 'So-Co-In' at the beginning of 1934" (*Apuntes*, no. 1733).

See also Miguel Deán Guelbenzu, AGP, RHF, T–04741/1, p. 9.

[269] *Apuntes*, no. 1290.

[270] *C 141* (6 Feb 1936).

[271] *Apuntes*, no. 1307.

[272] *C 144* (3 Mar 1936).

[273] Diary of the journey to Valencia, April 20–23, 1936, written by Father Josemaría and Ricardo during those days of their visit there. Original in AGP, RHF, D–15346.

[274] *Apuntes*, nos. 1323, 1331, 1332, 1347, 1351, and 1357.

[275] *C 162* (2 May 1936).

[276] *Apuntes*, no. 1334.

[277] The confiscation of the Santa Isabel Foundation and the expulsion of the nuns did not take effect immediately, so for several more weeks he was still able to celebrate Mass there. (See *C 163*, 1 Jun 1936, and *Apuntes*, nos. 1334–37.)

Concerning the murmurings against the Work, see *Apuntes*, nos. 1342 and 1345. Entry no. 1346, dated May 31, 1936, says, "Recently, that I know of, religious from three different orders have been *spreading rumors* about us. Opposition from the good? Works of the devil."

As for his priestly faculties, at the end of May the archbishop of Saragossa granted them fully and in perpetuity. (See *Apuntes*, no. 1344.)

[278] *Apuntes*, no. 1350.

[279] *Apuntes*, no. 1352.

[280] *Apuntes*, no. 1343.

[281] *Instruction* of 31 May 1936, no. 2.

[282] See ibid., no. 27.

[283] *Apuntes*, no. 1356.

[284] *Apuntes*, no. 1361.

[285] *C 165* (18 Jun 1936).

[286] *Apuntes*, no. 1373.

[287] *Apuntes,* no. 1365.
[288] *Apuntes,* no. 1369.
[289] *Apuntes,* no. 1371.
[290] *Apuntes,* no. 432.
[291] *Apuntes,* no. 1369.
[292] *Apuntes,* no. 1372.
[293] *Apuntes,* no. 1372.
[294] *Apuntes,* no. 1372.
[295] *Apuntes,* no. 1371.
[296] See *C 168* (1 Jul 1936), *C 169* (7 Jul 1936), and *C 170* (15 Jul 1936).
[297] See Francisco Botella, AGP, RHF, T–00159/1, p. 12, and Ricardo Fernández Vallespín, AGP, RHF, T–00162, pp. 31–32.

Index

Abraham, 386
academy-residence, 392
  atmosphere of, 430–32, 435
  Blessed Sacrament at, 419–21,
    434
  financial difficulties and, 402–4
  oratory of, 420–21
  problems with, 413–15
action, 277
actual sins, 387–88
Albás, Carlos (uncle), 11, 43, 85, 94,
  493n24
  Josemaría's law studies and, 123
  Josemaría's seminary studies
    and, 86, 92
  poor relations with, 131–32,
    139–40, 155, 544n177
Albás, Juan (great-uncle), 10
Albás, Mauricio (uncle), 41, 92
Albás, Mercedes (aunt), 85
Albás, Pascual (grandfather), 6, 10,
  22, 43
Albás, Vicente (uncle), 11, 492n24
Albás Linés, Manuel (great-grandfather), 10
Albás y Blanc, Candelaria (aunt), 85
Albás y Blanc, Dolores (mother),
  73–74
  baptism of, 461
  character of, 47
  childhood of, 492n17
  education of her children by,
    19–20
  family background of, 10–11,
    458–59
  family misfortune and, 40–45
  family relations of, 139–40

  health of, 305
  household of, 14–15, 19, 26–28,
    30–31, 52, 59–60, 108
  Josemaría's birth and, 6
  Josemaría's childhood illness
    and, 16–17
  Josemaría's first Mass and,
    144–45
  marriage of, 11, 21, 462–63
  Santiago's birth and, 78
  suffering of, 45, 154, 302
  See also Escrivás
Albás y Blanc, María de la
  Concepcíon (aunt), 10
Albás y Blanc, Mauricio (uncle), 85
Alcála Zamora, Niceto, 583n76
Alcolea, Felisa, 434
Alda, Archbishop, 89
Alfaro, Daniel, 136, 139
Alfonso the Wise, 62
Alfonso XIII, 265, 531n56, 561n40
Alphonsus Ligouri, Saint, 104
Alvarado, Margarita, 211
Amado Institute, 201
Amado Lóriga, Santiago, 171
anarcho-syndicalists, 373
Andrew Avelino, Saint, 198
anticlericalism, 266–76
  acts of, 271–74
  Catholic Church and, 270–71
  Foundation for the Sick and, 270
  Jesuits and, 267, 275–76
  of liberal bourgeoisie, 81–82
  press and, 271
Antonia, 336–37
apostolate
  among humble folk, 167–68